HISTORICAL STATISTICS OF CHILE

HISTORICAL STATISTICS OF CHILE

Demography and Labor Force

VOLUME 2

Compiled by
MARKOS J. MAMALAKIS

Greenwood Press
Westport, Connecticut • London, England

Library of Congress Cataloging in Publication Data

Mamalakis, Markos.
Historical statistics of Chile.

Bibliography: p.
1. Chile—Population—Statistics.
2. Chile—Statistics, Vital. 3. Labor supply—
Chile—Statistics. I. Title.
HA1007.M35 312'.0983 79-54051
ISBN 0-313-20854-9 (v. 2)

Library of Congress Catalog Card Number: 79-54051
ISBN: 0-313-20854-9

First published in 1980

Greenwood Press
A division of Congressional Information Service, Inc.
51 Riverside Avenue, Westport, Connecticut 06880

Printed in the United States of America

10 9 8 7 6 5 4 3 2 1

To Angelica

CONTENTS

ABBREVIATIONS

BCC	Banco Central de Chile (Central Bank of Chile).
BID	Banco Interamericano de Desarrollo (Interamerican Development Bank).
CEC	Comisión de Planeamiento Integral de la Educación Chilena (Commission for the Integrated Planning of Chilean Education).
CELADE	Centro Latinoaméricano de Demografía (Latin American Demographic Center).
CICRED	Committee for International Coordination of National Research in Demography.
CIEPLAN	Corporacion de Investigaciones Economicas para Latino-america (Corporation of Economic Research for Latin America).
CONCEM	Convenio Centro de Estudios Estadístico-Matemáticos Universidad de Chile (Contract with the Center for Statistical and Mathematical Studies of the University of Chile).
DEC	Dirección de Estadística y Censos (Bureau of Census and Statistics).
DERTO	Departamento de Relaciones del Trabajo y Desarrollo Organizacional (Department of Labor Relations and Organizational Development).
DGE	Dirección General de Estadística (Bureau of Census and Statistics).
ECLA	Economic Commission for Latin America.
EDESEC	Encuesta Demográfica y Socio-económica (Demographic and Socio-economic Survey).
FLACSO	Facultad Latinoamericana de Ciencias Sociales.
ICN	Interdepartmental Committee on Nutrition for National Defense.
IECH	Instituto de Economía Universidad de Chile, Santiago (Institute of Economics of the University of Chile) or Instituto de Economia y Planificación (Institute of Economics and Planning) or Departamento de Economía (Department of Economics).
INE	Instituto Nacional de Estadísticas (National Institute of Statistics).
MEP	Ministerio de Educación Pública (Ministry of Public Education).
ODEPLAN	Oficina de Planificación Nacional (National Planning Office).

PISPAL	Programa de Investigaciones Sociales Sobre Problemas de Población Relevantes para Politícas de Población in America Latina (Program of Social Research about Population Problems Relevant to Population Policies in Latin America).
PREALC	The Regional Employment Programme for Latin America and the Caribbean (Programa Regional de Empleo para America Latina y el Caribe).
SNE	Servicio Nacional de Estadística y Censos (National Service of Statistics and the Census).
SNS	Servicio Nacional de Salud (National Health Service).
SSE	Superintendencia. Sección Estadística (Superintendency Statistical Section).
SSS	Servicio de Seguro Social (Social Security Service).
UN	United Nations.
USA	United States of America.

TABLES

Chapter 6

Chapter 7

Chapter 8

Chapter 9

Chapter 10

Chapter 13

Chapter 14

Chapter 15

Chapter 16

Chapter 17

Chapter 18

MAJOR DATES AND EVENTS IN CHILEAN HISTORY

1536	Expedition to and discovery of Chile by Diego de Almagro
1540	Conquest of Chile by Pedro de Valdivia
1541	City of Santiago founded by Pedro de Valdivia
1817	Bernardo O'Higgins nominated head of state of independent Chile
1817	Defeat of Spaniards at Charabuco in Argentina by combined Argentine and Chilean army
1817-1823	Government of O'Higgins
1823-1826	Government of Ramón Freire
1823	Abolition of slavery in Chile
1827-1829	Government of Francisco A. Pinto
1830	Beginning of nitrate exports to Europe for industrial and agricultural uses
1831-1861	The era of Diego Portales and conservative hegemony
1831-1841	Presidency of José Joaquín Prieto
1836-1839	War against Peruvian-Bolivian Confederation
1843	Establishment of the University of Chile
1841-1851	Presidency of Manuel Bulnes Prieto
1849-1851	First railroad from Copiapó to Caldera built by Wheelwright
1851-1861	Presidency of Manuel Montt
1861-1871	Presidency of José Joaquín Pérez
1863	Establishment of Radical Party
1871-1876	Presidency of Federico Errázuriz Zañartu
1876-1881	Presidency of Aníbal Pinto
1879-1883	War of the Pacific with Chile defeating Peru and Bolivia. Conquest by Chile of mineral rich provinces of Tarapacá and Antofagasta
1881-1886	Presidency of Domingo Santa María
1883	Peace with Araucanian Indians
1886-1891	Presidency of José Manuel Balmaceda
1891-1920	Parliamentary Republic
1891-1896	Presidency of Jorge Montt
1896-1901	Presidency of Errazuriz Echaurren
1901-1906	Presidency of Germán Riesco
1906-1910	Presidency of Pedro Montt
1910-1915	Presidency of Ramón Barros Luco

1912	Formation of Socialist Party
1915-1920	Presidency of Juan Luis Sanfuentes
1920-1938	Political instability
1920-1924	Presidency of Arturo Alessandri, the Lion of Tarapacá. Social and economic reforms
1925-1927	Presidency of Emiliano Figueros Larraín
1927-1931	Military dictatorship of Carlos Ibañez del Campo
1929-1931	The Great Depression
July 1931 to June 1932	Presidency of Juan Esteban Montero Rodríguez
1932, June to September	Socialist Republic
1932-1938	Second Presidency of Arturo Allessandri
1938-1952	The Radical Presidencies
1938-1941	Presidency of Pedro Aguirre Cerda
1939	Major earthquake and creation of the Chilean Development Corporation, Corporación de Fomento de la Producción (CORFO)
1942-1946	Presidency of Juan Antonio Rios
1942	Chile declares war on Germany
1945	Gabriela Mistral awarded Nobel Prize for Literature
1946-1952	Presidency of Gabriel González Videla
1948	Communist Party declared illegal under law for the "defense of the democracy"
1952-1958	Presidency of General Carlos Ibañez del Campo. Populism of the Right
1958-1964	Presidency of Jorge Alessandri Rodriguez. Economic orthodoxy and prosperity
1960	Major earthquake in south
1964-1970	Presidency of Eduardo Frei Montalva. Gradual, democratic but accelerating reform under "Revolution in Freedom"
1967	Approval of agrarian reform law
1970-1973	Presidency of Salvador Allende Gossens. Marxist populism and revolutionary transformation
1971	Complete nationalization of copper, nitrate and iron mining
1971	Pablo Neruda receives Nobel Prize for Literature
1973	Military junta overthrows Allende
1973-1978	Desocialization and decontrol of Chilean economy
1978	Referendum on United Nations resolution about human rights in Chile

INTRODUCTION

The present volume, consisting of five parts, contains a systematic, comprehensive, and up-to-date presentation of the demographic and labor force statistics of Chile. It also describes and critically evaluates most of the statistics and presents selected information on data, documents, and studies underlying or related to demography and the labor force.

Part I on population contains five chapters dealing with population, natality and fertility, mortality, nuptiality, and age and sex composition of the Chilean population. Part II on migration, population projections, and education consists of four chapters dealing with internal migration, international migration, projections of the population of Chile by age, sex and regions, and educational attainment and institutions. Part III on labor force contains four chapters dealing with labor force countrywide, labor force of Santiago, unemployment and joblessness, and labor force participation rates. Part IV on wages, salaries, health and social security contains two chapters dealing with wages and salaries and health and social security. Finally, Part V deals with the regional distribution of the population and is composed of three chapters dealing with distribution of population by regions and provinces, urbanization, and size and growth of cities.

REASONS FOR AND OBJECTIVES OF THIS STUDY

Why should a collection and evaluation of the demographic and labor force statistics of Chile be undertaken? And, furthermore, are there any compelling reasons for bringing up to date and publishing the mimeographed version of the second volume of the *Historical Statistics of Chile,* which covered *Demography* and was prepared under the auspices of the Yale Economic Growth Center between 1963 and 1967? There are many reasons for bringing up to date and publishing the volume on *Demography and Labor Force,* the second of the *Historical Statistics of Chile.*

(1) The demand for the mimeographed version of the *Historical Statistics of Chile* has been uniformly strong from individual scholars, libraries, firms, governmental, and other agencies ever since this work was first completed in 1967. This demand has been a reflection of the strong and rising interest by historians, political scientists, demographers, sociologists, and other scholars in the long-term, as well as more recent political, social, economic, and demographic events and changes in Chile. Although it was the rise and fall of Salvador Allende that

aroused the great worldwide interest and outpouring of publications, President Eduardo Frei's Revolution in Peace, the unprecedented trade and market liberalization, and the private enterprise-based development strategies between 1973 and 1980 have also contributed to the sustained interest in Chile.

(2) Although the national accounts give a broad picture of the evolution of Chilean economic development from the standpoint of aggregate and sectoral income, they still provide only a partial, one-sided and therefore incomplete view. The other side of economic development is revealed through the examination of population and the various elements that compose it as well as link it to the creation of income and thus determination of economic welfare. Per capita income and its growth are notions linked as much to income as to population levels and changes. Indeed, per capita income and its growth cannot be computed without accurate estimates of the level and growth of population.

(3) As a perusal of the various chapters of the present volume will reveal, estimates of levels of population, employment, unemployment, and labor force and of changes thereof are likely to be subject to at least as much, if not more, error than income estimates. It is thus hoped that publication of the present volume will warn economists especially that they cannot assume that demographic variables and changes thereof are completely accurate, free of estimation errors and exogenous to the working of the economic system. The third reason for publishing the present volume on demography and labor force can be rephrased as follows: demographic variables are as important to the understanding of long-term Chilean economic development as the national accounts variables and therefore need to attract the same interest and be subjected to an equal degree of critical scrutiny by economists and other social scientists as income and national accounts.

(4) The "population crash," that is, the precipitous decline in Chile's birth rate and growth of population, beginning with 1962-63 can be expected to have profound repercussions on future health, education, employment, and income policies. Publication and systematic scrutiny of the demographic underpinnings of this population slowdown, namely births, deaths, and international migration, are advisable as well as necessary in order to determine the accuracy as well as shape of the alleged "birth crash" before compensatory strategies are formulated.

(5) Although by no means perfectly accurate or comprehensive in their coverage, major demographic time series of Chile nevertheless extend back far beyond 1940 when the country's national income estimates begin.

Demographic and labor force data thus provide historical evidence for understanding Chile's development process during periods for which no national income estimates are available.

(6) There exists a large number of empirical, methodological, and analytical demographic and labor force studies and/or statistical compendia. Although many of them are truly excellent in terms of the insights that they provide to our understanding of the functioning of Chile's economy and society, none of them is broad enough to create a comprehensive, in-depth vision of the working of the economic system. They are all partial. In contrast, the present volume hopes to provide statistical information that covers each and all major dimensions of Chile's demographic and labor force fabric and thereby reveals its total shape, design and strength rather than only part of it. Diverse demographic and labor force variables are considered by presenting historical statistical information pertaining to them and/or by linking inter-related series and/or by pointing out the need for more and better data. Lack of an integrated compendium of historical demographic information on Chile is a major rationale behind publication of this book. This volume hopes to present all major demographic and labor force data in an integrated manner that reveals a major segment of the Chilean economic physiognomy, exposes historical lacunae, and stimulates research to fill existing knowledge deficiencies.

(7) The present volume provides a major statistical foundation for the Mamalakis study on the *Growth and Structure of the Chilean Economy* (New Haven, Conn.: Yale University Press, 1976). Much of the discussion of that monograph on population, fertility, mortality, urbanization, education, labor force, and health was condensed because the more extensive statistics and discussion were contained in the "Demography" volume of the *Historical Statistics of Chile.* It was natural, therefore, that to many readers and reviewers the evolution of Chile's economic history presented in the monograph was incomplete without access to the complementary *Historical Statistics.* Publication of the present volume adds another step in correcting this deficiency.

Although this project began as a collection of the historical statistics that would provide the brick and mortar for a comprehensive economic history of Chile, it gathered its own strength and momentum with time and the actual form in which the volume of demography and labor force is being published is much broader than originally planned. Rather than being just a collection of statistics, it also provides much of the methodological, analytical, and institutional background information needed in using and improving these statistics and in understanding Chile's long-term economic development path.

RESEARCH BACKGROUND AND ACKNOWLEDGMENTS

The first and significantly shorter version of this volume was prepared during 1963-1967 while I was on the economics department faculty of Yale University and member of its Economic Growth Center. Much of the statistical information was compiled, like that of Volume I, *Historical Statistics of Chile: National Accounts,* during my eighteen-month stay at the Instituto de Economía of the University of Chile between 1964 and 1966. Without the generous support of Lloyd Reynolds, Gustav Ranis, Shane Hunt, Albert Berry, and Hugh Patrick, all of Yale, the first version, which provided the solid foundation for this volume, would not have been put together.

Generous assistance was also provided by Carlos Massad, Roberto Maldonado, Carlos Hurtado, Samuel Mardones, and Arturo Malbrán of the Instituto de Economía.

The present volume differs much more from its previous mimeographed version prepared under the auspices of the Yale Economic Growth Center than the first volume on National Accounts differs from its mimeographed version. The presently published volume on *Demography and Labor Force* bears only limited resemblance to its original version. The majority of the tables are either completely new or heavily revised and transformed versions of the original ones. Furthermore, tables and text have been organized in chapters that combine historical statistics with methodological introductions. And completely new chapters and sets of tables have also been added.

The present extended, up-to-date volume on Demography and Labor Force was made possible by a grant from the Tinker Foundation since the original Yale-sponsored version went only up to 1964. Special thanks and appreciation, therefore, go to the Tinker Foundation and to Martha Twitchell Muse, chairman and president, and Erika V.C. Bruce, program director, of the Tinker Foundation for their support and cooperation. Many thanks also go to Deans W. Halloran and G. Keulks and Associate Deans N. Hall and N. Laska at the University of Wisconsin-Milwaukee, College of Letters and Science and Graduate School, for the generous assistance; to Tong Hun Lee of the Department of Economics who greatly facilitated the completion of this volume; and to Donald Shea of the Latin American Center for his and the center's manifold assistance and cooperation.

A number of scholars made detailed comments suggesting means to improve and extend the early version. The most comprehensive and detailed comments and notes were made by Rolando Mellafe, a leading Chilean demographer. Most of his suggestions found their way into the text. Also extremely valuable were the comments and suggestions by Robert McCaa, of the University of Minnesota, Bruce Herrick, of the University of California, Los Angeles, and Ann Hagerman Johnson, of the University of California, Davis.

Many institutions and persons cooperated generously while I was gathering, evaluating, and organizing the data in Chile.

The most important source of demographic and labor force statistics in Chile is the National Institute of Statistics. The quantity and quality of data prepared and/or published by the National Institute of Statistics are impressive and among the very best in Latin America. Generous and continuous assistance was provided by Sergio Claparro Ruiz, National Director of the Institute, as well as Odette Tacla, Monica Correa, Héctor Kappes Barientos, Carlos Torres, Isabel Manzor, Maria E. Oliden, Ruben Ampuero, Raul Henriquez, and Guillermo Delano. Their support greatly expedited publication of this volume.

The Latin American Center of Demography (Centro Latinoamericano de Demografía-CELADE) has undertaken research and published first rate studies in almost every line of demography. Many, although by no means all of them, have been summarized or referred to here. Although the present volume contains the most comprehensive collection of demographic statistics on Chile and lengthy bibliographical notes, in many sections it remains but a modest guide to the more specialized literature of CELADE and other institutions. I would like to express here my appreciation for the help received from José Pujol, Carmen Arretx, Erica Taucher, and Betty Johnson de Vodanović, all of CELADE.

Continuous cooperation was also provided by Alberto Spottke, Rolando Rivas, Irene Ceron, Maria Luisa Duerr, Carolina Sánchez, and Olga Guarda Muñoz, all of the Planning Office; by Andrés Sanfuentes, Director of the Department of Economics and Planning of the University of Chile, and Carolina Sánchez Naranjo of the Social Security Service.

Peggy Limbacher and Joyce Miezin provided essential secretarial and organizational services. Jorge Domínguez assisted in preparing the first version while Ernesto Peralta, Carol Stolz, Ernesto Infante, Mauro Leos, Rosalinda Quintanilla, and Mayra Zermena, my research assistants in Milwaukee, as well as Michael Hensen and Jane Reiter, provided manifold clerical help.

Last but not least, many thanks go to my wife, Angelica, who assisted me throughout our sojourn in Chile in preparing the first set of tables.

However, the responsibility for the contents of this volume is exclusively mine.

Markos Mamalakis
May 1979

GLOSSARY

Abortion (Aborto) is defined, with reference to the woman, as any interruption of pregnancy before 28 weeks of gestation with a dead foetus. There are two major categories of abortion: spontaneous and induced. Induced abortions are those initiated by deliberate action undertaken with the intention of terminating pregnancy; all other abortions are considered as spontaneous.

Age pattern of fertility (Fecundidad por grupos de edad). The percent distribution of a set of age-specific fertility rates. It expresses the relative contribution of each age group to total fertility.

Age-specific fertility rate (Tasas de fecundidad por grupos de edad). The number of births during 1 year to women in a given 5-year age group per 1,000 women in the same age group (based on midyear population).

Age-specific marital fertility rate (Tasas de fecundidad de cas casadas, por grupos de edad). The number of births to married women in a given age group per 1,000 married women in the same age group.

Birth rate (Tasa de natalidad). The number of births during 1 year per 1,000 persons (based on midyear population). Also called crude birth rate.

Children ever born. The number of live births a woman has had, regardless of the woman's present or past marital status and regardless of whether the children are now living or dead, or living with or away from the mother.

Cohort (Coherte). A group of individuals who experience the same event in the same calendar period, such as the same year of birth or marriage.

Component method. A method of projecting the size of a population by age and sex, in which separate assumptions are made concerning the future fertility, mortality, and migration rates of the population.

Crude birth rate (CBR tasa bruta de natalidad). The number of live births, per year, per 1,000 of population.

Crude death rate (CDR = tasa bruta de mortalidad). The number of deaths, per year per 1,000 of population (based on midyear population). Also called general death rate or just death rate.

Death (Muerte o defuncion) is the permanent disappearance of all evidence of life at any time after live birth has taken place (post-natal cessation of vital functions without capability of resuscitation). This definition therefore excludes foetal deaths.

Divorce (Divorcio) is a final legal dissolution of a marriage, that is, that separation of husband and wife which confers on the parties the right to remarriage under civil, religious and/or other provisions, according to the laws of each country.

Ever-married women. All women who are now, or who have been, married. The category includes the currently married, those living in consensual unions, and the widowed, divorced, or separated.

Foetal death (Muerte fetal) is death prior to the complete expulsion or extraction from its mother of a product of conception, irrespective of the duration of pregnancy; the death is indicated by the fact that after such separation the foetus does not breathe or show any other evidence of life, such as beating of the heart, pulsation of the umbilical cord, or definite movement of voluntary muscles. Late foetal deaths are those of twenty-eight completed weeks of gestation or over. These are synonymous with the events reported under the pre-1950 term stillbirth.

General fertility rate (Tasa general de fecundidad). The number of live births per year, per 1,000 women, aged 15-49 years.

Gross reproduction rate (Tasa bruta de reproducción). The average number of daughters born per woman in a group of women passing through the childbearing years and experiencing a given set of age-specific fertility rates. This rate implicitly assumes that all the women live to the end of the childbearing years. (See also net reproduction rate.)

Growth rate (Tasa de crecimiento). The annual increase (or decrease) to the population resulting from a surplus or deficit of births over deaths and a surplus or deficit of migrants into or out of the country, expressed as a percentage of the base population.

Infant mortality rate (Tasa de mortalidad infantil). The number of deaths of children under 1 year of age per 1,000 live births in a calendar year.

Late foetal deaths (Muertes fetales tardías) are those of twenty-eight completed weeks of gestation or over. These are synonymous with the events reported under the pre-1950 term stillbirth.

Life expectancy at birth (Esperanza de vida al nacer). The average number of years to be lived by persons born in a certain year if mortality rates for each age group remain constant in the future.

Live birth (Nacidos vivos) is the complete expulsion or extraction from its mother of a product of conception, irrespective of the duration of pregnancy, which after such separation, breathes or shows any other evidence of life such as beating of the heart, pulsation of the umbilical cord, or definite movements of voluntary muscles, whether or not the umbilical cord has been cut or the placenta is attached; each product of such a birth is considered live-born regardless of gestational age.

Marriage (Matrimonio) is the act, ceremony or process by which the legal relationship of husband and wife is constituted. The legality of the union may be established by civil, religious, or other means as recognized by the laws of each country.

Median age of childbearing. The midpoint age that separates the younger half of all women giving birth in a given year from the older half.

Net reproduction rate (Tasa neta de reproducción). A refinement of the gross reproduction rate that allows for mortality of women from birth to the end of their reproductive years.

New acceptors. Persons accepting methods of contraception from family planning systems, including clients accepting contraceptive services for the first time; clients changing to another service organization; clients changing to a different contraceptive method; and clients resuming acceptance of contraceptive services after a lapse of 1 year.

Rate of natural increase (Crecimiento natural o vegetativo). The annual increase (or decrease) to the population resulting from a surplus or deficit of births over deaths, expressed as a percentage of the midyear population. The natural increase of the population does not include the migration of persons into or out of the country.

Rate of population growth (Tasa de crecimiento de la población). The rate of natural increase adjusted for migration, and expressed as a percentage of the total population in a given year.

Replacement level fertility. A level of fertility equivalent to a Net Reproduction Rate of 1.0 -- the level at which childbearing women, on the average, have enough daughters to replace themselves in the population.

Sex ratio at birth (Índice de masculinidad al nacer). The number of male births for each female birth.

Stationary population (Población estacionaria). A population that for a long time has had a constant replacement level fertility and therefore also has a growth rate equal to zero and a constant age composition.

Total fertility rate (TFR) (Tasa total de fecundidad). The average number of children that would be born per woman if all women lived to the end of their childbearing years and bore children according to a given set of age-specific fertility rates. It is five times the sum of the age-specific fertility rates, divided by 1,000.

United Nations Age-Sex Accuracy Index. An index developed by the United Nations to measure irregularities in age distributions in 5-year age groups. Index values of less than 20 usually describe "reasonably reliable" age distributions, values between 20 and 40 "fairly unreliable" age distributions, and values over 40 "quite unreliable" age distributions. The United Nations states that although high test scores may reflect actual irregularities in the age data caused by past demographic fluctuations or international migrations, usually, to a larger extent, they reflect errors in the age data.

BIBLIOGRAPHY

ALBERTS, JOOP (1977) Migración Hacia Areas Metropolitanas de América Latina. Un Estudio Comparativo. Santiago, Chile. CELADE, Serie E, Nº 24.

ALVAREZ, L. and J. M. PUJOL (1967) Chile: Tablas Abreviadas de Mortalidad por Regiones, 1960-1961. Santiago, Chile. CELADE, Serie A, Nº 76 (November). Pp. 1-102.

ARÉVALO, JORGE (1974) Migración Intercensal de Seis Países de América Latina. Santiago, Chile. CELADE (November), Serie A, Nº 127. Pp. 1-192.

ARRETX, CARMEN, ROLANDO MELLAFE and JORGE L. SOMOZA (1976a) Estimaciónes de Mortalidad en una Parroquia de Santiago a Partir de Información Sobre Orfandad. Ñuñoa 1866-1871. Santiago, Chile. CELADE (June). Pp. 1-26.

---(1976b) Mortality Estimates in a Parish of Santiago from Orphanhood Information. Ñuñoa 1866-1871. Santiago, Chile. CELADE (October). Pp. 1-19. Mimeo.

---(1976c) Estimaciones de Mortalidad: Religiosos de Chile en los Siglos XVIII y XIX. Santiago, Chile. CELADE (March). Pp. 1-44. Mimeo.

---(1977a) Adult Mortality Estimate Based on Information on Age Structure of Deaths. An Application to Data for San Felipe Around 1787. Santiago, Chile. CELADE (February). Pp. 1-24. Mimeo.

---(1977b) Estimación de la Mortalidad Adulta a Partir de Información sobre la Estructura por Edades de las Muertes. Aplicación a Datos de San Felipe en Torno a 1787. Santiago, Chile. CELADE (February). Pp. 1-28. Mimeo.

ARRETX, CARMEN, ARMANDO DE RAMÓN, ROLANDO MELLAFE, RENÉ SALINAS and JORGE L. SOMOZA (1977) Preliminary Report on Nupciality, Fertility and Mortality, Based on Histories of Chilean Families. With the collaboration of Raúl Cárdenas, Eduardo Cavieres, Antonia García, Isabel Grau, Gladys Lizama, Fabio Rodríguez, Hernán Orellana and Mariano Vásquez. Santiago, Chile. CELADE. Pp. 1-44.

ARRIAGA, E. A. (1968) New Life Tables for Latin American Populations in the Nineteenth and Twentieth Centuries. Berkeley, California.

AVILA, ROBERTO (1971) Evolución de los Efectivos Escolares de la Educación General Básica de Chile para el Período 1964-1969. Santiago, Chile. CELADE (September). Pp. 1-34.

BALLESTEROS, MARTO A. and TOM DAVIS (1963) The Growth of Output and Employment in Basic Sectors of the Chilean Economy, 1908-1957. Economic Development and Cultural Change. Vol. XI, No. 2, Part I (January).

BCC (1956) Boletín Mensual No. 334. Santiago, Chile, Imprenta Universitaria.

---(1963) Boletín Mensual No. 425. Santiago, Chile, Impresora Gutenberg.

---(1965) Boletín Mensual No. 448. Santiago, Chile, Impresora Gutenberg.

BEHM, HUGO R. (1962) Mortalidad Infantil y Nivel de Vida. Santiago, Chile. Ediciones de la Universidad de Chile. Pp. 1-134.

---(1964) Recent Mortality Trends in Chile. Vital and Health Statistics. Series 3, Number 2. National Center for Health Statistics. U.S. Department of Health and Welfare. Washington, D.C. (April). Pp. 1-33.

---(1978) Niveles, Tendencias y Diferenciales de la Mortalidad Infantil y Perinatal en el Mundo, Con Especial Referencia a la Situación en la América Latina. Con la colaboración de Domingo Primante. San José, Costa Rica. CELADE. Material de Enseñanza 1003 (March). Pp. 1-43.

BEHM, HUGO and MONICA CORREA (1977) La Mortalidad en los Primeros Años de Vida en Países de la América Latina. Chile. 1965-1966. San José, Costa Rica. CELADE, Serie A, No. 1030 (June). Pp. 1-60.

BRUTON, HENRY (1968) Productividad de la Educación en Chile. Santiago, Chile. Instituto de Economía y Planificación. Pp. 1-57.

BUCCHI PENSA, ELIANA (1939) Política, Legislación y Control de la Inmigración en Chile y Otros Estados Americanos. Santiago, Chile.

CABELLO, O., J. VILDÓSOLA and M. LATORRE (1947) Tablas de Vida para Chile 1920, 1930, 1940, in Revista Chilena de Higiene y Medicina Preventiva, Vol. VIII, N° 3 (September) 1946 and Vol. IX, N° 2 (June) 1947.

CAMISA, ZULMA (1977) La Nupcialidad de la Mujeres Solteras en la América Latina. San José, Costa Rica. (December) CELADE. Serie A, No. 1034. Pp. 1-140.

CARMAGNANI, MARCELLO (1967) Colonial Latin American Demography: Growth of Chilean Population, 1700-1830, Journal of Social History. Number 1. Pp. 179-91.

CARMAGNANI, MARCELLO and HERBERT S. KLEIN (1965) Demografía Histórica: La Población del Obispado de Santiago, 1777-78, Boletín de la Academia Chilena de la Historia. Number 72. Pp. 54-74.

CARNOY, MARTIN (1967) Tasas de Retorno a la Educación en América Latina. Cuadernos de Economía. No. 13.

CHILE. COMISIÓN CENTRAL DEL CENSO (1908) Censo de la República de Chile Levantado el 28 de Noviembre de 1907. Santiago de Chile. Sociedad Imprenta y Litografía Universo. Pp. I-XLVII plus 1-1320.

COLLVER, O. ANDREW (1965) Birth rates in Latin America: New Estimates of Historical Trends and Fluctuations. Berkeley, Institute of International Studies, University of California, Berkeley.

CONNING, ARTHUR M. (1969) Estimación de la Migración Interna Neta, Classificada por Edad y por Sexo, en las Provincias y Regiones de Chile durante los Años 1930-1940, 1940-1952, 1952-1960. Con una breve introducción referente a la metodología. Santiago, Chile. CELADE, Series D, No. 36. Pp. 1-103.

CONTRERAS ARIAS, JUAN; EUGENIO FLORES MARAMBIO; INÉS HERRERA CANALES; LEONARDO MAZZEI DEGRAZIA; ARÍSTIDES RIVERA NAVARRO and RODIA SEPÚLVEDA (1972) Fuentes para un Estudio de Demografía Histórica de Chile en el Siglo XVIII. Concepción. Universidad de Concepción, Instituto Central de Historia. Auspiciado por Centro Latinoamericano de Demografía.

CORBO, M. (1974) Schooling Experience and Wages in Santiago, Chile. Chicago, Illinois. University of Chicago.

CORFO (1954) National Accounts, Annex XI of Agricultural and Transport Development Program. Santiago, Chile. CORFO. Unpublished material.

---(1964) Proyecciones de Matrículas y Gastos en Educación. Santiago, Chile. CORFO. Pp. 1-176.

---(1965a)Departamento de Investigaciones Económicas. Estimaciones y Proyecciones Mediante Interpolación y Extrapolación de los Datos Censales Corregidos de la Población Ocupada a Mediados de Cada Año, 1940-1970. Santiago, Chile. CORFO.

---(1965b) Proyecciones Básicas de la Población Chilena. Clasificación por Sexos, por Edades, por Regiones, y Población Activa: 1960, 1965, 1970, 1975, 1980, y 2000. Projections of CELADE for the aforementioned years and interpolation of CORFO for the intermediate years. Santiago, Chile. CORFO.

CROCCO FERRARI, JUAN (1947) Ensayos Sobre la Población Chilena. Memoria para optar al grado de Licenciado en Economía y Comercio. Santiago, Chile. Universidad de Chile.

CSO (Caja de Seguro Obligatorio) (1949) Anuario Estadístico 1948. Santiago, Chile. Imprenta el Imparcial. CSO.

---(1951) Anuario Estadístico 1949. Santiago, Chile. Imprenta el Imparcial. CSO.

---(1952a) Anuario Estadístico 1950. Santiago, Chile. Imprenta de la Dirección General de Prisiones. CSO.

---(1952b) Anuario Estadístico 1951. Santiago, Chile. Imprenta de la Dirección General de Prisiones. CSO.

DE CASTRO SPIKULA, SERGIO (1979) Exposición Sobre el Estado de la Hacienda Pública Presentada por el Ministro de Hacienda Señor Sergio de Castro Spikula. Santiago, Chile. Ministerio de Hacienda. Dirección de Presupuestos. (January). Pp. 1-77.

DEPARTAMENTO DE DERECHO DEL TRABAJO Y SEGURIDAD SOCIAL UNIVERSIDAD CATÓLICA DE CHILE (1975) Guía de Leyes del Servicio Seguro Social. Santiago, Chile. Oficina Coordinadora de Investigación, Profesor Jaime Eyzaguirre. Pp. 1-206.

DEC (1925) Censo de Población de la República de Chile, Levantado el 15 de Diciembre de 1920. Santiago, Chile. Soc. Imp. y Litografía Universo. Pp. 1-610.

---(1933) Censo de la Población Tomo II. Santiago, Chile. DEC. (January).

---(1956) Demografía Año 1956. Santiago, Chile. DEC.

---(1958) Demografía Año 1958. Santiago, Chile. DEC.

---(1959) Demografía Año 1959. Santiago, Chile. DEC.

---(1960a) III Censo Nacional de Manufacturas, 1957. Santiago, Chile. DEC.

---(1960b) XIII Censo de Población, 29 de Noviembre de 1960. Serie A. Resumen del País. Santiago, Chile. Date of publication not available. Pp. 1-448.

---(1963a) Boletines Nos. 7-12. Santiago, Chile. DEC.

---(1963b) Demografía Año 1961. Santiago, Chile. DEC.

---(1964a) Población del País. Características Básicas de la Población, Censo 1960. Santiago, Chile. DEC.

---(1964b) Población Total por Provincias. Chile. 1885-1960. Santiago, Chile. DEC. Pp. 1-12.

---(1964c) Breves Consideraciones Sobre la Muestra de la Población del Censo de 1960, en Relación a las Características de Edad y Sexo. Santiago, Chile. DEC.

---(1964d) Demografía Año 1962. Santiago, Chile. DEC. Pp. 1-286.

---(1965a) Estadísticas de Turismo y Movimiento Internacional de Viajeros. Turismo 1965. Santiago, Chile. DEC. Pp. 1-395.

---(1966a) Estadísticas de Turismo y Movimiento Internacional de Viajeros. Turismo 1966. Santiago, Chile. DEC. Pp. 1-396.

---(1969) Demografía Año 1966. Santiago, Chile. DEC. Pp. 1-245.

---(1970) Demografía Año 1967. Santiago, Chile. DEC. Pp. 1-103.

DEC-CONCEM, Continuous Employment Survey (1966) Muestra Nacional de Hogares. Encuesta Continua de Mano de Obra. Julio-Octubre. Santiago, Chile. DEC-CONCEM. (December) Pp. 1-151.

---(1967) Muestra Nacional de Hogares. Encuesta Continua de Mano de Obra. Noviembre 1966-Febrero 1967. Santiago, Chile. DEC-CONCEM. (September). Pp. 1-118.

---(1968a) Muestra Nacional de Hogares. Encuesta Continua de Mano de Obra. Julio-Octubre. Santiago, Chile. DEC-CONCEM. (May). Pp. 1-134.

---(1968b) Muestra Nacional de Hogares. Encuesta Continua de Mano de Obra. Noviembre 1967-Febrero 1968. Santiago, Chile. DEC-CONCEM. (December). Pp. 1-134.

DEC-CONCEM, Continuous Supplementary Survey (1966) Muestra Nacional de Hogares. Encuesta Supplementaria Sobre Niveles de Instrucción y Calificación de la Mano de Obra. Julio-Octubre. Santiago, Chile. DEC-CONCEM. Pp. 1-35.

---(1967a) Muestra Nacional de Hogares. Encuesta Suplementaria Sobre Ahorro. Noviembre 1966-Febrero 1967. Santiago, Chile. DEC-CONCEM.

---(1967b) Encuesta Suplementaria Sobre Algunos Aspectos de Asistencia Médica y Hospitalaria de la Mano de Obra. Marzo-Junio 1967. Santiago, Chile. DEC-CONCEM. Pp. 1-59.

---(1967c) Muestra Nacional de Hogares. Encuesta Suplementaria Sobre Niveles de Instrucción y Calificación de la Mano de Obra. Julio-Octubre 1967. Santiago, Chile. DEC-CONCEM. Pp. 1-38.

---(1968) Encuesta Nacional Sobre Ingresos Familiares, Marzo-Junio. Santiago, Chile. DEC-CONCEM. Pp. 1-130.

DEC-CONCEM, Continuous Survey of Domestic Trade and Services (1964) Encuesta Continua de Comercio Interior y Servicios. Año 1964. Santiago, Chile. DEC-CONCEM. Pp. 1-45.

---(1965) Encuesta Continua de Comercio Interior y Servicios. Año 1965. Santiago, Chile. DEC-CONCEM. Pp. 1-61.

---(1966) Encuesta Continua de Comercio Interior y Servicios. Año 1966. Santiago, Chile. DEC-CONCEM. Pp. 1-70.

---(1967) Encuesta Continua de Comercio Interior y Servicios. Año 1967. Santiago, Chile. DEC-CONCEM. Pp. 1-64.

DGE (1931) X Censo de la Población of November 27, 1930. Vol. 1. Santiago, Chile. DGE. March, 1931.

---(1936) Demografía y Asistencia Social, Año 1935. Santiago, Chile. DGE.

---(1942) Política, Administración, Justicia y Educación, Año 1940.

---(1945) Estadística Chilena, Año 1945. Santiago, Chile. DGE.

---(1948) Estadística Chilena, Año 1948. Santiago, Chile. DGE.

---(1949) Demografía y Asistencia Social, Año 1946. Santiago, Chile. DGE.

---(1953a) Demografía y Asistencia Social, Año 1949. Santiago, Chile. DGE.

---(1953b) Estadística Chilena, Diciembre (Sinopsis) de 1952. Santiago, Chile. DGE.

DÍAZ VIAL, RAÚL (1962) La situación de los libres parroquiales. Revista de Estudios Históricos. No. 10. Pp. 109-122.

DIRECCIÓN GENERAL DE ESTADÍSTICA (1925) Censo de Población de la República de Chile. Levantado el 15 de Diciembre de 1920. Santiago de Chile. Soc. Imp. y Litografía Universo.

DODERO, CARLOS (1963) Desarrollo Económico de la Región de Concepción 1948-1964. Memoria de Prueba, Facultad de Ciencias Económicas y Administración, Universidad de Concepción. Concepción, Chile.

ELTON, CHARLOTTE (1978) Migración Femenina en América Latina. Factores Determinantes. Santiago, Chile. CELADE. Serie E, No. 26. Pp. 1-84.

FAO (1964) Production Yearbook, 1964. Rome, Italy. United Nations.

---(1971) Production Yearbook, 1971. Vol. 25. Rome, Italy. U.N.

FREEBURGER, ADELA R. and CHARLES C. HAUCH (1964) Education in Chile. Studies in Comparative Education. Washington, D.C. U.S. Department of Health, Education and Welfare. Pp. 1-42.

FUCARACCIO, ANGEL (1974) El Trabajo de la Mujer en Chile en 1970, Parte II, Resto Urbano del País. Santiago, Chile. CELADE. (November). Pp. 1-30.

GREGORY, PETER (1967) Industrial Wages in Chile. Ithaca, New York, New York State School of Industrial and Labor Relations, Cornell University. Pp. 1-113.

GUTIÉRREZ ROLDÁN, HÉCTOR (1968) La Integridad del Registro de Nacimientos en Chile, 1953-1963. Dpto. de Salud Pública y Med. Social. Santiago, Chile. Universidad de Chile.

---(1975) La Población de Chile. Paris, CICRED. Pp. 1-81.

HAGERMAN JOHNSON, ANN LOUISE (1978) Internal Migration in Chile to 1920: Its Relationship to the Labor Market, Agricultural Growth, and Urbanization. Davis, California. Department of History, University of California at Davis. Pp. 1-652.

HARBERGER, ARNOLD C. and MARCELO SELOWSKY (1966) Fuentes del Crecimiento Económico Chileno. Cuadernos de Economía. No. 10 (December).

HERRERA, LIGIA and WALDOMIRO PECHT (1976) Crecimiento Urbano de América Latina. Vol. I, pp. 1-549. Vol. 2. Mapas y Planos de Ciudades. Santiago, Chile. BID-CELADE. Serie E, No. 22. Con la colaboración de Fernando Olivares.

HERRICK, BRUCE H. (1965) Urban Migration and Economic Development in Chile. Cambridge, Mass. MIT University Press.

HURTADO, CARLOS (1966) Concentración de Población y Desarrollo Económico: El Caso Chileno. Santiago, Chile. IECH.

ICN (1961) Chile, Nutrition Survey, March-June 1960, Washington, D.C. United States Government Printing Office.

IECH (Universidad de Chile, Instituto de Economía or Instituto de Economía y Planificación or Departamento de Economía) (1959) La Migración Interna en Chile en el Período 1940-52. Santiago, Chile. IECH.

---(1961) Ocupación y Desocupación. Iquique, Antofagasta, La Serena-Coquimbo, Valparaíso-Viña del Mar, Gran Santiago, Concepción, Valdivia, Puerto Montt, Castro. Septiembre de 1961. Santiago, Chile. IECH (September). No. 44. Pp. 1-110.

---(1962a) Ocupación y Desocupación. Gran Santiago, Concepción. June 1962. Santiago, Chile. IECH.

---(1962b) Ocupación y Desocupación. Iquique, Antofagasta, La Serena-Coquimbo, Valparaíso-Viña del Mar, Gran Santiago, Concepción, Valdivia, Puerto Montt, Castro. Marzo de 1962. Santiago, Chile. IECH (May). No. 46. Pp. 1-117.

---(1963a) Ocupación y Desocupación. Valparaíso, Viña del Mar, Gran Santiago, Concepción. Marzo de 1963. Santiago, Chile. IECH (April). No. 57. Pp. 1-55.

---(1963b) Ocupación y Desocupación. Gran Santiago, Valparaíso-Viña del Mar, Conjunto Provincial Arauco, Bío-Bío, Concepción, Malleco, Ñuble. Septiembre de 1963. Santiago, Chile. IECH (October). No. 61. Pp. 1-74.

---(1964) Ocupación y Desocupación. Gran Santiago, Concepción-Talcahuano. Diciembre de 1963. Santiago, Chile. IECH (January). No. 63. Pp. 1-39.

---(1965) Ocupación y Desocupación. Gran Santiago. Santiago, Chile. IECH (March). No. 71. Pp. 1-37.

---(1967) Ocupación y Desocupación. Gran Santiago. Diciembre de 1966. Santiago, Chile. IECH (December). Pp. 1-70.

---(1968) Ocupación y Desocupación. Concepción-Talcahuano y Lota-Coronel. Octubre de 1968. Santiago, Chile. IECH (October). Pp. 1-72.

---(1970) Ocupación y Desocupación. Gran Santiago. Marzo de 1970. Santiago, Chile. IECH (March). Pp. 1-50.

---(1973a) Ocupación y Desocupación. Gran Santiago. Marzo de 1973. Santiago, Chile. IECH (March). Pp. 1-50.

---(1973b) Ocupación y Desocupación. Concepción-Talcuhuano y Lota-Coronel. Abril de 1973. Santiago, Chile. IECH (April). Pp. 1-70.

---(1976) Ocupación y Desocupación en el Gran Santiago. Marzo 1976. Santiago, Chile. IECH (March). Pp. 1-44.

---(1978a) Ocupación y Desocupación en el Gran Santiago. Diciembre 1977. Santiago, Chile. IECH (March). Pp. 1-33.

---(1978b) Ocupación y Desocupación. Sectores Urbanos de las Regiones IV a X, Excepto el Gran Santiago. Enero 1977-Enero 1978. Santiago, Chile. IECH (July). No. 59. Pp. 1-69.

INE (República de Chile, Ministerio de Economía, Fomento y Reconstrucción, Instituto Nacional de Estadísticas) (1967a) Estadísticas de Turismo y Movimiento Internacional de Viajeros. Año 1967. Santiago, Chile. INE. Pp. 1-123.

---(1970) Resultados Definitivos del Censo de Población, 1970. XIV Censo de Población y III de Vivienda 1970. Población. Total País. Santiago, Chile. INE. Date of publication not available. Pp. 1-157.

---(1971a) Demografía. Año 1968. Santiago, Chile. INE. Pp. 1-91.

---(1971b) Estadísticas de Turismo y Movimiento Internacional de Viajeros. Año 1971. Santiago, Chile. INE. Pp. 1-87.

---(1971c) Muestra Nacional de Hogares. Encuesta Continua de Mano de Obra. Enero-Junio de 1971. Santiago, Chile. INE (October). Pp. 1-127.

---(1971d) Muestra Nacional de Hogares. A-13. Encuesta Continua de Mano de Obra. Julio-Diciembre 1971. Santiago, Chile. INE (December). Pp. 1-127.

---(1972a) Educación y Cultura. Año 1972. Santiago, Chile. INE. Date of publication not available. Pp. 1-119.

---(1972b) Demografía. Año 1969. Santiago, Chile. INE. Pp. 1-72.

---(1972c) Características Básicas de la Población (Censo 1970) Resumen País XIV Censo de Población y III de Vivienda 1970. Santiago, Chile. INE. Pp. 1-56.

---(1975a) Estadísticas de Turismo 1975. Movimiento Internacional de Pasajeros y Comunicaciones. Santiago, Chile. INE. Pp. 1-109.

---(1976) Anuario Estadístico 1976. Santiago, Chile. INE. Pp. 1-365.

---(1977a) Anuario Estadístico, 1976. Santiago, Chile. INE. Date of publication not available. Pp. 1-365.

---(1977b) Compendio Estadístico 1977. Santiago, Chile. INE. Pp. 1-279.

---(1977c) Población, 1960-1975. Total País, Provincias y Area Metropolitana. Estimaciones por Sexo y Grupos de Edad al 30 Junio de Cada Año. Santiago, Chile. INE (June). Pp. 1-232.

---(1977d) Informativo Estadístico. Enero-Mayo Año 1977. Santiago, Chile. INE. Pp. 1-72.

---(1977e) Informativo Estadístico. Junio-Julio-Agosto-Septiembre Año 1977. Santiago, Chile. INE. Pp. 1-80.

---(1977f) Encuesta Nacional del Empleo. I Región Tarapacá. Octubre 1977. Santiago, Chile. INE (October). Pp. 1-11.

---(1977g) Encuesta Nacional del Empleo. II Región Antofagasta. Octubre 1977. Santiago, Chile. INE (October). Pp. 1-11.

---(1977h) Encuesta Nacional del Empleo. IV Región Coquimbo. Octubre 1977. Santiago, Chile. INE (October). Pp. 1-10.

---(1977i) Encuesta Nacional del Empleo. VII Región Maule. Octubre 1977. Santiago, Chile. INE (October). Pp. 1-11.

---(1977j) Encuesta Nacional del Empleo. VIII Región Bío-Bío. Octubre 1977. Santiago, Chile. INE (October). Pp. 1-13.

---(1977k) Encuesta Nacional del Empleo. XI Región Aysén del Gral. Carlos Ibañez del Campo. Octubre 1977. Santiago, Chile. INE (October). Pp. 1-10.

---(1977l) Encuesta Nacional del Empleo. III Región Atacama. Noviembre 1977. Santiago, Chile. INE (November). Pp. 1-10.

---(1977m) Encuesta Nacional del Empleo. VI Región Libertador Gral. Bernardo O'Higgins. Noviembre 1977. Santiago, Chile. INE (November). Pp. 1-10.

---(1977n) Encuesta Nacional del Empleo. IX Región de la Araucania. Noviembre 1977. Santiago, Chile. INE (November). Pp. 1-18.

---(1977o) Encuesta Nacional del Empleo. X Región De Los Lagos. Noviembre 1977. Santiago, Chile. INE (November). Pp. 1-12.

---(1977p) Encuesta Nacional del Empleo. XII Región Magallanes y Antárctica Chilena. Noviembre 1977. Santiago, Chile. INE (November). Pp. 1-12.

---(1977q) Encuesta Nacional del Empleo. V Región Aconcagua. Diciembre 1977. Santiago, Chile. INE (December). Pp. 1-10.

---(1977r) Encuesta Nacional del Empleo. Total Nacional Años 1975-1976-1977. Santiago, Chile. INE. Pp. 1-13.

---(1978a) Informativo Estadístico. Septiembre-Diciembre Año 1977. Santiago, Chile. INE (March). Pp. 1-76.

---(1978b) Compendio Estadístico 1978. Santiago, Chile. INE. Pp. 1-319.

---(1978c) Encuesta Nacional del Empleo. Gran Santiago. Octubre-Diciembre 1978. Santiago, Chile. INE. Pp. 1-19.

INE-CONCEM, Continuous Employment Survey (1971a) Encuesta Continua de Mano de Obra. Resultados del Gran Santiago. Santiago, Chile. INE-CONCEM. Pp. 1-41.

---(1971b) Encuesta Continua de Mano de Obra. Resultados del Gran Santiago. Santiago, Chile. INE-CONCEM (April-June). Pp. 1-41.

INE-CONCEM, Continuous Survey of Domestic Trade and Services (1968) Encuesta Continua de Comercio y Servicios. Año 1968. Santiago, Chile. INE-CONCEM. Pp. 1-65.

---(1969) Encuesta Continua de Comercio Interior y Servicios. Año 1969. Santiago, Chile. INE-CONCEM. Pp. 1-39.

LABARCA, AMANDA (1939) Historia de la Enseñanza en Chile. Santiago, Chile. Imprenta Universitaria.

LARRAÍN EUZAGUIRRE, IVÁN (1956) La Parroquia ante el derecho civil chileno. Santiago, Chile.

LEGARRETA, A., L. LÓPEZ and A. ALDEA (1973) Omisión del Registro de Defunciones de Niños Fallecidos en Maternidades. Boletín de la Organización Panamericana de la Salud. Vol. LXXV, No. 4 (October).

LIRA, LUIS FELIPE (1975a) Estructura Agraria y Población: Análisis del Caso Chileno. (Versión Preliminar). Santiago, Chile. CELADE-PISPAL. (April). Pp. 1-62.

---(1975b) Características Socio Económicas y Estructura de las Familias en la Ciudad de Santiago: Chile, 1970. Santiago, Chile. CELADE-PISPAL. (October). Pp. 1-35.

LIRA MONTT, LUIS (1965) Padrones del Reino de Chile Existentes en el Archivo de Indias, Revista de Estudios Históricos. Number 13. Pp. 85-88.

MAMALAKIS, MARKOS (1966a) La teoría de los choques entre sectores. Santiago, Chile. Instituto de Economía, Universidad de Chile. (March). Pp. 1-64.

---(1966b) La teoría de los choques entre sectores. El Trimestre Económico. Vol. XXXIII(2), Abril-Junio de 1966, Núm. 130. Pp. 187-222.

---(1969) The Theory of Sectoral Clashes. The Latin American Research Review, Vol. 4, No. 3, Fall. Pp. 9-46.

---(1971) The Theory of Sectoral Clashes and Coalitions Revisited. Latin American Research Review. Vol. VI, No. 3, Fall 1971. Pp. 89-126.

---(1972) Urbanization and Sectoral Transformation in Latin America, 1950-65, Actas y Memorias del XXXIX Congreso Internacional de Americanistas Lima 1970, Vol. 2, Simposio 2: Proceso de Urbanización en América desde sus orígenes hasta nuestro días. Lima, Perú. Instituto de Estudios Peruanos, 1972. Pp. 293-345.

---(1976a) Urbanización y transformación sectorial de América Latina, 1950-1965, El Trimestre Económico, Vol. XLIII(2). México, April-June 1976, No. 170.

---(1976b) Los Servicios en la ciudad latinoamericana contemporánea: el caso chileno, in Las ciudades de América Latina y sus áreas de influencia a través de la historia compiled by Jorge E. Hardoy and Richard P. Schaedel (Buenos Aires, Argentina: Sociedad Interamericana de Planificación, 1976).

---(1976c) Services in the Contemporary Latin American City: The Case of Chile, in Atti del XL Congresso Internazionale Degli Americanisti, Volume IV (Genova, Italy: Casa Editrice Tilgher).

---(1976d) The Growth and Structure of the Chilean Economy: From Independence to Allende. New Haven, Connecticut, Yale University Press.

---(1977) Urbanización y transformaciones sectoriales en Latinoamérica (1950-1970). Antecedentes e implicaciones para una reforma urbana, in Asentamientos urbanos y organización socioproductiva en la historia de América Latina, compiled by J. E. Hardoy and R. P. Schaedel (Buenos Aires, Argentina: Sociedad Interamericana de Planificación, May 1977).

---(1978a) Historical Statistics of Chile: An Introduction. Latin American Research Review, Volume XIII, No. 2. Pp. 127-137.

---(1978b) Services in the Contemporary Latin American City: The Case of Chile, in Urbanization in the Americas from its Beginnings to the Present. Richard P. Schaedel, Jorge E. Hardoy, Nora Scott Kinser, Editors. The Hague, Paris. Mouton Publishers, distributed in the USA and Canada by Aldine. Chicago.

---(1978c) Historical Statistics of Chile. National Accounts. Westport, Connecticut. London, England. Pp. 1-262.

MARIN LIRA, MARÍA ANGÉLICA (1975) Reconstitution de la Population Chilienne au XXe Siecle. Thèse de Doctorat de 3e Cycle presentée àl' Université de Paris I. Ecole des Hautes Etudes en Sciences Sociales. Paris. October 1975. Vol. I. Pp. 1-282.

McCAA, ROBERT (1976) Chile XI Censo de Población (1940). Santiago, Chile. CELADE. Pp. 1-335.

---(1978) Chilean Social and Demographic History: Sources, Issues, and Methods,' The Latin American Research Review, Vol. XIII, Number 2. Pp. 104-126.

MELLAFE, ROLANDO (1956) Problemas Demográficos Historia Colonial Hispanoamericana, Temas de Historia Económica Hispanoamericana, Colección Nova Americana, No. 1. Paris. Pp. 45-55.

---(1972) Descripción Tipológica de los Documentos Utiles para la Demografía Histórica Existente en los Archivos Latinoamericanos. Santiago, Chile. CELADE, Serie D, No. 71 (February).

MELLAFE, ROLANDO and JULIO MORALES (1975) Migraciones Rurales en Chile del Siglo XVII. Santiago, Chile. CELADE LS/5 (April).

MEP-CEC (1964) Algunos Antecedentes para el Planamiento Integral de la Educación Chilena. Santiago, Chile. MEP.

MEP (1977) Education in Chile. Chilean Report to the 36th Meeting of the International Conference on Education, Geneva, 1977. Educational Process 1974-1976, August 30th-September 8th. Santiago, Chile. MEP, Superintendencia de Educación. Pp. 1-58.

MEP-SSE (1974a) Sector Fiscal. Algunos Antecedentes Para el Estudio del Rendimiento Escolar: Destino de la Matrícula de Educación Básica Expresado en Valores Relativos y Absolutos, Por Grados - Según Provincia. Año 1968. Santiago, Chile. MEP-SSE. (April). Pp. 1-8 mimeo.

---(1974b) Sector Fiscal. Algunos Antecedentes Para el Estudio del Rendimiento Escolar: Destino de la Matrícula de Educación Básica Expresado en Valores Relativos y Absolutos, Por Grados - Según Provincia. Año 1972. Santiago, Chile. MEP-SSE. (April). Pp. 1-8 mimeo.

---(1974c) Sector Fiscal. Algunos Antecedentes Para el Estudio del Rendimiento Escolar: Destino de la Matrícula de Educación Básica Expresado en Valores Relativos y Absolutos, Por Grados - Según Provincia. Año 1971. Santiago, Chile. MEP-SSE. (April). Pp. 1-8 mimeo.

---(1974d) Sector Fiscal. Algunos Antecedentes Para el Estudio del Rendimiento Escolar: Destino de la Matrícula de Educación Básica Expresado en Valores Relativos y Absolutos, Por Grados - Según Provincia. Año 1966. Santiago, Chile. MEP-SSE. (April). Pp. 1-8 mimeo.

---(1974e) Sector Fiscal. Algunos Antecedentes Para el Estudio del Rendimiento Escolar: Destino de la Matrícula de Educación Básica Expresado en Valores Relativos y Absolutos, Por Grados - Según Provincia. Año 1973. Santiago, Chile. MEP-SSE. (June). Pp. 1-7 mimeo.

---(1974f) Sector Fiscal. Algunos Antecedentes Para el Estudio del Rendimiento Escolar: Destino de la Matrícula de Educación Básica Expresados en Valores Relativos y Absolutos Por Grados - Según Provincia. Año 1967. Santiago, Chile. MEP-SSE. (April). Pp. 1-8 mimeo.

---(1974g) Sector Fiscal. Algunos Antecedentes Para el Estudio del Rendimiento Escolar: Destino de la Matrícula de Educación Básica Expresado en Valores Relativos y Absolutos, Por Grados - Según Provincia. Año 1969. Santiago, Chile. MEP-SSE. (April). Pp. 1-7 mimeo.

---(1974h) Sector Fiscal y Particular, Número de Establecimientos de Educación Parvularia, Básica y Media Por Tipos, Modalidades y Ramas, Según Provincia. Año 1973. Santiago, Chile. MEP-SSE. (August). Pp. 1-5 mimeo.

---(1975a) Educación de Adultos. Informe de Matrícula y Número de Establecimientos de Educación Básica y Media Por Dependencia y Tipo de Enseñanza, Según Regiones. Año Escolar 1974. Santiago, Chile. MEP-SSE. (July). Pp. 1-14 mimeo.

---(1975b) Sector Fiscal. Antecedentes Sobre Rendimiento Escolar de la Educación Media Niños, Por Grado o Año de Estudio, Modalidades y Ramas de Enseñanza, Según Provincia. Año Escular 1971. Santiago, Chile. MEP-SSE. (July). Pp. 1-19 mimeo.

---(1975c) Educación de Niños. Número de Establecimientos por Regiones y Dependencia, Según Tipo de Educación. Año Escolar 1974. Santiago, Chile. MEP-SSE. (September). Pp. 1-8 mimeo.

---(1975d) Educación Básica Fiscal Niños. Algunos Antecedentes de Rendimiento Escolar. Periodo 1966-1969 y 1971-1973. Santiago, Chile. MEP-SSE. (January). Pp. 1-17 mimeo.

---(1975e) Sector Fiscal. Antecedentes Sobre Rendimiento Escolar de la Educación Media Niños, Por Grado o Año de Estudio, Modalidades y Ramas de Enseñanza, Según Provincia. Año Escolar 1973. Santiago, Chile. MEP-SSE. (April). Pp. 1-19 mimeo.

---(1975f) Educación Básica Niños. Matrícula Efectiva de Repitentes Por Grado o Año de Estudio y Sexo, Según Región y Dependencia. Año Escolar 1973. Santiago, Chile. MEP-SSE. (August). Pp. 1-6 mimeo.

---(1975g) Sector Fiscal. Antecedentes Sobre Rendimiento Escolar de la Educación Media Niños, Por Grado o Año de Estudio, Modalidades o Ramas de Enseñanza, Según Provincia. Año Escolar 1972. Santiago, Chile. MEP-SSE. (June). Pp. 1-19 mimeo.

---(1975h) Informe de Matrícula Inicial de Educación Pre-Básica, Básica Especial, Básica Regular y Media Niños, Por Región, Dependencia y Sexo. Año Escolar 1974. Santiago, Chile. MEP-SSE. (March). Pp. 1-18 mimeo.

---(1976a) Sector Fiscal. Alumnos Matriculados, Promovidos, Reprobados y Retirados y Tasas Respectivas de la Educación Básica y Media del Año Escolar 1974, Por Regiones y Provincias, Según Grado o Año de Estudio y Ramas de Enseñanza. Santiago, Chile. MEP-SSE. (July). Pp. 1-36 mimeo.

---(1976b) Sector Fiscal. Informe de Matrícula, Repitentes y Número de Cursos de la Enseñanza Pre-Básica, Básica Especial y Básica Regular Niños. Año Escolar 1975. Santiago, Chile. MEP-SSE. (June). Pp. 1-13 mimeo.

---(1976c) Sector Fiscal. Rendimiento Escolar de la Enseñanza Básica y Media, Por Región y Provincia, Según Grado o Año de Estudio. Año Escolar 1975. Santiago, Chile. MEP-SSE. (October). Pp. 1-34 mimeo.

---(1976d) Educación de Niños y Adultos, Número de Establecimientos Por Regiones y Dependencia, Según Tipo de Educación. Año Escolar 1976. Santiago, Chile. MEP-SSE. (November). Pp. 1-10 mimeo.

---(1976e) Educación de Niños. Número de Profesores Por Regiones y Dependencia, Según Tipo de Educación. Año Escolar 1976. Santiago, Chile. MEP-SSE. (December). Pp. 1-17 mimeo.

---(1976f) Area Metropolitana. Matrícula, Repitentes, Número de Cursos y de Establecimientos de la Enseñanza Pre-Básica, Básica y Media Niños. Año Escolar 1974. Santiago, Chile. MEP-SSE. (September). Pp. 1-24 mimeo.

---(1976g) Educación de Niños y Adultos. Informe de Matrícula de la Enseñanza Pre-Básica, Básica y Media, Por Region, Dependencia y Sexo Según Grado o Año de Estudio. Año Escolar 1976. Santiago, Chile. MEP-SSE. (November). Pp. 1-33 mimeo.

---(1976h) Total País. Matrícula, Repitentes, Número de Cursos y de Establecimientos de la Enseñanza Pre-Básica, Básica y Media Niños. Año Escolar 1974. Santiago, Chile. MEP-SSE. (September). Pp. 1-24 mimeo.

---(1977a) Región Metropolitana. Matrícula y Asistencia Media del Alumnado Fiscal de Enseñanza Pre-Básica, Especial y Básica Niños, Por Comuna, Según Grado o Año de Estudio. Año Escolar 1975. Santiago, Chile. MEP-SSE. (March). Pp. 1-7 mimeo.

MESA-LAGO, CARMELO (1978) Social Security in Latin America: Pressure Groups, Stratification and Inequality. Pittsburgh, Pennsylvania. University of Pittsburgh Press.

MIRÓ, CARMEN (1963) Algunos Problemas Relativos a la Evolución de los Resultados de los Censos de la Población. Santiago de Chile.

---(1965) La Población de América Latina en el Siglo XX, Santiago de Chile. CELADE. Serie A, No. 48 (September). Pp. 1-29.

MORALES, JULIO V. (1969) Chile: Nuevas Proyecciones de Población por Sexo y Grupos de Edades, 1960-2000. Santiago, Chile. CELADE (November). Pp. 1-25.

---(1974) Panorama de la Migración Internacional entre Países Latinoamericanos. Santiago, Chile. CELADE. Serie A, No. 121 (January).

ODEPLAN (1970) Recopilación de Antecedentes de Estudios de Recursos Humanos en Chile. Santiago, Chile. ODEPLAN (April). Pp. 1-139.

---(1971a) Los Recursos Humanos en el Desarrollo del País. Periodo 1960-1970. Santiago, Chile. ODEPLAN (January). Pp. 1-160.

---(1971b) 1971-76. Plan de la Economía Nacional: Antecedentes Sobre el Desarrollo Chileno. 1960-70. Santiago, Chile. ODEPLAN. Ser. 1, No. 1.

---(1971c) Población Ocupada por Sectores Económicos 1960-1970. Santiago, Chile. ODEPLAN (December).

---(1972) Disponibilidad y Utilización de Mano de Obra en Chile. (Balance de Mano de Obra 1970-1976). Santiago, Chile. ODEPLAN (June). Pp. 1-19.

---(1974) Primer Plan Nacional Indicativo de Desarrollo. 1975-1980. Versión Preliminar. Santiago, Chile. ODEPLAN (November). Pp. 1-260.

---(1975a) Proyección de la Población de Chile por Sexo y Grupos Quinquenales de Edad. 1950-2000. Santiago, Chile. ODEPLAN. Trabajo elaborado por la Oficina de Planificación Nacional (ODEPLAN) en colaboración con CELADE.

---(1975b) Serie de Población No. 2. Proyección de la Población a Nivel Nacional y Regional, por Sexo y Grupos Quinquenales de Edades. 1970-2000. Santiago, Chile. ODEPLAN (June). Pp. 1-73.

---(1975c) Tablas Abreviadas de Mortalidad a Nivel Nacional y Regional, 1969-1970. Santiago, Chile. ODEPLAN (July). Pp. 1-137.

---(1976a) Encuesta Demográfica y Socio-Económica. Santiago, Chile. ODEPLAN (July). Pp. 1-500.

---(1976b) Los Recursos Humanos y el Empleo en Chile. Santiago, Chile. ODEPLAN (January). Pp. 1-40 plus 22 tables.

ORTIZ, PURA (1976) Estructura Jurídico-Institucional del Estado Chileno, 1925-1973. Santiago, Chile. CELADE (April). Pp. 1-39.

PÉREZ ROSALES, VICENTE (1859) Ensayo Sobre Chile. Trans. Manuel Migriel. Santiago, Chile. Imprenta del Ferrocarril.

PREALC (1972) Creación de Empleos y Absorción del Desempleo en Chile. Ginebra PREALC. Pp. 1-57.

---(1978a) Sector Informal. Funcionamiento y Polfticas. Santiago, Chile. PREALC. Pp. 1-369.

---(1978b) Características Laborales y Educacionales de Migrantes y No Migrantes en Chile. PREALC. Pp. 1-44.

---(1978c) Fecundidad y Desarrollo Económico y Social en Chile, 1952-1970. PREALC (May). Pp. 1-52.

---(1978d) Antecedentes Sobre el Trabajo de los Menores en Chile. PREALC (November). Pp. 1-43.

---(1978e) Participación Femenina en la Actividad Económica en América Latina (Análisis Entadístico). PREALC (November). Pp. 1-36.

---(1978f) Employment in Latin America. New York, N.Y. PREALC. Pp. 1-193.

PISPAL (1977) Inventario de Investigaciones Sociales Relevantes Para Políticas de Población. Volumen III Chile. Santiago, Chile. CELADE, Unidad Central de PISPAL, FLACSO. Pp. 1-433.

PUJOL, JOSÉ M. (1976a) Chile: Proyecciones de la Población por Sexo y Grupos Quinquenales de Edades, 1950-2000. Santiago, Chile. CELADE (July). Pp. 1-23.

---(1976b) Chile: Tablas Abreviadas de Mortalidad a Nivel Nacional y Regional, 1969-1970. Santiago, Chile. CELADE (July). Pp. 1-74.

---(1976c) Chile: Proyección de la Población por Regiones Según Sexo y Grupos de Edades. 1970-2000. Santiago, Chile. CELADE (September). Pp. 1-44.

---(1976d) Chile: Proyección de la Población Urbana y Rural a Nivel Nacional y Regional, por Sexo y Grupos Quinquenales de Edades. 1970-2000. Santiago, Chile. CELADE (November). Pp. 1-63.

RACZYNSKI, DAGMAR (1978a) Empleo, Pobreza y Migraciones en Chile. Santiago, Chile. CIEPLAN (November).

---(1978b) Migraciones Internas en Chile: Metodología e Información Estadística. Santiago, Chile. CIEPLAN (October). Notas Técnicas No. 11.

REQUENA, MARIANO (1968) Correlación Social y Económica del Aborto Inducido en Santiago de Chile. Santiago, Chile. CELADE, Serie A, No. 62 (July). Pp. 1-27.

RIVERA NAVARRO, ARÍSTIDES; JUAN CONTRERAS ARIAS; RODIA ROMERO SEPÚLVEDA and EUGENIO FLORES MARAMBIO (1972) Prospección de las Fuentes Demográficas de la Provincia de Chiloé, 1567-1826. Mimeo versión Concepción. Instituto Central de Historia, Universidad de Concepción. Also published in Fuentes para la demografía histórica en América Latina. Mexico: CLACSO-CELADE, Comisión de Historia Económica.

SALAS SILVA, IRMA (1930) The Socio-Economic Composition of the Secondary School Population of Chile. Santiago, Chile. Imprenta Lagunas y Quevedo.

SALINAS MEZA, RENÉ (1970) La Población de Valparaíso en la Segunda Mitad del Siglo XVIII. Valparaíso, Universidad Católica.

---(1978) Fuentes para el Estudio de la Demografía Histórica en el Norte Chico Chileno (1600-1854). The Latin American Research Review, Vol. XIII, Number 2. Pp. 98-103.

SÁNCHEZ C, DOMINGO and GABRIELA SANTA MARÍA (1977) Contribuciones al Estudio de los Recursos Humanos en Chile Rural. Santiago, Chile. DERTO. University of Chile. Pp. 1-43.

SCHIEFELBEIN, ERNESTO (1976) Diagnóstico del Sistema Educacional Chileno en 1970. Santiago, Chile. Departamento de Economía, Universidad de Chile.

SCHIEFELBEIN, ERNESTO and CARLOS CLAVEL (1978) Stability over time of educational input-output relationships. Documento de Investigación N° 30, Diciembre de 1978. Santiago, Chile. Universidad de Chile, Departamento de Economía (December). Pp. 1-39.

SNE (1954) Educación, Justicia, Política y Administración. Año 1950. Santiago, Chile. SNE.

---(1955) Demografía. Año 1953. Santiago, Chile. SNE.

---(1956) XII Censo General de Población y I de Vivienda of April 24, 1952. Tomo I. Resumen del País. Santiago, Chile. SNE.

SNS (Servicio Nacional de Salud or Departamento de Planificación, Ministerio de Salud) (1964) Anuario 1962. Defunciones y Causas de Muerte. Volumen V. Santiago, Chile. SNS (March). Pp. 1-90 mimeo.

---(1971) Anuario 1970. Defunciones y Causas de Muerte. Santiago, Chile. SNS (July). Pp. 1-92.

---(1975a) Anuario 1974. Defunciones y Causas de Muerte. Santiago, Chile. SNS (July). Pp. 1-94 mimeo.

---(1975b) Anuario 1974. Nacimientos. Santiago, Chile. SNS (July). Pp. 1-21.

---(1976a) Anuario 1975. Defunciones y Causas de Muerte. Santiago, Chile. SNS (July). Pp. 1-97 mimeo.

---(1976b) Anuario 1975. Enfermedades de Notificación Obligatoria. Santiago, Chile. SNS (July). Pp. 1-43.

---(1977) Anuario 1976. Atenciones y Recursos. Santiago, Chile. SNS (May). Pp. 1-63.

---(1978a) Anuario 1977. Atenciones y Recursos. Santiago, Chile. SNS (May). Pp. 1-69.

---(1978b) Anuario 1977. Nacimientos. Santiago, Chile. SNS (June). Pp. 1-23.

---(1978c) Anuario 1977. Defunciones y Causas de Muerte. Santiago, Chile. SNS (June). Pp. 1-129 mimeo.

---(1978d) Anuario 1977. Enfermedades de Notificación Obligatoria. Santiago, Chile. SNS (June). Pp. 1-66.

---(1978e) Anuarios 77. Accidentes del Trabajo y Enfermedades Profesionales. Santiago, Chile. Departamento de Planificación. Ministerio de Salud (November). Pp. 1-19.

SOLBERG, CARL (1970) Immigration and Nationalism. Argentina and Chile, 1890-1914. Austin and London. The University of Texas Press.

SOMOZA, JORGE and ODETTE TACLA (1966) La Mortalidad en Chile Según las Tablas de Vida de 1920, 1930, 1940, 1952-1960. Santiago, Chile. CELADE. A No. 17. Pp. 1-39. Reprinted also in Chile, Serie I, N° 1. Santiago, Chile. CELADE, 1969. Pp. 255-285.

SOTO, ZAIDA (1978) América Latina: Actividades Desarrolladas por los Programas de Planificación de la Familia, 1976. Santiago, Chile. CELADE, Serie A, N° 163 (November). Pp. 1-69.

SPOTTKE, ALBERTO (1965) Estimaciones y Proyecciones Mediante Interpolación y Extrapolación de los Datos Censales Corregidos de la Población Ocupada a Mediados de Cada Año, 1940-1970. Santiago, Chile. CORFO.

SSS (Servicio de Seguro Social) (1958) Estadísticas 1952-1956. Santiago, Chile. SSS. Pp. 1-245.

---(1959) Estadísticas 1957-1959. Santiago, Chile. SSS. Pp. 1-157.

---(1960) Estadísticas 1960. Santiago, Chile. SSS. Pp. 1-94.

---(1961) Estadísticas 1961. Santiago, Chile. SSS. Pp. 1-100.

---(1962) Estadísticas 1962. Santiago, Chile. SSS. Pp. 1-98.

---(1963) Estadísticas 1963. Santiago, Chile. SSS. Pp. 1-99.

---(1964) Estadísticas 1964. Santiago, Chile. SSS. Pp. 1-100.

---(1965) Estadísticas 1965. Santiago, Chile. SSS. Pp. 1-110.

---(1967) Estadísticas 1967. Santiago, Chile. SSS. Pp. 1-110.

---(1968) Estadísticas 1968. Santiago, Chile. SSS. Pp. 1-112.

---(1969) Estadísticas 1969. Santiago, Chile. SSS. Pp. 1-114.

---(1970) Estadísticas 1970. Santiago, Chile. SSS. Pp. 23-90.

---(1971) Estadísticas 1971. Santiago, Chile. SSS. Pp. 1-112.

---(1972) Estadísticas 1972. Santiago, Chile. SSS. Pp. 1-102.

---(1973) Estadísticas 1973. Santiago, Chile. SSS. Pp. 1-100.

---(1974-75) Estadísticas 1974-1975. Santiago, Chile. SSS. Pp. 1-114.

---(1976) Estadísticas 1976. Santiago, Chile. SSS. Pp. 1-89.

SUPERINTENDENCIA DE SEGURIDAD SOCIAL (1977) Costo de la Seguridad Social Chilena. Santiago de Chile. Superintendencia de Seguridad Social. Pp. 1-27.

TACLA CHAMY, ODETTE (1975) Panorama Demográfico de Chile y Su Evolución en el Presente Siglo. Santiago, Chile. INE. Pp. 1-47.

TACLA CHAMY, ODETTE and JOSÉ M. PUJOL (1965) Chile: Tablas Abreviadas de Mortalidad, 1952-1953 y 1960-1961. Santiago, Chile. CELADE, C Nº 11. Pp. 1-46.

TAUCHER, ERICA (1975) Estudio de Casos, Chile, Sistema de Estadísticas de Servicio Para un Programa Maternoinfantil. Santiago, Chile. CELADE (September). Pp. 1-52.

---(1978a) Chile: Mortalidad desde 1955 a 1975. Tendencias y Causas. Santiago, Chile. CELADE (September). Pp. 1-83.

---(1978b) La Mortalidad en Chile desde 1955 a 1975: Tendencias y Causas. Notas de Población. Revista Latinoamericana de Demografía. San José, Costa Rica. Año VI, Nº 18 (December). Pp. 113-142.

UN (1950) Economic and Social Council. La Inmigración en Chile. E/CN 12/169/Add 2. New York, U.N.

---(1965) Demographic Yearbook 1964. New York. U.N.

---(1966) Demographic Yearbook 1965. New York. U.N.

---(1967) Demographic Yearbook 1966. New York. U.N.

---(1968) Demographic Yearbook 1967. New York. U.N.

---(1969a) Demographic Yearbook 1968. New York. U.N.

---(1969b) Principles and Recommendations for the 1970 Population Censuses. Second Printing with changes of a non-substantive nature. Statistical Papers Series M. No. 44. U.N. (July). Pp. 1-83.

---(1970) Demographic Yearbook 1969. New York. U.N.

---(1971a) Demographic Yearbook 1970. New York. U.N.

---(1971b) Indexes to the International Standard Industrial Classification of All Economic Activities. Statistical Papers Series M. No. 4, Rev. 2, Add 1. Indexed Edition. New York. U.N. (March). Pp. 1-247.

---(1972) Demographic Yearbook 1971. New York. U.N.

---(1973) Demographic Yearbook 1972. New York. U.N.

---(1974) Demographic Yearbook 1973. New York. U.N.

---(1975) Demographic Yearbook 1974. New York. U.N.

---(1976a) Demographic Yearbook 1975. New York. U.N.

---(1976b) Yearbook of Industrial Statistics (formerly The Growth of World Industry) 1974 Edition. Volume 1. General Industrial Statistics. ST/ESA/STAT/SER. P/12 (Vol. 1). New York. U.N. (May). Pp. 1-661.

---(1976c) Yearbook of National Accounts Statistics 1975. Volume 1 Individual Country Data. ST/ESA/STAT/SER. 0/5. New York. U.N. (July). Pp. 1-924.

---(1977) Demographic Yearbook 1976. New York. U.N.

UNIVERSITY OF CHILE (1974) Encuesta de Fecundidad en Santiago. Santiago, Chile. Universidad de Chile. Departamento de Salud Pública y Medicina Social. Pp. 1-145.

URÍZAR GARFIAZ, FERNANDO (1835) Repertorio Chileno. Santiago, Chile. Imprenta Araucana.

---(1845) Estadística de la República de Chile. Provincia de Maule. Tomo I. Santiago, Chile. Imprenta de los Tribunales.

USA BUREAU OF THE CENSUS (1978) Chile. Country Demographic Profiles. Washington, D.C. Superindendent of Documents, U.S. Government Printing Office (February). Pp. 1-20.

ABOUT THE AUTHOR

Markos J. Mamalakis, Professor of Economics at the University of Wisconsin-Milwaukee, has specialized in the study of economic development and Latin American economic history. Among his earlier publications are *Essays on Chilean Economy* (co-author) and *The Growth and Structure of the Chilean Economy: From Independence to Allende.*

PART I
POPULATION

1
POPULATION

The human resources of a nation provide the base for as well as the object of analysis of all social sciences. All academic disciplines have as their ultimate goal the improvement of the welfare of the population of a nation and of the world and relate, directly or indirectly, to people. An understanding, therefore, of the evolution of the population is a necessary precondition for social, political and economic decision making and planning, whether it refers to the present, short-, medium- or long-run.

The demographic profile of a nation includes such features as age, sex, education, labor force, health, births and deaths and so forth. Most of these features will be examined in subsequent chapters of this volume. In the present chapter is examined primarily the total population of Chile. A thorough understanding of this variable is important, among others, because per capita income, the most widely used indicator of the level and change in the economic welfare of a nation is calculated by dividing the value of all goods and services produced within a geographic region by population.[1]

POPULATION, 1835-2000

The population of Chile between 1835 and 1977 and projections up to the year 2000 are presented in Table 1.1. The area of Chile, population and density during census years from 1835 to 1970 and the population of Chile's twelve regions in 1970 are presented in Table 1.2. Total population figures are also presented in Table 3.3 of Chapter 3.

Even though all the population figures published in the present book have been elaborated by the National Institute of Statistics (the name of this office has changed over time), they display differences which are usually small. These differences reveal the fact that completely accurate, final historical population figures do not exist as yet and that even the latest estimates are likely to change as more demographic research on such population determinants as births, deaths and international migration is undertaken.

With a surface of 2,006,626 square kilometers (km^2), which includes 1,250,000 km^2 of Chilean Antarctic Territory, Chile occupies the southern region of the Andean system which dominates the western coast of South America.

The best descriptions of the demographic problems of Chile for the period since the Spanish conquest can be found in: Servicio Nacional de Estadística y Censos, "Reseña de la Historia Censal del País," XII Censo

---

[1]For an examination of the relationship between population and income growth in Chile over time see (Mamalakis: 1976d, chapter 1 and 1978c).

TABLE 1.1

Total Population, Chile, 1835-1975 and Projections, 1975-2000.
(Thousands of Inhabitants)[1]

Year	Population	Year	Population	Year	Population
1835	1,010[2]	1921	3,853	1962	7,961
1843	1,083	1922	3,907	1963	8,147
1854	1,439	1923	3,961	1964	8,330
1865	1,819	1924	4,017	1965	8,510
1875	2,076	1925	4,073	1966	8,686
1885	2,492[3]	1926	4,130	1967	8,859
1886	2,509	1927	4,188	1968	9,030
1887	2,539	1928	4,246	1969	9,199
1888	2,569	1929	4,305	1970	9,369
1889	2,600	1930	4,365	1971	9,539
1890	2,631	1931	4,429	1972	9,712
1891	2,662	1932	4,495	1973	9,888
1892	2,693	1933	4,563	1974	10,068
1893	2,725	1934	4,631	1975	10,253
1894	2,758	1935	4,700	1976	10,443
1895	2,790[3]	1936	4,771	1977	10,639
1896	2,823	1937	4,842	1978	10,840
1897	2,857	1938	4,914	1979	11,047
1898	2,890	1939	4,988	1980	11,260
1899	2,925	1940	5,063	1981	11,477
1900	2,959	1941	5,149	1982	11,699
1901	2,994	1942	5,244	1983	11,924
1902	3,030	1943	5,341	1984	12,153
1903	3,066	1944	5,440	1985	12,384
1904	3,102	1945	5,541	1986	12,617
1905	3,139	1946	5,643	1987	12,851
1906	3,176	1947	5,748	1988	13,085
1907	3,213[3]	1948	5,854	1989	13,320
1908	3,253	1949	5,962	1990	13,553
1909	3,294	1950	6,091	1991	13,787
1910	3,336	1951	6,252	1992	14,019
1911	3,378	1952	6,378	1993	14,251
1912	3,421	1953	6,493	1994	14,483
1913	3,465	1954	6,612	1995	14,714
1914	3,509	1955	6,743	1996	14,945
1915	3,553	1956	6,889	1997	15,176
1916	3,598	1957	7,048	1998	15,405
1917	3,644	1958	7,220	1999	15,631
1918	3,690	1959	7,400	2000	15,850
1919	3,737	1960	7,585		
1920	3,785[3]	1961	7,773		

Notes and Methodology: 1. Except for the census years, the figures of this table are estimates for June 30 each year prepared by the Section of Analysis and Measurement of Population of the National Institute of Statistics. To obtain the population year by year, the geometric annual intercensus rate of increase of the population was calculated. The formula used for this calculation was the following:

$$P_t = P_o(1+i)^t$$

where: P_t = population of the ultimate census, P_o = population of the preceding census, t = time that has intervened between censuses, i = annual geometric rate of increase.

2. The census of 1835 was initiated in 1834 and completed in the year 1835.

3. The censuses of 1885, 1895, 1907 and 1920 do not include the population of territories which in reality were not Chilean.

TABLE 1.1 (Cont'd)
Total Population, Chile, 1835-1975 and Projections, 1975-2000.
(Thousands of Inhabitants)[1]

Source: The information for the period 1885-1949 was obtained from DEC, Población Total por Provincias. Chile. 1885-1960 (Santiago, Chile: 1964), Table 3, pp. 4-10. The information for the five census years before 1885 was obtained from DEC, XIII Censo de Población, 29 de Noviembre de 1960. Serie A. Resumen del País (Santiago, Chile: DEC, 1968?), Table 1, p. 14. It is worth mentioning that the population figures for the census years 1885, 1895, 1907, 1920, 1930 and 1940 presented in (DEC: 1960b, 14) are slightly different from those presented in Table 1.1. The population figures for the period between 1950 and 2000, which are also discussed in the chapter on projections, were obtained from (ODEPLAN: 1975a, p. 25, Table 7).

TABLE 1.2

Area, Population, and Density by Census and Actual Regions. 1835-1970.

Census and Region	Area (km^2)	Population	Density (inhabitants per sq. kilometer)
	1,823,247.34[1]		
1835	573,247.00[2]	1,010,336	1.8
1843		1,083,801	1.9
1854		1,439,120	2.5
1865		1,819,223	3.2
1875		2,075,971	3.6
	2,006,626.34[1]		
1885	756,626.00[2]	2,507,005	3.3
1895		2,695,625	3.6
1907		3,231,022	4.3
1920		3,730,235	4.9
1930		4,287,445	5.7
1940		5,023,539	6.6
1952		5,932,995	7.8
1960		7,374,115	9.7
	2,006,626.34[1]		4.4[1]
1970	756,626.00[2]	8,884,768	11.7
I Tarapacá	58,072.70	174,981	3.0
II Antofagasta	125,306.30	251,906	2.0
III Atacama	78,267.50	152,616	1.9
IV Coquimbo	39,647.00	340,215	8.6
V Aconcagua	16,378.20	967,369	59.1
VI Of the Liberator General Bernardo O'Higgins	17,963.60	495,339	27.6
VII Maule	30,518.10	619,130	30.3
VIII Bío-Bío	36,007.24	1,253,345	34.8
IX Of the Araucania	32,471.80	599,899	18.5
X Of the Lakes	69,039.20	748,262	10.8
XI Aisén of General Carlos Ibañez del Campo	107,153.40	49,197	0.5
XII Magallanes and Chilean Antarctic	1,382,033.50	89,443	0.1
Metropolitan Region	13,807.80	3,143,066	227.6

Notes: 1. It includes the Antarctic Territory.
2. It excludes the Antarctic Territory and population densities are calculated with this area.

Source: National Institute of Statistics.

General de la Población y I de Vivienda, I (Santiago, Chile: Empresa Periodística "Gutenberg," 1956), pp. 11-46. This review of census history was written by Rolando Mellafe; Rolando Mellafe "Problemas Demográficos e Historia Colonial Hispanoamericana, Temas de História Económica Hispanoamericana, Colección Nova Americana, No. 1, pp. 45-55, Paris, 1956; Eugenio Pereira Salas, CORFO, "El Desenvolvimiento Histórico-Etnico de la Población," Geografía Económica de Chile (Santiago, Chile: CORFO, 1965) pp. 337-356; and Miguel Cruchaga, Estudio sobre la Organización Económica y la Hacienda Pública de Chile, I (Madrid: Editorial Reus, 1929), pp. 457-540. For an excellent brief summary of demographic trends and developments in the twentieth century see Odette Tacla Chamy, Panorama Demográfico de Chile y su Evolución en el Presente Siglo (Santiago, Chile: INE, 1975), pp. 1-46.

Population Estimates: From the Conquest to the Census of 1835

Like most other Latin American countries, Chile lacks reliable demographic information for the Indian and colonial periods. It appears that there were about one million Indians in Chile at the time of the Spanish conquest. It should be born in mind, however, that the estimated range is from 400,000 to 1,500,000. This Indian population was concentrated in the central part of Chile. Overall, there were four main Indian groups, according to the Geografía Económica de Chile: the Mapuches, between the Bío-Bío and Tolten rivers; the Pecunches in the north; the Behuenches in the Andes region, and the Huilliches, from the Cale-Calle river to the Corcovado Gulf.

There are two broad categories of deficiencies in all population estimates during the colonial period. First, most estimates were, at best, approximations based on the registrations in the parishes and in the municipalities (cabildos) which were not always accurate. The social composition of the colony and the semi-permanent state of war made it possible to have large segments of the population completely unaffiliated. Second, there were no uniform methods for census taking in the various parts of the country; classification varied widely, particularly those relating to ethnic groups.

It should be added here that during the XVII century and part of the XVIII century some primitive census operations called visits (visitas) were realized in the corregimientos of the country, that is, in the basic administrative units of that time. These "visitas" are rather incomplete and inefficient for demographic projects. However, some successful attempts have been made to utilize them, as for example in Rolando Mellafe and Julio Morales, Migraciones rurales en Chile del Siglo XVII (Santiago, Chile: CELADE, April 1975), LS/5.

At a more specific level, first, population estimates for the colonial period were based on the concept of neighbor or vecino. This implied both property ownership and the existence of a head of the family. Secondly, most surveys of the Indian population have counted only the head of the family. This necessitates multiplying the figures, either by 4, assuming a nuclear family (man, woman and two children), or by 20 assuming an extended kinship group. Since the population estimates give no clue as to what kind of head of family is being counted, the estimates of the Indian population are unreliable. Third, estimates of the Indian population made by religious authorities attempted to count only Christian Indians; in fact, they counted merely a limited amount of both Christians and non-Christians. And fourth, there is no account of internal migrations of Indians or Mestizos.

In addition to the study by Mellafe (1972) described in the chapter on internal migration, useful for the study of Chilean population history is Juan Contreras Arias, Eugenio Flores Marambio, Inés Herrera Canales, Leonardo Mazzei Degrazia, Arístides Rivera Navarro and Rodia Romero Sepúlveda, Fuentes para un estudio de demografía histórica de Chile en el siglo XVIII (Santiago, Chile: CELADE, 1972).

For making estimates of various structural aspects of demography in the colonial epoch, the most useful documentation is found in the parish registers of baptisms, marriages and deaths. These are very useful documents in spite of their obvious underregistration of deaths. Some Chilean parishes have continued documentation since the middle of the XVII century. A chronological description and listing of the locations where these documents can be found is provided by Raúl Díaz Vial, "La situación de los libros parroquiales", Revista de Estudios Históricos, No. 10, 1962, pp. 109-122; Iván Larrain Eyzaguirre, La parroquia ante el derecho civil chileno (Santiago,

Chile: 1956); Arístides Rivera Navarro, Juan Contreras Arias, Rodia Romero Sepúlveda and Eugenio Flores Marambio, "Prospección de las Fuentes Demográficas de la Provincia de Chiloé, 1567-1826" mimeographed version, Instituto Central de Historia, Universidad de Concepción, 1972, pp. 1-92; and René Salinas Meza and Robert McCaa "La documentación histórica-demográfica del 'Norte Chico', Chile" mimeographed, no date or place of publication, pp. 1-34 with both of the last two references published in Fuentes para la demografía histórica en America Latina (Mexico: CLACSO-CELADE, Comisión de Historia Económica, 1975) with introduction and coordination by Rolando Mellafe. Highly useful background information is contained in Robert McCaa, "Chilean Social and Demographic History: Sources, Issues, and Methods," The Latin American Research Review, Vol. XIII, Number 2, 1978, pp. 104-126 and in René Salinas Meza, "Fuentas para el Estudio de la Demografía Histórica en el Norte Chico Chileno (1600-1854)", The Latin American Research Review, Vol. XIII, Number 2, 1978, pp. 98-103.

The statistical elaboration of these is very risky, complex and uncertain. Various scholars have attempted such elaborations but up to now only a few studies have provided reliable results. Among others it is possible to cite René Salinas Meza, La población de Valparaíso en la segunda mitad del siglo XVIII (Valparaíso: Universidad Catolica, 1970) as well as (Arretx and others: 1976a; 1976b; 1977b) and Carmen Arretx, Armando De Romón, Rolando Mellafe, René Salinas and Jorge L. Somoza, Preliminary Report on Nupciality, Fertility and Mortality, Based on Histories of Chilean Families (mimeo), Santiago, Chile, 1977, pp. 1-44.

The most comprehensive educated guesses of the population of Chile between 1540 and 1620 were made by Rolando Mellafe and are presented in Table 1.3. The Mellafe estimates do not differ significantly from those made by Angel Rosemblat and presented in Table 1.4 but they are more detailed than those of Rosemblat.

Angel Rosemblat has given some population estimates for the earlier part of the colonial period in La Población Indígena y el Mestizaje en América, I, pp. 88, 59.

Ann Louise Hagerman Johnson has made a number of corrections and adjustments to the population figures of Chile from 1700 to 1895 in an effort to eliminate previous territorial, ethnic or categorical inconsistencies. The Hagerman Johnson figures are presented in Table 1.5.

The first general census undertaken in Chile was completed in 1778. Only the results for the Bishopric of Santiago, which extended from the Atacama desert to the Maule river, are available, as follows:

Whites	190,919
Negroes	25,508
Mestizos	20,651
Indians	22,568

In 1784, the Governor of Chiloé, Francisco Hurtado estimated the population of the province of Chiloé and surroundings, which at that time extended from Río Bueno to Cabo de Hornos, as follows:

Whites	15,076
Mestizos & Indians	11,627
	26,703

In 1791, Governor Ambrosio O'Higgins persuaded the ecclesiastical authorities to undertake a new census, which reported a population of 203,732 inhabitants for the Bishopric of Santiago and 104,114 for that of Concepción. The latter extended at that time from the Maule to the Valdivia rivers. In 1793, recount of the population in the Bishopric of Concepción reported 118,707 Christian inhabitants. These censuses reported only the "civilized" or "Christian" inhabitants of Chile. Therefore, Governor O'Higgins ordered a partial census of the non-Christian Indian population in the Araucanía. This census reported a population of 95,504 Indians. The population estimates for the 1778-1796 period are taken from (SNE: 1956, 16-17).

According to these figures, the combined population for the Bishoprics of Santiago and Concepción was 307,846 in 1791. This represented a decline for Santiago of 21.5% from the 1778 figures. The 1793 figures for Concepción on the other hand, represent a 14.0% increase over the 1791 figures. Since there is no evidence of massive population movements in the 1778-93 period, these differences among the three surveys should be taken as indicators of the inexactitude of these estimates. Taking the most updated population estimates, that is, 1784 for Chiloé, 1791 for Santiago, 1793 for Concepción, and 1796 for the Araucanía, one can calculate the counted population of Chile by the end of the eighteenth century at around 450,000 inhabitants. The real population may have been closer to 600,000. The Chilean Statistical and Census Bureau estimates that, of these, 350,000 were pure Indians, 160,000 were Mestizos (with

TABLE 1.3

Population of Chile Between 1540 and 1620.
Mellafe Estimates.

Years	Neighbors,[1] Spaniards and Europeans	White Mestizos	Blacks or Coloured Mestizos	Indians[2] Under National Jurisdiction	Indian[3] Population Outside National Jurisdiction	Total
1540	154		10		1,000,000	1,000,164
1570	7,000	10,000	7,000	450,000	150,000	624,000
1590	9,000	17,000	16,000	420,000	120,000	582,000
1600	10,000	20,000	19,000	230,000	270,000	549,000
1620	15,000	40,000	22,000	230,000	250,000	557,000

Notes: 1. Neighbors, Spaniards and Europeans is my translation of Rolando Mellafe's term "vecinos, españoles, europeos y criollos".

2. Indians under national domination is the English translation by Ann Louise Hagerman Johnson of Rolando Mellafe's Spanish term "Indios de Paz en encomiendas y otros". I have used the term Indians under national jurisdiction in the table because, I believe, it reflects more accurately the legal meaning of the term.

3. Indian population outside national jurisdiction is my English translation of Rolando Mellafe's term "Indios rebelados". Hagerman Johnson's translation is "Population of Araucanía outside national domination".

Source: Rolando Mellafe, La Introducción de la Esclavitud Negra en Chile. Tráfico y Rutas (Santiago, Chile: Universidad de Chile, 1959), p. 226.

TABLE 1.4

Population in 1570 and 1650.
Rosemblat Estimates.

Year	Whites	Negroes	Mestizos	Mulattoes	Indians	Total
1570	10,000		10,000		600,000	620,000
1650	15,000	5,000	8,000	2,000	520,000	550,000

Source: Extracted from Servicio Nacional de Estadística y Censos, XII Censo General de la Población y I de Vivienda, I (Santiago, Chile: Empresa Periodística "Gutenberg," 1956), pp. 14-17.

TABLE 1.5

The Population of Chile, 1700-1895, with Reference to Its Ethnic and Geographic Components. Hagerman Johnson Adjustments.

Year	Total Given Population	"Whites"	"Castas"	Indians Under National Domination	Population of Araucanía Outside National Domination	Population of Norte Grande	Adjusted National Population
1700	590,000	25,000	100,000	215,000	235,000	-	575,000
1790	600,000	50,000	200,000	160,000	190,000	10,000	610,000
1813	660,000	521,175		80,000	150,000	10,000	761,176
1835	1,010,336	1,010,335		1	150,000	10,000	1,170,336
1854	1,439,120	1,439,120		1	150,000	20,000	1,609,120
1875	2,075,971	2,075,971		1	109,500	50,000	2,235,471
1895	2,695,625	2,695,625		1	22,500	-	2,728,125

Notes: 1. Included in "Whites"-"Castas" population.

Source: Ann Louise Hagerman Johnson, 1978, 620.

the White element predominant), 40,000 were Negroes or Mulattoes and 50,000 were Whites (Spaniards or Creoles).

The population figures and estimates for the 1784, 1791, 1793 and 1796 population censuses or estimates are not totally reliable. There exist various distinct copies of these censuses, prepared during that period, each giving a different number for total population. Useful background information on this matter is provided by Marcello Carmagnani and Herbert S. Klein, "Demografía histórica: la población del obispado de Santiago, 1777-78," Boletín de la Academia Chilena de la Historia, No. 72, 1965, pp. 54-74, and by Luis Lira Montt Padrones del reino de Chile existentes en el Archivo de Indias," Revista de Estudios Históricos, No. 13, 1965, pp. 85-88.

About the population of Chile in the XVIII century and the first decades of the next there is available the estimate prepared by Marcello Carmagnani, "Colonial Latin American Demography: Growth of Chilean Population, 1700-1830," Journal of Social History, No. 1, 1967, pp. 179-91. However, according to Rolando Mellafe, the average annual population increase of 1.8 percent which Carmagnani obtains is unacceptably high while the method and sources used by him are insufficient.

The National Congress of 1811 ordered a general census whose implementation was interrupted by the Desastre de Rancagua. Only partial results are available for the 1813 census which was published as Censo de 1813, levantado por Juan Egaña de Orden de la Junta de Gobierno, formada por los señores Peres, Infante y Eyzaguirre. Santiago, Chile, 1953. The Bishopric of Santiago (without the city of Santiago, which was not surveyed at all) was reported to have a population of 295,528. There are two sets of figures for the population of Concepción in 1813, and no way of determining which one was more accurate. Estimating the population of the city of Santiago from the surveys of 1779, 1835, 1843 and 1854 at 60,000, then the total population of Chile, according to the lower figures for Concepción, was 646,848, and, according to the higher Concepción figures, it was 681,866.

THE CHILEAN CENSUSES

Chile has the largest series of data on population movements of all the Latin American countries. There have been fourteen censuses: 1831-35, 1843, 1854, 1865, 1875, 1885, 1895, 1907, 1920, 1930, 1940, 1952, 1960 and 1970.

The first general census of Chile was taken in two parts. In 1831, the provinces of Chiloé, Valdivia, Concepción and Maule and the department of Santiago were surveyed. In 1835, Talca, Colchagua, Aconcagua, Coquimbo and the districts of Santiago not surveyed in 1831 were included in the census. The population of the country, according to the 1831-35 census, was 1,010,332.

The 1831 (1831-1835) population census results are given by sex and marital status, for departments and provinces in Repertorio Chileno, (Santiago, Chile: Imprenta Araucana, 1835) published by Fernando Urízar Garfíaz, the official in charge of the census operation. Total population is given for departments and provinces for the 1843 census by Vicente Pérez Rosales, Ensayo sobre Chile, Trans. Manuel Miguel, (Santiago: Imprenta del Ferrocarril, 1959). More detailed data of the 1843 census but only for the province of Maule were published by Fernando Urizar Garfiaz, Estadística de la República de Chile. Provincia de Maule. Tomo I (Santiago, Chile: Imprenta de los Tribunales, 1845).

The second census was carried out in 1843 over the whole country. This work constitutes only one page of paper and one summary table without any specifications concerning the distribution of population in the districts, subdelegations, departments and provinces. The reported population was 1,083,801, an increase of 73,469 or 7.3%. The "Reseña de la Historia Censal del País," (SNE: 1956, 22,24) estimates at least a 10% error for each of these censuses.

No correction was ever made of the census of 1843 primarily because Chilean demographers wanted to undertake a more careful study of the problem. Mellafe now believes that the actual error is more than 10 percent and that the magnitude of this omission tends to diminish to the extent that the censuses are closer to the 1970 one. The problem of the colonial censuses as well as of all undertaken in the XIX century is that part of what seems as natural population growth is in reality an increase in the area covered by the census together with a decline in omission due to improved census techniques. Therefore, it is always very risky to compute the average annual growth or inter-census rate of increase. This is very important at least until the 1865 census. For more on this issue see Carmen Miró Algunos problemas relativos a la evolución de los resultados de los censos de población, Santiago de Chile, 1963 and Carmen Miró, La Población de America Latina en el Siglo XX, Santiago de Chile, 1965. It is important to take this into account when using the population figures and rates of growth of Andrew O. Collver, Birth Rates in Latin America: New Estimates of Historical Trends and Fluctuations, Berkeley, Institute of International Studies, University of California, Berkeley, 1965, or of E. A. Arriaga, New Life Tables for Latin American Populations in the Nineteenth and Twentieth Centuries, Berkeley, California, 1968.

The corrected figures would indicate that the population of the country was as follows:

1835	1,111,370
1843	1,192,181
Total Increase	80,811
% Increase	7.3%

In 1853, President Manuel Bulnes issued the Census Law which mandated that the country take a decennial census. There were five decennial censuses altogether in this first series: 1854, 1865, 1875, 1885 and 1895.

The operational deficiencies of this first series of five decennial censuses, from 1854 to 1895, can be summarized as follows:

1. Clear criteria to distinguish rural and urban areas were not developed until the 1907 census. Hence the 1854-95 censuses and, in particular, those prior to 1875, failed to classify large numbers of small and intermediate towns as either urban or rural, even though their inhabitants were included in the total population of the departments or provinces

2. In the censuses of 1854, 1865 and 1875, no provisions were made to count the male population engaged in seasonal work in the more remote areas; therefore, there were great differences in population by sex in several regions of the country which were apparent, not real; the 1854 census suffered from the highest rate of delinquency, as women sent their husbands into hiding, fearing higher taxes or military conscription

3. The determination of age was left up to the discretion of the census taker and was one of the less reliable items in this entire series of censuses

4. The question regarding civil state (married, single, etc.) made no allowances for counting persons in common law unions; this was a failure of all five censuses between 1854 and 1895

5. Occupations were computed alphabetically, as reported individually by the census takers; it was not until the 1875 census that categories were formed out of those occupations which, although reported under different names, were essentially the same; and it was not until the 1895 census that the 200

occupations were reduced to 26 basic occupational groups; furthermore, none of these censuses developed uniform criteria for the registering of these occupations; and

6. Place of birth (nacimiento) and country of citizenship (nacionalidad) were often confused when many assumed that the latter referred to their province of birth.

The structural problems or deficiencies of this first series of five decennial censuses, from 1854 to 1895, were those arising out of specific political circumstances or legal obstacles which surrounded the promulgation of each census law. They were as follows:

1. The annexation of the provinces of Tacna, Tarapacá and Antofagasta altered the figures for the censuses between 1885 and 1920 and were not fully adjusted;

2. The Indians were not included until the 1885 and 1895 censuses, and even then they were only partially counted. Only the Indians living in cities and their suburbs were counted. The Indians living in the countryside or even the Chileans found among them for commercial reasons on the day of the census were not included;

3. The war of 1879 and the revolution of 1891 brought about economic changes, social conflicts and migrations which must be taken into account when evaluating the 1885 and 1895 censuses; and

4. The results of the 1875 and 1885 censuses were falsified for electoral purposes, particularly in the latter which added as many as 90,000 non-existent inhabitants to the figures for the total population of the country. Corrections of the provincial and departmental sub-totals would require a comparative demographic regional study of that period in the light of the denunciations of census frauds which were made to the National Congress and to the Ministry of the Interior at that time.

However, according to Rolando Mellafe, the population recorded by the census was reduced for many departments so that it could be increased for political-electoral purposes in other departments, in such a way that the figure given for the total inhabitants of the country may be correct. In other words, the error would be exclusively in the spatial distribution of the population.

The information for the 1854-95 censuses, like that for the two previous ones, was gathered by the departmental statistical bureaus which did not have any technical assistants who specialized in census preparation or census taking. The only national coordination at this stage was provided by the general directives of the Ministry of the Interior. The tabulation, ordering and presentation of the census results, however, was in the hands of the National Statistical and Census Bureau which corrected, insofar as possible, the major inconsistencies in the local operations.

The basic items in all the censuses were: personal identification, sex, age, civil status, occupation, degree of education, nationality and physical defects. Besides the development of a census taking tradition, among the strong points of these censuses, one must cite the use of extensive preliminary studies, including sampling methods, and the attempts at maintaining some statistical continuity through demographic predictions.

The 1854 census was the third general one for Chile. Its goal was to provide information for public administration and mainly for the determination of seats for Congressional deputies per district, according to population.

The point of departure was the person's residence. This census was the first one to try to establish an equivalence between religious and civil inscriptions in an effort to move away from the custom of using religious parishes. Although this method was far from successful, the trend was begun when the enabling law ordered the establishment of census districts. The 1854 census was still taken and published (the total population was reported to be 1,439,069) according to parish districts. It was the 1865 census which was the first in which there was a total and definitive change to civil districts.

According to Collver (1965), the growth rate indicated by the difference between the census of 1854 and 1865 is much higher than the rate of growth after 1865. Although some of the difference may be due to immigration, there is no independent evidence of any such substantial migration. Pending the discovery of such evidence, Collver has therefore calculated that the 1854 census understated the population by 8.5%. Such an adjustment would give a population of 1,516,387 for 1854. Taking, then, the corrected figures for the 1843 and the 1854 censuses, we can calculate a population increase of 324,206 or 27.2%. This rate of growth appears still to be too high, but it is the best approximation available.

The fourth census was carried out in 1865. Cruchaga tells us that because of bad weather conditions in parts of the country on the day of the census, the inaccessibility of certain remote places, and the unwillingness of many Araucanos to be counted, the census figure of a population of 1,819,223 may have been underestimated by 10%. There was a registered increase of 380,156 or 26.4% over the raw figures of the 1843 census; using the Collver adjustment for the 1854 figures, the increase was 302,836 or 20.0%. The census was carried out by provinces. This was the first census which employed the techniques of demographic cartography and whose aim was to develop demographic maps of Chile and of each of the provinces. The 1865 census adopted various demographic techniques employed in Europe and which were particularly recommended by the Belgian Jacobo Quetelet in Lay de Vitalidad and in Teoría del Hombre Medio.

The fifth general census was raised in 1875. The population reported was 2,075,971, an increase of 256,748 or 14.1%. Since the counting of the Araucanos remained inadequate, Cruchaga suggests that the real total population may have been underestimated by 7%. The demographic map of Chile had to be adjusted to include the newly colonized territories of Angol and Magallanes. The main scientific principles for this census were drawn from Armando Pissis' Geografía Física de Chile.

The 1885 census reported a population of 2,507,005, an increase of 431,034 or 20.8% over the raw figures of the 1875 census. It was already mentioned before that the results of this census may be higher by at least 90,000 because of political considerations and fraud. Subtracting this amount, the population appears to be 2,417,005, with an increase of 341,034 or 16.4%. Collver indicates that the 1885 census returned a population which was 6% above the figure which would have been expected according to calculations based on the natural increase. Using this second suggested adjustment, the population would have been 2,356,585 with an increase of 307,244 or 14.8%. For the 1885 census, the demographic map of Chile had to be adjusted again to include the acquisition of the territories of Tacna (which was subsequently returned to Perú), Tarapacá and Antofagasta.

The 1895 census reported a population of 2,695,625, an increase of 188,620 or 7.5% over the 1885 raw census figures. Using the first set of corrected 1885 figures (subtracting 90,000) the increase is 278,620 or 11.5%. Using the second set of corrected figures (Collver, subtracting 6%), the increase is 339,040 or 14.4%. The questionnaire of the 1895 census was expanded to include not only the same questions as the previous censuses but also new questions inquiring about the citizenship of the sons of immigrants and about religion. The 1895 census adopted the recommendations of the Statistical Congress of St. Petersburg of 1872.

The First National Seminar on Population Statistics met in Santiago, Chile, from May 24 to July 1, 1954, under the auspices of the Inter-American Biostatistics Centre and of the Servicio Nacional de Estadística y Censos. Its Final Report (Document CIB: 1054:20:86) revised the figures for Chilean censuses since 1885. They did not adjust the census results prior to 1885, for their concern was centered on the more recent and less inaccurate period, which is also easier and more profitable to adjust. The 1885 figures were set at 2,492,000, a decrease of 15,005 or 0.6%. Under this third set of revised figures for this year (taking the 1875 figures unrevised as they are), the increase would have been 416,029 or 20.0%. It is this third set of corrected figures which appears in Table 1.1. The 1895 figures were revised upwards, for undernumeration, by 108,375 to 2,804,000. Using the Seminar's revised figures for 1885 and 1895, the increase by 1895 was 312,000 or 12.5%. The Seminar's belief was that the census programs for both 1885 and 1895 understated the real population of the country. The electoral fraud of 1885, which increased the population figures, has the effect of approximating more closely the real figures for the population of the country. Hence, a slight decrease in the 1885 figures and a substantial increase in the 1895 figures became the only necessary adjustments to obtain the real population figures for this decade.

The total population figures which appear in Tables 1.1, 1.2 and 3.3 are taken from different sources and, therefore, their usefulness varies accordingly. The information for the five census years 1835, 1843, 1854, 1865 and 1875, has not been revised in

TABLE 1.6

Total Population, Chile, 1570-1895, Revisions and Estimates.

	Population			Difference		% Growth	
Year	Estimates	Census	Revised	Census	Revised	Census	Revised
1570	620,000	-	-	-	-	-	-
1650	550,000	-	-	-	-	-	-
1800	600,000	-	-	-	-	-	-
1813	660,000	-	-	-	-	-	-
1835		1,010,332	1,111,370	-	-	-	-
1843		1,083,801	1,192,181	73,469	80,811	7.3	7.3
1854		1,439,067	1,516,387	355,319	324,206	32.8	27.2
1865		1,819,223	1,819,223	380,156	302,836	26.4	20.0
1875		2,075,971	2,075,971	256,748	256,748	14.1	14.1
1885		2,507,005	2,417,005[a]	431,034	341,034[a]	20.8	16.4[a]
		-	2,356,585[b]	-	307,244[b]	-	14.8[b]
		-	2,492,000[c]	-	416,029[c]	-	20.0[c]
1895		2,695,625	2,695,625	188,620	278,620[a]	7.5	11.5[a]
		-	2,695,625	-	359,040[b]	-	14.4[b]
		-	2,804,000[c]	-	312,000[c]	-	12.5[c]
		-	[1]2,790,000[d]	-	298,000[d]	-	12.0[d]

Notes: 1. These figures represent the population of the country as of June 30, 1895. Since the 1895 census was taken on November 28, the June 30 figure is but an operational adjustment of dates. These figures, however, are an adjustment from set c (2,804,000) which had undergone a substantive revision from the census figures (2,695,625).

Methodology and Sources: This is essentially a summary table. The 1570 and 1650 estimates are taken from: Angel Rosemblat, La Población Indígena y el Mestizaje en América, I, pp. 59, 88. These figures and those for 1800 and 1813 are found in (SNE: 1956, 14-17). The details concerning the compilation of the information for these estimates is presented in the main text of this chapter. The census figures for 1835-1895 were obtained from (SNE: 1956, 38). The census figures for 1835 and 1843 were revised by increasing them by 10%. The 1854 census figures were increased by 8.5%. There are three sets of corrected figures for 1885. The first, denoted by letter a, decreased the original figures by 90,000 or 4.4%; the second, denoted by letter b, decreased them by 150,420 or 6.0%; the third, denoted by letter c, decreased them by 15,005 or 0.6%. The 1895 figures were revised twice. The first revision, denoted by letter c, increased the figures by 4.0% or 108,375; the second, denoted by letter d, increased them by 94,375 or 3.5%. Letter c was the substantive revision. Letter d was merely the adjustment to the June 30 date. The census figures for 1865 and 1875 were not revised. The justification for these versions is found in the main text of this chapter. The source for the revisions of the census figures for the years 1835, 1843, 1885 (set a) and 1895 (set a) is SNE: 1956, 21-24, 30). The source for the revisions of the census figures for the years 1854, 1885 (set b) and 1895 (set b) is Collver (1965). The source for the 1895 revisions (set d) is found in Table 1.1. The difference and percentage for set d were calculated on the basis of 1885 set c which is also presented in Table 1.1. The differences between the figures of a given census or its revision and its immediate predecessor, or its revision were computed by the author. For example, the difference between the figures for the census of 1865 and those of 1854 are given in the raw of 1865, under "difference, c". Percentages were computed in relation to the previous census figures or their revisions. Hence they appear for the first time in the raw for 1843, based on the growth since 1835. Therefore

1. 1865 Difference c = 1865 Population c - 1854 Population c
2. 1865 % c = 1865 Difference c/1854 Population c
3. 1865 Difference R = 1865 Population R - 1854 Population R
4. 1865 % R = 1865 Difference R/1854 Population R

Whenever the figures for a given census were not revised, the census figures are repeated in the "revised" column. This occurs in 1865 and 1875. These figures are treated like the other revised figures to compute differences and percentages.

any way. Therefore, the preceding discussion must be born in mind--and caution exercised--when using them. The information beginning in 1885 has been substantially revised according to the recommendations of the First National Seminar on Population Statistics of 1954. The various sources are given in each table. However, Chilean censuses have been taken on different dates and at different times during the year. In order to make possible more accurate comparisons among different periods, the Dirección de Estadísticas has adjusted all the population figures since 1886 to a common date: June 30. The figures of Table 1.1 are as follows: up to 1885, they are not revised in any way and not adjusted to the June 30 date; the 1885 figures were revised according to the Population Seminar's recommendations, but not adjusted to the June 30 date; since 1886, the figures have been both substantially revised and operationally adjusted to June 30.

The reader should be aware, moreover, that only the total population figures have been revised. Many of the sub-components, including total population figures by province, have not been revised. Hence, caution is recommended in the use of these unrevised statistics.

In summary, the principle problems with the 1854-1895 censuses are enumeration difficulties (untrained enumerators, lack of administrative cartographs, dispersed and uneducated population, fraud, incorporation of new territories both in the North--Tarapacá and Antofagasta--and the Southern Frontier), quality of collected data (age: ignorance and information provided by second parties; marital status: common law unions not noted until 1952; occupation: no special attention to collecting accurate information), and published results (extraordinary, geographic and nationality detail, but no cross-classifications of demographic and social characteristics; occupation: no standards or continuity; place of birth data not published until 1952). Many censuses, however, are published in such detail that the researcher can go back and create his own groups.

A principle innovation in the twentieth century is that the bureau began to publish information on the enumeration process itself.

The first break in the decennial chain took place when no census could be carried out in 1905 because of administrative and economic difficulties. The 1907 census, however, became a landmark in Chilean demographic activities, serving as a model for future censuses. There was a long period of preparation preceding this census. Elaborate demographic maps were prepared to help the census takers; a preliminary housing census was carried out. The boundaries of census districts were revised. Clear criteria were at long last established to distinguish between urban and rural areas. The census takers received an intensive training course. Each provincial, departmental and municipal unit received extensive technical help. Enumeration schedules were made more complex in 1907; the enumerators used one sheet per house (where earlier the sheets were simply filled up with as many people as possible; one line per person). The enumerator had to fill out administrative details for each household instead of for every 20 people as in earlier censuses. Instructions were made much more explicit and enumerators encouraged to note the sex and marital status by letter codes. Specific instructions obliterated occupational differences which was unfortunate (e.g., "artesanos", "labradores", "empleados" without further indication). A question on "propiedad raiz" was also added. Steps were taken to count the entire Indian population. Therefore, most of the defects of the censuses of the nineteenth century were corrected. These healthier practices were maintained and improved in subsequent censuses.

There was no census in 1917 because Chile signed the statement of the Fourth Inter-American Conference (1910) which recommended that all the American states should take a census in 1920. The decennial pattern was reestablished thereafter. The 1930 census had to renew the entire work on demographic maps in order to conform to the new provisions of the Constitution of 1925. The 1952 census was the first Chilean census to follow the continental criteria for censuses established by the Inter-American demographic organisms and summarized in the Minimo Censal Interamericano. The effect of these international recommendations has been to make it possible to compare the census results among various Latin American countries.

Chile's First National Seminar on Population Statistics of 1954 reached the conclusion that censuses may show errors amounting to 5%, that approximately 5% of live births are not registered, and that about 1% of the deaths may escape registration. As indicated earlier, these errors have been corrected by the Chilean Statistical and Census Bureau and these revised figures have been included in Tables 1.1, 1.2 and 3.3. These revisions increased the registration of minors up to two years of age by 9.5% for the 1938-51 period and by 5% for the 1952-60 period. The effect of these revisions is to indicate that Chile's population growth since 1930 has been much greater than had been previously estimated. Writings prior to the 1954 Population Seminar consistently underestimated the population of the country. For example, Juan Crocco Ferrari, Ensayos sobre la Población Chilena, Memoria en Economía (Santiago, Chile: Universidad de Chile, 1947), pp. 1-362, indicated that the annual rate of population growth for Chile was less than 1%; the Population Seminar, however, calculated the annual growth rate to be 1.7% for the decade of the 1940's and 1.5% for the decade of the 1930's. Thus Crocco's predicted population figures for 1950, for example, were an underestimate of about 500,000 persons or about 8% of the real figures.

Of the seven censuses taken during this century (with the exception of the one of 1940), the total of persons utilized in the calculations was the one obtained directly from the enumeration. Only the result of the 1940 census already included an adjustment to correct the census omission. In reality, according to Juan Crocco (1947, 23), the enumerated population in the 1940 census was not 5,023,999 as the official publications indicate but, rather, 4,885,018.

Analysis of the results of the 1952 census seems to indicate that the omission of the census was relatively higher than that of the censuses of 1940 and 1960. In this, as in other cases, the total population calculated for 1952 on the basis of the previous censuses exceeds the value given by the census itself (Tacla: 1975, 4). Even though Tacla believes that the proportion of persons omitted by the 1952 census is higher than the previous and the 1960 census it cannot be precluded that further demographic research on international migration, births and deaths may alter this conclusion.

The first application of modern techniques of census evaluation in Latin America was undertaken in Chile with respect to the XIII Population Census and II of Housing of November 29, 1960. The direct method used consisted of the controlled retaking of the census in randomly selected zones with the goal of measuring the degree of accuracy of the figures given by the census. Special attention was paid to errors originating from census omission (persons or dwellings that should have been enumerated but were not) and those caused by overenumeration (duplication of persons or dwellings (Tacla: 1975, 4).

There have been allegations that the 1970 census has some limitations because it was taken on April 22 when Chile was in the midst of the political and social unrest that preceded the election to the presidency of Salvador Allende Gossens. The officials of the National Institute of Statistics deny the validity of these allegations.

The present chapter provides the most important and complete information from the Chilean censuses. However, for more demographic information, one may check other primary sources. Besides the publications mentioned previously in this chapter, statistical information on population is found in the various issues of Demografía (e.g. DEC: 1964d and INE: 1971). Statistics presented in Demografía include population by provinces estimated for the 30th of June of each year, population by sex and age estimated for June 30 of each year, by civil status (single, married, divorced) and age groups, total population since the nineteenth century (starting dates vary) and population in cities with 20,000 inhabitants or more. Population data are also found in the various issues of Demographic Yearbook published by the United Nations (e.g. UN: 1966 or UN: 1976a).

A BRIEF HISTORY OF THE STATISTICAL OFFICE OF CHILE

The name of the statistical office or census and statistics bureau of Chile has changed so many times and the office itself has played such an important role in Chilean statistical and economic development that a short history of its evolution may be of significant value in understanding the information presented in this book.

The official birthday of Chile's Office of Statistics ("Oficina Estadística"), the original institution that gradually developed into the present day National Institute of Statistics (Instituto Nacional de Estadísticas, INE) is considered to be September 17, 1847, the day of promulgation of the law creating it, signed by President don Manuel Bulnes.

However, even earlier, on

March 27, 1843, a decree had been dictated by the same President establishing an Office of Statistics ("Oficina de Estadística") dependent on the Ministry of the Interior, manned by two officials and having numerous obligations.

In 1853, an order was issued to undertake the first population census. The norms of generality contained in the respective legal text have made it into a fundamental law about this matter. Among other concepts included in its dispositions are the establishment of decennial census taking and compulsory giving of exact and timely data by private individuals when requested by the Service. These ideas were incorporated into subsequent laws and regulations.

The year 1927 marks the beginning of important reforms for the institution. In order to improve the demographic statistics, the authority of the civil register (Registro Civil) is reinforced, the celebration of religious marriages and baptisms is prohibited unless a certificate accrediting the civil marriage or birth inscription had been previously presented. In the same year, the Dirección General de Estadística (General Statistical Office) was reorganized, assuming the exclusive elaboration of all official statistics.

Two principles of maximum interest are incorporated in 1930: a) government divisions and state enterprises must adhere to the norms and instructions of the Service (Dirección) whenever they prepare their own statistics; and b) establishment of the "statistical secret" with obligatory character to the Service.

The subsequent organic laws of 1932, 1953 and 1960 have adapted the structure, authority and functions of this entity to the modern statistical concepts and the international norms and recommendations.

With respect to the names which this organism has had, they have been "Oficina de Estadística", "Dirección General de Estadística", "Servicio Nacional de Estadística", "Dirección de Estadística y Censos", and now, "Instituto Nacional de Estadísticas" (INE).

With respect to its connection with the other state agencies, it has been successively dependent on the Ministry of the Interior, of Development and the General Controller's Office (Contraloría General de la República) becoming an autonomous public service under the custody-supervision of the Ministry of Development. Finally, as of October 15, 1970, by Law N° 17,374, it is an autonomous institution dependent on the Ministry of Economy, Development and Reconstruction and is "a legal person of public law, functionally decentralized and with its own patrimony".

The names and dates in office of the directors of the National Institute of Statistics are presented below.

LIST OF DIRECTORS OF THE NATIONAL STATISTICAL INSTITUTE FROM ITS INCEPTION TO THE PRESENT

1.	Fernando Urizar Garfias	1843
2.	Jose Miguel de la Barra	1847
3.	Manuel Talavera	1850
4.	Santiago Lindsay	1858
5.	Joaquin Alvarez de Toledo	1872
6.	Francisco Solano Astaburuaga	1876
7.	Joaquin Alvarez de Toledo (acting)	1879
8.	Vicente Grez	1889
9.	Francisco de Beze	1911
10.	Valentin del Campo	1913
11.	Alberto Edwards	1916
12.	German Pedregal	1929
13.	Roberto Vergara Herrera	1933
14.	Emilio Rodriguez Mendoza	1938
15.	Carlos Roberto Gonzalez	1941
16.	Victor Masjuan	1945
17.	Rafael A. Gumucio	1945
18.	Aliro Feliu Vergara	1947
19.	Luis Carcamo Cantin	1948
20.	Omar Rojas M.	1960
21.	Sergio Chaparro Ruiz	1963
22.	Gaston Ormeño Toledo	1971
23.	Oscar Tapia Paul	1973
24.	Carlos Clavel	1973
25.	Abraham Perez Lizama	1973
26.	Eliana Carrasco	1974
27.	Sergio Chaparro Ruiz	1974

2
NATALITY AND FERTILITY

The crude birth rate of Chile fell from 38.1% in 1962, as can be seen in Table 2.1, to 22.6% in 1977, as can be observed in Table 3.3, a decline of 15.5 births per thousand inhabitants or by 68.5 percent within only fifteen years. During the preceding ninety years (from 1870 to 1961) the crude birth rate had declined by only 5% or, stated differently, had remained relatively stable fluctuating between 33.1% during the war year of 1943 and 43.6% in 1928, the peak of the prosperity of the 1920s. Part of these fluctuations in the crude birth rate can be attributed to statistical errors. More than half of the recent decline in natality occurred during the Presidency of Eduardo Frei (1964-1970) with further sharp reductions during the Presidency of Salvador Allende (1970-1973) and the Military Junta of General Augusto Pinochet (1973-). This decline in the birth rate has been more rapid and sharp than the previous decline in the death rate. There is the impression of a crash in natality that is brought about by, or at least coincides with, the social, economic and political upheavals under the administrations of Eduardo Frei, Salvador Allende and Augusto Pinochet.

CRUDE BIRTH RATE

Fertility is one variable that determines to a large extent the size, evolution and structure of the population. Fertility and natality influence the process of economic development since they shape the level and composition of the demand for goods and services and the supply of labor. Actual and future needs of public and private services in the areas of health, education and housing are closely linked to births and birth rates.

The crude birth rate, or just birth rate, is defined as the relation between the annual number of births and the population of the nation midyear expressed per 1,000 of inhabitants. Live births by sex and crude birth rates between 1870 and 1975 are presented in Table 2.1. Figures on natality between 1931 and 1977 are also presented in Table 3.3.

Natality has normally passed through at least three phases both in the industrially developed nations and the poorer, developing ones of Asia, Africa and Latin America. During the first phase birth rates are high ranging between 35% and 55%. Chile appears to have remained in this phase up to as recently as 1961. During the second phase birth rates declined to 10%-15% as a consequence of increased and extensive use of contraceptives. Social and cultural factors reflected in the matrimonial systems and marriage rates have affected decisively the behavior of fertility when birth control devices are absent. For example, the principle regulators of human fertility in the populations of the pre-industrial and pre-modern services epochs were the frequency of marriages, the age of matrimony, stability of marriage, sexual prohibitions,

TABLE 2.1

Live Births by Sex and Crude Birth Rates.
1870-1975.

Years	Live Births: Total	Live Births: Sex: Males	Live Births: Sex: Females	Crude Birth Rates (Per 1,000 Inhabitants)[1]
Averages				
1870-74	85,736	43,528	42,208	43.0
1875-79	84,466	43,013	41,453	39.1
1880-84	95,600	48,802	46,798	40.1
1885-89	78,079	40,210	37,869	30.5
1890-94	98,900	50,804	48,096	37.4
1895-99	105,459	54,285	51,174	37.7
1900	110,697	56,942	53,755	38.1
1901	115,745	59,539	56,206	39.3
1902	115,813	59,574	56,239	38.7
1903	115,524	59,424	56,100	38.0
1904	116,950	59,872	57,078	37.9
1905	119,650	62,185	57,465	38.2
1906	117,123	60,134	56,989	36.8
1907(Census)	126,104	64,537	61,567	38.8
1908	129,733	66,331	63,402	39.7
1909	129,333	66,166	63,167	39.1
1910	130,052	66,741	63,311	38.9
1911	133,468	69,035	64,433	39.4
1912	135,373	68,931	66,442	39.5
1913	140,525	71,609	68,916	40.6
1914	136,500	70,198	66,350	39.0
1915	136,597	70,050	66,547	38.6
1916	144,193	74,235	69,958	40.3
1917	149,161	76,246	72,915	41.2
1918	145,871	74,298	71,573	39.9
1919	144,980	74,362	70,618	39.2
1920(Census)	146,725	74,820	71,820	39.1
1921	147,795	75,319	72,476	39.2
1922	147,205	75,693	71,512	38.7
1923	151,805	77,635	74,170	39.5
1924	155,100	79,375	75,725	40.0
1925	156,225	80,161	76,064	39.8
1926	159,611	82,260	77,351	40.1
1927	172,673	89,645	83,028	42.8
1928	179,594	92,446	87,148	43.6
1929	176,030	91,655	84,375	41.9
1930(Census)	169,395	87,202	82,193	39.5
1931	129,488	77,164	72,324	34.6
1932	149,459	77,099	72,360	34.2
1933	147,733	76,276	71,459	33.4
1934	150,362	77,056	73,306	33.8
1935	153,151	78,689	74,462	34.1
1936	156,917	80,357	76,560	34.6
1937	153,354	78,743	74,611	33.5
1938	154,927	79,401	75,526	33.5
1939	163,589	83,765	79,824	35.2
1940(Census)	166,593	85,349	81,244	33.2
1941	165,004	83,980	81,024	32.6
1942	170,222	86,986	83,236	33.2
1943	172,095	87,880	84,215	33.1
1944	174,864	89,248	85,616	33.2
1945	178,292	91,459	86,833	33.3
1946	175,685	89,619	86,066	32.4
1947	207,133	104,291	101,855	36.0
1948	206,520	104,644	102,570	35.3

TABLE 2.1 (Cont'd)

Live Births by Sex and Crude Birth Rates.
1870-1975.

Years	Live Births			Crude Birth Rates (Per 1,000 Inhabitants)[1]
	Total	Sex		
		Males	Females	
1949	206,591	105,790	100,335	34.7
1950	188,323	95,450	92,873	34.6
1951	191,332	97,351	93,981	34.4
1952	195,470	99,476	95,994	34.5
1953	211,808	107,364	104,444	36.6
1954	209,920	106,028	103,892	35.5
1955	225,352	114,312	111,040	36.6
1956	237,268	120,260	117,008	37.3
1957	249,609	127,389	122,220	38.4
1958	250,247	127,432	122,815	37.8
1959	254,274	129,289	124,985	37.3
1960	260,653	132,518	128,135	37.8 (34.4)[2]
1961	269,273	136,649	132,624	38.1 (34.7)
1962	274,440	139,715	134,725	38.1 (34.5)
1963	277,144	140,886	136,258	37.7 (34.0)
1964	275,323	139,853	135,470	36.4 (33.1)
1965	274,580	139,832	134,748	35.5 (32.3)
1966	268,233	136,795	131,438	33.9 (30.9)
1967	259,729	132,556	127,173	30.9 (29.3)
1968	248,934	126,492	122,442	29.0 (27.6)
1969	239,549	121,810	117,739	27.4 (26.0)
1970	238,669	121,558	117,111	26.8 (25.5)
1971	247,970	126,446	121,524	27.3 (26.0)
1972	256,097	130,839	125,258	27.7 (26.3)
1973	255,037	130,911	124,126	27.1 (25.8)
1974	244,127	124,824	119,303	25.4 (24.2)
1975	233,711	119,975	113,736	25.0 (22.8)

Notes: 1. The crude birth rates were calculated by using the "corrected" figures of live births.

2. The figures of crude birth rates found in parentheses were estimated by taking as a basis total population statistics from República de Chile, Ministerio de Economía, Fomento y Reconstrucción, Instituto Nacional de Estadísticas, Población 1960-1975, Total País, Provincias y Area Metropolitana (Santiago, Chile: INE, 1977), pp. 1-16 and included in the present volume's table on population births, live births according to legitimacy, 1870-1975.

Sources: National Health Service is the source for the statistical information for 1974 and 1975. The total of live births for 1947-1949 was obtained from Demografía Año 1962, table 7, p. 32. Live births calculated from 1938 to 1949 by increasing the registrations of minors up to two years of age by 9.5% and from 1952 onwards by increasing by 5% the number of live births during a year, registered between the first of January of that year and the thirty-first of March of the following year. The birth rate for 1947-1962 was obtained from the same source, table 8, p. 33. There is a substantial jump in the birth rate between 1946 and 1947 caused by the upward revision in the number of live births. Since the series on dead births was not revised there was a simultaneous drop in the ratio of these births per thousand of live births. In the present table the time series before 1947 were not presented in their revised forms mainly because the later revisions were limited to only some series. Their introduction would have, therefore, made the unrevised series, which are the majority, valueless. A complete set of

TABLE 2.1 (Cont'd)

Live Births by Sex and Crude Birth Rates.
1870-1975.

Sources (cont'd): the revised figures is found elsewhere in this publication. The information for children born alive was obtained for 1947, 1948 and 1949 from República de Chile, Ministerio de Economía, D.G.E., Demografía y Asistencia Social, Año 1949 (Santiago, Chile: Dirección General de Estadística, 1953), p. 11. The figures on live births, total and of males and females, since 1950 were obtained directly from the National Institute of Statistics. For the years between 1950 and 1960 the figures on total births differ substantially from earlier figures found in the table of the present volume on population births, live births according to legitimacy, 1870-1970 and in the official documents listed in the sources of said table.

TABLE 2.2

Chile: Percentage of Underreporting
of Births by Sex and Region. 1960-1970 Period.

Region	Province	Males	Females
	Total of Country	4.71	5.28
I	Tarapacá	14.98	13.98
II	Antofagasta	1.00	2.99
III	Atacama	2.00	2.00
IV	Coquimbo	2.01	1.99
V	Aconcagua and Valparaíso (including the department of San Antonio)	1.00	2.00
VI	O'Higgins and Colchagua	2.00	4.00
VII	Curicó, Talca, Maule and Linares	6.00	3.00
VIII	Ñuble, Concepción, Arauco and Bío-Bío	5.00	5.00
IX	Cautín and Malleco	25.01	25.00
X	Valdivia, Osorno, Llanquihue and Chiloé	17.00	18.00
XI	Aysén	21.94	20.03
XII	Magallanes	8.96	8.96
Metropolitan Region of Santiago (excluding the department of San Antonio)		2.00	2.00

Source: Pujol, 1976b, p. 11 and ODEPLAN, 1975c, p. 10.

lactation periods and so forth.

In Chile, the decline in the birth rate has to be explained, at least in part, in terms of induced abortions and modern contraceptive practices. Since 1962 the Chilean Government introduced a health policy, as part of its maternal-child program, which aimed to disseminate through the National Health Service contraceptive practices as a means of preventing the ever higher incidence of abortion by ever wider segments of the female population (Tacla: 1975, 16).

During the third phase the crude birth rate stabilizes at a low level of approximately 10% and is equal to or only slightly higher than the crude death rate. During this third phase, population is stationary or experiences only mild natural rate of increase. During the fourth phase the crude death rate exceeds the crude birth rate. Other configurations between the crude birth and death rates are possible but not very likely.

QUALITY OF BIRTH RECORDS

The various analyses and research projects trying to determine the completeness of the Chilean birth records seem to conclude, according to Tacla (1975, 1), that an important number is registered late and that a proportion of births is totally omitted. In view of these facts both the National Institute of Statistics (INE) and the National Health Service (SNS) proceed to correct the registered births in an effort to prepare time series which reflect reality more accurately, especially when birth rates are calculated (Tacla: 1975, 1). Unfortunately, the methods used by various scholars and different agencies in making adjustments to the raw official data on births have not been uniform. As a consequence, available time series on Chilean births display significant differences even though these have been reduced for recent years due to increased inter-agency collaboration.

According to a study by H. Gutierrez (cited in Tacla: 1975, 2) "La Integridad del Registro de Nacimientos en Chile, 1953-1963" Depto de Salud Pública y Med Social, Universidad de Chile, Santiago, Chile, 1968, which used the so-called late registrations (inscripciones tardías") method, the birth records covered an average of 90.3% of all births during 1953-1966. This signifies an underreporting of births of the official registers of 10 percent.

Figures of the percentage of underregistration of births by sex and region during the 1960-1970 period are presented in Table 2.2. These figures provide a good indication of the magnitude of omission of births and of the subsequent adjustments made by the National Institute of Statistics.

Both the National Health Service (SNS) and the National Statistical Institute (INE) publish data on births with those of INE being higher because they have been corrected for errors and omissions.

The figures on live births presented in Table 3.3 have been corrected for underregistration by the National Health Service. These corrections affect live births since 1953 with the coefficient of correction for each year being (in parentheses): 1954 (10.6), 1955 (8.6), 1956 (7.9), 1957 (8.2), 1958 (8.6), 1959 (8.1), 1960 (9.2), 1961 (9.1), 1962 (9.5), 1963 (9.6), 1964 (9.2), 1965 (9.2), 1966 (8.9), 1967 (8.9), 1968 (8.9), 1969 (8.9), 1970 (8.9), 1971 (8.9), 1972 (8.9), 1973 (8.9), 1974-76 (8.9) (SNS: 1978c).

Depending on what statistics of total population and births are used, different estimates of the crude birth rate can be obtained. Two different estimates of the crude birth rate for the 1960-1975 period are presented in Table 2.1. The first estimate was provided by the National Institute of Statistics while the second was calculated by the author using official time series published by INE. It should be noted that the trends displayed by the two estimates are very similar and that the differences in the absolute level could be explained by the use of different total population time series.

FERTILITY

The term fertility is used in its strictest sense when we consider the frequency of births in a population of women during their childbearing age (15 to 49 years). The global fertility rate is defined as the number of children born to a woman during her childbearing age, that is by the time she is fifty years old. In Chile, the average number of children born to a woman declined from five to three between 1959 and 1979 as a consequence of the tremendous impact that the political, social (urbanization, emancipation of women), economic (improved education, higher labor force participation, improved distribution of assets and income between 1967 and 1974), and cultural transformations have had on the female segment of the population. This decline was facilitated by the diffusion of family planning campaigns.

The age-specific fertility rates permit the calculation of the gross and net reproduction rates which constitute the most refined index of the crude birth rate.

The gross reproduction rate is the average number of daughters born per woman in a group of women passing through the childbearing years and experiencing a given set of age-specific fertility rates. This rate implicitly assumes that all the women live to the end of the childbearing years. The net reproduction rate is a refinement of the gross reproduction rate to the end of their reproducible years.

Age specific fertility rates for 1960, 1965 and 1970 are presented in Table 2.3 and for the 1950-1980 period in Table 2.4.

TABLE 2.3

Chile: Fertility Rates by Age of Mother: 1960, 1965 and 1970 (per 10,000 women).

Age of Mother	Fertility Rates (nfx)[1]		
	1960	1965	1970
15-19	80.58	79.54	73.47
20-24	229.21	222.77	185.19
25-29	261.59	224.22	181.31
30-34	223.17	190.20	127.18
35-39	153.52	143.73	86.63
40-44	67.54	55.65	44.36
45-49	15.09	10.35	6.51

Notes: 1. nfs stands for the number of children (n) born to the women in a specific age group (x).

Source: Tacla, 1975, 16.

TABLE 2.4

Age-Specific Fertility Rates, 1950-1980.

Period/Age	15-19	20-24	25-29	30-34	35-39	40-44	45-49
1950-1955	0.0780	0.2266	0.2319	0.1905	0.1435	0.0700	0.0189
1955-1960	0.0853	0.2257	0.2770	0.2165	0.1465	0.0708	0.0171
1960-1965	0.0817	0.2219	0.2475	0.2277	0.1415	0.0623	0.0126
1965-1970	0.0789	0.2079	0.2018	0.1464	0.1129	0.0528	0.0084
1970-1975	0.0712	0.1878	0.1822	0.1322	0.1019	0.0477	0.0076
1975-1980	0.0662	0.1831	0.1769	0.1257	0.0928	0.0427	0.0067

Source: ODEPLAN, 1975a, 19.

The study of the levels and trends in fertility of a country is of vital importance in trying to predict tendencies of future population increases.

As can be observed from Tables 2.3 and 2.4, the form of the age-specific fertility rates has changed over time rising for all age cohorts (except that of 45-49) between 1950-55 and 1955-60 and falling after that. In 1960 and 1965 (Table 2.3) the maximum value of the series corresponded to the 25-29 age group. In contrast, in 1970, the maximum value is registered in the group with 20-24 years of age. Furthermore, as can be observed in both Tables 2.3 and 2.4, a clear tendency of falling fertility in all age groups sets in between 1965 and 1970 being the strongest in the older age groups, especially in 1970. This indicates that even though the fertility of the younger age groups has declined, it has increased in recent years in relation to the other age cohorts.

From the information presented in Table 2.3, Tacla determined the gross reproduction rates for 1960 (2.51), 1965 (2.26) and 1970 (1.80) (Tacla: 1975, 17).

The gross reproduction rate describes the conditions of replacement of one generation by another on the assumption that mortality is zero. The gross reproduction rate is a rate of the moment since it describes actual fertility conditions. However, it has the important defect that it lumps together different fertility experiences and, furthermore, does not take into account mortality which is another major limitation.

Gross reproduction rates for 1970-75 and 1975-80 for Chile as a whole and its three major regions (North, South and Metropolitan) are presented in Table 2.5.

TABLE 2.5

Gross Reproduction Rates by Zones, 1970-1980.

Period	Zone			Total of Country
	North	Metropolitan	South	
1970-1975	1.74	1.58	2.08	1.80
1975-1980	1.65	1.50	1.97	1.71

Source: ODEPLAN: 1975b, 8.

A variety of hypotheses about net reproduction rates in Chile, elaborated by CELADE, is found in (Tacla: 1975, 42). According to the third hypothesis, which is the one recommended as being the most accurate, the net reproduction rates in Chile during the respective time periods were, in parentheses, 1950-55 (1.86), 1955-60 (2.07), 1960-65 (2.03), 1965-70 (1.70), 1970-75 (1.58) and 1975-80 (1.54).

In summary, fertility and the gross and net reproduction rates have declined in recent years, although fertility not necessarily with the same speed for all age groups.

BIRTHS: LEGITIMACY, AGE OF MOTHER, ORDER OF BIRTH AND MONTH OF BIRTH

Time series of live births according to legitimacy between 1870 and 1975 are presented in Table 2.6. More detailed information on live births according to age group of mother and legitimacy is presented in Table 2.7. for the years between 1950 and 1959 and in Table 2.8 for the years between 1960 and 1975.

The number of illegitimate children accounted for 34 percent of total births in 1926 (calculated from Table 2.6), 17 percent in 1965 and 20 percent in 1975. Chile has always had a major problem with illegitimacy and also the large number of mothers and legitimate children abandoned by their fathers.

Details information on live births according to order of birth and sex for the period between 1960 and 1975 is presented in Table 2.9. As this table reveals, the number of first- and second-born children has increased substantially between 1960 and 1973. The absolute number of third- to tenth-born children, however, started declining in 1962 or 1963 and has fallen often sharply ever since. This evidence suggests that the recent decline in the crude birth rate can be explained by the sharp decline of women bearing three or more children.

Information on live births according to month of birth for the 1960-1975 period is presented in Table 2.10.

Statistics on live births by month of occurrence and province are also found in Demografía.

It can be added here that the National Health Service (SNS) has always tabulated births according to legitimacy and illegitimacy (e.g. SNS: 1978b, 20-22). The National Institute of Statistics (INE) used the classification legitimacy-illegitimacy until 1969 and since then has reported births according to civil status of mother. The time series of births published by SNS and INE are different, especially during earlier years, with those published by INE being slightly higher.

The SNS publication on Nacimientos (e.g. SNS: 1978b) provides detailed information of live births by province of residence, according to type of professional attention and location of delivery (hospital or other facility), according to month of birth, age of mother and order of birth, and according to sex and legitimacy. It also provides data on children born dead according to sex, causes of death, legitimacy, place of birth (home or hospital), and type of birth (single or twin).

TABLE 2.6

Population Births. Live Births According to Legitimacy. 1870-1975.

Years	Children Born Alive					
	Legitimate[1]		Illegitimate		Unknown[2]	Total
	Male	Female	Male	Female		
Averages						
1870-74	63,932		21,804			85,736
1875-79	65,112		19,354			84,466
1880-84	72,583		23,017			95,600
1885-89	58,139		19,940			78,079
1890-94	66,899		32,001			98,900
1895-99	71,845		33,614			105,459
1900	76,713		33,984			110,697
1901	76,160		39,585			115,745
1902	76,203		39,610			115,813
1903	37,972	35,624	21,452	20,476		115,524
1904	37,217	35,199	22,655	21,879		116,950
1905	42,168	38,153	20,017	19,312		119,650
1906	37,088	35,838	23,046	21,151		117,123
1907	41,275	39,508	23,262	22,059		126,104
1908	41,945	40,141	24,386	23,261		129,733
1909	41,147	39,495	25,019	23,672		129,333
1910	41,946	39,895	24,795	23,416		130,052
1911	42,352	39,999	26,683	24,434		133,468
1912	43,091	41,572	25,840	24,870		135,373
1913	44,829	42,880	26,780	26,036		140,525
1914	44,084	41,385	26,114	24,967		136,500
1915	44,338	41,894	25,712	24,653		136,597
1916	46,057	43,149	28,178	26,809		144,193
1917	46,487	44,340	29,759	28,575		149,161
1918	45,940	44,099	28,358	27,474		145,871
1919	45,789	43,485	28,573	27,133		144,980
1920	46,479	44,920	28,341	26,985		146,725
1921	47,170	45,481	28,149	26,995		147,795
1922	48,447	45,560	27,246	25,952		147,205
1923	49,376	47,153	28,259	27,017		151,805
1924	50,820	48,450	28,555	27,275		155,100
1925	51,911	49,195	28,250	26,869		156,225
1926	53,655	50,209	28,605	27,142		159,611
1927	58,227	53,894	31,418	29,134		172,673
1928	59,860	56,026	32,586	31,122		179,594
1929	62,340	57,825	29,315	26,550		176,030
1930	61,377	56,770	25,825	25,423		169,395
1931	54,848	50,858	22,316	21,466		149,488
1932	55,888	51,020	22,211	21,340		149,459
1933	53,603	50,014	22,673	21,443		147,733
1934	54,329	51,407	22,727	21,899		150,362
1935	55,135	51,861	23,554	22,601		153,151
1936	56,683	53,731	23,674	22,829		156,917
1937	56,112	53,082	22,631	21,529		153,354
1938	57,173	54,513	22,228	21,013		154,927
1939	61,587	58,346	22,178	21,478		163,589
1940	64,084	60,959	21,265	20,285		166,593
1941	63,143	60,763	20,837	20,288		165,004
1942	65,922	62,944	21,064	20,292		170,222
1943	67,318	64,685	20,562	19,530		172,095
1944	69,213	66,036	20,035	19,580		174,864
1945	70,085	66,454	21,374	20,379		178,292
1946	69,881	67,230	19,738	18,836		175,685
1947	81,726	80,621	22,565	21,234	987	207,133
1948	82,864	81,629	21,780	20,944	697	206,520

TABLE 2.6

Population Births. Live Births According to Legitimacy.
1870-1975.

	Children Born Alive					
	Legitimate[1]		Illegitimate		Unknown[2]	Total
	Male	Female	Male	Female		
1949	83,638	79,003	22,152	21,332	466	206,591
1950	83,092	81,368	21,426	20,238	458	206,582
1951	85,376	82,934	21,223	19,975	286	209,794
1952	85,495	83,178	20,673	19,730	16,682	225,758
1953	93,214	90,961	19,519	18,706	556	222,956
1954	91,937	90,137	19,394	18,949	551	220,968
1955	99,782	96,929	20,246	19,663	593	237,213
1956	105,572	102,675	20,701	20,183	625	249,756
1957	111,429	106,826	22,329	21,503	659	262,746
1958	112,704	108,863	21,009	20,093	749	263,418
1959	113,355	109,793	22,400	21,441	668	267,657
1960[3]	219,176		41,477			260,653
1961	226,774		42,499			269,273
1962	229,555		44,885			274,440
1963	231,374		45,770			277,144
1964	229,485		45,838			275,323
1965	227,718		46,862			274,580
1966	222,380		45,853			268,233
1967	213,758		45,971			259,729
1968	203,432		43,608		1,894	248,934
1969	194,147		43,758		1,644	239,549
1970	190,626		44,302		3,741	238,669
1971	198,674		49,296			247,970
1972	206,145		49,952			256,097
1973	204,078		50,959			255,037
1974	191,803		47,507		4,817	244,127
1975	183,099		46,434		4,178	233,711

Notes: 1. Between 1960 and 1968 the information of this table refers to legitimacy of babies born alive. From 1969 to 1973 the information refers to the marital (civil) status of the mother. The National Health Service (SNS) has always tabulated births according to legitimacy and illegitimacy. The National Statistical Institute has tabulated births according to legitimacy and illegitimacy up to 1969 and since then according to civil status of the mother.

2. The figures for the years between 1947 and 1959 were obtained as the statistical discrepancy between the sum of legitimate and illegitimate births, on one hand, and the total, on the other hand. The term "unknown" means that the status of the child as legitimate or illegitimate is unknown.

3. For the period 1960-1975 the source of the information on legitimacy of live births is the National Health Service (SNS).

Sources: The statistical information used in this table for 1870-1946 inclusive was obtained from Demografía y Asistencia Social, Año 1946 (Santiago, Chile: Dirección de Estadística y Censos, 1949), pp. 1-2. The total of live births for 1947-1960 was obtained from Demografía Año 1962, table 7, p. 32. Live births were calculated from 1938 to 1951 by increasing the registrations of minors up to two years of age by 9.5% and from 1952 onwards by increasing by 5% the number of live births during a year, registered between the first of January of that year and the thirty-first of March of the following year. The information for children born alive was obtained for 1947, 1948 and 1949 from

TABLE 2.6

Population Births. Live Births According to Legitimacy. 1870-1975.

Sources (cont'd): República de Chile, Ministerio de Economía, D.G.E. Demografía y Asistencia Social, Año 1949 (Santiago, Chile: Dirección General de Estadística, 1953), p. 11. For 1950, 1951, and 1952, República de Chile, Ministerio de Economía, D.G.E., Estadística Chilena, Diciembre (sinopsis) de 1952 (Santiago, Chile: Dirección General de Estadística, 1953), p. 602. For 1953, República de Chile, Ministerio de Economía, Demografía Año 1953 (Santiago, Chile: Servicio Nacional de Estadística y Censos, 1955), p. 22. For 1954, 1955, 1956, 1957, and 1958, República de Chile, Ministerio de Economía, D.E. y C., Demografía Año 1958 (Santiago, Chile: Dirección de Estadística y Censos, 1962), p. 24. For the year 1959, Demografía Año 1961, p. 22. The statistical information for the 1960-1975 period was obtained from the National Institute of Statistics.

TABLE 2.7

Live Births According to Age Group of Mother and Legitimacy. 1950-1959.

Age Groups of Mother and Legitimacy	Legitimacy									
	1950	1951	1952	1953	1954	1955	1956	1957	1958	1959
Total	188,323	191,332	195,470	211,808	209,920	225,352	237,268	249,609	250,247	254,274
Under 15 years	-	-	454	528	491	557	514	463	463	585
15-19 years	-	-	19,223	20,206	20,476	22,293	24,144	25,509	25,691	26,301
20-24 years	-	-	54,002	56,684	.56,146	57,759	59,577	62,287	62,007	63,068
25-29 years	-	-	46,861	52,892	53,352	60,062	65,117	68,002	66,840	65,918
30-34 years	-	-	33,510	36,842	36,791	40,128	42,518	46,062	47,811	51,019
35-39 years	-	-	23,468	25,578	23,908	25,895	26,729	28,443	28,997	29,439
40-44 years	-	-	9,544	11,053	10,561	11,399	11,526	11,870	11,910	11,793
45-49 years	-	-	1,703	1,880	1,737	1,944	1,969	2,024	`2,000	1,842
50 years and over	-	-	461	474	410	427	418	447	439	342
Unknown	-	-	6,244	5,671	6,048	4,888	4,756	4,502	4,089	3,967
Legitimate	150,192	153,708	158,327	175,404	173,403	187,343	198,331	207,862	211,102	212,521
Under 15 years	-	-	317	348	298	372	333	276	269	369
15-19 years	-	-	13,198	14,184	14,389	15,850	17,425	18,215	18,587	18,591
20-24 years	-	-	43,591	46,767	46,257	47,846	49,580	51,575	52,124	52,466
25-29 years	-	-	40,056	45,992	46,282	52,287	56,783	59,177	58,792	57,660
30-34 years	-	-	29,318	32,392	32,274	35,140	37,594	40,508	42,309	44,750
35-39 years	-	-	20,498	22,554	20,846	22,669	23,337	24,748	25,479	25,637
40-44 years	-	-	8,476	9,951	9,413	10,072	10,225	10,488	10,712	10,431
45-49 years	-	-	1,509	1,689	1,524	1,716	1,756	1,774	1,780	1,651
50 years and over	-	-	387	428	362	366	372	382	378	301
Unknown	-	-	977	1,099	1,758	1,025	926	719	672	665
Illegitimate	38,131	37,624	37,143	36,404	36,517	38,009	38,937	41,747	39,145	41,753
Under 15 years	-	-	137	180	193	185	181	187	194	216
15-19 years	-	-	6,025	6,022	6,087	6,443	6,719	7,294	7,104	7,710
20-24 years	-	-	10,411	9,917	9,889	9,913	9,997	10,712	9,883	10,602
25-29 years	-	-	6,805	6,900	7,070	7,775	8,334	8,825	8,048	8,258
30-34 years	-	-	4,192	4,450	4,517	4,988	4,924	5,554	5,502	6,269
35-39 years	-	-	2,970	3,024	3,062	3,226	3,392	3,695	3,518	3,802
40-44 years	-	-	1,068	1,102	1,148	1,327	1,301	1,382	1,198	1,362
45-49 years	-	-	194	191	213	228	213	250	220	191
50 years and over	-	-	74	46	48	61	46	65	61	41
Unknown	-	-	5,267	4,572	4,290	3,863	3,830	3,783	3,417	3,302

Source: National Institute of Statistics.

TABLE 2.8

Live Births According to Age and Marital Status of Mother and Legitimacy, 1960-1975.

Age Groups and Marital Status of Mother	Legitimacy(1)								or
	1960	1961	1962	1963	1964	1965	1966	1967	1968
TOTAL	260,653	269,273	274,440	277,144	275,323	274,580	268,233	259,729	248,934
Under 15 years	599	667	608	696	692	685	686	763	677
15 to 19 years	26,876	28,452	28,818	30,335	30,474	31,475	31,872	32,519	31,520
20 to 24 years	65,595	66,860	69,779	74,659	75,604	75,643	75,254	75,342	73,593
25 to 29 years	66,288	68,661	68,279	65,975	66,201	66,437	65,801	63,137	60,958
30 to 34 years	53,491	56,519	57,588	55,174	52,138	49,313	45,606	42,397	38,941
35 to 39 years	30,459	31,326	31,728	32,945	33,197	34,119	32,781	30,127	26,768
40 to 44 years	11,531	11,225	12,057	12,244	11,955	11,951	11,682	11,136	10,962
45 to 49 years	1,891	1,742	1,776	1,614	1,540	1,636	1,549	1,437	1,374
50 years or more	430	394	302	277	281	248	205	206	182
Unknown-M(2)	3,493	3,427	3,505	3,225	3,241	3,073	2,797	2,615	3,959
Married									
Legitimate	219,176	226,774	229,555	231,374	229,485	227,718	222,380	213,758	203,432
Under 15 years	379	408	328	363	377	379	360	408	327
15 to 19 years	19,102	20,465	20,799	21,441	21,600	22,309	22,706	23,044	22,005
20 to 24 years	54,617	56,375	57,563	62,023	62,885	62,698	62,406	62,047	60,483
25 to 29 years	58,235	59,697	59,483	57,452	57,723	57,699	57,126	54,481	52,328
30 to 34 years	47,061	49,585	50,364	48,138	45,320	42,792	39,512	36,545	33,270
35 to 39 years	26,765	27,643	27,706	28,507	28,648	29,158	28,036	25,596	22,570
40 to 44 years	10,139	9,964	10,614	10,781	10,448	10,308	10,136	9,565	9,411
45 to 49 years	1,690	1,542	1,515	1,442	1,358	1,427	1,348	1,283	1,167
50 years and over	350	349	265	247	252	223	180	183	150
Unknown-M	838	746	918	980	874	725	570	606	1,721
Not Married									
Illegitimate	41,477	42,499	44,885	45,770	45,838	46,862	45,853	45,971	43,608
Under 15 years	220	259	280	333	315	306	326	355	345
15 to 19 years	7,774	7,987	8,019	8,894	8,874	9,166	9,166	9,475	9,427
20 to 24 years	10,978	10,485	12,216	12,636	12,719	12,945	12,848	13,295	12,900
25 to 29 years	8,053	8,964	8,796	8,523	8,478	8,738	8,675	8,656	8,452
30 to 34 years	6,430	6,934	7,224	7,036	6,818	6,521	6,094	5,852	5,560
35 to 39 years	3,694	3,683	4,022	4,438	4,549	4,961	4,745	4,531	4,109
40 to 44 years	1,392	1,261	1,443	1,463	1,507	1,643	1,546	1,571	1,530
45 to 49 years	201	200	261	172	182	209	20	204	204
50 years and over	80	45	37	30	29	25	25	23	27
Unknown	2,655	2,681	2,587	2,245	2,367	2,348	2,227	2,009	1,054

TABLE 2.8 (Cont'd)

Live Births According to Age and Marital Status of Mother and Legitimacy, 1960-1975.

Age Groups and Marital Status of Mother	Marital Status of Mother						
	1969	1970	1971	1972	1973	1974 (3)	1975 (3)
TOTAL	239,549	238,669	247,970	256,097	255,037	244,127	233,711
Under 15 years	746	674	721	823	789		
15 to 19 years	31,922	33,198	36,730	39,839	40,241		
20 to 24 years	71,258	72,123	76,695	80,430	82,108		
25 to 29 years	58,752	59,539	62,813	64,624	63,949		
30 to 34 years	37,167	36,262	38,411	38,937	38,499		
35 to 39 years	24,386	22,006	21,491	20,788	19,880		
40 to 44 years	10,323	9,942	9,646	9,243	8,317		
45 to 49 years	1,319	1,306	1,288	1,234	1,112		
50 years or more	161	186	175	179	142		
Unknown-M (2)	3,515	3,433	-	-	-		
Married	194,147	190,626	198,674	206,145	204,078		
Legitimate						191,803	183,099
Under 15 years	394	350	371	418	405		
15 to 19 years	22,000	22,769	25,066	27,517	27,723		
20 to 24 years	58,224	57,897	61,529	64,848	66,071		
25 to 29 years	50,081	50,263	52,951	54,973	53,856		
30 to 34 years	31,708	30,398	31,982	32,487	31,862		
35 to 39 years	20,396	18,218	17,556	17,087	16,287		
40 to 44 years	8,756	8,263	7,963	7,603	6,818		
45 to 49 years	1,135	1,096	1,100	1,061	931		
50 years and over	139	159	156	151	115		
Unknown-M	1,314	1,213	-	-	-		
Not married	43,458	44,302	49,296	49,952	50,959		
Illegitimate						47,507	46,434
Under 15 years	352	319	350	405	384		
15 to 19 years	9,901	10,121	11,664	12,322	12,508		
20 to 24 years	12,991	13,628	15,166	15,582	16,037		
25 to 29 years	8,639	8,701	9,862	9,651	10,093		
30 to 34 years	5,435	5,516	6,429	6,450	6,637		
35 to 39 years	3,982	3,577	3,935	3,701	3,593		
40 to 44 years	1,555	1,595	1,683	1,640	1,499		
45 to 49 years	182	194	188	173	181		
50 years and over	22	21	19	28	27		
Unknown	699	630	-	-	-		

TABLE 2.8 (Cont'd)

Live Births According to Age and Marital Status of Mother and Legitimacy, 1960-1975.

Age Groups and Marital Status of Mother	Legitimacy[1]								or
	1960	1961	1962	1963	1964	1965	1966	1967	1968
Unknown-C[2]	-	-	-	-	-	-	-	-	1,894
Under 15 years	-	-	-	-	-	-	-	-	5
15 to 19 years	-	-	-	-	-	-	-	-	88
20 to 24 years	-	-	-	-	-	-	-	-	210
25 to 29 years	-	-	-	-	-	-	-	-	178
30 to 34 years	-	-	-	-	-	-	-	-	111
35 to 39 years	-	-	-	-	-	-	-	-	89
40 to 44 years	-	-	-	-	-	-	-	-	21
45 to 49 years	-	-	-	-	-	-	-	-	3
50 years and over	-	-	-	-	-	-	-	-	5
Unknown-M	-	-	-	-	-	-	-	-	1,184

TABLE 2.8 (Cont'd)

Live Births According to Age and Marital Status of Mother and Legitimacy, 1960-1975.

Age Groups and Marital Status of Mother	Marital Status of Mother						
	1969	1970	1971	1972	1973	1974[3]	1975[3]
Unknown-C[2]	1,644	3,741	-	-	-	4,817	4,178
Under 15 years	-	5	-	-	-		
15 to 19 years	21	308	-	-	-		
20 to 24 years	43	598	-	-	-		
25 to 29 years	32	575	-	-	-		
30 to 34 years	24	348	-	-	-		
35 to 39 years	8	211	-	-	-		
40 to 44 years	12	84	-	-	-		
45 to 49 years	2	16	-	-	-		
50 years and over	-	6	-	-	-		
Unknown-M	1,502	1,590	-	-	-		

Source: National Statistical Institute of Chile.

Notes: (1) Between 1960 and 1968 the information of this table refers to legitimacy of babies born alive. From 1969 to 1973 the information refers to the marital (civil) status of the mother. The National Health Service (SNS) has always tabulated births according to legitimacy and illegitimacy. The National Statistical Institute has tabulated births according to legitimacy and illegitimacy up to 1969 and since then according to civil status of the mother.

(2) The term "unknown-M" (ignorada) means that the age of the mother who has made a declaration of a birth is unknown. The term "unknown-C" (ignorado) means that the status of the child as legitimate or illegitimate is unknown.

(3) The source of the information on legitimacy of live births is the National Health Service (SNS).

TABLE 2.9

Live Births According to Order of Birth and Sex. 1960-1975.

Sex and Years	Total	Order of Birth										
		1	2	3	4	5	6	7	8	9	10 and More	Unknown
Total												
1960	260,653	60,772	45,515	38,983	30,800	23,205	18,223	12,843	9,313	6,727	11,997	2,275
1961	269,273	61,737	47,196	39,872	31,948	24,196	18,438	13,645	9,993	7,159	13,616	1,473
1962	274,440	63,532	48,198	40,582	32,910	23,777	18,566	13,973	10,231	7,267	13,720	1,684
1963	277,144	62,987	49,073	39,422	31,113	24,731	19,219	14,364	10,868	8,027	15,354	1,986
1964	275,323	62,767	49,966	39,240	30,311	23,721	18,903	14,331	10,945	7,947	15,322	1,870
1965	274,580	66,414	49,815	38,659	29,499	22,637	18,156	14,012	10,901	7,986	15,830	671
1966	268,233	68,194	50,470	37,227	28,046	22,235	16,784	12,555	10,031	7,401	14,879	411
1967	259,729	70,437	50,490	35,312	26,202	19,425	15,046	11,911	9,203	6,856	14,351	496
1968	248,934	70,402	50,915	34,349	24,176	17,418	13,600	10,353	8,176	6,112	13,232	201
1969	239,549	71,663	51,429	33,565	22,178	15,653	11,917	8,981	7,107	5,339	11,657	60
1970	238,669	74,183	53,232	33,870	21,813	14,677	11,053	8,186	6,250	4,646	10,241	518
1971	247,970	78,795	56,191	35,852	22,548	14,714	10,660	7,807	5,848	4,505	9,417	1,633
1972	256,097	85,320	59,659	36,935	22,482	14,522	9,988	7,332	5,512	4,114	8,672	1,561
1973	255,037	87,931	60,760	36,703	21,833	13,842	9,677	6,675	5,016	3,681	7,443	1,476
1974	244,127											
1975	233,711											
Males												
1960	132,518	31,145	23,279	19,823	15,571	11,701	9,126	6,564	4,752	3,371	6,041	1,145
1961	136,649	31,472	24,065	20,147	16,171	12,282	9,381	6,926	5,016	3,576	6,854	759
1962	139,715	32,937	24,071	20,376	16,936	12,194	9,485	7,185	5,135	3,602	6,909	885
1963	140,886	32,186	25,104	20,169	15,615	12,467	9,734	7,292	5,470	4,073	7,746	1,030
1964	139,853	31,921	25,637	19,034	15,244	12,011	9,567	7,271	5,535	4,022	7,756	955
1965	139,832	34,022	25,524	19,507	15,017	11,504	9,256	7,063	5,536	4,057	7,999	347
1966	136,795	35,229	25,583	18,822	14,385	11,758	8,588	6,076	5,115	3,739	7,295	205
1967	132,556	36,448	25,696	17,910	13,296	9,778	7,724	6,051	4,658	3,473	7,310	212
1968	126,492	36,132	25,743	17,472	12,138	8,807	6,922	5,229	4,124	3,128	6,689	108
1969	121,810	36,280	26,384	17,020	11,261	7,931	6,069	4,490	3,667	2,716	5,965	27
1970	121,558	37,968	27,181	17,303	11,062	7,451	5,611	4,149	3,110	2,271	5,174	278
1971	126,446	40,348	28,659	18,208	11,515	7,408	5,446	4,017	2,984	2,243	4,766	852
1972	130,839	43,889	30,429	18,963	11,346	7,334	5,036	3,711	2,814	2,033	4,414	870
1973	130,911	45,244	31,207	18,775	11,178	7,014	4,954	3,401	2,571	1,898	3,854	815
1974	124,824											
1975	119,975											

TABLE 2.9 (Cont'd)

Live Births According to Order of Birth and Sex.
1960-1975.

Sex and Years	Total	Order of Birth										
		1	2	3	4	5	6	7	8	9	10 and More	Unknown
Females												
1960	128,135	29,627	22,236	19,160	15,229	11,504	9,097	6,279	4,561	3,356	5,956	1,130
1961	132,624	30,265	23,131	19,725	15,777	11,914	9,057	6,719	4,977	3,583	6,762	714
1962	134,725	30,595	24,127	20,206	15,974	11,583	9,081	6,788	5,096	3,665	6,811	799
1963	136,258	30,801	23,969	19,253	15,498	12,264	9,485	7,072	5,398	3,954	7,608	956
1964	135,470	30,846	24,329	19,306	15,067	11,710	9,336	7,060	5,410	3,925	7,566	915
1965	134,748	32,392	24,291	19,152	14,482	11,133	8,900	6,949	5,365	3,929	7,831	324
1966	131,438	32,965	24,887	18,405	13,661	10,477	8,196	6,479	4,916	3,662	7,584	206
1967	127,173	33,989	24,794	17,402	12,906	9,647	7,322	5,860	4,545	3,383	7,041	284
1968	122,442	34,270	25,172	16,877	12,038	8,611	6,678	5,124	4,052	2,984	6,543	93
1969	117,739	35,383	25,045	16,545	10,917	7,722	5,848	4,491	3,440	2,623	5,692	33
1970	117,111	36,215	26,051	16,567	10,751	7,226	5,442	4,037	3,140	2,375	5,067	240
1971	121,524	38,447	27,532	17,644	11,033	7,306	5,214	3,790	2,864	2,262	4,651	781
1972	125,258	41,431	29,230	17,972	11,136	7,188	4,952	3,621	2,698	2,081	4,258	691
1973	124,126	42,687	29,553	17,928	10,655	6,828	4,723	3,274	2,445	1,783	3,589	661
1974	119,303											
1975	113,736											

Source: The source for the data of all years except 1974 and 1975 is the National Institute of Statistics. The information for the years 1974 and 1975 was obtained from Chile's National Health Service.

TABLE 2.10

Live Births According to Month of Birth.
1960-1975.

Years	Total	Month of Birth											
		January	February	March	April	May	June	July	August	September	October	November	December
1960	260,653	21,616	18,794	20,187	19,608	20,761	20,988	21,730	23,302	24,132	25,217	22,571	21,747
1961	269,273	22,938	19,506	20,931	20,508	21,176	22,045	23,073	24,067	25,026	25,358	23,043	21,602
1962	274,440	23,452	19,955	22,097	20,279	19,542	23,108	23,605	24,321	25,851	25,537	23,499	23,194
1963	277,144	23,630	20,516	22,627	22,038	22,762	23,186	23,340	24,163	24,752	24,954	22,903	22,273
1964	275,323	22,821	20,009	21,344	21,034	22,570	23,291	23,571	24,007	24,997	25,448	23,541	22,690
1965	274,580	23,376	20,148	22,205	21,627	22,271	22,391	23,460	23,925	24,812	25,013	23,328	22,024
1966	268,233	22,387	19,947	21,812	20,323	21,304	22,235	23,196	23,634	24,378	24,409	22,921	21,687
1967	259,729	23,041	19,480	20,671	19,172	20,737	21,825	22,089	22,534	23,374	23,375	22,029	21,402
1968	248,934	21,670	19,866	20,990	20,696	20,370	20,319	20,673	21,193	21,794	21,753	20,491	19,119
1969	239,549	20,541	17,850	20,037	19,580	20,498	20,394	20,580	20,035	20,802	20,750	19,537	18,945
1970	238,669	20,318	17,373	19,204	18,169	19,071	19,494	19,905	20,731	22,097	21,628	20,565	20,114
1971	247,970	21,294	18,054	17,891	19,186	19,886	20,470	20,726	21,998	22,882	22,931	21,885	20,767
1972	256,097	22,593	20,169	21,402	20,240	20,775	20,838	21,610	21,914	22,788	22,733	20,472	20,563
1973	255,037	22,685	19,378	21,012	20,114	20,321	20,402	21,239	21,584	22,834	23,035	21,618	20,815
1974	244,127	22,472	18,902	20,101	18,639	19,220	18,593	19,812	20,943	21,976	22,632	21,090	19,747
1975	233,711	21,432	18,279	19,771	19,042	19,744	19,801	19,529	19,241	20,471	20,712	18,493	17,196

Source: The source for all data except for 1974 and 1975 is the National Institute of Statistics. The statistical information for 1974 and 1975 was the National Health Service.

3
MORTALITY

One of the elements that intervenes in a dominant manner in the demographic growth of the population is mortality. Mortality is also closely related to the socioeconomic development of a country. Its careful study is, therefore, necessary in understanding past demographic and economic growth and in planning future changes. It is also important to obtain an as accurate measure of mortality as possible.

GENERAL AND INFANT MORTALITY

The crude death rate, also referred to as the general death rate or just death rate, is the relation between the number of deaths occurring during a period and the midyear population of the same period, expressed in 1,000 inhabitants. General mortality is measured by the crude death rate. General deaths according to sex, crude death rates and the rate of natural population increase between 1870 and 1977 are presented in Table 3.1.

Crude mortality displays high levels between 1870 and 1925 with crude death rates remaining close to 30 deaths per 1,000 inhabitants. There exist some significant variations in the death rates between years (e.g. 28.1% in 1904 versus 35.2% in 1905) but they do not lead to a trend. General mortality, as seen in Table 3.1, was 26.7% during 1870-74 and 32.0% in 1923. Since 1925 crude mortality experiences a significant and continuous decline due to progress in preventive as well as general medicine, extensive implementation of governmental programs of public health and general socioeconomic development.

Two periods of decline occur since 1925. From 1925-29 to 1940 crude death rates fluctuate between 21.5 to 27.7 per thousand. And, then, when during a continuously declining trend between 1945 and 1965 the death rate falls by almost 50 percent from 20.0% in 1945 to 10.8% in 1965. A further significant decline was registered in recent years with the crude death rate falling to 7.0% in 1977. The figures of crude deaths and death rates presented in Table 3.1 are those prepared by the National Institute of Statistics and are slightly higher than those published by the National Health Service and presented in Table 3.3

In addition to the crude death rate it is of interest to examine infant deaths and infant mortality especially since these have displayed very high levels in Chile. The infant mortality rate is the relation between deaths of children under one year of age and the number of births that occurred during a specific year, expressed per thousand.

Infant mortality has undergone, as can be seen from Table 3.2, a sharp decline from a level of 338% during 1890-94 to 55.4% in 1975. It needs to be mentioned that the rates of infant mortality presented in Table 3.2 are significantly higher than those prepared by Cabello et al. (1947) and

TABLE 3.1

Population Deaths. General Deaths According to Sex, Crude Death Rates and Rate of Natural Population Increase. 1870-1977.

	Deaths				
	Overall Total (including those under one year)				
Years	Male	Female	Total	Per Thousand Population	Rate of Natural Population Increase
Averages					
1870-74	27,091	26,258	53,349	26.7	16.3
1875-79	30,847	30,104	60,951	28.2	10.9
1880-84	32,292	31,412	63,704	26.7	13.4
1885-89	39,359	36,729	76,088	29.7	0.8
1890-94	48,320	44,631	92,951	35.1	2.3
1895-99	43,358	40,250	83,608	29.9	7.8
1900	65,940	50,372	104,312	35.9	2.2
1901	55,950	52,249	108,199	36.7	2.3
1902	44,526	41,581	86,107	28.8	9.9
1903	44,914	41,459	86,373	28.4	9.6
1904	44,254	42,376	86,630	28.1	9.8
1905	56,407	53,869	110,276	35.2	3.0
1906	53,931	50,959	104,890	33.0	3.8
1907	49,092	47,359	96,451	29.7	9.1
1908	53,593	50,633	104,226	31.9	7.8
1909	54,661	50,046	104,707	31.7	7.4
1910	54,695	51,378	106,073	31.7	7.3
1911	55,642	52,174	107,816	31.9	7.5
1912	53,173	50,732	103,905	30.3	9.2
1913	54,995	52,205	107,200	31.0	9.6
1914	51,580	48,479	100,059	28.6	10.4
1915	49,756	46,960	96,716	27.3	11.3
1916	50,791	49,065	99,856	27.9	12.4
1917	54,617	52,582	107,199	29.6	11.6
1918	56,088	52,579	108,667	29.7	10.2
1919	69,854	67,684	137,538	37.2	2.0
1920	58,624	56,804	115,428	30.7	8.4
1921	63,148	61,049	124,197	32.9	6.3
1922	56,102	52,654	108,756	28.6	10.1
1923	65,810	61,567	126,877	32.0	6.5
1924	59,013	55,159	114,172	29.5	10.5
1925	55,225	53,562	108,787	27.7	12.1
1926	55,093	53,158	108,251	27.2	12.9
1927	53,734	51,819	105,553	26.2	16.6
1928	51,923	49,805	101,728	24.7	18.9
1929	56,465	53,601	110,066	26.2	15.7
1930	53,938	51,202	105,140	24.5	15.0
1931	48,796	46,393	95,189	22.0	12.6
1932	52,369	47,303	99,664	22.8	11.4
1933	61,694	56,738	118,432	26.8	6.6
1934	61,148	57,930	119,078	26.8	7.0
1935	57,245	55,199	112,364	25.0	9.1
1936	58,623	55,769	114,392	25.3	9.3
1937	56,662	53,133	108,795	24.0	9.5
1938	58,706	55,013	113,719	24.6	8.9
1939	58,594	55,547	114,141	24.6	10.6
1940	55,242	52,529	107,771	21.5	11.7
1941	51,545	48,546	100,091	19.8	12.8
1942	53,857	50,265	104,122	20.3	12.9
1943	53,079	50,156	103,235	19.9	13.2
1944	53,901	49,153	103,054	19.5	13.7
1945	56,427	50,637	107,064	20.0	13.3
1946	49,145	44,402	93,547	17.0	15.4

TABLE 3.1 (Cont'd)

Population Deaths. General Deaths According to Sex,
Crude Death Rates and Rate of Natural Population Increase. 1870-1977.

	Deaths				
	Overall Total (including those under one year)				
Years	Male	Female	Total	Per Thousand Population	Rate of Natural Population Increase
1947	48,180	44,301	92,481	16.1	19.9
1948	50,940	46,730	97,670	16.7	18.6
1949	54,425	48,959	103,364	17.3	17.4
1950[1]	48,499	42,681	91,180	15.0	19.0
1951	49,102	43,626	92,728	15.0	19.2
1952	43,099	38,867	81,966	13.0	19.7
1953	42,057	38,011	80,068	12.4	22.2
1954	45,058	39,461	84,519	12.8	20.7
1955	47,407	40,436	87,843	13.0	22.1
1956	45,353	38,846	84,199	12.1	22.1
1957	48,686	42,820	91,506	12.9	22.2
1958	47,985	40,945	88,930	12.2	23.9
1959	50,867	43,624	94,491	12.7	23.2
1960	51,592	43,914	95,486	12.3	23.2
1961	49,206	42,142	91,348	11.5	24.2
1962	51,976	43,078	94,874	11.6	23.9
1950[1]	33,114	29,224	62,338	10.2	24.4
1951	33,858	30,451	64,309	10.3	24.1
1952	43,099	38,867	81,966	12.9	21.6
1953	42,057	38,011	80,068	12.4	24.2
1954	45,058	39,461	84,519	12.8	22.7
1955	47,407	40,436	87,843	13.0	23.6
1956	45,353	38,846	84,199	12.2	25.1
1957	48,686	42,820	91,506	12.9	25.5
1958	47,985	40,945	88,930	12.3	25.5
1959	50,867	43,624	94,491	12.7	24.6
1960	51,572	43,914	95,486	12.6	25.2(21.8)[3]
1961	49,206	42,142	91,348	11.8	26.3(22.9)
1962	51,796	43,078	94,874	11.9	26.2(22.6)
1963	53,877	44,416	98,293	12.1	25.6(21.9)
1964	51,195	42,863	94,058	11.3	25.1(21.8)
1965	49,305	42,343	91,648	10.8	24.7(21.5)
1966	49,824	41,262	91,086	10.5	23.4(20.4)
1967	47,857	38,983	86,840	9.8	21.1(19.5)
1968	46,149	38,284	84,433	9.4	19.6(18.2)
1969	46,320	38,016	84,336	9.2	18.2(16.8)
1970	45,278	37,736	83,014	8.9	17.9(16.6)
1971	45,893	37,563	83,456	8.7	18.6(17.3)
1972	49,089	38,340	87,429	9.0	18.7(17.3)
1973	45,708	35,286	80,994	8.2	18.9(17.6)
1974	42,713	35,571	78,284	7.4	18.0(16.8)
1975[2]	40,863	33,319	74,182	7.2	17.8(15.6)
1975*[2]			76,178	7.4	19.7
1976			81,380	7.8	16.1
1977			74,584	7.0	15.4

Notes: 1. The present table includes two sets of time series for male and female general deaths, crude death rates and rates of natural increase of the population between 1950 and 1962. The two sets are presented here so that the reader and researcher can be aware of the different population estimates available and of changes in such estimates over time. The second and more recent estimate can also be considered as the more reliable one.

TABLE 3.1 (Cont'd)

Population Deaths. General Deaths According to Sex,
Crude Death Rates and Rate of Natural Population Increase. 1870-1977.

Notes: 2. The first set of figures for 1975 was obtained from the National Health Service. The second set of figures for 1975 was obtained from the National Institute of Statistics. See also sources of this table.

3. The figures of the rate of natural population increase in parentheses (1960-1974) were obtained as the difference between the crude death rate and crude birth rates obtained by taking as a basis those figures of total population published in República de Chile, Ministerio de Economía, Fomento y Reconstrucción, Instituto Nacional de Estadísticas. Población 1960-1975, Total País, Provincias y Area Metropolitana (Santiago, Chile: INE, 1977), pp. 1-16 and included in the present volume's table on population births, live births according to legitimacy, 1870-1975.

Sources: The information for the period 1870-1946 was obtained from República de Chile, D.G.E., Demografía y Asistencia Social Año 1946 (Santiago, Chile: Dirección General de Estadística 1949), pp. 1-2. The information about deaths and death rates for the period 1947-1962 was obtained from Demografía Año 1962 (Santiago, Chile: Dirección de Estadística y Censos, 1964), tables 7 and 8, pp. 32-33. Mortality rates have changed over time because of upward revision in the figures of live births. In the present table a discontinuity exists in the figures between 1946 and 1947 and the upward revision of the time series on live births causes a sudden drop in the mortality rates. The various mortality rates were calculated by using the population and birth figures of the table that gives population, birth, and birth rates or have been provided by INE. The more recent data for the 1950-1975 period was obtained from the National Institute of Statistics. The source for the information for 1974 and 1975 is the National Health Service. The figures for 1975*, 1976 and 1977 were obtained from INE, Informativo Estadístico, Septiembre-Diciembre Año 1977 (Santiago, Chile: INE, 1978), table 1, p. 1.

TABLE 3.2

Population Deaths. Deaths Between Birth and One Year of Age by Sex and Infant Mortality Rates, 1870-1975.

Years	Deaths					
	Less Than One Month Old			Less Than One Year Old		
	Male	Female	Per 1,000 of Live Births	Male	Female	Per 1,000 of Live Births
Averages						
1890-94	-		-	33,433		338.0
1895-99	-		-	30,562		290.0
1900	-		-	37,917		343.0
1901	-		-	39,330		340.0
1902	-		-	31,299		270.0
1903	-		-	16,003	14,464	264.0
1904	-		-	17,317	16,082	286.0
1905	-		-	15,555	14,294	249.0
1906	-		-	20,050	18,271	327.0
1907	-		-	19,023	18,506	298.0
1908	-		-	21,789	19,441	318.0
1909	-		-	21,339	19,398	315.0
1910	-		-	18,217	16,540	267.0
1911	-		-	23,124	21,300	333.0
1912	-		-	20,079	18,737	287.0
1913	-		-	20,836	19,299	266.0
1914	-		-	18,184	16,598	255.0
1915	18,584		136.0	18,300	16,444	254.0
1916	19,028		132.0	18,369	16,428	241.0
1917	21,239		142.0	21,140	19,029	269.0
1918	20,150		138.0	19,388	17,763	255.0
1919	22,243		153.0	23,340	21,084	306.0
1920	19,856		135.0	20,044	18,610	263.0
1921	20,063		136.0	21,412	19,739	278.0
1922	17,694		120.0	18,716	16,648	270.0
1923	20,965		138.8	22,732	20,233	283.0
1924	20,231		130.0	21,677	19,620	266.0
1925	19,358		124.0	21,017	19,259	258.0
1926	19,138		120.0	21,205	18,848	251.0
1927	18,564		108.0	20,594	18,453	226.0
1928	17,589		98.0	20,183	17,820	212.0
1929	9,457	8,043	99.0	21,351	18,130	224.0
1930	8,980	7,842	99.0	21,099	18,615	234.0
1931	8,153	7,132	102.0	18,559	16,304	232.0
1932	8,346	7,217	104.0	18,831	16,286	235.0
1933	8,905	7,824	113.0	20,155	17,951	258.0
1934	9,398	8,559	119.0	20,720	18,663	262.0
1935	9,318	8,376	116.0	20,213	18,219	251.0
1936	9,077	8,135	110.0	20,774	18,795	252.0
1937	8,620	7,554	105.0	19,411	17,503	241.0
1938	8,253	7,141	99.0	19,612	16,900	236.0
1939	7,779	6,908	90.0	19,404	17,332	225.0
1940	7,532	6,622	85.0	19,089	17,101	217.0
1941	6,935	6,151	79.0	17,494	15,539	200.0
1942	6,762	5,917	74.0	17,578	15,568	195.0
1943	6,689	5,923	73.0	17,541	15,837	194.0
1944	6,961	5,849	73.0	16,836	14,780	181.0
1945	6,724	5,824	70.0	17,453	15,378	184.0
1946	6,021	5,027	63.0	15,047	12,982	160.0
1947	11,327		54.1	30,048		145.1
1948	11,108		53.8	30,358		147.0
1949	11,814		57.2	32.064		155.2
1950[1]	10,706		51.8	28,792		139.4
1951	10,338		49.3	28,419		135.5

TABLE 3.2 (Cont'd)

Population Deaths. Deaths Between Birth and One Year of Age by Sex and Infant Mortality Rates, 1870-1975.

Years	Deaths: Less Than One Month Old			Deaths: Less Than One Year Old		
	Male	Female	Per 1,000 of Live Births	Male	Female	Per 1,000 of Live Births
1952	9,561		46.5	26,594		129.2
1953	9,270		41.6	25,058		112.4
1954	9,255		41.9	27,645		125.1
1955	9,511		40.1	28,426		119.8
1956	8,930		35.8	27,572		110.4
1957	9,324		35.5	30,062		114.4
1958	9,383		35.6	31,947		121.3
1959	9,582		35.8	31,441		117.5
1960	9,934		36.2	34,314		125.1
1961	10,047		35.4	31,505		111.2
1962	10,154		35.1	44,105		119.6
1950[2]				15,385	13,457	136.8
1951				15,244	13,175	132.6
1952				14,341	12,253	121.5
1953				13,529	11,529	105.6
1954				15,029	12,616	117.7
1955				15,447	12,979	115.2
1956				14,854	12,718	107.0
1957				16,224	13,838	110.6
1958				17,404	14,543	116.7
1959				17,103	14,339	113.6
1960				18,624	15,690	119.5
1961				17,091	14,414	106.4
1962				18,083	15,022	109.2
1963				16,700	14,037	100.3
1964				17,048	14,396	103.7
1965				15,965	13,444	97.3
1966				15,939	13,074	98.5
1967				14,124	11,776	94.7
1968				12,393	10,404	87.0
1969				11,423	9,525	83.1
1970				11,411	9,238	82.2
1971				10,494	8,802	73.9
1972				10,814	8,786	72.7
1973				9,872	7,785	65.8
1974[2]				9,412	7,539	63.3
1975[2]				7,916	6,301	55.4

Notes: 1. The deaths of male and female infants (less than one year) and the infant mortality rates are presented for the 1950-1962 period twice. This procedure was adopted in order to demonstrate that the figures published by the various Chilean statistical agencies have changed over time though, in general, not substantially.

2. The more recent corrected information for the 1950-1962 period should be considered as more reliable than the earlier estimates also found in this table.

Sources: The information for the period 1870-1946 was obtained from República de Chile, D.G.E. Demografía y Asistencia Social Año 1946 (Santiago, Chile: Dirección General de Estadística 1949), pp. 1-2. The information about deaths and death rates for the period 1947-1962 was obtained from Demografía Año 1962 (Santiago, Chile: Dirección de Estadística y Censos, 1964), tables 7 and 8, pp. 32-33. The absolute values of infant

TABLE 3.2 (Cont'd)

Population Deaths. Deaths Between Birth and One Year of Age by Sex and Infant Mortality Rates, 1870-1975.

Sources (cont'd): (below one year) and neo-natal (below one month or twenty-eight days) mortality have remained relatively stable in the various publications. They should therefore be considered rather reliable. The mortality rates, nevertheless, have changed because of the upward revision in the figures of live births. In the present table a discontinuity exists in the figures between 1946 and 1947 and the upward revision of the time series on live births causes a sudden drop in the mortality rates. The various mortality rates were calculated by using the population and birth figures of the table that gives population, birth, and birth rates. The more recent data for the 1950-1975 period was obtained from the National Institute of Statistics. The source for the information for 1974 and 1975 is the National Health Service.

Tacla and Pujol (1965) and also found in Somoza and Tacla (1966: 24).

Thus, infant mortality for males, according to Somoza and Tacla (1966: 24)(always per thousand) was 263.96 during 1919-22 (central moment 31-XII-1920), 205.44 during 1939-42 (central moment 31-XII-1940) and 122.24 during 1960-61 (central moment 31-XII-1960). With 1960 as the base year, the index of masculine infant mortality declined from 215.9 during 1919-22 to 100.0 during 1960-61. Infant mortality of females was 248.66 during 1919-22 (the central moments are the same as those given earlier), 188.48 during 1939-42 and 107.19 during 1960-61 (Somoza and Tacla: 1966, 24 and 1969, 271). With 1960 again as the base year, female infant mortality declined from 232.0 during 1919-22 to 100.0 during 1960-61.

Neo-natal mortality is another important indicator of the level of development achieved by a nation. The neo-natal mortality rate is the relation between deaths of children under 30 (earlier 28) days old and the number of births that occurred during a specific year, expressed per thousand. As can be seen in Tables 3.2 and 3.3, the neo-natal death rate declined from 136.0% in 1915 to 20.9% in 1977.

The probabilities of death between birth and one year of age by sex and region are presented in Table 3.4. This measure corresponds to the infant mortality rate. There is an inverse relationship between the level of infant mortality and life expectancy. Thus, region X, which according to Table 3.8 had one of the lowest life expectancies in 1969-70, has at 117.4% the highest level of infant mortality. The Metropolitan Area has, with 57.5 deaths per thousand, the lowest infant mortality and is followed closely by those of regions I and XII. However, Chile's nationwide infant mortality rate presented in Tables 3.2 and 3.3 as well as the lowest one for Santiago found in Table 3.5 are significantly above the levels encountered in developed countries, which are close to 10-15 per thousand.

Deaths: Accuracy of the Data

The generally accepted opinion among demographers and other specialists on mortality data is that death records are reasonably complete. Although it is also generally agreed that there exists a certain percentage of omission, the lack of adequate background information has made it impossible to estimate the magnitude of this omission and take it into account in the calculations of population and mortality rates (Tacla: 1975, 2).

Though Chile's infant mortality rate has been and still remains very high for the country's income and general development level, even so the official figures seem to underestimate its true level due to underreporting.

According to a study by Hugo R. Behm on "Mortalidad infantil y nivel de vida" (infant mortality and standard of living), Ediciones de la Universidad de Chile, Santiago, Chile, 1962, it would not be exaggerated to think of the possibility that some infants are not buried in official cemeteries in remote rural areas, especially during the winter (Tacla: 1975, 2).

TABLE 3.3

Population, Natality, Neo-Natal Mortality, Infant Mortality and General Mortality. Chile 1931-1970.

Years	Population (In thousands of Inhabitants)	Natality		Mortality					
				Neo-Natal		Infant		General	
		Live Births	Rate[1]	Deaths -28 Days	Rate[2]	Deaths -1 Year	Rate[2]	Total Deaths	Rate[1]
1931	4,429	180,305	40.7	15,285	84.8	34,663	192.2	95,189	21.5
1932	4,495	182,827	40.7	15,563	85.1	35,117	192.2	99,664	22.2
1933	4,563	181,589	39.8	16,729	92.1	38,106	209.8	118,432	26.0
1934	4,631	181,653	39.2	17,957	98.8	39,383	216.8	119,078	25.7
1935	4,700	179,120	38.1	17,694	98.8	38,432	214.6	112,364	23.9
1936	4,771	174,766	36.6	17,212	98.5	39,569	226.4	114,392	24.0
1937	4,842	169,280	35.0	15,923	94.1	36,420	215.1	109,132	22.5
1938	4,914	171,172	34.8	15,288	89.3	35,946	210.0	112,658	22.9
1939	4,988	180,742	36.2	14,575	80.6	36,317	200.9	113,244	22.7
1940	5,063	184,061	36.4	13,961	75.8	35,482	192.8	107,771	21.3
1941	5,149	182,305	35.4	13,095	71.8	32,578	178.7	100,091	19.4
1942	5,244	188,070	35.9	12,473	66.3	32,676	173.7	104,122	19.9
1943	5,341	190,143	35.6	12,379	65.1	32,867	172.8	103,325	19.3
1944	5,440	193,204	35.5	12,524	64.8	31,222	161.6	103,054	18.9
1945	5,541	196,944	35.5	12,245	62.2	32,399	164.5	105,903	19.1
1946	5,643	194,111	34.4	10,817	55.7	27,717	142.8	92,664	16.4
1947	5,748	206,391	35.9	11,001	53.3	29,468	142.8	92,026	16.0
1948	5,854	208,815	35.7	11,031	52.8	30,474	145.9	98,405	16.8
1949	5,962	209,619	35.2	11,340	54.1	31,499	150.3	102,234	17.1
1950	6,073	208,092	34.3	10,483	50.4	28,345	136.2	90,081	14.8
1951	6,185	209,509	33.9	10,056	48.0	27,551	131.5	91,473	14.8
1952	6,295	218,036	34.6	9,528	43.7	25,696	117.8	80,251	12.7
1953	6,437	229,699	35.7	9,168	39.9	24,544	106.9	78,508	12.2
1954	6,597	230,484	34.9	9,461	41.0	27,804	120.7	84,635	12.8
1955	6,761	243,118	36.0	9,720	40.0	28,320	116.5	87,386	12.9
1956	6,944	254,519	36.6	9,118	35.8	27,509	108.1	83,744	12.1
1957	7,121	266,776	37.5	9,502	35.6	30,008	112.5	91,073	12.8
1958	7,298	270,018	37.0	9,452	35.0	31,914	118.1	88,611	12.1
1959	7,465	271,816	36.4	9,694	35.7	31,043	114.2	93,292	12.5
1960	7,628	282,681	37.0	9,965	35.2	34,003	120.3	93,625	12.3
1961	7,858	290,412	37.0	10,367	35.7	31,638	108.9	91,551	11.6
1962	8,029	304,930	38.0	10,333	33.9	32,920	108.0	94,569	11.8
1963	8,222	309,908	37.7	11,053	35.7	31,044	100.2	98,901	12.0
1964	8,450	306,050	36.2	10,411	34.0	31,495	102.9	94,111	11.0

TABLE 3.3 (Cont'd)

Population, Natality, Neo-Natal Mortality, Infant Mortality and General Mortality. Chile 1931-1970.

Years	Population (In thousands of Inhabitants)	Natality		Mortality					
				Neo-Natal		Infant		General	
		Live Births	Rate[1]	Deaths -28 Days	Rate[2]	Deaths -1 Year	Rate[2]	Total Deaths	Rate[1]
1965	8,484	308,014	36.3	10,318	33.5	29,394	95.4	91,491	10.8
1966	8,661	295,761	34.1	10,297	34.8	28,909	97.7	90,488	10.4
1967	8,838	277,009	31.3	9,512	34.3	26,127	94.3	86,987	9.8
1968	9,015	273,296	30.3	8,646	31.6	22,807	83.5	84,560	9.4
1969	9,192	268,807	29.2	8,357	31.1	21,156	78.7	84,680	9.2
1970	9,369	261,609	27.9	8,195	31.3	20,750	79.3	83,166	8.9
1971	9,545	273,518	28.7	7,743	28.3	19,271	70.5	83,240	8.7
1972	9,722	277,891	28.6	8,062	29.0	19,752	71.1	88,658	9.1
1973	9,899	276,650	27.9	7,450	27.0	18,029	65.2	82,988	8.4
1974	10,076	267,977	26.6	6,903	25.8	16,951	63.3	78,284	7.8
1975	10,253	256,543	25.0	6,369	24.8	14,217	55.4	74,182	7.2
1976	10,454	247,722	23.7	5,848	23.6	13,374	54.0	79,389	7.6
1977	10,655	240,463	22.6	5,037	20.9	11,429	47.5	73,541	6.9

Notes: 1. Rate per 1,000 inhabitants.
2. Rate per 1,000 live births.

Source: Servicio Nacional de Salud, Dirección General, Departamento Técnico, Anuario 1970, Defunciones y Causas de Muente (Santiago, Chile: SNS, July 1971), p. 1, for the period 1931-1964 and SNS, Anuario 1977, Defunciones y Causasdde Muerte (Santiago, Chile: SNS, June 1978), Table 1, p. 4 for the 1965-77 period.

TABLE 3.4

Chile: Probability of Death Between 0 and 1 Year (Infant Mortality Rate), by Sex and According to Region, 1969-1970. (Per Thousand)

Region	Province	Males	Females	Both Sexes
	Total of Country	89.2	75.4	82.5
I	Tarapacá	60.4	55.6	58.1
II	Antofagasta	97.9	74.3	86.4
III	Atacama	94.6	90.7	92.7
IV	Coquimbo	90.8	78.7	84.9
V	Aconcagua and Valparaíso (including the department of San Antonio)	63.5	54.6	59.1
VI	O'Higgins and Colchagua	87.5	72.4	80.1
VII	Curicó, Talca, Maule and Linares	105.5	97.4	101.5
VIII	Ñuble, Concepción, Arauco and Bío-Bío	114.3	101.2	107.9
IX	Cautín and Malleco	115.4	99.4	107.6
X	Valdivia, Osorno, Llanquihue and Chiloé	124.4	110.0	117.4
XI	Aysén	95.3	75.5	85.6
XII	Magallanes	63.3	53.5	58.5
Metropolitan Region of Santiago (excluding the department of San Antonio)		64.4	50.2	57.5

Source: Pujol, 1976b, p. 22 and ODEPLAN, 1975c, p. 23.

Strong support to the hypothesis that infant deaths have been underreported was given by the Pan-American Health Organization. As part of the Interamerican Research on Childhood Mortality during the years 1968-1970, a study was made of a sample of deaths of children under five years of age residing in Great Santiago and four rural communities in the Northern Hospital Area (Area Hospitaloria Norte) and the findings were published in an article by A. Legarreta, L. López and A. Aldea on "Omisión del Registro de Defunciones de Niños Fallecidos en Maternidades" (Omission in the registration of children dying in maternity wards), Boletín de la Organización Panamericana de la Salud, Vol. LXXV, No. 4, October 1973.

The researchers of the Pan-American Health Organization found in their first year of the investigation of death rates of children under one year of age that Santiago had the surprisingly low infant mortality rate of around six deaths per one thousand live births, which compared favorably to the figure of ten per thousand in the USA. Rather than attributing the low recorded infant deaths in Santiago to superior medical services, the researchers considered the hypothesis that this phenomenon was caused by omissions in the registration of deaths of infants that survived a few hours or days (Tacla: 1975, 2).

Their subsequent findings confirmed the underregistration hypothesis. It was determined that the omission in the registration of deaths of children under 28 days of age was 56.1 percent. Furthermore, with respect to the relationship between the degree of omission and survival of the children, it was determined that for children that had survived for a few minutes, the underregistration amounted to 78 percent. These figures tend to decline as the child survives for longer periods but tend to remain high, since slightly more than one third of the children that died after having lived for eight days or more were not registered legally (Tacla: 1952, 2).

The results obtained from this investigation are, according to Tacla, who is a leading demographer with the National Institute of Statistics, of transcendental importance because they are bound to shape the official statistics published by the National Institute of Statistics and the National Health Service on the basis of information supplied to them by the Servicio de Registro Civil e Identificación (Civil Registration and Identification Service) which collects the data (Tacla: 1975, 3). Correction of the omission is bound to bring along an increase in the published rates of infant mortality. To the extent that infant deaths are underreported while births are reported accurately, the rate of natural population increase may be exaggerated. However, to the extent that infant deaths relate to children whose birth was not recorded in the first place, improved registration will mean an increase of both the crude birth and infant mortality rates.

Even though the statistics on births are corrected in order to incorporate in the calculations those that are hypothetically registered late, no effort had been made until 1975 by either the National Health Service or the National Institute of Statistics to correct the death rates for an underestimate of infant deaths (Tacla: 1975, 3). It is further more possible, due to the social upheaval between 1969 and 1975, that the rather sharp decline in infant mortality in recent years is in part explained by an increase in underregistration of infant deaths.

In its publications Defunciones y Causes de Muerte, e.g. SNS: 1978c, publishes time series of population, mortality (live births and rate), mortality (neo-natal, infant and general). Deaths are recorded according to province of residence, type (with or without medical certification), age and sex, month of occurrence, causes of death (by single type and group and age for each group). Special, detailed tables provide information for tuberculosis and cancer as causes of death according to month, province, age groups, localities and sex (SNS: 1978c, 107-129).

MORTALITY AND LIFE EXPECTANCY

The values of the crude death are strongly affected by the age structure of the population. Even though, therefore, they can be used to make intertemporal comparisons within a country such as Chile, they are normally avoided in making comparisons in the conditions of mortality between countries or regions. Thus, as an example, (Tacla: 1975, 9) even with equal sanitary conditions, the country with a larger proportion of elderly will have a higher mortality than another with a younger age structure (for example the cases of France and the United States of America). It then becomes more appropriate to analyze mortality by sex and age since it varies according to these variables.

A summary and purified measure that permits the study of the evolution of mortality by sex and age is the life expectancy at birth. The life expectancy at birth, or average life, is the average number of years of life corresponding to each member of a recently born generation if the time that the whole generation is expected to live with the level of mortality of the table is divided uniformly among the individuals that form the generation (Tacla: 1975, 9).

In a 1976 study, Pujol (1976b) elaborated mortality tables for Chile and for each of the 13 regions in which Chile had been divided for administrative reasons by 1976. This study contains sex-specific tables covering the period 1969-1970. The basic data came from the Population Census (April 22, 1970) and from vital statistics for deaths and births published by the National Institute of Statistics.

Pujol used two methods. One for the population under five years of age, and the other for the population over five. The method used for the first group is called that of "inter-related births". By means of this method death probabilities are calculated on the basis of birth (previously adjusted) and death data from vital statistics. For the second group (over five), death probabilities were derived from age-specific mortality rates by means of the Reed and Merrel equations.

The mortality table is an instrument that permits the measurement of mortality through its different functions. A synthetic measure of the mortality table is the expectancy of life at birth which represents the average number of years which a newly born infant is expected to live subject to the mortality risks expressed in the table. This measure has the advantage of not being affected, as we have already mentioned, by the age structure of the population, as it happens with the crude mortality rate and other synthetic measures.

The mortality tables constructed by Pujol (1976b), ODEPLAN and CELADE (ODEPLAN: 1975c) demonstrate in a systematic manner that the levels of female mortality by age are below those of the male population. Life expectancy at birth by sex for Chile since 1920 is presented in Table 3.5. Comparing life expectancy at birth by sex it becomes evident that (a) the life expectancy of females always exceeds that of males and (b) that the differences between sexes have increased systematically over the years.

TABLE 3.5

Life Expectancy at Birth by Sex.
(In Years)

Period of Table	Males	Females	Difference
1919-1922[a]	30.90	32.21	1.31
1929-1932[a]	39.47	41.75	2.28
1939-1942[a]	40.65	43.06	2.41
1952-1953[b]	52.95	56.83	3.88
1960-1961[b]	54.35	59.90	5.55
1969-1970	58.50	64.68	6.18

a. Cabello O., Vildósola, J. and Latorre, M., "Tablas de vida para Chile 1920, 1930, 1940", in Revista Chilena de Higiene y Medicina Preventiva, Vol. VIII, Nº 3, September, 1946, and Vol. IX, Nº 2, June, 1947.

b. Tacla O. and Pujol, J. M., Chile: Tablas abreviadas de mortalidad, 1952-1953 y 1960-1961, CELADE, Serie C, Nº 11, September, 1968.

Source: Pujol, 1976b, p. 17 and ODEPLAN, 1975c, p. 17.

TABLE 3.6

Annual Increase of Life Expectancy at Birth.
(In Years)

Period	Males	Females
1920-1930	0.86	0.95
1930-1940	0.12	0.13
1940-1952	1.02	1.15
1952-1960	0.18	0.38
1960-1970	0.42	0.48

Source: Pujol, 1976b, p. 18 and ODEPLAN, 1975c, p. 18.

Contained in Table 3.6 is the annual increase experienced by life expectancy at birth for each sex. As Table 3.6 clearly demonstrates the increase experienced by the life expectancy at birth of females has been larger than that observed by the life expectancy of males.

Life expectancies at birth by sex and the differences between sexes at the regional level are presented in Tables 3.7 and 3.8. As demonstrated in Table 3.8, the regions with the highest life expectancy are the I, XII and the Metropolitan while Regions VIII and IX have the lowest. It is worth noting that during 1960-61 there were interregional differences of more than 10 years while, in contrast, the largest difference in 1969-1970 was of the order of six years (between Region IX and Region XII). Another notable fact is that the differences between the female and male life expectancies in 1969-70 ranged between 3.7 (IX region) and 7.9 (II region) years.

If the figures by sex are examined, it can be observed that the highest value for men corresponds to region XII both in 1960-61 and 1969-1970 and that the lowest in 1969-1970 corresponds to region VIII, which is approximately the same region that had the lowest life expectancy in 1960-61. The highest value for women is found in the Metropolitan Area and the lowest in region IX. In general, it can be said that no significant differences have been produced in the ranking of the different provinces in terms of life expectancy between 1960-1 and 1969-70.

Although there has been a significant decline in mortality in Chile as expressed by the rise in life expectancy for males from 30.90 years during 1919-22 to 58.50 during 1969-70 and for females from 32.21 during 1919-22 to 64.68 during 1969-70, "male life expectancy would have to rise an addi-

TABLE 3.7

Chile: Life Expectancy at Birth by Sex at the National and Regional Level,1960-1961. (In Years)

Region	Province	Males (1)	Females (2)	Both Sexes (3)	Difference (2)-(1)
	Total of Country	54.35	59.90	57.06	5.55
I	Tarapacá	56.71	63.22	59.55	6.51
II	Antofagasta	55.31	60.01	57.42	4.70
III	Atacama and Coquimbo	54.98	59.52	57.09	4.54
IV	Aconcagua and Valparaíso	56.51	62.26	59.38	5.71
V	O'Higgins and Colchagua	54.44	59.82	56.96	5.38
VI	Curicó, Talca, Maule and Linares	52.01	58.14	54.64	6.13
VII	Ñuble, Concepción, Arauco, Bío-Bío and Malleco	50.38	56.00	53.08	5.62
VIII	Cautín, Valdivia and Osorno	52.70	55.93	54.20	3.23
IX	Llanquihue, Chiloé and Aysén	54.42	58.20	56.38	3.88
X	Magallanes	60.77	66.13	63.16	5.36
Metropolitan Region of Santiago		56.62	63.08	59.92	6.46

Source: L. Alvarez and J. M. Pujol, Chile: Tablas Abreviadas de Mortalidad por Regiones, 1960-1961 (Santiago, Chile: CELADE, Serie A, Nº 76, November, 1967), Pujol, 1976b, p. 20 and ODEPLAN, 1975c, p. 20.

TABLE 3.8

Chile: Life Expectancy at Birth by Sex at the National and Regional Level, 1969-1970. (In Years)

Region	Province	Males (1)	Females (2)	Both Sexes (3)	Difference (2)-(1)
	Total of Country	58.50	64.68	61.50	6.18
I	Tarapacá	61.93	67.21	64.50	5.28
II	Antofagasta	56.52	64.39	60.35	7.87
III	Atacama	59.12	64.45	61.70	5.33
IV	Coquimbo	61.53	65.49	63.45	3.96
V	Aconcagua and Valparaíso (including the Department of San Antonio)	61.10	67.04	63.99	5.94
VI	O'Higgins and Colchagua	59.25	64.43	61.77	5.18
VII	Curicó, Talca, Maule and Linares	56.70	62.38	59.46	5.68
VIII	Ñuble, Concepción, Arauco and Bío-Bío	54.98	61.83	58.30	6.85
IX	Cautín and Malleco	57.04	60.78	58.86	3.74
X	Valdivia, Osorno, Llanquihue and Chiloé	56.63	61.38	58.94	4.75
XI	Aysén	59.85	64.80	62.24	4.95
XII	Magallanes	61.96	67.26	64.54	5.30
Metropolitan Region of Santiago (excluding the Department of San Antonio)		60.71	68.12	64.31	7.41

Source: Pujol, 1976b, p. 19 and ODEPLAN, 1975c, p. 19.

tional 10.9 years and that of women 11.9 years to reach the level of France in 1968" (Tacla: 1975, 11).

SOME EVIDENCE ON ABORTION

Since abortion is a factor in preventing births or a cause of death of the unborn infant (nasciturus) and thus a determinant of population growth, it is important to provide some statistical evidence on abortion gathered in a study of Requena (1968) and also summarize its major findings.

The total number of pregnancies examined by Requena and the spontaneous and induced abortions, both in absolute numbers and percentages, are presented in Table 3.9. This table also contains the findings of an earlier study on abortion by R. Armijo and T. Monreal ("Epidemiología del Aborto Provocado en Santiago," Documentos, Escuela de Salubridad. Santiago, Chile). Statistics on the age of the mother at the time of conception and the type of termination of pregnancies are presented in Table 3.10. Requena provides a total of 23 tables examining the relationship between abortion and a variety of socioeconomic characteristics. The major findings of this study are the following. The percentage of pregnancies that ended in induced abortions in the sample of Quinta Normal is significantly higher than that encountered in the total Santiago population. This is in part explained by the influence of socioeconomic factors since this sample includes exclusively the low socioeconomic stratum. Furthermore, women can be classified into three categories: (a) the first would include women that practice no birth control whatsoever and have a large family; (b) the second would be composed of women that have had numerous spontaneous abortions due to pathological factors and therefore have no need to practice any type of birth control; (c) in the third group are those women who desire to limit the size of their family and do this primarily by means of induced abortions.

TABLE 3.9

Number of Pregnancies and Percentage of All Abortions, Spontaneous and Induced. Findings of Requena and Armijo-Monreal.

	Findings of Requena				Findings of Armijo-Monreal			
	Number		Percentage		Number		Percentage	
Pregnancies	2,617				4,577			
Abortions	903		34.5		1,310		28.6	
Spontaneous		295		11.3		548		12.0
Induced		608		23.2		762		16.6

Source: Mariano Requena, 1968, p. 7.

TABLE 3.10

Percentage Distribution of 2,617 Pregnancies According to Type of Termination and the Age of Mother at the Time of Conception. (Quinta Normal, 1962-63).

Age	Number	Percentage	Total Result			
			Born Alive	Stillborn	Spontaneous	Induced
15-19	272	10.4	80.2	2.2	5.5	12.1
20-24	871	33.3	69.1	1.3	8.4	21.2
25-29	788	30.1	60.3	0.8	10.0	28.9
30-34	463	17.7	56.8	1.3	17.9	24.0
35 and more	199	7.6	61.3	0.5	16.1	22.1
Unknown	24	0.9	-	-	-	-
Total	2,617	100.0	64.3	1.2	11.3	23.2

Source: Mariano Requena, 1968, p. 8.

The civil status, education and frequency of sexual relations did not demonstrate any relationship with the risk of inducing abortions. The woman working as an untrained laborer has a higher risk of abortion than the housewife, office worker or professional. It was also found that the risk was higher when the husband or cohabitant was unemployed.

The Catholic woman has the same risk as the woman without religion and a higher one than Protestant women. Rather curiously, the risk of inducing abortions rises in the Catholic woman to the extent that her religious fervor is higher, measured on the basis of the frequency with which she attends religious services. Furthermore, the longer the time a woman has lived in Santiago the higher the risk that she will resort to induced abortion. Also, the risk of inducing an abortion is higher in the higher socioeconomic strata represented in the sample.

Finally, those women who mentioned that they had practiced some form of contraception have a higher risk of induced abortion than those who did not practice birth control. It was demonstrated that the great majority of birth control methods were inefficient.

ESTIMATES OF MORTALITY IN THE XVIII AND XIX CENTURIES

Carmen Arretx, Rolando Mellafe and Jorge L. Somoza have published a series of short monographs on mortality estimates in the eighteenth and nineteenth century. The have utilized modern methods of historical demography to prepare, in spite of major difficulties and some shortcomings, some first rate and highly informative studies.

In their first study (Arretx, Mellafe, Somoza: 1976c) they obtained life tables for adults in the XVIII and XIX centuries on the basis of records of the first three religious orders in Santiago (one of nuns and two of monks). This group of members of Chilean religious orders presented excellent conditions for estimating life expectancy.

The whole sample comprised 585 cases with 285 men and 300 women who lived between the years 1655 and 1933. According to the results, life expectancy for a female in Chile in the first half of the XIX Century at the age of 25 was of 35.72 years and for a man of 33.04 years. The life expectancy results obtained for Chile in the aforementioned period were compared with life expectancy known to prevail in Holland and Sweden at the same period and there were found no differences.

Another study made use of historical data available in the Parish of Ñuñoa during 1866-1871 when this area was a satellite town of Santiago. The group investigated was one of peasants and was strongly affected by immigration coming from the whole country (Arretx, Mellafe, Somoza: 1976a and 1976b). Data were drawn from marriage records of orphans which in this case contain, besides the age of the couple, information on whether the parents of the newly married were dead or alive. The method of Louis Henry (1960) ("Mesure Indirecte de la Mortalité des adultes," Population, XV, June-July 1960, N° 3) and William Brass and Ken Hill (1973) (Estimating Adult Mortality from Orphanhood, International Union for the Scientific Study of Population, International Population Conference, Liege, 1973) were applied to this information on orphanhood to obtain adult mortality indicators. Results from this study are consistent with the mortality estimates for monks within the same period made in the first study, as well as with mortality for European population at the same time. In fact, with information on orphanhood and on monks, values for expectation of life at age 30 are of 31 years for both sexes, in the same order of magnitude as those for the European population.

The data gathered in this study from marriage records of the parish of Ñuñoa between 1869 and 1871 about the condition of orphanhood of newly married permitted the derivation of estimates on adult mortality by sex which correspond to the mid nineteenth century. The data collected seem to be consistent and have only one defect which is often found in modern-day data of this type: The incidence of maternal orphanhood in the youngest group considered — people aged 15-19 — is apparently underestimated. The estimates showed that male mortality was higher than female mortality and placed the level of mortality in the expected order of magnitude.

These findings are of approximately the same order as the aforementioned mortality among members of religious orders in Santiago between approximately 1757 and 1867. These estimates, by sex, are presented in Table 3.11 together with the values of expectation of life drawn from European life tables in the nineteenth century and the values of expectation of life calcu-

TABLE 3.11

Expectation of Life at Ages 30, 40, 50 and 60 in Selected Life Tables

	Expectation of life at age:			
	30	40	50	60
		Men		
Orphans: Ñuñoa (1869-1871)				
- Method of Henry	30.0	23.5	17.4	12.0
- Method of Brass-Hill	29.7	23.0	16.5	11.0
Members of Chilean religious orders (1757-1867)	29.0	21.9	16.1	11.6
Sweden (1816-1840)	30.3	23.7	17.6	12.1
Netherlands (1816-1825)	27.6	21.9	16.4	11.6
England and Wales (1841)	33.1	23.5	17.5	12.0
		Women		
Orphans: Ñuñoa (1869-1871)				
- Method of Henry	32.7	26.2	19.6	13.4
- Method of Brass-Hill	31.7	24.7	18.1	12.2
Members of Chilean religious orders (1757-1867)	32.3	25.7	19.7	14.6
Sweden (1816-1840)	33.4	26.4	19.6	13.2
Netherlands (1816-1825)	30.7	24.8	18.7	12.8
England and Wales (1841)	34.3	27.7	21.1	14.4

Source: Arretx, Mellafe and Somoza, 1976b, 13.

lated from marriage records of Ñuñoa orphans.

The figures in the table show that mortality estimates from information on orphanhood were very similar to those registered in other populations in the same period. It is interesting to note that although the group of religious members was not representative of the population of Chile, both groups have similar mortality levels.

In the third study, Arretx, Mellafe and Somoza (1977a) have drawn on data from registers of deaths (registros parroquiales de defunciones) from the parish (Parroquía) of San Felipe and on population censuses taken in that area in 1787 to make estimates of adult mortality. These estimates were made on the basis of information on age structure of annual deaths and population and by using a basic relation which, even though valid strictly in a stable population demographic model, was sufficiently robust to be extended to actual populations.

Furthermore, Arretx, Mellafe and Somoza compared the resulting estimates of mortality in terms of a life table for the age interval 10-60 with their earlier mortality estimates for the three religious orders in Santiago and for the group of peasants in the parish of Ñuñoa for periods covering approximately from the mid XVIII century to the mid XIX century. The mortality estimated for San Felipe is higher than the mortality of these two populations.

Data for deaths by age were drawn from Defunction Books (libros de defunciones) of the white population of the San Felipe parish from 1780 to 1787. Thus, their mortality estimates are of a white rural country population that could easily be typical of the Central Valley of Chile in the last decades of the Eighteenth Century.

The research was made with calculations relating exclusively to information about the white or mestizo European population which was referred to in the various documents of that epoch with terms such as Spaniards, American Spaniards, whites, mestizos and so forth. Expressions such as Indians, coloured mestizos (mestizos de color), zambos, mulattoes, coloured breeds (castas de color) and so forth were used for those society groups that were ostensibly Indian or mestizos of African descent. When, then, mortality rates by age were calculated by relating the number of registered annual deaths to the number of enumerated persons, Arretx, Mellafe and Somoza obtained apparently exaggerated values. The data of the registers and of the census could be conciliated if only 60 percent of the registered deaths were taken into account. As this and the earlier studies indicate, the most serious obstacle to high quality studies in Chilean historical demography is the lack of reliable time series or cross section statistical information.

NATURAL POPULATION INCREASE

Most of the official statistics indicate that Chile has not been a country of large scale immigration such as Argentina. The statistical evidence on international in- and out-migration from Chile is presented in Chapter 7. Here, following the concensus of demographers in Chile, it is assumed that international migration has not been a significant determinant of population. The rate of natural population increase for the period between 1870 and 1975, which is presented in Table 3.1, is therefore determined by the interaction between natality and mortality.

The rate of natural population increase was "relatively" stable until 1940. There were some significant fluctuations before 1940 but they did not seem to establish a clearcut trend, even though there was a mild rise since 1907. According to the averages calculated by Odette Tacla (1975, 6) the annual rate of natural population increase rose from 1.1% during 1907-1920, to 1.4% during 1920-1930, to 1.6% during 1930-1940, to 2.0% during 1940-1952 and 2.5% during 1952-1960 (the crude birth experienced its sharpest decline during 1940-1960), and then fell to 2.3% during the 1960-1970 decade when the birth rate decline set in. If the figures of Table 3.3 are used, the rate of natural population increase had fallen to 1.57% in 1977.

Depending on what official population figures are used different estimates of the rate of natural population increase are obtained. Two such estimates are presented in Table 3.1 for the period between 1960 and 1975.

LATE FOETAL DEATHS

Late foetal deaths are those of at least 28 weeks gestation. Late foetal deaths by sex and late foetal death ratios for the period between 1903 and 1975 are presented in Table 3.12.

TABLE 3.12

Late Foetal Deaths by Sex and Late Foetal Death Ratios, 1903-1975.[2]

Years	Total	Sex		Late Foetal Death Rates Per 1000 Live Births[1]
		Males	Females	
1903	2,545	1,392	1,153	21.6
1904	2,843	1,531	1,312	23.7
1905	2,900	1,572	1,321	23.7
1906	2,947	1,589	1,358	24.5
1907	2,775	1,512	1,263	21.5
1908	3,476	1,913	1,563	26.1
1909	3,543	1,919	1,624	26.7
1910	3,471	1,920	1,551	26.0
1911	3,611	2,004	1,607	26.3
1912	3,842	2,147	1,695	27.6
1913	4,013	2,201	1,812	27.8
1914	3,993	2,202	1,791	28.4
1915	3,525	2,017	1,508	25.2
1916	3,513	1,950	1,563	23.8
1917	3,864	2,152	1,712	25.3
1918	3,834	2,117	1,717	25.6
1919	3,914	2,183	1,731	26.3
1920	4,122	2,257	1,865	27.3
1921	4,116	2,304	1,812	27.1
1922	4,358	2,374	1,984	28.8
1923	4,521	2,468	2,053	28.9
1924	4,670	2,592	2,078	29.2
1925	4,757	2,581	2,176	29.5
1926	4,738	2,081	2,057	28.8
1927	5,203	2,849	2,354	29.3
1928	5,560	3,150	2,410	30.0
1929	6,036	3,360	2,676	32.2
1930	5,866	3,310	2,556	33.5
1931	5,863	3,252	2,611	37.7
1932	5,943	3,261	2,682	38.2
1933	6,489	3,585	2,904	42.1
1934	7,336	4,160	3,176	46.5
1935	7,848	4,279	3,569	48.7
1936	7,877	4,341	3,536	47.8
1937	8,224	4,545	3,679	50.9
1938	8,239	4,454	3,785	50.5
1939	7,955	4,395	3,560	46.4
1940	8,047	4,478	3,569	46.1
1941	8,171	4,541	3,660	47.2
1942	8,179	4,540	3,639	45.8
1943	8,150	4,533	3,617	45.2
1944	7,253	4,018	3,235	39.8
1945	7,521	4,120	3,401	40.5
1946	7,192	4,053	3,139	39.3
1947	7,114	3,937	3,177	34.3
1948	7,412	4,079	3,333	35.9
1949	7,493	4,061	3,432	36.3
1950	7,490	4,111	3,379	35.5
1951	7,382	3,943	3,439	34.5
1952	7,423	4,138	3,285	33.9
1953	7,489	4,114	3,375	31.6
1954	7,132	3,937	3,195	30.4
1955	6,995	3,886	3,109	28.4
1956	7,209	3,995	3,214	28.0
1957	7,461	4,222	3,239	27.4
1958	7,018	3,882	3,136	25.6
1959	7,171	3,915	3,256	25.9
1960	7,269	4,028	3,241	25.3
1961	7,442	4,085	3,357	25.1

TABLE 3.12 (Cont'd)

Late Foetal Deaths by Sex and Late Foetal Death Ratios, 1903-1975.[2]

Years	Total	Sex		Late Foetal Death Rates Per 1000 Live Births[1]
		Males	Females	
1962	7,294	4,015	3,279	24.1
1963	7,395	3,936	3,459	24.1
1964	6,839	3,690	3,149	22.6
1965	6,657	3,538	3,119	22.0
1966	6,940	3,579	3,361	23.6
1967	6,550	...	...	24.0
1968	5,572	...	...	21.3
1969	4,987	2,553	2,434	19.8
1970	4,884	2,501	2,383	19.4
1971	5,015	2,467	2,548	19.2
1972	5,603	2,792	2,811	20.8
1973	4,538	2,290	2,248	16.9
1974	4,596	2,386	2,250	17.2
1975	4,274	2,097	2,177	16.7

Notes: 1. Late foetal death rates were calculated by using corrected data on live births.

2. Late foetal deaths are those of at least 28 weeks gestation. Foetal deaths of unknown gestational age are included. Ratios are the number of late foetal deaths per 1,000 live births.

Sources: The information concerning late foetal deaths for the years between 1870 and 1946 inclusive was obtained from DEC, Demografía y Asistencia Social, Año 1946 (Santiago, Chile: DEC, 1949), pp. 1-2. For the years 1953, 1954, 1955 and 1956 it was obtained from Demografía Año 1956, p. 91. For the years 1957, 1958, 1959, from Demografía Año 1959, and for 1960, 1961, and 1962, from Demografía Año 1962, p. 269. The number of late foetal deaths for the 1947-1962 period was also obtained from Demografía Año 1962, table 7, p. 32. There is no conflict or discontinuity between the earlier and later figures of this series. The rate of late foetal deaths is not, however, a consistent series. Before 1946, the denominator of this ratio is the total live and dead births. After 1946, the denominator is live births only. The figures for this ratio for the 1947-1962 period were obtained from Demografía Año 1962, table 8, p. 33. The information for the years between 1962 and 1973 was obtained from the National Institute of Statistics. The data for 1974 and 1975 was obtained from the National Health Service.

4
NUPTIALITY

Marriage is an institution that reflects the social and political development of a nation and is an integral part of economic development. The nature and stability of marriage, the role and contributions of each partner at different phases of the marriage are factors influencing and being affected by economic development. Such variables as infant mortality, health, education, nutrition and subsequent achievement of children, causes of death and patterns of migration are influenced by the level and nature of nupciality.

MARRIAGES AND MARRIAGE RATES

According to the United Nations Demographic Yearbook (UN: 1977) "marriage is defined as the act, ceremony or process by which the legal relationship of husband and wife is constituted. The legality of the union may be established by civil, religious, or other means as recognized by the laws of each country" (UN: 1977, 33).

The total population of Chile, the number of marriages and marriage rates between 1870 and 1975 are presented in Table 4.1. The total number of marriages rose almost continuously since 1870 reaching its peak of 85,577 in 1972 but declining rather sharply since then to 76,205 in 1975. The marriage rate displays some long swings rising from 3 per thousand during 1885-89 to 11.6 per thousand in 1928 and 10.0 per thousand in 1929, the golden years of Chile's mineral-based export-led growth. The marriage rate displays some shorter, approximately 15-year swings, since 1929 with peaks in 1939 (9.6%), 1955 (8.9%) and 1971 (8.9%) and troughs in 1932 (6.6%), 1951 (7.5%), and 1962 (6.7%).

The marriage statistics presented in Tables 4.1, 4.2, 4.3, 4.4, 4.5 and 4.6 include both first marriages and remarriages after widowhood, separation or annulment. These statistics refer to the number of marriages performed, and not to the number of persons marrying.

The marital status of the Chilean population of 15 years and over by sex and age groups for the 1952, 1960 and 1970 censuses is presented in Table 4.2. It is of interest to note that in all three censuses the number of women reporting to be married exceeds the number of men reporting to be married (by approximately 21,000 in 1952 and 1960 and by 11,000 in 1970). This can be explained either by the fact that many husbands may have emigrated and are located in foreign countries or because males underreport and females overreport marriages.

The age classification of Table 4.2 is the following: 5-year age groups from 15-19 through 60-64 years and 65 years and over.

Table 4.2 provides data on the marital status of the population 15 years of age and older according to whether they are single (never married), married, living together or in common-

TABLE 4.1

Total Population, Number of Marriages, and Marriage Rates, 1870-1975.

Years	Population (average)	Marriages No.	Marriages Marriage Rates 0/00
Averages			
1870-74	1,995,498	15,473	7.8
1875-79	2,159,415	14,605	6.8
1880-84	2,383,008	14,621	6.1
1885-89	2,563,313	7,614	3.0
1890-94	2,645,408	11,921	4.5
1895-99	2,795,202	13,675	4.9
1900	2,902,368	13,331	4.6
1901	2,946,629	17,740	6.0
1902	2,991,917	16,751	5.6
1903	3,037,893	15,912	5.2
1904	3,084,068	16,295	5.3
1905	3,130,945	17,220	5.5
1906	3,178,534	18,507	5.8
1907 (Census)	3,249,279	21,271	6.5
1908	3,268,684	21,491	6.6
1909	3,307,493	19,637	5.9
1910	3,346,302	19,326	5.8
1911	3,385,111	19,814	5.9
1912	3,423,920	21,258	6.2
1913	3,462,729	21,461	6.2
1914	3,501,538	19,002	5.4
1915	3,540,347	19,150	5.4
1916	3,579,156	20,121	5.6
1917	3,617,965	21,379	5.9
1918	3,656,774	21,614	5.9
1919	3,695,583	21,471	5.8
1920 (Census)	3,753,799	24,932	6.6
1921	3,773,955	24,954	6.6
1922	3,801,292	25,023	6.6
1923	3,847,071	25,912	6.7
1924	3,874,008	28,276	7.3
1925	3,929,086	28,726	7.3
1926	3,976,983	30,344	7.6
1927	4,033,767	32,278	8.0
1928	4,118,095	47,671	11.6
1929	4,119,167	42,004	10.0
1930 (Census)	4,287,445	39,202	9.1
1931	4,321,995	29,052	6.7
1932	4,375,070	28,813	6.6
1933	4,420,363	29,562	6.7
1934	4,446,617	30,017	6.8
1935	4,485,792	32,661	7.3
1936	4,530,051	34,201	7.5
1937	4,572,147	38,082	8.3
1938	4,618,869	37,487	8.1
1939	4,645,510	44,767	9.6
1940 (Census)	5,023,539	42,187	8.4
1941	5,057,064	42,390	8.4
1942	5,130,089	43,559	8.5
1943	5,199,036	43,004	8.3
1944	5,272,784	43,358	8.2
1945	5,349,209	42,488	7.9
1946	5,429,866	42,564	7.8
1947	5,748,000	45,248	7.9
1948	5,854,000	46,414	7.9
1949	5,962,000	46,260	7.8
1950	6,073,000	46,001	7.6
1951	6,185,000	46,195	7.5
1952	6,295,000	48,327	7.7
1953	6,437,000	54,354	8.4
1954	6,597,000	54,563	8.3
1955	6,761,000	59,929	8.9
1956	6,944,000	58,470	8.4
1957	7,121,000	53,783	7.6
1958	7,298,000	52,803	7.2
1959	7,465,000	55,364	7.4
1960	7,585,350	55,865	7.2
1961	7,770,270	57,394	7.2
1962	7,955,190	54,948	6.7
1963	8,140,110	56,863	7.4
1964	8,325,030	60,370	7.3
1965	8,509,950	64,922	7.6
1966	8,681,671	66,155	7.6
1967	8,853,393	65,199	7.4
1968	9,025,115	65,375	7.2
1969	9,196,837	66,893	7.3
1970	9,368,558	71,631	7.6
1971	9,545,449	84,747	8.9
1972	9,722,341	85,577	8.8
1973	9,899,231	83,550	8.4
1974	10,076,123	79,954	7.9
1975	10,253,014	76,205	7.4

Sources: The statistical information used in this table for 1870-1946 inclusive, was obtained from Demográfia y Asistencia Social, Año 1946 (Santiago, Chile: Dirección de Estadística y Censos, 1949), pp. 1-2. The number of marriages from 1946 to 1962 was obtained from Demográfia Año 1962 (Santiago, Chile: Dirección de Estadística y Censos, 1964), table no. 7, p. 32. The marriage rate for the period from 1946 through 1962 was obtained from Demográfia Año 1962, table no. 8, p. 33. The time series on the number of marriages is consistent and reliable. Because the population figures used to obtain the marriage rates up to and including 1946 were not corrected and those used to obtain the marriage rates after 1946 were corrected, the rates for before and after 1946 are not strictly comparable. The population statistics for the years 1947-59 were obtained from Demográfia Año 1962, table 1, p. 1. The figures of total population from 1960 to 1975 were obtained from República de Chile, Ministerio de Economía, Fomento y

TABLE 4.1 (Cont'd)

Total Population, Number of Marriages, and Marriage Rates, 1870-1975.

Sources (cont'd): Reconstrucción, Instituto Nacional de Estadísticas. Población 1960-1975, Total País, Provincias y Area Metropolitana (Santiago, Chile: INE, 1977), pp. 1-16. The number of marriages from 1947 to 1975 were obtained from the National Institute of Statistics. Marriage rates from 1962 to 1975 were estimated by dividing the number of marriages of each year by the average total population of the same year. These rates are estimated per 1,000 inhabitants.

law marriage, widowed, separated or with marriage annulment and marital status unknown. Annulment is defined as the invalidation or voiding of a marriage by a competent authority, according to the laws of Chile, which confers on the parties the status of never having been married to each other.

The number of marriages by age of groom are presented in Table 4.3 for the period between 1964 and 1973. The number of marriages by age of bride between 1964 and 1973 is presented in Table 4.4.

Age is defined as age at last birthday or completed years. The age classification used in this table is the following: under 15 years, 5-year age groups through 70-74 years, 75 years and over and age unknown. The same classification is used for both grooms and brides.

The number of marriages according to regions and provinces between 1969 and 1973 is presented in Table 4.5. And the number of marriages and marriage rates according to regions between 1969 and 1973 are presented in Table 4.6.

A variety of aspects of nupciality in Chile, but with figures not as recent as those presented in this chapter are discussed in Zulma Camisa, La Nupcialidad de las miyeres solteras en la América Latina (San José, Costa Rica: CELADE 1977) Serie A No. 1034. A highly informative historical study of Chilean population which contains a short section on nuptiality is by Héctor Gutiérrez Roldan, La Población de Chile (Paris, France: Committee for International Coordination of National Research in Demography, 1975), pp. 51-53.

The figures on Chile confirm that females tend to marry earlier than males. Thus among those who were legally married in 1970, 8 per cent of the males did so before becoming 20 years old. In contrast, before the same age, the proportion corresponding to women was 30.5 per cent. Although nupciality is early for both sexes, it is much earlier for females. Of the total number of marriages contracted in 1970, 52.9 per cent corresponded to males and 69.1 per cent to females of less than 25 years old (Gutiérrez: 1975, 52). It can be expected that the 1980 census will show a significant delay in the average age at which males and females entered into a marriage. The decline in fertility experienced between 1970 and 1979 is likely to have resulted from later marriages as well as increased use of family control devices by married females.

TABLE 4.2

Total Population 15 Years of Age and Over by Sex, According to Age Groups and Marital Status. 1952, 1960, and 1970: Census Data.

Age Groups and Marital Status	1952		1960		1970	
	Male	Female	Male	Female	Male	Female
Total	1,796,635	1,919,873	2,144,688	2,306.909	2,592,586	2,811,040
15-19 years	282,200	291,717	354,554	370,253	446,729	466,736
20-24 years	275,467	299,570	287,637	310,762	370,653	398,383
25-29 years	213,144	234,918	251,833	275,172	301,862	324,130
30-34 years	185,795	195,565	246,879	260,273	249,409	267,312
35-39 years	179,374	197,677	199,965	215,448	247,473	267,078
40-44 years	163,939	159,245	178,478	185,401	223,014	232,778
45-49 years	127,714	133,484	157,143	167,091	172,260	184,593
50-54 years	114,819	116,571	137,561	141,015	149,338	163,277
55-59 years	79,281	81,813	103,319	109,013	127,242	141,449
60-64 years	69,019	78,450	86,342	96,713	105,715	117,484
65 and over	105,883	130,863	140,977	175,768	198,891	247,820
Single	771,176	715,726	876,434	827,865	1,026,414	988,601
15-19 years	278,672	265,544	349,924	334,903	437,451	420,684
20-24 years	217,196	174,207	221,303	177,477	272,587	223,068
25-29 years	97,546	81,201	104,965	89,134	113,252	97,726
30-34 years	51,965	45,481	60,272	54,837	62,387	52,355
35-39 years	36,188	36,396	37,027	36,810	37,322	40,432
40-44 years	26,939	26,619	27,323	28,068	28,450	30,866
45-49 years	18,010	21,027	21,231	23,947	19,944	23,687
50-54 years	14,721	18,919	17,015	21,279	16,138	21,151
55-59 years	9,264	12,769	11,765	16,616	13,161	18,759
60-64 years	8,675	12,850	10,152	15,796	11,055	16,800
65 and over	12,000	20,713	15,457	28,998	24,687	43,073
Married	876,379	897,470	1,102,821	1,124,578	1,389,863	1,401,117
15-19 years	2,726	22,709	3,921	31,682	7,070	40,524
20-24 years	51,820	111,710	60,215	120,934	90,302	161,133
25-29 years	104,401	136,297	135,256	107,557	177,080	207,330
30-34 years	120,397	130,442	171,208	181,150	184,446	192,409
35-39 years	128,167	135,581	147,575	152,163	194,949	198,831
40-44 years	121,099	105,985	134,889	128,380	178,404	168,111
45-49 years	95,168	84,138	120,148	110,641	137,193	126,717
50-54 years	84,711	65,834	104,324	84,253	117,322	102,688
55-59 years	58,058	41,251	77,202	58,287	98,976	80,226
60-64 years	47,020	31,152	61,049	42,132	78,361	55,482
65 and over	62,812	32,371	87,036	47,399	125,760	69,666

TABLE 4.2 (Cont'd)

Total Population 15 Years of Age and Over by Sex, According to Age Groups and Marital Status. 1952, 1960, and 1970: Census Data.

Age Groups and Marital Status	1952		1960		1970	
	Male	Female	Male	Female	Male	Female
Living Together "Common Law Marriage"	61,091	65,645	71,835	76,932	60,766	70,958
15-19 years	523	2,712	553	2,912	1,498	3,950
20-24 years	5,020	9,632	4,905	8,620	5,872	8,991
25-29 years	8,007	10,549	8,687	10,906	7,932	9,817
30-34 years	9,043	9,680	10,640	12,168	7,962	9,492
35-39 years	9,386	10,520	9,848	11,158	8,485	10,083
40-44 years	8,517	7,818	9,073	9,248	7,370	8,607
45-49 years	6,243	5,624	7,764	7,662	6,033	6,201
50-54 years	5,107	3,616	6,678	5,580	4,856	4,616
55-59 years	3,272	2,108	4,878	3,368	3,738	3,554
60-64 years	2,732	1,691	3,830	2,446	2,951	2,367
65 and over	3,241	1,695	4,979	2,864	4,069	3,280
Widowed			68,657	222,148	79,764	271,693
	70,826	204,792				
15-19 years	61	200	52	189	220	524
20-24 years	451	1,229	284	960	456	1,419
25-29 years	1,413	2,978	845	2,321	878	2,803
30-34 years	2,277	5,500	1,649	4,804	1,397	4,978
35-39 years	3,362	9,782	2,422	7,797	2,521	8,927
40-44 years	5,168	14,012	4,018	12,261	4,070	13,870
45-49 years	6,260	18,358	5,069	17,843	4,998	18,420
50-54 years	8,497	24,512	6,765	24,015	7,027	26,168
55-59 years	7,519	23,290	7,378	26,398	8,003	31,870
60-64 years	9,490	30,837	9,458	32,872	10,512	37,711
65 and over	26,328	74,094	30,717	92,688	39,682	125,003

TABLE 4.2 (Cont'd)

Total Population 15 Years of Age and Over by Sex, According to Age Groups and Marital Status. 1952, 1960, and 1970: Census Data.

Age Groups and Marital Status	1952		1960		1970	
	Male	Female	Male	Female	Male	Female
Separated-Annulment	15,232	34,710	24,508	55,254	35,779	78,671
15-19 years	88	446	76	554	490	1,054
20-24 years	703	2,536	847	2,749	1,436	3,772
25-29 years	1,556	3,776	2,045	5,247	2,720	6,454
30-34 years	1,916	4,328	3,047	7,295	3,237	8,078
35-39 years	2,088	5,266	3,059	7,515	4,196	10,805
40-44 years	2,040	4,673	3,132	7,437	4,720	11,324
45-49 years	1,720	4,234	2,909	6,993	4,092	9,568
50-54 years	1,670	3,563	2,740	5,876	3,995	8,654
55-59 years	1,094	2,300	2,079	4,336	3,364	7,040
60-64 years	1,005	1,810	1,829	3,454	2,836	5,124
65 and over	1,352	1,778	2,745	3,798	4,693	6,798
Unknown	1,931	1,530	433	132	-	-
15-19 years	130	106	28	13	-	-
20-24 years	277	256	83	22	-	-
25-29 years	221	117	36	1	-	-
30-34 years	197	134	63	19	-	-
35-39 years	183	132	34	5	-	-
40-44 years	176	138	43	7	-	-
45-49 years	313	103	22	5	-	-
50-54 years	113	127	39	12	-	-
55-59 years	74	95	17	8	-	-
60-64 years	97	110	24	13	-	-
65 and over	150	232	44	21	-	-

Source: The figures for the years 1952 and 1970 were obtained from the National Institute of Statistics of Chile. The figures for the year 1960 were obtained from República de Chile, Censo Población 1960, Resumen País (Santiago, Chile: Dirección de Estadística y Censos), table 1.4.1, pp. 152-154.

TABLE 4.3

Marriages According to Age Group of Groom.
1964-1973.

Age Groups of Consort	Marriages									
	1964	1965	1966	1967	1968	1969	1970	1971	1972	1973
Total	60,370	64,922	66,155	65,199	65,375	66,893	71,631	84,747	85,577	83,550
Under 15 years	7	10	17	12	12	5	10	20	10	5
15-19 years	4,651	4,912	5,409	5,297	5,219	5,405	5,699	7,073	7,367	7,529
20-24 years	24,627	26,757	27,600	28,114	27,983	29,494	31,906	37,226	38,596	37,737
25-29 years	15,049	16,401	16,829	16,478	16,239	17,258	18,965	22,446	22,079	21,407
30-34 years	6,927	7,039	6,701	6,303	6,588	6,289	6,347	7,930	7,858	7,630
35-39 years	3,223	3,567	3,581	3,239	3,427	2,855	3,035	3,555	3,312	3,155
40-44 years	1,819	1,860	1,804	1,723	1,772	1,686	1,703	2,228	2,104	2,002
45-49 years	1,163	1,223	1,127	1,070	1,024	1,015	1,052	1,286	1,237	1,227
50-54 years	896	956	870	845	770	767	724	918	903	848
55-59 years	637	667	693	597	603	612	565	729	684	616
60-64 years	526	548	500	489	482	471	509	600	532	534
65-69 years	382	425	411	458	408	399	409	426	417	389
70-74 years	198	270	281	264	244	242	286	337	273	255
75 years and over	165	186	235	201	191	204	191	273	205	216
Unknown	100	101	97	109	413	191	230	-	-	-

Source: National Institute of Statistics.

TABLE 4.4

Marriages According to Age Group of Bride.
1964-1973.

Age Group of Wife	Marriages									
	1964	1965	1966	1967	1968	1969	1970	1971	1972	1973
Total	60,370	64,922	66,155	65,199	65,375	66,893	71,631	84,747	85,577	83,550
Under 15 years	911	1,026	1,018	987	977	1,026	1,039	1,332	1,331	1,210
15-19 years	16,981	17,804	18,780	18,488	18,467	18,956	20,742	24,553	25,670	25,694
20-24 years	21,987	23,860	24,543	24,722	24,827	25,920	27,690	32,250	32,600	31,733
25-29 years	9,515	10,735	10,635	10,502	10,505	10,934	11,575	13,969	13,946	13,340
30-34 years	4,583	4,645	4,463	4,257	4,055	4,123	4,400	5,502	5,238	5,138
35-39 years	2,483	2,703	2,609	2,447	2,312	2,109	2,165	2,621	2,455	2,332
40-44 years	1,439	1,522	1,519	1,343	1,373	1,389	1,396	1,735	1,661	1,579
45-49 years	905	956	900	876	830	766	852	986	1,022	955
50-54 years	610	687	639	597	545	538	554	653	663	649
55-59 years	367	367	430	400	384	378	416	470	431	399
60-64 years	242	291	253	250	237	232	241	335	286	272
65-69 years	110	144	170	138	153	142	132	189	146	128
70-74 years	78	77	81	61	81	65	63	97	78	74
75 years and older	37	50	42	38	41	31	25	55	50	47
Unknown	122	55	73	93	588	284	341	-	-	-

Source: National Institute of Statistics.

TABLE 4.5

Marriages According to Regions and Provinces.
1969-1973.

	Regions and Provinces	Marriages 1969	1970	1971	1972	1973
	Total	66,893	71,631	84,747	85,577	83,550
I	Tarapacá	1,327	1,495	1,949	2,083	1,856
	Arica	757	840	1,181	1,248	1,149
	Iquique	570	655	768	835	707
II	Antofagasta	2,086	2,375	2,587	2,810	2,538
	Tocopilla	343	321	355	361	314
	Antofagasta	1,206	1,438	1,489	1,675	1,501
	El Loa	537	616	743	774	723
III	Atacama	1,164	1,207	1,370	1,367	1,322
	Chañaral	322	344	364	375	337
	Copiapó	530	548	597	624	588
	Huasco	312	315	409	368	397
IV	Coquimbo	2,189	2,337	2,751	2,752	2,849
	Elqui	1,204	1,286	1,499	1,455	1,534
	Limarí	613	664	802	806	796
	Choapa	372	387	450	491	519
V	Aconcagua	7,606	8,035	9,208	9,615	9,291
	Valparaíso	4,563	4,711	5,490	5,703	5,600
	San Antonio	550	662	694	699	711
	Quillota	1,153	1,235	1,397	1,508	1,454
	Petorca	304	314	371	407	368
	San Felipe	618	656	775	750	690
	Los Andes	411	448	467	528	461
	Isla de Pascua	7	9	14	20	7
VI	Of the Liberator General Bernardo O'Higgins	3,604	3,707	4,360	4,434	4,343
	Chapoal	2,490	2,446	2,917	2,992	2,921
	Colchagua	1,114	1,261	1,443	1,442	1,422
VII	Maule	4,151	4,361	5,286	5,261	5,345
	Cuvicó	1,097	1,125	1,374	1,330	1,424
	Talca	1,626	1,726	2,159	2,161	2,126
	Linares	1,428	1,510	1,753	1,770	1,795
VIII	Bío-Bío	8,489	8,965	10,606	11,068	10,966
	Ñuble	2,032	2,102	2,527	2,542	2,454
	Concepción	4,176	4,421	5,157	5,553	5,549
	Aráuco	686	721	945	936	991
	Bío-Bío	1,595	1,721	1,977	2,037	1,972
IX	Of the Araucania	3,499	3,694	4,959	5,025	5,113
	Malleco	955	1,007	1,419	1,437	1,480
	Cautín	2,544	2,687	3,540	3,588	3,633
X	Of the Lakes	4,652	5,134	6,418	6,459	6,348
	Valdivia	1,696	1,871	2,397	2,442	2,303
	Osorno	1,095	1,177	1,483	1,434	1,471
	Llanguihue	1,235	1,380	1,750	1,780	1,695
	Chiloé	626	706	788	803	879
XI	Aisen of General Carlos Ibañez Del Campo	358	312	427	446	420
	Aisén	302	263	345	374	366
	General Carrera	41	43	66	64	46
	Capitan Prat	15	6	16	8	8
XII	Magallanes and Chilean Antarctica	760	808	924	997	974
	Ultima Esperanza	134	142	211	179	237
	Magallanes	586	625	674	776	707
	Tierra del Fuego	39	37	38	41	30
	Chilean Antarctica	1	4	1	1	-
	Metropolitan Region	27,008	29,201	33,902	33,260	32,185

Source: National Institute of Statistics.

TABLE 4.6

Marriages and Marriage Rates According to Regions. 1969-1973.

Regions	Marriages									
	Absolute Numbers					Rates Per 1000 Inhabitants				
	1969	1970	1971	1972	1973	1969	1970	1971	1972	1973
Total	66,893	71,631	84,747	85,577	83,550	7.3	7.6	8.9	8.8	8.4
I Tarapacá	1,327	1,495	1,949	2,083	1,856	7.4	8.1	10.3	10.7	9.3
II Antofagasta	2,086	2,375	2,587	2,810	2,538	8.0	8.9	9.6	10.2	9.1
III Atacama	1,964	1,207	1,370	1,367	1,322	7.4	7.5	8.3	8.1	7.7
IV Coquimbo	2,189	2,337	2,751	2,752	2,849	6.2	6.5	7.6	7.5	7.6
V Aconcagua	7,606	8,035	9,208	9,615	9,291	7.6	7.9	8.8	9.1	8.6
VI Of the Liberator General Bernardo O'Higgins	3,604	3,707	4,360	4,434	4,343	7.0	7.1	8.3	8.3	8.1
VII Maule	4,151	4,361	5,286	5,261	5,345	6.4	6.7	8.0	7.9	8.0
VIII Bío-Bío	8,489	8,965	10,606	11,068	10,966	8.5	6.8	7.9	8.2	8.0
IX Of the Arucania	3,499	3,694	4,959	5,025	5,113	5.6	5.9	7.8	7.9	8.0
X Of the Lakes	4,652	5,134	6,418	6,459	6,348	6.0	6.5	8.1	8.0	7.8
XI Aisén of General Carlos Ibañez del Campo	358	312	427	446	420	7.1	6.0	8.1	8.5	7.6
XII Magallanes and Chilean Antarctica	760	808	924	997	974	8.2	8.5	9.6	10.2	9.8
Metropolitan Region	27,008	29,201	33,902	33,260	32,185	8.4	8.8	9.9	9.5	8.9

Source: National Institute of Statistics.

5
AGE AND SEX COMPOSITION OF THE CHILEAN POPULATION

The age structure of the population exerts an important influence on the process of economic development. The number and share of children in the total population shape the demand for education, influence female participation rates and can shape a household's capacity to save. The supply of labor is determined by the age as well as sex structure of the population. The level as well as sectoral, commodity and consumption-investment composition of aggregate demand and the supply of labor and capital are closely linked to the age and sex composition of the population.

In the present chapter I present various tables about the age structure of the Chilean population.

Age is defined as age at last birthday or completed years. Table 5.1 provides the population of Chile by age groups for the 1885-1970 censuses and for 1975 and 1980. The age classification used in Table 5.1 includes 12 categories as follows: begins with 0-9 years group and continues with 10-year groups to 90-99 and ends with 100 and over and age unknown.

The population of Chile according to sex and age groups for the censuses of 1920, 1930, 1940, 1952, 1960 and 1970 is presented in Tables 5.2 to 5.7. These tables provide the absolute as well as relative numbers of males and females in each age group. The age classification used in Tables 5.2 to 5.7 includes 16 categories as follows: begins with 0-4 group and continues with 5-year groups to 70-74 and ends with 75 and over.

THE PYRAMIDAL AGE STRUCTURE

The age structure revealed by the distribution of the Chilean population according to quinquennial age groups has the distinct form of a pyramid for the censuses of 1930 and 1960. The percentage of the population in the 0-4 age group is larger than the percentage of the population in the 5-9 age group which is larger than the percentage in the 10-14 group and so forth. Thus, in the 1930 census the percentage of the population in the 0-4 age group is 13.6 while in the 5-9 age group it is 12.3. The only census with a clear indication of a weakening of the pyramidal age structure of the Chilean population is that of 1970 in which the percentage of the population in the 0-4 age group (12.2 per cent) is smaller than the percentage of the population in the 5-9 age group (13.7 per cent). The proportion of the population in each successive age group declines, often sharply. The proportion of the population in the 0-4 age group is also smaller than the percentage in the 5-9 age group in the censuses of 1920 and 1940 and is the same in the 1952 census, as can be observed in Tables 5.2, 5.4 and 5.5, but this phenomenon can be explained largely by the general underreporting of children in the 0-4 age group. In contrast, it is the sharp decline in fertility since the early 1960s that can be considered as the major force leading to a weakening of the pyramidal

TABLE 5.1

Comparative Table of Population by Age Groups.
Census Years, 1885-1970, and 1975 and 1980.[1]

Age Groups	1885	1895	1907	1920	1930	1940	1952	1960	1970	1975	1980
Total	2,497,797	2,687,984	3,220,531	3,714,887	4,287,445	5,023,539	5,932,995	7,374,115	8,884,768	10,253,014	11,259,871
0- 9	734,071	790,750	833,793	971,945	1,125,284	1,256,860	1,558,116	2,086,209	2,366,764	2,433,731	2,613,030
10-19	540,016	586,697	714,940	832,977	937,814	1,122,100	1,222,355	1,561,116	2,027,843	2,343,523	2,396,802
20-29	492,469	505,412	578,246	663,815	778,599	883,831	1,019,495	1,125,404	1,395,028	1,724,116	1,997,388
30-39	322,535	340,728	399,384	481,585	557,986	673,397	755,735	922,565	1,031,272	1,294,069	1,505,048
40-49	197,006	217,360	292,448	337,658	395,277	484,660	582,303	688,113	812,645	971,489	1,052,242
50-59	119,831	138,044	196,390	208,792	248,402	308,610	391,090	490,908	581,306	693,405	800,938
60-69	54,113	66,246	122,142	131,559	149,507	184,593	239,749	311,275	395,069	481,770	528,147
70-79	25,485	29,069	53,831	57,638	65,314	77,064	103,101	136,160	187,477[2]	239,587[2]	278,578[2]
80-89	9,013	9,669	21,633	22,040	22,223	24,908	31,879	42,949	87,364[2]	71,324[2]	87,698[2]
90-99	2,760	3,083	6,270	5,613	5,801	6,291	6,715	7,923			
100 or more	498	926	1,454	1,265	1,238	1,225	1,431	1,493			
Age unknown	-	-	-	-	-	-	21,026	-			

Notes: 1. Since it was impossible to obtain the age distribution of the population of the department of Arica, this is not included in the province of Tarapacá in the censuses of 1885, 1895, 1907 and 1920.

2. The figures for the years 1970, 1975 and 1980 are for 80 years or more.

Sources: The information for the census years 1885-1952 was derived from República de Chile, Servicio Nacional de Estadística y Censos, XII Censo General de Población y I de Vivienda, Tomo I. Resumen del País, 1952 (Santiago, Chile: Servicio Nacional de Estadística y Censos, 1956), table 7, p. 43. The 1960 census figures were obtained from República de Chile, DEC, Censo Población 1960, Resumen País (Santiago, Chile: DEC, 1960), table 1.1.3, p. 127. The 1970 census figures were obtained from INE, Población, Total País. XIV Censo de Población y III de Vivienda 1970 (Santiago, Chile: Imprenta INE, 1970), table 3, pp. 1-4. The estimates for the years 1975 and 1980 were obtained from INE, Anuario Estadístico, 1976 (Santiago, Chile: INE, 1977), pp. 20-21.

TABLE 5.2

Population According to Sex and Age Groups.
Absolute and Relative Numbers.
1920 Census.

Age Groups	Absolute Numbers			Relative Numbers		
	Total	Males	Females	Total	Males	Females
Total	3,753,799	1,865,827	1,887,972	100.0	100.0	100.0
0- 4	474,041	238,901	235,140	12.6	12.8	12.5
5- 9	506,648	256,659	249,989	13.5	13.8	13.2
10-14	442,022	225,570	216,452	11.8	12.1	11.5
15-19	398,186	193,618	204,568	10.6	10.4	10.8
20-24	353,550	173,497	180,053	9.4	9.3	9.5
25-29	318,914	154,504	164,410	8.5	8.3	8.7
30-34	251,977	124,772	127,205	6.7	6.7	6.7
35-39	235,788	118,293	117,495	6.3	6.3	6.2
40-44	202,317	102,077	100,240	5.4	5.5	5.3
45-49	139,692	71,406	68,286	3.7	3.8	3.6
50-54	134,489	65,152	69,337	3.6	3.5	3.7
55-59	76,236	38,858	37,378	2.0	2.1	2.0
60-64	93,740	43,493	50,247	2.5	2.3	2.7
65-69	38,872	19,143	19,729	1.1	1.0	1.1
70-74	42,065	19,678	22,387	1.1	1.0	1.2
75 and over	45,262	20,206	25,056	1.2	1.1	1.3

Source: National Institute of Statistics.

TABLE 5.3

Population According to Sex and Age Groups.
Absolute and Relative Numbers.
1930 Census.

Age Groups	Absolute Numbers			Relative Numbers		
	Total	Males	Females	Total	Males	Females
Total	4,287,445	2,122,709	2,164,736	100.0	100.0	100.0
0- 4	589,920	296,218	293,702	13.8	14.0	13.6
5- 9	535,364	269,859	265,505	12.5	12.7	12.3
10-14	468,495	237,661	230,834	10.9	11.2	10.7
15-19	469,319	229,000	240,319	10.9	10.8	11.1
20-24	416,854	205,558	211,296	9.7	9.7	9.8
25-29	361,744	172,169	189,575	8.4	8.1	8.8
30-34	288,576	145,344	143,232	6.9	6.9	6.6
35-39	269,410	132,304	137,106	6.3	6.2	6.3
40-44	217,770	109,976	107,794	5.1	5.2	5.0
45-49	177,507	89,793	87,714	4.1	4.2	4.0
50-54	149,473	73,737	75,736	3.5	3.5	3.5
55-59	98,929	49,384	49,545	2.3	2.3	2.3
60-64	96,457	44,304	52,153	2.2	2.1	2.4
65-69	53,050	26,185	26,865	1.2	1.2	1.2
70-74	44,270	19,776	24,494	1.0	0.9	1.1
75 and over	50,307	21,441	28,866	1.2	1.0	1.3

Source: National Institute of Statistics.

TABLE 5.4

Population According to Sex and Age Groups.
Absolute and Relative Numbers.
1940 Census.

Age Groups	Absolute Numbers			Relative Numbers		
	Total	Males	Females	Total	Males	Females
Total	5,023,539	2,489,926	2,533,613	100.0	100.0	100.0
0- 4	622,003	313,667	308,336	12.4	12.6	12.2
5- 9	634,857	321,952	312,905	12.6	12.9	12.4
10-14	609,297	306,807	302,490	12.1	12.3	11.9
15-19	512,803	256,321	256,482	10.2	10.3	10.1
20-24	456,930	218,871	238,059	9.1	8.8	9.4
25-29	426,901	204,395	222,506	8.5	8.2	8.8
30-34	352,405	177,431	174,974	7.0	7.1	6.9
35-39	320,992	155,405	165,587	6.4	6.3	6.5
40-44	268,675	136,983	131,692	5.3	5.5	5.2
45-49	215,985	109,145	106,840	4.3	4.4	4.2
50-54	174,021	86,081	87,940	3.5	3.5	3.5
55-59	134,589	68,181	66,408	2.7	2.7	2.6
60-64	118,223	55,443	62,780	2.4	2.2	2.5
65-69	66,370	32,586	33,784	1.3	1.3	1.3
70-74	51,099	22,562	28,537	1.0	0.9	1.1
75 and over	58,389	24,096	34,293	1.2	1.0	1.4

Source: These figures were obtained from Chile, XI Censo de Población (1940). Recopilación de Cifras Publicadas por la Dirección de Estadística y Censos (Santiago, Chile: Centro Latinoamericano de Demografía, CELADE), p. 335.

TABLE 5.5

Population According to Sex and Age Groups.
Absolute and Relative Numbers.
1952 Census.

	Absolute Numbers			Relative Numbers		
	Total	Males	Females	Total	Males	Females
Total	5,932,995	2,912,558	3,020,437	100.0	100.0	100.0
0- 4	781,925	393,432	388,493	13.2	13.5	12.9
5- 9	781,763	393,597	388,166	13.2	13.5	12.9
10-14	652,799	328,894	323,905	11.0	11.3	10.7
15-19	573,917	282,200	291,717	9.7	9.7	9.7
20-24	575,037	275,467	299,570	9.7	9.5	9.9
25-29	448,062	213,144	234,918	7.5	7.3	7.8
30-34	381,360	185,795	195,565	6.4	6.4	6.5
35-39	377,051	179,374	197,677	6.3	6.2	6.5
40-44	323,184	163,939	159,245	5.4	5.6	5.3
45-49	261,198	127,714	133,484	4.4	4.4	4.4
50-54	231,390	114,819	116,571	3.9	3.9	3.8
55-59	161,094	79,281	81,813	2.7	2.7	2.7
60-64	147,469	69,019	78,450	2.5	2.4	2.6
65-69	93,125	44,488	48,637	1.6	1.5	1.6
70-74	68,474	30,863	37,611	1.2	1.1	1.2
75 and over	75,147	30,532	44,615	1.3	1.0	1.5

Note: There were 21,060 persons that appeared with age unknown in the 1952 census. There were 12,698 males and 8,328 females, for a total of 21,026. They have been pro-rated in the present table.

Source: These figures were obtained from República de Chile, Censo Población 1960, Resumen País (Santiago, Chile: Dirección de Estadística y Censos, 1960), table no. 1.1.3, p. 127.

TABLE 5.6

Population According to Sex and Age Groups.
Absolute and Relative Numbers.
1960 Census.

Age Groups	Absolute Numbers			Relative Numbers		
	Total	Males	Females	Total	Males	Females
Total	7,374,115	3,612,807	3,761,308	100.0	100.0	100.0
0- 4	1,104,720	554,796	549,924	15.0	15.4	14.6
5- 9	981,489	492,442	489,047	13.3	13.6	13.0
10-14	836,309	420,881	415,428	11.3	11.6	11.1
15-19	724,807	354,554	370,253	9.8	9.8	9.8
20-24	598,399	287,637	310,762	8.1	8.0	8.3
25-29	527,005	251,833	275,172	7.2	7.0	7.3
30-34	507,152	246,879	260,273	6.9	6.8	6.9
35-39	415,413	199,965	215,448	5.6	5.5	5.7
40-44	363,879	178,478	185,401	4.9	4.9	4.9
45-49	324,234	157,143	167,091	4.4	4.3	4.5
50-54	278,576	137,561	141,015	3.8	3.8	3.8
55-59	212,332	103,319	109,013	2.9	2.9	2.9
60-64	183,055	86,342	96,713	2.5	2.4	2.6
65-69	128,220	60,615	67,605	1.7	1.7	1.8
70-74	84,455	38,032	46,423	1.2	1.1	1.2
75 and over	104,070	42,330	61,740	1.4	1.2	1.6

Source: These figures were obtained from República de Chile, Censo Población 1960, Resumen País (Santiago, Chile: Dirección de Estadística y Censos, 1960), table no. 1.1.3, p. 127.

TABLE 5.7

Population According to Sex and Age Groups.
Absolute and Relative Numbers.
1970 Census.

Age Groups	Absolute Numbers			Relative Numbers		
	Total	Males	Females	Total	Males	Females
Total	8,884,768	4,343,512	4,541,256	100.0	100.0	100.0
0- 4	1,122,834	567,233	555,601	12.6	13.1	12.2
5- 9	1,243,930	624,134	619,796	14.0	14.4	13.7
10-14	1,114,378	559,559	554,819	12.6	12.9	12.2
15-19	913,465	446,729	466,736	10.3	10.3	10.3
20-24	769,036	370,653	398,383	8.7	8.5	8.8
25-29	625,992	301,862	324,130	7.1	7.0	7.1
30-34	516,721	249,409	267,312	5.8	5.7	5.9
35-39	514,551	247,473	267,078	5.8	5.7	5.9
40-44	455,792	223,014	232,778	5.1	5.1	5.1
45-49	356,853	172,260	184,593	4.0	4.0	4.1
50-54	312,615	149,338	163,277	3.5	3.4	3.6
55-59	268,691	127,242	141,449	3.0	2.9	3.1
60-64	223,199	105,715	117,484	2.5	2.4	2.6
65-69	171,870	79,614	92,256	1.9	1.8	2.0
70-74	117,772	53,660	64,112	1.3	1.3	1.4
75 and over	157,069	65,617	91,452	1.8	1.5	2.0

Source: These figures were obtained from República de Chile, Población, Total País. XIV Censo de Población y III de Vivienda 1970 (Santiago, Chile: Instituto Nacional de Estadísticas, 1970), table 3, pp. 1-4.

age composition of the population in the census of 1970 of Chile. However, a clear change in the age structure is likely to become evident only in the 1980 census.

The base of the age pyramid has been very broad in all censuses between 1920 and 1970. Thus the percentage of the population in the 0-9 age group ranged between 24.6 per cent (1940) and 27.6 per cent (1960) while the percentage in the 0-19 age group ranged between 46.6 per cent (1940) and 48.5 per cent (1960). The Chilean population had the typical features of a young population with some early signals of ageing evident only in the 1970 census.

Some alterations in the structure of the age pyramid can be explained in terms of poor declarations of age, a preference in declaring an age that ends in zero or five or can reflect changes in mortality and fertility in previous decades. International migration can also influence the age structure of the population but this factor is believed not to have been very important in Chile (see for more comments in the chapter on international migration).

The population of Chile according to age and sex groups for the censuses of 1952, 1960 and 1970 is presented in Table 5.8. The age classification used in Table 5.8 includes 17 categories as follows: begins with the 0-4 group and continues with 5-year age groups to 75-79 and ends with 80 and over. The population of Chile according to age and sex (the same age classification as Table 5.8) for each year between 1960 and 1975 is presented in Table 5.9.

Masculinity, Ageing and Dependency

The sex structure or sex distribution of the population is generally measured by the ratio of the total number of one sex to the total number of the other sex. When the male sex is considered, we often speak of the masculinity of the population. The masculinity proportion is the proportion of males in the total population. The sex ratio is the ratio of the number of one sex to that of the other. The ratio of the number of men to the number of women is called the masculinity ratio or the masculinity index.

The masculinity index according to quinquennial age groups for 1960, 1965, 1970, 1975 and 1980 is presented in Table 5.10. As can be observed from Table 5.10 as well as from Tables 5.2 to 5.8, in the younger ages the masculine group is larger because of the larger number of live births of this sex. However, the higher mortality of males contributes to an ever higher ratio of females. With rising life expectancy, the masculinity ratio has fallen because of the ever rising gap in the life expectancy between males and females.

The masculinity ratio is higher in nations with heavy immigration since immigrants tend to be males. In the case of Chile Marin Lira (1975, 97) has estimated masculinity ratios excluding and including Chilean emigrants to Argentina for 1960 and these are presented in Table 5.11.

The ageing index is the proportion of persons 65 years of age and over per 100 persons in the 0-14 age cohort.

As the figures presented in Tables 5.12 and 5.13 indicate there can be observed a mild ageing trend in Chile between 1960 and 1975. The total ageing index rose from 11.04 in 1960 to 14.29 in 1975 while the ageing index for females rose during the same period from 12.64 to 16.67.

The dependency index measures the relationship between the economically active and inactive segments of the population. The higher the value of the dependency index the heavier the economic burden carried by the economically active segment of the population. The dependency index or ratio is defined as the proportion of persons in the 0-14 years age cohort plus the persons in the 65 years and over age cohort for each 100 persons 15-64 years of age. As can be observed in Table 5.12, the dependency index for Chile as a whole fell from 67.8 in 1976 to 66.8 in 1977.

A number of aspects of the age and sex structure of the Chilean population are discussed in Marin Lira (1975) and in Gutiérrez Roldan (1975).

TABLE 5.8

Total Population According to Age and Sex Groups
1952, 1960, and 1970: Census Data.

Age and Sex Groups	1952 Total	1960 Total	1970 Total
Total	5,932,995	7,374,115	8,884,768
0- 4	781,925	1,104,720	1,122,834
5- 9	781,763	981,489	1,243,930
10-14	652,799	836,309	1,114,378
15-19	573,917	724,807	913,465
20-24	575,037	598,399	769,036
25-29	448,062	527,005	625,992
30-34	381,360	507,152	616,721
35-39	377,051	415,413	614,551
40-44	323,184	363,879	455,792
45-49	261,198	324,234	366,853
50-54	231,390	278,576	312,615
55-59	161,094	212,332	268,691
60-64	147,469	183,055	223,199
65-69	93,125	128,220	171,870
70-74	68,474	84,455	117,772
75-79	34,986	51,705	89,705
80 and over	40,161	52,305	87,304
Males	2,912,558	3,612,807	4,343,512
0- 4	393,432	554,796	667,233
5- 9	393,597	492,442	624,134
10-14	328,894	420,881	559,559
15-19	282,200	354,554	446,729
20-24	275,407	287,637	370,653
25-29	213,144	251,833	301,862
30-34	185,795	246,879	249,409
35-39	179,374	199,965	247,473
40-44	163,939	178,478	223,014
45-49	127,714	157,143	172,260
50-54	114,819	137,561	149,338
55-59	79,281	103,319	127,242
60-64	69,019	86,342	105,715
65-69	44,488	60,615	79,614
70-74	30,863	38,032	53,660
75-79	15,457	22,740	31,021
80 and over	15,075	19,590	34,596
Females	3,020,437	3,761,308	4,541,256
0- 4	388,493	549,924	555,601
5- 9	388,166	489,047	619,796
10-14	323,905	415,428	554,819
15-19	291,717	370,253	466,736
20-24	299,570	310,762	398,383
25-29	234,918	275,172	324,130
30-34	195,565	260,273	267,312
35-39	197,677	215,448	267,078
40-44	159,245	185,401	232,778
45-49	133,091	167,091	184,593
50-54	116,571	131,015	163,277
55-59	81,813	109,013	141,449
60-64	78,450	96,713	117,484
65-69	48,637	67,605	92,256
70-74	37,611	46,423	64,112
75-79	19,529	28,965	38,684
80 and over	25,086	32,775	52,768

Source: National Institute of Statistics.

TABLE 5.9

Population of Chile by Age Groups and Sex, 1960-1975.
Census Data for 1960 and 1970 and Estimates for the Other Years.

Age Group	1960			1961		
	Total	Male	Female	Total	Male	Female
Total	7,585,350	3,758,757	3,826,593	7,770,270	3,849,238	3,921,032
0- 4	1,167,797	588,553	579,244	1,187,161	598,302	588,859
5- 9	940,036	474,034	466,002	979,291	493,560	485,731
10-14	861,632	433,137	428,495	875,441	440,245	435,196
15-19	757,637	380,814	376,823	776,244	390,026	386,218
20-24	625,128	313,856	311,272	648,229	325,279	322,950
25-29	542,375	271,562	270,813	555,923	278,293	277,630
30-34	519,346	258,932	260,414	521,129	259,832	261,297
35-39	421,947	209,577	212,370	438,391	217,660	220,731
40-44	376,502	185,408	191,094	382,628	188,490	194,138
45-49	336,026	163,833	172,193	340,803	166,173	174,630
50-54	290,850	141,748	149,102	296,136	143,930	152,206
55-59	225,726	106,881	118,845	234,399	111,271	123,128
60-64	192,587	88,892	103,695	194,533	89,817	104,716
65-69	139,408	62,369	77,039	144,364	64,545	79,819
70-74	95,638	42,193	53,445	98,580	43,179	55,401
75-79	50,564	20,800	29,764	54,063	22,281	31,782
80 and more	42,151	16,168	25,983	42,955	16,355	26,600

Age Group	1962			1963		
	Total	Male	Female	Total	Male	Female
Total	7,955,190	3,939,719	4,015,471	8,140,110	4,030,200	4,109,910
0- 4	1,206,525	608,051	598,474	1,225,890	617,800	608,090
5- 9	1,018,546	513,085	505,461	1,057,801	532,611	525,190
10-14	889,251	447,354	441,897	903,059	454,462	448,597
15-19	794,851	399,238	395,613	813,458	408,450	405,008
20-24	671,329	336,701	334,628	694,429	348,124	346,305
25-29	569,469	285,023	284,446	583,017	291,754	291,263
30-34	522,911	260,732	262,179	524,695	261,633	263,062
35-39	454,835	225,743	229,092	471,278	233,825	237,453
40-44	388,755	191,572	197,183	394,881	194,654	200,227
45-49	345,581	168,513	177,068	350,360	170,854	179,506
50-54	301,423	146,113	155,310	306,711	148,296	158,415
55-59	243,072	115,661	127,411	251,746	120,051	131,695
60-64	196,479	90,742	105,737	198,423	91,666	106,757
65-69	149,319	66,721	82,598	154,274	68,896	85,378
70-74	101,521	44,165	57,356	104,463	45,151	59,312
75-79	57,562	23,762	33,800	61,060	25,243	35,817
80 and more	43,761	16,543	27,218	44,565	16,730	27,835

TABLE 5.9 (Cont'd)

Population of Chile by Age Groups and Sex, 1960-1975
Census Data for 1960 and 1970 and Estimates for the Other Years.

Age Group	1964			1965		
	Total	Male	Female	Total	Male	Female
Total	8,325,030	4,120,681	4,204,349	8,509,950	4,211,162	4,298,788
0- 4	1,245,254	627,549	617,705	1,264,618	637,298	627,320
5- 9	1,097,055	552,136	544,919	1,136,311	571,662	564,649
10-14	916,869	461,571	455,298	930,678	463,679	461,999
15-19	832,065	417,662	414,403	850,672	426,874	423,798
20-24	717,529	359,546	357,983	740,630	370,969	369,661
25-29	596,563	298,484	298,079	610,111	305,215	304,896
30-34	526,477	262,533	263,944	528,260	263,433	264,827
35-39	487,723	241,908	245,815	504,167	249,991	254,176
40-44	401,007	197,736	203,271	407,133	200,818	206,315
45-49	355,138	173,194	181,944	359,915	175,534	184,381
50-54	311,998	150,479	161,519	317,284	152,661	164,623
55-59	260,419	124,441	135,978	269,092	128,831	140,261
60-64	200,369	92,591	107,778	202,315	93,516	108,799
65-69	159,229	71,072	88,157	164,185	73,248	90,937
70-74	107,405	46,137	61,268	110,346	47,123	63,223
75-79	64,559	26,724	37,835	68,058	28,205	39,853
80 and more	45,371	16,918	28,453	46,175	17,105	29,070

Age Group	1966			1967		
	Total	Male	Female	Total	Male	Female
Total	8,681,671	4,294,686	4,386,985	8,853,393	4,378,210	4,475,183
0- 4	1,252,759	631,418	621,341	1,240,899	625,538	615,361
5- 9	1,156,217	581,663	574,554	1,176,125	591,665	584,460
10-14	969,905	488,179	481,726	1,009,133	507,679	501,454
15-19	864,602	434,036	430,566	878,533	441,199	437,334
20-24	759,328	380,216	379,112	778,026	389,462	388,564
25-29	633,191	316,608	316,586	656,276	328,001	328,275
30-34	541,893	270,191	271,702	555,527	276,949	278,578
35-39	506,278	251,056	255,222	508,390	252,121	256,269
40-44	423,496	208,823	214,673	439,859	216,828	223,031
45-49	366,225	178,687	187,538	372,535	181,840	190,695
50-54	322,285	155,087	167,198	327,287	157,514	169,773
55-59	274,541	131,074	143,467	279,989	133,316	146,673
60-64	210,667	97,619	113,048	219,018	101,722	117,296
65-69	166,385	74,221	92,164	168,584	75,193	93,391
70-74	114,786	48,934	65,852	119,226	50,746	68,480
75-79	70,536	28,954	41,582	73,013	29,702	43,311
80 and more	48,574	17,920	30,654	50,973	18,735	32,238

TABLE 5.9 (Cont'd)

Population of Chile by Age Groups and Sex, 1960-1975.
Census Data for 1960 and 1970 and Estimates for the Other Years.

Age Group	1968			1969		
	Total	Male	Female	Total	Male	Female
Total	9,025,115	4,461,735	4,563,380	9,196,837	4,545,259	4,651,578
0- 4	1,229,041	619,659	609,382	1,217,181	613,779	603,402
5- 9	1,196,031	601,666	594,365	1,215,938	611,668	604,270
10-14	1,048,359	527,178	521,181	1,087,587	546,678	540,909
15-19	892,464	448,361	444,103	906,395	455,524	450,871
20-24	796,725	398,709	398,016	815,423	407,955	407,468
25-29	679,360	339,395	339,965	702,442	350,788	351,654
30-34	569,161	283,708	285,453	582,795	290,466	292,329
35-39	510,501	253,186	257,315	512,613	254,251	258,361
40-44	456,221	224,832	231,389	472,584	232,837	239,747
45-49	378,844	184,993	193,851	385,154	188,146	197,008
50-54	332,287	159,940	172,347	337,289	162,367	174,922
55-59	285,438	135,559	149,879	290,887	137,801	153,086
60-64	227,369	105,824	121,545	235,720	109,927	125,793
65-69	170,786	76,167	94,619	172,985	77,139	95,846
70-74	123,666	52,557	71,109	128,106	54,369	73,737
75-79	75,489	30,450	45,039	77,966	31,198	46,768
80 and more	53,373	19,551	33,822	55,772	20,366	35,406

Age Group	1970			1971		
	Total	Male	Female	Total	Male	Female
Total	9,368,558	4,628,783	4,739,775	9,545,449	4,714,979	4,830,470
0- 4	1,205,322	607,899	597,423	1,214,289	612,233	602,056
5- 9	1,235,844	621,669	614,175	1,225,389	616,459	608,930
10-14	1,126,814	566,178	560,636	1,146,871	576,246	570,625
15-19	920,325	462,686	457,639	959,545	482,166	477,379
20-24	834,121	417,202	416,919	848,229	424,444	423,785
25-29	725,525	362,181	363,344	744,312	371,462	372,850
30-34	596,428	297,224	299,204	619,423	308,557	310,866
35-39	514,724	255,316	259,408	528,312	262,047	266,265
40-44	488,947	240,842	248,105	491,199	242,001	249,198
45-49	391,464	191,299	200,165	407,428	199,084	208,344
50-54	342,290	164,793	177,497	348,438	167,870	180,568
55-59	296,336	140,044	156,292	301,144	142,380	158,764
60-64	244,072	114,030	130,042	249,182	116,128	133,054
65-69	175,185	78,112	97,073	182,578	81,659	100,919
70-74	132,546	56,180	76,366	134,481	57,023	77,458
75-79	80,444	31,947	48,497	83,828	33,253	50,575
80 and more	58,171	21,181	36,990	60,801	21,967	38,834

TABLE 5.9 (Cont'd)

Population of Chile by Age Groups and Sex, 1960-1975.
Census Data for 1960 and 1970 and Estimates for the Other Years.

Age Group	1972			1973		
	Total	Male	Female	Total	Male	Female
Total	9,722,341	4,801,176	4,921,165	9,899,231	4,887,370	5,011,861
0- 4	1,223,258	616,569	606,689	1,232,224	620,903	611,321
5- 9	1,214,934	611,249	603,685	1,204,480	606,039	598,441
10-14	1,166,928	586,314	580,614	1,186,985	596,382	590,603
15-19	998,765	501,646	497,119	1,037,984	521,125	516,859
20-24	862,336	431,685	430,651	876,442	438,926	437,516
25-29	763,099	380,743	382,356	781,886	390,024	391,862
30-34	642,418	319,890	322,528	665,413	331,224	334,189
35-39	541,900	268,778	273,122	555,489	275,509	279,980
40-44	493,451	243,160	250,291	495,702	244,318	251,384
45-49	423,392	206,869	216,523	439,357	214,654	224,703
50-54	354,586	170,947	183,639	360,733	174,023	186,710
55-59	305,952	144,716	161,236	310,761	147,053	163,708
60-64	254,292	118,226	136,066	259,401	120,323	139,078
65-69	189,971	85,206	104,765	197,364	88,753	108,611
70-74	136,416	57,866	78,550	138,350	58,708	79,642
75-79	87,212	34,559	52,653	90,598	35,866	54,732
80 and more	63,431	22,753	40,678	66,062	23,540	42,522

Age Group	1974			1975		
	Total	Male	Female	Total	Male	Female
Total	10,076,123	7,973,566	5,102,557	10,253,014	5,059,762	5,193,252
0- 4	1,241,192	625,239	615,953	1,250,158	629,572	620,586
5- 9	1,194,028	600,831	593,197	1,183,573	595,621	587,952
10-14	1,207,044	606,451	600,593	1,227,101	616,519	610,582
15-19	1,077,202	540,604	536,598	1,116,422	560,084	556,338
20-24	890,549	446,168	444,381	904,656	453,409	451,247
25-29	800,673	399,305	401,368	819,460	408,586	410,874
30-34	688,408	342,558	345,850	711,403	353,891	357,512
35-39	569,078	282,240	286,838	582,666	288,971	293,695
40-44	497,953	245,476	252,477	500,205	246,635	253,570
45-49	455,319	222,436	232,883	471,284	230,222	241,062
50-54	366,879	177,098	189,781	373,028	180,176	192,852
55-59	315,569	149,390	166,179	320,377	151,726	168,651
60-64	264,509	122,420	142,089	269,619	124,518	145,101
65-69	204,758	92,300	112,458	212,151	95,847	116,304
70-74	140,284	59,550	80,734	142,219	60,393	81,826
75-79	93,984	37,173	56,811	97,368	38,479	58,889
80 and more	68,694	24,327	44,367	71,324	25,113	46,211

Source: República de Chile, Ministerio de Economía, Fomento y Reconstrucción. Instituto Nacional de Estadísticas, Población 1960-1975, Total País, Provincias y Area Metropolitana, Estimaciones por Sexo y Grupos de Edad al 30 de Junio de Cada Año (Santiago, Chile: INE, 1977), pp. 1-16.

TABLE 5.10

Masculinity Index in Chile According to Quinquennial Age Groups, 1960, 1965, 1970, 1975, 1980.

Age Groups	1960			1965			1970		
	Males	Females	Index	Males	Females	Index	Males	Females	Index
0- 4	588,553	579,244	101.6	637,298	627,320	101.6	607,899	597,423	101.8
5- 9	474,034	466,002	101.7	571,662	564,649	101.2	621,669	614,175	101.2
10-14	433,137	428,495	101.1	468,679	461,999	101.4	566,178	560,636	101.0
15-19	380,814	376,823	101.1	426,874	423,798	100.7	462,686	457,639	101.1
20-24	313,856	311,272	100.8	370,969	369,661	100.4	417,202	416,919	100.1
25-29	271,562	270,813	100.3	305,215	304,896	100.1	362,181	363,344	99.7
30-34	258,932	260,414	99.4	263,433	264,827	99.5	297,224	299,204	99.3
35-39	209,577	212,370	98.7	249,991	254,176	98.4	255,316	259,408	98.4
40-44	185,408	191,094	97.0	200,818	206,315	97.3	240,842	248,105	97.1
45-49	163,833	172,193	95.1	175,534	184,381	95.2	191,299	200,165	95.6
50-54	141,748	149,102	95.1	152,661	164,623	92.7	164,793	177,497	92.8
55-59	106,881	118,845	89.9	128,831	140,261	91.9	140,044	156,292	89.6
60-64	88,892	103,695	85.7	93,516	108,799	86.0	114,030	130,042	87.7
65-69	62,369	77,039	81.0	73,248	90,937	80.5	78,112	97,073	80.5
70-74	42,193	53,445	78.9	47,123	63,223	74.5	56,180	76,366	73.6
75-79	20,800	29,764	69.9	28,205	39,853	70.8	31,947	48,497	65.9
80 and over	16,168	25,983	62.2	17,105	29,070	58.8	21,181	36,990	57.3
Total	3,758,757	3,826,593	98.2	4,211,162	4,298,788	98.0	4,628,783	4,739,775	97.7

TABLE 5.10 (Cont'd)

Masculinity Index in Chile According to Quinquennial Age Groups, 1960, 1965, 1970, 1975, 1980.

Age Groups	1975			1980		
	Males	Females	Index	Males	Females	Index
0- 4	629,572	620,586	101.4	694,454	685,556	101.3
5- 9	595,621	587,952	101.3	619,611	613,409	101.0
10-14	616,519	610,582	101.0	592,088	585,538	101.1
15-19	560,084	556,338	100.7	611,867	607,389	100.7
20-24	453,409	451,247	100.5	552,866	551,456	100.3
25-29	408,586	410,874	99.4	446,514	446,552	100.0
30-34	353,891	357,512	99.0	401,258	405,813	98.9
35-39	288,971	293,695	98.4	345,881	352,096	98.2
40-44	246,635	253,570	97.3	280,437	287,956	97.4
45-49	230,222	241,062	95.5	236,845	247,004	95.9
50-54	180,176	192,852	93.4	217,874	232,764	93.6
55-59	151,726	168,651	90.0	166,720	183,580	90.8
60-64	124,518	145,101	85.8	135,631	156,931	86.4
65-69	95,847	116,304	82.4	105,398	130,187	81.0
70-74	60,393	81,826	73.8	74,786	98,492	75.9
75-79	38,479	58,889	65.3	41,830	63,470	65.9
80 and over	25,113	46,211	54.3	30,436	57,262	53.2
Total	5,059,762	5,193,252	97.4	5,554,416	5,705,455	97.4

Source: National Institute of Statistics.

TABLE 5.11

Masculinity Ratios of Chile in 1960
Excluding and Including Emigrants to Argentina.

Age Groups	Masculinity Ratios	
	of population enumerated in Chile	of Chileans in Chile as well as emigrants to Argentina
0- 4	100.9	100.9
5- 9	100.7	100.7
10-14	101.3	101.3
15-19	95.7	95.9
20-24	92.5	93.8
25-29	91.5	93.1
30-34	94.8	96.5
35-39	92.8	94.3
40-44	96.3	97.5
45-49	94.0	95.2
50-54	97.5	98.8
55-59	94.8	96.2
60-64	89.3	90.5
65-69	89.7	90.8
70-74	81.9	82.9
75-79	78.5	79.2
80 and over	59.8	60.2
Unknown		
Total	96.1	96.7

Source: Marin Lira, 1975, 97.

TABLE 5.12

Masculinity, Ageing and Dependency Indices
Estimated for June 30 of 1976 and 1977 According to Regions

Regions	Masculinity Index[1]		Ageing Index[2]		Dependency Index[3]	
	1976	1977	1976	1977	1976	1977
Country Total	97.4	97.4	14.6	14.9	67.8	66.8
I Tarapacá	106.3	106.2	14.0	14.3	59.9	59.0
II Antofagasta	103.2	103.0	12.7	12.9	60.3	59.4
III Atacama	105.9	105.7	10.7	10.9	70.4	69.3
IV Coquimbo	96.7	96.7	15.1	15.3	81.4	80.2
V Aconcagua	96.1	96.1	17.2	17.5	63.5	62.5
VI Of the Liberator General Bernardo O'Higgins	104.4	104.4	15.3	15.7	72.8	71.5
VII Maule	102.6	102.6	15.7	16.1	75.3	74.0
VIII Bío-Bío	99.3	99.2	13.0	13.3	72.4	71.1
IX Of the Araucanía	100.2	100.2	15.2	15.5	74.4	73.2
X Of the Lakes	101.7	101.7	14.1	14.5	75.3	74.0
XI Aisén of General Carlos Ibañez del Campo	119.4	120.0	9.3	9.6	70.5	69.1
XII Magallanes and Chilean Antarctic	109.4	109.2	18.9	19.4	49.1	48.2
Metropolitan Region	92.2	92.3	14.6	14.9	63.3	62.6

Notes: 1. The masculinity index is defined as the proportion of the total number of males to the total number of females expressed per 100.

2. The ageing index is the proportion of persons 65 years and over per 100 persons between 0 and 14 years of age.

3. The dependency index is defined as the proportion of persons of 0-14 years of age plus the persons of 65 years and over for each 100 persons of 15 to 64 years of age which, in theory, is considered the economically active population.

Source: National Institute of Statistics.

TABLE 5.13

Ageing Index According to Sex, 1960, 1965, 1970, 1975 and 1980.

	Total for Country		
	Total	Males	Females
1960			
0-14	2,969,465	1,495,724	1,473,741
65 and over	327,761	141,530	186,231
AI[1]	11.04	9.46	12.64
1965			
0-14	3,331,607	1,677,639	1,653,968
65 and over	388,764	165,681	223,083
AI	11.67	9.88	13.49
1970			
0-14	3,567,980	1,795,746	1,772,234
65 and over	446,346	187,420	258,926
AI	12.51	10.44	14.61
1975			
0-14	3,660,832	1,841,712	1,819,120
65 and over	523,062	219,832	303,230
AI	14.29	11.94	16.67
1980			
0-14	3,790,576	1,906,073	1,884,503
65 and over	601,861	252,450	349,411
AI	15.88	13.24	18.54

Notes: 1. AI stands for ageing index. The ageing index is, $AI = \frac{P.^{65 \text{ and over}}}{P.^{0-14}} \times 100$ where P. stands for population.

Source: National Institute of Statistics.

PART II
MIGRATION, POPULATION PROJECTIONS AND EDUCATION

6
INTERNAL MIGRATION

INTRODUCTION

The spatial distribution of the population within Chile and changes in this distribution has been determined by birth and death rates and international migration as well as internal migration. In many regions, provinces and cities domestic (in or out) migration has actually been as critical a demographic factor in shaping total population growth as the natural population increase.

Internal migration in Chile, as elsewhere, can be and has been explained by many factors. The absolute level of internal migration is determined by the size and natural rate of increase of the total population. What has introduced a new dimension to domestic migration in Chile as compared to the patterns observed in Great Britain and Europe is the fact that the annual increments in its total population have exceeded the increases historically observed in present day developed countries. With population increasing within each region, province, rural area and city due to natural factors more rapidly than the production of goods and services, the potentially migrant population has often been quite large. Important in Chile is the fact that a population surplus has existed not only in selected localities or regions but has been prevalent throughout the country during prolonged periods. Internal migration has, therefore, been often influenced as much by the presence or absence of population or labor surplus in a region, city or rural area as by the degree of the relative magnitude of the population/labor surplus and the relative level of absolute economic development and modernization achieved by each region or province.

A central feature of underdevelopment in Chile is the wide spectrum of economic development level or stage achieved by the various geographic segments of the nation. Not less important is the fact that domestic migration has not eliminated or even reduced regional, provincial or urban-rural income and development differentials and that in some instances such migration may have strengthened such inequalities.

Domestic migration has been shaped by and has influenced the features of the processes of production, distribution and capital formation in Chile (Mamalakis: 1976b, 1976c, and 1976d, Ch. 14). Most of the models of internal migration consider such factors as distance, education, and absolute as well as relative income levels in trying to explain population movements. There does not exist as yet, however, a general, comprehensive model that incorporates and permits testing of the importance of major production, distribution and capital formation variables in explaining directly or indirectly domestic demographic movements. Until such a model is developed, our understanding of the forces that shape domestic migration will be incomplete and any domestic migration policy will be flawed.

In addition to the major statistical studies described later on in this chapter, the following studies examine the patterns and determinants of internal migration: (1) Bruce H. Herrick, Urban Migration and Economic Development in Chile (Cambridge, Mass: MIT University Press, 1965); (2) Carlos Hurtado, Concentración de Población y Desarrollo Económico: El Caso Chileno (Santiago, Chile: IECH, 1966); (3) IECH, La Migración Interna en Chile en el Período 1940-52 (Santiago, Chile: IECH, 1959); (4) Dagmar Raczynski, Empleo, Pobreza y Migraciones en Chile (Santiago, Chile: CIEPLAN, November 1978); (5) Dagmar Raczynski, Migraciones Internas en Chile: Metodología e Información Estadística (Santiago, Chile: CIEPLAN, October 1978), Notas Técnicas N° 11.

MIGRATION: SOME DEFINITIONS

Migration is a form of geographical mobility or spatial mobility between one geographical unit and another, generally involving a change of residence from the place of origin or place of departure to the place of destination or place of arrival. Such migration is called permanent migration and should be distinguished from other forms of movement which do not involve a permanent change of residence. Migration within a given state, which consists of movement between different parts of that state, is called internal migration.

The term migratory movement is used for that section of total population which is due to migration. The total of arrivals of immigrants and departures of emigrants is called gross migration or the volume of migration. Net migration is the difference between the total number of persons arriving and the total number leaving; it is also referred to as the balance of migration. If the number entering exceeds the number leaving, there is net immigration. In the reverse case there is net emigration.

Internal Migration During the Colonial Period

Although it is true that there do not exist direct registers of internal migration in the XVII or XVIII centuries, there exist nevertheless documents which are useful in making indirect estimates such as the visitas (visits) of the colonial period or the marriage records of the parish books. These generally state the origin or geographic place of origin of the contracting parties. A general description of the different types of documents useful for an examination of the history of population in Chile and other parts of Latin America during the colonial period is Rolando Mellafe, Descripción tipológica de los documentos útiles para la demografía histórica existente en los archivos latino americanos (Santiago, Chile: CELADE, Serie D, No. 71, February, 1972).

Net Domestic Migration Between 1855 and 1970: The Hagerman Series

Excellent studies on domestic migration by age and sex in Chile for the decades between 1930 and 1970 are those by Conning (1969) and Arévalo (1974). Subsequent sections of this chapter are devoted to these studies.

Age-sex specific net migration rates by provinces for the periods between 1855 and 1970 are found in (1) Ann Louise Hagerman Johnson, "Internal Migration in Chile to 1920: Its Relationship to the Labor Market, Agricultural Growth, and Urbanization," unpublished Ph.D. dissertation, Department of History, University of California at Davis, 1978, for the periods between 1855 and 1920; and (2) The complete time series on net migration rates for the total population, selected provinces and selected decades is reproduced, with adjustments for changes in techniques of calculation and with estimates of migration between 1920 and 1930 in Ann Hagerman Johnson, with the assistance of Rolando Mellafe and Arnold J. Bauer, "Internal Migration in Chile: 1854-1970, Estimation of Age-Sex Specific Migration by Provinces and an Analysis of the Relationships Between Internal Migration and the Growth Distribution."

The total amount of net migration by sex for the intercensual periods from 1855 to 1970 is presented in Table 6.1. Net migration rates for selected provinces and decades are presented in Table 6.2.

Domestic Migration by Regions Between 1930 and 1960: The Conning Series

Net domestic migration estimates classified according to age and sex in the provinces and regions of Chile during the years 1930-1940, 1940-1952 and 1952-1960 are found in the solid study by Arthur M. Conning, Estimación de la migración interna neta, clasificada por edad y por sexo, en las provincias y regiones de Chile durante los años 1930-1940, 1940-1952 y

TABLE 6.1

Total Amount of Net Migration by Sex, Intercensual Periods 1855 to 1970.

Period	Both Sexes	Men	Women
1855-1865	42,557	23,612	18,945
1865-1875	72,353	40,633	31,720
1895-1905	150,545	80,490	70,055
1905-1915	138,590	70,139	68,451
1930-1940	166,030	75,009	91,020
1940-1950	266,299	121,006	145,293
1950-1960	302,931	132,560	170,371
1960-1970	398,416	183,565	214,851

Source: This table was prepared by Ann Louise Hagerman Johnson and is found in her thesis (Hagerman Johnson: 1978, 166). The detailed original sources of this table are as follows: The information for 1855-1915 was obtained from (Hagerman Johnson: 1978, Appendix 2). Since Chile grew territorially and new areas were enumerated in successive censuses, the figures here are for different areas for different dates. To simplify the problem of territorial change and the distortion of more complete enumeration, the sum of all out-migrants, by sex, is given here. The periods 1875-1885 and 1885-1895 are not included here because the distortions in the 1885 census caused distortions in net migration rates for the preceding and following decades. Net migration rates between 1920 and 1930 have not been calculated because boundary changes in that decade makes it almost impossible to adjust population to comparable territorial units. The information for 1930-1940 was obtained from Arthur M. Conning, *Estimación de la migración interna neta, clasificada por edad y por sexo, en las provincias y regiones de Chile durante los años 1930-1940, 1940-1952, 1952-1960*, CELADE Series D N36. The figure here is the sum of all positive migration. The net migration figures for 1940-1970 were obtained from Jorge Arévalo, *Migración intercensal de seis países de América Latina*, CELADE (November, 1974). The figure here is the sum of all positive migration.

TABLE 6.2

Net Migration Rates, Total Population, Selected Provinces, Selected Decades.

	Net Migration Rates Per 1,000 Population		
Province	1855-1865	1895-1905	1960-1970
Coquimbo	4.01	-12.35	-14.94
Aconcagua	-10.98	- 6.63	- 3.99
Colchagua	- 3.08	-16.73	-17.35
Maule	-15.03	-22.56	-18.64
Linares	2.43	- 9.93	-15.75
Ñuble	- 2.51	- 8.71	- 9.77
Arauco	45.53	-12.27	-14.64
Cautín	-	- 1.66	-15.36
Valdivia	- 3.19	35.08	-18.56
Chiloé	-11.71	-11.22	-10.26

Sources: For 1855-1865 and 1895-1905 Hagerman Johnson: 1978, Appendix 2, and for 1960-1970, Arévalo: 1974.

TABLE 6.3

Net Number of Migrants in Chile's Six Regions[1] and the Country by Age and Sex Cohorts, 1930-1940.

Age in 1930	Age in 1940	Region 1	Region 2	Region 3	Region 4	Region 5	Region 6	Country
				Males				
5- 9	15-19	-2,917	77	5,138	-2,819	769	-248	11,967
10-14	20-24	-1,089	-710	5,760	-3,981	481	-462	12,482
15-19	25-29	-1,861	-91	5,642	-3,902	233	-21	11,750
20-24	30-34	-4,489	938	5,345	-2,419	263	362	13,816
25-29	35-39	-5,799	1,252	4,741	-987	423	369	13,571
30-34	40-44	-5,192	1,157	3,546	-435	575	348	11,252
35-39	45-49	-4,052	1,067	2,519	-453	570	349	9,010
40-44	50-54	-3,096	974	1,827	-457	474	277	7,105
45-49	55-59	-2,246	724	1,258	-290	370	185	5,073
50-54	60-64	-1,423	352	763	-64	256	117	2,974
55-59	65-69	-716	128	420	-44	156	55	1,520
60-64	70-74	-349	33	237	-96	126	49	890
65 and over	75 and over	-274	-141	-181	148	372	76	1,192
Total		-33,503	5,761	37,014	-15,798	5,068	1,457	98,602
				Females				
5- 9	15-19	-3,815	206	7,882	-4,110	-276	113	16,402
10-14	20-24	-2,930	-313	8,640	-5,139	-278	20	17,319
15-19	25-29	-2,388	-133	7,107	-4,427	-312	152	14,519
20-24	30-34	-2,373	254	5,405	-3,086	-427	226	11,770
25-29	35-39	-2,443	495	4,162	-2,170	-189	146	9,605
30-34	40-44	-2,336	487	2,903	-1,428	222	152	7,527
35-39	45-49	-2,056	397	2,378	-1,139	216	204	6,391
40-44	50-54	-1,516	312	2,207	-1,209	28	177	5,449
45-49	55-59	-1,008	181	1,589	-913	49	103	3,842
50-54	60-64	-733	67	807	-327	111	75	2,122
55-59	65-69	-446	35	313	-114	147	65	1,120
60-64	70-74	-226	34	62	-90	185	35	633
65 and over	75 and over	-246	-56	-381	118	443	122	1,366
Total		-22,516	1,967	43,075	-24,034	-80	1,589	93,261

Notes: 1. The regions are composed of provinces as follows: Region 1: Tarapacá and Antofagasta; Region 2: Atacama and Coquimbo; Region 3: Aconcagua, Valparaíso, Santiago, O'Higgins, Colchagua, Maule, Talca, Linares, Ñuble, and Curicó; Region 4: Concepción, Arauco, Bío-Bío, Malleco and Cautín; Region 5: Valdivia, Osorno and Llanquihue; Region 6: Chiloé, Aisén and Magallanes.

Source: Conning: 1969, 42.

TABLE 6.3 (Cont'd)

Net Number of Migrants in Chile's Six Regions[1] and the Country by Age and Sex Cohorts, 1940-1952.

Age in 1940	Age in 1952	Region 1	Region 2	Region 3	Region 4	Region 5	Region 6	Country
				Males				
5- 9	17-21	2,317	-4,316	9,969	-5,982	-872	-1,116	24,572
10-14	22-26	3,679	-5,070	11,727	-7,353	-1,874	-1,108	30,811
15-19	27-31	2,697	-3,707	10,098	-6,657	-1,830	-602	25,592
20-24	32-36	815	-1,912	7,201	-4,664	-1,235	-205	16,032
25-29	37-41	-198	-1,207	4,913	-2,788	-598	-122	9,826
30-34	42-46	-506	-978	3,323	-1,687	-99	-53	6,646
35-39	47-51	-603	-610	2,408	-1,331	102	33	5,087
40-44	52-56	-601	-384	1,844	-1,035	144	33	4,041
45-49	57-61	-592	-282	1,348	-566	106	-14	2,908
50-54	62-66	-522	-215	919	-241	82	-23	2,002
55-59	67-71	-376	-169	644	-238	102	37	1,567
60-64	72-76	-244	-118	425	-251	114	73	1,225
65 and over	77 and over	-155	-151	268	-212	201	49	1,037
Total		5,711	-19,120	55,087	-33,004	-5,656	-3,017	121,595
				Females				
5- 9	17-21	-279	-4,257	15,864	-8,562	-1,905	-862	31,729
10-14	22-26	6	-4,506	17,072	-9,459	-2,186	-926	34,155
15-19	27-31	348	-3,203	12,980	-7,445	-1,973	-708	26,658
20-24	32-36	289	-1,875	8,390	-4,806	-1,421	-577	17,359
25-29	37-41	-87	-1,150	5,494	-3,086	-637	-535	10,988
30-34	42-46	-337	-918	4,075	-2,273	-150	-398	8,150
35-39	47-51	-408	-847	3,627	-1,963	-197	-213	7,254
40-44	52-56	-467	-650	3,067	-1,568	-251	-131	6,135
45-49	57-61	-440	-427	2,193	-996	-184	-146	4,386
50-54	62-66	-343	-294	1,363	-489	-84	-154	2,726
55-59	67-71	-267	-176	873	-371	18	-77	1,781
60-64	72-76	-177	-97	515	-301	75	-15	1,180
65 and over	77 and over	-197	-328	70	182	188	86	1,051
Total		-2,358	-18,728	75,584	-41,136	-8,707	-4,656	151,168

Notes: 1. The provinces included in the various regions were as follows: Region 1: Tarapacá and Antofagasta; Region 2: Atacama and Coquimbo; Region 3: Aconcagua, Valparaíso, Santiago, O'Higgins, Colchagua, Maule, Talca, Linares, Ñuble, Curicó; Region 4: Concepción, Arauco, Bío-Bío, Malleco, Cautín; Region 5: Valdivia, Osorno, Llanquihue; Region 6: Chiloé, Aisén, Magallanes.

Source: Conning: 1969, 64-65.

TABLE 6.3 (Cont'd)

Net Number of Migrants in Chile's Six Regions[1] and the Country by Age and Sex Cohorts, 1952-1960.

Age in 1952	Age in 1960	Region 1	Region 2	Region 3	Region 4	Region 5	Region 6	Country
				Males				
7-11	15-19	817	-1,733	10,501	-5,083	-3,745	-757	22,635
12-16	20-24	1,396	-1,893	12,182	-6,662	-4,343	-679	27,156
17-21	25-29	61	-613	9,714	-5,711	-3,464	-12	19,575
22-26	30-34	-1,400	684	5,931	-3,499	-1,987	-271	13,773
27-31	35-39	-1,489	830	3,415	-1,739	-1,044	-25	8,542
32-36	40-44	-1,051	476	2,466	-1,171	-636	-84	5,885
37-41	45-49	-914	257	2,258	-1,068	-421	-112	5,030
42-46	50-54	-789	187	1,846	-748	-321	-174	4,066
47-51	55-59	-678	179	1,273	-373	-212	-190	2,905
52-56	60-64	-616	96	980	-200	-102	-157	2,152
57-61	65-69	-508	-8	810	-161	-41	-91	1,620
62-66	70-74	-337	-38	495	-124	19	-15	1,028
67 and over	75 and over	-147	35	154	-58	36	-20	449
Total		-5,656	-1,541	52,026	-26,597	-16,261	-1,971	104,051
				Females				
7-11	15-19	-438	-2,187	15,081	-7,021	-4,583	-853	30,162
12-16	20-24	145	-2,237	15,776	-7,909	-4,874	-901	31,842
17-21	25-29	415	-1,098	11,115	-5,809	-3,882	-741	23,059
22-26	30-34	179	-222	6,589	-3,439	-2,588	-519	13,536
27-31	35-39	-304	-10	4,119	-1,951	-1,424	-430	8,237
32-36	40-44	-417	-87	3,316	-1,557	-888	-368	6,632
37-41	45-49	-423	-214	3,390	-1,637	-867	-249	6,781
42-46	50-54	-418	-187	2,971	-1,448	-769	-149	5,942
47-51	55-59	-332	-74	1,899	-857	-486	-150	3,797
52-56	60-64	-278	-89	1,378	-516	-294	-200	2,756
57-61	65-69	-190	-87	1,212	-551	-207	-176	2,424
62-66	70-74	-82	-42	788	-443	-125	-97	1,576
67 and over	75 and over	-32	-56	721	-386	-170	-78	1,442
Total		-2,173	-6,590	68,354	-33,524	-21,157	-4,910	136,707

Notes: 1. The provinces included in each region are as follows: Region 1: Tarapacá and Antofagasta; Region 2: Atacama and Coquimbo; Region 3: Aconcagua, Valparaíso, Santiago, O'Higgins, Colchagua, Maule, Talca, Linares, Ñuble, Curicó; Region 4: Concepción, Arauco, Bío-Bío, Malleco, Cautín; Region 5: Valdivia, Osorno, Llanquihue; Region 6: Chiloé, Aisén, Magallanes.

Source: Conning: 1969, 42.

1952-1960, Con una breve introducción referente a la metodología (Santiago, Chile: CELADE, 1969), pp. 1-103. For a detailed description of the method used by Conning (he uses the method of survival coefficients) see Conning (1969, 1-21).

Domestic Migration by Provinces Between 1940 and 1970: The Arévalo Series

Another solid study of internal migration in Chile is that by Jorge Arévalo, Migración Intercensal de Seis Países de América Latina (Santiago, Chile: CELADE, November 1974) Series A, Nº 127. Chile is one of six countries for which Arévalo examines internal migration. Arévalo provides statistical information on net domestic migrants and annual rates of net domestic migration according to sex, age and provinces of Chile during 1940-50, 1950-60 and 1960-70 (Arévalo: 1974, 113-137). Arévalo presents also a detailed methodology of his study. Net domestic migration and annual rates of net domestic migration by age and province during 1940-50, 1950-60 and 1960-70 are presented for both sexes and for 5-year age groups in Table 6.4. The age classification used in this table includes 11 categories as follows: it begins with 10-14 and continues with 5-year groups to 55-59 and ends with 60 and over. The age is that of the migrants at the end of the period.

Santiago and Valparaíso are the only two provinces with consistent, positive immigration throughout 1940-1970. Another feature that stands out is the wide spectrum of rates of net emigration from the various provinces.

Arévalo uses the method of survival relations to estimate the number of net migrants encountered in a territorial division during a specific time period. Net migration is the balance between immigrants and emigrants since the method does not permit a distinction between the two groups. This method compares the observed number of persons of a cohort at the end of the period of observation with the expected number of survivors of the same cohort which is determined by multiplying the number of persons observed at the beginning of the period by an appropriate survival relation. The difference between the number observed at the end of the period and the expected, is the quantity of net migrants at the end of the interval.

The data required under this method are the number of persons residing in the same territorial division in two dates classified by age and survival relations applicable to the different cohorts.

Arévalo engages into an extensive discussion of the three implicit assumptions of the direct or forward survival method that he uses. The implicit assumptions of this method are: First, that the population is closed that is not affected by international migration. Second, that the degree of enumeration integrity of a cohort during a census is the same in the territorial division under consideration and in the country as a whole. Third, the survival relations in the territorial division under consideration are the same as the national ones. Among Arévalo's conclusion is "that the method of survival relations, in its direct version, substitutes the number of deaths of the immigrants for those of the emigrants" (Arévalo: 1974, 5). Arévalo introduces some modifications and concludes that the estimates of domestic migration obtained in his study are rather accurate.

Rural-Urban Migration in Central Chile

An attempt to examine the relationship between agrarian reform and migration from rural to urban areas was made by (Lira: 1975). According to Lira's study net migration out of rural areas of Central Chile (Aconcagua to Ñuble) increased during the 1960-70 period over that of 1950-60 as illustrated in Table 6.5. Even though it was not possible to isolate the exact contribution which agrarian reform had made to this increase, Lira advances the hypothesis that the requirements stipulated by the Christian Democratic reform to become a recipient of land (asentado) may have contributed to the abandonment of rural areas by certain types of workers. On the basis of the findings, Lira argues that different types of agrarian reform can produce different effects on the rural-urban migration. It is thus possible that the agrarian reform of the Popular Unity Government of Salvador Allende retained more agricultural population than the Christian Democratic reform primarily because it insured the indiscriminate participation of all agricultural workers (campesinos) in the new agricultural establishments (asentamiento) (Lira: 1975, 61). Among the factors that push, expel labor out of rural areas, Lira examines the land tenure system, the lack of employment opportunities and agricultural modernization and reviews the relevant literature and empirical evidence on Chile.

TABLE 6.4

Chile. Net Domestic Migrants and Annual Rates of Net Domestic Migration According to Age, Decades and Provinces. From 1940 to 1970. Both Sexes.

Age at end of the Period	Net Migrants of the Period:			Net Annual Rates of Migration (per thousand) of the Period:		
	1940-50	1950-60	1960-70	1940-50	1950-60	1960-70
			1 - Tarapacá			
Total	-3,585	-1,060	24,129	-4.58	-1.16	18.57
10-14	-1,173	-877	3,843	-10.81	-6.45	18.54
15-19	-320	901	6,314	-3.20	7.66	33.58
20-24	-493	429	4,078	-4.73	4.41	26.93
25-29	170	103	2,118	2.05	1.12	16.79
30-34	188	214	2,401	2.88	2.29	22.85
35-39	-578	-331	1,903	-8.56	-4.34	17.35
40-44	-890	-281	1,806	-14.46	-4.51	17.58
45-49	-383	-254	944	-7.58	-4.60	12.74
50-54	-116	-236	270	-2.70	-4.81	4.67
55-59	68	-289	-165	2.11	-7.46	-3.43
60 and over	-58	-439	617	-0.87	-4.84	4.88
			2 - Antofagasta			
Total	12,298	-6,030	-5,625	9.54	-3.81	-2.75
10-14	753	-2,644	-3,232	4.28	-11.46	-9.56
15-19	979	-349	197	6.47	-1.80	0.70
20-24	4,333	1,942	2,583	24.57	11.05	11.24
25-29	4,651	2,943	1,888	33.36	18.45	9.86
30-34	1,973	-552	1,729	16.21	-3.13	9.48
35-39	614	-1,773	-749	5.36	-12.44	-4.03
40-44	-373	-1,708	-1,311	-3.63	-14.47	-7.90
45-49	-66	-1,256	-1,413	-0.78	-13.02	-12.02
50-54	-26	-803	-1,163	-0.36	-9.49	-12.14
55-59	-188	-602	-1,875	-3.66	-9.13	-25.87
60 and over	-352	-1,228	-2,279	-3.53	-8.91	-12.40
			3 - Atacama			
Total	-13,844	6,803	5,414	-21.19	8.88	4.76
10-14	-1,515	-96	-396	-14.92	-0.79	-1.92
15-19	-1,975	81	135	-22.74	0.76	0.82
20-24	-1,896	1,404	1,968	-22.51	14.95	15.14
25-29	-1,519	2,207	4,155	-23.38	26.79	34.38
30-34	-1,110	1,468	355	-20.06	19.62	3.68
35-39	-1,557	908	598	-27.29	15.69	5.71
40-44	-1,659	527	-801	-32.33	10.43	-10.32
45-49	-1,083	323	-125	-25.67	7.23	-2.17
50-54	-485	191	-157	-14.43	4.92	-3.23
55-59	-350	69	-150	-14.78	2.24	-3.64
60 and over	-695	-279	-168	-12.94	-4.19	-1.75
			4 - Coquimbo			
Total	-25,494	-24,655	-41,318	-12.93	-11.04	-14.94
10-14	-2,458	-2,138	-5,154	-7.10	-5.49	-9.72
15-19	-4,943	-4,448	-9,521	-16.51	-13.15	-22.22
20-24	-8,219	-7,957	-11,000	-31.78	-29.59	-34.17
25-29	-5,409	-6,000	-7,250	-28.23	-26.70	-27.57
30-34	-1,228	-1,770	-2,609	-8.31	-9.45	-12.93
35-39	-705	-609	-1,282	-4.89	-4.06	-6.24
40-44	-629	-692	-2,210	-4.82	-5.22	-13.31
45-49	-499	-454	-342	-4.43	-3.77	-2.53
50-54	-113	-192	-153	-1.17	-1.72	-1.28
55-59	-305	218	-1,062	-4.36	2.37	-10.42
60 and over	-986	-613	-735	-5.46	-2.76	-2.47

TABLE 6.4 (Cont'd)

Chile. Net Domestic Migrants and Annual Rates of Net Domestic Migration According to Age, Decades and Provinces. From 1940 to 1970. Both Sexes.

Age at end of the Period	Net Migrants of the Period:			Net Annual Rates of Migration (per thousand) of the Period:		
	1940-50	1950-60	1960-70	1940-50	1950-60	1960-70
			5 - Aconcagua			
Total	-7,891	-13,519	-5,295	-8.17	-12.51	-3.99
10-14	-676	-1,302	-495	-4.41	-7.58	-2.22
15-19	-2,361	-2,201	103	-17.45	-13.99	0.53
20-24	-1,430	-2,869	-1,785	-11.00	-23.12	-11.47
25-29	-1,468	-1,842	-2,576	-15.70	-17.51	-20.51
30-34	-561	-2,268	-91	-6.96	-22.77	-0.88
35-39	-210	-562	-180	-2.68	-7.28	-1.73
40-44	-242	-638	96	-3.59	-8.92	1.08
45-49	-141	-513	1,315	-2.55	-7.92	17.33
50-54	-207	-462	247	-4.30	-8.28	3.81
55-59	-61	-288	-62	-1.70	-6.61	-1.10
60 and over	-534	-574	-1,867	-5.98	-5.27	-13.92
			6 - Valparaíso			
Total	14,576	17,356	34,568	3.97	3.87	5.69
10-14	2,753	2,121	4,525	5.76	3.39	4.65
15-19	2,272	3,101	7,059	5.05	5.58	9.01
20-24	4,032	3,792	5,647	8.59	8.01	8.54
25-29	3,139	3,175	4,394	8.16	7.15	7.80
30-34	1,602	1,688	1,681	4.76	3.75	3.57
35-39	737	289	4,457	2.25	0.77	8.52
40-44	-267	336	1,767	-0.92	1.01	3.80
45-49	592	681	182	2.53	2.33	0.51
50-54	170	1,236	1,734	0.82	4.78	5.42
55-59	165	419	861	1.10	2.11	3.16
60 and over	-619	518	2,261	-1.85	1.13	3.36
			7 - Santiago			
Total	206,212	255,138	327,057	17.61	15.59	13.15
10-14	22,739	25,246	34,449	15.15	10.80	8.38
15-19	32,346	46,383	63,260	23.35	22.48	19.23
20-24	49,979	55,821	84,552	33.16	31.49	29.37
25-29	34,888	43,829	55,514	27.51	26.47	22.63
30-34	19,472	23,544	25,843	17.15	13.82	12.58
35-39	12,827	13,025	14,406	11.54	9.25	6.81
40-44	7,656	9,237	10,943	8.11	7.51	5.87
45-49	7,125	9,074	9,937	9.44	8.47	6.99
50-54	6,185	8,941	7,324	9.59	9.83	5.98
55-59	4,302	5,094	6,927	9.61	7.50	6.60
60 and over	8,693	14,944	13,902	8.89	9.88	5.82
			8 - O'Higgins			
Total	-11,619	-19,935	-7,588	-7.06	-10.49	-3.08
10-14	-1,791	-2,470	-366	-6.85	-7.61	-0.81
15-19	-3,315	-5,056	-3,943	-14.92	-18.77	-10.73
20-24	-3,012	-3,875	-4,022	-14.38	-18.10	-13.84
25-29	-1,427	-2,020	-879	-8.78	-11.20	-3.87
30-34	-636	-1,225	544	-4.54	-7.24	2.94
35-39	-347	-756	1,270	-2.54	-5.37	6.63
40-44	-408	-884	6	-3.46	-6.95	0.03
45-49	-127	-862	585	-1.32	-7.62	4.48
50-54	-209	-728	-408	-2.47	-7.42	-3.64
55-59	-74	-701	116	-1.21	-9.34	1.16
60 and over	-273	-1,358	-491	-1.75	-7.15	-1.99

TABLE 6.4 (Cont'd)

Chile. Net Domestic Migrants and Annual Rates of Net Domestic Migration According to Age, Decades and Provinces. From 1940 to 1970. Both Sexes.

Age at end of the Period	Net Migrants of the Period:			Net Annual Rates of Migration (per thousand) of the Period:		
	1940-50	1950-60	1960-70	1940-50	1950-60	1960-70
			9 - Colchagua			
Total	-12,333	-15,158	-24,346	-11.68	-12.88	-17.35
10-14	-1,266	-1,233	-2,002	-7.39	-6.08	-7.39
15-19	-2,410	-3,874	-6,063	-16.60	-22.85	-29.71
20-24	-3,237	-3,488	-6,503	-23.98	-25.86	-39.89
25-29	-2,508	-2,566	-3,202	-23.88	-23.21	-25.39
30-34	-947	-1,212	-2,109	-11.07	-11.99	-21.22
35-39	-471	-591	-1,536	-5.75	-7.12	-15.58
40-44	-349	-476	-155	-4.91	-6.32	-1.65
45-49	-328	-427	-396	-5.72	-6.34	-5.45
50-54	-74	-290	55	-1.36	-4.87	0.81
55-59	-131	-195	-519	-3.45	-4.33	-9.18
60 and over	-612	-806	-1,916	-5.58	-6.36	-12.73
			10 - Curicó			
Total	-4,986	-6,375	-11,879	-7.50	-8.32	-12.41
10-14	-499	-258	-767	-4.81	-1.96	-4.22
15-19	-535	-1,207	-1,959	-6.08	-10.97	-13.27
20-24	-1,240	-1,281	-3,454	-14.94	-14.70	-30.85
25-29	-1,129	-1,509	-2,081	-17.18	-21.11	-23.65
30-34	-579	-644	-905	-10.47	-9.75	-12.73
35-39	-19	-173	-305	-0.35	-3.14	-4.48
40-44	-50	-104	-300	-1.08	-2.08	-4.92
45-49	-254	-200	107	-6.58	-4.44	2.10
50-54	-254	-210	-702	-6.95	-5.32	-16.60
55-59	-102	-131	-120	-4.02	-4.34	-3.05
60 and over	-325	-658	-1,393	-4.82	-8.24	-14.54
			11 - Talca			
Total	-8,913	-11,535	-19,217	-6.91	-7.74	-10.19
10-14	-919	-888	-3,563	-4.71	-3.50	-10.49
15-19	-763	-2,171	-3,486	-4.55	-10.31	-12.08
20-24	-2,092	-2,029	-2,940	-13.06	-12.24	-12.60
25-29	-2,138	-2,138	-3,304	-16.43	-15.15	-19.14
30-34	-623	-858	-1,286	-5.73	-6.56	-9.23
35-39	-513	-211	-1,798	-4.86	-1.92	-13.54
40-44	-110	-414	-641	-1.17	-4.17	-5.23
45-49	-415	-562	-1,082	-5.45	-6.45	-11.27
50-54	-382	-688	-503	-5.50	-8.78	-5.73
55-59	-233	-361	-96	-4.70	-6.08	-1.26
60 and over	-725	-1,215	-518	-5.60	-7.90	-2.63
			12 - Maule			
Total	-6,662	-7,332	-13,034	-11.78	-11.98	-18.64
10-14	-464	-635	-1,889	-5.17	-6.54	-15.99
15-19	-1,484	-1,555	-3,044	-19.44	-18.23	-31.45
20-24	-2,262	-2,017	-3,763	-32.97	-28.54	-50.42
25-29	-1,581	-1,686	-2,400	-29.40	-30.33	-39.09
30-34	-442	-461	-1,347	-9.82	-9.34	-26.92
35-39	-318	-192	-568	-7.58	-4.60	-11.75
40-44	-64	-242	-142	-1.74	-6.06	-3.08
45-49	-57	-75	-402	-1.89	-2.15	-11.20
50-54	58	-143	-499	1.92	-4.57	-14.93
55-59	16	20	440	0.73	0.80	13.13
60 and over	-64	-350	580	-0.93	-4.47	5.96

TABLE 6.4 (Cont'd)

Chile. Net Domestic Migrants and Annual Rates of Net Domestic Migration According to Age, Decades and Provinces. From 1940 to 1970. Both Sexes.

Age at end of the Period	Net Migrants of the Period:			Net Annual Rates of Migration (per thousand) of the Period:		
	1940-50	1950-60	1960-70	1940-50	1950-60	1960-70
			13 - Linares			
Total	-10,739	-11,327	-24,036	-9.81	-9.05	-15.75
10-14	-1,300	-1,065	-3,194	-7.41	-5.00	-11.34
15-19	-1,977	-2,607	-5,010	-13.62	-14.38	-22.14
20-24	-3,135	-2,516	-4,914	-22.38	-17.52	-26.99
25-29	-2,270	-1,820	-3,207	-20.74	-15.66	-22.40
30-34	-877	-993	-1,591	-9.90	-9.25	-13.87
35-39	-383	-286	-700	-4.35	-3.19	-6.19
40-44	224	-100	-1,419	2.97	-1.24	-15.00
45-49	-266	-264	-1,159	-4.26	-3.57	-15.17
50-54	-375	-573	-840	-6.40	-8.90	-12.00
55-59	-161	-260	-898	-3.93	-5.28	-14.64
60 and over	-219	-843	-1,104	-1.99	-6.40	-6.77
			14 - Ñuble			
Total	-26,883	-24,620	-25,584	-13.85	-11.50	-9.77
10-14	-1,752	-860	-1,035	-5.45	-2.37	-2.18
15-19	-4,902	-5,494	-5,468	-18.36	-17.52	-14.16
20-24	-7,753	-6,812	-8,079	-31.87	-26.75	-25.61
25-29	-4,997	-5,244	-5,419	-26.22	-26.43	-22.24
30-34	-2,857	-1,955	-2,543	-18.43	-11.19	-13.12
35-39	-1,808	-931	-596	-11.51	-6.24	-3.23
40-44	-508	-222	-974	-3.83	-1.65	-6.12
45-49	-613	-529	-682	-5.53	-4.18	-5.20
50-54	-758	-637	-312	-7.44	-5.72	-2.55
55-59	-235	-228	645	-3.20	-2.59	-5.57
60 and over	-700	-1,708	-1,121	-3.72	-7.54	-3.88
			15 - Concepción			
Total	26,378	13,853	-21,962	9.62	3.80	-4.33
10-14	4,123	2,266	-2,713	10.07	3.77	-2.86
15-19	5,555	3,927	-583	15.67	7.67	-0.75
20-24	8,138	5,910	-1,714	22.18	13.84	-2.85
25-29	4,320	3,760	-1,510	14.40	10.07	-3.04
30-34	1,630	226	-3,647	6.40	0.61	-8.88
35-39	1,070	-153	-3,224	4.29	-0.51	-7.85
40-44	1,033	-159	-1,082	5.17	-0.62	-2.98
45-49	-43	-633	-2,693	-0.26	-2.88	-10.21
50-54	178	-703	-819	1.31	-3.97	-3.55
55-59	158	-35	-1,886	1.66	-0.26	-10.09
60 and over	207	-562	-2,091	0.96	-1.91	-5.03
			16 - Arauco			
Total	-7,172	-5,044	-11,742	-13.53	-8.08	-14.64
10-14	-957	-390	-1,480	-10.18	-3.40	-9.45
15-19	-1,566	-1,479	-3,056	-19.71	-15.38	-23.86
20-24	-2,168	-1,429	-2,756	-30.06	-18.97	-28.05
25-29	-913	-915	-1,525	-16.37	-14.81	-19.96
30-34	-824	-283	-872	-19.22	-5.25	-14.66
35-39	-294	-200	-444	-6.94	-4.29	-7.40
40-44	-66	45	-471	-1.96	1.20	-9.47
45-49	-67	-219	-203	-2.38	-6.33	-4.89
50-54	-215	-98	-114	-9.04	-3.40	-3.31
55-59	-63	-34	-364	-3.55	-1.49	-12.74
60 and over	-39	-42	-457	-0.89	-0.76	-6.28

TABLE 6.4 (Cont'd)

Chile. Net Domestic Migrants and Annual Rates of Net Domestic Migration According to Age, Decades and Provinces. From 1940 to 1970. Both Sexes.

Age at end of the Period	Net Migrants of the Period:			Net Annual Rates of Migration (per thousand) of the Period:		
	1940-50	1950-60	1960-70	1940-50	1950-60	1960-70
			17 - Bío-Bío			
Total	-13,411	-8,029	-18,738	-13.10	-6.68	-12.26
10-14	-1,879	-157	-2,114	-10.23	-0.74	-7.36
15-19	-2,315	-2,388	-3,891	-15.25	-12.91	-16.85
20-24	-3,617	-2,574	-6,489	-26.78	-17.37	-36.43
25-29	-2,680	-2,048	-1,602	-25.79	-17.11	-10.28
30-34	-1,456	-536	-944	-17.44	-5.21	-7.74
35-39	-572	-43	-739	-6.88	-0.51	-6.41
40-44	-55	271	-647	-0.80	3.63	-6.71
45-49	-371	-17	-404	-6.66	-0.24	-5.32
50-54	-271	-252	-844	-5.57	-4.32	-12.72
55-59	-99	95	-415	-2.90	2.11	-6.77
60 and over	-96	-380	-649	-1.16	-3.59	-4.52
			18 - Malleco			
Total	-20,375	-23,001	-33,451	-16.68	-17.32	-22.07
10-14	-2,524	-2,112	-4,064	-11.62	-9.06	-14.77
15-19	-2,728	-3,631	-6,627	-14.74	-17.73	-28.68
20-24	-5,061	-5,402	-7,216	-30.72	-33.33	-38.88
25-29	-3,734	-4,905	-6,779	-29.59	-36.53	-47.46
30-34	-2,144	-2,406	-2,516	-21.48	-21.14	-22.07
35-39	-1,150	-1,125	-2,169	-11.73	-11.93	-19.99
40-44	-790	-843	-966	-9.51	-10.35	-10.03
45-49	-595	-598	-393	-8.99	-7.70	-4.87
50-54	-657	-784	-1,096	-11.56	-11.94	-16.55
55-59	-557	-434	-482	-13.75	-8.67	-7.38
60 and over	-435	-761	-1,143	-4.69	-6.55	-7.51
			19 - Cautín			
Total	-62,270	-54,779	-54,326	-21.36	-17.90	-15.36
10-14	-7,990	-3,720	-2,142	-15.00	-7.05	-3.36
15-19	-8,328	-8,642	-8,766	-18.76	-18.50	-16.41
20-24	-14,316	-14,827	-16,017	-36.63	-38.38	-37.50
25-29	-10,771	-12,178	-14,680	-35.17	-39.04	-44.75
30-34	-6,927	-5,955	-6,492	-28.34	-23.07	-25.42
35-39	-4,538	-2,672	-2,454	-19.00	-12.08	-9.40
40-44	-2,704	-1,387	-1,047	-13.94	-7.13	-4.72
45-49	-2,171	-1,751	-1,874	-14.33	-9.73	-10.17
50-54	-1,698	-1,495	-747	-13.12	-9.88	-4.37
55-59	-1,261	-994	-208	-14.09	-8.93	-1.34
60 and over	-1,566	-1,158	101	-7.17	-4.32	0.27
			20 - Valdivia			
Total	-3,654	-26,924	-42,630	-2.26	-14.02	-18.56
10-14	-87	-3,226	-5,758	-0.31	-9.57	-13.03
15-19	312	-4,920	-8,659	1.30	-17.30	-25.36
20-24	-1,745	-5,171	-8,164	-8.11	-22.26	-29.27
25-29	-1,260	-5,169	-6,385	-7.26	-26.20	-29.84
30-34	-1,193	-2,930	-4,105	-8.58	-17.07	-23.74
35-39	-387	-1,604	-2,891	-2.85	-10.88	-16.81
40-44	498	-880	-1,753	4.52	-7.12	-11.91
45-49	-97	-791	-1,106	-1.09	-7.01	-8.89
50-54	130	-863	-1,301	1.73	-9.12	-12.50
55-59	-237	-637	-838	-4.42	-9.11	-8.86
60 and over	412	-733	-1,670	3.52	-4.61	-7.83

TABLE 6.4 (Cont'd)

Chile. Net Domestic Migrants and Annual Rates of Net Domestic Migration According to Age, Decades and Provinces. From 1940 to 1970. Both Sexes.

Age at end of the Period	Net Migrants of the Period:			Net Annual Rates of Migration (per thousand) of the Period:		
	1940-50	1950-60	1960-70	1940-50	1950-60	1960-70
			21 - Osorno			
Total	-5,061	-8,444	-13,205	-5.67	-8.01	-9.99
10-14	-1,144	-1,096	-763	-7.41	-6.20	-3.09
15-19	-229	-979	-1,868	-1.73	-6.42	-9.86
20-24	-706	-1,563	-3,924	-5.82	-12.05	-25.97
25-29	-942	-1,875	-2,851	-9.88	-16.74	-22.75
30-34	-865	-1,206	-1,961	-11.26	-12.04	-18.79
35-39	-586	-655	-965	-8.02	-8.09	-9.04
40-44	-150	-339	-455	-2.47	-4.98	-4.99
45-49	-176	-227	-567	-3.68	-3.77	-8.16
50-54	-110	-353	-50	-2.65	-6.94	-0.81
55-59	-92	-157	-141	-3.30	-4.13	-2.67
60 and over	-61	6	340	-0.90	0.06	2.69
			22 - Llanquihue			
Total	-5,015	-8,958	-11,012	-5.13	-7.49	-7.06
10-14	-1,140	-1,206	-860	-6.18	-5.50	-2.92
15-19	-230	-1,443	-2,769	-1.58	-8.03	-11.78
20-24	-1,660	-2,697	-3,322	-12.92	-17.76	-16.99
25-29	-1,033	-2,375	-2,599	-10.54	-19.49	-17.30
30-34	-859	-914	-928	-10.62	-8.80	-7.42
35-39	-388	-319	-422	-5.09	-3.76	-3.59
40-44	-111	-108	-634	-1.66	-1.47	-6.64
45-49	109	59	-173	2.15	0.90	-2.26
50-54	-134	-74	769	-3.01	-1.28	10.80
55-59	247	115	117	7.86	2.68	1.95
60 and over	184	4	-191	2.37	0.03	-1.33
			23 - Chiloé			
Total	-13,148	-19,791	-9,345	-16.37	-24.34	-10.26
10-14	-1,362	-1,958	-258	-9.74	-14.25	-1.60
15-19	-1,777	-2,557	-3,087	-15.43	-21.79	-24.39
20-24	-3,919	-5,111	-3,800	-40.46	-52.42	-35.18
25-29	-2,830	-4,386	-2,236	-36.51	-57.14	-25.42
30-34	-987	-1,686	56	-16.37	-27.58	0.82
35-39	-1,083	-1,124	-459	-18.02	-21.06	-7.99
40-44	-512	-832	509	-9.63	-17.05	10.67
45-49	-226	-460	254	-5.36	-10.13	5.56
50-54	57	-340	41	1.45	-7.93	0.98
55-59	-107	-286	4	-3.80	-8.81	0.10
60 and over	-402	-1,051	-449	-4.48	-10.76	-3.88
			24 - Aysén			
Total	2,609	2,769	-535	16.57	11.65	-1.49
10-14	200	315	-644	7.15	7.36	-9.70
15-19	358	228	-377	15.16	6.55	-6.70
20-24	525	479	15	26.26	16.42	0.33
25-29	536	440	648	31.97	17.10	17.38
30-34	325	426	473	23.33	18.88	14.81
35-39	140	157	-178	10.10	8.33	-6.04
40-44	152	198	-400	12.27	12.41	-17.75
45-49	150	138	-128	16.83	10.29	-7.25
50-54	45	143	-111	5.56	11.67	-7.32
55-59	42	45	259	9.11	5.47	18.39
60 and over	136	200	-92	15.46	12.67	-3.46

TABLE 6.4 (Cont'd)

Chile. Net Domestic Migrants and Annual Rates of Net Domestic Migration According to Age, Decades and Provinces. From 1940 to 1970. Both Sexes.

Age at end of the Period	Net Migrants of the Period:			Net Annual Rates of Migration (per thousand) of the Period:		
	1940-50	1950-60	1960-70	1940-50	1950-60	1960-70
			25 - Magallanes			
Total	1,874	8,012	7,248	4.43	15.18	9.90
10-14	-95	230	738	-1.88	3.75	7.44
15-19	35	1,309	1,610	0.77	22.04	19.54
20-24	1,117	2,427	1,573	21.04	41.69	22.45
25-29	1,015	2,685	2,123	22.30	48.61	29.07
30-34	228	1,112	1,042	5.22	18.99	14.65
35-39	-82	413	-698	-1.95	8.41	-9.79
40-44	-119	44	469	-3.18	1.01	7.09
45-49	-30	157	10	-1.07	4.23	0.20
50-54	-37	-168	-452	-1.50	-5.33	-11.84
55-59	-97	-60	60	-5.44	-2.65	1.73
60 and over	-61	-137	773	-1.78	-2.80	10.23

Source: Jorge Arévalo, Migración Intercensal de Seis Países de América Latina (Santiago, Chile: CELADE, November 1974), pp. 113-137.

TABLE 6.5

Central Zone. Net Migration Rates Out of Rural Areas by Provinces of Persons With 15 Years of Age or Older During 1950-60 and 1960-70.

Provinces	Rates per Thousand	
	1950-60	1960-70
Aconcagua	-54.78	-29.65
Valparaíso	-36.23	-39.66
Santiago	-26.43	-58.54
O'Higgins	-30.10	-19.65
Colchagua	-28.00	-32.25
Curicó	-18.07	-33.23
Talca	-18.03	-35.82
Maule	-20.94	-31.52
Linares	-21.66	-31.11
Ñuble	-44.21	-32.72

Source: LIRA: 1975a, 42.

Note: A negative sign next to a number indicates that the number of emigrants from the rural areas exceeds the number of immigrants thus giving rise to a net negative migratory balance for the rural zones.

Since it was impossible to estimate directly rural outmigration, Lira proceeded to make an indirect estimate by using the data of the 1952, 1960 and 1970 censuses. The periods examined were those of 1950-60, with little or no land reform, and 1960-70 during which most of the land reform took place, and included the provinces from Aconcagua until Ñuble where 70.3 per cent of the expropriated agricultural land was concentrated. Differences in migration according to age are presented in Table 6.6.

TABLE 6.6

Central Zone. Net Migration Rates Out of Rural Areas by Provinces and According to Age Groups of Persons With 15 Years of Age or Older During 1950-60 and 1960-70.

	Age Groups (Rates Per Thousand)					
	15-24	25-34	35-44	45-54	55-64	65 and over
Aconcagua						
1950-60	-59.68	-63.69	-40.86	-51.08	-50.70	-42.65
1960-70	-39.09	-40.78	-19.64	-19.31	-18.40	- 6.61
Valparaíso						
1950-60	-43.01	-42.43	-27.70	-33.09	-28.49	-20.13
1960-70	-48.27	-47.94	-30.34	-34.22	-28.44	-22.02
Santiago						
1950-60	-35.06	-25.40	-15.64	-25.18	-22.44	-21.24
1960-70	-64.52	-61.65	-50.81	-57.46	-56.35	-42.55
O'Higgins						
1950-60	-53.79	-47.63	-30.18	-40.06	-39.28	-29.30
1960-70	-33.23	-28.94	- 6.38	- 9.33	- 4.82	+ 4.24
Colchagua						
1950-60	-41.47	-33.35	-14.78	-19.94	-19.41	- 8.48
1960-70	-47.35	-45.05	-17.96	-18.84	-15.75	- 5.20
Curicó						
1950-60	-28.82	-23.66	-45.07	-10.52	-12.39	- 6.21
1960-70	-45.55	-50.18	-18.01	-19.52	-23.66	-10.81
Talca						
1950-60	-27.89	-21.60	- 4.23	-17.75	-10.60	- 6.49
1960-70	-47.01	-44.95	-23.44	-28.11	-22.91	-14.48
Maule						
1950-60	-33.45	-26.38	-10.61	-13.17	-11.09	- 5.97
1960-70	-50.13	-41.98	-14.20	-18.07	-14.58	-12.19
Linares						
1950-60	-32.68	-24.21	- 8.54	-18.61	-12.76	-14.17
1960-70	-43.11	-43.44	-17.82	-18.58	-18.10	- 9.22
Ñuble						
1950-60	-35.91	-30.58	- 7.82	-14.51	-11.39	- 7.63
1960-70	-49.06	-46.19	-16.56	-17.62	-14.41	- 7.09

Source: Lira: 1975a, 44.

Population According to Province of Birth and Residence

Intercensual migration rates are calculated on the basis of census information about the province of residence and the province of birth of the country's inhabitants. Total population according to province of birth and by province of residence for 1952 is presented in Table 6.7, for the 1960 census in Table 6.8, and for the 1970 census in Table 6.9.

TABLE 6.7

Total Population of the Country According to Province of Birth and Residence, 1952.

Province of Birth	All Provinces	Province of Residence				
		Tarapacá	Antofagasta	Atacama	Coquimbo	Aconcagua
Republic	5,932,995	102,789	184,824	80,113	262,169	128,378
Tarapacá	122,770	75,580	10,066	1,281	3,098	697
Antofagasta	162,024	4,374	108,708	4,231	6,690	886
Atacama	96,083	1,756	12,565	59,880	5,943	580
Coquimbo	331,004	5,885	29,484	8,751	232,040	3,447
Aconcagua	171,897	602	1,391	592	1,686	102,600
Valparaíso	432,310	2,158	3,476	690	2,075	6,514
Santiago	1,249,503	2,524	5,382	1,684	4,469	6,909
O'Higgins	240,171	278	723	276	473	796
Colchagua	195,068	358	549	144	370	549
Curicó	108,568	291	806	127	292	337
Talca	192,062	411	1,135	191	426	521
Maule	115,957	226	608	136	197	338
Linares	166,234	194	308	105	311	296
Ñuble	335,581	344	776	311	465	705
Concepción	363,361	526	1,009	230	565	521
Arauco	103,831	81	153	47	87	121
Bío-Bío	179,753	145	248	82	236	322
Malleco	187,990	180	290	66	207	267
Cautín	407,598	248	500	134	361	402
Valdivia	216,765	160	388	92	239	273
Osorno	132,795	47	117	18	90	94
Llanquihue	135,740	66	140	27	81	89
Chiloé	132,660	107	590	32	69	68
Aisén	12,635	9	24	11	21	13
Magallanes	36,757	53	120	18	63	71
Foreign country	103,878	6,186	5,268	957	1,615	962

Province of Birth	Province of Residence						
	Valparaíso	Santiago	O'Higgins	Colchagua	Curicó	Talca	Maule
Republic	498,254	1,754,954	224,593	139,531	89,432	173,693	72,181
Tarapacá	6,760	21,001	598	258	293	376	88
Antofagasta	7,387	23,907	980	297	414	644	138
Atacama	3,276	9,968	396	148	121	186	66
Coquimbo	15,588	30,796	913	261	320	520	80
Aconcagua	30,042	30,322	1,011	388	280	523	105
Valparaíso	340,442	62,832	1,740	731	626	1,046	276
Santiago	35,006	1,132,506	16,638	5,986	3,738	5,899	1,407
O'Higgins	3,918	53,227	169,800	3,565	1,048	1,982	222
Colchagua	3,665	48,325	12,820	119,375	4,190	1,940	190
Curicó	2,276	23,677	2,879	3,263	66,983	4,767	240
Talca	3,635	35,064	2,856	1,240	5,745	130,549	1,554
Maule	3,818	20,080	1,292	449	655	8,525	63,950
Linares	2,011	26,295	1,843	529	924	6,198	1,195
Ñuble	4,808	51,695	4,570	771	1,228	3,788	1,226
Concepción	8,717	31,720	1,127	421	521	1,475	442
Arauco	1,140	5,592	167	106	156	285	98
Bío-Bío	1,814	15,870	738	214	307	795	127
Malleco	1,792	16,526	793	250	345	809	126
Cautín	3,086	32,471	1,053	360	498	1,073	196
Valdivia	2,140	12,663	396	166	208	504	113
Osorno	749	5,263	195	68	71	450	51
Llanquihue	1,463	3,957	126	57	55	121	38
Chiloé	1,515	2,484	95	45	48	74	25
Aisén	58	277	16	5	8	20	19
Magallanes	1,556	2,986	64	19	33	55	18
Foreign country	11,562	55,450	1,487	563	617	1,089	191

TABLE 6.7 (Cont'd)

Total Population of the Country According to Province of Birth and Residence, 1952.

Province of Birth	Province of Residence						
	Linares	Ñuble	Concepción	Arauco	Bío-Bío	Malleco	Cautín
Republic	146,257	251,342	411,566	72,289	138,292	159,419	365,072
Tarapacá	214	278	1,098	25	115	123	241
Antofagasta	255	357	1,352	78	114	147	287
Atacama	112	135	417	26	61	69	152
Coquimbo	273	360	1,124	29	112	151	266
Aconcagua	247	216	794	46	99	111	233
Valparaíso	554	800	4,287	96	290	292	737
Santiago	3,562	4,140	8,032	405	1,390	1,677	2,880
O'Higgins	692	885	1,037	45	242	172	268
Colchagua	601	366	590	43	155	148	237
Curicó	587	444	619	34	119	187	287
Talca	3,845	953	1,875	94	266	375	581
Maule	6,654	2,498	3,399	118	278	672	1,230
Linares	119,048	2,619	1,861	82	378	532	791
Ñuble	4,075	221,572	21,994	417	2,621	3,938	6,668
Concepción	1,357	6,507	288,593	3,149	3,329	4,233	4,492
Arauco	313	613	23,109	62,239	573	2,573	4,232
Bío-Bío	739	2,549	14,270	1,297	120,587	8,383	7,322
Malleco	722	1,776	12,596	2,536	4,093	125,005	14,578
Cautín	1,065	1,990	13,210	990	1,942	8,023	307,678
Valdivia	300	544	4,249	256	525	992	6,073
Osorno	124	379	1,180	43	231	275	1,562
Llanquihue	85	188	1,136	31	100	170	833
Chiloé	79	98	610	36	55	95	470
Aisén	10	9	40	4	10	18	63
Magallanes	46	77	581	14	39	51	138
Foreign country	696	989	3,513	156	568	1,007	2,773

Province of Birth	Province of Residence					
	Valdivia	Osorno	Llanquihue	Chiloé	Aisén	Magallanes
Republic	232,647	123,059	139,986	100,687	26,262	55,206
Tarapacá	164	85	126	31	36	138
Antofagasta	315	92	123	46	35	167
Atacama	78	34	21	29	13	51
Coquimbo	208	93	98	26	53	126
Aconcagua	212	76	93	31	47	150
Valparaíso	728	258	463	159	138	902
Santiago	1,777	937	902	327	482	844
O'Higgins	228	105	56	21	60	52
Colchagua	177	103	48	23	37	69
Curicó	147	78	54	8	22	44
Talca	292	162	106	21	75	88
Maule	404	82	122	44	70	112
Linares	312	120	115	30	64	73
Ñuble	2,134	473	363	99	305	235
Concepción	2,129	641	548	183	211	715
Arauco	1,548	193	152	61	74	118
Bío-Bío	2,407	331	362	114	350	144
Malleco	3,503	577	378	148	292	135
Cautín	25,918	2,302	1,867	514	1,328	389
Valdivia	173,430	7,451	2,872	614	1,183	934
Osorno	10,032	100,361	9,408	718	773	496
Llanquihue	2,637	5,428	111,894	2,368	2,292	2,358
Chiloé	1,690	1,781	8,148	93,960	5,796	14,690
Aisén	77	67	192	82	11,515	67
Magallanes	225	134	430	360	187	29,419
Foreign country	1,875	1,095	1,045	670	824	2,690

Source: República de Chile, Servicio Nacional de Estadística y Censos, XII Censo General de Población y I de Vivienda, Levantado el 24 de Abril de 1952. Resumen del País (Santiago, Chile: SNE, 1956), pp. 119-120.

TABLE 6.8

Total Population According to Province of Birth, by Province of Residence. 1960 Census.

Province of Residence	Total	Province of Birth							
		Tarapacá	Antofagasta	Atacama	Coquimbo	Aconcagua	Valparaíso	Santiago	O'Higgins
Total	7,269,262	143,075	204,770	118,277	389,939	189,139	549,229	1,797,212	287,794
Tarapacá	116,952	88,872	5,871	1,836	5,319	747	3,155	5,966	425
Antofagasta	209,841	11,097	140,030	11,420	27,886	1,208	3,516	6,613	685
Atacama	115,105	2,158	6,600	80,501	16,913	1,056	1,233	3,127	470
Coquimbo	307,089	3,688	7,761	6,650	274,725	1,992	2,210	5,483	480
Aconcagua	139,646	736	902	498	3,307	114,712	7,165	6,464	743
Valparaíso	606,306	7,398	8,420	3,321	17,382	31,263	440,195	40,514	4,332
Santiago	2,379,421	24,649	29,327	12,133	39,095	33,569	74,633	1,653,744	67,263
O'Higgins	258,223	606	891	360	936	1,220	2,173	19,210	200,506
Colchagua	157,972	266	266	120	238	368	703	6,415	4,454
Curicó	105,234	254	442	99	285	261	602	4,269	1,294
Talca	205,179	394	601	148	492	392	1,095	6,668	2,035
Maule	79,559	54	112	48	86	85	307	1,503	291
Linares	170,598	204	270	73	251	271	709	4,407	892
Ñuble	284,760	329	386	122	454	291	915	5,636	1,226
Concepción	536,291	1,052	1,395	432	1,123	614	4,674	9,969	1,230
Arauco	89,316	32	67	29	53	27	160	549	47
Bío-Bío	168,038	147	154	56	183	149	386	2,389	313
Malleco	173,503	135	113	41	126	100	299	1,956	186
Cautín	392,217	240	268	120	272	219	761	4,105	299
Valdivia	258,204	168	200	71	232	122	560	2,266	216
Osorno	143,001	84	93	29	117	66	268	1,278	94
Llanquihua	166,630	131	126	40	113	86	602	1,409	86
Chiloé	98,549	48	69	23	36	27	125	336	20
Aysén	36,975	68	67	16	70	49	196	807	67
Magallanes	70,619	264	339	91	245	245	2,579	2,115	139
Unknown	34	1	-	-	-	-	8	14	1

TABLE 6.8 (Cont'd)

Total Population According to Province of Birth, by Province of Residence. 1960 Census.

Province of Residence	Province of Birth								
	Colchagua	Curicó	Talca	Maule	Linares	Ñuble	Concepción	Arauco	Bío-Bío
Total	220,416	128,870	227,310	122,690	196,147	357,951	488,629	120,381	207,472
Tarapacá	391	307	411	216	271	492	739	125	212
Antofagasta	458	669	924	550	363	713	908	142	255
Atacama	234	187	298	159	230	366	334	61	184
Coquimbo	292	232	371	165	270	413	594	113	215
Aconcagua	569	288	409	249	343	607	555	123	289
Valparaíso	3,666	2,271	3,694	3,328	2,161	5,422	11,097	1,240	2,237
Santiago	54,806	28,052	40,353	23,502	32,415	65,433	42,268	7,846	21,677
O'Higgins	12,934	3,175	2,639	1,209	1,862	4,360	1,479	256	910
Colchagua	136,794	3,493	1,288	349	466	762	418	104	251
Curicó	5,182	80,478	6,714	608	983	1,125	534	109	376
Talca	2,237	6,627	159,551	8,196	6,590	3,770	1,590	257	1,026
Maule	162	309	1,464	71,181	1,460	1,137	437	89	178
Linares	587	735	4,171	5,549	141,965	4,256	1,577	290	1,136
Ñuble	537	527	1,051	2,108	2,590	249,420	8,649	827	2,783
Concepción	608	596	1,854	2,976	1,928	24,441	395,514	23,279	16,383
Arauco	51	55	76	89	79	480	4,505	77,231	1,121
Bío-Bío	186	169	438	249	452	2,774	5,139	875	143,563
Malleco	112	143	241	421	364	2,525	3,196	2,479	6,506
Cautín	184	183	475	859	620	4,345	4,298	3,208	5,003
Valdivia	118	130	387	295	298	1,551	1,811	1,104	1,805
Osorno	84	93	145	98	93	426	644	155	319
Llanquihue	76	45	136	94	123	357	625	161	369
Chiloé	22	22	23	30	31	86	135	58	104
Aysén	45	21	68	73	50	281	264	100	356
Magallanes	79	63	129	137	140	409	1,319	148	213
Unknown	2	-	-	-	-	-	-	1	1

TABLE 6.8 (Cont'd)

Total Population According to Province of Birth, by Province of Residence. 1960 Census.

Province of Residence	Province of Birth								
	Malleco	Cautín	Valdivia	Osorno	Llanquihue	Chiloé	Aysén	Megallanes	Unknown
Total	221,508	473,710	271,356	162,009	169,410	134,386	21,896	47,262	424
Tarapacá	271	505	312	131	120	122	22	92	22
Antofagasta	302	583	454	165	217	546	22	107	8
Atacama	172	312	211	132	49	46	27	36	9
Coquimbo	273	452	322	128	94	68	25	66	7
Aconcagua	320	491	378	129	158	86	33	92	-
Valparaíso	2,252	4,275	3,617	1,216	2,550	1,915	108	2,382	50
Santiago	23,720	54,981	23,765	9,789	7,846	3,848	680	3,882	145
O'Higgins	824	1,340	576	280	200	168	35	65	9
Colchagua	300	389	247	72	95	66	10	28	10
Curicó	350	629	318	118	84	47	15	43	15
Talca	930	1,334	595	261	165	100	30	82	13
Maule	127	263	106	74	38	23	8	17	-
Linares	960	1,238	495	206	185	104	16	44	7
Ñuble	2,149	2,861	980	454	202	112	36	90	25
Concepción	17,928	18,523	7,013	1,882	1,422	638	112	681	24
Arauco	2,909	1,183	351	95	55	43	1	10	18
Bío-Bío	6,045	2,676	976	403	159	67	13	51	26
Malleco	144,946	7,583	1,199	404	205	109	64	47	3
Cautín	12,397	342,847	8,025	1,907	938	385	87	154	18
Valdivia	2,636	23,838	204,942	10,991	2,542	1,624	98	195	4
Osorno	556	2,466	9,446	118,711	6,064	1,501	65	105	1
Llanquihue	467	2,114	3,390	11,401	136,308	7,517	340	506	8
Chiloé	131	469	730	930	2,814	91,780	169	331	-
Aysén	288	1,632	1,670	1,265	3,155	6,433	19,681	253	-
Magallanes	253	725	1,236	865	3,745	17,038	199	37,902	2
Unknown	2	1	2	-	-	-	-	1	-

Source: National Institute of Statistics

TABLE 6.9

Total Population According to Habitual, Actual Province of Residence, by Province of Birth. 1970 Census.

Province of Birth	Population									
		Province of Habitual Actual Residence								
	Total	Tarapacá	Anto-fagasta	Atacama	Coquimbo	Aconcagua	Val-paraíso	Santiago	O'Higgins	Colchagua
	Tarapacá to Colchagua									
Total Both Sexes	5,507,080	184,139	251,023	152,045	338,873	164,310	736,708	3,208,553	303,503	167,926
Tarapacá	166,113	116,977	9,784	1,985	3,269	770	6,801	25,592	702	233
Antofagasta	240,818	11,487	169,007	7,703	9,073	913	9,040	32,313	1,045	232
Atacama	148,540	3,173	11,971	105,489	8,872	671	3,817	13,914	508	125
Coquimbo	429,498	9,200	28,984	23,538	295,744	3,850	21,240	45,203	1,468	271
Aconcagua	199,330	1,122	1,013	890	1,679	128,668	29,796	34,449	1,365	348
Valparaíso	645,536	5,933	4,354	2,011	3,351	8,935	532,051	85,481	2,692	728
Santiago	2,297,185	14,364	9,591	4,301	7,252	8,208	48,404	2,174,057	24,073	6,935
O'Higgins	328,789	990	741	474	543	1,275	5,085	81,849	233,312	4,520
Colchagua	221,930	539	446	230	313	513	3,515	59,371	12,167	144,836
Curicó	43,355	670	638	272	259	312	2,254	32,303	3,238	3,409
Talca	59,091	868	888	283	465	458	3,779	48,065	3,066	1,219
Maule	30,139	422	489	133	176	275	2,955	24,191	1,222	276
Linares	52,519	698	446	223	397	471	2,634	44,524	2,547	579
Ñuble	91,981	973	754	384	482	611	5,568	78,121	4,360	728
Concepción	81,130	1,633	1,199	525	633	631	13,478	60,385	2,179	467
Arauco	13,705	240	145	115	105	146	1,374	11,144	359	77
Bío-Bío	36,724	444	307	156	284	396	2,376	31,315	1,172	274
Malleco	44,038	664	530	204	361	462	3,000	37,280	1,145	392
Cautín	97,033	1,194	790	386	497	655	5,186	86,074	1,771	480
Valdivia	47,623	1,814	615	353	344	459	4,413	38,447	921	257
Osorno	20,236	340	376	118	146	215	1,700	16,721	494	126
Llanquihue	18,173	399	305	107	169	178	3,362	13,279	273	101
Chiloé	7,505	281	448	57	99	80	1,790	4,507	182	61
Aysén	1,717	72	29	17	29	71	203	1,223	48	25
Magallanes	9,457	187	177	46	98	98	3,160	5,528	118	45
Foreign Country	73,710	6,435	3,682	788	1,435	962	8,389	50,344	1,321	354
Unknown	101,205	3,020	3,314	1,252	2,798	4,027	11,338	72,873	1,755	828

TABLE 6.9 (Cont'd)

Total Population According to Habitual, Actual Province of Residence, by Province of Birth. 1970 Census.

Province of Birth	Population									
		Province of Habitual Actual Residence								
	Total Curicó to Malleco	Curicó	Talca	Maule	Linares	Ñuble	Concepción	Arauco	Bío-Bío	Malleco
Total Both Sexes	2,038,364	114,046	230,665	82,676	188,206	314,974	642,163	97,173	192,357	176,104
Tarapacá	2,748	236	360	91	190	335	1,237	49	147	103
Antofagasta	3,503	372	572	145	206	344	1,519	74	148	123
Atacama	1,230	90	163	52	75	158	557	29	57	49
Coquimbo	3,161	245	421	97	214	389	1,345	74	195	181
Aconcagua	2,213	190	402	146	195	249	701	75	138	117
Valparaíso	10,627	585	1,140	359	574	918	6,029	194	504	324
Santiago	48,738	4,687	7,693	1,844	4,954	7,202	15,249	926	3,810	2,373
O'Higgins	8,299	1,395	2,002	324	776	1,477	1,597	95	459	174
Colchagua	8,973	4,360	2,052	192	582	485	847	62	254	139
Curicó	98,109	88,603	6,787	304	716	519	821	84	165	110
Talca	199,434	6,705	180,724	1,820	4,820	2,010	2,332	112	635	276
Maule	88,191	623	7,197	70,524	4,943	1,724	2,534	121	243	282
Linares	174,116	948	7,488	1,589	157,117	3,115	2,690	144	679	346
Ñuble	307,121	967	3,034	1,267	3,702	269,105	24,344	499	2,479	1,724
Concepción	507,932	554	1,762	826	1,606	10,269	476,546	5,681	7,181	3,507
Arauco	107,930	115	258	157	321	737	21,591	81,310	834	2,607
Bío-Bío	190,056	295	1,091	345	1,119	4,017	17,373	1,219	158,961	5,636
Malleco	183,087	445	1,141	316	1,078	2,674	21,497	3,015	7,603	145,318
Cautín	37,621	551	1,508	460	1,288	2,967	18,654	1,244	3,319	7,630
Valdivia	14,985	326	895	244	721	1,467	7,881	500	1,620	1,331
Osorno	4,713	149	375	84	258	619	2,265	115	436	412
Llanquihue	3,425	122	251	44	234	424	1,719	110	249	272
Chiloé	1,290	42	81	41	65	154	598	64	96	149
Aysén	384	13	37	6	20	38	135	15	39	81
Magallanes	1,416	33	87	29	74	141	886	38	52	76
Foreign Country	6,639	380	642	131	658	705	3,019	124	489	491
Unknown	22,423	1,015	2,502	1,239	1,700	2,732	8,197	1,200	1,565	2,273

TABLE 6.9 (Cont'd)

Total Population According to Habitual, Actual Province of Residence, by Province of Birth. 1970 Census.

Province of Birth	Population									
		Province of Habitual Actual Residence								
	Total Cautín to Unknown	Cautín	Valdivia	Osorno	Llanquihue	Chiloé	Aysén	Megallanes	Foreign Country	Unknown
Total Both Sexes	1,339,324	420,248	277,351	158,977	196,910	109,754	48,496	87,916	3,387	36,285
Tarapacá	1,238	287	200	108	139	90	111	212	73	18
Antofagasta	1,322	292	216	97	161	102	86	295	64	9
Atacama	547	142	107	48	48	38	44	91	26	3
Coquimbo	1,319	326	249	149	122	67	100	256	36	14
Aconcagua	1,176	201	223	74	89	52	89	215	83	150
Valparaíso	6,410	932	773	344	721	267	364	2,791	199	19
Santiago	22,879	7,492	4,274	2,213	2,555	990	1,420	3,570	306	59
O'Higgins	1,461	468	298	124	159	77	114	190	27	4
Colchagua	966	246	183	102	148	44	75	124	42	2
Curicó	963	280	218	120	80	85	37	118	13	12
Talca	1,711	558	306	222	190	82	131	200	15	7
Maule	1,554	644	226	109	96	49	57	172	5	196
Linares	1,942	736	437	153	211	84	93	205	18	5
Ñuble	6,404	3,508	1,197	390	430	134	306	421	18	5
Concepción	10,750	5,114	1,832	662	788	234	361	1,669	53	37
Arauco	4,094	2,445	800	130	113	72	84	115	8	327
Bío-Bío	7,044	4,086	1,525	353	411	112	293	233	14	17
Malleco	18,528	12,977	2,994	713	656	220	405	392	35	136
Cautín	380,783	354,339	18,693	2,201	2,228	765	1,535	879	111	32
Valdivia	253,809	10,981	223,380	10,507	4,686	1,186	1,564	1,391	67	47
Osorno	158,970	2,324	10,530	129,089	12,969	1,309	1,367	1,205	35	142
Llanquihue	181,972	1,433	2,812	6,300	157,745	4,300	3,559	5,136	57	630
Chiloé	130,807	483	1,334	1,230	6,919	96,458	6,236	17,427	113	607
Aysén	30,134	200	208	176	585	366	28,217	338	23	21
Magallanes	49,890	257	275	201	719	619	253	47,429	54	83
Foreign Country	10,092	2,119	1,300	780	841	698	803	1,967	1,560	24
Unknown	52,559	7,383	2,761	2,382	3,101	1,254	792	875	332	33,679

Source: República de Chile, INE, Población, Total País, XIV Censo de Población y III de Vivienda, 1970 (Santiago, Chile: INE, 1970), pp. 13, 16 and 19.

7

INTERNATIONAL MIGRATION

International migration can be an important element in the process of economic development. Countries with surplus labor tend to experience emigration. Underpopulated nations tend to attract immigrants. Immigrants can affect capital formation by bringing capital resources along with them, by being more parsimonious than the native population or by producing more and better capital goods in their adopted country. Immigrants can and have shaped income distribution by creating profits or, through their high skills and education, earning wage and salaries that exceed the average levels within the nation. In addition to immigrants, foreigners resident within the nation shape economic development by being active in agricultural, mineral, industrial and service activities.

MOVEMENT OF FOREIGNERS EXCLUDING TOURISTS

Arrivals and departures of foreigners for the period between 1908 and 1975 (along with the difference) are presented in Table 7.1. These figures show a net influx of foreigners into Chile during most of the years between 1908 and 1975. Only the years between 1957 and 1961 are an exception showing a major exodus of foreigners.

As foreigners are classified, according to Chilean law, the following are categories of individuals: (a) Official residents. Among these are included the members of the diplomatic and consular corps accredited to the Chilean Government and of the international organizations recognized by Chile. Such a status can also be acquired by their family members, administrative and service personnel and other persons determined as such by the Ministry of Foreign Affairs. (b) Temporary resident. This group includes the persons having as their goal to reside in Chile and enter the country with a temporary residence visa. (c) Resident subject to contract. Included here are foreigners (and the members of their families) who come to Chile to work under contract. (d) Student resident. In this category are included individuals who came to study at various institutions or centers in Chile. (e) Permanent residents are those who reside indefinitely in the country and can pursue any type of legal activity. (f) Immigrant is the foreigner who enters Chile with the visa of an immigrant and with the intention of residing indefinitely in the country in order to pursue an economic activity.

The estimated number of immigrants entering Chile between 1849 and 1906 (not all years are covered) is presented in Table 7.2. Only two years (1889 and 1890) stand out as registering significant immigration. Immigration into Chile, a medium-sized country, never approached the magnitude of migration into Argentina, a large nation, which had a much higher land/labor ratio than Chile. The figures on estimated number of immigrants entering Chile between 1849 and 1906 presented in Table 7.2 are not comparable to the

TABLE 7.1

Movement of Foreigners

Year	Arrivals	Departures	Difference	Year	Arrivals	Departures	Difference
1908	25,775	12,759	+13,016	1942	53,649	55,796	-2,147
1909	19,014	15,867	+3,147	1943	72,164	73,276	-1,112
1910	25,788	16,798	+8,990	1944	68,250	66,909	+1,341
1911	24,845	23,841	+1,004	1945	84,729	84,425	+304
1912	27,645	15,482	+12,163	1946	121,888	116,373	+5,515
1913	35,393	28,248	+7,145	1947	122,542	115,559	+6,943
1914	47,147	21,054	+26,093	1948	121,334	106,627	+14,707
1915	17,326	10,408	+6,918	1949	104,491	102,745	+1,746
1916	25,878	24,919	+959	1950	102,489	95,320	+7,169
1917	30,076	19,009	+11,067	1951	104,203	102,468	+1,735
1918	17,953	19,438	-1,485	1952	97,553	90,507	+7,046
1919	15,658	15,124	+534	1953	93,810	89,896	+3,914
1920	22,122	18,391	+3,731	1954	117,352	118,269	-917
1921	21,926	15,072	+6,854	1955	124,993	118,201	+6,972
1922	19,528	15,489	+4,039	1956	156,056	151,900	+4,147
1923	21,998	17,283	+4,715	1957	164,456	172,945	-8,489
1924	37,054	29,166	+7,888	1958	149,808	165,786	-15,978
1925	32,255	25,234	+7,021	1959	164,107	169,775	-5,668
1926	27,060	26,837	+223	1960	169,116	184,760	-15,644
1927	23,683	24,282	-599	1961	167,789	180,837	-13,048
1928	22,395	21,667	+728	1962	159,995	158,726	+1,269
1929	37,988	33,356	+4,632	1963			
1930	39,860	37,860	+1,410	1964			
1931	29,195	29,888	-693	1965	134,400	133,294	+1,106
1932	25,151	25,878	-728	1966	144,096	140,230	+3,866
1933	35,396	23,671	+1,725	1967	178,025	173,913	+4,112
1934	26,550	26,901	-351	1968	194,693	188,999	+5,694
1935	31,524	29,536	+1,988	1969	205,730	197,507	+8,223
1936	35,313	32,032	+3,281	1970	224,595	216,709	+7,886
1937	40,085	36,821	+3,264	1971	288,235	275,914	+12,321
1938	48,221	44,751	+3,470	1972	209,556	203,938	+5,618
1939	54,486	47,960	+6,526	1973	194,967	189,417	+5,550
1940	46,368	45,576	+792	1974	224,606	221,652	+2,954
1941	49,790	52,511	-2,721	1975	256,860	247,697	+9,163

Source: The information for the period between 1908-1935 was obtained from República de Chile, D.G.E., Demografía y Asistencia Social Año 1935 (Chile: Dirección General de Estadística), Volume I, 1936, Table 46, p. 69. Time series information for the period since 1955 was obtained from D.G.E. Estadística Chilena, Año 1945 (Santiago, Chile: Dirección General de Estadística), p. 567, for the years 1936-37; Estadística Chilena, Ibid., Enero-Febrero 1948, for the years 1938-1947; D.E.C. Sinopsis 1952 (Santiago, Chile: D.E.C. 1953) for the period 1948-1953; D.E.C. Boletín No. 7-11, Julio-Noviembre 1962 (Santiago, Chile: D.E.C., 1963), p. 178, for the period 1954-1961; and Boletín No. 12, Synopsis, December 1962, Ibid., p. 340, for 1962.

Note: This information has been published in various publications of the Chilean Bureau of Census and Statistics. The title and description of the relevant table has changed over time even though the underlying information has remained the same. Originally, it appeared in the Bureau's publication Demografía y Asistencia Social, cited in the previous paragraph, under the title Movimiento de Pasajeros Entrados y Salidos del País. In the forties, the title was changed to Pasajeros Entrados y Salidos y Movimiento Migratorio and used in the Bureau's publication Estadística Chilena, Año XII - Nos. 1-2, 1948. In the fifties it received the title Movimiento Migratorio which is used in the Bureau's monthly bulletin, Boletín, cited in the source of this table. The information for the period between 1965 and 1975 was given to the author directly by the Instituto Nacional de Estadísticas but is also found in the publications described in the text of the chapter.

figures on movement of foreigners presented in Table 7.1.

For an historical examination of immigration and the role of foreigners in Chile see Carl Solberg, Immigration and Nationalism. Argentina and Chile, 1890-1914 (Austin and London: The University of Texas Press, 1970); UN. Consejo Económico y Social La Immigración en Chile (New York: UN, E/CN.12/169/Add.2.1 May 1950) and Markos Mamalakis (1976d, 38-45; 47-64; 256-266).

TABLE 7.2

Estimated Number of Immigrants Entering Chile: 1849-1906

Year	Number of Immigrants	Year	Number of Immigrants
1849	85	1886	905
1851	102	1887	808
1852	212	1888	805
1853	51	1889	10,413
1854	35	1890	11,001
1856	460	1891	318
1857	180	1892	286
1858	9	1893	405
1859	11	1894	395
1860	93	1896	1,114
1861	11	1897	970
1862	32	1898	564
1863	12	1899	548
1864	155	1900	936
1866	26	1901	1,449
1869	7	1902	864
1882	2,466	1905	293
1885	1,837	1906	1,442

Source: Política, legislación y control de la immigración en Chile y otros estados americanos, by Eliana Bucchi Pensa, Santiago, 1939. Also, United Nations, Economic and Social Council, La Immigración en Chile, Table 62, Migración E/CN.12/169/Add. 2, 1 May 1950.

MOVEMENT OF CHILEANS AND TOURISTS

Arrivals and departures of Chileans and tourists between 1960 and 1973 are presented in Table 7.3. Tourists are the foreigners who enter Chile for no longer than 90 days for reasons of health, pleasure, sports, study, business, religion, family and so forth without intention of immigrating or assuming residence or developing remunerative activities. In each year since 1960 the arrivals of tourists have exceeded departures, often by large numbers. The number of tourist arrivals exceeded departures between 1960 and 1975 by more than 140 thousand suggesting that many tourists may have changed status after their arrival or that the figures are subject to limitations.

Detailed information on arrivals and departures of tourists according to nationality, sex, income, route used, age, and profession (often on a monthly basis) is presented in DEC, Estadísticas de Turismo y Movimiento Internacional de Viajeros (e.g. DEC: 1965a and DEC: 1966a) and the similar publication published by INE (1967a; 1971b and 1975a).

Information on arrivals and departures of Chileans according to age, sex, profession or occupation, income, route used and country of origin and destination is also provided in the aforementioned publications (e.g. DEC: 1966a and INE: 1975a).

These same publications on tourism and international movement of passengers also provide detailed information on the arrivals and departures of foreigners by nationality (monthly), type of visitor, sex, route used and place of entry and exit (e.g. INE: 1975a).

The statistics on arrivals and departures of Chileans between 1965 and

1975, which are presented in Table 7.3, show a marked and continuous outflow. Thus, while there is an overall net influx of foreigners including tourists, into Chile, there is an exodus of Chileans to other nations and continents. Since international migration provides a weak link in Chile's demographic panorama, a comprehensive examination of the statistics and other evidence is both desirable and necessary.

TABLE 7.3

Arrivals and Departures of Chileans and Tourists, 1960-1973.

Year	Chileans		Tourists	
	Arrivals	Departures	Arrivals	Departures
1960	-	-	63,469	50,193
1961	-	-	67,403	53,683
1962	-	-	76,670	67,383
1963	-	-	74,885	67,767
1964	-	-	100,294	93,613
1965	78,711	86,158	117,220	114,979
1966	94,515	99,477	124,469	118,128
1967	130,501	134,839	155,189	148,982
1968	138,720	144,000	170,310	162,362
1969	150,675	159,804	181,182	170,336
1970	188,791	214,594	198,824	185,443
1971	162,236	171,934	261,214	246,560
1972	148,884	157,971	177,928	169,780
1973	151,868	171,848	168,241	155,919
1974	211,449	260,451	204,524	199,421
1975	370,158	438,964	235,624	224,240

Source: National Institute of Statistics.

INTERNATIONAL MIGRATION: QUALITY OF INFORMATION

The major sources for the study of international migration are the movements of persons between countries captured through continuous statistics and the data contained in the population censuses about persons born outside Chile's national territory. Both sources have major limitations not only because of the scarce information which they provide but also because they suffer from omission (Tacla: 1975, 3). In general, according to Tacla, the continuous statistics record only departures and arrivals of passengers without specifying either the nature of the movement to which they refer or such basic characteristics of this movement as age, sex, economic activity and so forth. This is not true, however, as it was already pointed out before, for arrivals and departures of foreigners, tourists and Chileans in recent decades.

The most serious problem according to Tacla (1975, 3) is that of omission. For almost a century there exists the belief and evidence that an important number of Chileans emigrate to other countries. The best known and documented migration is that of Chileans from the Austral provinces to Argentina seeking seasonal or permanent employment. Such outmigration may be underestimated according to Tacla either because undocumented migrants elude the controls of the international police where such movements are recorded for statistical purposes or because such statistical records are not kept in border points (Tacla: 1975, 3).

Outmigration received a special impetus during 1970-1975. First came the exodus of those middle and upper class Chileans who wanted to escape the socialist state being established by Salvador Allende. Colonies of Chileans were established or strengthened in Argentina (Mendoza and elsewhere), Australia, Mexico, Venezuela, Central America, the United States and Europe. Much larger numbers, however, fled Chile after Allende's overthrow by the Military Junta on September 11, 1973. Large numbers of Chileans settled in Buenos Aires, Argentina, in England, Sweden, Italy, East and West Germany and elsewhere throughout South and

Central Latin America, North America and Europe. Since 1974 some of those who fled the country during the Allende years and the Military Junta have returned to Chile. It is also alleged that Argentina forced many Chilean workers to return to Chile when the tensions between the two countries increased during 1978. Official records about the international migration movements of the 1969-1979 decade are the meager ones up to 1975 presented in this chapter. It is hypothesized here that migration out of Chile may have been much higher than generally believed ever since (or even before) 1955 and that it may have been sufficiently high to affect such figures as birth rates, population growth and population projections.

According to Tacla, the total number of Chileans who had emigrated and were residing abroad in 1950 amounted to 70-80 thousand persons with approximately 60 thousand located in Argentina (Tacla: 1975, 18).

The net migratory balance of Chile with Argentina during the 1960-70 period gives a total of 47 thousand Chileans who had arrived since 1960. In contrast, the continuous statistics registered a total of 82.6 thousand immigrants giving rise to a difference of 34,900 persons between one register and the other (Tacla: 1975, 18). According to Julio Morales, who compiled these figures (Morales, 1974), a significant part of those who had entered Argentina legally were with expired entry visas or permits on the date of the census and attempted to avoid the censual count or declared to be natives of Argentina in order to avoid possible sanctions (Tacla: 1975, 18).

According to an estimate by the International Catholic Commission on Migration (Comisión Católica Internacional de Migración-CCIM), cited by Morales and Tacla (1975, 18) there were 350,000 Chileans in Argentina in 1970. This estimate, which is considered as highly inflated by many demographers, exceeds by 217,000 persons the estimate made by Morales of Chileans found in Argentina in 1970 which gave a total of 133,000. The Morales estimate was based on the sample survey of the 1970 census of Argentina.

The concensus among demographers is that the census figures of Argentina underestimate the number of Chilean immigrants but not by as much as the Catholic Commission estimate seems to indicate.

INTERNATIONAL MIGRATION: THE *CELADE-ODEPLAN* ESTIMATES FOR 1950-1980

International migration (immigrants less emigrants) according to sex and five-year age groups for quinquennial periods between 1950 and 1980 is presented in Table 7.4. The age classification used in Table 7.4 includes 17 categories as follows: it begins with the 0-4 group and continues with 5-year groups to 75-79 and ends with 80 or more. The figures presented in Table 7.4 are the migration estimates recommended as most plausible by CELADE and ODEPLAN. These figures suggest a declining trend in the exodus of Chileans between 1950 and 1980 and zero net international migration after 1980.

Although these trends are suggested as plausible, international migration after 1980 will be affected by the existence of a labor surplus or shortage as a consequence of the liberal free market and opening to global markets policies since 1974, the birth rate and political relations between Chile, on the one hand, and Argentina, Bolivia and Peru, on the other hand.

It should be pointed out that it has been impossible to reconcile the international migration estimates for 1950-1980 prepared jointly by CELADE and ODEPLAN with the continuous statistics on arrivals and departures of foreigners, Chileans and tourists recorded by the National Institute of Statistics.

FOREIGNERS RESIDENT IN CHILE. CENSUS DATA

The number of foreigners resident in Chile during the census years starting with 1854 and up to 1930 (and also for 1949) according to their nationality is presented in Table 7.5. The most important groups of foreigners resident in Chile between 1854 and 1949 include the Spaniards, Germans, Bolivians, Peruvians and Italians. The number of foreigners resident in Chile according to sex and origin by continent and country during the census of 1960 is presented in Table 7.6. Finally, the number of foreigners resident in Chile according to age groups and continent and country of birth during the census of 1970 is presented in Table 7.7.

TABLE 7.4

International Migration (Immigrants Less Emigrants) by Sex and Quinquennial Age-Groups, 1950-1980.[1] According to Migration Hypothesis Recommended by CELADE and ODEPLAN in 1975.

Age	1950-1955		1955-1960		1960-1965		1965-1970		1970-1975		1975-1980	
	Male	Female	Male	Female	Male	Female	Male	Female	Male	Female	Male	Female
Total	-24,000	-16,000	-24,000	-16,000	-20,000	-13,000	-20,000	-13,000	-20,000	-13,000	-10,000	-6,500
0- 4	-1,100	-1,050	-1,100	-1,050	-1,050	-700	-1,050	-700	-1,050	-700	-520	-350
5- 9	-1,200	-1,150	-1,200	-1,150	-1,500	-1,000	-1,500	-1,000	-1,500	-1,000	-750	-500
10-14	-1,300	-1,300	-1,300	-1,300	-1,700	-1,100	-1,700	-1,100	-1,700	-1,100	-850	-550
15-19	-2,200	-1,550	-2,200	-1,550	-2,300	-1,500	-2,300	-1,500	-2,300	-1,500	-1,150	-750
20-24	-3,100	-1,850	-3,100	-1,850	-4,400	-2,900	-4,400	-2,900	-4,400	-2,900	-2,200	-1,450
25-29	-3,200	-1,800	-3,200	-1,800	-2,700	-1,800	-2,700	-1,800	-2,700	-1,800	-1,350	-900
30-34	-2,800	-1,550	-2,800	-1,550	-1,850	-1,250	-1,850	-1,250	-1,850	-1,250	-930	-620
35-39	-2,050	-1,250	-2,050	-1,250	-1,450	-800	-1,450	-800	-1,450	-800	-720	-400
40-44	-1,750	-1,100	-1,750	-1,100	-950	-650	-950	-650	-950	-650	-500	-320
45-49	-1,500	-900	-1,500	-900	-800	-550	-800	-550	-800	-550	-400	-280
50-54	-1,250	-750	-1,250	-750	-500	-300	-500	-300	-500	-300	-250	-150
55-59	-950	-550	-950	-550	-350	-150	-350	-150	-350	-150	-170	-80
60-64	-700	-450	-700	-450	-145	-100	-145	-100	-145	-100	-70	-50
65-69	-450	-300	-450	-300	-120	-80	-120	-80	-120	-180	-60	-40
70-74	-250	-200	-250	-200	-85	-60	-85	-60	-85	-60	-40	-30
75-79	-130	-130	-130	-130	-60	-30	-60	-30	-60	-30	-30	-20
80 and more	-70	-120	-70	-120	-40	-30	-40	-30	-40	-30	-10	-10

Note: 1. It is hypothesized that no migration will take place between 1980 and 2000.

Source: República de Chile, ODEPLAN, Proyección de la Población de Chile por Sexo y Grupos Quinquenales de Edad, 1950-2000 (Santiago, Chile: ODEPLAN, May, 1975), table 2, pp. 17-18.

TABLE 7.5

Foreigners Resident in Chile.[a]

Nationalities	Annual Census								
	1854	1865	1875	1885	1895	1907	1920	1930	1949a
Germans	1,929	3,619	4,033	6,808	7,560	10,724	8,950	10,861	20,052
Arabs	-	-	-	-	-	-	1,849	1,634	-
Argentines	10,551	8,100	7,000	9,835	7,507	6,956	7,362	7,048	8,405
Austro-Hungarians	25	36	375	674	1,550	3,813	1,573	651	788
Belgians	33	56	86	90	278	391	387	334	452
Bolivians	133	192	278	13,146	8,669	21,968	15,552	10,366	5,606
Brasilians	32	45	45	85	94	189	290	724	568
Canadians	-	-	-	-	-	-	-	-	194
Cubans	-	-	-	-	-	-	-	-	358
Colombians	41	51	50	134	143	213	217	252	988
Costa-Ricans	-	-	-	-	-	-	-	-	155
Czechs	-	-	-	-	-	-	-	325	1,150
Chinese	72	83	122	1,164	999	1,920	1,954	1,605	1,799
Danes	50	128	131	193	241	372	337	272	316
Ecuadorians	113	126	92	334	421	597	711	947	1,096
Slavs	-	-	-	-	-	-	1,354	-	-
Spaniards	915	1,150	1,072	2,508	8,494	18,755	25,962	23,439	26,757
North-Americans	683	803	907	924	745	1,055	1,908	2,078	4,440
French	1,650	2,330	3,192	4,198	8,266	9,800	7,215	5,007	4,074
Greeks	3	9	47	109	137	319	522	674	736
Dutch	24	37	76	66	98	524	492	485	908
Hungarians	-	-	-	-	-	-	-	170	1,560
British	1,940	2,972	4,109	5,310	6,838	9,845	7,220	5,292	4,639
Italians	406	980	1,926	4,114	7,797	13,023	12,358	11,070	14,098
Japanese	-	-	2	51	20	209	557	670	526
Libanese	-	-	-	-	-	-	-	-	908
Mexicans	58	71	95	110	123	173	183	209	352
Norwegians	1	22	85	217	221	662	319	220	199
Palestinians	-	-	-	-	-	-	1,164	3,156	3,855
Panamanians	-	-	-	-	-	-	-	-	263
Paraguayans	-	-	-	-	-	-	-	-	149
Peruvians	599	571	802	34,901	15,999	27,140	12,991	6,223	4,060
Poles	-	-	-	-	-	-	181	601	2,055
Portuguese	168	300	308	331	237	296	403	303	219
Rumanians	-	-	-	-	-	-	144	651	1,644
Russians	20	27	50	109	234	660	1,320	1,343	1,823
Serbs	-	-	-	-	-	-	1,432	-	-
Syrians	-	-	-	-	-	-	1,204	1,345	1,590
Swedes	22	65	85	217	211	376	242	181	285

TABLE 7.5 (Cont'd)

Foreigners Resident in Chile.[a]

Nationalities	Annual Census								
	1854	1865	1875	1885	1895	1907	1920	1930	1949
Swiss	31	79	124	1,275	1,653	2,080	1,677	1,374	1,423
Turks	2	3	3	29	76	1,729	1,282	526	451
Uruguayans	21	9	45	94	186	335	407	411	691
Yugoslavs	-	-	-	-	-	-	-	4,064	4,666
Venezuelans	-	-	-	-	-	-	-	-	564
Other Nationalities	137	118	59	51	259	401	717	952	1,186
Total	19,669	21,982	25,199	87,077	79,056	134,524	120,436	105,463	124,049

[a]No group of less than 100 is specified.

Source: Dirección General de Estadística y Dirección General de Identificación y Pasaportes; and, United Nations, Economic and Social Council, Immigration in Chile. (E/CN.12/169/Add. 2, 1 May 1950). Table 62-C.

TABLE 7.6

Foreign Population (Aliens) Resident in Chile According to Sex and According to Their Origin by Continents and Countries. 1960 Census.

Continents and Countries	Foreign Population		
	Total	Males	Females
Total	104,685	58,749	45,936
North America	3,426	1,873	1,553
Greenland	8	2	6
San Pedro and Miguelón	23	15	8
Canada	208	132	76
United States of America	2,975	1,627	1,348
Mexico	212	97	115
Central America and West Indies	899	501	398
Guatemala	67	37	30
Belize	15	10	5
El Salvador	81	45	36
Honduras	61	35	26
Nicaragua	49	33	16
Costa Rica	90	56	34
Panama	159	86	73
Panama Canal Zone	19	6	13
Cuba	224	128	96
Dominican Republic	40	14	26
Haiti	47	26	21
Barbados (West Indies)	1	-	1
Jamaica and its dependencies (West Indies)	3	2	1
Trinidad and Tobago (West Indies)	3	3	-
Guadalupe and dependencies	4	2	2
Martinique	2	2	-
Netherland Antilles	4	3	1
Puerto Rico	30	13	17
South America	27,353	14,211	13,142
Colombia	645	310	335
Ecuador	946	549	397
Venezuela	411	212	199
Brasil	616	310	306
Uruguay	531	262	269
Argentina	11,876	5,737	6,139
Bolivia	8,517	4,951	3,566
Paraguay	206	105	101
Peru	3,583	1,764	1,819
Guayana (British)	12	5	7
Malvinas Islands and its dependencies	7	4	2
Surinam	3	1	2
Europe	63,735	36,578	27,157
Albania	37	21	16
Germany, Federal Republic of	11,809	6,434	5,375
German Democratic Republic	90	52	38
Andorra	2	1	1
Austria	1,424	750	674
Belgium-Luxemburg	469	251	218
Bulgaria	76	59	17
Chechoslovakia	857	471	386
Vatican City	8	4	4
Denmark	146	92	54
Spain	21,777	12,585	9,192
Faeroe Islands	4	2	2
Finland	38	23	15
France	2,845	1,387	1,458
Gibraltar	9	4	5
Greece	524	395	129
Hungary	1,524	838	686
Ireland	81	42	39
Iceland	10	5	5
Italy	11,459	7,085	4,374
Malta	10	6	4
Netherlands, The	510	321	189
Channel Islands	6	4	2
Norway	110	58	52
Poland	1,522	837	685
Portugal	186	103	83
United Kingdom	1,924	1,052	872
Romania	1,352	719	633
Sweden	157	92	65
Switzerland	943	496	447
Yugoslavia	3,826	2,389	1,437

TABLE 7.6 (Cont'd)

Foreign Population (Aliens) Resident in Chile According to Sex and According to Their Origin by Continents and Countries. 1960 Census.

Continents and Countries	Foreign Population Total	Males	Females
Asia	6,507	4,186	2,321
Aden (Colony and protectorate)	6	4	2
Afghanistan	1	1	-
Burma	2	1	1
Borneo	1	-	1
Brunei	2	2	-
Bhutan	1	-	1
Ceylon	3	2	1
China, People's Republic of	611	519	92
China, Republic of (Taiwan-Formoso)	356	285	71
Cyprus	12	9	3
Countries subjected to a state of truce)	1	-	1
Philippines	15	8	7
Hong-Kong	5	2	3
India	63	50	13
Portuguese India	10	9	1
Indonesia	24	10	14
Iraq	7	4	3
Iran	12	9	3
Israel	399	235	164
Jammu	9	6	3
Japan	430	340	90
Jordan	247	151	96
Lao People's Democratic Republic	7	-	7
Lebanon	731	478	253
Macao	1	1	-
New Guinea	5	3	2
Pakistan	17	17	-
Quatar	1	1	-
Saudia Arabia	57	43	14
Singapore	2	2	-
Syrian Arab Republic	2,996	1,732	1,264
Thailand	1	1	-

Continents and Countries	Foreign Population Total	Males	Females
Turkey	383	197	18
Yemen Arab Republic	89	64	25
Union of Soviet Socialist Republic, Africa	2,003	1,050	953
USSR	1,752	943	839
French Equatorial Africa	10	2	8
French West Africa	13	3	10
Guinea	2	2	0
Alhucemas Islands	2	-	2
Algeria	17	6	11
Cape Verde Islands	7	7	0
Cameroon	6	4	2
Comoras Islands	4	1	3
Belgian Congo-Rwanda-Urundi	4	4	0
Egypt-Arab Republic of	120	70	50
Ethiopia	7	5	2
Ghana	1	1	0
Kenya	1	1	0
Lybian Arab Republic	7	5	2
Morocco	14	6	8
Nigeria	2	1	1
Sudan	2	1	1
Tanganyika	2	2	0
Tunisia	14	7	7
South Africa	16	9	7
Oceania	66	26	40
Australia	43	16	27
Cook Islands	1	-	1
Gilbert and Ellice Islands	1	-	1
Hawaiian Islands	2	2	-
Nauru Volcano	1	1	-
New Guinea-Australian Administration	1	-	1
New Zealand	9	3	6
French Oceania	1	-	1
North American Oceania	7	4	3
Other Countries	696	324	372

Source: National Institute of Statistics

TABLE 7.7

Population Born Abroad According to Age Groups and Continent and Country of Birth. Census of 1970.

Continents and Countries Where Foreigners Were Born	Population Born Abroad						
		Age Groups					
	Total	Less Than 15	15 to 24 Years	25 to 34 Years	35 to 54 Years	55 to 74 Years	75 and More
Country Total							
Total Both Sexes	90,441	10,254	8,573	10,904	25,920	27,385	7,405
1--North America	4,536	1,421	645	771	1,205	416	78
Canada	358	48	28	70	157	51	4
U.S.A.	3,828	1,277	575	626	970	321	59
Greenland	11	3	1	3	3	0	1
Mexico	335	92	41	72	74	43	13
San Pedro and Miquelón	4	1	0	0	1	1	1
2--Central America	1,180	243	218	221	332	140	26
Costa Rica	108	33	14	24	30	5	2
Cuba	250	56	14	36	87	45	12
El Salvador	113	23	26	22	29	13	0
Guatemala	67	14	12	11	19	10	1
Haiti	52	6	7	10	19	10	0
Honduras	123	20	24	29	43	7	0
British Honduras (Belice)	16	2	6	1	3	3	1
Nicaragua	60	14	12	13	16	4	1
Panama	223	35	80	35	46	23	4
Puerto Rico	64	18	7	10	15	10	4
Dominican Republic	81	17	16	24	18	6	0
Canal Zone	11	1	0	2	3	4	1
Other Countries of Central America	12	4	0	4	4	0	0
3--South America	29,641	6,321	4,899	4,303	8,234	4,826	1,058
Argentina	13,674	3,890	1,783	1,401	3,758	2,423	419
Bolivia	7,666	1,011	1,993	1,590	1,862	920	290
Brasil	955	218	147	210	207	152	21
Colombia	825	177	116	169	264	88	11
Ecuador	1,018	123	147	204	300	203	41
Guyana	11	1	3	1	5	0	1
Paraguay	304	45	61	67	83	42	6
Peru	3,930	507	469	448	1,425	856	225
Uruguay	805	157	103	151	247	110	37
Venezuela	405	182	71	57	73	19	3
Other Countries of South America	48	10	6	5	10	13	4

TABLE 7.7 (Cont'd)

Population Born Abroad According to Age Groups and Continent and Country of Birth. Census of 1970.

Continents and Countries Where Foreigners Were Born	Population Born Abroad						
		Age Groups					
	Total	Less Than 15	15 to 24 Years	25 to 34 Years	35 to 54 Years	55 to 74 Years	75 and More
4--Europe	48,232	1,765	2,318	5,006	14,559	19,206	5,378
Albania	79	7	11	11	26	19	5
West Germany	7,905	459	305	909	2,072	3,180	980
East Germany	855	52	26	102	198	383	94
Austria	1,020	23	110	85	262	439	101
Belgium	546	44	35	84	196	149	38
Bulgaria	89	9	6	7	37	25	5
Czechoslovakia	685	27	25	74	243	286	30
Denmark	140	13	4	37	42	35	9
Scotland	288	12	11	21	90	106	48
Spain	16,628	321	744	1,628	5,157	6,896	1,882
Finland	161	34	17	24	51	27	8
France	2,469	238	173	374	697	621	366
Greece	337	8	10	22	118	145	34
Holland	540	45	20	100	208	126	41
Hungary	980	7	57	76	372	405	63
England	1,251	147	78	151	357	351	167
Ireland	97	2	7	20	34	25	9
Iceland	13	1	3	1	2	6	0
Italy	8,225	135	447	837	2,632	3,300	874
Malta	20	0	6	3	5	5	1
Norway	274	59	31	40	72	48	24
Poland	1,031	7	18	45	353	534	74
Portugal	118	4	8	11	20	67	8
Romania	925	11	30	54	336	440	54
Sweden	157	32	13	34	46	19	13
Switzerland	670	47	35	75	178	249	86
Yugoslavia	2,668	20	85	174	744	1,291	354
Other Countries of Europe	61	1	3	7	11	29	10
5--Asia	5,036	343	353	418	1,175	2,087	660
Saudi Arabia	507	76	33	34	107	176	81
Mainland China	496	29	31	48	115	213	60
China-Taiwan (Formosa)	173	4	18	25	52	57	17
Cyprus	25	0	6	3	9	6	1
India	69	7	17	9	27	6	3
Indonesia	23	7	0	2	13	0	1
Iran	10	3	1	0	2	4	0

TABLE 7.7 (Cont'd)

Population Born Abroad According to Age Groups and Continent and Country of Birth. Census of 1970.

Continents and Countries Where Foreigners Were Born	Population Born Abroad						
		Age Groups					
	Total	Less Than 15	15 to 24 Years	25 to 34 Years	35 to 54 Years	55 to 74 Years	75 and More
Israel	378	54	55	34	69	121	45
Japan	302	33	14	58	75	91	31
Jordan	689	27	84	68	154	282	74
Lebanon	461	33	26	38	109	189	66
Pakistan	18	5	3	2	4	4	0
Soviet Union	1,091	29	10	39	232	590	191
Turkey	302	11	27	20	86	128	30
Other Countries of Asia	492	25	28	38	121	220	60
5--Africa	1,599	83	117	147	366	686	200
Algeria	73	12	8	12	23	11	7
Ethiopia	6	0	0	4	1	0	1
Morocco	49	8	9	8	14	8	2
Egypt	1,347	28	93	101	308	636	181
Tunisia	11	1	0	4	2	2	2
Other Countries of Africa	113	34	7	18	18	29	7
7--The Pacific	217	78	23	38	49	24	5
Australia	210	76	23	35	48	23	5
Other Countries of the Pacific	7	2	0	3	1	1	0

Source: INE: 1970, pp. 22-24.

8
PROJECTIONS OF THE POPULATION OF CHILE BY AGE, SEX AND REGIONS

INTRODUCTION

Demographic variables have been undergoing significant changes in Chile during the last three decades and are expected to undergo further transformation in the decades to come. These demographic changes are expected to influence almost all economic aspects of Chilean life. Furthermore, as Chile moves from its present status of intermediate economic development to the level of an advanced, modern, ever-changing economy, the evolution of its demographic characteristics is likely to be affected by economic factors. Demographic projections, even though of a tentative if not speculative nature, are therefore a necessary ingredient of medium and long-term economic planning.

The projections presented in the present chapter are the best available as of early 1979. Most of the tables with projections include some historical data, normally for the base period. The methodological notes also have a historical dimension since they include a methodological discussion of estimations of base year data. The statistics and methology of the present chapter complement the information and analysis of such variables as mortality, fertility, domestic and international migration, and regional distribution of the population found in other chapters of this monograph.

The Chilean Development Corporation (CORFO), the Latin American Demographic Center (CELADE), the Chilean Planning Office (ODEPLAN) and the National Institute of Statistics (INE) (as well as numerous other agencies and individuals) have prepared and published projections of a variety of demographic and economic data. Such projections became an integral part of Chile's numerous development plans.

In the mimeographed version of the present volume the following projections can be found: (1) projection of the population of Chile by sex and age groups: 1960-2000; (2) projection of the population of Chile for individual age years for ages from five to twenty four years: 1960-1980; (3) projection of the population of Chile by sex: 1960-1980; and (4) projection of the Chilean population by regions (according to CORFO classification) and quinquennial age groups: 1960, 1965, 1970, 1975 and 1980. These early projections, which are found also in (CORFO: 1965b), are not included in the present volume because they are incomplete and out of date. They predicted population levels significantly above the levels realized in 1975 or 1977 or being currently projected for the 1980-2000 period. Other earlier projections (e.g. Morales: 1969) also overestimated population increases. The lower than expected levels of population and population growth can be explained in terms of more rapidly than expected falling birth rates, larger than expected international emigration, higher than anticipated mortality rates and/or not completely accurate population estimates for 1940, 1950 and 1960.

The importance of each one of these factors is examined either later in this chapter or elsewhere in this volume.

AGGREGATE POPULATION PROJECTIONS

The population projections, by age groups and sex, presented in tables 8.1, 8.2, 8.3 and 8.4 of the present chapter are for the period between 1950 and 2000 and were prepared by ODEPLAN with the assistance of CELADE. They are based on statistics derived from the 1970 population census, statistics on births and deaths and information about international migration. These projections, as well as most of the methodological discussion presented here, were obtained from ODEPLAN, Proyección de Población de Chile por Sexo y Grupos Quiquenales de Edad. 1950-2000 (Santiago, Chile: ODEPLAN, 1975).

The new projections are the result of a careful examination of the evolution of the population during 1950-1970 and the formulation of hypotheses about future trends of the variables determining population changes, namely hypotheses about fertility, mortality and international migration. As any estimate, these projections are not sure predictions but expected values with margins of error; they will be a good approximation of reality to the extent that the underlying hypotheses are satisfied.

The projections presented in (ODEPLAN: 1975a) and published here are a revision of earlier ones prepared by ODEPLAN with the advice of CELADE. They became necessary due to the appearance of new information, after the earlier ones had been prepared, about international migration between 1950 and 1970 and because new evidence suggested that the projection of mortality for the 1995-2000 quinquennium was not very realistic.

Projections of Total Population

The population projections found in Table 8.1 cover the 1950-2000 period, that is, present a description of the evolution of the population of Chile between 1950 and 1970 and since that year they are projections properly speaking supported by alternative hypotheses about the variables determining change.

TABLE 8.1

Total Population of Chile 1950-2000

Year	Total Population	Year	Total Population
1950	6,090,833	1975	10,253,015
1951	6,251,933	1976	10,443,240
1952	6,377,619	1977	10,639,033
1953	6,492,774	1978	10,840,489
1954	6,612,138	1979	11,047,519
1955	6,743,269	1980	11,259,871
1956	6,888,843	1981	11,477,150
1957	7,048,426	1982	11,698,844
1958	7,219,783	1983	11,924,349
1959	7,399,842	1984	12,152,999
1960	7,585,349	1985	12,384,093
1961	7,773,314	1986	12,616,930
1962	7,961,258	1987	12,850,839
1963	8,147,349	1988	13,085,215
1964	8,330,423	1989	13,319,549
1965	8,509,950	1990	13,553,459
1966	8,685,954	1991	13,786,715
1967	8,858,908	1992	14,019,246
1968	9,029,621	1993	14,251,136
1969	9,199,122	1994	14,482,584
1970	9,368,559	1995	14,713,816
1971	9,539,108	1996	14,944,948
1972	9,711,891	1997	15,175,744
1973	9,887,925	1998	15,405,283
1974	10,068,073	1999	15,631,459
		2000	15,850,308

Source: ODEPLAN, 1975a, p. 25.

Projection of Aggregate Mortality Rates

In population projections it is common to formulate only one assumption about the future evolution of mortality (ODEPLAN: 1975a,2). In the Chilean case, as presented in table 8.3, it is assumed that mortality will continue on a declining trend and that a life expectancy at birth of slightly more than 70 years for both sexes will be reached during the last quinquennium (1995-2000) of the projection. This level corresponds to those found around 1970 in countries such as the Federal Republic of Germany, Italy and Belgium.

Projections of Aggregate Fertility Rates

Unlike the case of mortality, various hypotheses are made about the future development of fertility with the result that significantly different population projections are obtained. The diverse alternatives of future fertility define the interval within which the real values will, most likely, be located. The projections presented here were chosen from those made on the basis of five alternative fertility hypotheses. The first, which served purely theoretical purposes, assumes that the fertility will remain constant throughout the period of the projection at the level established for the 1970-1975 quinquennium and that it corresponds to 3.7 children per woman during her childbearing age.

The second alternative assumed an evolution such that fertility would slowly decline to a final level of 3 children per woman in the 1995-2000 five-year period. The third alternative, which gave rise to the time series found in table 8.2 and is being referred to in the tables as the one recommended by ODEPLAN-CELADE, presents perhaps, the behavior of fertility which would most likely materialize in view of past trends. Fertility would continue a downward trend reaching a level of 2.7 children per woman in the 1995-2000 quinquennium. This is similar to the level observed in countries of Southern Europe in 1975.

The fourth alternative implies a much sharper decline than the third, with fertility estimated to be of 2.4 children per woman towards the end of the projection. Finally, the fifth alternative, which like the first, was formulated for purely theoretical purposes assumes that towards 1995-2000 each woman would have had at the end of her childbearing age an average of 2.04 children. This level combined with the mortality assumed to prevail during that period could possibly lead to zero population growth or a stationary population for Chile.

International Migration

Examining international migration, the 1950-1970 ODEPLAN-CELADE projections (which are presented along with the projections in the chapter on international migration) were largely based on the population census of the Argentine Republic and displayed a mildly declining trend. It was estimated that there were 80 thousand Chilean emigrants to Argentina during the 1950-1960 decade and that during the 1960-1970 decade 66 thousand Chileans had emigrated. Furthermore, the ODEPLAN-CELADE researchers established that the emigration during the 1970-1975 quinquennium would be similar to that estimated for the preceding five-year period. This emigration would be reduced by half during the 1975-1980 five-year period, and finally reach zero from 1980 onwards. There exists no solid basis, according to ODEPLAN-CELADE, to justify this hypothesis, but it is considered reasonable and does not exert a strong influence over the results of these projections. As explained in the chapter on international migration, the estimates of past, present and future inter-country migratory movements are at best incomplete. Emigration out of Chile to countries other than Argentina ever since 1950 but especially during 1970-75 seems to have been significant. A projection of international migration for the 1980-2000 period that is based exclusively on Argentine census data is bound to be incomplete and partial. The international migration estimates and projections can be considered as vulnerable and subject to significant changes if and when a more solid statistical base is developed in order to revise and update present information and projections.

The ODEPLAN-CELADE researchers admit the importance of international migration but only for historical trends. It is their belief that: "it is not possible to state, however, the same (that international migration does not matter) when it is attempted to describe the evolution of the Chilean population between 1950 and 1970. By not considering emigration, as was the case with all previous studies, population estimates were obtained which exceeded the figures given in the more recent censuses. This difference (projection less census) was invariably attributed to defects in the enumeration

TABLE 8.2

Age-Specific Fertility Rates, 1950-2000.
Fertility Hypothesis Recommended by CELADE and ODEPLAN in 1975.

Period/Age	15-19	20-24	25-29	30-34	35-39	40-44	45-49
1950-1955	0.0780	0.2266	0.2319	0.1905	0.1435	0.0700	0.0189
1955-1960	0.0853	0.2257	0.2770	0.2165	0.1465	0.0708	0.0171
1960-1965	0.0817	0.2219	0.2475	0.2277	0.1415	0.0623	0.0126
1965-1970	0.0789	0.2079	0.2018	0.1464	0.1129	0.0528	0.0084
1970-1975	0.0712	0.1878	0.1822	0.1322	0.1019	0.0477	0.0076
1975-1980	0.0662	0.1831	0.1769	0.1257	0.0928	0.0427	0.0067
1980-1985	0.0611	0.1785	0.1716	0.1192	0.0836	0.0377	0.0058
1985-1990	0.0561	0.1738	0.1664	0.1128	0.0745	0.0328	0.0048
1990-1995	0.0510	0.1692	0.1611	0.1063	0.0653	0.0278	0.0039
1995-2000	0.0460	0.1645	0.1558	0.0998	0.0562	0.0228	0.0030

Source: República de Chile, ODEPLAN, Proyección de la Población de Chile por Sexo y Grupos Quinquenales de Edad, 1950-2000 (Santiago, Chile: ODEPLAN, May, 1975), table 3, p. 19.

TABLE 8.3

Expectation of Life at Birth According to Mortality
Hypothesis Recommended by CELADE and ODEPLAN in 1975.
In Years 1950-2000.

Period/Sex	Expectation of Life at Birth		
	Males	Females	Total Persons
1950-1955	52.26	56.04	54.12
1955-1960	53.74	58.56	56.11
1960-1965	55.02	60.40	57.66
1965-1970	57.64	63.61	60.57
1970-1975	59.53	65.70	62.56
1975-1980	61.30	67.60	64.40
1980-1985	62.97	69.31	66.09
1985-1990	64.53	70.85	67.64
1990-1995	65.99	72.25	69.07
1995-2000	67.36	73.52	70.39

Source: República de Chile, ODEPLAN, Proyección de la Población de Chile por Sexo y Grupos Quinquenales de Edad, 1950-2000 (Santiago, Chile: ODEPLAN, May, 1975), table 4, p. 20.

TABLE 8.4

Projection of the Population of Chile by Sex and Five-Year Age Groups. 1950-2000. Hypothesis Recommended by ODEPLAN-CELADE.

Males

Age/ Year	1950	1955	1960	1965	1970	1975
Total	3,024,918	3,346,147	3,758,757	4,211,162	4,628,783	5,059,762
0- 4	453,126	489,075	588,553	637,298	607,899	629,572
5	83,716	91,507	100,388	122,197	125,755	118,182
6	81,060	89,550	96,940	118,642	125,615	118,108
7	78,340	87,613	94,218	114,631	124,888	118,685
8	75,599	85,674	92,084	110,321	123,606	119,701
9	72,882	83,712	90,404	105,870	121,805	120,944
5- 9	391,598	438,056	474,034	571,662	621,669	595,621
10	70,195	81,786	89,171	101,157	119,653	122,458
11	67,543	79,955	88,381	96,063	117,320	124,286
12	65,159	77,793	87,243	92,134	114,162	124,942
13	63,161	75,118	85,358	90,085	109,942	123,705
14	61,482	72,149	82,984	89,240	105,101	121,128
10-14	327,540	386,801	433,137	468,679	566,178	616,519
15	59,821	69,302	80,839	88,214	100,209	118,665
16	58,109	66,505	78,853	87,292	95,022	116,241
17	56,966	63,986	76,552	85,997	90,962	112,963
18	56,627	61,906	73,793	83,952	88,755	108,603
19	56,753	60,172	70,177	81,420	87,737	103,612
15-19	288,277	321,871	380,814	426,874	462,686	560,084
20	56,875	58,428	67,850	79,090	86,519	98,557
21	57,214	56,616	64,953	76,890	85,378	93,185
22	56,696	55,381	62,354	74,482	83,946	89,011
23	54,782	54,966	60,228	71,719	81,901	86,802
24	52,009	55,029	58,472	68,809	79,457	85,855
20-24	277,576	280,420	313,856	370,969	417,202	453,409
25-29	227,147	268,328	271,562	305,215	362,181	408,586
30-34	203,599	218,323	258,932	263,433	297,224	353,891
35-39	183,830	194,824	209,577	249,991	255,316	288,971
40-44	164,008	174,302	185,408	200,818	240,842	246,635
45-49	129,456	153,455	163,833	175,534	191,299	230,222
50-54	114,918	118,776	141,748	152,661	164,793	180,176
55-59	89,228	102,698	106,881	128,831	140,044	151,726
60-64	69,886	76,485	88,892	93,516	114,030	124,518
65-69	42,483	56,334	62,369	73,248	78,112	95,847
70-74	33,820	31,344	42,193	47,123	56,180	60,393
75-79	17,689	22,126	20,800	28,205	31,947	38,479
80 +	10,737	12,929	16,168	17,105	21,181	25,113

TABLE 8.4 (Cont'd)

Projection of the Population of Chile by Sex and Five-Year Age Groups. 1950-2000. Hypothesis Recommended by ODEPLAN-CELADE.

Males

Age/ Year	1980	1985	1990	1995	2000
Total	5,554,416	6,109,765	6,687,885	7,261,638	7,823,223
0- 4	694,454	757,589	794,351	804,427	808,337
5	128,401	143,406	154,541	159,609	160,349
6	125,784	140,322	152,475	158,785	160,103
7	123,544	137,199	150,201	157,780	159,865
8	121,683	134,096	147,752	156,588	159,596
9	120,199	131,076	145,157	155,203	159,260
5- 9	619,611	686,099	750,127	787,965	799,174
10	118,892	128,146	142,486	153,663	158,855
11	117,558	125,314	139,805	152,005	158,383
12	117,212	122,907	136,957	150,011	157,617
13	118,257	121,089	133,894	147,591	156,444
14	120,088	119,764	130,762	144,867	154,939
10-14	592,008	617,220	683,904	748,139	786,239
15	121,742	118,470	127,760	142,120	153,329
16	123,471	117,060	124,860	139,377	151,614
17	124,014	116,633	122,387	136,471	149,567
18	122,664	117,613	120,529	133,375	147,112
19	119,976	119,384	119,177	130,222	144,363
15-19	611,867	589,160	614,714	681,565	745,984
20	117,385	120,961	117,837	127,183	141,578
21	114,814	122,602	116,371	124,233	138,788
22	111,444	123,068	115,832	121,714	135,840
23	107,080	121,659	116,792	119,815	132,710
24	102,142	118,927	118,491	118,425	129,528
20-24	552,866	607,217	585,372	611,370	678,443
25-29	446,514	547,055	601,740	580,853	607,335
30-34	401,258	440,375	540,463	595,404	575,521
35-39	345,881	393,843	433,104	532,513	587,622
40-44	280,437	337,092	384,737	424,026	522,433
45-49	236,845	270,524	326,076	373,164	412,336
50-54	217,874	225,128	257,985	311,977	358,170
55-59	166,720	202,593	210,173	241,820	293,604
60-64	135,631	149,849	183,022	190,856	220,740
65-69	105,398	115,628	128,617	158,177	166,098
70-74	74,786	82,993	91,856	103,102	127,967
75-79	41,830	52,395	58,794	65,819	74,745
80 +	30,436	35,005	42,850	50,461	58,475

TABLE 8.4 (Cont'd)

Projection of the Population of Chile by Sex and Five-Year Age Groups. 1950-2000. Hypothesis Recommended by ODEPLAN-CELADE.

Females

Age/ Year	1950	1955	1960	1965	1970	1975
Total	3,065,915	3,397,120	3,826,593	4,298,788	4,739,775	5,193,252
0- 4	447,144	479,622	579,244	627,320	597,423	620,586
5	82,579	90,319	98,542	120,727	124,044	116,530
6	79,923	88,466	95,193	117,232	124,019	116,512
7	77,198	86,591	92,594	113,250	123,397	117,148
8	74,449	84,682	90,602	108,948	122,214	118,226
9	71,723	82,723	89,071	104,493	120,501	119,535
5- 9	385,873	432,781	466,002	564,649	614,175	587,952
10	69,025	80,775	88,002	99,757	118,438	121,116
11	66,363	78,898	87,397	94,612	116,204	123,011
12	63,976	76,707	86,389	90,701	113,105	123,144
13	61,989	74,040	84,547	88,785	108,882	122,596
14	60,328	71,104	82,159	88,143	104,007	120,115
10-14	321,682	381,525	428,495	461,999	560,636	610,582
15	58,690	68,280	80,008	87,305	99,085	117,752
16	57,001	65,504	78,014	86,575	93,851	115,439
17	55,896	63,016	75,723	85,436	89,834	112,247
18	55,617	60,982	73,012	83,483	87,809	107,933
19	55,818	59,306	70,065	80,999	87,060	102,967
15-19	283,022	317,089	376,823	423,798	457,639	556,338
20	56,018	57,623	67,202	78,728	86,095	97,941
21	56,444	55,873	64,368	76,587	85,215	92,587
22	56,003	54,710	61,836	74,209	83,982	88,495
23	54,144	54,378	59,776	71,506	82,026	86,466
24	51,415	54,532	58,089	68,631	79,600	85,758
20-24	274,024	277,116	311,272	369,661	416,919	451,247
25-29	225,191	267,122	270,813	304,896	363,344	410,874
30-34	204,380	218,655	260,414	264,827	299,204	357,512
35-39	186,543	197,734	212,370	254,176	259,408	293,695
40-44	164,697	179,453	191,094	206,315	248,105	253,570
45-49	135,405	157,119	172,193	184,381	200,165	241,062
50-54	124,061	127,503	149,102	164,623	177,497	192,852
55-59	99,723	114,539	118,845	140,261	156,292	168,651
60-64	77,988	89,045	103,695	108,799	130,042	145,101
65-69	51,789	66,219	77,039	90,937	97,073	116,304
70-74	42,534	40,744	53,445	63,223	76,366	81,826
75-79	24,371	30,133	29,764	39,853	48,497	58,889
80 +	17,488	20,721	25,983	29,070	36,990	46,211

TABLE 8.4 (Cont'd)

Projection of the Population of Chile by Sex and Five-Year Age Groups. 1950-2000. Hypothesis Recommended by ODEPLAN-CELADE.

Females

Age/ Year	1980	1985	1990	1995	2000
Total	5,705,455	6,274,330	6,865,575	7,452,179	8,027,089
0- 4	685,556	748,271	784,583	794,091	797,212
5	127,115	142,031	153,094	158,051	158,623
6	124,549	139,047	151,133	157,337	158,490
7	122,328	136,001	148,946	156,422	158,347
8	120,461	132,956	146,564	155,303	158,159
9	118,957	129,976	144,022	153,979	157,892
5- 9	613,409	680,010	743,759	781,092	791,510
10	117,612	127,075	141,388	152,486	157,546
11	116,222	124,267	138,730	150,862	157,121
12	115,859	121,863	135,908	148,906	156,405
13	116,957	120,024	132,885	146,538	155,292
14	118,888	118,665	129,799	143,873	153,854
10-14	585,538	611,894	678,711	742,666	780,217
15	120,633	117,340	126,840	141,178	152,306
16	122,451	115,894	123,986	138,481	150,649
17	123,101	115,476	121,540	135,625	148,663
18	121,877	116,532	119,676	132,583	146,276
19	119,327	118,428	118,303	129,486	143,598
15-19	607,389	583,670	610,346	677,353	741,492
20	116,883	120,126	116,952	126,506	140,883
21	114,474	121,889	115,474	123,626	138,162
22	111,223	122,489	115,018	121,153	135,282
23	106,905	121,227	116,031	119,265	132,220
24	101,972	118,646	117,879	117,867	129,105
20-24	551,456	604,377	581,353	608,417	675,653
25-29	446,552	547,640	600,956	578,673	606,142
30-34	405,813	442,444	543,379	597,032	575,514
35-39	352,096	400,797	437,670	538,304	592,244
40-44	287,956	346,188	394,753	431,796	531,936
45-49	247,004	281,296	338,814	387,095	424,240
50-54	232,764	239,063	272,798	329,297	377,081
55-59	183,580	222,094	228,623	261,550	316,580
60-64	156,931	171,288	207,807	214,585	246,315
65-69	130,187	141,308	154,810	188,576	195,565
70-74	98,492	110,797	120,872	133,138	163,100
75-79	63,470	76,890	87,062	95,638	106,107
80 +	57,262	66,303	79,279	92,876	106,181

TABLE 8.4 (Cont'd)

Projection of the Population of Chile by Sex and Five-Year Age Groups. 1950-2000. Hypothesis Recommended by ODEPLAN-CELADE.

Both Sexes

Age/ Year	1950	1955	1960	1965	1970	1975
Total	6,090,833	6,743,267	7,585,350	8,509,950	9,368,558	10,253,014
0- 4	900,270	968,697	1,167,797	1,264,618	1,205,322	1,250,158
5	166,296	181,825	198,929	242,924	249,799	234,712
6	160,983	178,016	192,133	235,874	249,634	234,621
7	155,538	174,205	186,812	227,881	248,285	235,834
8	150,049	170,356	182,686	219,269	245,820	237,928
9	144,606	166,435	179,475	210,364	242,306	240,479
5- 9	777,471	870,837	940,036	1,136,311	1,235,844	1,183,573
10	139,220	162,561	177,174	200,915	238,091	243,574
11	133,906	158,853	175,778	190,674	233,524	247,297
12	129,135	154,501	173,632	182,835	227,266	248,685
13	125,150	149,157	169,905	178,870	218,824	246,301
14	121,810	143,253	165,143	177,383	209,108	241,243
10-14	649,222	768,326	861,632	930,678	1,126,814	1,227,101
15	118,511	137,583	160,847	175,519	199,294	236,418
16	115,110	132,009	156,868	173,868	188,873	231,680
17	112,862	127,003	152,275	171,432	180,796	225,210
18	112,244	122,888	146,805	167,435	176,565	216,536
19	112,572	119,478	140,842	162,419	174,797	206,579
15-19	571,299	638,960	757,637	850,672	920,325	1,116,422
20	112,893	116,051	135,052	157,818	172,614	196,497
21	113,658	112,490	129,321	153,477	170,594	185,772
22	112,699	110,091	124,191	148,671	167,929	177,505
23	108,926	109,344	120,005	143,225	163,928	173,268
24	103,424	109,561	116,560	137,439	159,057	171,614
20-24	551,600	557,536	625,128	740,630	834,121	904,656
25-29	452,338	535,450	542,375	610,111	725,525	819,460
30-34	407,979	436,978	519,346	528,260	596,428	711,403
35-39	370,373	392,558	421,947	504,167	514,724	582,666
40-44	328,705	353,755	376,502	407,133	488,947	500,205
45-49	264,861	310,574	336,026	359,915	391,464	471,284
50-54	238,979	246,279	290,850	317,284	342,290	373,028
55-59	188,951	217,237	225,726	269,092	296,336	320,377
60-64	147,874	165,530	192,587	202,315	244,072	269,619
65-69	94,272	122,553	139,408	164,185	175,185	212,151
70-74	76,354	72,088	95,638	110,346	132,546	142,219
75-79	42,060	52,259	50,564	68,058	80,444	97,368
80 +	28,225	33,650	42,151	46,175	58,171	71,324

Source: República de Chile, Junta de Gobierno, Oficina de Planificación Nacional, Proyección de la Población de Chile per Sexo y Grupos Quinquenales de Edad. 1950-2000 (Santiago, Chile: ODEPLAN, May 1975), pp. 22-24.

TABLE 8.4 (Cont'd)

Projection of the Population of Chile by Sex and Five-Year Age Groups. 1950-2000. Hypothesis Recommended by ODEPLAN-CELADE.

Both Sexes

Age/ Year	1980	1985	1990	1995	2000
Total	11,259,871	12,384,095	13,553,460	14,713,817	15,850,312
0- 4	1,380,010	1,505,860	1,578,934	1,598,518	1,605,549
5	255,516	285,436	307,635	317,660	318,972
6	250,333	279,369	303,608	316,122	318,593
7	245,872	273,200	299,147	314,202	318,212
8	242,143	267,052	294,316	311,891	317,755
9	239,156	261,051	289,179	309,182	317,152
5- 9	1,233,020	1,366,109	1,493,886	1,569,057	1,590,684
10	236,504	255,220	283,874	306,149	316,401
11	233,780	249,582	278,536	302,867	315,504
12	233,071	244,770	272,865	298,918	314,022
13	235,215	241,112	266,779	294,129	311,736
14	238,976	238,429	260,561	288,740	308,793
10-14	1,177,546	1,229,114	1,362,615	1,490,805	1,566,456
15	242,375	235,810	254,600	283,298	305,634
16	245,922	232,955	248,846	277,858	302,262
17	247,115	232,109	243,927	272,096	298,230
18	244,541	234,145	240,206	265,957	293,388
19	239,303	237,812	237,480	259,708	287,961
15-19	1,219,256	1,172,830	1,225,060	1,358,918	1,487,476
20	234,268	241,087	234,788	253,689	282,462
21	229,288	244,491	231,845	247,859	276,950
22	222,667	245,557	230,900	242,867	271,122
23	213,985	242,886	232,823	239,080	264,930
24	204,113	237,572	236,370	236,292	258,632
20-24	1,104,322	1,211,594	1,166,725	1,219,787	1,354,096
25-29	893,066	1,094,695	1,202,696	1,159,526	1,213,477
30-34	807,071	882,819	1,083,842	1,192,436	1,151,035
35-39	697,977	794,640	870,774	1,070,817	1,179,866
40-44	568,393	683,280	779,490	855,822	1,054,369
45-49	483,849	551,820	664,890	760,259	836,576
50-54	450,638	464,191	530,783	641,274	735,251
55-59	350,300	424,687	438,796	503,370	610,184
60-64	292,562	321,137	390,829	405,441	467,055
65-69	235,585	256,936	283,427	346,753	361,663
70-74	173,278	193,790	212,728	236,240	291,067
75-79	105,300	129,285	145,856	161,457	180,852
80 +	87,698	101,308	122,129	143,337	164,656

TABLE 8.5

Demographic Indicators Estimated Between 1950-55 and 1995-2000.
(Hypothesis Recommended by ODEPLAN and CELADE in 1975)

Demographic Indicators	1950-55	1955-60	1960-65	1965-70	1970-75	1975-80	1980-85	1985-90	1990-95	1995-2000
Fertility										
Births per Year: B	225,608	268,331	286,931	267,854	273,381	297,293	320,359	332,568	333,893	333,027
Crude Birth Rate: b(0/00)	35.16	37.45	35.65	29.96	27.87	27.64	27.10	25.64	23.62	21.79
General Fertility Rate	4.80	5.19	4.98	4.05	3.65	3.47	3.29	3.11	2.92	2.74
Mortality										
Deaths per Year: D	87,121	91,915	95,411	89,532	89,890	92,621	95,515	98,695	101,822	105,729
Crude Death Rate: d(0/00)	13.58	12.83	11.86	10.02	9.16	8.61	8.08	7.61	7.20	6.92
Natural Increase										
Natural Increase per Year	138,487	176,416	191,520	178,322	183,491	204,672	224,844	233,873	232,071	227,298
Rate of Natural Increase (0/00)	21.58	24.62	23.79	19.94	18.71	19.03	19.02	18.03	16.42	14.87
Migration										
Migration per Year: M	8,000	-8,000	-6,600	-6,600	-6,600	-3,300	-	-	-	-
Migration Rates: m (0/00)	-1.25	-1.12	-0.82	-0.74	-0.67	-0.31	-	-	-	-
Total Increase										
Increase per Year: B-D±M	130,487	168,416	184,920	171,722	176,891	201,372	224,844	233,873	232,071	227,298
Rate of Total Increase: r (0/00)	20.33	23.50	22.97	19.20	18.04	18.72	19.02	18.03	16.42	14.87
Population Composition by Age										
C (0-14) (%)	38.44	38.91	39.15	38.62	36.90	34.68	33.39	32.92	32.18	30.85
C (15-64) (%)	57.50	56.85	56.40	56.72	58.16	60.09	61.19	61.52	61.98	62.98
C (65 and over) (%)	4.06	4.24	4.45	4.66	4.94	5.23	5.42	5.56	5.84	6.17
Dependency Index										
[C(10-14)+C(65 and over)]/C(15-64) %	73.91	75.91	77.28	76.32	71.96	66.45	63.44	62.58	61.37	58.80

Source: Oficina de Planificación Nacional (ODEPLAN), Proyección de la Población de Chile por Sexo y Grupos Quinquenales de Edad, 1950-2000 (Santiago, Chile: ODEPLAN, May 1975), p. 21.

of the census. However, counting now with better information about international migration it has been possible to describe, possibly with greater realism, the demographic evolution during the 1950-1970 period. As a consequence, a population estimate for 1970 was obtained which was close to the figure given by the census. In the conclusion of our earlier study the 1970 population was being exaggerated by not taking into account the small but systematic effect of emigration." (ODEPLAN: 1975a, 4).

The projections of the population of Chile by sex and five-year age groups according to the hypothesis recommended by ODEPLAN-CELADE are found in Table 8.4. Furthermore, summary statistical information on demographic indicators estimated for the period between 1950 and 2000 is presented in Table 8.5.

Findings of the Projections

Some of the findings of the projections included in tables 8.1, 8.2, 8.3, 8.4 and 8.5 are:

1. Annual births, which are implicit in the projection, show a growth in absolute numbers until the 1990-1995 quinquennium, in spite of the hypothesis of declining fertility. This is the consequence of an age distribution of the population with a growth potential that cannot be counterbalanced by the presumed decline in fertility. In contrast, the crude birth rates display a systematic decline throughout the period of the projection.

2. Annual deaths also rise in absolute terms, although at a lesser degree than that of births and in spite of the assumption of declining mortality. Again, this phenomenon reflects the influence of the age structure of the population.

3. The estimated annual increase of approximately 177 thousand persons for the 1970-1975 quinquennium would reach its maximum value of approximately 234 thousand persons during the 1985-1990 quinquennium. It is estimated on the basis of the adopted hypotheses about fertility, mortality and international migration that the annual increase would be around 227 thousand persons during the last quinquennium of the projection.

4. Finally, the age structure of the population would experience a gradual aging process, that is, the proportion of the population under 15 years of age would be relatively less important. From a level of approximately 37% during the 1970-1975 period, it would decline to close to 31% in the last quinquennium of the projection.

The CELADE-Pujol Projections

Most of the recent mortality, fertility, international migration and population projections were made by or under supervision of José M. Pujol of CELADE. Some of the CELADE projections are, therefore, identical to those published by ODEPLAN and found in the present chapter. The 1976 study by Pujol (1976a) contains much the same statistical information as that by ODEPLAN (ODEPLAN: 1975a). In the first half of the paper the evolution of the population between 1950 and 1970 is assessed, using information from the 1950, 1960 and 1970 censuses and from vital statistics of the same period. Census data from other Latin American countries were also used, in particular from Argentina, and continuous statistics from the United States (Pujol: 1976a, 12) in an effort to detect and measure international migration.

Once fertility, mortality and international migration were estimated and their evolution was established for the period between 1950 and 1970, Pujol made projections until the year 2000. One mortality variability hypothesis was established, one international migration variability hypothesis was formulated, and five fertility variability hypotheses were defined, the first and fifth being of rather theoretical character. The third hypothesis is the recommended one, the results of which were accepted by ODEPLAN and also published in this chapter. It is worth noting that while the international migration figures in Pujol (1976a, 12) and ODEPLAN (1975a) are identical, they are identified as emigration to Argentina in (ODEPLAN: 1975a) but as emigration to all other countries in (Pujol: 1976a, 12). The Pujol study (1976a, 12) contains more detailed methodological information than the ODEPLAN (1975a) study.

In addition to the possibility that the international migration hypothesis is subject to a significant margin of error, the assumptions about trends in mortality may also need revision. This will be particularly true if currently estimated infant mortality rates underestimate infant deaths (as believed by some) and currently available overall mortality figures are subsequently revised upwards (see more in the chapter on mortality).

URBAN-RURAL POPULATION PROJECTIONS

José Pujol also made projections of the urban and rural population at the national and regional level, by sex and according to quinquennial age groups for the period between 1970 and 2000 (Pujol: 1976d). The work was carried out in two stages. The country's urban and rural population was projected in the first stage and, in the second, projections were elaborated for the regions.

By means of the "method of components" urban and rural population for the country, by sex and age, was projected. In order to use this methodology urban mortality tables, by sex were constructed through the use of correlations between mortality, urbanization and literacy. Urban fertility was estimated by means of differentials based upon born children data derived from the 1960 and 1970 censuses. Migration was established using the 1952, 1960 and 1970 censuses, and urban mortality and fertility estimates were made for the period between 1950 and 1970. Thus, intercensal migration values were obtained. Urban population projections were obtained after projecting mortality, fertility and migration. The difference between this projection and the country's total population corresponds to the rural population.

Total values for regions, by sex, were estimated, in first place, to obtain regional projections. In this case, the methodology put forward by the United Nations was used. The methodology of the "square table" was used to establish age-groups (Pujol: 1976d).

POPULATION PROJECTIONS BY REGIONS, SEX AND AGE

Chile's projections, at the regional level, were elaborated by José Pujol in 1976 by means of breaking the country up into three geographical zones: the Metropolitan and those of the North and South. The purpose for this was to apply the component projection methodology. In other words, to project populations for each zone by means of hypotheses of mortality, fertility and migration variations.

In order to estimate the demographic variables corresponding to years around 1970, mortality tables by zones were built; fertility was estimated through birth data according to mother's age on a zone level. Internal migration was calculated based on data from the 1970 census which refer to the place of residence five years before the census was taken, place of residence at the moment the census was taken, and place of birth. International migration hypotheses were adopted according to those elaborated for the country's total population projection.

Hypotheses about quinquennial changes were made for each variable. At the end of each quinquennium the sum of the population by zone, according to sex and age, was made coincident with the projection elaborated for the whole country. Finally, the population projections by zones were disaggregated into regions by using the square table method (Pujol: 1976c). Exactly the same projections and methodology found in (Pujol: 1976c) are also presented in (ODEPLAN: 1975b).

Life Expectancy at Birth by Zones

In order to estimate future levels of mortality for each of the three regions, it was assumed by Pujol (1976c, 5-6) that by 1995-2000 the conditions of life of the population would have become uniform in the various zones as far as the incidence of mortality is concerned. For this reason, the hypothesis was formulated that for the 1995-2000 period the level and structure of mortality would be the same within each zone and that these would correspond to those of the country as a whole. In other words, there were adopted for the three zones for the 1995-2000 period the mortality tables corresponding to the country as a whole and which appear in an implicit form in the studies on projections of population for the total country (ODEPLAN: 1975a, and Pujol: 1976a). These projections of life expectancy at birth by zones and sex, along with the actual figures for 1970-1975, are presented in Table 8.6

TABLE 8.6

Chile: Life Expectancy at Birth by Zones and According to Sex. 1970-2000.

Zone	Sex	Period 1970-1975	1975-1980	1980 1985	1985-1990	1990-1995	1995-2000
North	Males	60.87	62.23	63.57	64.86	66.13	67.36
	Females	66.83	68.34	69.75	71.08	72.34	73.52
Metro-politan	Males	61.34	62.58	63.80	65.01	66.19	67.36
	Females	68.67	69.72	70.73	71.70	72.63	73.52
South	Males	57.66	59.90	61.98	63.91	65.70	67.36
	Females	63.43	65.91	68.13	70.12	71.91	73.52
Country Total	Males	59.53	61.30	62.97	64.53	65.99	67.36
	Females	65.70	67.60	69.31	70.85	72.25	73.52

Source: Pujol, 1976c, 4.

Estimation and Projections of Fertility by Zones

In order to calculate fertility between 1970 and 2000, fertility was first estimated for the 1970-1975 period and, then, projections were made for the 1975-2000 period.

Unpublished information about births by provinces and according to age of mother for the year 1971 were obtained from the National Institute of Statistics. Then fertility rates by age and zones for the 1970-1975 period were calculated by grouping this information in zones and relating it with the average female population during the same period. These rates were subject to two limitations. The dates in the numerator were not the same with those of the denominator and, more important, no correction had been made for underreporting of births. Since, however, the objective was to determine differences in fertility by zones, this information was satisfactory for making projections.

The fertility rates obtained were then adjusted in a manner making them consistent with the specific fertility rates of the projection of the total country during the 1970-1975 period, that is in a manner making the sum of births by zone consistent with total births for the country. This way specific fertility rates, adjusted by zone, were obtained for 1970-1975, the initial period of the projection.

Once fertility for the initial period was fixed, fertility during the final 1995-2000 period was established. In respect to fertility it was accepted that differences by zones would persist and it was therefore assumed that the gross reproduction rates would maintain approximately the same differences, in relative terms, during 1995-2000, as those existing at the beginning of the projection, declining in the same manner as those for the country as a whole. It was furthermore assumed that the changes in such gross rates in the intermediate periods would be linear. The gross reproduction rates by zones are presented in Table 8.7.

At the beginning of the projection each zone had its own structure of age-specific fertility rates. It was hypothesized by Pujol, however, that in the final 1995-2000 period all would have the same structure and that this would correspond to the projection for the country as a whole. The projections for the age-specific fertility rates by zones for the 1975-2000 period are found in (Pujol: 1976c, 40).

TABLE 8.7

Chile: Gross Reproduction Rates According to Zones. 1970-2000.

Period	Zone			Total for Chile
	North	Metropolitan	South	
1970-1975	1.74	1.58	2.08	1.80
1975-1980	1.65	1.50	1.97	1.71
1980-1985	1.56	1.42	1.86	1.62
1985-1990	1.48	1.35	1.75	1.53
1990-1995	1.39	1.27	1.64	1.44
1995-2000	1.30	1.20	1.53	1.35

Source: Pujol, 1976c, 6.

Estimation of Migration During 1965-1970 and Hypothesis About Its Evolution During 1970-2000

One of the major problems in projecting population at the regional level is to establish the domestic migration since solid continuous statistics of this phenomenon are not available and the questions needed to detect it are not included in the censuses. Even though the 1970 census of Chile had asked a question that could serve to detect migration, the findings had not been fully tabulated by 1976, when Pujol made the projections included in this chapter. The information available included only tabulations of immigrants by sex, by large age groups and by province.

It would have been desirable to dispose of, in addition, the place of origin of these immigrants in order to calculate net migratory balances by zones. In order to complete the information Pujol found it necessary to work with the crossed tabulations of the place of birth and the place of habitual residence. With these tabulations it was possible to calculate the immigrants and emigrants in each zone and thus the migratory balance. Since what was needed was a migratory balance during 1965-1970, these estimates were adjusted to the migration data of the 1965-1970 period. It was thus possible to obtain an estimate of the total migratory balance by zones for the reference period.

Subsequently the age and sex structure of the immigrants between 1965 and 1970 was utilized to obtain the zonal migratory balance by sex and quinquennial age groups.

The net migratory balance from the North was found to be practically nil during 1965-1970 and it was assumed that it would remain so in the future. The net migration from the South to the Metropolitan Zone was estimated at approximately 200,000 persons during the 1965-1970 quinquennium (Pujol: 1976, 7). Furthermore, even though the figures suggested an increase in the migratory flow to the Metropolitan Zone during 1965-1970, this was considered a transitory phenomenon. Therefore the hypothesis formulated for the 1970-1975 period was that the total number of migrants had been around 150,000 persons.

Since it was difficult to fix a total of migrants for each one of the quinquennia, Pujol chose to fix the total population of the Metropolitan Zone in the year 2000, assuming that in that year it would represent 42.5 percent of the country's total. Combining then the hypotheses that absolute migratory balance during 1970-1975 was about 150,000 persons and that the percentage represented by the Metropolitan Zone in the total population for the country in the year 2000 would be 42.5 percent, it was possible to establish a sequence of the percentages this zone would represent in the intermediate years of 1975, 1980, 1985, 1990 and 1995 and thus subsequently establish a migratory balance. The age structure adopted for these migrants was the same as that encountered in 1970. The sequence of net migration and the rate of net domestic migration between 1970 and 2000 are presented in Table 8.8.

Should Chile achieve between 1976 and 2000 a continuously rapid rate of growth in both gross and per capita income through the elimination of trade barriers, increase in agricultural and mineral exports and a decentralization of all activities, the share of population in Santiago's Metropolitan zone may be below the 42.5 percent level assumed by Pujol for the year 2000. Should that

TABLE 8.8

Metropolitan Zone: Net Domestic Migration by Sex and Five-year Period and Annual Rate of Migration. 1970-2000.

Period	Domestic Migration			Annual Rate of Internal Migration (Per thousand)
	Males	Females	Total	
1970-1975	66,700	78,300	145,000	8.12
1975-1980	73,600	86,400	160,000	7.86
1980-1985	79,120	92,880	172,000	7.43
1985-1990	80,500	94,500	175,000	6.69
1990-1995	78,200	91,800	170,000	5.82
1995-2000	68,080	79,920	148,000	4.59

Source: Pujol, 1976c, 8.

prove to be the case, the pattern of domestic migration could differ significantly from that envisaged by the specialists in the year 1976.

International Migration

As we have already seen before, the projection of the population of Chile was made by assuming the existence of a positive net international emigration until 1980 and none between 1980 and 2000. This obviously will have repercussions on the population estimates by zones and regions. Pujol assumed that half of the immigrants would move into the Metropolitan Zone and the other half to the South. The overall figures are presented in table 8.9 while the sex and age distribution of international migration is found in (Pujol: 1976c, 13).

TABLE 8.9

Chile: Net International Migration by Zones and According to Sex. 1970-1980.[1]

Zone	1970-1975			1975-1980		
	Males	Females	Total	Males	Females	Total
North	-	-	-	-	-	-
Metropolitan	-10,000	- 6,500	-16,500	- 5,000	-3,250	- 8,250
South	-10,000	- 6,500	-16,500	- 5,000	-3,250	- 8,250
Country	-20,000	-13,000	-33,000	-10,000	-6,500	-16,500

Note: 1. In the population projection for Chile it was assumed that net international migration during the 1980-2000 period would be nil.

Source: Pujol, 1976c, 9.

Projection of Population by Zones

The projection of the population for the North was made by utilizing mortality and fertility since there was no migration. In order to calculate the population in the Metropolitan and Southern Zones the element of migration was added.

In order to achieve coherence between the projections by zones and the projection for the country as a whole it became necessary to make adjustments in each step of the zonal projections. When projections were made for the three zones from 1970 to 1975, the figures obtained for the country as a whole from the two projections were compared and the differences (always relatively small since the methodologies were consistent) encountered with respect to the country projection were prorated among the zones. The figures for total population by zone and sex between 1970 and 2000 are presented in Table 8.10, while the more detailed information for quinquennial age groups is found in (Pujol: 1976c, 42-44).

TABLE 8.10

Chile: Total Population by Zone and Sex. 1970-2000.

Sex	1970	1975	1980	1985	1990	1995	2000
Northern Zone							
Males	994,769	1,087,307	1,190,203	1,302,748	1,418,782	1,534,454	1,645,017
Females	1,003,149	1,099,480	1,206,102	1,322,036	1,441,351	1,559,034	1,673,647
Both Sexes	1,997,918	2,186,787	2,396,305	2,624,784	2,860,133	3,093,488	3,318,664
Metropolitan Zone							
Males	1,598,126	1,825,243	2,084,674	2,372,155	2,670,929	2,974,706	3,266,044
Females	1,737,238	1,980,716	2,253,837	2,553,868	2,864,590	3,175,801	3,476,005
Both Sexes	3,335,364	3,805,959	4,338,511	4,926,023	5,535,519	6,150,507	6,742,049
Southern Zone							
Males	2,035,888	2,147,212	2,279,539	2,434,862	2,598,174	2,752,478	2,912,162
Females	1,999,388	2,113,056	2,245,516	2,398,426	2,559,634	2,717,344	2,877,437
Both Sexes	4,035,276	4,260,268	4,525,055	4,833,288	5,157,808	5,469,822	5,789,599
Country							
Males	4,628,783	5,059,762	5,554,416	6,109,765	6,687,885	7,261,638	7,823,223
Females	4,739,775	5,193,252	5,705,455	6,274,330	6,965,575	7,452,179	8,027,089
Both Sexes	9,368,558	10,253,014	11,259,871	12,384,095	13,553,460	14,713,817	15,850,312

Source: Pujol, 1976c, 12.

Projection of the Population by Regions

Once the projections at the zone level were made and adjusted to the figures of the projection for the country, the zone of the North as well as that of the South were divided into the corresponding regions by using the square table method. Total population by sex and region was projected until the year 2000 by extrapolating the percentages which each region represented with respect to the corresponding zone, by sex. The basic information used was that of the censuses of 1940, 1952, 1960 and 1970 with the percentages projected up to the year 2000. Between 1970 and 2000 the percentages were interpolated in a linear form.

The percentages and totals of the population by region and sex corresponding to 1970 and the year 2000 are presented in Table 8.11. Detailed information for the intervening periods by sex and quinquennial age groups is found in (Pujol: 1976c, 14-26).

TABLE 8.11

Chile: Total Population by Region and Sex and Percentages Within the Corresponding Zones. 1970 and 2000.

Region	1970				2000			
	Males		Females		Males		Females	
	Absolute Figures	Per-centage	Absolute Figures	Per-centage	Absolute Figures	Per-centage	Absolute Figures	Per centage
Zone: North								
Region I	95,715	9.62	89,300	8.90	193,289	11.75	184,101	11.00
II	136,274	13.70	129,982	12.96	205,627	12.50	207,532	12.40
III	83,329	8.38	77,649	7.74	148,874	9.05	143,934	8.60
IV	175,292	17.62	181,733	18.12	259,913	15.80	267,784	16.00
V	504,159	50.68	524,485	52.28	837,314	50.90	870,296	52.00
Total	994,769	100.00	1,003,149	100.00	1,645,017	100.00	1,673,647	100.00
Zone: South								
Region VI	257,291	12.64	243,274	12.17	369,845	12.70	359,680	12.50
VII	329,439	16.18	321,759	16.09	460,122	15.80	444,564	15.45
VIII	658,685	32.35	660,259	33.02	990,135	34.00	1,009,880	35.10
IX	315,635	15.50	314,909	15.75	384,405	13.20	385,576	13.40
X	396,883	19.50	390,473	19.53	570,784	19.60	558,223	19.40
XI	27,676	1.36	23,813	1.19	56,787	1.95	43,162	1.50
XII	50,279	2.47	44,901	2.25	80,084	2.75	76,252	2.65
Total	2,035,888	100.00	1,999,388	100.00	2,912,162	100.00	2,877,437	100.00
Metropolitan Zone								
	1,598,126		1,737,238		3,266,044		3,476,005	
Total Country	4,628,783		4,739,775		7,823,223		8,027,089	

Source: Pujol, 1976c, 13.

9
EDUCATIONAL ATTAINMENT AND INSTITUTIONS

INTRODUCTION

Investment in human capital (education) is a central determinant of a nation's development path and prospects. The quality of labor, which is heavily determined by education, shapes the productivity of the labor force, the pattern of income distribution and such other variables as labor force participation, migration movements and the quality of social and political institutions. In addition, the endowment of human capital and the speed at which this capital grows determine an economic system's response to outside shocks as well as a nation's consumption or investment absorptive capacity. Human capital is thus a major determinant of the capacity of an economy to transform, modernize and absorb both internal and external shocks and stimuli with a minimum of social and political dislocations. In the present chapter the reader will find a description of the major features of education in Chile and the most important statistical evidence on educational attainment and institutions.

HISTORICAL BACKGROUND

The history of Chilean education[1] has been quite a long one. The first schools appeared in Chile during the colonial period, most of them run by the Roman Catholic Church. They concentrated on primary and secondary education, with highly selective standards for the latter. The Real Universidad de San Felipe was authorized by King Felipe IV of Spain in 1738; it opened in 1747. Like in most universities in the world at that time, philosophy and theology were the core of the curriculum. Laymen as well as clergy taught there. The historical evolution of Chile's universities is described in a subsequent section.

In 1813, the Instituto de Educación e Industria Popular (later called Instituto Nacional) opened in Santiago, the first real public secondary school. During the early Republican period, however, the educational quality of the Universidad de San Felipe declined until it was dissolved in 1837.

There were, however, according to Labarca, several limitations to the country's intellectual development: 1. Education did not emphasize intellectual pursuits or the development of the liberal arts; legal, medical, and other similar studies began upon termination of secondary school training; 2. The secondary schools were exclusively preparatory for university studies; there were no vocational or technical schools for preparation for intermediate-

---

[1]Most of this information is taken from: Amanda Labarca, Historia de la Enseñanza en Chile (Santiago, Chile: Imprenta Universitaria, 1939). See also for additional aspects of education in Chile (Mamalakis: 1976d, 74-78, 276).

skills professions; and 3. The secondary schools limited their function to academic instruction; no attempts were made at furthering civic responsibilities or developing other aspects of the personality.

An analysis of the educational conditions of Chile in 1850 indicated that only 1% of the population or 10,000 were enrolled in primary schools; and only 2,000 or 0.2% were in secondary schools. Moreover, as can be seen from Table 9.1, 49.3% of all secondary school students were enrolled in private or religious schools in 1854, which suggests that education was primarily the privilege of the wealthy.

TABLE 9.1

Secondary School Enrollment in 1854.

	Number of Schools		Number of Pupils		Total Enrollment
	Men	Women	Men	Women	
Public Schools	17	3	2,026	132	2,158
Private Schools	10	15	782	969	1,751
Religious Schools	5	-	349	-	349
Total	32	18	3,157	1,101	4,258

Source: Labarca: 1939, 122.

Under President Manuel Montt, there was an expansion of educational facilities. School buildings and enrollment were tripled during the 1850's. The law of 1860 provided that every citizen had a right to free elementary education; it ordered that a primary school for boys and a primary school for girls be established in each department with more than 2,000 inhabitants; and that a secondary school be established in each provincial capital.

In the 1880's, under liberal and positivist influences, the entire direction of Chilean education was changed to conform to Germany's educational methods and goals; German professors were imported to teach in the secondary schools and in the University. Thus, the German immigration into the country, although limited in number, was to shape the thinking of the country at least for a generation. The decade of the 1880's broke with the Spanish methods and goals; the decade of the 1890's was characterized by German intellectual domination of Chilean education. However, at the same time the quality and quantity of the educational establishment was vastly improved. The educational budget, which was $1,083,944 in 1879 rose to $5,641,120 in 1892, or 520.4%. This was used primarily to build new schools and to import German teachers.

Characteristics of Chilean Education in 1900

The characteristics of Chilean education by 1900 were as follows: 1. There was no real educational tradition in the country; 2. The educational system was centralized, because it was supervised and administered from the national capital; it was uniform, because all the educational programs are the same. Private secondary schools were free to develop their own curricula and to choose textbooks and teachers; their students, however, had to take the State exams administered by the University if they wanted to receive their secondary school degree. This arrangement continued into the twentieth century. Public education was financed entirely out of funds from the national government; 3. There was no real coordination or continuity between primary and secondary schools; 4. Vocational and technical schools were scarce and primitive; 5. The academic preparation of the students for University education remained exclusively the goals of secondary schooling; and 6. There were no formal programs of extracurricular activities. The population of Chile, according to the raw figures of the 1895 census, was over one and one-half million people. Only 12.8% of these were in school.

Table 9.2 indicates that only 8.6% of all enrolled students or 0.83% of the population of the country went beyond primary school in 1900. The table also shows that one-third of all primary school students were in private and religious schools.

TABLE 9.2

Total School Enrollment in 1900.

	Number of Students		% Composition	
Primary Schools	170,909		91.4	
Public		114,410[1]		66.9[1]
Private		30,215		17.7
Religious		26,284		15.4
Secondary Schools	11,719		6.3	
Vocational Schools	1,856		1.0	
Teachers Schools	760		0.4	
Religious Seminaries	591		0.3	
University	1,106		0.6	
Total	187,087		100.0	

Note: 1. These three separate figures refer to primary school enrollment.

Source: Labarca: 1939, 216.

At the beginning of the twentieth century, a nationalistic reaction set in. The aim was to rescue Chilean public education from its foreign orientation and to re-direct it to fulfill national goals. The main problem was illiteracy. According to the 1907 census, 62.5% of the country's children (approximately one million), were growing up without any instruction. The same census revealed that 60% of the population was illiterate. Finally, the 1920 Education Law made primary school compulsory for everyone. The law also provided for the expansion of educational facilities. The educational budget was increased as follows:

TABLE 9.3

Educational Budgets, 1900-1930 (Current Prices).

Year	Millions of Pesos	Index, base 1900=100
1900	8.0	100
1905	15.6	196
1910	26.3	331
1915	32.8	412
1920	45.0	566
1925	85.5	1,075
1930	164.3	2,064
1935	168.3	2,115

Source: Labarca: 1939, 275. Indexes calculated by the author.

The reduction in the proportion of illiterates, however, was a slow process. In 1854, 86.5% of the country was illiterate; half a century later, in 1907, it had only declined to 60.0%, or a rate of less than 0.5 percentage points per year. By 1930, however, it declined to 44.0%. Considerable progress had been made during the second quarter of the twentieth century. Literacy in 1940 stood at 79.9%, declining by 1.5 percentage points each year during the 1930's. In 1960 it was 83.6% (see Table 9.4). However, as recently as 1952, the rate of illiteracy was four times higher in the rural area (where a third of the inhabitants remained illiterate) than in the urban areas.

As illustrated in Table 9.4, which contains the most comprehensive, corrected time series on literacy, 89 per cent of the population with 15 or more years was literate. The figures presented in Table 9.4 differ slightly from some of those of Labarca presented in the text due to differences in coverage or definition. Statistical information on the literacy of the population in 1930, 1952, 1960 and 1970 according to age and sex or urban-rural location is found in Tables 9.5, 9.6, 9.7 and 9.15.

TABLE 9.4

Literacy of the Population Since 1854 and up to 1970 and Percentage of Literates.[1]

Year	Literates	Illiterates	Total	% of Literates		
				Male	Female	Total
1854	193,898	1,245,222	1,439,120	17.3	9.7	13.5
1865	309,309	1,509,914	1,819,223	20.2	13.8	17.0
1875	477,321	1,598,650	2,075,971	26.2	19.8	22.9
1885	731,263	1,796,057	2,527,320	31.7	26.2	28.9
1895	855,495	1,832,490	2,687,985	34.3	29.2	31.8
1907[2,3]	1,014,847	1,002,247	2,017,094	n.a.	n.a.	50.3
1920[2]	1,465,918	848,864	2,314,782	n.a.	n.a.	63.3
1930	1,945,944	658,480	2,604,424	n.a.	n.a.	74.7
1940	2,248,982	836,101	3,085,083	75.2	70.7	72.9
1952	2,954,431	728,360	3,682,791	82.0	78.6	80.2
1960	3,720,324	730,038	4,450,362	84.8	82.4	83.6
1970	4,808,877	594,749	5,403,626	89.8	88.2	89.0

Notes: 1. Since 1907 the literacy figures refer to that segment of the population with 15 or more years.

2. The censuses of 1907 and 1920 exclude the population of the province of Tacna which was returned to Peru by Chile in 1929.

3. The figures for 1907, 1920, 1930, 1940, 1952, 1960, and 1970 exclude those persons whose literacy condition is ignored. These persons represent at most 1.1% of the total.

Sources: The figures for the years 1854, 1865, 1875, 1885, and 1895 were obtained from República de Chile, X Censo de la Población 1930 (Santiago, Chile: Dirección General de Estadística, January 1933), Vol. II, p. XI. The figures for the years 1907, 1920 and 1930 were obtained from República de Chile, Censo Población 1960, Resumen País (Santiago, Chile: Dirección de Estadística y Censos, 1960), p. 69. The figures for the year 1940 were obtained from Chile, XI Censo de Población (1940), Recopilación de Cifras Publicadas por la Dirección de Estadística y Censos (Chile, Santiago: Centro Latinoamericano de Demografía, CELADE), p. 15. The figures for the year 1952 were obtained from República de Chile, XII Censo General de Población y I de Vivienda (Santiago, Chile: Servicio Nacional de Estadísticas y Censos, 1952), p. 159. The figures for the year 1960 were obtained from República de Chile, Censo de Población 1960 (Santiago, Chile: Dirección de Estadística y Censos, 1960), p. 208. The figures for the year 1970 were obtained from República de Chile, Población Total País, XIV Censo de Población y Vivienda 1970 (Chile, Santiago: Instituto Nacional de Estadísticas, 1970), p. 43.

TABLE 9.5

Literacy of the Population in 1930, Classified by Age and Sex.

Years of Age	A. Literates[1]	B. Illiterates	C. Unknown[2]	D. Total	% of Illiterates in Total $\frac{B}{A+B}$ Male	Female	Total
8	44,141	39,245	23,771	107,157	46.7	47.4	47.1
9	52,883	25,689	11,001	89,573	32.8	32.5	32.7
10	72,931	25,616	5,860	104,407	25.9	26.1	26.0
11	62,090	15,674	3,111	80,875	20.3	20.0	20.2
12	81,593	19,376	3,300	104,269	19.4	19.0	19.2
13	70,035	12,598	2,406	85,039	15.8	14.7	15.2
14	76,911	14,410	2,584	93,905	16.2	15.3	15.8
15	74,147	14,476	2,542	91,165	16.7	16.0	16.3
16	76,339	15,127	2,741	94,207	16.9	16.2	16.5
17	73,722	13,928	2,757	90,407	16.7	15.1	15.9
18	87,129	21,153	3,288	111,570	20.4	18.7	19.5
19	65,170	14,310	2,490	81,970	19.3	16.7	18.0
20-29	600,767	151,125	26,706	778,598	18.5	21.6	20.1
30-39	410,354	128,375	19,257	557,986	20.4	27.2	23.8
40-49	271,479	111,140	12,658	395,277	24.5	33.7	29.0
50-59	158,820	81,567	8,015	248,402	29.4	38.4	33.9
60 or more	128,017	107,279	8,788	244,084	40.8	49.6	45.6
Total	2,406,528	811,088	1,069,829	4,287,445	23.1	27.2	25.2

Notes: 1. Literates are defined as those able to read.
2. The total number of persons whose literacy is unknown is larger than the sum of the column because in the original table from which this information was extracted, persons between the ages of 0 and 7 were also classified as persons with literacy unknown. For the same reason, there is a similar discrepancy in the fourth column giving the total number of persons.

Source: República de Chile. Dirección General de Estadística. X Censo de la Población del 27 de Noviembre, 1930. Volumen II. (Santiago de Chile: Dirección General de Estadística, 1931), table 16, p. 309.

TABLE 9.6

Population of 15 Years or More, Urban and Rural, and Illiterate by Provinces, 1952.

	Population of 15 Years or More				Illiterates							
	Total	Urban	Rural	% Rural	Total	% Rural	Urban	%	Rural	%	Unknown	%
Tarapacá	67,626	41,000	25,961	38.3	7,149	10.5	2,437	5.9	4,710	18.1	665	0.98
Antofagasta	121,927	107,452	13,570	11.1	11,033	9.0	8,015	7.4	3,018	22.2	905	0.74
Atacama	48,607	25,126	23,235	47.8	8,156	16.7	2,643	10.5	5,513	23.7	246	0.50
Coquimbo	153,749	64,996	87,578	56.9	41,540	27.0	8,161	12.5	33,379	38.1	1,175	0.76
Aconcagua	79,016	32,909	45,650	57.7	18,797	23.8	4,213	12.8	14,584	31.9	477	0.60
Valparaíso	332,802	285,962	44,081	13.2	32,938	9.9	19,766	6.9	13,172	29.8	2,759	0.82
Santiago	1,168,819	1,021,477	135,298	11.5	123,122	10.5	79,759	7.8	43,383	32.0	11,790	1.0
O'Higgins	135,819	56,837	78,088	57.5	37,287	27.4	8,472	14.9	28,815	36.9	894	0.65
Colchagua	83,336	23,084	59,648	71.5	30,459	36.5	4,015	17.4	26,444	44.3	604	0.72
Curicó	54,245	21,077	32,722	60.3	17,895	32.9	3,374	6.2	14,521	44.3	446	0.82
Talca	106,277	43,192	61,505	57.8	32,548	30.6	6,658	15.4	25,890	42.0	1,580	1.48
Maule	44,441	16,619	27,425	61.7	14,214	31.9	3,047	18.3	11,167	40.7	397	0.89
Linares	88,099	27,707	59,334	67.3	27,751	31.5	4,756	17.1	22,995	38.7	1,058	1.20
Ñuble	149,943	53,957	94,883	63.2	50,035	33.3	10,065	18.6	39,970	42.1	1,103	0.73
Concepción	254,921	195,482	57,355	22.5	48,867	19.1	27,183	13.9	21,684	37.8	2,084	0.81
Arauco	41,448	12,268	29,002	69.9	14,900	35.9	2,864	23.3	12,036	41.5	178	0.42
Bío-Bío	80,060	26,531	52,707	65.8	25,908	32.2	4,887	18.4	21,021	39.8	822	1.02
Malleco	93,161	37,524	54,605	58.6	32,181	34.5	6,808	18.1	25,373	46.4	1,032	1.10
Cautín	213,782	75,000	136,174	63.7	63,806	29.8	10,087	13.4	53,719	39.4	2,608	1.21
Valdivia	137,230	53,750	81,853	59.6	34,795	25.3	7,149	13.3	27,646	33.7	1,627	1.18
Osorno	74,317	31,778	41,913	56.4	17,544	23.6	4,378	13.7	13,166	31.4	626	0.84
Llanguihue	80,310	27,506	52,244	65.2	18,771	23.3	3,500	12.7	15,271	29.2	560	0.69
Chiloé	60,331	11,444	48,500	80.3	14,218	23.5	1,393	12.1	12,825	12.1	387	0.64
Aysén	15,388	6,743	8,391	54.5	3,269	21.2	958	14.2	2,311	27.5	254	1.65
Magallanes	39,007	30,582	8,363	21.4	2,943	7.5	2,240	7.3	703	8.4	62	0.15
Total	3,724,407	2,330,003	1,360,065	36.5	730,124	19.6	236,808	10.1	493,316	36.3	34,339	0.92

Source: Ministerio de Educación Pública. Comisión de Planeamiento Integral de la Educación Chilena. Algunos Antecedentes para el Planeamiento Integral de la Educación Chilena. (Santiago, Chile: Ministerio de Educación Pública, 1964), table XIV, p. 255.

Note: This table is divided in two parts. The first refers to the population by provinces and according to urban and rural areas. The last column of the first part gives the percentage of rural in total population. The second part of the table presents the total of illiterates by provinces and the number of illiterates in the urban and rural population. The respective percentages refer to the population totals of fifteen years and over.

TABLE 9.7

Population of 15 Years or More, Urban and Rural, and Illiterate by Provinces, 1960.

Provinces	Population of 15 Years or More				Illiterates							
	Total	Urban	Rural	% Rural	Total	%	Urban	%	Rural	%	Un-known	%
Tarapacá	77,534	67,301	10,178	13.1	6,110	7.8	3,598	5.3	2,512	24.6	55	0.07
Antofagasta	131,969	124,575	7,471	5.5	9,647	7.3	8,133	6.5	1,514	20.2	23	0.01
Antacama	69,143	49,866	19,245	27.8	9,232	13.3	4,450	8.9	4,782	24.8	32	0.04
Coquimbo	174,377	94,825	79,493	45.5	40,795	23.4	11,765	12.4	29,038	36.5	59	0.03
Aconcagua	84,967	49,065	35,884	42.2	17,201	20.2	6,477	13.2	10,724	29.8	18	0.02
Valparaíso	394,331	354,345	39,937	10.1	31,810	8.0	21,238	5.9	10,572	26.4	49	0.01
Santiago	1,545,778	1,397,626	137,514	8.9	138,010	8.9	98,790	7.0	39,220	28.5	638	0.04
O'Higgins	149,549	82,886	66,617	44.5	33,867	22.6	11,562	13.9	22,305	33.4	46	0.03
Colchagua	90,643	31,664	58,965	65.0	29,168	32.1	5,357	16.9	23,811	40.3	14	0.01
Curicó	60,626	26,163	34,445	56.8	17,784	29.3	3,678	14.0	14,106	40.9	18	0.02
Talca	118,871	54,340	64,501	54.2	32,511	27.3	7,121	13.1	25,390	39.3	30	0.02
Maule	47,985	19,765	28,206	58.7	13,755	28.6	3,008	15.2	10,747	38.1	14	0.02
Linares	99,140	37,744	61,383	61.9	28,052	28.3	5,954	15.7	22,098	36.0	13	0.01
Ñuble	166,567	68,534	98,015	58.8	49,099	29.5	11,300	16.4	37,799	38.5	18	0.01
Concepción	314,556	258,749	55,790	17.7	49,539	15.7	29,556	11.4	19,983	35.8	17	0.005
Arauco	49,273	18,092	31,173	63.2	15,274	30.9	3,946	21.8	11,328	36.3	8	0.016
Bío-Bío	96,176	37,310	58,855	61.2	28,160	29.2	6,320	16.9	21,840	37.1	11	0.01
Malleco	99,848	46,797	53,032	53.1	30,051	30.1	7,954	16.9	22,097	41.6	19	0.01
Cautín	229,686	93,050	136,542	59.4	60,895	26.5	11,335	12.1	49,560	36.3	94	0.04
Valdivia	147,864	68,324	71,521	53.7	32,702	22.1	8,527	12.4	24,175	30.4	19	0.01
Osorno	84,910	40,721	44,185	52.0	17,552	20.6	5,475	13.4	12,077	27.3	4	0.004
Llanquihue	95,129	41,276	53,836	56.6	19,369	20.3	5,424	13.1	13,945	25.9	17	0.01
Chiloé	58,339	13,363	44,971	77.0	12,433	21.3	1,678	12.5	10,755	23.9	5	0.008
Aysén	21,212	11,251	9,961	46.9	3,908	18.4	1,498	13.2	2,418	24.2	0	-
Magallanes	51,124	41,246	9,864	19.3	3,114	6.1	2,445	5.9	669	6.7	14	0.02
Total	4,449,597	3,128,778	1,319,584	29.6	730,038	16.4	286,581	9.1	443,457	33.6	1,235	0.02

Source: Ministerio de Educación Pública. Comisión de Planeamiento Integral de la Educación Chilena. Algunos Antecedentes para el Planeamiento Integral de la Educación Chilena (Santiago, Chile: Ministerio de Educación Pública, 1964), table XIV, p. 255.

Note: This table is divided in two parts. The first refers to the population by provinces and by urban and rural areas. The last column of the first part gives the percentage of rural in total population. The second part of the table presents the total of illiterates in the urban and rural population. The percentages refer to the respective totals of population of fifteen years and over.

The Educational Pyramid

Beyond literacy, at more advanced educational levels, there has also been progress. The number of students in grammar and secondary schools jumped from 774,000 in 1943 to 1,292,000 in 1957. There is, however, an uneven distribution between the two components of these figures. In 1943-45, elementary school enrollment was six times greater than secondary school enrollment; in 1955-57, it was 4.5 times greater. Therefore, although progress was made, the educational pyramid was still very broad at the bottom, but thinning out very quickly at the secondary school level. The mass of the Chilean population may not yet be fully equipped for some years for an efficient introduction of modern technology. The secondary school system was traditionally divided into two parts. The humanistic curriculum or liceo was a prerequisite for University studies. It also increasingly became a prerequisite for most kinds of non-specialized work. It is also apparent that for social prestige reasons, many parents have preferred, throughout the twentieth century, to send their children to the liceo rather than to any other kind of school. The other branch of the secondary school system was the professional school whose aim was to train technical personnel, and which included commercial institutes, teacher training schools and vocational schools. This school performed fundamental service for economic development. However, enrollment in professional schools as a percentage of total secondary school enrollment declined from 44.7% in 1943-45 to 36.4% in 1955-57, and although vocational schools were the most important of the professional schools, their relative share of professional school students declined from 48.3% in 1943-45 to 45.3% in 1955-57. Tables 9.10, 9.11, 9.12, 9.13 and 9.16 show that the Chilean educational pyramid narrows even further prior to the beginning of University training, suggesting again that even as late as 1970 or 1976 the upper strata of the country were not ready for a full mobilization of modern technology.

THE CHILEAN SCHOOL SYSTEM DURING 1974-1976

The Chilean Normal School System contained during 1974-1976 the following levels: (1) Pre-school (pre-escolar) or pre-basic education provided in the pre-schools (parvularios) of the National Corporation of Play Schools of the Ministry of Education (Junta Nacional de Jardines Infantiles del Ministerio de Educación) and various other public and private institutions (Law N° 17.301 of 1970 and Supreme Degree of Education N° 1.576 of 1971). Pre-school education contains the following sublevels: (a) 0 to 2 years (creche) (sala cuna) (day care centers), (b) 2-4 years (pre-school or nursery) (nivel medio) and (c) 4 years until they reach basic education (kindergarten) (nivel de transición). All recent Chilean governments have paid special attention to pre-school education with emphasis on the poorest income strata. This has been related to an attempt, albeit not totally successful, to prevent malnutrition of the young and poor attention or child abuse.

(2) Basic Education (Educación Basíca), which lasts eight years, from 1st to 8th grade and leads to a basic education finishing certificate. It is divided into universal basic (basíca común) and special basic education, which in turn includes special, home and consolidated schools (escuelas especiales o diferenciales; escuelas hogares y escuelas consolidadas).

(3) High School Education which exists in two variations or types. The arts and science path (científico-humanista) is similar to the European Gymnasium or Lycée aiming to prepare the student to enter higher education or integrate himself to the socio-economic development of the nation. This path leads to a high school certificate. The technical and professional path includes (a) commercial training (accounting, sales and publicity, and secretarial studies), (b) industrial training (mechanics, electricity, building, textiles), (c) technical training (knitting, weaving, clothing, alimentation, social welfare, craftsmanship and decoration, pre-school and, cooperative studies, beauty and cosmetics), (d) agricultural training (cattle raising, fruit arboriculture, forestry, crop plantation and agro-industries). The objective of technical professional education is to prepare middle level technicians in agricultural, commercial, industrial and technical specialties according to the qualitative and quantitative requirements of the professional market. Technical-professional education leads to specialized certificates, such as e.g. the high school and technical certificate in accounting, or, in secretarial studies, or, in mechanics, or, in crop plantation and

and agroindustries and so forth.

The Chilean arts and sciences or scientifico-humanistic high-school education is excellent in arts and humanities but has proved inadequate in the technical areas. A deliberate attempt has been made, at least since 1960, to reduce the deep regional differences in high-school education.

(4) Higher Level Education which has as its objective the formation of high level professionals in a broad range of specialties according to the interests of the student and with the social, economic and cultural needs of Chile.

Detailed information on education in Chile during 1974-1976 can be found in Ministerio de Educación Pública, Education in Chile, Chilean Report to the 36th Meeting of the International Conference on Education, Geneva, 1977. Educational Process 1974-1976, August 30th-September 8th (Santiago, Chile: MEP, Superintendencia de Educación, 1977), pp. 1-58. The material of the present section was extracted largely from this publication.

A bibliography on, and a description of education in Chile in 1964 is found in Adela R. Freeburger and Charles C. Hauch, Education in Chile, Studies in Comparative Education, (Washington, D.C.: U.S. Department of Health, Education and Welfare, 1964), pp. 1-42.

University Enrollment in 1938

Tables 9.10 to 9.14, 9.16 and 9.17 provide all the important contemporary information on primary, secondary and University enrollment. It may be useful, nevertheless, to look at the breakdown of University enrollment in 1938 presented in Table 9.8.

TABLE 9.8

University Enrollment in 1938

Schools	Enrollment of Chilean Students	% Composition
Law	1,309	24.4
Commerce and Industrial Economics	178	3.3
Education	600	11.2
Physical Education	181	3.4
Medicine	784	14.6
Chemistry and Pharmacy	165	3.1
Dentistry	218	4.1
Nursing	80	1.4
Obstetrics	69	1.3
Engineering	320	6.0
Architecture	99	1.8
Public Works	66	1.3
Agriculture	171	3.2
Veterinary	64	1.2
Practical Agricultural	119	2.2
Fine Arts	148	2.8
Applied Arts	285	5.3
Music	509	9.4
Total	5,365	100.0

Source and Methodology: Labarca: 1939, 351. The first column includes only Chilean nationals. There were 536 foreign students enrolled in the University, who are not included in this table, 209 of these were in the School of Medicine.

Table 9.8 shows that one out of every four Chilean students in the University in 1938 (including the schools in Santiago and in Valparaíso) was studying law. In 1940, the agricultural sector contributed 14.9% of gross domestic product (in 1961 prices). However, in 1938, the Schools of Agriculture, Veterinary and Practical Agriculture had only 6.6% of total University enrollment. The decline in Chilean agriculture, which contributed 9.1% of GDP in 1963 (1961 prices), may be partly attributed to that sector's intellectual and technical starvation. And for a country which would enbark upon an industrialization policy, it seems clear that the lawyers could issue the general guidelines but it is uncertain whether there would be enough engineers, trained economists, and businessmen equipped to carry these out in an efficient fashion.

Finally, Table 9.9 shows a comparative educational table for the 1930's.

TABLE 9.9

Student Enrollment in Eight Countries

Country and Year	Population	Primary School Enrollment	% of Population	Secondary School Enrollment	% of Population	Higher Education Enrollment	% of Population
1	2	3		4			5
Chile (1936)	4,530,051	568,700	12.6	41,893	.9	6,444	.1
Argentina (1933)	2,028,646	1,043,747	13.7	56,624	.5	22,086	.2
Costa Rica (1933)	471,524	53,707	11.4	-	-	-	-
U.S.A. (1930)	122,775,146	18,276,125	14.9	4,708,494	3.8	989,757	.8
England & Wales (1934)	48,783,471	5,689,383	11.7	545,850	1.1	52,249	.1
France (1933)	41,834,923	5,320,559	12.7	290,776	.7	72,249	.2
Belgium (1932)	8,213,449	1,085,152	13.2	166,694	2.0	9,914	.1
Norway (1931)	2,817,124	408,708	14.5	40,315	1.4	-	-

Source: Labarca: 1939, 361.

The reader should be warned that the date for Chilean figures is 1936, while the dates for the other countries are 1931-33, and 1930 for the United States. While Chile by 1936 was pulling out of the depression, the figures for the other countries and, in particular, for the United States, came at the time when the depression had the greatest impact upon educational development.

For a study of problems in Chilean education at this time, one should consult Irma Salas Silva, The Socio-Economic Composition of the Secondary School Population of Chile (Santiago, Chile: Imprenta Lagunas y Quevedo, 1930) which gives some clues as to the failure of Chilean education to respond to the social needs of the country and to the pressures of economic development.

CHILEAN UNIVERSITIES: A HISTORICAL OUTLINE

In 1979 Chile has eight universities -- two state and six private -- with campuses in twenty cities. They are: the University of Chile (a state university), founded in 1842; the Catholic University of Chile, 1888; the University of Concepción, 1919; the Catholic University of Valparaíso, 1928; the Federico Santa María Technical University, 1926; the State Technical University (a state university), 1947; the Southern University of Chile, 1954; and the University of the North, 1956.

The presidents of these eight universities comprise the Council of Presidents of the Chilean Universities, whose purpose is to promote coordination between these different establishments with a view to enhancing the efficiency and quality of instruction.

Although various institutions of higher learning existed in Chile during the seventeenth and eighteenth centuries, the country's first university, the University of San Felipe, was established by King Philip of Spain in 1738. This university was legally abolished in 1839, a decision influenced in great part by Chileans who visited the Old World and returned with the desire to spread European culture in Chile.

Thus, on November 19, 1842, in compliance with a law of the Republic, the University of Chile was founded. Under the guidance of its first rector, the internationally known humanist and jurist Andrés Bello, the University was successful in its mission at this crucial time in the nation's cultural development.

In 1931, under the Organic Statute of University Education, the University of Chile was granted administrative and teaching autonomy. This new autonomy led to significant growth in the educational milieu, with the up-grading and intensification of university research and extension programs.

The University of Chile is currently governed by the Organic Statute of June 4, 1971. Its total student enrollment in 1978 was 54,000, its total full- and part-time teaching staff 10,000 and its total budget in US dollars $115 million.

A variety of factors, based either on ideology or on regional development and needs, gradually led to the establishment of seven other Chilean universities.

In keeping with the ideas of Pope Leo XIII, who called for a greater participation by Catholics in the challenges of the times, the second Chilean university, the Catholic University of Chile, was founded on June 21, 1888.

In 1931, the state granted the University full academic autonomy. At the same time, Pope Pius XI declared it a Pontifical university, which involves a special relationship with the Vatican. The total student enrollment of the Catholic University of Chile in 1978 was 14,474, its total full- and part-time teaching staff 1,934 and its total budget for 1978 in US dollars $30 million. The Catholic University of Chile is divided into faculties, defined along lines of the general major disciplines. Faculties, in turn, are subdivided into schools, institutes and centers. Schools are oriented toward preparing professionals in a specific discipline; institutes engage principally in the advance of an art or science; and centers are dedicated to the in-depth study and teaching of a specific interdisciplinary field. In addition to the basic bachelor's degree (bachillerato), the University awards Master's and Doctor's degrees in general disciplines, such as sciences, arts, philosophy and law.

The third Chilean university, the University of Concepción, came into existence on March 17, 1919. Under government Decree N°1038 of 1920, it was granted legal recognition and validity and became a Private Law corporation governed by its own by-laws. This institution was the result of the efforts made by the people of the central southern city of Concepción to further cultural development of the region. Two years after its founding, the Lottery of Concepción was created which provided the university with steady income and thus helped it to make rapid progress.

The total student enrollment of the University of Concepción in 1978 was 13,012, its total number of full- and part-time teaching staff was 1,676 and its budget $29 million US dollars. Research projects carried out by the University of Concepción focus principally on the study of renewable and non-renewable natural resources, pollution, and means of preventing pollution of the region's resources.

On March 15, 1928, an endowment from the Isabel Caces de Brown Foundation permitted the establishment of the Catholic University of Valparaíso in accordance with Decree of the Bishopric of the city of Valparaíso. The University's legal personality was recognized under Supreme Decree 5.879 of 1929, and in 1961 its by-laws were approved and it was officially recognized as an autonomous Catholic university.

The Bishop of the city of Valparaíso acts as Grand Chancellor of the University, overseeing its Christian principles and expressing confidence in its president by approving his designation.

Located in Chile's principal port city, this university has devoted much of its curriculum to sea studies. Its total student enrollment in 1978 was 7,031, its total number of full-time, part-time, and teachers and assistants hired by the hour was 950 and its budget $10 million US dollars.

On March 31, 1926, the Federico Santa María Technical University was founded through an endowment from Federico Santa María, a public figure in Chile, after whom the school was named. This university seeks to meet the need for technical and professional training as well as scientific and technological development, particularly in the field of engineering. It was officially recognized by the state on April 27, 1926.

The will bequeathing funds for this university established the goal of helping to raise the socio-economic level of the most disadvantaged sectors of Valparaíso. With a budget of $9 million US dollars in 1978, it had a total student enrollment of 3,815 and a total full- and part-time teaching faculty of 338.

On April 9, 1947, a stage in the development of professional and technological education of the nation was completed with the establishment of the State Technical University. The decree giving legal life to this institution made it possible to merge several existing technical and engineering academic units into State Technical. In 1952, the University obtained its first Organic Statute and officially initiated its activities, reiterating its objective of promoting scientific and technological research into the nation's economic problems and the improved utilization of natural resources. In 1978, it had a total student enrollment of 29,728, a total full- and part-time teaching staff of 2,960 and a budget of $29 million US dollars.

As the result of the efforts of a group of professionals in the southern city of Valdivia, the Southern University of Chile ("Universidad Austral de Chile") was founded in February 1954. On September 7, 1954, its by-laws were officially approved and it was granted legal status.

The University was originally funded by the generous support of its founding members as well as professionals and private industry of the region. In 1955, it obtained a share in the profits of the national lottery, and later was granted government subsidies under the Annual National Budget Law.

The University campus is located about one third of a mile from downtown Valdivia. With a total student enrollment of 8,307 in 1978, the Southern University of Chile had a total number of full- and part-time teaching staff of 778 and a budget of $14 million US dollars.

Finally, the University of the North was founded on May 31, 1956, and officially recognized by the state on January 31, 1964. Its main campus is situated in the northern city of Antofagasta. Originally part of the Catholic University of Valparaiso, it became an independent university with its legal recognition in 1964 and thus became eligible for state funding allocated for expansion of the nation's universities.

Because of its geographical location, the University of the North has placed special emphasis on the study of the sea, natural resources, and arid zones, as well as on mineralogy, anthropology, and archaeology. Its total student enrollment in 1978 was 5,898, its total full- and part-time teaching staff was 571 and its budget $13.5 million US dollars. All Chilean Universities were suffering from a severe financial crisis throughout the price stabilization efforts of the Military Junta during 1974-1977. Their financial position improved mildly in 1978.

Most of the above information was obtained from Report on Chilean University Life. Number One, Winter 1979 (Washington, D.C.: Embassy of Chile) edited by Mario Correa, Cultural Attache, pp. 1-11.

Student Enrollment: 1960 to 1977

The spectacular rise in student enrollment between 1960 and 1977 is revealed by Tables 9.16 and 9.17. The sharpest increases were those experienced by high school and University enrollments.

TABLE 9.10

Primary, Secondary, Special and University Education, 1940.

Type of Education	Registered			Average Attendance		
	Male	Female	Total	Male	Female	Total
I Primary Education						
A. Public						
Independent daily schools	249,457	244,838	494,295	203,325	200,665	403,990
Daily schools attached to teachers' colleges	1,137	2,142	3,279	1,019	1,949	2,968
Schools attached to secondary schools for boys	7,505	753	8,258	6,867	681	7,548
Schools attached to secondary schools for girls	29	7,114	7,143	26	6,264	6,290
Night schools	5,981	1,939	7,920	4,298	1,271	5,569
Night schools attached to teachers' colleges	321	148	469	205	77	282
Schools for blind, deaf, dumb, and mentally retarded	242	66	308	224	56	280
Total	264,672	257,000	521,672	215,964	210,963	426,927
B. Municipal						
Primary daily schools	2,417	1,933	4,350	1,790	1,456	3,246
Primary night schools	1,264	44	1,308	814	38	852
Total	3,681	1,977	5,658	2,604	1,494	4,098
C. Private						
Independent daily schools	49,262	40,503	89,765	41,897	34,540	76,437
Kindergarten	596	885	1,481	472	656	1,128
Schools for blind, deaf, dumb, and mentally retarded	56	73	129	56	71	127
Schools attached to secondary schools for men and coeducational	12,681	2,226	14,907	11,363	1,979	13,342
Schools attached to secondary schools for girls	543	10,018	10,561	456	8,720	9,176
Night schools	4,949	336	5,285	3,493	259	3,752
Total	68,087	54,041	122,128	57,737	46,225	103,962
Total Primary Education	336,440	313,018	649,458	276,305	258,682	534,987
II Secondary Education						
A. Public						
Secondary schools for boys and girls	17,274	13,864	31,138	15,629	12,380	28,009
Total	17,274	13,864	31,138	15,629	12,380	28,009
B. Private						
Secondary schools for boys and coeducational	9,278	1,063	10,341	8,616	974	9,590
Night secondary schools	605	102	707	495	71	566
Secondary schools for girls	-	7,203	7,203	-	6,456	6,456
Total	9,883	8,368	18,251	9,111	7,501	16,612
Total Secondary Education	27,157	22,232	49,389	24,740	19,881	49,621

TABLE 9.10 (Cont'd)

Primary, Secondary, Special and University Education, 1940.

Type of Education	Registered			Average Attendance		
	Male	Female	Total	Male	Female	Total
III Special Education						
A. Agricultural						
Public applied agricultural schools	559	-	559	511	-	511
Private applied agricultural schools	259	-	259	249	-	249
Total	818	-	818	760	-	760
B. Vocational						
Public workshops and vocational schools	2,616	14,817	17,433	2,102	12,021	14,123
Total	2,616	14,817	17,433	2,102	12,021	14,123
C. Industrial						
Public industrial schools	2,283	-	2,283	1,920	-	1,920
Public mineral schools	932	-	932	882	-	882
	550	-	550	526	-	526
Total	3,765	-	3,765	3,328	-	3,328
D. Technical for Women						
Public, independent technical schools	-	4,309	4,309	-	3,303	3,303
Public technical schools attached to secondary schools	-	1,032	1,032	-	850	850
Private technical schools	-	267	267	-	262	262
Total	-	5,608	5,608	-	4,415	4,415
E. Commercial						
Public commercial institutes	2,982	2,593	5,575	2,745	2,373	5,118
Private commercial colleges	373	361	734	365	340	705
Total	3,355	2,954	6,309	3,110	2,713	5,823
F. Fine Art Schools						
National Conservatory of Music (public)	163	391	554	-	-	-
Academy of Fine Arts (public)	93	132	225	-	-	-
Secondary Institute of Fine Arts (public)	15	67	82	-	-	-
Applied School of Arts (public)	142	132	274	-	-	-
Private Conservatory of Music	98	310	408	80	273	353
Total	511	1,032	1,543	80	273	353
G. Primary Teachers Training College						
Primary Teachers Training College (public)	577	1,368	1,945	548	1,283	1,831
Primary Teachers Training College (private)	-	230	230	-	221	221
Total	577	1,598	2,175	548	1,504	2,052

TABLE 9.10 (Cont'd)

Primary, Secondary, Special and University Education, 1940.

Type of Education	Registered			Average Attendance		
	Male	Female	Total	Male	Female	Total
H. Health and Welfare						
Obstetric and Pediatric schools (public)	-	61	61	-	-	-
Nursing schools (public)	-	99	99	-	-	-
Social Welfare schools (private)	-	225	225	-	211	211
Total	-	385	385	-	211	211
Total Special Education	11,642	26,234	37,876	-	-	-
IV University Education						
Public Universities	3,483	1,075	4,558	-	-	-
Private Universities	1,566	278	1,844	-	-	-
Total University Education	5,049	1,353	6,402	-	-	-
General Total 1940	380,288	362,837	743,125	-	-	-
General Total 1939	352,176	334,879	687,055	-	-	-
General Total 1938	359,432	338,940	698,372	-	-	-

Notes: I have used the term secondary public schools for what is in Chile described as lyceos. The term escuela normal, which means primary teachers' training college, has been translated as teachers' college.

Source: República de Chile, Dirección General de Estadística. Politica, Administración, Justicia y Educación, Año 1940 (Chile: Dirección General de Estadística, 1942), p. 73.

TABLE 9.11

Primary, Secondary, Special and University Education, 1950.

Type of Education	Number of Operating Establishments	Registered			Average Attendance		
		Male	Female	Total	Male	Female	Total
I Primary Education							
A. Public							
Independent daily schools	3,683	272,878	262,359	535,237	219,659	216,381	436,040
Daily schools attached to teachers' colleges	14	3,615	3,429	7,044	3,197	3,004	6,201
Schools attached to secondary schools for boys	34	5,963	-	5,963	5,510	-	5,510
Schools attached to secondary schools for girls	35	-	7,078	7,078	-	6,258	6,258
Schools attached to coeducational public schools	22	1,154	975	2,129	1,069	908	1,977
Daily schools for adults	32	576	627	1,203	467	569	1,036
Night schools for adults	306	10,577	4,656	15,203	7,652	3,694	11,346
Schools for blind, deaf, and dumb, mentally retarded	1	131	29	160	105	25	130
Jail schools	34	3,326	-	3,326	3,153	-	3,153
Total	4,161	298,190	279,153	577,343	240,812	230,849	471,661
B. Private							
Independent daily schools	1,838	95,964	81,973	177,937	81,153	71,250	152,403
Schools attached to secondary schools for boys	56	14,398	-	14,398	13,272	-	13,272
Schools attached to secondary schools for girls	78	-	14,144	14,144	-	12,792	12,792
Schools attached to coeducational secondary schools	58	4,010	4,388	8,398	3,653	3,976	7,629
Night schools for adults	90	3,559	1,511	5,070	2,703	1,348	4,051
Schools for blind, deaf, and dumb, mentally retarded	3	173	127	300	42	80	122
Total	2,123	118,104	102,143	220,247	100,823	89,446	190,262
Total Primary	6,283	416,294	381,296	797,590	341,635	320,285	661,920
II Secondary Education							
A. Public							
Secondary schools for boys	34	20,007	-	20,007	17,950	-	17,950
Secondary schools for girls	36	-	21,368	21,368	-	18,997	18,997
Coeducational secondary schools	30	5,154	4,895	10,049	4,628	4,445	9,073
Total	100	25,161	26,263	51,424	22,578	23,442	46,020

TABLE 9.11 (Cont'd)

Primary, Secondary, Special and University Education, 1950.

Type of Education	Number of Operating Establishments	Registered			Average Attendance		
		Male	Female	Total	Male	Female	Total
B. Private							
Secondary schools for boys	60	9,964	-	9,964	9,432	-	9,432
Secondary schools for girls	94	-	11,604	11,604	-	10,683	10,683
Coeducational secondary schools	54	2,114	2,081	4,195	1,975	1,945	3,920
Night secondary schools	15	2,609	1,141	3,750	2,039	890	2,929
Total	223	14,687	14,826	29,513	13,446	13,518	26,964
Total Secondary Education	323	39,848	41,089	80,937	36,024	36,960	72,984
III Special Education							
A. Agricultural							
Public, applied agricultural schools	6	477	-	477	378	-	378
Private, applied agricultural schools	8	458	-	458	430	-	430
Total	14	935	-	935	808	-	808
B. Vocational							
Public workshop and vocational schools	51	3,953	24,588	28,541	3,460	20,441	23,901
Manual training (handicraft) schools (public)	30	4,249	-	4,249	3,920	-	3,920
Total	81	8,202	24,588	32,790	7,380	20,441	27,821
C. Mining and Industrial							
Public industrial schools	18	4,997	-	4,997	4,429	-	4,429
Private industrial schools	7	914	-	914	827	-	827
Public mining schools	3	1,270	-	1,270	1,235	-	1,235
Total	28	7,181	-	7,181	6,491	-	6,491
D. Technical Education for Women							
Technical, independent public schools	15	-	6,802	6,802	-	5,271	5,271
Public technical schools attached to secondary schools	17	-	1,012	1,012	-	820	820
Total	32	-	7,814	7,814	-	6,091	6,091
E. Commercial							
Public, commercial institutes	24	6,209	5,099	11,308	5,552	4,576	10,128
Private commercial institutes	7	288	689	977	145	461	606
Total	31	6,497	5,788	12,285	5,697	5,037	10,734

TABLE 9.11 (Cont'd)

Primary, Secondary, Special and University Education, 1950.

Type of Education	Number of Operating Establishments	Registered			Average Attendance		
		Male	Female	Total	Male	Female	Total
F. Fine Art Schools							
National Conservatory of Music (public)	1	393	614	1,007	-	-	-
Secondary Institute of Fine Arts (public)	1	21	104	125	-	-	-
Academy of Fine Arts (public)	1	163	228	391	-	-	-
School of Decorative Art (public)	1	168	202	370	-	-	-
Private Conservatories of Music	4	66	291	357	66	287	353
Total	8	811	1,439	2,250	66	287	353
G. Primary Teachers Training College							
Primary teachers training colleges (public)	14	1,778	2,131	3,909	1,680	1,940	3,620
Primary teachers training colleges (private)	1	-	277	277	-	257	257
Total	15	1,778	2,408	4,186	1,680	2,197	3,877
H. Health and Welfare							
Obstetric and Pediatric Schools (public)	1	-	99	99	-	99	99
Nursing and Welfare Visiting Nursing Schools (public)	3	-	128	128	-	-	-
Social Welfare Schools (private)	4	-	303	303	-	270	270
Total	8	-	530	530	-	369	369
I. Military							
Military Academy	1	310	-	310	307	-	307
Naval Academy	1	334	-	334	316	-	316
Air Force Academy	1	42	-	42	36	-	36
Police Academy	1	785	-	785	-	-	-
Total	4	1,471	-	1,471	659	-	659
Total Special Education	221	26,875	42,567	69,442	22,781	34,422	57,203
IV University Education							
Public Universities	12	4,724	2,179	6,903	-	-	-
Private Universities	23	3,132	954	4,086	-	-	-
Total University Education	35	7,856	3,133	10,989	-	-	-

TABLE 9.11 (Cont'd)

Primary, Secondary, Special and University Education, 1950.

Type of Education	Number of Operating Establishments	Registered			Average Attendance		
		Male	Female	Total	Male	Female	Total
Total 1950	6,863	490,873	468,085	958,958	-	-	-
Total 1949	6,698	478,889	454,416	933,305	-	-	-
Total 1948	6,486	462,941	436,716	899,657	-	-	-
Total 1947	6,156	444,316	415,398	859,714	-	-	-
Total 1946	6,035	433,542	403,881	837,423	-	-	-

Note: I have used the term secondary public schools for what is in Chile described as lyceos. The term escuela normal, which means primary teacher's training college, has been translated as teachers college.

Source: República de Chile, Servicio Nacional de Estadística y Censos, Educación, Justicia, Politica y Administracion, Año 1950 (Chile: Servicio Nacional de Estadística, 1954), p. 1.

TABLE 9.12

Population Six Years and Over According to Level of Education, by Age Groups. 1952 Census.

Age Groups	Population of Six Years and Over						
	Total	Level of Education					
		No Schooling	Primary	Secondary	University	Special	Unknown
Total	4,903,522	1,170,735	2,776,059	665,657	79,246	121,074	90,751
6- 9 years	534,215	291,815	239,676	-	-	108	2,616
10-14 years	652,799	121,480	472,008	49,700	-	5,814	3,797
15-19 years	573,917	83,610	345,360	104,947	5,372	27,011	7,617
20-24 years	575,037	82,340	343,570	100,235	14,844	23,018	11,030
25-29 years	448,062	72,623	258,724	81,683	10,920	14,783	9,329
30-34 years	381,360	64,941	218,788	69,666	9,683	9,809	8,473
35-39 years	377,051	69,860	212,992	66,394	9,717	9,363	8,725
40-44 years	323,184	69,630	175,836	53,387	7,815	8,578	7,938
45-49 years	261,198	61,347	137,683	41,994	6,276	7,042	6,856
50-54 years	231,390	59,529	119,356	34,459	5,607	5,981	6,458
55-59 years	161,094	45,679	81,345	22,118	3,402	3,806	4,744
60-64 years	147,469	51,630	69,014	17,088	2,378	2,667	4,692
65 years and over	236,746	96,251	101,707	23,986	3,232	3,094	8,476

Source: National Institute of Statistics.

TABLE 9.13

Total Population 5 Years of Age and Over by Age Groups, According to Level of Education and the Highest School-Year Completed. Census, 1960.

Level of Education and the Highest School-Year Completed	Population 5 Years and Over					
	Total	Age Groups				
		5-9	10-14	15-19	20-24	25 and over
Total	6,269,395	981,489	836,309	724,807	598,399	3,128,391
No Schooling	1,596,335	731,686	114,106	68,236	69,362	612,945
Primary	3,363,046	245,905	678,275	422,656	334,689	1,681,521
1 year	357,969	150,450	99,793	16,077	10,689	80,960
2-4 years	1,814,147	95,455	421,983	202,353	167,658	926,698
5-6 years	1,190,930	-	156,499	204,226	156,342	673,863
Unknown						
Secondary	942,564	-	36,318	178,864	132,904	594,478
1 year	183,876	-	24,486	48,655	24,518	86,217
2-4 years	512,018	-	11,483	105,527	68,187	326,821
5-6 years	246,670	-	349	24,682	40,199	181,440
Unknown						
Commercial	85,378	-	2,068	18,863	14,373	50,074
1 year	10,804	-	1,674	5,595	970	2,565
2-4 years	47,928	-	388	12,032	7,983	27,525
5-7 years	26,646	-	6	1,236	5,420	19,984
Unknown						
Industrial	36,592	-	791	10,741	7,901	17,159
1 year	6,419	-	664	3,727	905	1,123
2-4 years	26,754	-	125	6,855	6,321	13,453
5 years	3,419	-	2	159	675	2,583
Unknown						
Technical						
Females	36,059	-	840	11,297	7,572	16,350
1 year	6,867	-	658	4,268	711	1,230
2-4 years	26,213	-	179	6,814	6,094	13,126
5 years	2,979	-	3	215	767	1,994
Unknown						

TABLE 9.13 (Cont'd)

Total Population 5 Years of Age and Over by Age Groups, According to Level of Education and the Highest School-Year Completed. Census, 1960.

Level of Education and the Highest School-Year Completed	Population 5 Years and Over					
	Total	Age Groups				
		5-9	10-14	15-19	20-24	25 and over
Agricultural	4,299	-	112	1,316	728	2,143
1 year	699	-	63	474	73	89
2-4 years	2,820	-	47	807	484	1,482
5 years	780	-	2	35	171	572
Unknown						
University	81,967	-	-	2,060	15,068	64,839
1 year	9,875	-	-	1,523	4,238	4,114
2-4 years	35,590	-	-	525	9,170	25,895
5-6 years	36,502	-	-	12	1,660	34,830
Unknown						
Others (Not Specified)	48,355	1	354	4,211	8,139	35,650
Special	396	13	93	97	50	143
Unknown	74,404	3,884	3,352	6,466	7,613	53,089

Source: National Institute of Statistics.

TABLE 9.14

Total Population 5 Years of Age and Over by Age Groups, According to Level of Education and the Highest School-Year Completed. Census, 1970.

Level of Education and the Highest School-Year Completed	Population 5 Years and Over						
	Total	Age Groups					
		5-9	10-14	15-19	20-24	25-29	30 and over
Total	7,761,934	1,243,930	1,114,378	913,465	769,036	625,992	3,095,133
No Schooling	1,151,976	587,418	44,347	26,043	33,012	36,896	424,260
Primary	4,795,880	632,193	1,049,621	581,831	403,707	337,136	1,791,392
1 year	585,294	317,809	74,216	21,302	19,365	17,685	134,917
2-4 years	2,169,054	304,790	525,138	164,438	151,444	140,715	882,529
5-6 years	1,689,449	1,377	324,067	231,863	210,860	171,170	750,112
7-8 years	325,540	-	125,022	162,027	19,653	5,574	13,264
Unknown	26,543	8,217	1,178	2,201	2,385	1,992	10,570
Secondary	1,262,215	-	17,866	254,130	206,929	160,935	622,355
1 year	236,009	-	13,390	88,358	35,197	24,286	74,768
2-4 years	638,987	-	4,308	113,350	102,995	83,622	334,712
5-6 years	379,903	-	-	51,806	67,643	52,008	208,446
Unknown	7,316	-	166	616	1,094	1,009	4,429
Commercial School	129,373	-	475	17,062	28,799	21,733	61,304
1 year	10,978	-	326	3,884	2,355	1,505	2,908
2-4 years	71,765	-	145	8,407	16,194	13,271	33,748
5-6 years	45,595	-	-	4,726	10,069	6,792	24,003
Unknown	1,035	-	4	45	121	160	645
Industrial School	70,536	-	329	12,573	16,458	11,634	29,542
1 year	7,775	-	241	3,602	1,451	797	1,684
2-4 years	42,819	-	86	6,699	9,244	7,180	19,610
5-6 years	19,412	-	-	2,220	5,662	3,553	7,977
Unknown	530	-	2	52	101	104	271
Farm School	11,792	-	71	1,822	3,141	1,927	4,831
1 year	1,005	-	27	433	267	87	191
2-4 years	5,983	-	41	884	1,404	880	2,774
5-6 years	4,684	-	-	446	1,447	932	1,803
Unknown	120	-	3	9	23	22	63

TABLE 9.14 (Cont'd)

Total Population 5 Years of Age and Over by Age Groups, According to Level of Education and the Highest School-Year Completed. Census, 1970.

Level of Education and the Highest School-Year Completed	Population 5 Years and Over						
	Total	Age Groups					
		5-9	10-14	15-19	20-24	25-29	30 and over
Technical							
Females	57,548	-	223	8,123	15,587	10,020	23,595
1 year	4,743	-	126	1,699	1,101	528	1,289
2-4 years	36,388	-	88	4,599	9,308	6,401	15,992
5-6 years	15,939	-	-	1,767	5,071	3,009	6,092
Unknown	478	-	9	58	107	82	222
Normal School	51,035	-	32	1,688	8,144	9,380	31,791
1 year	2,385	-	14	389	1,039	262	681
2-4 years	13,621	-	16	378	2,746	2,567	7,913
5-6 years	34,337	-	-	909	4,275	6,427	22,726
Unknown	692	-	2	11	84	124	471
University	205,550	-	-	10,016	53,140	36,331	106,063
1 year	32,240	-	-	7,384	13,834	3,597	7,925
2-4 years	94,495	-	-	2,492	33,481	17,940	40,582
5-6 years	61,487	-	-	-	4,835	11,976	44,576
7-8 years	13,809	-	-	-	415	2,282	11,112
Unknown	3,519	-	-	140	475	536	2,368
Unknown	26,029	24,319	1,414	177	119	-	-

Source: National Institute of Statistics.

TABLE 9.15

Total Population 15 Years of Age and Over by Sex, According to Age Groups and Literacy Condition. 1952, 1960 and 1970: Census Data.

Age Groups and Literacy Condition	1952		1960		1970	
	Male	Female	Male	Female	Male	Female
Total	1,796,635	1,919,873	2,144,688	2,306,909	2,592,586	2,811,040
15-19	282,200	291,717	354,554	370,253	446,729	466,736
20-24	275,467	299,570	287,637	310,762	370,653	398,383
25-29	213,144	234,918	251,833	275,172	301,862	324,130
30-34	185,795	195,565	246,879	260,273	249,409	267,312
35-39	179,374	197,677	199,965	236,448	247,473	267,078
40-44	163,939	159,245	178,478	185,401	223,014	232,778
45-49	127,714	133,484	157,143	167,091	172,260	184,593
50-54	114,819	116,571	137,561	141,015	149,338	163,277
55-59	79,281	81,813	103,319	109,013	127,242	141,449
60-64	69,019	78,450	86,342	96,713	105,715	117,484
65 and Over	105,883	136,863	140,977	175,768	198,891	247,820
Literate	1,464,374	1,500,582	1,819,387	1,900,937	2,329,649	2,479,228
15-19	238,616	252,983	319,054	337,469	428,802	449,880
20-24	238,906	258,818	254,522	275,179	350,709	376,628
25-29	180,931	195,275	222,724	240,916	281,204	300,446
30-34	159,180	159,880	216,074	223,529	228,403	241,199
35-39	149,775	158,025	170,172	177,378	224,329	230,977
40-44	133,178	120,873	150,826	150,996	198,012	201,791
45-49	101,868	98,359	130,666	133,289	149,174	154,941
50-54	89,792	82,385	111,433	106,841	128,134	135,122
55-59	60,021	55,600	81,435	79,621	106,049	114,456
60-64	48,633	47,363	65,289	66,625	84,697	89,856
65 and Over	67,474	73,221	97,212	109,094	150,076	177,932
Illiterate	321,894	408,999	324,450	405,588	262,937	331,812
15-19	42,176	37,645	35,396	32,747	17,927	16,856
20-24	37,054	41,365	32,994	35,531	19,884	21,755
25-29	31,063	38,628	29,020	34,211	20,658	23,684
30-34	27,612	34,820	30,709	36,707	21,006	26,113
35-39	28,674	38,733	29,703	38,026	23,144	30,101
40-44	29,823	37,465	27,567	34,371	25,002	30,987
45-49	25,141	34,443	26,413	33,775	23,086	29,652
50-54	24,306	33,514	26,073	34,162	21,204	28,155
55-59	18,810	25,727	21,843	29,373	21,193	26,993
60-64	19,883	30,462	21,040	30,068	21,018	27,628
65 and Over	37,352	56,197	43,692	66,629	48,815	69,888

TABLE 9.15 (Cont'd)

Total Population 15 Years of Age and Over by Sex, According to Age Groups and Literacy Condition. 1952, 1960 and 1970: Census Data.

Age Groups and Literacy Condition	1952		1960		1970	
	Male	Female	Male	Female	Male	Female
Unknown	10,367	10,292	851	384	-	-
15-19	1,408	1,289	104	37	-	-
20-24	1,507	1,387	121	52	-	-
25-29	1,150	1,015	89	45	-	-
30-34	1,003	805	96	37	-	-
35-39	925	919	90	44	-	-
40-44	938	907	85	34	-	-
45-49	705	682	64	27	-	-
50-54	721	672	55	22	-	-
55-59	450	486	41	21	-	-
60-64	503	625	33	20	-	-
65 and Over	1,057	1,445	73	45	-	-

Source: National Institute of Statistics

TABLE 9.16

School Enrollment According to Sector, Level of Education and Sex 1960-1976.

Years/Sex	Students Enrolled				
	Total				
	Total	Pre Elementary	Elementary	Inter-mediate	Higher Education
Total					
1960	1,506,287[1]	27,641	1,193,360	259,270	26,016
1961	1,596,786[2]	34,005	1,255,992	280,052	26,737
1962	1,698,279[3]	39,432	1,344,362	286,436	28,416
1963	1,773,752	40,432	1,400,276	303,090	29,954
1964	1,837,381	44,053	1,435,807	323,304	34,217
1965	1,990,961[4]	48,701	1,545,469	357,494	39,297
1966	2,064,251[5]	51,543	1,589,232	379,337	44,139
1967	2,195,894	54,413	1,860,661	231,535	49,285
1968	2,339,155	57,581	1,954,087	265,243	62,244
1969	2,440,239	56,276	2,003,798	310,093	70,072
1970	2,523,605	58,990	2,078,874	308,762	76,979
1971	2,836,470	68,820	2,242,070	425,977	99,603
1972	2,985,455[6]	77,999	2,310,307	471,156	125,993
1973	3,101,195	79,483	2,375,214	506,503	139,995
1974	3,172,851	93,385	2,403,248	532,252	143,966
1975	3,164,697[7]	92,954	2,389,269	535,425	147,049
1976	3,146,239	100,802	2,353,384	557,904	134,149
Males					
1960	755,660	12,868	612,765	117,292	12,735
1961	804,935	15,494	633,363	143,337	12,741
1962	850,244	18,499	669,757	147,110	14,878
1963	889,331	19,194	697,021	153,850	19,266
1964	929,689	20,628	724,346	163,498	21,217
1965	1,019,541	23,269	795,705	182,041	18,526
1966	1,049,180	24,527	809,331	191,373	23,949
1967	1,119,847	26,077	945,078	115,249	33,443
1968	1,190,874	26,881	996,073	130,719	37,201
1969	1,240,533	26,298	1,020,263	151,745	42,227
1970	1,274,791	28,174	1,055,454	143,695	47,468
1971	1,443,675	32,991	1,040,417	208,728	61,539
1972	1,504,443	38,292	1,175,841	230,266	60,044
1973	1,573,098	39,321	1,199,648	248,166	85,963
1974	1,517,589	45,646	1,215,531	256,412	...
1975	1,579,302	45,490	1,213,337	261,444	59,031
1976	1,585,710	49,607	1,191,646	267,304	77,153
Females					
1960	722,258	14,773	572,789	127,338	7,358
1961	785,518	18,511	622,629	136,715	7,663
1962	843,244	20,566	674,605	139,326	8,747
1963	884,421	21,238	703,255	149,240	10,688
1964	907,692	23,425	711,461	159,806	13,000
1965	961,479	25,432	749,764	174,673	11,610
1966	994,937	27,016	766,088	187,964	13,869
1967	1,076,047	28,336	915,583	116,286	15,842
1968	1,148,281	30,700	958,014	134,524	25,043
1969	1,199,706	29,978	983,535	158,348	27,845
1970	1,248,814	30,816	1,023,420	165,067	29,511
1971	1,392,795	35,829	1,101,653	217,249	38,064
1972	1,455,030	39,707	1,134,466	240,890	39,967
1973	1,528,097	40,162	1,175,566	258,337	54,032
1974	1,511,296	47,739	1,187,717	275,840	...
1975	1,550,854	47,464	1,175,932	273,981	53,477
1976	1,560,529	51,195	1,161,738	290,600	56,996

TABLE 9.16 (Cont'd)

School Enrollment According to Sector, Level of Education and Sex 1960-1976.

Years/Sex	Students Enrolled				
	Enrollment in Private Schools				
	Total	Pre Elementary	Elementary	Inter-mediate	Higher Education
Total					
1960	483,368	4,901	357,346	111,753	9,368
1961	496,693	6,519	358,171	121,875	10,128
1962	525,555	7,033	386,977	119,961	11,584
1963	539,033	6,873	397,773	122,665	11,722
1964	548,081	7,564	401,809	125,262	13,446
1965	559,176	5,133	407,188	131,656	15,199
1966	522,097	10,207	374,880	120,681	16,329
1967	547,374	11,397	455,180	62,592	18,205
1968	565,170	12,858	470,323	60,741	21,248
1969	575,832	14,021	473,926	64,010	23,875
1970	576,605	15,668	464,574	70,251	26,112
1971	610,098	20,201	477,762	80,461	31,674
1972	628,334	24,757	480,181	84,856	38,540
1973	620,981	21,875	473,258	84,050	41,798
1974	618,559	29,182	454,267	86,858	48,252
1975	584,921	26,548	422,818	84,557	50,998
1976	538,482	22,910	375,073	93,599	46,900
Males					
1960	244,485	2,489	181,866	55,848	4,282
1961	251,491	2,153	182,078	61,508	4,752
1962	265,615	3,516	193,412	62,107	6,580
1963	271,222	3,398	197,363	62,627	7,834
1964	274,893	2,664	199,563	63,435	8,231
1965	276,612	2,729	203,254	67,050	3,479
1966	256,880	4,926	185,541	60,049	6,364
1967	268,638	5,705	218,728	30,164	14,041
1968	276,202	6,160	227,970	29,400	12,672
1969	274,412	6,578	227,291	31,328	14,215
1970	277,324	7,895	220,924	32,486	16,019
1971	295,256	9,851	227,100	38,591	19,714
1972	288,101	12,695	228,123	40,175	7,108
1973	300,958	11,367	224,838	39,624	25,129
1974	270,185	14,119	215,010	41,056	...
1975	278,568	13,019	199,266	40,018	26,265
1976	256,687	11,204	174,455	44,579	26,449
Females					
1960	232,930	2,412	173,980	54,469	2,069
1961	242,106	3,366	176,093	60,367	2,280
1962	258,398	3,517	193,565	57,854	3,462
1963	267,811	3,475	300,410	60,038	3,888
1964	273,188	3,900	302,246	61,827	5,215
1965	272,623	2,404	203,834	63,826	2,559
1966	258,896	5,281	189,339	60,632	3,644
1967	278,736	5,692	236,452	32,428	4,164
1968	288,968	6,698	242,353	31,341	8,576
1969	296,420	7,443	246,635	32,682	9,660
1970	299,281	7,773	243,650	37,765	10,093
1971	314,842	10,350	250,662	41,870	11,960
1972	314,251	12,062	252,058	44,681	5,450
1973	320,023	10,508	248,420	44,426	16,669
1974	300,122	15,063	239,257	45,802	...
1975	304,086	13,529	223,552	44,539	22,466
1976	281,795	11,706	200,618	49,020	20,451

TABLE 9.16 (Cont'd)

School Enrollment According to Sector, Level of Education and Sex
1960-1976.

Years/Sex	Students Enrolled				
	Enrollment in Public Schools				
	Total	Pre Elementary	Elementary	Inter-mediate	Higher Education
Total					
1960	1,022,919	22,740	836,014	147,517	16,648
1961	1,100,093	27,486	897,821	158,177	16,609
1962	1,172,724	32,032	957,385	166,475	16,832
1963	1,234,719	33,559	1,002,503	180,425	18,232
1964	1,289,300	36,489	1,033,998	198,042	20,771
1965	1,431,785	43,568	1,138,281	225,838	24,098
1966	1,542,154	41,336	1,214,352	258,656	27,810
1967	1,648,520	43,016	1,405,481	168,943	31,080
1968	1,773,985	44,723	1,483,764	204,502	40,996
1969	1,864,407	42,255	1,529,872	246,083	46,197
1970	1,947,000	43,322	1,614,300	238,511	50,867
1971	2,226,372	48,619	1,764,308	345,516	67,929
1972	2,357,121	53,242	1,830,126	386,300	87,453
1973	2,480,214	57,608	1,901,956	422,453	98,197
1974	2,554,292	64,203	1,948,981	445,394	95,714
1975	2,579,776	66,406	1,966,451	450,868	96,051
1976	2,607,757	77,892	1,978,311	464,305	87,249
Males					
1960	511,175	10,379	430,899	61,444	8,453
1961	553,444	12,341	451,285	81,829	7,989
1962	584,629	14,983	476,345	85,003	8,298
1963	618,109	15,796	499,658	91,223	11,432
1964	654,796	16,964	524,783	100,063	12,986
1965	742,929	20,540	592,351	114,991	15,047
1966	792,300	19,601	623,790	131,324	17,585
1967	851,209	20,372	726,350	85,085	19,402
1968	914,672	20,721	768,103	101,319	24,529
1969	961,121	19,720	792,972	120,417	28,012
1970	997,467	20,279	834,530	111,209	31,449
1971	1,148,419	23,140	913,317	170,137	41,825
1972	1,216,342	25,597	947,718	190,091	52,936
1973	1,272,140	27,954	974,810	208,542	60,834
1974	1,247,404	31,527	1,000,521	215,356	...
1975	1,300,734	32,471	1,014,071	221,426	32,766
1976	1,329,023	38,403	1,017,191	222,725	50,704
Females					
1960	489,328	12,361	398,809	72,869	5,289
1961	543,412	15,145	446,536	76,348	5,383
1962	584,846	17,049	481,040	81,472	5,285
1963	616,610	17,763	502,845	89,202	6,800
1964	634,504	19,525	509,215	97,979	7,785
1965	688,856	23,028	545,930	110,847	9,051
1966	736,041	21,735	576,749	127,332	10,225
1967	797,311	22,644	679,131	83,858	11,678
1968	859,313	24,002	715,661	103,183	16,467
1969	903,286	22,535	736,900	125,666	18,185
1970	949,533	23,043	779,770	127,302	19,418
1971	1,077,953	25,479	850,991	175,379	26,104
1972	1,140,779	27,645	882,408	196,209	34,517
1973	1,208,074	29,654	927,146	213,911	37,363
1974	1,211,174	32,676	948,460	230,038	...
1975	1,246,768	33,935	952,380	229,442	31,011
1976	1,278,734	39,489	961,120	241,580	36,545

TABLE 9.16 (Cont'd)

School Enrollment According to Sector, Level of Education and Sex
1960-1976.

Notes: 1. This figure includes 28,369 students classified as follows. (a) Elementary education: 7,806 students with 6,306 attending public schools and 1,500 attending private schools. (b) Intermediate education: 14,640 students with 13,204 attending public schools and 1,436 attending private schools. (c) Higher education: 5,923 students with 2,906 attending public institutions and 3,017 attending private institutions. The classification of these students according to sex is not known.

2. This figure includes 6,333 students attending institutions of higher education (3,237 attending public and 3,096 attending private ones) whose classification by sex is unknown.

3. This figure includes 4,791 students attending institutions of higher education (3,249 attending institutions of the public sector and 1,542 attending institutions of the private sector) whose classification by sex is unknown.

4. This figure includes 9,941 students (780 receiving technical professional education and 9,161 receiving higher education, with both corresponding to the private sector) whose classification by sex is unknown.

5. This figure includes 20,134 students (13,813 belonging to the public elementary education level and 6,321 belonging to the private higher education level) whose classification by sex is unknown.

6. This figure includes 25,982 students pertaining to the private higher education level whose classification by sex is unknown.

7. This figure includes 34,541 students of the higher education level (32,274 of the public sector and 2,267 of the private sector) whose sex classification is unknown.

Source: National Institute of Statistics.

TABLE 9.17

Student Enrollment in Chile by Sex, Level of Education and According to Sector That Provides the Education. 1977 School Year.

Level and Sector of Education	Student Enrollment		
	Total	Males	Females
Country Total	3,237,444	1,565,698	1,540,080
Public Sector	2,648,813	1,309,681	1,256,881
Private Sector	588,631	256,017	283,199
Pre-Elementary Education	148,181	72,922	75,259
Public	119,411	59,090	60,321
Private	28,770	13,832	14,938
Special Elementary Education	23,125	13,604	9,521
Public	22,435	13,202	9,233
Private	690	402	288
Regular Elementary Education	2,348,120	1,193,061	1,155,059
Public	1,939,920	1,000,435	939,485
Private	408,200	192,626	215,574
High School Education	586,352	286,111	300,241
Scientific-Humanist	384,160	171,443	212,717
Public	309,713	136,728	172,985
Private	74,447	34,715	39,732
Technical Professional	202,192	114,668	87,524
Public	175,083	100,226	74,857
Private	27,109	14,442	12,667
Higher Education (P)	131,666	-	-
Public (P)	82,251	-	-
Private (P)	49,415	-	-

Notes: P stands for preliminary.

Source: INE, Compendio Estadístico 1978 (Santiago, Chile: INE, 1978), p. 101.

ENROLLMENT IN SCHOOLS FOR CHILDREN AND ADULTS

Enrollment of All Students

Very comprehensive statistical information on the enrollment of children as well as adults in pre-elementary, elementary (special and regular) and high schools in 1975 and 1976 (as well as percentage changes) by sex, type and grade and according to region and dependency (private versus public) is contained in (MEP-SSE: 1976g). The detailed data on enrollment of adults in 1976 (MEP-SSE: 1976g, 22-31) complement the statistics for 1973 and 1974 found in (MEP-SSE: 1975a). A comparison of these two documents reveals a very sharp and continuous (more than 75%) increase in adult student enrollment between 1973 and 1976, most of it in elementary education. The weakest part of adult education is in vocational, especially technical and agricultural training.

Detailed statistical information of enrollment in pre-elementary (includes only those students attended by establishments depending on the Ministry of Education), special and regular elementary, and high school education in 1973 (only aggregate data), and 1974 by sex, type, and grade and according to region and dependency (private versus public) is provided in (MEP-SSE: 1975h).

Enrollment of Elementary School Students Repeating Classes

Effective enrollment of students who had to repeat a grade in private and public schools in 1973 is given in (MEP-SSE: 1975f). Repeaters are classified by grade or year of studies and sex and according to region and dependency. Enrollment of repeaters includes students who failed to be promoted in the preceding or earlier years and decided to enroll in 1973.

Adult Education

Statistical information on adult education in 1973 and 1974 is found in (MEP-SSE: 1975a). This document contains detailed data on adult education according to whether it is public or private, primary (basic) or high-school (intermediate) as well as by sex and distribution by regions and provinces.

Detailed information is also provided on the public and private establishments providing adult education in the nation's regions and provinces.

Major features of adult education in Chile in 1973 and 1974 are: (1) more than 95 per cent is public; (2) enrollment rose sharply, by more than 22 per cent, between 1973 and 1974; (3) enrollment was divided evenly between primary and high-school education; (4) high-school adult education was concentrated heavily (more than 75 per cent) in the scientific-humanistic areas; (5) agricultural adult education remained grossly neglected both in 1973 and 1974. It accounted for less than twenty per cent of one per cent of total adult education and was being provided exclusively by private establishments.

Metropolitan Region

Detailed statistical information on enrollment, average attendance and percentage of attendance of students attending pre-elementary, special and elementary public schools in the Metropolitan Region during the school year of 1975, according to school year and community, is furnished in (MEP-SSE: 1977a).

PROGRESS OF STUDENTS

Public Elementary Education

The education of progress achieved by the 1,241 million students (91% coverage) attending elementary (primary) public schools in 1966 is described in detail in (MEP-SSE: 1974d).

The educational progress achieved by students attending primary public schools in 1968 is outlined in (MEP-SSE: 1974a). This document provides absolute and relative figures on promotion, repetition and desertion according to grades (first to eighth) and provinces. Because no data was available for the provinces of Maule and Bío-Bío, this study covers only 75% of the students enrolled in primary education.

In 1968, among 1.463 million students enrolled in primary public education, 1.2 million was promoted, .168 million had to repeat and .089 dropped out of school.

A study of educational progress achieved by students attending public primary schools in 1971 (MEP-SSE: 1974c) was successful in covering 94 per cent of all students enrolled and includes the provinces of Maule and Bío-Bío. This document supplies absolute and relative figures on promotion, repetition and desertion for 1.717 million students attending primary public schools in 1971 according to grade and by provinces. The overall promotion rate in 1971 was 85 per cent [as compared to 82 per cent in 1968 (MEP-SSE: 1974a, 2)], the rate of repetition 11 per cent (12% in 1968) and the drop-out rate 4 per cent (6% in 1968) (MEP-SSE: 1974c, 2 and MEP-SSE: 1974a, 2).

A similar study of educational progress achieved by students attending public primary schools in 1972 (MEP-SSE: 1974b) (with a 95 per cent coverage and the same features as the study for 1971, MEP-SSE: 1974c) suggests a mild reversal in trends. Out of a total of 1.777 million primary school students covered, 81% were promoted, 13% had to repeat and 6% dropped out of school (MEP-SSE: 1974b, 2).

By 1973, 1.840 million students were enrolled in public elementary schools. Detailed absolute and relative statistics on promotion (79% were promoted in 1973), repetition (15%) and desertion (6%) by grade and provinces in 1973 are found in (MEP-SSE: 1974e) which covered 94% of all students enrolled. In comparison, the study for 1967 (MEP-SSE: 1974f), which had a coverage of only 79%, deals with 1.374 million students enrolled in public primary schools (82% were promoted, 13% repeated and 5% deserted school in 1967). A similar study for 1969, with a coverage of only 79% of students enrolled in public primary schools, reveals total enrollment of 1.502 million of which 83% was promoted, 11% had to repeat and 6% left school (MEP-SSE: 1974g, 2,4). In 1969, the rate of promotion in the first grade ranged between 62% (28% had to repeat) in Maule and 88% in Tarapacá (where only 6% had to repeat) (MEP-SSE: 1974g, 1).

Comprehensive coverage of selected time series about educational progress of students attending public elementary schools during 1966-1969 and 1971-1973 (absolute as well as relative values of promotion, repetition and desertion) by grade and province is found in (MEP-SSE: 1975d).

Public High School Education

The progress achieved by high school students attending public schools in 1971 is outlined in detail in (MEP-SSE: 1975b). This document provides statistical information on the absolute numbers and rates of promotion, repetition and dropping out (desertion) by students attending public high schools by grade, year of studies, type of studies and provinces.

According to this study (a) the drop-out rate declines in higher grades; (b) the country-wide promotion rate in 1971 for students attending public high schools was 80%, the rate of repetition 13% and the school desertion rate 7%; (c) the number of students receiving agricultural vocational training was below 1% of the total enrollment.

Similar detailed statistical information about progress achieved by students attending high schools during the year 1972 is available in (MEP-SSE: 1975g).

The progress achieved by high school students attending public schools in 1973 is presented in similar detail in (MEP-SSE: 1975e). The country-wide promotion rate in 1973 for students attending public high schools was 73%, the rate of repetition was 15% and the desertion rate 12% (MEP-SSE: 1975e, 5). The number of students receiving vocational training in agriculture was just 1% of total high school enrollment.

Public Elementary and High School Education

Statistical information on educational progress of students enrolled in public elementary and high schools in 1974 (absolute as well as relative values of enrollment, promotion, repetition and dropping out by grade, region and province) is found in (MEP-SSE: 1976a, 3). Worth noting are the following facts: (1) primary school enrollment was higher in 1974 than in 1975; (2) 23.6 per cent of all high school students had to repeat classes in 1974 as compared to 19.5 per cent in 1975; (3) the rate at which students were being promoted in the technical-professional fields was significantly lower in 1974 than in 1975. E.g. it was only 50.2% in commercial high schools (65.3% in 1975) and 58.9% in agricultural high schools (72.5% in 1975) (MEP-SSE: 1976a, 3 and MEP-SSE: 1976c, 4).

In 1976 the Ministry of Education released a study outlining the educational progress of students attending both primary and secondary (high) schools in 1975 (MEP-SSE: 1976c). This document provides detailed data on absolute and relative values on total student enrollment, promotion, repetition (reprobación) and drop out (retiro) by year of school, by region and by province. Of a total of 1.878 million students attending public primary schools, 78.8% were promoted, 14% had to repeat and 6.2% dropped out of school. This performance was worse than in 1972, 1971 or 1968. Among 364,740 students attending public high schools, 72.2% were promoted, 14% had to repeat and 6.2% dropped out of school (MEP-SSE: 1976c, 4).

A striking feature of the school enrollment figures presented in (MEP-SSE: 1976c) and Table 9.16 of this chapter is the small number of public grammar school students receiving any type of high school or intermediate training (high school enrollment in 1975 was below 20% of elementary school enrollment) and the inadequate educational framework for vocational training.

QUALITY OF EDUCATION: SELECTED AREAS

Quality of Education Throughout Chile

Novel statistics relating to the quality of education throughout Chile in pre-elementary, elementary and high-schools in 1974 are included in (MEP-SSE: 1976h). These include the number of urban and rural courses in pre-elementary, special and elementary education grouped according to the average number of students, type of education and grade. Among Chile's total urban courses of 52,076, 3,553 had more than 50 students while 14,494 courses had 41-50 students. Among the nation's 16,697 rural courses, 1,121 had more than 50 while 1,834 had 41-50 students (MEP-SSE: 1976h, 10). Also presented in this document is the number of heterogeneous courses (a total of 7,844 in Chile in 1974 of which 7,205 were rural) according to the various grades taught simultaneously by only one teacher.

Finally, it provides information on urban and rural pre-elementary, special, elementary and high school establishments (independent, annexes and sections) according to the highest grade taught and a classification of enrollment, courses and teachers in urban and rural elementary education establishments according to the average size of enrollment (MEP-SSE: 1976h, 22).

Quality of Education in Metropolitan Area

Novel aspects of education, which permit the quantification of phenomena related to the quality of education, are presented in the collection of tables about enrollment, repeaters, and number of courses and establishments providing pre-elementary, elementary and high school education to children in the Santiago Metropolitan Area during 1974 found in (MEP-SSE: 1976f).

This publication gives the number of heterogeneous courses, that is, courses composed of groups of students belonging to different grades or years of study but attended simultaneously by only one teacher. Thus, there were 18,718 homogeneous and 443 heterogeneous courses offered in elementary education in the Metropolitan Region in 1974 (MEP-SSE: 1976f, 10-11). Also new in this publication is the number of courses in each grade classified by size (1-10, 11-20, ..., >50). While there was a total of 20,997 courses offered at the pre-elementary, special and elementary (homogeneous and heterogeneous) education level (19,661 urban and 1,336 rural), the average number of students per course was often high. As an example, with the average number of students per course given in parentheses, among urban courses there were 2,387 (>50), 7,582 (41-50), 6,484 (31-40), while among urban courses there were 78 (>50), 200 (41-50) and 398 (31-40) (MEP-SSE: 1976f, 10). Large average class size emerges, therefore, as a major problem of Chilean education and as an obstacle to providing quality elementary education.

Another novel type of information found in this document is the number of elementary and high schools classified according to the highest grade attended as well as the number of elementary schools classified according to the size of their enrollment (MEP-SSE: 1976f, 16-24).

Number of Teachers

Statistics on the number of teachers in private and public schools for children (from pre-elementary to high schools) during the 1976 school year according to sex and modes of teaching are found in (MEP-SSE: 1976e). The figures on numbers of teachers have to be used with caution if the aggregate quantity or supply of teachers is to be calculated since some teach in more than one school. However, these figures are reliable if such statistics as student/teacher ratios by course are to be estimated.

Courses Offered and Students Repeating Classes

Detailed statistical information on the number of students repeating classes and the number of courses offered in public pre-primary, special primary and regular primary schools by sex, grade, regions and provinces in 1975 is given in (MEP-SSE: 1976b). Out of a total enrollment of 1,877,716 students attending regular public primary schools, 261,710 students were repeaters (MEP-SSE: 1976b, 4,7). The document also provides information on public high school enrollment and courses offered by type of training, grade or age of studies, according to regions and provinces during the 1975 school year (MEP-SSE: 1976b, 8-11).

NUMBER OF EDUCATIONAL ESTABLISHMENTS

The number of establishments providing education for children and adults during the 1973, 1974 and 1976 school years is found in (MEP-SSE: 1974h; MEP-SSE: 1975c and MEP-SSE: 1976d). All three documents contain detailed information on the number of private and public educational establishments and sections operating in each one of them by region and mode (pre-elementary, elementary, high school and other) as well as type (scientific-humanist and technical-professional high school) education but for different years. Detailed information on the number, regional distribution and type of public educational establishments is found, however, only in (MEP-SSE: 1976d, 10). The number and type of children's schools in Chile in 1976 are found in Table 9.18.

TABLE 9.18

Education of Children. Number of Establishments and Sections by Dependency and According to Type of Education. 1976 School Year.

Type of Education	Total for Country					
	Total		Public		Private	
	E	S	E	S	E	S
Overall Total	8,900	2,232	6,901	1,640	1,999	592
Pre-Elementary Education	122	1,734	54	1,270	68	464
Elementary Education	8,050	329	6,448	208	1,602	121
-Special Elementary	101	122	93	122	8	-
-Regular Elementary	7,949	207	6,355	86	1,594	121
-General 1st Class	1,624	-	1,624	-	-	-
-General 2nd Class	4,443	-	4,443	-	-	-
-General Without Category	1,802	-	211	-	1,591	-
-Consolidated	-	30	-	30	-	-
-Household	42	-	39	-	3	-
-Other	38	177	38	56	-	121
High School Education	700	169	371	162	329	7
-Scientific-Humanistic	500	97	234	96	266	1
-Technical-Professional	200	72	137	66	63	6
-Commercial	55	25	46	22	9	3
-Industrial	75	24	56	24	19	-
-Technical	45	22	27	19	18	3
-Agricultural	25	1	8	1	17	-
Other Types	28	-	28	-	-	-
-Artistic Development	17	-	17	-	-	-
-Sports	7	-	7	-	-	-
-Other	4	-	4	-	-	-

Notes: E stands for the actual establishments.
S stands for sections of the establishments providing the type of education indicated.

Source: República de Chile, Ministerio de Educación Pública, Superintendencia, Sección Estadística, Educación de Niños y Adultos, Número de Establecimientos Por Regiones y Dependencia, Según Tipo de Educación, Año Escolar 1976 (Santiago, Chile: MEP:SSE, 1976), p. 3.

PART III
LABOR FORCE

10
LABOR FORCE: COUNTRYWIDE

DATA

INTRODUCTION

The age, sex, sectoral and occupational structure of the labor force is an indicator of a country's level of economic development. Economic development is measured by the level of labor productivity and has as its goal a continuous rise in the productivity of all members of the labor force and improved economic welfare of all inhabitants of a nation. The quality of the labor force shapes technological progress, income distribution and capital formation. In turn, income distribution and capital formation influence the level, quality and nature of the labor force, the inactive population and their various components.

Whether the goal is to determine the welfare level of the population, or to understand the historical process of economic development, or to develop short-, medium-, or long-term strategies to improve the economic welfare of the economically active and inactive segments of the population, reliable and up-to-date statistical information on the labor force, the inactive population, employment and unemployment and other components of the labor force are necessary. The statistics relating to various dimensions of the Chilean labor force that are important to historians, economists, planners, sociologists and so forth are too numerous to be included in one volume, let alone in one or a few chapters. Presented, therefore, in Chapters 10, 11, 12 and 13 of this volume are only those aggregate or long-term statistics that are indispensable and, to some extent, almost sufficient in understanding the central forces of the evolution of Chile's labor force.

The Continuous Labor Force Surveys

Continuous and comprehensive series on the labor force, employment and unemployment for Chile as a whole are available only since 1966. The continuous survey of the labor force was started in 1966 as part of the national sample of households which, in turn, was carried out within the series of sample investigations. The overall project was carried out initially under a contract between the Dirección de Estadística y Censos and the Centro de Estudios Estadístico-Matemáticos of the University of Chile. They were subsequently carried out by the National Institute of Statistics.

A detailed description of the objectives, concepts and instruments of the overall sample investigations, of the objective of the continuous labor force survey and of the characteristics to be studied and definitions utilized in the labor force survey is found in DEC-CONCEM, Continuous Employment Survey, Muestra Nacional de Hogares. Encuesta Continua de Mano de Obra. Julio-Octubre (Santiago, Chile: DEC-

CONCEM, December 1966). Data for subsequent years along with condensed or updated methodological notes are found in DEC-CONCEM. Continuous Employment Survey (1967; 1968a; 1968b) and in INE (1971c and 1971d). A variety of tables based on these continuous labor force surveys are included in Chapters 10, 11, 12 and 13.

The Economically Active Population: 1940-1970

The active population of Chile in 1952 by type of economic activity and occupational position and provinces according to the census of 1952 corrected and centered in June is presented in Table 10.1. The economic activities included are those of agriculture, fishing, mining, industry, construction, electricity, water, gas and sanitary services, trade, transport, storage and communications and services. The active population figures found in Table 10.1 are also classified by occupational position or employment status. In the classification of Table 10.1 employers (empleadores) are distinguished from employees on the one hand and from workers on own account or independent workers (trabajadores por cuenta propia) on the other. Workers on own account do not employ labor for pay, but they, as well as employers, may be assisted by unpaid family workers or family helpers (familiares no remunerados) who are distinguished as a separate group in Table 10.1. Employees in Chile have been traditionally divided into salaried employees (empleados) and wage employees (obreros).

Although salaried employees were originally the non-manual workers or clerical and office workers and wage employees were the manual workers or operatives, in subsequent years the distinction became increasingly legal in nature. Since the benefits received by the salaried employees were substantially better and broader than those received by wage employees, many unions aimed at and succeeded in changing the classification of their members from the wage to the salaried employee group.

For a discussion of the nature and changes in the structure of the labor force in Chile, the growth in productivity of labor, employment and unemployment and so forth, the reader is referred to (Mamalakis: 1976d) and the studies cited in it.

The active population of Chile in 1960 by type of economic activity, occupational status and provinces according to the census of 1960 corrected and centered in June is presented in Table 10.2.

Estimates and projections of the active population of Chile between 1940 and 1970 by type of activity and occupational position in the middle of each year are presented in Table 10.3. These estimates, projections and interpolations were prepared by Alberto Spottke of CORFO and ODEPLAN.

The economically active population of twelve years and over according to sex and type of economic activity for the census years of 1952, 1960 and 1970 is presented in Table 10.4. A comparison between the census figures for 1952, 1960 and 1970 presented in Tables 10.1, 10.2, 10.3 and 10.4 reveals that the latest, revised estimates of Chile's active population prepared by the National Institute of Statistics and presented in Table 10.4 give figures that are lower than those found in the earlier estimates. The downward correction in the figures for the economically active population is strongest for 1970 and reflects changes in or statistical problems with the figures of natality, mortality and international migration, as explained in earlier chapters.

There exists the need for a major, comprehensive study of the figures of population and economically active labor force for as many census and non-census years as possible, for a study which would incorporate such factors as domestic and international migration as well as births and deaths. The National Institute of Statistics needs additional resources to improve the coverage and quality of its on-going surveys and in order to undertake some new, special ones required to fill existing gaps in statistical information. Hopefully, a high quality population census for 1980 will provide the information needed to adjust and correct annual data for the years since the 1970 census.

Economically Active Population: Sex and Occupational Categories

Absolute and relative figures of the economically active population of twelve years and over according to sex and broad occupational categories for the census years of 1952, 1960 and 1970 are presented in Table 10.5. Furthermore, figures on the Chilean population of twelve years of age and over by sex and according to age groups and economic activity for the census years of

TABLE 10.1

Active Population in 1952 by Type of Activity, Occupational Position and Provinces, According to the Census of the Same Year Corrected and Centered in June.

1952	Agriculture 01/03					
	Employers 1	Own-Account Workers 2	Salaried Employees 3	Wage Employees 4	Unpaid Family Workers 5	Total 6
1 Tarapacá	110	2,341	95	1,997	869	5,412
2 Antofagasta	29	528	45	753	115	1,470
3 Atacama	258	919	139	3,107	200	4,623
4 Coquimbo	670	9,178	703	19,715	2,334	32,600
5 Aconcagua	284	3,308	739	16,839	740	21,910
6 Valparaíso	366	4,181	1,100	19,705	733	26,085
7 Santiago	1,999	7,652	3,945	58,973	2,860	75,429
8 O'Higgins	620	3,913	1,341	35,825	523	42,222
9 Colchagua	480	2,754	1,167	27,867	352	32,620
10 Curicó	432	2,248	773	15,055	348	18,856
11 Talca	564	4,015	1,624	20,054	708	32,965
12 Maule	381	4,019	588	8,854	631	14,473
13 Linares	770	4,433	1,766	24,586	869	32,424
14 Ñuble	1,481	13,723	1,767	34,921	2,749	54,641
15 Concepción	958	5,170	882	16,904	1,334	25,249
16 Auraco	319	2,842	317	8,673	786	12,937
17 Bío-Bío	944	5,903	1,124	20,947	1,266	30,184
18 Malleco	714	9,300	918	17,229	2,090	30,311
19 Cautín	1,807	32,027	1,749	28,528	6,698	70,809
20 Valdivia	1,373	9,465	1,367	24,991	2,047	39,243
21 Osorno	1,282	4,389	859	15,536	886	22,952
22 Llanquihue	993	10,631	551	12,109	3,180	27,464
23 Chiloé	106	16,617	132	3,884	5,393	26,132
24 Aisén	148	1,615	142	2,169	464	4,538
25 Magallanes	198	254	358	4,697	34	5,541
Country	17,286	161,426	24,251	449,418	38,209	691,090

TABLE 10.1 (Cont'd)

Active Population in 1952 by Type of Activity, Occupational Position and Provinces, According to the Census of the Same Year Corrected and Centered in June.

1952	Fishing 04					
	Employers 1	Own-Account Workers 2	Salaried Employees 3	Wage Employees 4	Unpaid Family Workers 5	Total 6
1 Tarapacá	4	351	23	247	10	635
2 Antofagasta	2	270	7	127	1	407
3 Atacama	1	71	1	25	1	99
4 Coquimbo	1	393	7	130	43	574
5 Aconcagua	-	70	1	14	1	86
6 Valparaíso	4	667	45	629	26	1,371
7 Santiago	4	267	59	197	15	542
8 O'Higgins	-	1	-	1	-	2
9 Colchagua	1	92	2	8	6	109
10 Curicó	-	20	1	19	3	43
11 Talca	-	4	-	1	-	5
12 Maule	-	93	2	29	6	130
13 Linares	-	8	-	2	-	10
14 Ñuble	-	17	-	3	-	20
15 Concepción	5	1,359	27	401	82	1,874
16 Auraco	1	449	-	14	17	481
17 Bío-Bío	-	2	-	1	-	3
18 Malleco	-	-	-	3	-	3
19 Cautín	1	249	1	53	7	311
20 Valdivia	5	379	2	20	17	423
21 Osorno	-	-	-	12	-	12
22 Llanquihue	8	556	13	265	44	886
23 Chiloé	5	421	3	246	20	695
24 Aisén	-	89	-	42	18	149
25 Magallanes	-	50	1	8	-	59
Country	42	5,878	195	2,497	317	8,929

TABLE 10.1 (Cont'd)

Active Population in 1952 by Type of Activity, Occupational Position and Provinces, According to the Census of the Same Year Corrected and Centered in June.

1952	Mining 1					
	Employers 1	Own-Account Workers 2	Salaried Employees 3	Wage Employees 4	Unpaid Family Workers 5	Total 6
1 Tarapacá	33	85	1,181	8,594	10	9,903
2 Antofagasta	60	235	5,148	28,584	11	34,038
3 Atacama	139	968	875	9,012	51	11,045
4 Coquimbo	107	1,384	588	7,214	108	9,401
5 Aconcagua	16	58	169	1,793	4	2,040
6 Valparaíso	21	41	376	2,061	7	2,506
7 Santiago	117	447	1,142	3,522	26	5,254
8 O'Higgins	8	56	1,328	6,269	4	7,665
9 Colchagua	11	40	21	233	2	307
10 Curicó	2	13	2	28	1	46
11 Talca	9	16	19	469	-	513
12 Maule	1	2	9	68	1	81
13 Linares	-	2	9	50	-	61
14 Ñuble	4	8	17	68	2	99
15 Concepción	26	36	1,099	17,357	5	18,523
16 Auraco	8	14	151	3,147	1	3,321
17 Bío-Bío	-	1	6	13	-	20
18 Malleco	7	21	10	107	4	149
19 Cautín	6	23	22	228	6	285
20 Valdivia	6	39	45	736	-	826
21 Osorno	-	13	2	47	5	67
22 Llanquihue	7	3	6	19	1	36
23 Chiloé	3	-	1	15	-	19
24 Aisén	1	5	61	364	-	431
25 Magallanes	11	19	418	2,051	1	2,500
Country	603	3,529	12,705	92,049	250	109,136

TABLE 10.1 (Cont'd)

Active Population in 1952 by Type of Activity, Occupational Position and Provinces, According to the Census of the Same Year Corrected and Centered in June.

1952	Industry 2-3					
	Employers 1	Own-Account Workers 2	Salaried Employees 3	Wage Employees 4	Unpaid Family Workers 5	Total 6
1 Tarapacá	83	1,810	390	2,075	35	4,393
2 Antofagasta	125	3,256	842	3,331	69	7,623
3 Atacama	56	1,315	270	1,277	56	2,974
4 Coquimbo	215	4,958	730	3,444	223	9,570
5 Aconcagua	127	2,450	587	3,077	90	6,331
6 Valparaíso	941	10,971	6,770	27,206	301	46,189
7 Santiago	6,526	40,139	33,581	134,623	1,537	216,406
8 O'Higgins	167	4,089	622	3,879	141	8,898
9 Colchagua	106	2,502	367	1,854	82	4,911
10 Curicó	86	1,572	274	1,320	36	3,288
11 Talca	192	3,223	978	4,225	26	8,644
12 Maule	47	1,593	173	695	73	2,581
13 Linares	141	2,827	444	1,654	72	5,138
14 Ñuble	215	4,928	589	3,127	273	9,132
15 Concepción	491	7,216	4,389	24,914	239	37,254
16 Auraco	40	1,024	120	847	35	2,066
17 Bío-Bío	116	1,956	304	2,110	66	4,552
18 Malleco	110	2,762	567	3,352	116	6,907
19 Cautín	487	6,898	1,317	6,162	313	15,177
20 Valdivia	312	3,799	1,320	10,639	91	16,161
21 Osorno	235	2,561	721	3,975	67	7,559
22 Llanquihue	229	2,452	511	3,202	175	6,569
23 Chiloé	63	1,786	113	934	60	2,956
24 Aisén	33	440	61	527	37	1,098
25 Magallanes	128	1,198	329	2,284	9	3,948
Country	11,271	117,725	56,369	250,738	4,222	440,325

TABLE 10.1 (Cont'd)

Active Population in 1952 by Type of Activity, Occupational Position and Provinces, According to the Census of the Same Year Corrected and Centered in June.

1952	Construction 4					
	Employers 1	Own-Account Workers 2	Salaried Employees 3	Wage Employees 4	Unpaid Family Workers 5	Total 6
1 Tarapacá	10	180	118	1,376	2	1,686
2 Antofagasta	22	274	401	3,391	1	4,089
3 Atacama	12	68	64	630	-	774
4 Coquimbo	70	328	593	6,885	17	7,893
5 Aconcagua	22	205	168	1,677	12	2,084
6 Valparaíso	127	1,782	703	9,252	14	11,878
7 Santiago	799	6,396	3,767	35,376	68	46,406
8 O'Higgins	18	312	213	2,519	7	3,069
9 Colchagua	20	237	61	933	5	1,256
10 Curicó	4	195	53	872	1	1,125
11 Talca	29	381	121	1,728	4	2,263
12 Maule	16	107	66	955	2	1,146
13 Linares	21	299	145	1,632	15	2,112
14 Ñuble	37	355	201	2,733	12	3,338
15 Concepción	76	674	318	5,143	13	6,224
16 Auraco	7	61	30	498	1	597
17 Bío-Bío	19	205	103	1,147	1	1,475
18 Malleco	11	193	111	1,325	11	1,651
19 Cautín	41	384	145	2,348	4	2,922
20 Valdivia	38	281	140	2,006	1	2,466
21 Osorno	56	180	123	1,519	4	1,882
22 Llanquihue	14	160	130	1,305	8	1,617
23 Chiloé	5	74	39	749	2	869
24 Aisén	2	31	43	541	-	617
25 Magallanes	29	114	59	1,117	-	1,319
Country	1,505	13,476	7,915	87,657	205	110,758

TABLE 10.1 (Cont'd)

Active Population in 1952 by Type of Activity, Occupational Position and Provinces, According to the Census of the Same Year Corrected and Centered in June.

1952	Electricity, Water, Gas and Sanitary Services 5					
	Employers 1	Own-Account Workers 2	Salaried Employees 3	Wage Employees 4	Unpaid Family Workers 5	Total 6
1 Tarapacá	1	1	99	269	-	370
2 Antofagasta	2	3	104	284	-	393
3 Atacama	-	3	42	67	-	112
4 Coquimbo	3	8	200	1,767	1	1,979
5 Aconcagua	3	1	74	194	-	272
6 Valparaíso	-	9	697	2,071	2	2,779
7 Santiago	21	86	3,106	5,980	3	9,199
8 O'Higgins	-	1	115	363	1	480
9 Colchagua	1	3	61	120	-	185
10 Curicó	-	1	57	113	-	171
11 Talca	2	2	322	1,658	-	1,984
12 Maule	-	1	46	82	-	129
13 Linares	-	2	59	126	-	155
14 Ñuble	3	2	100	246	1	352
15 Concepción	4	5	332	879	2	1,222
16 Auraco	-	2	15	86	-	103
17 Bío-Bío	1	2	80	400	-	483
18 Malleco	-	1	72	153	2	228
19 Cautín	1	4	127	338	1	471
20 Valdivia	1	6	87	230	-	324
21 Osorno	2	1	80	169	-	252
22 Llanquihue	1	-	44	109	-	154
23 Chiloé	1	-	14	40	-	55
24 Aisén	-	-	7	26	-	33
25 Magallanes	2	1	45	187	-	235
Country	52	145	5,985	15,957	13	22,152

TABLE 10.1 (Cont'd)

Active Population in 1952 by Type of Activity, Occupational Position and Provinces, According to the Census of the Same Year Corrected and Centered in June.

1952	Trade 6					
	Employers 1	Own-Account Workers 2	Salaried Employees 3	Wage Employees 4	Unpaid Family Workers 5	Total 6
1 Tarapacá	101	2,211	1,023	554	155	4,044
2 Antofagasta	224	2,875	1,846	786	164	5,895
3 Atacama	76	1,269	649	345	83	2,422
4 Coquimbo	229	4,815	1,762	738	465	8,009
5 Aconcagua	150	2,388	1,022	359	209	4,128
6 Valparaíso	1,094	11,007	10,647	3,669	750	27,167
7 Santiago	4,770	39,859	44,507	13,234	3,432	105,800
8 O'Higgins	235	4,065	1,410	629	297	6,636
9 Colchagua	127	2,029	684	276	135	3,251
10 Curicó	131	1,506	801	236	116	2,790
11 Talca	138	2,940	1,446	683	135	5,392
12 Maule	36	1,026	301	73	92	1,528
13 Linares	155	2,260	831	354	142	3,742
14 Ñuble	217	3,664	1,440	545	372	6,288
15 Concepción	600	7,407	4,854	2,152	609	15,622
16 Auraco	41	1,103	240	125	74	1,583
17 Bío-Bío	111	1,741	701	292	130	2,975
18 Malleco	80	2,150	767	374	151	3,522
19 Cautín	438	5,137	2,531	1,304	310	9,720
20 Valdivia	287	2,936	1,871	1,106	201	6,401
21 Osorno	230	1,437	1,224	443	70	3,404
22 Llanquihue	191	1,610	977	413	138	3,329
23 Chiloé	39	951	190	47	43	1,270
24 Aisén	40	333	128	56	27	584
25 Magallanes	148	826	955	339	25	2,293
Country	9,938	107,543	82,807	29,182	8,325	237,795

TABLE 10.1 (Cont'd)

Active Population in 1952 By Type of Activity, Occupational Position and Provinces, According to the Census of the Same Year Corrected and Centered in June.

1952	Transport, Storage and Communications 7					
	Employers 1	Own-Account Workers 2	Salaried Employees 3	Wage Employees 4	Unpaid Family Workers 5	Total 6
1 Tarapacá	17	471	1,248	2,273	2	4,011
2 Antofagasta	24	656	2,497	3,912	11	7,100
3 Atacama	6	281	607	1,136	4	2,034
4 Coquimbo	45	577	1,538	2,119	20	4,299
5 Aconcagua	18	300	753	819	6	1,896
6 Valparaíso	107	1,493	6,648	6,501	15	14,764
7 Santiago	473	6,065	19,424	8,757	74	34,293
8 O'Higgins	14	485	803	766	8	2,076
9 Colchagua	12	233	529	480	3	1,257
10 Curicó	13	179	386	293	6	877
11 Talca	28	353	931	606	4	1,922
12 Maule	6	132	210	171	-	519
13 Linares	9	217	523	339	5	1,093
14 Ñuble	23	343	811	605	13	1,795
15 Concepción	40	749	2,889	3,097	19	6,794
16 Auraco	4	69	173	359	-	605
17 Bío-Bío	4	187	410	454	1	1,056
18 Malleco	9	208	838	683	8	1,746
19 Cautín	30	480	1,456	1,137	10	3,113
20 Valdivia	35	445	1,437	2,138	13	4,068
21 Osorno	20	239	561	632	2	1,454
22 Llanquihue	32	281	701	848	9	1,871
23 Chiloé	22	104	369	378	6	879
24 Aisén	6	85	107	244	3	445
25 Magallanes	15	413	563	1,423	4	2,418
Country	1,012	15,045	46,412	40,170	246	102,385

TABLE 10.1 (Cont'd)

Active Population in 1952 by Type of Activity, Occupational Position and Provinces, According to the Census of the Same Year Corrected and Centered in June.

	Services 8						
	Employers 1	Own-Account Workers 2	Salaried Employees 3	Wage Employees 4	Unpaid Family Workers 5	Total 6	Overall Total 7
1 Tarapacá	56	1,068	6,177	2,286	53	9,640	40,094
2 Antofagasta	115	1,904	7,058	4,683	65	13,825	74,840
3 Atacama	52	1,015	1,966	2,146	68	5,247	29,330
4 Coquimbo	147	2,583	4,834	8,018	149	15,731	90,056
5 Aconcagua	92	1,249	5,035	4,302	86	10,764	49,511
6 Valparaíso	608	6,343	27,483	25,293	314	60,041	192,780
7 Santiago	2,399	23,764	80,410	108,824	1,079	216,476	709,805
8 O'Higgins	154	2,384	3,593	6,614	133	12,878	83,926
9 Colchagua	65	1,147	2,149	3,840	41	7,242	51,138
10 Curicó	40	939	1,806	3,146	33	5,964	33,160
11 Talca	96	1,485	3,374	5,769	38	10,762	64,450
12 Maule	24	481	1,571	2,210	12	4,298	24,885
13 Linares	63	1,054	3,072	4,314	35	8,538	53,305
14 Ñuble	90	1,796	4,132	8,301	79	14,398	90,063
15 Concepción	235	3,670	15,222	17,933	113	37,173	149,935
16 Auraco	23	416	899	1,721	19	3,078	24,771
17 Bío-Bío	49	792	2,497	4,196	36	7,570	48,318
18 Malleco	40	1,147	3,310	4,632	37	9,166	53,683
19 Cautín	141	2,482	6,160	11,358	71	20,212	123,020
20 Valdivia	124	1,542	4,274	8,327	49	14,316	84,228
21 Osorno	103	977	2,201	5,623	30	8,934	46,516
22 Llanquihue	98	869	2,493	4,657	22	8,139	50,065
23 Chiloé	13	424	1,424	2,549	13	4,423	37,298
24 Aisén	13	296	1,084	887	16	2,296	10,191
25 Magallanes	67	819	3,504	2,296	14	6,700	25,013
Country	4,907	60,646	195,728	253,425	2,605	517,811	2,240,381

TABLE 10.1 (Cont'd)

Active Population in 1952 by Type of Activity, Occupational Position and Provinces, According to the Census of the Same Year Corrected and Centered in June.

1952	Active Population by Occupational Position and by Provinces					
	Employers 1	Own Account Workers 2	Salaried Employees 3	Wage Employees 4	Unpaid Family Workers 5	Total 6
1 Tarapacá	415	8,518	10,354	19,671	1,136	40,094
2 Antofagasta	603	10,001	17,948	45,851	437	74,840
3 Atacama	600	5,909	4,613	17,745	463	29,330
4 Coquimbo	1,487	24,224	10,955	50,030	3,360	90,056
5 Aconcagua	712	10,029	8,548	29,074	1,148	49,511
6 Valparaíso	3,268	36,494	54,469	96,387	2,162	192,780
7 Santiago	17,111	124,673	189,941	368,986	9,094	709,805
8 O'Higgins	1,216	15,306	9,425	56,865	1,114	83,926
9 Colchagua	823	9,037	5,041	35,611	626	51,138
10 Curicó	708	6,673	4,153	21,082	544	33,160
11 Talca	1,108	12,419	8,815	41,193	915	64,450
12 Maule	511	7,454	2,966	13,137	817	24,885
13 Linares	1,159	11,102	6,849	33,059	1,138	53,305
14 Ñuble	2,070	24,836	9,057	50,599	3,501	90,063
15 Concepción	2,435	26,289	30,012	88,785	2,416	149,935
16 Auraco	443	5,980	1,945	15,470	933	24,771
17 Bío-Bío	1,244	10,789	5,225	29,560	1,500	48,318
18 Malleco	971	15,782	6,653	27,858	2,419	53,683
19 Cautín	2,952	47,684	13,508	51,456	7,420	123,020
20 Valdivia	2,181	18,892	10,543	50,193	2,419	84,228
21 Osorno	1,928	9,797	5,771	27,956	1,064	46,516
22 Llanquihue	1,573	16,562	5,426	22,927	3,577	50,065
23 Chiloé	257	20,377	2,285	8,842	5,537	37,298
24 Aisén	243	2,894	1,633	4,856	565	10,191
25 Magallanes	598	3,694	6,232	14,402	87	25,013
Country	46,616	485,413	432,367	1,221,593	54,392	2,240,381

Source: Planning Office of the Presidency of the Republic. The help of Alberto Spottke in preparing this table is greatly appreciated.

TABLE 10.2

Active Population in 1960 by Type of Activity, Occupational Position and Provinces, According to the Census of the Same Year Corrected and Centered in June.

1960	Agriculture, Forestry, Hunting and Fishing 01/04						
	Employers 1	Own-Account Workers 2	Salaried Employees 3	Wage Employees 4	Paid Family Workers 5	Unpaid Family Workers 6	Total 7
1 Tarapacá	49	3,181	136	2,188	91	426	6,071
2 Antofagasta	17	1,329	45	733	28	72	2,224
3 Atacama	57	1,815	114	2,648	157	163	4,954
4 Coquimbo	311	10,375	709	18,625	881	2,247	33,148
5 Aconcagua	156	2,976	589	16,742	536	526	21,525
6 Valparaíso	311	4,488	840	20,948	423	389	27,399
7 Santiago	1,786	8,250	3,770	61,588	882	688	76,964
8 O'Higgins	708	3,346	1,006	34,480	457	297	40,294
9 Colchagua	264	3,229	1,096	26,686	358	393	32,026
10 Curicó	171	2,185	852	15,933	356	298	19,795
11 Talca	308	4,056	1,569	27,789	556	634	34,912
12 Maule	403	3,821	421	9,167	596	1,067	15,475
13 Linares	334	4,482	1,380	25,655	791	510	33,152
14 Ñuble	778	12,759	1,577	35,865	2,052	3,212	56,243
15 Concepción	420	8,160	525	17,308	675	1,546	28,634
16 Auraco	127	3,145	262	7,807	988	576	12,905
17 Bío-Bío	405	5,951	1,246	21,128	1,019	1,303	31,052
18 Malleco	415	8,363	850	16,557	1,223	1,593	29,001
19 Cautín	795	30,520	1,425	25,264	4,368	8,474	70,846
20 Valdivia	668	10,329	1,219	23,860	951	1,597	38,624
21 Osorno	956	4,364	667	15,525	604	1,345	23,461
22 Llanquihue	824	9,367	393	12,009	816	3,103	26,512
23 Chiloé	2,750	10,443	63	2,879	700	4,328	21,163
24 Aisén	87	2,167	164	2,555	202	473	5,648
25 Magallanes	104	510	330	3,994	79	22	5,039
Country	13,204	159,611	21,248	447,933	19,789	35,282	697,067

TABLE 10.2 (Cont'd)

Active Population in 1960 by Type of Activity, Occupational Position and Provinces, According to the Census of the Same Year Corrected and Centered in June.

1960	Mining 1						
	Employers 1	Own-Account Workers 2	Salaried Employees 3	Wage Employees 4	Paid Family Workers 5	Unpaid Family Workers 6	Total 7
1 Tarapacá	12	59	427	2,150	2	-	2,650
2 Antofagasta	29	131	4,292	18,723	5	-	23,180
3 Atacama	67	1,079	1,850	11,721	43	10	14,770
4 Coquimbo	45	970	1,064	9,174	13	18	11,284
5 Aconcagua	4	27	161	1,453	3	-	1,648
6 Valparaíso	19	38	187	1,253	-	1	1,498
7 Santiago	102	417	1,080	3,065	7	13	4,684
8 O'Higgins	5	62	1,347	5,893	-	-	7,307
9 Colchagua	3	39	5	292	7	4	350
10 Curicó	-	7	3	17	-	-	27
11 Talca	-	16	8	100	-	-	124
12 Maule	1	1	-	36	-	-	38
13 Linares	-	19	4	47	-	-	70
14 Ñuble	1	7	6	94	-	-	108
15 Concepción	6	69	1,245	13,920	-	-	15,220
16 Auraco	-	3	204	4,419	-	1	4,627
17 Bío-Bío	-	4	4	131	2	-	141
18 Malleco	-	15	8	95	-	1	119
19 Cautín	-	17	7	201	-	-	225
20 Valdivia	1	7	35	231	-	1	275
21 Osorno	1	37	7	13	-	-	58
22 Llanquihue	2	3	10	21	-	1	37
23 Chiloé	3	12	3	7	-	4	29
24 Aisén	-	1	64	421	-	-	486
25 Magallanes	5	35	855	2,134	-	-	3,029
Country	306	3,055	12,876	75,611	82	54	91,984

TABLE 10.2 (Cont'd)

Active Population in 1960 by Type of Activity, Occupational Position and Provinces, According to the Census of the Same Year Corrected and Centered in June.

1960	Industry 2-3						
	Employers 1	Own-Account Workers 2	Salaried Employees 3	Wage Employees 4	Paid Family Workers 5	Unpaid Family Workers 6	Total 7
1 Tarapacá	116	1,620	799	3,452	18	7	6,012
2 Antofagasta	86	2,422	897	4,656	45	22	8,128
3 Atacama	30	1,346	506	2,133	16	7	4,038
4 Coquimbo	114	3,854	739	3,633	79	65	8,484
5 Aconcagua	82	1,858	467	2,818	38	24	5,287
6 Valparaíso	710	8,919	6,971	26,344	207	86	43,237
7 Santiago	5,948	36,744	37,644	151,592	952	377	233,257
8 O'Higgins	110	2,517	693	3,565	51	33	6,969
9 Colchagua	43	1,669	477	1,915	39	19	4,162
10 Curicó	37	1,180	458	1,030	34	20	2,759
11 Talca	91	2,569	1,130	4,107	70	20	7,987
12 Maule	51	906	126	757	19	7	1,866
13 Linares	64	1,871	678	1,940	73	26	4,652
14 Ñuble	150	3,351	685	3,328	108	49	7,671
15 Concepción	386	6,541	4,942	28,183	121	62	40,235
16 Auraco	9	770	95	956	30	12	1,872
17 Bío-Bío	52	1,832	776	3,437	44	30	6,171
18 Malleco	106	1,966	507	2,873	37	27	5,516
19 Cautín	254	4,591	1,229	6,043	103	154	12,374
20 Valdivia	119	3,159	942	5,898	53	35	10,206
21 Osorno	95	2,563	604	3,752	78	34	7,126
22 Llanquihue	110	2,615	585	3,656	65	148	7,179
23 Chiloé	47	981	64	783	17	34	1,926
24 Aisén	16	516	95	757	22	12	1,418
25 Magallanes	52	1,070	399	1,998	24	13	3,556
Country	8,878	97,430	62,508	269,606	2,343	1,323	442,088

TABLE 10.2 (Cont'd)

Active Population in 1960 by Type of Activity, Occupation Position and Provinces, According to the Census of the Same Year Corrected and Centered in June.

1960	Construction 4						
	Employers 1	Own-Account Workers 2	Salaried Employees 3	Wage Employees 4	Paid Family Workers 5	Unpaid Family Workers 6	Total 7
1 Tarapacá	33	375	329	3,624	3	1	4,365
2 Antofagasta	19	260	350	4,206	7	4	4,846
3 Atacama	7	192	223	1,939	-	-	2,361
4 Coquimbo	8	430	263	2,541	12	3	3,257
5 Aconcagua	10	243	83	1,200	1	2	1,539
6 Valparaíso	68	1,438	568	8,464	18	2	10,558
7 Santiago	575	5,663	3,785	39,137	61	14	49,235
8 O'Higgins	23	311	178	3,197	5	2	3,716
9 Colchagua	3	242	92	805	7	7	1,156
10 Curicó	6	159	87	715	3	1	971
11 Talca	10	327	171	2,408	5	-	2,921
12 Maule	5	72	41	782	1	3	904
13 Linares	3	297	236	2,167	3	4	2,710
14 Ñuble	3	457	263	2,886	18	4	3,631
15 Concepción	57	960	645	9,527	19	5	11,213
16 Auraco	2	82	57	803	3	-	947
17 Bío-Bío	8	129	161	2,413	1	1	2,713
18 Malleco	15	243	130	1,890	-	-	2,278
19 Cautín	15	354	260	3,463	3	2	4,097
20 Valdivia	23	363	396	5,812	5	3	6,602
21 Osorno	13	268	140	2,477	2	1	2,901
22 Llanquihue	14	306	202	3,033	6	4	3,565
23 Chiloé	4	184	90	890	-	2	1,170
24 Aisén	1	72	45	489	-	1	608
25 Magallanes	14	181	144	1,877	1	-	2,217
Country	939	13,608	8,939	106,745	184	66	130,481

TABLE 10.2 (Cont'd)

Active Population in 1960 by Type of Activity, Occupational Position and Provinces, According to the Census of the Same Year Corrected and Centered in June.

1960	Electricity, Water, Gas and Sanitary Services 5						
	Employers 1	Own-Account Workers 2	Salaried Employees 3	Wage Employees 4	Paid Family Workers 5	Unpaid Family Workers 6	Total 7
1 Tarapacá	1	-	76	223	-	-	300
2 Antofagasta	1	5	199	412	-	-	617
3 Atacama	-	3	49	116	-	-	168
4 Coquimbo	-	5	162	398	-	-	565
5 Aconcagua	-	2	95	140	-	-	237
6 Valparaíso	4	33	686	1,484	1	-	2,208
7 Santiago	12	157	4,331	5,169	2	1	9,672
8 O'Higgins	1	3	133	285	-	-	422
9 Colchagua	-	-	52	68	-	-	120
10 Curicó	-	2	60	71	-	-	133
11 Talca	1	10	261	491	-	-	763
12 Maule	-	3	47	111	-	-	161
13 Linares	-	7	62	93	-	-	162
14 Ñuble	-	6	142	267	-	-	415
15 Concepción	1	13	388	752	-	1	1,155
16 Auraco	1	-	24	55	-	-	80
17 Bío-Bío	1	1	95	444	-	-	541
18 Malleco	-	-	77	67	-	-	144
19 Cautín	2	2	155	267	-	-	426
20 Valdivia	1	4	115	560	-	-	680
21 Osorno	2	1	76	139	-	-	218
22 Llanquihue	1	5	33	82	-	-	121
23 Chiloé	-	1	36	77	-	-	114
24 Aisén	-	1	29	132	-	-	162
25 Magallanes	1	1	78	181	-	-	261
Country	30	265	7,461	12,084	3	2	19,845

TABLE 10.2 (Cont'd)

Active Population in 1960 by Type of Activity, Occupational Position and Provinces, According to the Census of the Same Year Corrected and Centered in June.

1960	Trade 6						
	Employers 1	Own-Account Workers 2	Salaried Employees 3	Wage Employees 4	Paid Family Workers 5	Unpaid Family Workers 6	Total 7
1 Tarapacá	177	3,064	1,638	435	61	31	5,406
2 Antofagasta	107	3,397	2,079	976	66	69	6,694
3 Atacama	42	1,952	783	400	38	44	3,259
4 Coquimbo	124	5,327	1,557	771	126	131	8,036
5 Aconcagua	44	2,280	705	385	73	80	3,567
6 Valparaíso	982	11,822	9,899	3,989	389	301	27,382
7 Santiago	3,740	52,223	47,388	16,310	1,457	1,058	122,176
8 O'Higgins	135	3,709	1,248	620	66	51	5,829
9 Colchagua	40	1,861	619	250	56	48	2,874
10 Curicó	75	1,423	819	211	28	28	2,584
11 Talca	87	2,822	1,281	459	86	41	4,776
12 Maule	39	937	241	76	33	24	1,350
13 Linares	58	1,983	804	280	46	47	3,218
14 Ñuble	116	3,405	1,355	546	130	92	5,644
15 Concepción	439	8,306	4,375	1,788	215	205	15,328
16 Auraco	13	1,100	174	80	22	13	1,402
17 Bío-Bío	49	1,717	805	245	37	62	2,915
18 Malleco	88	2,026	727	227	44	55	3,167
19 Cautín	132	5,050	2,124	571	102	110	8,089
20 Valdivia	132	2,848	1,497	472	58	44	5,051
21 Osorno	113	1,635	1,144	484	55	21	3,452
22 Llanquihue	143	1,803	990	397	43	37	3,413
23 Chiloé	36	769	184	53	9	29	1,080
24 Aisén	9	474	264	61	6	18	832
25 Magallanes	103	961	1,324	408	37	26	2,859
Country	7,023	122,894	84,024	30,494	3,283	2,665	250,383

TABLE 10.2 (Cont'd)

Active Population in 1960 by Type of Activity, Occupational Position and Provinces, According to the Census of the Same Year Corrected and Centered in June.

1960	Transport, Storage and Communications 7						
	Employers 1	Own-Account Workers 2	Salaried Employees 3	Wage Employees 4	Paid Family Workers 5	Unpaid Family Workers 6	Total 7
1 Tarapacá	12	883	1,795	2,282	13	4	4,989
2 Antofagasta	20	884	2,670	4,276	37	12	7,899
3 Atacama	8	622	1,018	1,445	20	5	3,118
4 Coquimbo	19	939	1,771	2,056	47	21	4,853
5 Aconcagua	10	398	679	753	23	7	1,870
6 Valparaíso	103	2,107	7,821	7,002	58	20	17,111
7 Santiago	404	8,240	23,582	10,116	166	47	42,555
8 O'Higgins	9	557	730	786	14	5	2,101
9 Colchagua	5	305	547	421	10	7	1,295
10 Curicó	2	236	378	255	6	2	879
11 Talca	12	499	929	687	12	2	2,141
12 Maule	2	165	220	211	6	-	604
13 Linares	13	329	563	398	23	8	1,334
14 Ñuble	10	429	881	745	10	12	2,087
15 Concepción	43	1,151	3,023	4,055	26	5	8,303
16 Auraco	-	106	221	503	1	-	831
17 Bío-Bío	4	337	516	748	10	3	1,618
18 Malleco	2	291	675	1,001	5	3	1,977
19 Cautín	15	623	1,569	1,495	6	1	3,709
20 Valdivia	11	590	1,276	2,564	13	3	4,457
21 Osorno	19	404	488	969	4	-	1,884
22 Llanquihue	48	430	915	1,440	16	6	2,855
23 Chiloé	17	113	265	347	5	4	751
24 Aisén	-	168	214	208	4	5	599
25 Magallanes	7	568	573	812	15	2	1,977
Country	795	21,374	53,319	45,575	550	184	121,797

TABLE 10.2 (Cont'd)

Active Population in 1960 by Type of Activity, Occupational Position and Provinces, According to the Census of the Same Year Corrected and Centered in June.

1960	Services 8							Over-all Total
	Employers 1	Own-Account Workers 2	Salaried Employees 3	Wage Employees 4	Paid Family Workers 5	Unpaid Family Workers 6	Total 7	
1 Tarapacá	87	840	7,183	3,110	9	9	11,238	41,031
2 Antofagasta	92	1,384	7,652	5,493	40	26	14,687	68,275
3 Atacama	36	836	2,557	2,563	13	10	6,015	38,683
4 Coquimbo	66	1,779	5,663	7,575	45	41	15,169	84,796
5 Aconcagua	37	715	4,548	3,537	22	15	8,874	44,547
6 Valparaíso	452	4,707	30,321	26,710	104	103	62,397	191,790
7 Santiago	1,875	19,375	117,304	125,106	358	232	264,250	802,793
8 O'Higgins	101	1,457	4,198	6,096	29	23	11,904	78,542
9 Colchagua	23	732	2,416	3,491	18	-	6,680	48,663
10 Curicó	23	451	2,313	2,886	7	15	5,695	32,843
11 Talca	45	1,131	4,320	5,854	22	13	11,385	65,009
12 Maule	22	284	1,671	1,860	5	3	3,845	24,243
13 Linares	34	670	3,425	4,495	14	18	8,656	53,954
14 Ñuble	42	1,130	4,949	7,647	20	13	13,801	89,600
15 Concepción	213	2,785	17,204	17,595	54	19	37,870	157,958
16 Auraco	10	258	1,179	1,750	6	4	3,207	25,871
17 Bío-Bío	35	575	2,674	4,482	4	12	7,782	52,933
18 Malleco	31	679	3,614	4,463	14	10	8,811	51,013
19 Cautín	66	1,272	6,986	10,912	20	17	19,273	119,039
20 Valdivia	68	1,024	4,737	7,640	13	15	13,497	79,392
21 Osorno	49	586	2,583	5,721	9	4	8,952	48,052
22 Llanquihue	42	612	3,095	5,017	15	4	8,785	52,467
23 Chiloé	18	259	1,735	2,187	4	3	4,206	30,439
24 Aisén	17	271	1,510	1,083	5	4	2,890	12,643
25 Magallanes	43	589	7,698	2,768	12	13	11,123	30,061
Country	3,527	44,401	251,535	270,041	862	626	570,992	2,324,637

TABLE 10.2 (Cont'd)

Active Population in 1960 by Type of Activity, Occupational Position and Provinces, According to the Census of the Same Year Corrected and Centered in June.

1960	Active Population by Occupational Position and by Provinces						
	Employers 1	Own-Account Workers 2	Salaried Employees 3	Wage Employees 4	Paid Family Workers 5	Unpaid Family Workers 6	Total 7
1 Tarapacá	487	10,022	12,383	17,464	197	478	41,031
2 Antofagasta	371	9,812	18,184	39,475	228	205	68,275
3 Atacama	247	7,845	7,100	22,965	287	239	38,683
4 Coquimbo	687	23,679	11,928	44,773	1,203	2,526	84,796
5 Aconcagua	343	8,499	7,327	27,028	696	654	44,547
6 Valparaíso	2,649	33,552	57,293	96,194	1,200	902	191,790
7 Santiago	14,442	131,069	238,884	412,083	3,885	2,430	802,793
8 O'Higgins	1,092	11,982	9,533	54,922	622	411	78,542
9 Colchagua	381	8,077	5,304	33,927	495	478	48,663
10 Curicó	314	5,643	4,970	21,118	434	364	32,843
11 Talca	554	11,430	9,669	41,895	751	710	65,009
12 Maule	523	6,189	2,767	13,000	660	1,101	24,243
13 Linares	506	9,658	7,152	35,075	950	613	53,954
14 Ñuble	1,100	21,544	9,858	51,378	2,338	3,382	89,600
15 Concepción	1,565	27,965	32,347	93,128	1,110	1,843	157,958
16 Auraco	162	5,459	2,216	16,373	1,050	606	25,871
17 Bío-Bío	554	10,546	6,277	33,028	1,117	1,411	52,933
18 Malleco	657	25,808	6,587	27,173	1,323	1,689	51,013
19 Cautín	1,279	42,429	13,755	48,216	4,602	8,758	119,039
20 Valdivia	1,023	18,324	10,217	47,037	1,093	1,698	79,392
21 Osorno	1,248	9,858	5,709	29,080	752	1,405	48,052
22 Llanquihue	1,184	15,141	6,223	25,655	961	3,303	52,467
23 Chiloé	2,875	12,762	2,440	7,223	735	4,404	30,439
24 Aisén	130	3,670	2,385	5,706	239	513	12,643
25 Magallanes	329	3,915	11,401	14,167	168	77	30,061
Country	34,702	462,638	501,910	1,258,088	27,096	40,202	2,324,637

Source: The Planning Office of the Presidency of the Republic. The help of Alberto Spottke in preparing this table is greatly appreciated.

TABLE 10.3

Estimates and Projections of Active Population by Type of Activity and Occupational Position in the Middle of Each Year.
(Exponential Interpolations and Extrapolations of Corrected and Centered Census Figures)
1940-1970.

Activity and Occupational Position	1940	1941	1942	1943	1944	1945	1946	1947	1948
Agriculture									
Employers	17,026	17,063	17,106	17,143	17,179	17,223	17,260	17,297	17,340
Own-Account Workers	158,895	159,256	159,616	159,983	160,344	160,705	161,066	161,428	161,790
Salaried Employees	22,665	22,768	22,881	22,987	23,095	23,209	23,317	23,426	23,542
Wage Employees	456,008	458,181	460,350	462,536	464,738	466,937	469,160	471,392	473,622
Total	654,594	657,268	659,953	662,649	665,356	668,074	670,803	673,543	676,294
Fishing									
Employers	22	23	25	26	28	30	32	34	36
Own-Account Workers	2,877	3,060	3,253	3,459	3,676	3,906	4,150	4,410	4,684
Salaried Employees	142	146	151	155	159	164	169	173	178
Wage Employees	2,018	2,078	2,138	2,200	2,263	2,326	2,390	2,454	2,520
Total	5,059	5,307	5,567	5,840	6,126	6,426	6,741	7,071	7,418
Mining									
Employers	357	377	398	418	439	461	483	504	526
Own-Account Workers	2,059	2,177	2,296	2,416	2,538	2,661	2,786	2,913	3,041
Salaried Employees	11,923	11,988	12,053	12,118	12,184	12,249	12,316	12,382	12,448
Wage Employees	86,119	86,584	87,051	87,523	87,995	88,471	88,947	89,428	89,911
Total	100,458	101,126	101,798	102,475	103,156	103,842	104,532	105,227	105,926
Industry									
Employers	8,840	9,041	9,245	9,451	9,664	9,881	10,102	10,328	10,558
Own-Account Workers	91,959	94,041	96,165	98,332	100,542	102,795	105,093	107,439	109,828
Salaried Employees	37,516	38,789	40,104	41,460	42,865	44,317	45,817	47,368	48,970
Wage Employees	168,840	174,564	180,481	186,601	192,920	199,451	206,201	213,172	220,380
Total	307,155	316,435	325,995	335,844	345,991	356,444	367,213	378,307	389,736
Construction									
Employers	600	652	709	768	833	902	976	1,054	1,139
Own-Account Workers	5,368	5,837	6,339	6,877	7,454	8,070	8,729	9,435	10,189
Salaried Employees	4,573	4,784	5,005	5,236	5,478	5,730	5,995	6,271	6,560
Wage Employees	50,531	52,865	55,305	57,858	60,525	63,317	66,235	69,288	72,479
Total	61,072	64,138	67,358	70,739	74,290	78,019	81,935	86,048	90,367

TABLE 10.3 (Cont'd)

Estimates and Projections of Active Population by Type of Activity and Occupational Position in the Middle of Each Year.
(Exponential Interpolations and Extrapolations of Corrected and Centered Census Figures)
1940-1970.

Activity and Occupational Position	1940	1941	1942	1943	1944	1945	1946	1947	1948
Electricity									
Employers	103	103	102	100	99	96	93	89	84
Own-Account Workers	286	285	282	279	273	266	258	246	233
Salaried Employees	2,830	3,010	3,202	3,406	3,623	3,853	4,099	4,360	4,637
Wage Employees	7,513	7,991	8,500	9,041	9,616	10,229	10,878	11,572	12,309
Total	10,732	11,389	12,086	12,826	13,611	14,444	15,328	16,267	17,263
Commerce[1]									
Employers	9,287	9,369	9,450	9,529	9,606	9,682	9,755	9,828	9,895
Own-Account Workers	100,281	101,171	102,043	102,900	103,736	104,551	105,344	106,114	106,857
Salaried Employees	47,711	50,055	52,482	55,000	57,608	60,313	63,113	66,016	69,026
Wage Employees	21,584	22,642	23,743	24,879	26,061	27,283	28,552	29,862	31,222
Total	178,863	183,237	187,718	192,308	197,011	201,829	206,764	211,820	217,000
Transport									
Employers	692	716	740	767	793	820	848	877	906
Own-Account Workers	10,264	10,622	10,992	11,372	11,763	12,166	12,582	13,009	13,449
Salaried Employees	36,358	37,081	37,818	38,568	39,336	40,118	40,914	41,727	42,556
Wage Employees	31,194	31,815	32,448	33,093	33,750	34,420	35,104	35,801	36,512
Total	78,508	80,234	81,998	83,800	85,642	87,524	89,448	91,414	93,423
Services									
Employers	2,877	3,022	3,169	3,327	3,486	3,652	3,825	4,005	4,191
Own-Account Workers	35,453	37,212	39,036	40,938	42,915	44,968	47,106	49,330	51,636
Salaried Employees	143,234	146,913	150,694	154,567	158,539	162,612	166,793	171,076	175,468
Wage Employees	186,721	191,524	196,451	201,498	206,679	211,995	217,438	223,023	228,757
Total	368,285	378,671	389,350	400,330	411,619	423,619	435,162	447,434	460,052
Total	1,764,726	1,797,805	1,831,823	1,866,811	1,902,802	1,939,829	1,977,926	2,017,131	2,057,479
Employers	39,804	40,366	40,944	41,529	42,127	42,747	43,374	44,016	44,675
Own-Account Workers	407,442	413,661	420,022	426,556	433,241	440,088	447,114	454,324	461,707
Salaried Employees	306,952	315,534	324,390	333,497	342,887	352,565	362,533	372,799	383,385
Wage Employees	1,010,528	1,028,244	1,046,467	1,065,229	1,084,547	1,104,429	1,124,905	1,145,992	1,167,712

Notes: 1. Commerce includes wholesale and retail trade banking and real estate.

TABLE 10.3 (Cont'd)

Estimates and Projections of Active Population by Type of Activity and Occupational Position in the Middle of Each Year.
(Exponential Interpolations and Extrapolations of Corrected and Centered Census Figures)
1940-1970.

Activity and Occupational Position	1949	1950	1951	1952	1953	1954	1955	1956	1957
Agriculture									
Employers	17,377	17,414	17,458	17,493	17,503	17,511	17,519	17,534	17,542
Own-Account Workers	162,159	162,521	162,884	163,247	163,361	163,481	163,595	163,704	163,815
Salaried Employees	23,652	23,762	23,879	23,990	24,503	25,011	25,529	26,043	26,568
Wage Employees	475,369	478,134	480,395	482,683	484,269	485,863	487,462	489,067	490,675
Total	679,057	681,831	684,616	687,413	689,636	691,866	694,103	696,348	698,600
Fishing									
Employers	38	40	42	45	49	54	59	65	71
Own-Account Workers	4,976	5,284	5,610	5,956	6,539	7,179	7,881	8,652	9,498
Salaried Employees	183	187	192	197	216	238	261	286	314
Wage Employees	2,585	2,652	2,719	2,786	3,059	3,357	3,686	4,047	4,443
Total	7,782	8,163	8,563	8,984	9,863	10,828	11,887	13,050	14,326
Mining									
Employers	549	572	594	618	612	606	600	594	588
Own-Account Workers	3,170	3,302	3,434	3,569	3,535	3,501	3,466	3,432	3,398
Salaried Employees	12,516	12,583	12,652	12,719	12,990	13,261	13,533	13,805	14,078
Wage Employees	90,395	90,882	91,372	91,863	91,731	91,599	91,467	91,334	91,200
Total	106,630	107,339	108,052	108,769	108,868	108,967	109,066	109,165	109,264
Industry									
Employers	10,739	11,028	11,271	11,521	11,412	11,300	11,192	11,080	10,971
Own-Account Workers	112,262	114,744	117,274	119,848	118,708	117,563	116,415	115,263	114,108
Salaried Employees	50,623	52,334	54,102	55,929	57,119	58,306	59,501	60,695	61,896
Wage Employees	227,837	235,535	243,491	251,713	252,373	253,044	253,707	254,380	255,047
Total	401,511	413,641	426,138	439,011	439,612	440,213	440,815	441,418	442,022
Construction									
Employers	1,229	1,326	1,428	1,538	1,548	1,552	1,551	1,541	1,526
Own-Account Workers	10,995	11,857	12,777	13,760	13,846	13,885	13,869	13,791	13,645
Salaried Employees	6,862	7,178	7,509	7,854	8,060	8,259	8,448	8,629	8,797
Wage Employees	75,817	79,306	82,956	86,773	93,644	101,043	109,011	117,589	126,819
Total	94,903	99,667	104,670	109,925	117,098	124,739	132,879	141,550	150,787

TABLE 10.3 (Cont'd)

Estimates and Projections of Active Population by Type of Activity and Occupational Position in the Middle of Each Year.
(Exponential Interpolations and Extrapolations of Corrected and Centered Census Figures)
1940-1970.

Activity and Occupational Position	1949	1950	1951	1952	1953	1954	1955	1956	1957
Electricity									
Employers	78	72	64	55	56	57	58	59	61
Own-Account Workers	217	199	177	152	155	158	161	164	167
Salaried Employees	4,932	5,247	5,580	5,936	6,046	6,159	6,274	6,391	6,510
Wage Employees	13,093	13,924	14,811	15,754	16,048	16,347	16,652	16,962	17,278
Total	18,320	19,442	20,632	21,897	22,305	22,721	23,145	23,576	24,016
Commerce									
Employers	9,964	10,027	10,088	10,145	10,051	9,958	9,861	9,765	9,665
Own-Account Workers	107,576	108,262	108,922	109,545	108,532	107,507	106,471	105,424	104,364
Salaried Employees	72,136	75,362	78,700	82,159	83,867	85,592	87,330	89,083	90,849
Wage Employees	32,630	34,091	35,601	37,165	37,665	38,164	38,671	39,178	39,694
Total	222,306	227,742	233,311	239,014	240,115	241,221	242,333	243,450	244,572
Transport									
Employers	938	969	1,000	1,034	1,031	1,026	1,019	1,010	999
Own-Account Workers	13,902	14,370	14,850	15,345	15,289	15,210	15,108	14,979	14,821
Salaried Employees	43,400	44,262	45,140	46,035	46,990	47,954	48,928	49,911	50,903
Wage Employees	37,236	37,974	38,730	39,497	42,193	45,032	48,017	51,158	54,461
Total	95,476	97,575	99,720	101,911	105,503	109,222	113,072	117,058	121,184
Services									
Employers	4,390	4,591	4,801	5,017	4,981	4,940	4,896	4,849	4,793
Own-Account Workers	54,636	56,535	59,124	61,817	61,363	60,868	60,334	59,753	59,135
Salaried Employees	179,972	184,595	189,330	194,187	198,067	202,029	206,070	210,197	214,400
Wage Employees	234,625	240,643	246,824	253,152	259,341	265,672	272,148	278,773	285,557
Total	473,025	486,364	500,079	514,173	523,752	533,509	543,448	553,572	563,885
Total	2,099,010	2,141,764	2,185,781	2,231,097	2,256,752	2,283,286	2,310,748	2,339,187	2,368,656
Employers	45,352	46,039	46,746	47,466	47,243	47,004	46,755	46,497	46,216
Own-Account Workers	469,295	477,074	485,052	493,239	491,328	489,352	487,298	485,162	482,951
Salaried Employees	394,276	405,510	417,084	429,006	437,858	446,809	455,874	465,040	474,315
Wage Employees	1,190,087	1,213,141	1,236,899	1,261,386	1,280,323	1,300,121	1,320,821	1,342,488	1,365,174

TABLE 10.3 (Cont'd)

Estimates and Projections of Active Population by Type of Activity and Occupational Position in the Middle of Each Year.
(Exponential Interpolations and Extrapolations of Corrected and Centered Census Figures)
1940-1970.

Activity and Occupational Position	1958	1959	1960	1961	1962	1963	1964	1965	1966
Agriculture									
Employers	17,550	17,557	17,565	17,572	17,579	17,586	17,600	17,607	17,613
Own-Account Workers	163,931	164,039	164,149	164,254	164,367	164,471	164,574	164,676	164,784
Salaried Employees	27,088	27,619	28,146	28,683	29,216	29,759	30,298	30,848	31,393
Wage Employees	492,290	493,911	495,547	497,179	498,815	500,457	502,104	503,756	505,385
Total	700,859	703,126	705,407	707,688	709,977	712,273	714,576	716,887	719,205
Fishing									
Employers	78	86	94	103	113	124	136	149	163
Own-Account Workers	10,427	11,447	12,565	13,794	15,143	16,625	18,251	20,036	21,996
Salaried Employees	345	379	416	457	502	551	604	664	729
Wage Employees	4,877	5,353	5,876	6,450	7,081	7,773	8,534	9,368	10,284
Total	15,727	17,265	18,951	20,804	22,837	25,073	27,525	30,217	33,172
Mining									
Employers	582	576	570	564	558	551	545	539	533
Own-Account Workers	3,364	3,329	3,294	3,260	3,226	3,190	3,156	3,121	3,087
Salaried Employees	14,350	14,624	14,898	15,173	15,447	15,723	15,999	16,276	16,552
Wage Employees	91,067	90,933	90,799	90,663	90,528	90,395	90,259	90,123	89,987
Total	109,363	109,462	109,561	109,660	109,759	109,859	109,959	110,059	110,159
Industry									
Employers	10,858	10,748	10,634	10,525	10,410	10,299	10,184	10,073	9,957
Own-Account Workers	112,950	111,784	110,620	109,450	108,282	107,102	105,928	104,741	103,560
Salaried Employees	63,096	64,304	65,512	66,725	67,938	69,158	70,378	71,605	72,831
Wage Employees	255,723	256,397	257,075	257,748	258,426	259,106	259,790	260,467	261,149
Total	442,627	443,233	443,841	444,448	445,056	445,665	446,275	446,886	447,497
Construction									
Employers	1,500	1,466	1,420	1,513	1,611	1,716	1,828	1,948	2,075
Own-Account Workers	13,422	13,110	12,700	13,529	14,412	15,353	16,355	17,422	18,559
Salaried Employees	8,950	9,084	9,200	9,800	10,439	11,120	11,846	12,619	13,442
Wage Employees	136,754	147,447	158,951	169,323	180,373	192,143	204,680	218,035	232,263
Total	160,626	171,107	182,271	194,165	206,835	220,332	234,709	250,024	266,339

TABLE 10.3 (Cont'd)

Estimates and Projections of Active Population by Type of Activity and Occupational Position in the Middle of Each Year.
(Exponential Interpolations and Extrapolations of Corrected and Centered Census Figures)
1940-1970.

Activity and Occupational Position	1958	1959	1960	1961	1962	1963	1964	1965	1966
Electricity									
Employers	62	63	64	65	66	68	69	70	71
Own-Account Workers	170	174	177	180	184	187	191	195	198
Salaried Employees	6,631	6,754	6,880	7,008	7,139	7,271	7,407	7,545	7,686
Wage Employees	17,601	17,929	18,263	18,604	18,950	19,304	19,663	20,030	20,404
Total	24,464	24,920	25,384	25,857	26,339	26,830	27,330	27,840	28,359
Commerce									
Employers	9,565	9,466	9,363	9,259	9,153	9,047	8,942	8,834	8,724
Own-Account Workers	103,292	102,208	101,110	100,003	98,838	97,705	96,560	95,402	94,232
Salaried Employees	92,629	94,425	96,235	98,058	99,854	101,706	103,576	105,458	107,356
Wage Employees	40,213	40,732	41,260	41,791	42,302	42,842	43,380	43,927	44,478
Total	245,699	246,831	247,968	249,111	250,147	251,300	252,458	253,621	254,790
Transport									
Employers	986	971	954	988	1,023	1,059	1,097	1,136	1,175
Own-Account Workers	14,634	14,415	14,164	14,663	15,180	15,715	16,269	16,842	17,436
Salaried Employees	51,905	52,910	53,923	55,824	57,792	59,829	61,937	64,121	66,381
Wage Employees	57,931	61,582	65,416	67,722	70,109	72,581	75,140	77,788	80,531
Total	125,456	129,878	134,457	139,197	144,104	149,184	154,443	159,887	165,523
Services									
Employers	4,739	4,681	4,618	4,553	4,483	4,410	4,331	4,242	4,155
Own-Account Workers	58,473	57,766	57,012	56,211	55,360	54,457	53,502	52,492	51,426
Salaried Employees	218,688	223,060	227,525	232,075	236,714	241,452	246,277	251,199	256,225
Wage Employees	292,490	299,584	306,840	314,259	321,851	329,610	337,555	345,686	353,990
Total	574,390	585,091	595,995	607,098	618,408	629,929	641,665	653,619	665,796
Total	2,399,211	2,430,913	2,463,835	2,498,028	2,533,464	2,570,445	2,608,940	2,649,040	2,690,340
Employers	45,920	45,614	45,282	45,142	44,996	44,860	44,732	44,598	44,466
Own-Account Workers	480,663	478,272	475,791	475,344	474,992	474,805	474,786	474,927	475,278
Salaried Employees	483,682	493,159	502,735	513,803	525,041	536,569	548,322	560,335	572,595
Wage Employees	1,388,946	1,413,868	1,440,027	1,463,739	1,488,435	1,514,211	1,541,100	1,569,180	1,598,471

TABLE 10.3 (Cont'd)

Estimates and Projections of Active Population by Type of Activity and Occupational Position in the Middle of Each Year.
(Exponential Interpolations and Extrapolations of Corrected and Centered Census Figures) 1940-1970.

Activity and Occupational Position	1967	1968	1969	1970
Agriculture				
Employers	17,620	17,626	17,632	17,638
Own-Account Workers	164,884	164,983	165,081	165,185
Salaried Employees	31,949	32,501	33,064	33,623
Wage Employees	507,078	508,754	510,428	512,108
Total	721,531	723,864	726,205	728,554
Fishing				
Employers	179	196	215	236
Own-Account Workers	24,147	26,509	29,102	31,948
Salaried Employees	800	878	964	1,059
Wage Employees	11,290	12,394	13,606	14,936
Total	36,416	39,977	43,887	48,179
Mining				
Employers	527	521	515	509
Own-Account Workers	3,051	3,016	2,981	2,946
Salaried Employees	16,830	17,079	17,386	17,665
Wage Employees	89,851	89,713	89,577	89,439
Total	110,259	110,359	110,459	110,559
Industry				
Employers	9,845	9,728	9,616	9,498
Own-Account Workers	102,366	101,178	99,977	98,782
Salaried Employees	74,063	75,296	76,535	77,774
Wage Employees	261,835	262,520	263,208	263,897
Total	448,109	448,722	449,336	449,951
Construction				
Employers	2,210	2,354	2,508	2,672
Own-Account Workers	19,769	21,059	22,434	23,897
Salaried Employees	14,319	15,254	16,249	17,309
Wage Employees	247,420	263,564	280,761	299,082
Total	283,718	302,231	321,952	342,960

TABLE 10.3 (Cont'd)

Estimates and Projections of Active Population by Type of Activity and Occupational Position in the Middle of Each Year.
(Exponential Interpolations and Extrapolations of Corrected and Centered Census Figures)
1940-1970.

Activity and Occupational Position	1967	1968	1969	1970
Electricity				
Employers	73	74	76	77
Own-Account Workers	202	206	210	214
Salaried Employees	7,828	7,974	8,123	8,274
Wage Employees	20,784	21,172	21,566	21,969
Total	28,887	29,426	29,975	30,534
Commerce				
Employers	8,616	8,504	8,390	8,279
Own-Account Workers	93,048	91,851	90,642	89,420
Salaried Employees	109,271	111,199	113,143	115,101
Wage Employees	45,029	45,589	46,153	46,718
Total	255,964	257,143	258,328	259,518
Transport				
Employers	1,217	1,260	1,304	1,350
Own-Account Workers	18,051	18,687	19,346	20,028
Salaried Employees	68,721	71,144	73,651	76,248
Wage Employees	83,369	86,307	89,350	92,499
Total	171,358	177,398	183,651	190,125
Services				
Employers	4,062	3,965	3,863	3,756
Own-Account Workers	50,302	49,111	47,866	46,557
Salaried Employees	261,338	266,566	271,891	277,329
Wage Employees	362,498	371,193	380,084	389,173
Total	678,200	690,835	703,704	716,815
Total	2,734,442	2,779,955	2,827,497	2,877,195
Employers	44,349	44,228	44,119	44,015
Own-Account Workers	475,820	476,600	477,639	478,877
Salaried Employees	585,119	597,891	611,006	624,382
Wage Employees	1,629,154	1,661,206	1,694,733	1,729,821

Source: CORFO, Departamento de Investigaciones Económicas, Estimaciones y Proyecciones Mediante Interpolación y Extrapolación de los Datos Censales Corregidos de la Población Ocupada a Mediados de Cada Ano, 1940-1970 (Santiago, Chile: CORFO, 1965), pp. 1-6, mimeographed. Alberto Spottke of the Chilean Development Corporation prepared this publication.

TABLE 10.4

Economically Active Population of 12 Years and Over According to Sex and Type of Economic Activity, 1952, 1960, 1970. Census Data.

Economic Activity	1952		1960		1970	
	Males	Females	Males	Females	Males	Females
(Absolute Numbers)						
Total	1,616,152	539,141	1,854,366	534,301	2,079,359	616,207
Agriculture, Hunting, Forestry and Fishing	605,970	42,084	632,673	23,706	551,576	18,579
Mining and Quarrying	99,011	2,357	89,503	1,609	79,494	1,716
Industry	276,863	131,850	327,022	101,840	336,990	109,505
Electricity, Water, Gas and Sanitary Services	19,782	682	18,043	823	18,818	1,186
Construction	101,132	1,185	134,874	884	171,695	3,471
Trade	166,906	55,974	182,361	58,657	209,604	92,453
Transport, Storage and Communications	89,668	5,606	111,588	6,353	153,974	11,568
Finance, Insurance, Real Estate and Business Services	-	-	-	-	35,311	9,830
Communal, Social and Personal Services	192,757	286,156	232,178	312,092	335,976	313,252
Insufficiently Specified Activities	64,063	13,247	37,499	7,614	185,921	54,647
Unknown	-	-	82,625	20,723	-	-
(Relative Numbers)						
Total	100.0	100.0	100.0	100.0	100.0	100.0
Agriculture, Hunting, Forestry and Fishing	37.6	7.8	34.4	4.4	26.5	3.0
Mining and Quarrying	6.1	0.4	4.8	0.3	3.8	0.2
Industry	17.1	24.5	17.6	19.1	16.2	17.8
Electricity, Water, Gas and Sanitary Services	1.2	0.1	1.0	0.1	0.9	0.2
Construction	6.3	0.2	7.3	0.2	8.3	0.6
Trade	10.3	10.4	9.8	11.0	10.1	15.0
Transport, Storage and Communications	5.5	1.0	6.0	1.2	7.4	1.9
Finance, Insurance, Real Estate and Business Services	-	-	-	-	1.7	1.6
Communal, Social and Personal Services	11.9	53.1	12.5	58.4	16.2	50.8
Insufficiently Specified Activities	4.0	2.5	2.0	1.4	8.9	8.9
Unknown	-	-	4.6	3.9	-	-

Source: *National Institute of Statistics.*

TABLE 10.5

Economically Active Population of 12 Years and Over, According to Sex and Broad Occupational Categories. 1952, 1960, 1970. Census Years.

Broad Occupational Categories	1952		1960		1970	
	Males	Females	Males	Females	Males	Females
(Absolute Numbers)						
Total	1,616,152	539,141	1,854,366	534,301	2,079,359	616,207
Professionals, Technicians and Similar	52,019	40,176	59,470	58,733	77,887	73,690
Managers, Administrators and Similar	98,400	39,216	38,292	7,660	38,346	7,842
Office Employees and Similar	116,100	44,521	113,234	48,792	157,585	74,992
Salesmen and Similar	40,509	14,292	122,975	45,244	136,379	54,452
Farmers, Fishermen and Similar	570,271	38,119	633,931	23,274	541,517	17,131
Transport Drivers and Similar	51,930	455	77,326	425	100,697	841
Artisans and Operators	394,050	118,748	341,897	81,600	367,420	77,334
Other Artisans and Mining Operators, Quarrymen and Similar	59,606	438	55,263	227	129,364	12,071
Workers and Laborers Not Specified	35,410	4,709	189,493	21,635	163,385	12,978
Workers in Personal Services	81,277	218,791	94,492	227,027	100,116	205,543
Other Workers Not Specified	116,580	19,676	127,993	19,684	266,663	79,333
(Relative Numbers)						
Total	100.0	100.0	100.0	100.0	100.0	100.0
Professionals, Technicians and Similar	3.2	7.5	3.2	11.0	3.7	12.0
Managers, Administrators and Similar	6.1	7.3	2.1	1.4	1.8	1.2
Office Employees and Similar	7.2	8.3	6.1	9.1	7.8	12.1
Salesmen and Similar	2.5	2.6	6.6	8.4	6.6	8.8
Farmers, Fishermen and Similar	35.3	7.0	34.2	4.4	26.0	2.8
Transport Drivers and Similar	3.2	0.1	4.2	0.1	4.8	0.1
Artisans and Operators	24.4	22.0	18.4	15.3	17.7	12.6
Other Artisans and Mining Operators, Quarrymen and Similar	3.7	0.1	3.0	0.0	6.2	2.0
Workers and Laborers Not Specified	2.2	0.9	10.2	4.1	7.8	2.1
Workers in Personal Services	5.0	40.6	5.1	42.5	4.8	33.4
Other Workers Not Specified	7.2	3.6	6.9	3.7	12.8	12.9

Source: National Institute of Statistics.

TABLE 10.6

Population 12 Years of Age and Over by Sex, According to Age Group and Economic Activity. 1952, 1960, and 1970: Census Data.

Age Groups and Economic Activity	1952		1960		1970	
	Male	Female	Male	Female	Male	Female
Total	1,988,326	2,107,488	2,393,543	2,552,524	2,921,698	3,138,022
12-14	191,691	187,615	248,855	245,815	329,112	326,982
15-19	282,200	291,717	354,554	370,253	446,729	466,736
20-24	275,467	299,570	287,637	310,762	370,653	398,383
25-29	213,144	234,918	251,833	275,172	301,862	324,130
30-34	185,795	195,565	246,879	260,273	249,409	267,312
35-39	179,374	197,677	199,965	215,448	247,473	207,078
40-44	163,939	159,245	178,478	185,401	223,014	232,778
45-49	127,714	133,484	157,143	167,091	172,260	184,593
50-54	114,819	116,571	137,561	143,015	149,338	163,277
55-59	79,281	81,813	103,319	109,013	127,242	141,449
60-64	69,019	78,450	86,342	96,713	105,715	117,484
65 and over	105,883	130,863	140,977	175,768	198,891	247,820
Active	1,617,814	538,944	1,854,366	534,301	2,079,359	616,207
12-14	25,480	10,915	29,416	9,610	18,966	7,376
15-19	186,940	82,980	218,669	87,140	202,375	77,646
20-24	252,676	105,165	263,356	100,840	314,477	126,613
25-29	205,803	71,517	244,184	76,829	289,882	95,926
30-34	180,867	54,853	240,802	61,815	243,318	68,129
35-39	174,763	54,479	194,037	48,519	240,983	65,445
40-44	158,883	43,940	170,776	41,102	214,292	33,522
45-49	121,453	35,455	146,714	35,599	160,955	39,325
50-54	105,826	28,647	121,091	27,395	131,323	31,414
55-59	71,417	18,353	86,502	18,280	104,392	21,816
60-64	59,417	15,309	66,346	13,293	75,473	13,001
65 and over	74,289	17,331	72,473	13,879	82,923	15,994

TABLE 10.6 (Cont'd)

Population 12 Years of Age and Over by Sex, According to Age Group and Economic Activity 1952, 1960, and 1970: Census Data.

Age Groups and Economic Activity	1952		1960		1970	
	Male	Female	Male	Female	Male	Female
Inactive	370,512	1,568,544	539,177	2,018,223	819,278	2,509,166
12-14	166,211	176,700	219,439	236,005	307,703	318,102
15-19	95,260	208,737	135,885	283,113	239,722	387,063
20-24	22,791	194,405	24,281	209,922	53,189	270,095
25-29	7,341	103,401	7,649	198,343	10,021	227,302
30-34	4,928	140,712	6,077	198,458	4,684	198,520
35-39	4,611	143,198	5,928	166,929	5,016	201,032
40-44	5,056	115,305	7,702	144,299	7,520	178,773
45-49	6,261	98,029	10,429	131,492	10,297	144,821
50-54	8,993	87,924	16,470	113,620	17,046	131,364
55-59	7,864	63,460	16,817	90,733	22,021	119,205
60-64	9,602	63,141	19,990	83,420	29,274	103,974
65 and over	31,594	113,532	68,504	161,889	112,785	228,915
Not Reported	-	-	-	-	23,061	12,649
12-14	-	-	-	-	2,443	1,504
15-19	-	-	-	-	4,632	2,027
20-24	-	-	-	-	2,987	1,675
25-29	-	-	-	-	1,959	902
30-34	-	-	-	-	1,407	663
35-39	-	-	-	-	1,474	601
40-44	-	-	-	-	1,202	483
45-49	-	-	-	-	1,008	447
50-54	-	-	-	-	969	499
55-59	-	-	-	-	829	428
60-64	-	-	-	-	968	509
65 and over	-	-	-	-	3,183	2,911

Source: National Institute of Statistics.

1952, 1960 and 1970 are presented in Table 10.6.

Seasonal Labor Input in Agriculture

Finally, the seasonal labor input in agriculture by province and region for 1970 is presented in Table 10.7. The absolute figures of Table 10.7 refer to thousands of eight-hour working days during the agricultural year of 1970 and the percentages to the relative monthly magnitude of these working days as compared to the annual total agricultural labor input. The figures of Table 10.7 show the seasonal variations in the labor inputs in agriculture and the differences in such seasonal variations between regions and provinces.

Human Resources in Chile

There exist many studies in Chile examining the issue or issues of human resources. To review or even cite these studies is beyond the scope of this volume. The reader can get a picture of the issues of human resources which have been of concern to Chileans, obtain a solid statistical base and find leads to other studies on human resources by consulting the following studies (ODEPLAN: 1970; ODEPLAN: 1971a; ODEPLAN: 1971b; ODEPLAN: 1971c; ODEPLAN: 1972; ODEPLAN: 1976a and 1976b; ODEPLAN: 1974).

Towards a Comprehensive Employment Strategy

Although the issues of human resources, labor force, employment, unemployment, migration and so forth are of central importance to the theory and policy of economic development, only in recent years has a concerted effort been made to examine them empirically and to link them to economic development within an acceptable economic framework. Significant progress has been made in examining selected labor force issues.

The prevailing labor theory and the presently recommended employment strategies do not distinguish between production, distribution and capital formation aspects of employment and frequently end up in making contradictory or incomplete recommendations.

For a complete, comprehensive and efficient employment strategy to be formulated and implemented, the production, distribution and capital formation dimensions of such a strategy (and also of the underlying labor theory) need to be identified, distinguished and made consistent as recommended in (Mamalakis: 1976d). Additional research is needed to link the various aspects of income distribution (Mamalakis: 1976d, 46-68, 211-243) to those of employment, and the various dimensions of capital formation to those of employment (Mamalakis: 1976, 69-85, 244-290) and then integrate them to the issues of production.

Some, unfortunately still limited, progress has been made in this difficult and complex area. For a picture of the current state of affairs of the employment theory and policy in Latin America see the informative study by PREALC, Employment in Latin America (New York and London: Praeger Publishers). The Regional Employment Programme for Latin America and the Caribbean (PREALC) has prepared and/or published numerous articles, reports and books relating to employment in Latin America which illustrate both the progress made in understanding the employment issues and the still rudimentary theoretical and analytical state of affairs of the labor-economic development nexus.

For an examination of the still conceptually highly controversial, "informal sector" in Latin America as well as in Chile see (PREALC: 1978a). Other PREALC studies of general interest or specifically relating to Chile and its labor force-employment are (PREALC: 1978b; 1978c; 1978d and 1978e).

TABLE 10.7

Seasonal Labor Input in Agriculture by Province and Region.
Agricultural Year of 1970.
Thousands of Eight-Hour Working Days and Monthly Percentages.

	May	June	July	August	September	October	November
I Tarapacá	24,28	21,86	24,23	44,21	40,13	63,50	82,90
%	4.6	4.2	4.6	8.5	7.7	12.2	15.9
II Antofagasta	15,24	5,25	15,72	6,29	16,06	13,24	23,58
%	1.1	3.1	9.4	3.8	9.6	7.9	14.1
III Atacama	62,69	72,68	77,04	96,92	93,33	95,56	95,69
%	7.0	8.1	8.6	10.8	10.4	10.6	10.6
IV Coquimbo	266,50	236,69	286,04	352,66	325,07	449,44	472,06
%	6.5	5.8	7.0	8.7	8.0	11.0	11.6
V Aconcagua	156,46	154,42	172,34	142,02	238,54	267,47	272,96
Valparaíso	153,80	164,01	145,78	214,56	324,67	405,66	351,68
Total	310,26	318,43	318,12	356,58	563,11	673,13	624,64
%	4.8	5.0	5.0	5.6	8.8	10.5	9.7
Metropolitan Area of Santiago	368,19	365,73	362,16	526,90	665,38	849,04	762,41
%	4.3	4.2	4.2	6.1	7.7	9.9	8.8
VI O'Higgins	271,54	266,69	158,95	260,26	328,95	528,09	447,15
Colchagua	234,27	288,15	162,70	178,92	233,40	323,89	282,52
Total	505,81	554,84	321,65	439,18	562,35	851,98	729,67
%	5.6	6.1	3.6	4.9	6.2	9.4	8.1
VII Curricó	110,33	106,49	86,33	102,17	211,01	256,14	229,03
Talca	212,04	226,42	194,12	270,55	340,12	454,93	445,43
Maule	94,31	77,64	101,60	56,89	75,79	79,34	86,92
Linares	211,00	228,84	105,09	249,87	330,26	450,89	442,05
Total	627,68	639,44	487,14	679,48	957,18	1,241,30	1,203,43
%	4.5	4.6	3.5	4.9	6.9	9.0	8.7
VIII Ñuble	322,47	275,03	195,33	358,22	380,20	496,22	529,11
Concepción	59,04	121,63	66,59	171,05	181,23	183,98	186,82
Arauco	25,82	19,36	17,40	32,58	48,40	68,31	85,22
Bío-Bío	232,55	208,36	140,81	171,30	227,50	347,30	436,11
Total	639,88	624,38	420,13	733,15	837,33	1,095,81	1,237,26
%	4.9	4.8	3.2	5.6	6.4	8.4	9.5
IX Malleco	212,25	136,18	81,76	129,15	247,44	100,12	204,40
Cautín	838,45	643,54	375,32	455,91	463,16	442,09	758,35
Total	1,050,70	779,72	457,08	585,06	710,60	542,21	962,75
%	9.9	7.3	4.3	5.5	6.7	5.1	9.1
X Valdivia	761,29	223,71	87,52	110,27	721,05	357,63	528,37
Osorno	314,20	147,56	87,91	97,22	86,94	156,28	296,60
Llanquihue	339,97	119,06	66,09	80,27	87,09	167,23	203,02
Chiloé	96,84	87,63	32,35	31,72	355,35	174,86	306,61
Total	1,512,30	577,96	273,87	319,48	1,250,43	856,00	1,334,60
%	14.0	5.3	2.5	3.0	11.6	7.9	12.4
XI Aysén	51,15	15,05	7,38	11,33	55,89	59,85	109,18
%	8.3	2.4	1.2	1.8	9.1	9.7	17.7
XII Magallanes	29,48	11,40	5,62	7,45	35,85	34,48	64,16
%	8.2	3.2	1.5	2.1	9.9	9.6	17.8
General Total	5,464,16	4,223,43	3,056,18	4,158,69	6,112,71	6,825,54	7,702,33

TABLE 10.7 (Cont'd)

Seasonal Labor Input in Agriculture by Province and Region.
Agricultural Year of 1970.
Thousands of Eight-Hour Working Days and Monthly Percentages.

	December	January	February	March	April	Total
I Tarapacá	42,04	33,75	53,07	64,20	27,51	521,68
%	8.0	6.5	10.2	12.3	5.3	100.0
II Antofagasta	12,24	18,17	15,95	19,57	5,47	166,79
%	7.3	10.9	9.6	11.7	3.3	100.0
III Atacama	67,80	70,34	41,66	73,72	50,77	898,20
%	7.5	7.8	4.6	8.2	5.6	100.0
IV Coquimbo	318,20	411,38	297,36	437,65	211,32	4,064,37
%	7.8	10.1	7.3	10.8	5.2	100.0
V Aconcagua	305,85	351,62	248,35	311,92	245,81	2,867,76
Valparaíso	390,55	403,18	324,28	306,58	351,10	3,535,85
Total	696,40	754,80	572,63	618,50	596,91	6,403,61
%	10.9	11.8	8.9	9.6	9.3	100.0
Metropolitan Area of Santiago	1,085,78	1,008,84	686,87	1,090,78	837,94	8,610,02
%	12.6	11.7	8.0	12.7	9.7	100.0
VI O'Higgins	586,49	518,04	385,62	766,07	670,27	5,188,12
Colchagua	396,77	493,37	244,47	531,90	464,87	3,835,23
Total	983,26	1,011,41	630,09	1,297,97	1,135,14	9,023,35
%	10.9	11.2	7.0	14.4	12.6	100.0
VII Curricó	269,40	283,22	183,16	455,10	255,19	2,547,57
Talca	515,25	569,39	273,56	1,388,14	537,16	5,427,16
Maule	40,37	60,79	59,83	155,45	244,44	1,433,37
Linares	500,89	472,36	233,30	653,57	493,96	4,372,08
Total	1,325,91	1,385,76	749,85	2,652,26	1,530,75	13,780,18
%	9.6	10.0	5.4	19.2	11.1	100.0
VIII Ñuble	645,97	923,73	434,74	798,22	877,82	6,237,06
Concepción	152,44	126,50	109,76	268,64	349,41	1,977,09
Arauco	74,22	65,35	49,31	176,62	153,52	816,11
Bío-Bío	449,83	528,94	369,06	410,83	416,26	3,948,85
Total	1,322,46	1,644,52	962,87	1,654,31	1,797,01	12,979,11
%	10.2	12.7	7.4	12.7	13.8	100.0
IX Malleco	201,62	421,08	276,25	268,20	131,36	2,409,81
Cautín	1,053,14	912,17	933,46	669,34	639,57	8,184,50
Total	1,254,76	1,333,25	1,209,71	937,54	770,93	10,594,31
%	11.8	12.6	11.4	8.8	7.3	100.0
X Valdivia	631,00	327,71	227,37	242,11	481,70	4,699,73
Osorno	291,42	155,46	328,34	172,80	208,42	2,343,15
Llanquihue	163,81	100,48	132,75	146,03	248,82	1,854,62
Chiloé	139,91	32,27	102,60	236,29	298,58	1,893,01
Total	1,226,14	615,92	791,06	797,23	1,237,52	10,790,51
%	11.4	5.7	7.3	7.4	11.5	100.0
XI Aysén	75,16	63,65	38,20	56,49	73,86	617,19
%	12.2	10.3	6.2	9.2	12.0	100.0
XII Magallanes	42,15	33,84	18,79	32,76	43,85	359,83
%	11.7	9.4	5.2	9.1	12.2	100.0
General Total	8,452,30	8,385,63	6,068,11	9,723,98	8,318,98	78,809,15

Source: This table was prepared by the Planning Office of the Presidency of the Republic of Chile by elaborating statistical information collected by the National Institute of Statistics in its agricultural surveys and the national agricultural census of 1965. Also used were data brought up to date by the Institute of Natural Resources (IREN: Instituto de Recursos Naturales).

11
LABOR FORCE OF SANTIAGO

The Instituto de Economía Employment-Unemployment Surveys

The largest, most comprehensive time series of labor force, employment, unemployment and related time series for the City of Santiago have been compiled and published since 1956 by the Instituto de Economía of the University of Chile. The employment-unemployment surveys of the Instituto de Economía were normally confined to the Greater Santiago area and published in the series Ocupación y Desocupación Gran Santiago (Santiago, Chile: IECH) (See for example IECH: 1962a; IECH: 1976 and IECH: 1978a.) Occasionally the Instituto de Economía undertook employment-unemployment surveys in urban areas outside Santiago. For example, the Instituto de Economía undertook employment-unemployment surveys for Iquique, Antofagasta, La Serena-Coquimbo, Valparaíso-Viña del Mar, Gran Santiago, Concepción, Valdivia, Puerto Montt and Castro in September of 1961 and March of 1962 (see IECH: 1961 and IECH: 1962b). It has also undertaken special employment-unemployment surveys in Concepción-Talcahuano and Lota-Coronel (IECH: 1968 and IECH: 1973b), in Gran Santiago, Concepción-Talcahuano (IECH: 1964), in Valparaíso, Viña del Mar, Gran Santiago, Concepción (IECH: 1963a), in Gran Santiago, Valparaíso-Viña del Mar, Conjunto Provincial Arauco, Bío-Bío, Concepción, Malleco, Ñuble (IECH: 1963b) and more recently undertook a countryside survey, the findings of which were published in Ocupación y Desocupación. Sectores Urbanos de las Regiones IV a X, excepto el Gran Santiago. Enero 1977-Enero 1978 (IECH: 1978b).

Coverage and Definitions of the Santiago Employment-Unemployment Surveys

The definitions used by the employment-unemployment surveys of the Institute of Economics of the University of Chile for Santiago and other urban areas of Chile have changed mildly over time. Those presented below were valid as of December 1977.

Greater Santiago. The geographic territory of the survey comprises, in its urban parts, the communities (comunas) listed below:

1. Santiago
2. Ñuñoa
3. La Reina
4. Providencia
5. Las Condes
6. San Miguel
7. La Florida
8. La Granja
9. La Cisterna
10. San Bernardo
11. Conchalí
12. Quinta Normal
13. Renca
14. Pudahuel
15. Maipú
16. Puente Alto
17. Quilicura

Family Group. Understood as family group has been a collection of people linked by consanguinity, marriage or other legal relationships who habitually share the same dwelling and cook in common. The dwelling could be a house, an apartment in a building, apartment or room in a house, and so forth. Included in the family group have been relatives and domestic servants, who work and live with them. Married sons and daughters who live with their parents are considered as a separate family only if they cook separately. Persons residing in a place only sporadically or temporarily, are not surveyed, even if linked by marriage or legal consanguinity.

Dwellings that do not include family groups, such as hotels, hospitals, colleges, boarding schools, barracks, and so forth, are not included in the surveys. However, pensions have been surveyed as follows: The individual pensioners whose pension included meals have been included in the family group formed by the owners of the pension. Individual pensioners who hired only boarding have been surveyed as a separate group. Married couples or families that hire boarding with or without meals, have been considered as separate family groups. Two or more persons with no family links who share the same room, have been surveyed in the same family group as the owners of the pension, when boarding and meals were hired, or as a separate family group if they do not eat in the pension.

In the case of the private houses in which a family has pensioners, the same criterion as in the case of pensioners was adopted. Private houses in which there was not a family and where the rooms were rented individually to persons or groups of persons, have been considered, by analogy, as if they were apartment buildings. Persons living in the same house or apartment have been considered as one family group even if there was no blood, marriage or other legal link.

The labor force (fuerza de trabajo) comprises the population of fourteen years or more, employed and unemployed.

Employed persons are those who, during the week covered by the survey, were found (1) working; that is, were performing some work for pay or profit or were working without compensation in the business of a family member living in the same dwelling; (2) employed but not working; that is, were neither working nor looking for employment but had a job or business from which they were temporarily absent due to illness, vacation or inclement weather.

Unemployed persons (personas desocupadas) are those not working but actively seeking work during the week covered by the survey. Unemployed persons are distinguished into two groups: those seeking employment for the first time (new entrants to the labor force), and those who have lost their employment and are seeking a new job. This last group of persons constitutes the jobless (cesantes).

Inactives or persons outside the labor force (inactivos o personas fuera de la fuerza de trabajo) are all those of fourteen or more years not included in the category of employed or unemployed.

This group is divided into (1) persons dedicated to household activities, (2) students, (3) rentiers, (4) retired or pensioners, (5) the sick and invalid, (6) the elderly who are unable to work, and (7) those who do not work nor seek employment for other reasons distinct of those already mentioned.

Economic Activity. In order to classify the economic activity performed by the labor force the following classification was used.

0. Agriculture, hunting, forestry and fishing. 00. Agriculture and hunting. 01. Forestry and extraction of wood. 02. Fishing.

1. Mining and quarrying. 10. Exploitation of coal mines. 11. Production of crude oil and natural gas. 12. Extraction of metallic minerals. 13. Extraction of other minerals.

2. Manufacturing industries. 20. Food products, beverages and tobacco. 21. Textiles, wearing apparel and leather industries. 22. Wood industry and products. 23. Production of paper and paper products; printing and publishing. 24. Production of chemical substances and chemical products derived from petroleum and coal, rubber and plastic products. 25. Production of mineral non metallic products, excluding the derivatives from petroleum and coal. 26. Basic metallic industries. 27. Production of metallic products, machinery and equipment. 28. Other manufacturing industries.

3. Construction. 30. Construction.

4. Commerce. 40. Wholesale. 41. Retail. 42. Restaurants and hotels.

5. Government and financial services. 50. Public administration and defense. 51. Financial establishments. 52. Insurance. 53. Real estate and services given to enterprises.

6. Personal and household serv-

ices. 60. Repair services. 61. Laundries and laundry services, and cleaning establishments. 62. Domestic services. 63. Personal and other services.

7. Social and community services. 70. Sanitation services. 71. Educational services. 72. Health services. 73. Social assistance agencies. 74. Amusement services. 75. Other community and social services.

8. Transport, storage, communication and public utility services. 80. Transport and storage. 81. Communications. 82. Electricity, gas and steam. 83. Water power services and delivery of water.

9. Inadequately specified activities. 91. Inadequately specified activities.

Sample Error of the Sample. Because only a sample of all family groups of the city of Great Santiago is studied it is necessary to generalize the figures drawn from the survey in order to estimate employment and unemployment in all the population. For this reason, in analyzing the changes in values among periods it is necessary to take into account the existence of a margin of error which is typical of any sampling process. The margins of error for the variables estimated in the survey of employment and unemployment in Great Santiago have been calculated considering a level of confidence of 95 per cent. This means that if we use the estimate provided by the sample to construct a confidence interval of the type: estimate-percentage of error, then in 95 out of every 100 times the real population value will be included in that interval. For example, an estimate was obtained in December of 1977 for the proportion of men in the population of Great Santiago which was equal to 47.2 with a margin of error equal to 2 per cent of this value. Therefore, it can be affirmed that the true proportion of men is one of the values falling between 46.3 (47.2-0.9) and 48.1 (47.2+0.9) and the risk that such a proportion will fall outside these limits is only 5 per cent.

The word "error" must not be understood as a mistake, but in a statistical sense of a variation within certain limits.

Some illustrative margins of sample errors, expressed as percentages of each sample statistic of Great Santiago, include: population of 14 years and over, 2%; men, 2%; labor force, 2%; unemployed in the labor force, 9%; inactives with desire to work, 11%.

Composition of Population and Labor Force

The composition of the population of Great Santiago between 1956 and 1978 is presented in Table 11.1. In Table 11.1 total population is subdivided into male and female and into population under 14 years and population of 14 years and over. The population of 14 years and over is subsequently divided into the labor force and the inactives.

The persons in the labor force are further subdivided into those employed and those unemployed. Employed persons are classified into those at work and those temporarily absent. The unemployed are further subdivided into jobless and new entrants.

Hours Worked Per Week

The total numbers of persons employed and at work in Santiago are presented in Table 11.2 according to the number of hours which they worked during a week between 1956 and 1978. Working persons are classified according to whether they worked 1-10 hours, 11-20, 21-34, and 35-48 hours and persons for which no information was available. Also given in Table 11.2 is the average weekly number of hours worked.

TABLE 11.1

Composition of the Population
Great Santiago, 1956-1978.
(Thousands of Persons)

	October 1956	June 1957	June 1958	March 1959	June 1959	April 1960	June 1960	September 1960[1]	September 1960[2]
Total Population	1,701,2	1,745,0	1,813,2	1,866,4	1,884,1	1,945,5	1,957,8	1,977,0	1,977,0
Men	780,7	798,0	824,4	846,0	863,3	893,9	878,1	888,9	889,6
Women	920,5	947,0	988,8	1,020,4	1,020,8	1,051,6	1,079,7	1,088,1	1,087,4
Under 14 years	562,7	581,0	613,4	621,1	624,7	631,3	634,4	622,5	626,6
Population of 14 years and over	1,138,5	1,164,0	1,199,8	1,245,3	1,259,4	1,314,2	1,323,4	1,354,5	1,350,4
Labor force	639,0	651,5	666,6	679,3	678,8	707,7	715,0	738,0	725,3
Inactives	499,4	512,5	533,2	566,0	580,5	606,5	608,4	616,5	625,1
Labor Force	639,0	651,5	666,6	679,3	678,8	707,7	715,0	738,0	725,3
Employed	596,5	609,8	603,5	608,4	628,6	655,8	657,7	685,2	672,1
At work	588,0	597,3	589,1	566,0	610,5	637,9	636,7	667,9	655,0
Temporarily absent	8,5	12,5	14,4	42,4	18,1	17,9	21,0	17,3	17,2
Unemployed	42,5	41,7	63,1	70,9	50,2	51,9	57,3	52,8	53,2
Jobless	37,8	32,0	54,2	62,5	43,3	44,3	47,4	47,8	44,6
New entrants	4,7	9,7	8,9	8,4	6,9	7,6	9,8	5,0	8,6

	December 1960	March 1961	June 1961	September 1961	December 1961	March 1962	June 1962	September 1962	October 1962[3]
Total Population	1,996,1	2,014,5	2,033,1	2,051,8	2,070,7	2,089,8	2,109,1	2,128,5	2,128,5
Men	905,8	905,8	920,7	926,5	950,8	945,8	965,0	974,1	970,6
Women	1,090,3	1,108,7	1,112,5	1,125,4	1,119,9	1,144,1	1,144,2	1,154,5	1,157,9
Under 14 years	631,5	636,4	651,7	663,6	657,4	669,1	675,9	694,8	704,5
Population of 14 years and over	1,364,6	1,378,2	1,381,5	1,388,2	1,413,4	1,420,8	1,433,3	1,433,8	1,424,0
Labor force	736,7	741,0	724,0	729,6	741,9	761,6	754,5	773,7	757,7
Inactives	627,9	637,2	657,6	658,7	671,6	659,2	678,8	660,2	666,2
Labor Force	736,7	741,0	724,0	729,6	741,9	761,6	754,5	773,7	757,7
Employed	684,9	684,5	672,8	679,5	705,0	714,7	711,5	740,8	725,9
At work	662,3	662,1	652,9	652,8	674,7	689,3	679,5	721,2	714,5
Temporarily absent	22,6	22,4	19,9	26,7	30,3	25,5	32,1	19,6	11,4
Unemployed	51,8	56,5	51,2	50,1	36,9	47,0	13,0	33,0	32,0
Jobless	45,8	45,7	43,6	42,8	31,5	36,2	35,3	27,5	28,4
New entrants	6,0	10,9	7,6	7,3	5,5	10,8	7,7	5,5	3,8

TABLE 11.1 (Cont'd)

Composition of the Population
Great Santiago, 1956-1978.
(Thousands of Persons)

	December 1962	March 1963	June 1963	September 1963	December 1963[4]	December 1963[5]	March 1964	June 1964	September 1964[6]
Total Population	2,148,1	2,167,9	2,187,9	2,208,1	2,258,5	2,258,5	2,279,3	2,300,3	2,321,5
Men	984,3	988,6	995,3	1,009,1	1,034,4	1,038,9	1,057,6	1,068,8	1,058,6
Women	1,163,9	1,179,3	1,192,7	1,199,0	1,224,1	1,219,6	1,221,7	1,231,6	1,262,9
Under 14 years	693,2	700,2	711,9	715,4	734,0	754,3	765,8	787,4	712,7
Population of 14 years and over	1,455,0	1,467,7	1,476,1	1,492,7	1,524,5	1,504,2	1,513,5	1,512,9	1,608,8
Labor force	774,1	778,3	775,3	788,3	786,0	779,2	790,9	793,6	877,5
Inactives	681,0	687,2	700,9	704,4	738,5	725,0	720,3	719,3	731,3
Labor Force	774,1	778,3	775,3	788,3	786,0	779,2	790,9	793,6	877,5
Employed	737,1	735,5	735,2	747,3	757,7	745,7	750,6	754,5	833,6
At work	704,3	709,0	710,7	723,7	731,8	713,7	730,0	729,4	810,8
Temporarily absent	32,8	26,5	24,5	22,9	25,9	31,9	21,4	25,1	22,8
Unemployed	37,1	42,8	40,2	41,0	28,3	33,5	40,3	39,2	43,9
Jobless	33,3	33,5	32,7	34,7	24,4	28,8	33,2	31,3	36,9
New entrants	3,8	9,3	7,5	6,3	4,0	4,7	7,1	7,9	7,0

	September 1964	December 1964	March 1965	June 1965	September 1965	December 1965	March 1966	June 1966	September 1966
Total Population	2,321,5	2,342,9	2,364,5	2,386,3	2,408,3	2,430,5	2,452,9	2,475,5	2,498,3
Men	1,077,2	1,089,4	1,092,4	1,109,6	1,112,6	1,132,6	1,133,2	1,142,4	1,164,2
Women	1,244,3	1,253,5	1,272,1	1,276,7	1,295,7	1,297,9	1,319,7	1,333,2	1,334,1
Under 14 years	782,3	801,3	808,7	830,4	826,0	838,5	848,7	852,0	846,9
Population of 14 years and over	1,539,2	1,541,6	1,555,8	1,555,9	1,582,3	1,592,0	1,604,2	1,623,6	1,651,4
Labor force	814,8	794,2	825,2	828,0	840,5	845,8	841,3	854,6	874,4
Inactives	724,3	747,4	730,6	725,4	741,8	746,2	762,9	769,0	777,0
Labor Force	814,8	794,2	825,2	828,0	840,5	845,8	841,3	854,6	874,4
Employed	764,3	756,1	774,9	786,6	790,9	806,1	801,8	803,6	828,1
At work	743,1	725,1	753,4	768,4	774,9	783,2	777,4	787,0	809,7
Temporarily absent	21,2	31,0	22,3	17,4	16,0	22,8	24,4	16,6	18,4
Unemployed	50,5	38,1	50,3	41,4	49,6	39,8	39,5	51,1	46,3
Jobless	41,6	32,6	41,3	31,5	41,2	33,0	32,0	40,2	39,3
New entrants	9,0	5,6	9,1	9,9	8,4	6,8	7,6	10,9	7,0

TABLE 11.1 (Cont'd)

Composition of the Population
Great Santiago, 1956-1978.
(Thousands of Persons)

	December 1966	March 1967[7]	March 1967[8]	June 1967	September 1967	December 1967	March 1968	June 1968	September 1968
Total Population	2,521,3	2,544,5	2,544,5	2,568,0	2,591,7	2,615,6	2,639,7	2,664,0	2,688,6
Men	1,174,9	1,178,1	1,188,3	1,201,8	1,212,9	1,224,1	1,230,1	1,247,1	1,258,4
Women	1,346,4	1,366,4	1,356,2	1,366,2	1,378,8	1,391,5	1,409,6	1,417,0	1,430,2
Under 14 years	839,6	834,6	870,2	880,8	878,6	873,6	911,0	911,9	896,1
Population of 14 years and over	1,681,7	1,709,9	1,674,3	1,687,2	1,713,1	1,742,0	1,728,7	1,752,1	1,792,5
Labor force	895,1	900,8	877,9	898,8	914,9	920,7	902,7	929,1	943,2
Inactives	789,2	809,2	799,0	785,8	880,8	821,3	826,0	823,1	849,3
Labor Force	895,1	900,8	877,9	898,8	914,9	920,7	902,7	929,1	943,2
Employed	846,7	851,3	822,5	845,8	861,8	861,8	852,4	869,7	879,5
At work	825,3	817,0	791,9	817,0	840,8	820,3	810,5	843,1	855,8
Temporarily absent	21,5	34,2	30,7	28,8	21,0	41,4	41,9	26,7	23,7
Unemployed	48,3	49,5	55,3	53,0	53,1	58,9	50,3	59,4	63,6
Jobless	38,5	40,5	46,5	44,0	45,7	48,8	40,8	48,3	52,2
New entrants	9,8	9,0	7,9	9,0	7,3	10,1	9,6	11,2	11,4

	December 1968	March 1969	June 1969	September 1969	December 1969	March 1970	June 1970	September 1970	December 1970
Total Population	2,713,4	2,738,4	2,763,6	2,789,1	2,814,8	2,840,7	2,866,9	2,893,3	2,920,0
Men	1,257,1	1,273,4	1,293,7	1,299,7	1,310,6	1,319,2	1,327,7	1,350,2	1,376,7
Women	1,456,3	1,465,0	1,469,9	1,489,4	1,504,2	1,521,5	1,539,2	1,543,1	1,543,3
Under 14 years	877,8	903,7	923,4	906,5	906,3	917,5	907,3	918,6	927,4
Population of 14 years and over	1,835,6	1,834,7	1,840,3	1,882,6	1,908,5	1,923,2	1,959,6	1,974,7	1,992,6
Labor force	965,1	953,0	968,1	992,9	1,012,6	987,4	1,023,4	1,021,0	1,034,1
Inactives	870,5	884,5	872,2	892,5	895,9	935,8	936,2	953,7	958,4
Labor Force	965,1	953,0	968,1	992,9	1,012,6	987,4	1,023,4	1,021,0	1,034,1
Employed	912,9	888,2	899,0	940,3	958,0	920,0	951,9	955,3	948,8
At work	881,0	857,7	866,7	915,5	919,1	873,6	915,7	921,2	906,6
Temporarily absent	31,9	30,5	32,3	24,8	38,9	46,4	36,2	34,2	42,1
Unemployed	52,2	64,8	69,1	52,6	54,7	67,5	71,5	65,6	85,4
Jobless	43,4	50,5	53,2	43,7	44,0	52,6	57,3	54,1	68,2
New entrants	8,8	15,2	15,9	8,9	10,7	14,9	14,2	11,6	17,2

TABLE 11.1 (Cont'd)

Composition of the Population
Great Santiago, 1956-1978.
(Thousands of Persons)

	March 1971	June 1971	September 1971	December 1971	March 1972	June 1972	September 1972	December 1972	March 1973
Total Population	2,946,9	2,974,1	3,001,5	3,029,2	3,057,1	3,085,3	3,113,7	3,142,4	3,171,4
Men	1,392,9	1,406,3	1,412,3	1,437,7	1,443,1	1,459,6	1,477,0	1,496,3	1,498,9
Women	1,554,1	1,567,9	1,589,2	1,591,5	1,614,0	1,625,7	1,636,7	1,646,1	1,672,5
Under 14 years	938,5	920,5	927,1	963,7	943,7	909,9	962,1	970,2	910,2
Population of 14 years and over	2,008,4	2,053,7	2,074,4	2,065,5	2,113,4	2,175,4	2,151,6	2,172,2	2,261,2
Labor force	1,031,4	1,073,8	1,061,8	1,059,4	1,060,6	1,105,3	1,065,9	1,079,4	1,104,1
Inactives	977,0	979,9	1,012,6	1,006,1	1,052,8	1,070,1	1,085,7	1,092,8	1,157,1
Labor Force	1,031,4	1,073,8	1,061,8	1,059,4	1,060,6	1,105,3	1,065,9	1,079,4	1,104,1
Employed	946,4	1,018,0	1,011,1	1,019,3	1,010,2	1,064,7	1,034,0	1,040,9	1,062,5
At work	913,1	989,1	980,3	990,2	974,7	1,032,7	971,2	1,004,0	1,016,2
Temporarily absent	33,3	29,0	30,8	29,1	35,5	32,0	62,8	36,9	46,3
Unemployed	85,0	55,8	50,7	40,1	50,4	40,7	31,9	38,5	41,6
Jobless	63,9	43,2	38,3	29,7	38,8	24,9	23,3	29,7	27,3
New entrants	21,2	11,4	12,4	10,4	11,6	15,8	8,6	8,8	14,3

	June 1973	December 1973	March 1974	June 1974	September 1974	December 1974	March 1975	June 1975	September 1975
Total Population	3,200,6	3,382,0	3,413,2	3,444,7	3,476,5	3,508,5	3,540,8	3,573,4	3,606,5
Men	1,549,7	1,637,5	1,642,3	1,646,6	1,665,3	1,661,9	1,693,7	1,729,7	1,723,6
Women	1,650,9	1,744,5	1,770,9	1,798,1	1,811,2	1,846,6	1,847,1	1,843,7	1,882,7
Under 14 years	880,8	1,094,5	1,119,8	1,113,9	1,140,0	1,109,3	1,104,0	1,077,7	1,097,1
Population of 14 years and over	2,319,8	2,287,5	2,293,4	2,330,8	2,336,5	2,399,2	2,436,8	2,495,7	2,509,2
Labor force	1,135,0	1,180,3	1,179,2	1,182,9	1,198,7	1,228,6	1,230,9	1,226,7	1,223,3
Inactives	1,184,8	1,107,2	1,114,2	1,147,9	1,137,8	1,170,6	1,205,9	1,269,0	1,285,9
Labor Force	1,135,0	1,180,3	1,179,2	1,182,9	1,198,7	1,228,6	1,230,9	1,226,7	1,223,3
Employed	1,099,8	1,097,6	1,070,3	1,060,6	1,086,1	1,109,3	1,067,2	1,029,5	1,019,9
At work	1,069,2	1,059,1	1,036,2	1,009,0	1,049,5	1,083,5	1,037,0	1,004,0	1,001,2
Temporarily absent	30,6	38,5	34,0	51,6	36,6	25,9	30,2	25,6	18,7
Unemployed	35,2	82,8	109,0	122,3	112,6	119,2	163,7	197,2	203,5
Jobless	23,4	58,8	75,4	88,5	81,1	75,4	112,1	147,7	153,7
New entrants	11,8	23,9	33,6	33,7	31,5	43,8	51,6	49,4	49,7

TABLE 11.1 (Cont'd)

Composition of the Population
Great Santiago, 1956-1978.
(Thousands of Persons)

	December 1975	March 1976	June 1976	July 1976[9]	August 1976	September 1976	December 1976	March 1977	June 1977
Total Population	3,639,5	3,673,0	3,706,9	3,718,4	3,729,8	3,741,1	3,775,6	3,810,3	3,845,5
Men	1,742,5	1,760,3	1,761,2	1,798,0	1,795,3	1,784,7	1,791,0	1,799,6	1,806,8
Women	1,897,0	1,912,7	1,945,7	1,920,4	1,934,5	1,956,4	1,984,6	2,010,7	2,038,7
Under 14 years	1,116,0	1,123,5	1,106,7	1,108,0	1,141,1	1,121,6	1,128,7	1,139,1	1,171,2
Population of 14 years and over	2,523,5	2,549,5	2,600,3	2,610,4	2,588,7	2,619,5	2,646,9	2,671,2	2,674,3
Labor force	1,280,2	1,298,7	1,333,5	1,284,4	1,291,4	1,291,5	1,317,5	1,336,6	1,368,8
Inactives	1,243,3	1,250,7	1,266,7	1,326,1	1,297,3	1,328,0	1,329,4	1,334,5	1,305,5
Labor Force	1,280,2	1,298,7	1,333,5	1,284,4	1,291,4	1,291,5	1,317,5	1,336,6	1,368,8
Employed	1,041,2	1,041,1	1,093,0	1,074,6	1,071,9	1,089,2	1,138,3	1,151,4	1,190,4
At work	1,016,4	1,017,3	1,065,9	1,040,7	1,056,1	1,070,8	1,121,8	1,130,5	1,162,8
Temporarily absent	24,8	23,7	27,1	33,9	15,8	18,4	16,5	20,9	27,6
Unemployed	239,0	257,6	240,5	209,8	219,5	202,3	179,2	185,2	178,4
Jobless	176,6	191,7	178,6	152,4	161,0	157,0	131,6	126,6	139,2
New entrants	62,3	66,0	61,9	57,3	58,5	45,3	47,6	58,6	39,2

	September 1977	December 1977	March 1978	June 1978
Total Population	3,880,9	3,916,7	3,952,8	3,989,2
Men	1,829,6	1,846,9	1,869,5	1,892,9
Women	2,051,3	2,069,8	2,083,3	2,096,3
Under 14 years	1,162,9	1,163,8	1,158,2	1,167,0
Population of 14 years and over	2,718,0	2,752,9	2,794,6	2,822,2
Labor force	1,371,3	1,374,9	1,417,2	1,426,9
Inactives	1,346,7	1,378,0	1,377,3	1,395,3
Labor Force	1,371,3	1,374,9	1,417,2	1,426,9
Employed	1,195,6	1,193,9	1,208,9	1,244,8
At work	1,174,9	1,175,2	1,189,5	1,224,1
Temporarily absent	20,7	18,8	19,4	20,7
Unemployed	175,8	180,9	208,4	182,1
Jobless	137,3	135,8	158,2	134,3
New entrants	38,5	45,2	50,1	47,8

TABLE 11.1 (Cont'd)

Composition of the Population
Great Santiago, 1956-1978.
(Thousands of Persons)

Notes:
1. Survey based on a sample designed in 1956.
2. Survey based on a sample designed in 1960.
3. Survey based on half of the sample interviewed in September, 1962.
4. Survey based on a sample designed in 1960.
5. Survey based on a sample designed in 1963.
6. Survey with special question about inactives.
7. Survey based on a sample designed in 1963.
8. Survey based on a sample designed in 1967.
9. Data corrected in March of 1976.

Sources: The data for the October 1956 - June 1962 period are found in Universidad de Chile, Instituto de Economía, <u>Occupación y Desocupación, Gran Santiago</u>. <u>Concepción</u>. Publication No. 48 (Santiago: June 1962), table 1, p. 15. The data for the September 1962 - December 1966 period are found in Universidad de Chile, Instituto de Economía, <u>Ocupación y Desocupación, Gran Santiago</u>, publication No. 91 (Santiago: December 1966), table 1, p. 7. The data for the March 1967 - March 1970 period are found in Universidad de Chile, Instituto de Economía y Planificación, <u>Ocupación y Desocupación, Gran Santiago</u>, Publication no. 116 (Santiago: March 1970), table 1, p. 6. The data for the June 1970 - March 1973 period are found in Universidad de Chile, Instituto de Economía y Planificación, <u>Ocupación y Desocupación, Gran Santiago</u>, inscription No. 41275 (Santiago: March 1973), table 1, p. 13. The data for the December 1973 - March 1976 period are found in Universidad de Chile, Facultad de Ciencias Económicas y Administratives, Departamento de Economía, <u>Ocupación y Desocupación, en el Gran Santiago</u>, Publication no. 32 (Santiago: March 1976), table 1, p. 7. The data for the June 1976 - June 1978 period are found in Universidad de Chile, Facultad de Ciencias Económicas y Administrativas, Departamento de Economía, <u>Ocupación y Disocupación en el Gran Santiago</u>, Publication no. 58 (Santiago: June 1978), table 1, p. 5. Given that data-gathering is an ongoing process there exist some, sometimes significant, differences between the data appearing in the sources listed above and those published in the present table. The data of the present table has been corrected on the basis of recent information supplied by the Instituto de Economía.

TABLE 11.2

Weekly Hours of Work
Great Santiago, 1956-1978.
(Thousands of Persons)

	October 1956	June 1957	June 1958	March 1959	June 1959	April 1960	June 1960	September 1960[2]	September 1960[3]
Total of Persons Working[1]	588,0	597,3	589,1	566,0	614,7	638,8	638,5	-	655,6
1-10 hours	4,9	4,4	6,5	4,3	6,2	5,0	7,5	-	4,8
11-20 hours	51,5	11,7	16,8	18,6	18,1	18,1	17,2	-	15,0
21-34 hours		28,9	40,1	42,6	41,6	47,4	38,9	-	33,6
35-48 hours	525,1	367,7	341,5	321,6	350,3	353,3	356,2	-	366,6
49 hours and over		172,9	181,3	178,0	192,2	212,1	215,7	-	230,6
No data available	6,5	11,8	2,7	0,9	6,3	3,0	2,9	-	5,1
Average weekly hours of work	49,6	49,4	48,9	49,5	49,8	50,3	49,2	-	50,3

	December 1960	March 1961	June 1961	September 1961	December 1961	March 1962	June 1962	September 1962	October 1962[5]
Total of Persons Working	664,9	665,9	654,7	654,2	676,3	691,2	680,8	722,9	-
1-10 hours	5,5	7,9	6,7	5,3	7,4	6,6	8,2	8,1	-
11-20 hours	16,0	16,0	18,7	13,9	25,0	16,2	18,1	21,2	-
21-34 hours	34,7	41,9	35,4	31,0	76,5	45,5	48,3	47,2	-
35-48 hours	384,3	365,2	348,7	362,9	333,4	366,3	360,9	385,5	-
49 hours and over	214,7	233,1	240,6	238,4	232,1	254,8	244,4	258,4	-
No data available	9,6	2,0	4,9	2,9	2,1	2,0	1,1	2,7	-
Average weekly hours of work	52,1	50,6	51,0	51,6	47,2	51,1	49,4	50,8	-

	December 1962	March 1963	June 1963	September 1963	December 1963[6]	December 1963[7]	March 1964	June 1964	September 1964[8]
Total of Persons Working	706,2	710,6	712,8	726,3	732,3	714,6	732,1	731,4	811,8
1-10 hours	10,0	7,1	9,3	8,0	11,7	10,7	7,3	7,9	12,2
11-20 hours	22,1	15,6	27,1	23,2	22,0	28,6	19,8	18,8	17,9
21-34 hours	93,2	37,7	83,6	45,0	99,6	88,6	42,5	41,5	43,8
35-48 hours	340,1	375,9	360,5	369,7	367,6	364,4	395,3	397,5	449,7
49 hours and over	238,6	271,4	228,4	279,6	227,7	219,4	266,5	262,0	283,3
No data available	2,5	2,1	4,2	0,7	3,7	2,9	1,5	3,9	4,9
Average weekly hours of work	47,6	51,7	46,8	51,1	45,7	45,6	50,4	50,6	50,5

TABLE 11.2 (Cont'd)

Weekly Hours of Work
Great Santiago, 1956-1978.
(Thousands of Persons)

	September 1964	December 1964	March 1965	June 1965	September 1965	December 1965	March 1966	June 1966	September 1966
Total of Persons Working	744,2	725,2	754,4	771,4	775,1	784,0	777,8	789,2	810,6
1-10 hours	6,1	8,3	6,8	7,7	13,2	6,3	9,3	10,1	6,5
11-20 hours	17,7	26,3	18,1	17,0	23,3	27,4	17,1	24,0	22,7
21-34 hours	37,7	185,0	41,5	49,4	42,6	56,4	42,0	48,4	42,2
35-48 hours	436,9	328,7	425,5	429,7	439,5	465,7	465,1	483,9	490,4
49 hours and over	245,1	203,1	262,5	266,9	257,3	227,4	243,5	222,6	248,9
No data available	0,6	1,5	-	x	-	0,8	x	0,4	-
Average weekly hours of work	50,3	43,6	50,3	50,3	49,5	46,0	50,0	49,0	49,8
	December 1966	**March 1967[10]**	**March 1967[11]**	**June 1967**	**September 1967**	**December 1967**	**March 1968**	**June 1968**	**September 1968**
Total of Persons Working[9]	825,7	816,7	794,5	822,6	844,3	825,9	824,2	851,2	860,5
1-10 hours	9,1	12,3	15,9	13,2	10,1	9,9	15,5	16,3	17,3
11-20 hours	20,6	45,7	37,3	33,7	31,2	34,7	33,0	29,2	26,4
21-34 hours	52,0	392,0	374,2	53,5	50,7	173,4	56,8	52,6	49,7
35-48 hours	488,0	204,2	210,5	477,9	483,8	338,6	444,5	472,3	489,2
49 hours and over	255,1	162,5	154,9	244,3	268,5	258,5	273,2	280,0	274,7
No data available	x	-	0,8	x	0,8	2,5	1,2	1,0	3,2
Average weekly hours of work	48,9	40,0	40,0	48,2	48,7	45,7	48,9	48,1	48,0
	December 1968	**March 1969**	**June 1969**	**September 1969**	**December 1969**	**March 1970**	**June 1970**	**September 1970**	**December 1970**
Total of Persons Working	888,1	863,9	874,3	923,3	924,2	879,3	926,1	929,1	919,6
1-10 hours	14,9	10,4	14,9	12,9	17,2	12,2	14,3	17,2	17,9
11-20 hours	38,0	30,2	38,0	27,7	50,6	43,3	33,3	32,2	45,8
21-34 hours	189,9	57,0	55,8	57,2	217,8	376,5	72,0	52,3	341,7
35-48 hours	380,3	461,3	477,2	481,0	367,3	247,0	490,4	510,2	284,0
49 hours and over	262,0	305,0	285,1	343,5	269,0	199,8	315,3	315,7	229,3
No data available	3,0	0,9	3,5	0,9	2,3	0,4	0,7	1,6	0,9
Average weekly hours of work	44,5	49,2	49,2	49,5	44,2	41,7	48,7	48,6	42,0

TABLE 11.2 (Cont'd)

Weekly Hours of Work
Great Santiago, 1956-1978.
(Thousands of Persons)

	March 1971	June 1971	September 1971	December 1971	March 1972	June 1972	September 1972	December 1972	March 1973
Total of Persons Working	925,3	1,003,4	988,7	994,3	983,1	1,038,3	977,6	1,010,8	1,020,3
1-10 hours	12,0	16,0	16,9	10,0	6,9	16,0	9,5	12,6	8,1
11-20 hours	27,1	30,3	29,9	31,4	30,6	35,5	28,8	31,6	29,9
21-34 hours	65,5	73,4	74,9	93,7	57,3	73,8	57,8	70,8	62,8
35-48 hours	508,3	565,5	571,7	568,2	570,4	606,2	607,5	595,7	653,0
49 hours and over	312,1	316,7	294,7	290,2	317,9	306,8	273,8	300,1	265,7
No data available	0,4	0,6	0,6	0,8	-	-	0,2	-	0,8
Average weekly hours of work	48,5	48,4	46,5	45,8	48,3	47,4	47,1	47,7	46,9

	June 1973	December 1973	March 1974	June 1974	September 1974	December 1974	March 1975	June 1975	September 1975
Total of Persons Working	1,073,6	1,064,5	1,047,0	1,039,5	1,061,5	1,090,4	1,047,7	1,020,0	1,009,9
1-10 hours	16,0	24,8	19,0	36,0	25,5	18,2	24,9	28,0	24,9
11-20 hours	44,0	36,2	39,9	46,9	40,4	42,9	35,6	35,2	36,5
21-34 hours	83,8	67,6	60,1	76,6	72,7	69,0	67,5	57,5	63,9
35-48 hours	659,3	604,6	628,1	594,7	567,5	617,8	624,6	575,5	562,3
49 hours and over	270,5	329,9	295,2	273,0	350,4	338,8	291,5	316,9	319,7
No data available	-	1,3	4,7	12,4	5,1	3,8	3,6	6,9	2,6
Average weekly hours of work	46,1	48,5	46,1	45,6	47,6	47,5	46,9	47,4	48,5

	December 1975	March 1976[12]	June 1976	July 1976	August 1976	September 1976	December 1976	March 1977	June 1977
Total of Persons Working	1,034,3	1,038,1	1,087,9	1,051,9	1,070,7	1,085,1	1,133,9	1,139,9	1,180,4
1-10 hours	26,2	17,0	31,9	15,4	19,0	14,6	18,0	19,4	22,2
11-20 hours	33,1	37,0	51,5	37,3	38,8	42,3	39,3	42,4	51,3
21-34 hours	64,5	67,5	74,3	64,4	69,4	68,0	67,9	64,3	78,1
35-48 hours	577,6	608,0	578,9	606,6	619,4	644,7	648,0	633,8	655,9
49 hours and over	333,0	308,6	351,0	327,8	323,7	315,6	358,9	379,8	362,7
No data available	-	-	0,3	0,5	0,5	-	1,7	0,3	0,3
Average weekly hours of work	47,7	47,6	46,6	47,5	47,1	48,2	48,0	47,7	46,7

TABLE 11.2 (Cont'd)

Weekly Hours of Work
Great Santiago, 1956-1978.
(Thousands of Persons)

	September 1977	December 1977	March 1978	June 1978
Total of Persons Working	1,192,9	1,183,6	1,199,7	1,233,1
1-10 hours	21,0	22,2	12,7	18,8
11-20 hours	49,9	44,9	43,4	44,5
21-34 hours	75,9	62,6	66,8	71,0
35-48 hours	644,4	678,1	687,6	693,7
49 hours and over	401,4	375,9	389,2	405,1
No data available	0,3	-	-	-
Average weekly hours of work	47,3	47,4	47,9	47,4

Notes:
1. In the survey from October 1956 to March 1959 only employed persons working are included. The survey from June 1959 to September 1960 includes also the jobless who are holding temporary jobs while in the process of seeking stable employment.
2. Survey based on sample designed in 1956.
3. Survey based on sample designed in 1960.
4. Between September 1962 and March 1967 it includes the employed persons currently working and the jobless who are holding temporary jobs while in the process of seeking stable employment.
5. Survey based on half of the sample interviewed in September 1962.
6. Survey based on sample designed in 1960.
7. Survey based on sample designed in 1963.
8. Survey with a special question about inactives.
9. Included in the survey of March 1967[10] are employed persons working and the jobless who are holding temporary jobs while in the process of seeking stable employment. The surveys from March 1967[11] onwards include also the jobless and the temporary inactive ones who worked some hours during the week of reference, before passing on to this condition.
10. Survey based on sample designed in 1963.
11. Survey based on sample designed in 1967.
12. The figures for the period between December 1973 and March 1976 are those that were corrected in March of 1976.

Sources: The data for the period between October 1956 and March 1959 reflect corrected statistical information given to the author directly by the Instituto de Economía. The data for the March 1959 - June 1962 period are found in Universidad de Chile, Instituto de Economía, Ocupación y Desocupación, Gran Santiago. Concepción. Publication No. 48 (Santiago: June 1962), table 3, p. 17. The data for the September 1962 - December 1966 period are found in Universidad de Chile, Instituto de Economía, Ocupación y Desocupación, Gran Santiago, Publication no. 91 (Santiago: December 1966), table 3, p. 11. The data for the March 1967 -

TABLE 11.2 (Cont'd)

Weekly Hours of Work
Great Santiago, 1956-1978.
(Thousands of Persons)

Sources (Cont'd): March 1970 period are found in Universidad de Chile, Instituto de Economía y Planificación, Ocupación y Desocupación, Gran Santiago, Publication no. 116 (Santiago: March 1970), table 3, p. 8. The data for the June 1970 - March 1973 period are found in Universidad de Chile, Instituto de Economía y Planificación, Ocupación y Desocupación, Gran Santiago, inscription no. 41275 (Santiago: March 1973), table 3, p. 15. The data for the December 1973 - March 1976 period are found in Universidad de Chile, Facultad de Ciencias Económicas y Administrativas, Departamento de Economía, Ocupación y Desocupación en el Gran Santiago, publication no. 32 (Santiago: March 1976), table 2, p. 9. The data for the June 1976 - June 1978 period are found in Universidad de Chile, Facultad de Ciencias Económicas y Administrativas, Departamento de Economía, Ocupación y Desocupación en el Gran Santiago, Publication no. 58 (Santiago: June 1978), table 2, p. 7. The reader should be cautioned that the data of the present table, which reflect the latest, revised and corrected figures prepared by the Instituto-Departamento de Economía of the University of Chile, may differ, sometimes significantly, from the statistical information found in the sources listed above.

Labor Force and Employment by Type of Economic Activity

The absolute figures on Greater Santiago's labor force by type of economic activity between 1956 and 1978 are presented in Table 11.3. The economic activities into which the labor force is subdivided are the goods producing (which are further subdivided into agriculture, hunting, forestry and fishing; mining and quarrying; manufacturing; and construction), service producing (which are subdivided into commerce; governmental and financial services; personal and housing-household services; and community and social services), transportation, storage, communications and public utilities, activities not adequately specified and, finally, new entrants to the labor force. Between 1956 and 1978, the only category of the labor force that displays an unusual growth is that of new entrants to the labor force, rising almost tenfold between October 1956 and June 1978. The sharpest increase in the number of new entrants to the labor force between 1956 and 1978 (a fourfold one) occurs between June 1973 (11.8 thousand) and June 1978 (47.8 thousand). The peak, however, in the number of new entrants to the labor force is reached in March of 1976 (66.0 thousand).

Employment in the Greater Santiago area between 1956 and 1978 according to economic activity (the same categories as in Table 11.3) is presented in Table 11.4.

Occupational Status

The labor force of Great Santiago according to occupational status between 1959 and 1978 is presented in Table 11.5. The employed population of Great Santiago according to occupational status is presented, in thousands of persons, for the period between 1959 and 1978 in Table 11.6. The occupational status categories of Table 11.5 are those of employers, own-account workers, salaried employees, wage employees, unpaid family members, persons for which no data is available and new entrants to the labor force (or new entrants without a job). The occupational status classification of Table 11.6 is the same as that of Table 11.5 except that it does omit the category "new entrants to the labor force."

Preferences for Work of Inactives

The preferences for work of the inactive population of Greater Santiago between 1964 and 1978 are presented in Table 11.7. The figures of Table 11.7 are in thousands of persons. The total inactive population is divided into persons with a desire to work, persons without a desire to work and those for which no information was available. Those persons with a desire to work are classified into five categories according to whether they desire to work (a) the entire year 40 or more hours; (b) the entire year from 20 to 39 hours, (c) the entire year less than 20 hours, (d) an unspecified schedule or (e) some months a year.

The Santiago Labor Force Time Series of the National Institute of Statistics

The population of the Greater Santiago area according to sex and employment situation between 1966 and 1977 is given in Table 11.8. The total population is first divided into two groups by sex and then into persons under twelve years of age and twelve years of age and over. Then, those with twelve years of age and over are divided into those belonging to the labor force and those not included in the labor force. Table 11.8 gives population and labor force for the Greater Santiago area in absolute figures and in percentages.

The most striking feature of the figures presented in Table 11.8 is the decline in the share of the labor force from 51.5 per cent of the Greater Santiago population of twelve years and over in July-October 1966 to 42.2 per cent in October-December 1977 and a corresponding rise of the inactive population, in the same periods, from 48.5 per cent to 57.8 per cent.

The Greater Santiago labor force according to occupational group between 1966 and 1977 is presented both in absolute figures and in percentages in Table 11.9. The most notable event revealed by Table 11.9 is the decline in the percentage importance of blue collar workers or wage employees.

TABLE 11.3

Labor Force by Economic Activity
Great Santiago, 1956-1978.
(Thousands of Persons)

Economic Activity	October 1956	June 1957	June 1958	March 1959	June 1959	April 1960	June 1960	September 1960[1]
Total Labor Force	639,0	651,5	666,6	679,3	678,8	707,7	715,0	-
Goods Producing Activities	270,9	249,9	264,0	265,2	258,6	282,8	270,7	-
Agriculture, Hunting, Forestry and Fishing	6,7	6,2	7,0	5,4	7,0	6,1	5,4	-
Mining and Quarrying	3,9	2,9	3,4	3,2	2,1	2,8	2,5	-
Manufacturing	209,7	197,7	208,1	208,1	206,3	224,1	214,4	-
Construction	50,6	43,1	45,5	48,5	43,2	49,8	48,4	-
Service Producing Activities	315,7	347,6	347,4	360,5	362,1	368,4	390,9	-
Commerce	91,7	100,2	92,5	109,2	102,2	103,0	102,9	-
Governmental and Financial Services	47,3	48,2	47,0	48,5	50,4	49,3	53,0	-
Personal and Housing Services	176,7	199,2	207,9	134,1	145,5	216,1	235,0	-
Community and Social Services					68,6	64,0		-
Transportation, Storage, Communications and Public Utilities	44,1	40,9	45,8	44,8	50,6	48,7	43,2	-
Activities not adequately specified	3,6	3,4	0,5	0,4	0,7	0,2	0,4	-
New entrants to the labor force	4,7	9,7	8,9	8,4	6,9	7,6	9,8	-

1. Survey based on a sample designed in 1956.

TABLE 11.3 (Cont'd)

Labor Force by Economic Activity
Great Santiago, 1956-1978.
(Thousands of Persons)

Economic Activity	September 1960[2]	December 1960	March 1961	June 1961	September 1961	December 1961	March 1962	June 1962
Total Labor Force	725,3	736,7	741,0	724,0	729,6	741,9	761,6	754,5
Goods Producing Activities	255,5	256,7	258,6	240,2	255,5	267,5	264,3	254,1
Agriculture, Hunting, Forestry and Fishing	7,0	7,2	7,3	7,8	7,1	5,8	6,3	7,2
Mining and Quarrying	2,3	4,0	4,0	4,3	4,1	4,1	4,0	2,6
Manufacturing	201,4	200,5	207,6	189,1	202,2	210,2	205,4	201,3
Construction	44,7	45,0	39,7	39,1	42,1	47,4	48,6	43,2
Service Producing Activities	407,0	419,6	422,1	424,6	416,6	416,4	436,6	440,9
Commerce	102,7	108,2	107,4	105,0	108,0	113,2	122,9	126,9
Governmental and Financial Services	59,9	57,2	58,5	64,3	55,0	55,8	53,9	60,8
Personal and Housing Services	148,0	143,9	142,7	144,8	139,1	131,4	141,1	143,0
Community and Social Services	96,4	110,3	113,5	110,7	114,5	116,0	118,7	110,4
Transportation, Storage, Communications and Public Utilities	52,1	52,9	49,4	50,6	49,7	51,8	50,3	51,5
Activities not adequately specified	2,1	1,3	0,4	1,1	0,7	1,1	-	0,4
New entrants to the labor force	8,6	6,0	10,9	7,6	7,3	5,5	10,8	7,7

2. Survey based on a sample designed in 1960.

TABLE 11.3 (Cont'd)

Labor Force by Economic Activity
Great Santiago, 1956-1978.
(Thousands of Persons)

Economic Activity	September 1962	October 1962[3]	December 1962	March 1963	June 1963	September 1963	December 1963[4]	December 1963[5]
Total Labor Force	773,7	758,0	774,1	778,3	775,3	788,3	785,6	779,2
Goods Producing Activities	266,2	282,0	264,6	263,2	252,0	257,7	266,3	288,7
Agriculture, Hunting, Forestry and Fishing	7,0	4,5	7,5	8,6	8,5	8,0	5,5	7,0
Mining and Quarrying	3,0	2,3	1,7	1,7	1,7	1,8	2,4	2,5
Manufacturing	210,5	223,6	209,9	207,9	199,3	203,6	209,8	220,7
Construction	45,7	51,5	45,5	45,0	42,8	44,3	48,7	58,5
Service Producing Activities	448,1	424,5	454,5	455,3	457,9	468,5	459,6	434,3
Commerce	123,7	122,0	128,9	121,2	123,5	130,1	128,8	121,6
Governmental and Financial Services	59,6	51,5	60,9	66,3	61,7	63,6	57,3	60,2
Personal and Housing Services	147,3	144,8	149,4	152,1	151,9	149,6	150,8	135,0
Community and Social Services	117,5	106,1	115,3	115,7	120,9	125,2	122,6	117,5
Transportation, Storage, Communications and Public Utilities	53,0	47,0	50,4	49,1	57,7	54,8	53,4	51,2
Activities not adequately specified	1,2	0,8	1,0	0,7	0,4	0,2	0,8	0,1
New entrants to the labor force	5,5	3,8	3,8	9,3	7,5	6,3	4,7	4,7

3. Survey based on half of the sample interviewed in September of 1962.
4. Survey based on a sample designed in 1960.
5. Survey based on a sample designed in 1963.

TABLE 11.3 (Cont'd)

Labor Force by Economic Activity
Great Santiago, 1956-1978.
(Thousands of Persons)

Economic Activity	March 1964	June 1964	September 1964[6]	September 1964	December 1964	March 1965	June 1965	September 1965
Total Labor Force	790,9	793,6	877,7	814,5	794,2	825,2	828,0	840,5
Goods Producing Activities	294,3	290,1	302,8	303,4	286,9	297,6	308,2	307,3
Agriculture, Hunting, Forestry and Fishing	9,5	8,1	5,3	12,6	7,3	8,0	6,0	8,2
Mining and Quarrying	2,6	3,3	1,8	2,8	2,0	1,8	3,3	2,6
Manufacturing	215,7	218,1	242,2	228,6	222,0	239,3	244,8	247,5
Construction	66,5	60,7	53,5	59,5	55,6	48,5	54,1	49,0
Service Producing Activities	438,9	445,6	513,5	448,3	451,0	466,1	461,0	469,8
Commerce	118,4	120,1	145,7	114,0	128,0	121,4	123,2	121,8
Governmental and Financial Services	56,3	60,5	66,7	61,1	62,8	68,5	68,7	69,4
Personal and Housing Services	131,8	137,0	163,3	141,4	129,3	141,0	138,9	146,3
Community and Social Services	132,4	128,0	137,8	131,8	130,9	135,2	130,2	132,3
Transportation, Storage, Communications and Public Utilities	51,5	49,7	53,5	52,6	50,1	53,2	49,0	55,0
Activities not adequately specified	-	0,5	0,9	1,5	-	-	-	-
New entrants to the labor force	7,1	7,9	7,0	8,7	5,6	9,1	9,9	8,4

6. Survey with a special question about inactives.

TABLE 11.3 (Cont'd)

Labor Force by Economic Activity
Great Santiago, 1956-1978.
(Thousands of Persons)

Economic Activity	December 1965	March 1966	June 1966	September 1966	December 1966	March 1967[7]	March 1967[8]	June 1967
Total Labor Force	845,8	841,3	854,6	874,4	895,1	900,2	877,9	898,8
Goods Producing Activities	310,9	302,1	317,4	316,2	319,8	314,2	307,3	333,5
Agriculture, Hunting, Forestry and Fishing	6,7	7,8	6,3	8,3	7,9	7,2	7,0	10,8
Mining and Quarrying	2,9	3,4	3,0	3,0	3,7	3,6	2,6	1,8
Manufacturing	245,6	232,5	247,0	249,9	257,9	258,4	237,0	258,9
Construction	55,7	58,4	61,2	55,0	50,3	45,0	59,7	62,9
Service Producing Activities	475,2	479,0	473,8	496,9	500,1	511,3	502,2	497,0
Commerce	129,5	127,1	129,6	131,1	139,5	143,1	130,8	133,9
Governmental and Financial Services	68,0	71,2	72,2	80,3	77,7	73,8	79,9	81,8
Personal and Housing Services	136,1	137,5	139,0	136,9	147,3	151,2	144,9	133,9
Community and Social Services	141,6	143,2	133,2	148,6	135,6	143,1	147,5	146,5
Transportation, Storage, Communications and Public Utilities	52,1	52,6	52,2	55,1	63,4	65,7	60,6	59,3
Activities not adequately specified	x	-	0,4	-	-	-	0,9	-
New entrants to the labor force	6,8	7,6	10,9	7,0	9,8	9,0	7,9	9,0

7. Survey based on a sample designed in 1963.
8. Survey based on a sample designed in 1967.

TABLE 11.3 (Cont'd)

Labor Force by Economic Activity
Great Santiago, 1956-1978.
(Thousands of Persons)

Economic Activity	September 1967	December 1967	March 1968	June 1968	September 1968	December 1968	March 1969	June 1969
Total Labor Force	914,9	920,7	902,7	929,1	943,2	965,1	953,0	968,1
Goods Producing Activities	330,3	330,5	308,2	327,1	341,4	326,6	309,7	331,4
Agriculture, Hunting, Forestry and Fishing	11,0	11,0	8,6	11,4	12,4	8,8	10,5	7,6
Mining and Quarrying	3,7	3,7	3,5	2,5	2,0	3,6	2,9	2,6
Manufacturing	264,4	261,5	244,0	261,2	275,1	256,7	249,7	265,4
Construction	51,2	54,3	52,2	52,1	51,9	57,5	47,7	55,8
Service Producing Activities	516,0	519,3	521,3	523,7	526,3	559,5	556,6	551,1
Commerce	132,7	137,2	140,0	134,1	135,4	154,0	146,8	159,8
Governmental and Financial Services	77,8	78,3	79,7	77,9	81,4	87,8	82,9	74,5
Personal and Housing Services	146,4	149,2	140,3	149,7	151,3	155,5	157,2	142,9
Community and Social Services	159,2	154,7	161,3	162,1	158,2	162,3	169,6	174,0
Transportation, Storage, Communications and Public Utilities	62,2	59,8	63,0	67,2	64,0	68,2	69,6	69,0
Activities not adequately specified	x	x	0,7	-	-	2,0	1,0	0,9
New entrants to the labor force	7,3	10,1	9,6	11,2	11,4	8,8	15,2	15,9

TABLE 11.3 (Cont'd)

Labor Force by Economic Activity
Great Santiago, 1956-1978.
(Thousands of Persons)

Economic Activity	September 1969	December 1969	March 1970	June 1970	September 1970	December 1970	March 1971	June 1971
Total Labor Force	992,9	1,012,6	987,4	1,023,4	1,021,0	1,034,1	1,031,4	1,073,8
Goods Producing Activities	346,5	332,1	314,0	353,1	353,5	338,2	338,6	350,9
Agriculture, Hunting, Forestry and Fishing	6,0	5,8	6,6	4,7	5,6	5,7	3,9	7,7
Mining and Quarrying	2,0	3,5	3,4	3,8	3,1	2,7	4,2	4,9
Manufacturing	284,0	271,1	247,4	279,2	281,5	268,3	271,4	279,7
Construction	53,6	51,7	56,6	65,6	63,3	61,5	59,1	58,8
Service Producing Activities	561,0	599,8	585,0	586,2	577,8	601,6	589,0	634,5
Commerce	153,9	155,1	143,0	148,2	159,1	164,0	146,8	157,4
Governmental and Financial Services	81,4	91,4	95,2	84,2	87,1	92,9	100,5	100,9
Personal and Housing Services	158,9	167,2	157,9	157,3	145,0	156,3	150,0	164,7
Community and Social Services	166,8	186,2	189,0	196,6	186,6	188,4	191,7	211,5
Transportation, Storage, Communications and Public Utilities	74,5	69,3	71,9	68,8	76,1	77,0	82,6	75,9
Activities not adequately specified	2,0	0,7	1,6	1,1	2,0	0,2	-	-
New entrants to the labor force	8,9	10,7	14,9	14,2	11,6	17,2	21,2	11,4

TABLE 11.3 (Cont'd)

Labor Force by Economic Activity
Great Santiago, 1956-1978.
(Thousands of Persons)

Economic Activity	September 1971	December 1971	March 1972	June 1972	September 1972	December 1972	March 1973	June 1973
Total Labor Force	1,061,8	1,059,4	1,060,6	1,105,3	1,065,9	1,079,4	1,104,1	1,135,0
Goods Producing Activities	363,6	375,0	351,7	356,2	365,2	358,5	366,9	375,9
Agriculture, Hunting, Forestry and Fishing	6,6	6,3	7,1	6,2	4,7	9,4	9,1	4,4
Mining and Quarrying	3,8	2,5	2,7	4,2	3,3	3,7	3,0	2,0
Manufacturing	288,5	297,9	285,2	289,5	300,8	295,8	301,0	320,3
Construction	64,8	68,3	56,9	56,3	56,4	49,5	53,9	49,2
Service Producing Activities	607,4	593,6	615,1	657,0	616,5	628,2	635,0	660,7
Commerce	157,6	155,0	154,9	174,8	167,4	163,5	156,4	170,2
Governmental and Financial Services	99,2	106,6	107,2	106,4	93,7	117,7	119,2	106,6
Personal and Housing Services	160,6	137,6	151,7	153,6	153,1	137,8	145,3	156,4
Community and Social Services	190,1	194,4	201,3	222,2	202,3	209,1	214,0	227,4
Transportation, Storage, Communications and Public Utilities	77,4	79,8	81,6	75,0	75,3	83,9	87,1	85,6
Activities not adequately specified	0,9	0,6	0,6	1,4	0,4	-	0,8	1,0
New entrants to the labor force	12,4	10,4	11,6	15,8	8,6	8,8	14,3	11,8

TABLE 11.3 (Cont'd)

Labor Force by Economic Activity
Great Santiago, 1956-1978.
(Thousands of Persons)

Economic Activity	December 1973	March 1974	June 1974	September 1974	December 1974	March 1975	June 1975	September 1975
Total Labor Force	1,180,3	1,179,2	1,182,9	1,198,7	1,228,6	1,230,9	1,226,7	1,223,3
Goods Producing Activities	466,6	454,6	458,5	463,0	492,3	464,2	448,4	440,3
Agriculture, Hunting, Forestry and Fishing	21,2	15,3	19,8	19,3	24,2	20,7	16,0	18,2
Mining and Quarrying	6,5	7,7	8,7	4,8	7,7	6,9	7,9	8,1
Manufacturing	351,6	336,5	337,7	338,6	358,0	338,5	322,3	320,0
Construction	87,2	95,1	92,2	100,4	102,5	98,1	102,3	94,0
Service Producing Activities	592,5	595,7	588,2	606,2	602,9	613,9	631,8	633,8
Commerce	184,1	183,6	179,0	194,2	180,5	191,2	202,8	190,7
Governmental and Financial Services	87,5	90,9	86,5	98,2	105,6	115,2	118,5	115,8
Personal and Housing Services	181,6	176,8	182,8	172,8	168,1	169,6	179,5	181,4
Community and Social Services	139,4	144,4	139,9	141,0	148,7	137,8	131,0	145,9
Transportation, Storage, Communications and Public Utilities	89,5	91,1	97,7	90,5	84,3	95,0	94,6	98,3
Activities not adequately specified	7,8	4,2	4,7	7,5	5,3	6,2	2,5	1,2
New entrants to the labor force	23,9	33,6	33,7	31,5	43,8	51,6	49,4	49,7

TABLE 11.3 (Cont'd)

Labor Force by Economic Activity
Great Santiago, 1956-1978.
(Thousands of Persons)

Economic Activity	December 1975	March 1976	June 1976	July 1976	August 1976	September 1976	December 1976	March 1977
Total Labor Force	1,280,2	1,298,7	1,333,5	1,284,4	1,291,4	1,291,5	1,317,5	1,336,6
Goods Producing Activities	450,3	450,6	472,2	461,7	454,3	468,6	461,4	435,5
Agriculture, Hunting, Forestry and Fishing	20,3	21,0	20,7	19,5	16,3	19,6	17,0	11,5
Mining and Quarrying	5,9	5,0	5,9	7,3	6,9	7,0	6,9	6,3
Manufacturing	339,3	330,4	354,8	347,6	338,5	345,0	350,3	344,0
Construction	84,8	94,2	90,9	87,3	92,6	96,9	87,1	73,8
Service Producing Activities	657,7	682,0	705,5	663,9	689,3	682,5	695,7	723,2
Commerce	190,3	211,4	232,8	203,5	201,2	201,3	197,5	209,3
Governmental and Financial Services	128,7	128,7	118,8	136,0	146,4	128,6	126,6	133,7
Personal and Housing Services	182,8	183,2	205,4	179,0	195,5	201,8	211,8	216,6
Community and Social Services	155,9	158,7	148,6	145,4	146,2	150,7	159,7	163,7
Transportation, Storage, Communications and Public Utilities	104,9	100,0	93,1	97,7	87,9	92,6	109,1	115,4
Activities not adequately specified	5,0	0,3	0,8	3,6	1,5	2,5	3,7	3,9
New entrants to the labor force	62,3	66,0	61,9	57,3	58,5	45,3	47,6	58,6

TABLE 11.3 (Cont'd)

Labor Force by Economic Activity
Great Santiago, 1956-1978.
(Thousands of Persons)

Economic Activity	June 1977	September 1977	December 1977	March 1978	June 1978
Total Labor Force	1,368,8	1,371,3	1,374,9	1,417,2	1,426,9
Goods Producing Activities	485,3	465,2	496,6	472,0	488,4
Agriculture, Hunting, Forestry and Fishing	18,1	18,1	18,2	15,6	16,4
Mining and Quarrying	6,2	4,8	7,1	8,4	7,6
Manufacturing	370,5	347,8	371,6	353,9	360,9
Construction	90,5	94,5	99,6	94,1	103,5
Service Producing Activities	744,0	771,6	735,9	802,7	787,0
Commerce	239,4	245,9	221,6	231,3	238,6
Governmental and Financial Services	133,8	138,1	130,0	150,4	152,6
Personal and Housing Services	208,9	226,2	219,8	242,9	227,1
Community and Social Services	161,9	161,4	164,6	178,2	168,7
Transportation, Storage, Communications and Public Utilities	98,1	90,5	97,2	91,1	101,6
Activities not adequately specified	2,2	5,6	-	1,3	2,2
New entrants to the labor force	39,2	38,5	45,2	50,1	47,8

Sources: The data for the period between October 1956 and December 1966 reflect corrected statistical information given to the author directly by the Instituto de Economía. It is also important to mention that the time series of this table, which are the latest, revised and corrected ones prepared by the Instituto-Departamento de Economía of the University of Chile, do differ, sometimes substantially and especially for earlier time periods, from the statistical information presented in the sources listed below. The data for the March 1967 - March 1970 period are found in Universidad de Chile, Instituto de Economía y Planificación, Ocupación y Desocupación, Gran Santiago, publication No. 116 (Santiago: March 1970), table 5, p. 10. The data for the June 1970 - March 1973 period are found in Universidad de Chile, Instituto de Economía y Planificación, Ocupación y Desocupación, Gran Santiago, inscription No. 41275 (Santiago: March 1973), table 5, p. 17. The data for the December 1973 - March 1976 period are found in Universidad de Chile, Facultad de Ciencias Económicas y Administrativas, Departamento de Economía, Ocupación y Desocupación en el Gran Santiago, publication No. 32 (Santiago: March 1976), table 3, p. 11. The data for the June 1976 - June 1978 period are found in Universidad de Chile, Facultad de Ciencias Económicas y Administrativas, Departamento de Economía, Ocupación y Desocupación en el Gran Santiago, publication No. 58 (Santiago: June 1978), table 3, p. 9.

TABLE 11.4

Employment by Economic Activity
Great Santiago, 1956-1978.
(Thousands of Persons)

Economic Activity	October 1956	June 1956	June 1958	March 1959	June 1959	April 1960	June 1960	September 1960[1]
Total Employment	596,5	609,8	603,5	608,4	628,6	655,8	657,7	-
Goods Producing Activities	247,3	229,3	233,0	228,0	237,0	256,9	244,6	-
Agriculture, Hunting, Forestry and Fishing	6,2	5,2	5,7	4,8	6,7	5,2	5,2	-
Mining and Quarrying	3,3	2,8	2,4	2,2	1,6	2,2	2,3	-
Manufacturing	196,2	186,4	191,1	183,4	193,8	208,0	196,6	-
Construction	41,6	35,0	33,8	37,6	34,9	41,5	40,5	-
Service Producing Activities	304,0	338,7	328,5	339,1	344,8	352,0	372,6	-
Commerce	88,4	97,5	87,3	102,1	96,9	98,0	98,3	-
Governmental and Financial Services	45,3	47,0	44,9	47,6	48,8	47,8	50,7	-
Personal and Housing Services	170,3	194,1	196,2	124,1	137,6	206,2	223,6	-
Community and Social Services				65,3	61,5			-
Transportation, Storage, Communication and Public Utilities	42,2	38,9	41,7	41,1	46,2	46,7	40,1	-
Activities not adequately specified	3,0	2,9	0,3	0,2	0,7	0,2	0,4	-

1. Survey based on a sample designed in 1956.

TABLE 11.4 (Cont'd)

Employment by Economic Activity
Great Santiago, 1956-1978.
(Thousands of Persons)

Economic Activity	September 1960[2]	December 1960	March 1961	June 1961	September 1961	December 1961	March 1962	June 1962
Total Employment	672,1	684,9	684,5	672,8	679,5	705,0	714,7	711,5
Goods Producing Activities	231,9	234,1	233,7	216,0	234,1	249,4	244,3	234,9
Agriculture, Hunting, Forestry and Fishing	6,4	6,7	6,5	6,5	6,3	5,3	5,3	6,4
Mining and Quarrying	2,1	3,7	3,3	3,8	3,1	3,5	2,7	2,6
Manufacturing	186,8	187,5	192,2	174,2	188,8	198,2	192,8	188,5
Construction	36,5	36,2	31,7	31,6	35,9	42,4	43,5	37,6
Service Producing Activities	390,5	400,5	404,2	408,3	398,1	404,6	422,4	426,6
Commerce	97,2	103,0	102,0	101,2	102,1	108,8	118,7	122,0
Governmental and Financial Services	58,8	55,4	56,5	62,3	53,6	54,6	53,4	59,9
Personal and Housing Services	143,6	138,2	138,1	138,9	134,9	129,1	137,3	139,0
Community and Social Services	90,9	103,8	107,6	106,0	107,5	112,1	113,0	105,8
Transportation, Storage, Communication and Public Utilities	48,4	49,2	47,0	47,9	47,0	50,2	48,3	49,8
Activities not adequately specified	1,4	1,1	-	0,8	0,5	1,1	-	0,4

2. Survey based on a sample designed in 1960.

TABLE 11.4 (Cont'd)

Employment by Economic Activity
Great Santiago, 1956-1978.
(Thousands of Persons)

Economic Activity	September 1962	October 1962[3]	December 1962	March 1963	June 1963	September 1963	December 1963[4]	December 1963[5]
Total Employment	740,8	726,0	737,1	735,5	735,2	747,3	757,5	745,7
Goods Producing Activities	249,5	267,2	246,0	247,1	252,9	239,9	250,7	272,8
Agriculture, Hunting, Forestry and Fishing	6,2	4,4	7,2	8,1	7,3	7,5	5,3	6,7
Mining and Quarrying	2,4	1,5	1,5	1,5	1,7	1,5	1,5	2,2
Manufacturing	199,3	214,2	199,2	195,6	188,6	191,3	199,2	211,0
Construction	41,6	47,2	38,2	41,9	39,2	39,6	44,7	52,9
Service Producing Activities	439,0	412,4	442,1	439,1	443,7	455,1	453,7	423,6
Commerce	120,7	117,6	125,6	116,2	119,3	124,8	126,5	118,6
Governmental and Financial Services	59,1	51,5	59,4	65,5	60,6	62,8	57,6	59,7
Personal and Housing Services	145,8	141,6	146,8	147,8	147,6	147,2	149,2	132,0
Community and Social Services	113,4	101,6	110,3	109,6	116,2	120,3	120,4	113,3
Transportation, Storage, Communication and Public Utilities	51,5	45,7	48,2	47,8	54,6	51,6	51,5	49,2
Activities not adequately specified	1,2	0,7	1,0	0,7	0,4	-	1,5	x

3. Survey based on half of the sample interviewed in September of 1962.
4. Survey based on a sample designed in 1960.
5. Survey based on a sample designed in 1963.

TABLE 11.4 (Cont'd)

Employment by Economic Activity
Great Santiago, 1956-1978.
(Thousands of Persons)

Economic Activity	March 1964	June 1964	September 1964[6]	September 1964	December 1964	March 1965	June 1965	September 1965
Total Employment	750,6	754,5	833,9	764,4	756,1	774,9	786,6	790,9
Goods Producing Activities	274,0	271,9	282,7	279,3	266,2	274,2	291,0	287,1
Agriculture, Hunting, Forestry and Fishing	9,0	7,6	4,2	12,4	6,8	7,7	5,5	7,1
Mining and Quarrying	2,3	3,0	1,7	2,3	1,5	1,5	3,1	2,4
Manufacturing	203,4	207,9	229,3	214,7	211,0	225,5	235,2	236,5
Construction	59,3	53,6	47,5	49,9	46,9	39,5	47,2	41,1
Service Producing Activities	427,0	434,8	498,7	432,7	440,8	451,0	449,2	451,6
Commerce	114,8	116,3	140,9	108,3	124,8	117,0	119,6	116,3
Governmental and Financial Services	55,5	59,3	65,9	60,6	62,0	67,4	68,4	68,0
Personal and Housing Services	129,1	134,1	160,1	137,0	127,0	137,2	136,1	140,8
Community and Social Services	127,6	125,2	131,8	126,8	127,0	129,4	125,1	126,5
Transportation, Storage, Communications and Public Utilities	50,3	47,4	51,7	50,9	48,4	50,4	46,4	52,2
Activities not adequately specified	-	0,5	0,8	1,5	-	-	-	-

6. Survey with a special question about inactives.

TABLE 11.4 (Cont'd)

Employment by Economic Activity
Great Santiago, 1956-1978.
(Thousands of Persons)

Economic Activity	December 1965	March 1966	June 1966	September 1966	December 1966	March 1967[7]	March 1967[8]	June 1967
Total Employment	806,1	801,8	803,6	828,1	846,7	850,6	822,5	845,8
Goods Producing Activities	293,4	286,2	296,6	294,8	300,5	292,6	280,5	307,0
Agriculture, Hunting, Forestry and Fishing	5,6	7,2	5,2	8,3	7,6	6,8	6,6	9,3
Mining and Quarrying	2,4	3,2	2,5	2,5	3,4	3,4	2,5	0,8
Manufacturing	235,4	222,1	234,1	238,5	247,2	245,0	223,7	245,3
Construction	50,0	53,7	54,9	45,5	42,3	37,4	47,7	51,6
Service Producing Activities	461,9	465,1	457,1	482,0	485,1	495,9	484,5	482,1
Commerce	125,8	121,9	123,6	126,7	134,6	139,5	125,8	129,4
Governmental and Financial Services	66,9	70,6	71,6	79,5	76,2	72,3	78,1	81,2
Personal and Housing Services	132,2	133,9	135,2	132,5	141,4	146,3	139,8	130,3
Community and Social Services	137,0	138,7	126,9	143,3	132,9	137,8	139,8	141,2
Transportation, Storage, Communications and Public Utilities	50,0	50,5	49,6	52,2	59,3	62,1	56,8	56,7
Activities not adequately specified	x	-	0,4	-	-	-	0,8	-

7. Survey based on a sample designed in 1963.
8. Survey based on a sample designed in 1967.

TABLE 11.4 (Cont'd)

Employment by Economic Activity
Great Santiago, 1956-1978.
(Thousands of Persons)

Economic Activity	September 1967	December 1967	March 1968	June 1968	September 1968	December 1968	March 1969	June 1969
Total Employment	861,8	861,8	852,4	869,7	879,5	912,9	888,2	899,0
Goods Producing Activities	305,1	302,5	285,9	299,0	312,2	303,2	289,6	307,7
Agriculture, Hunting, Forestry and Fishing	10,3	9,5	7,3	9,5	11,1	8,3	9,8	6,8
Mining and Quarrying	3,4	2,6	3,3	2,4	1,7	2,9	3,6	2,6
Manufacturing	249,9	243,9	231,2	274,4	258,6	244,5	237,1	252,3
Construction	41,4	46,5	44,1	39,8	40,8	47,5	40,0	46,2
Service Producing Activities	498,1	501,6	504,6	506,4	507,2	541,9	530,3	524,8
Commerce	128,4	133,6	134,5	128,8	129,0	148,9	141,2	153,4
Governmental and Financial Services	76,7	76,7	78,9	76,1	79,4	86,6	81,7	72,9
Personal and Housing Services	141,3	145,6	136,2	146,1	147,0	151,6	150,1	134,4
Community and Social Services	151,7	145,6	155,0	155,6	151,8	154,8	158,1	164,1
Transportation, Storage, Communications and Public Utilities	57,7	56,9	61,2	64,4	60,1	66,0	66,6	65,7
Activities not adequately specified	x	x	0,7	-	-	1,9	1,8	0,9

TABLE 11.4 (Cont'd)

Employment by Economic Activity
Great Santiago, 1956-1978.
(Thousands of Persons)

Economic Activity	September 1969	December 1969	March 1970	June 1970	September 1970	December 1970	March 1971	June 1971
Total Employment	940,3	958,0	920,0	951,9	955,3	948,8	946,4	1,018,0
Goods Producing Activities	325,3	309,4	285,1	322,9	325,3	301,5	300,0	326,6
Agriculture, Hunting, Forestry and Fishing	5,6	4,9	6,4	3,8	5,2	4,2	3,7	6,4
Mining and Quarrying	2,8	3,2	3,4	3,4	2,4	2,2	3,5	3,9
Manufacturing	269,9	260,0	230,5	261,4	266,7	250,5	249,2	266,5
Construction	47,0	41,3	44,8	54,3	51,0	44,7	43,6	49,8
Service Producing Activities	541,6	582,3	565,6	563,7	556,0	575,5	568,6	619,1
Commerce	148,6	151,0	138,5	142,8	153,5	157,8	143,2	152,1
Governmental and Financial Services	79,9	90,5	94,5	83,5	85,7	91,6	99,2	99,8
Personal and Housing Services	154,2	162,4	152,4	150,5	140,3	149,8	141,7	162,1
Community and Social Services	158,9	178,3	180,3	186,9	176,5	176,4	184,6	205,2
Transportation, Storage, Communications and Public Utilities	71,5	65,8	67,7	64,5	72,1	71,5	77,8	72,5
Activities not adequately specified	1,9	0,5	1,6	0,9	2,0	0,2	-	-

TABLE 11.4 (Cont'd)

Employment by Economic Activity
Great Santiago, 1956-1978.
(Thousands of Persons)

Economic Activity	September 1971	December 1971	March 1972	June 1972	September 1972	December 1972	March 1973	June 1973
Total Employment	1,011,1	1,019,3	1,010,2	1,064,7	1,034,0	1,040,9	1,062,5	1,099,8
Goods Producing Activities	344,5	359,5	332,8	344,4	353,9	342,2	354,4	365,9
Agriculture, Hunting, Forestry and Fishing	5,8	5,5	6,9	6,2	4,5	9,0	9,1	4,4
Mining and Quarrying	3,6	2,5	2,5	3,7	3,3	3,5	2,8	2,0
Manufacturing	278,6	289,8	272,0	282,2	293,3	285,0	292,2	311,9
Construction	56,5	61,7	51,4	52,4	52,9	44,6	50,3	47,6
Service Producing Activities	591,1	580,7	598,7	646,2	606,8	618,0	622,3	648,7
Commerce	152,5	151,8	151,9	171,5	163,2	160,0	153,6	165,8
Governmental and Financial Services	96,9	106,0	106,4	106,0	93,5	117,0	118,4	105,0
Personal and Housing Services	157,0	134,0	147,9	150,9	150,5	135,4	142,4	154,8
Community and Social Services	184,6	188,9	192,6	217,8	199,5	205,6	207,9	223,0
Transportation, Storage, Communications and Public Utilities	74,6	78,6	78,3	72,7	72,9	80,8	84,9	84,2
Activities not adequately specified	0,9	0,6	0,4	1,4	0,4	-	0,8	1,0

TABLE 11.4 (Cont'd)

Employment by Economic Activity
Great Santiago, 1956-1978.
(Thousands of Persons)

Economic Activity	December 1973[9]	March 1974	June 1974	September 1974	December 1974	March 1975	June 1975	September 1975
Total Employment	1,097,6	1,070,3	1,060,6	1,086,1	1,109,3	1,067,2	1,029,5	1,019,9
Goods Producing Activities	438,9	415,1	414,1	420,4	452,5	401,7	364,1	353,4
Agriculture, Hunting, Forestry and Fishing	20,1	14,3	17,6	16,8	22,0	18,8	14,0	17,1
Mining and Quarrying	5,6	5,9	6,9	4,3	7,2	6,4	6,9	7,1
Manufacturing	334,4	310,9	310,7	312,6	333,3	301,7	273,1	265,0
Construction	77,8	84,1	78,9	86,6	90,0	74,8	70,1	64,2
Service Producing Activities	568,6	565,7	550,3	576,4	572,0	570,7	577,0	580,0
Commerce	174,9	173,5	169,1	184,6	171,0	176,3	187,6	171,7
Governmental and Financial Services	85,9	88,8	82,6	95,1	102,2	110,2	111,6	109,7
Personal and Housing Services	172,7	164,8	165,9	160,8	156,6	152,5	155,1	162,0
Community and Social Services	135,1	138,5	132,7	136,0	142,2	131,6	122,7	136,7
Transportation, Storage, Communications and Public Utilities	84,1	85,2	91,5	82,5	80,0	88,9	86,0	85,3
Activities not adequately specified	6,9	4,2	4,7	6,7	4,8	5,9	2,5	1,2

9. The figures for the period between December 1973 and March 1976 are those that were corrected in March of 1976.

TABLE 11.4 (Cont'd)

Employment by Economic Activity
Great Santiago, 1956-1978.
(Thousands of Persons)

Economic Activity	December 1975	March 1976	June 1976	July 1976	August 1976	September 1976	December 1976	March 1977
Total Employment	1,041,2	1,041,1	1,093,0	1,074,6	1,071,9	1,089,2	1,138,3	1,151,4
Goods Producing Activities	358,2	348,9	373,8	378,6	368,8	381,3	392,5	375,4
Agriculture, Hunting, Forestry and Fishing	16,5	17,0	16,1	16,4	14,3	16,9	14,6	10,7
Mining and Quarrying	5,2	4,5	4,8	7,0	5,7	5,5	6,4	5,5
Manufacturing	285,3	270,6	294,4	298,6	287,4	296,2	306,6	304,5
Construction	51,2	56,7	58,5	56,6	61,5	62,7	64,9	54,7
Service Producing Activities	587,3	604,8	634,4	605,1	623,9	622,9	641,9	667,5
Commerce	169,3	184,9	208,9	185,0	177,3	184,5	182,7	190,7
Governmental and Financial Services	111,5	119,5	112,6	124,3	138,7	120,3	117,5	126,1
Personal and Housing Services	161,5	156,4	171,9	157,6	170,1	175,2	189,1	197,2
Community and Social Services	145,0	143,9	141,1	138,1	137,8	143,0	152,6	153,5
Transportation, Storage, Communications and Public Utilities	92,1	87,2	84,2	87,8	78,0	82,8	100,5	104,9
Activities not adequately specified	3,5	0,3	0,5	3,1	1,2	2,3	3,5	3,7

TABLE 11.4 (Cont'd)

Employment by Economic Activity
Great Santiago, 1956-1978.
(Thousands of Persons)

Economic Activity	June 1977	September 1977	December 1977	March 1978	June 1978
Total Employment	1,190,4	1,195,6	1,193,9	1,208,9	1,244,8
Goods Producing Activities	411,3	389,5	421,0	401,3	424,0
Agriculture, Hunting, Forestry and Fishing	16,2	14,6	15,8	13,7	13,4
Mining and Quarrying	5,1	3,7	5,3	6,7	7,1
Manufacturing	327,8	306,9	325,9	307,5	325,9
Construction	62,2	64,3	74,0	73,3	77,5
Service Producing Activities	687,5	717,9	684,4	724,3	725,6
Commerce	220,0	230,2	207,9	208,6	216,8
Governmental and Financial Services	125,1	130,4	122,0	139,4	140,9
Personal and Housing Services	189,4	207,4	203,7	213,0	209,9
Community and Social Services	153,0	150,0	150,8	163,3	158,1
Transportation, Storage, Communications and Public Utilities	90,0	83,4	88,5	82,5	93,4
Activities not adequately specified	1,6	4,8	-	0,8	1,9

Sources: The statistical information for the period between October 1956 and June 1978 reflects corrected data given to the author directly by the Instituto de Economía. The time series of this table, which are the latest, revised and corrected ones prepared by the Instituto-Departamento de Economía of the University of Chile, differ, sometimes substantially, and especially for earlier time periods, from the statistical information presented in the sources listed below. The data for the March 1959 - June 1962 period are found in Universidad de Chile, Instituto de Economía, Ocupación y Desocupación, Gran Santiago, publication No. 48 (Santiago: June 1962), table 5, p. 19. The data for the September 1962 - December 1966 period are found in Universidad de Chile, Instituto de Economía, Ocupación y Desocupación, Gran Santiago, publication No. 91 (Santiago: December 1966), table 5, p. 15. The data for the March 1967 - March 1970 period are found in Universidad de Chile, Instituto de Economía y Planificación, Ocupación y Desocupación, Gran Santiago, publication No. 116 (Santiago: March 1970), table 7, p. 12. The data for the June 1970 - March 1973 period are found in Universidad de Chile, Instituto de Economía y Planificación, Ocupación y Desocupación, Gran Santiago, inscription No. 41275 (Santiago: March 1973), table 7, p. 19. The data for the December 1973 - March 1976 period are found in Universidad de Chile, Facultad de Ciencias Económicas y Administrativas, Departamento de Economía, Ocupación y Desocupación en el Gran Santiago, publication No. 32 (Santiago: March 1976), table 4, p. 13. The data for the June 1976 - June 1978 period are found in Universidad de Chile, Facultad de Ciencias Económicas y Administrativas, Departamento de Economía, Ocupación y Desocupación en el Gran Santiago, publication No. 58 (Santiago: June 1978), table 4, p. 11.

TABLE 11.5

Labor Force According to Occupational Status
Great Santiago, 1959-1978.
(Thousands of Persons)

Status	March 1959	June 1959	April 1960	June 1960	September 1960[1]	September 1960[2]	December 1960	March 1961	June 1961	September 1961
Total Labor Force	679,3	678,8	707,7	715,0	-	725,3	736,7	741,0	724,0	722,3
Employers	20,8	26,4	26,0	17,3	-	20,1	28,7	26,9	19,1	25,7
Own-Account Workers	126,5	125,6	138,1	148,0	-	133,2	127,0	120,9	132,6	127,7
Salaried Employees	192,3	180,4	186,4	187,6	-	221,1	220,1	229,9	220,7	226,0
Wage Employees	313,8	325,2	336,5	333,9	-	329,2	343,4	339,5	331,3	331,3
Unpaid Family Workers	17,5	14,1	12,9	18,0	-	11,6	11,2	12,9	11,9	11,4
No Data Available	-	0,2	0,2	0,4	-	1,5	0,3	0,2	1,1	0,4
New Entrants Without a Job	8,4	6,9	7,6	9,8	-	8,6	6,0	10,9	7,6	7,3

Status	December 1961	March 1962	June 1962	September 1962	October 1962[3]	December 1962	March 1963	June 1963	September 1963	December 1963[4]
Total Labor Force	741,9	761,6	754,5	737,7	-	774,1	778,3	775,3	788,3	785,6
Employers	26,4	28,5	26,3	24,2	-	23,5	23,7	25,0	24,9	24,4
Own-Account Workers	130,3	139,1	144,1	146,8	-	143,9	140,5	145,5	146,4	139,8
Salaried Employees	227,4	221,9	220,2	239,2	-	247,3	240,3	235,9	257,8	261,6
Wage Employees	335,6	347,0	342,1	338,3	-	335,7	344,0	336,9	336,6	334,7
Unpaid Family Workers	16,5	14,4	14,0	19,4	-	20,1	19,9	23,5	16,6	19,6
No Data Available	0,4	0,2	0,2	0,5	-	-	-	1,3	-	0,8
New Entrants Without a Job	5,5	10,8	7,7	5,5	-	3,8	9,3	7,5	6,3	4,7

1. Survey based on a sample designed in 1956.
2. Survey based on a sample designed in 1960.
3. Survey based on half of the sample interviewed in September of 1962.
4. Survey based on a sample designed in 1960.

TABLE 11.5 (Cont'd)

Labor Force According to Occupational Status
Great Santiago, 1959-1978.
(Thousands of Persons)

Status	December 1963[5]	March 1964	June 1964	September 1964[6]	September 1964	December 1964	March 1965	June 1965	September 1965
Total Labor Force	779,2	790,9	793,6	877,7	814,5	794,2	825,2	828,0	840,5
Employers	16,4	19,0	18,3	25,5	16,3	20,4	17,8	16,8	17,4
Own-Account Workers	139,4	142,2	140,9	156,2	138,8	143,4	143,1	150,6	147,4
Salaried Employees	232,0	237,8	242,2	283,5	245,4	251,2	257,7	248,7	264,6
Wage Employees	368,9	368,4	368,2	386,2	389,2	358,6	378,2	384,1	386,1
Unpaid Family Workers	17,9	17,3	16,3	19,3	16,0	14,4	18,6	19,1	16,6
No Data Available	-	-	-	-	-	-	-	-	-
New Entrants Without a Job	4,7	7,1	7,9	7,0	8,7	5,6	9,1	9,9	8,4

Status	December 1965	March 1966	June 1966	September 1966	December 1966	March 1967[7]	March 1967[8]	June 1967	September 1967
Total Labor Force	845,8	841,3	854,6	874,4	895,1	900,2	877,9	898,8	914,9
Employers	18,8	19,2	17,2	20,1	19,5	18,9	17,6	18,0	19,2
Own-Account Workers	154,9	152,0	155,0	170,7	168,1	166,5	153,6	164,5	162,9
Salaries Employees	271,9	268,5	261,5	284,3	286,5	284,5	288,8	283,1	290,9
Wage Employees	373,1	381,1	387,4	379,0	394,0	405,1	395,9	409,9	417,2
Unpaid Family Workers	20,2	12,8	22,7	13,2	17,1	16,2	13,2	14,4	17,4
No Data Available	-	-	-	-	-	-	0,9	-	-
New Entrants Without a Job	6,8	7,6	10,9	7,0	9,8	9,0	7,9	9,0	7,3

5. Survey based on a sample designed in 1963.
6. Survey with a special question about inactives.
7. Survey based on a sample designed in 1963.
8. Survey based on a sample designed in 1967.

TABLE 11.5 (Cont'd)

Labor Force According to Occupational Status
Great Santiago, 1959-1978.
(Thousands of Persons)

Status	December 1967	March 1968	June 1968	September 1968	December 1968	March 1969	June 1969	September 1969	December 1969
Total Labor Force	920,7	902,7	929,1	943,2	965,1	953,0	968,1	992,9	1,012,6
Employers	22,1	21,5	21,3	27,4	22,6	21,9	20,8	24,8	28,0
Own-Account Workers	154,7	150,4	176,4	162,2	172,8	165,8	185,1	183,7	184,1
Salaried Employees	310,3	303,1	313,1	318,1	346,9	330,7	324,5	357,4	374,3
Wage Employees	405,1	403,6	391,9	408,3	395,7	399,3	394,9	401,1	397,8
Unpaid Family Workers	18,4	14,5	15,3	15,8	18,3	21,0	27,2	16,9	17,8
No Data Available	-	0,2	-	-	-	-	-	-	-
New Entrants Without a Job	10,1	9,6	11,2	11,4	8,8	15,2	15,9	8,9	10,7

Status	March 1970	June 1970	September 1970	December 1970	March 1971	June 1971	September 1971	December 1971	March 1972
Total Labor Force	987,4	1,023,4	1,021,0	1,034,1	1,031,4	1,073 8	1,061,8	1,059,4	1,060,6
Employers	19,4	22,0	19,7	19,5	22,3	25,1	25,0	22,9	26,9
Own-Account Workers	163,2	187,2	185,3	178,6	180,2	204,5	172,2	188,7	196,8
Salaries Employees	385,8	358,5	375,5	412,8	410,0	422,8	420,0	412,8	399,8
Wage Employees	387,7	419,1	404,8	384,2	373,9	380,1	413,2	401,3	403,7
Unpaid Family Workers	16,5	22,4	23,9	21,9	23,9	28,8	19,0	23,1	21,8
No Data Available	-	-	0,2	-	-	-	-	0,2	-
New Entrants Without a Job	14,9	14,2	11,6	17,2	21,2	12,7	12,4	10,4	11,6

TABLE 11.5 (Cont'd)

Labor Force According to Occupational Status
Great Santiago, 1959-1978.
(Thousands of Persons)

Status	June 1972	September 1972	December 1972	March 1973	June 1973	December 1973[9]	March 1974	June 1974	September 1974
Total Labor Force	1,105,3	1,065,9	1,079,4	1,104,1	1,135,0	1,180,3	1,179,2	1,182,9	1,198,7
Employers	28,3	23,0	21,4	24,6	26,2	21,7	27,0	25,5	23,8
Own-Account Workers	206,6	196,8	200,3	217,8	233,8	260,4	225,2	242,3	235,6
Salaried Employees	458,9	424,7	456,6	461,9	464,3	417,4	406,0	409,7	433,7
Wage Employees	364,9	396,3	370,5	365,5	370,7	435,9	469,4	445,6	447,9
Unpaid Family Workers	30,8	16,5	21,8	20,0	28,2	21,0	17,1	23,1	24,1
No Data Available	-	-	-	-	-	-	0,9	3,0	2,2
New Entrants Without a Job	15,8	8,6	8,8	14,3	11,8	23,9	33,6	33,7	31,5

Status	December 1974	March 1975	June 1975	September 1975	December 1975	March 1976	June 1976	July 1976	August 1976
Total Labor Force	1,228,6	1,230,9	1,226,7	1,223,3	1,280,2	1,298,7	1,333,5	1,284,4	1,291,4
Employers	23,9	25,9	23,4	21,8	24,8	25,5	35,4	27,9	23,5
Own-Account Workers	223,2	227,8	241,4	222,2	220,1	214,2	261,5	236,1	229,8
Salaried Employees	461,6	453,5	442,0	472,5	462,9	477,1	438,2	449,8	445,1
Wage Employees	456,1	450,2	445,4	436,5	490,7	494,8	508,4	486,2	518,7
Unpaid Family Workers	18,0	20,0	25,1	20,1	18,4	21,2	28,2	27,1	15,8
No Data Available	1,9	1,9	-	0,5	0,9	-	-	-	-
New Entrants Without a Job	43,8	51,6	49,4	49,7	62,3	66,0	61,9	57,3	58,5

9. The figures for the period between December 1973 and March 1976 are those that were corrected in March of 1976.

TABLE 11.5 (Cont'd)

Labor Force According to Occupational Status
Great Santiago, 1959-1978.
(Thousands of Persons)

Status	September 1976	December 1976	March 1977	June 1977	September 1977	December 1977	March 1978	June 1978
Total Labor Force	1,291,5	1,317,5	1,336,6	1,368,8	1,371,3	1,374,9	1,417,2	1,426,9
Employers	32,5	28,6	25,6	29,7	28,4	30,9	20,5	32,8
Own-Account Workers	233,8	220,5	209,5	241,3	241,9	251,7	248,8	267,3
Salaried Employees	420,0	452,5	525,2	467,2	498,6	487,3	486,6	494,9
Wage Employees	542,8	545,6	499,9	560,2	539,8	538,9	587,3	561,3
Unpaid Family Workers	17,1	22,7	17,0	31,1	24,2	20,9	24,0	22,9
No Data Available	-	-	0,8	-	-	-	-	-
New Entrants Without a Job	45,3	47,6	58,6	39,2	38,5	45,2	50,1	47,8

Sources: The statistical information for the period between March 1959 and June 1978 reflects corrected data given to the author directly by the Instituto de Economía. The time series of this table, which are the latest, revised and corrected ones prepared by the Instituto-Departamento de Economía of the University of Chile, differ, sometimes substantially, and especially for earlier time periods, from the statistical information presented in the sources listed below. The data for the March 1967 - March 1970 period are found in Universidad de Chile, Instituto de Economía y Planificación, Ocupación y Desocupación, Gran Santiago, publication No. 116 (Santiago: March 1970), table 12, p. 17. The data for the June 1970 - March 1973 period are found in Universidad de Chile, Instituto de Economía y Planificación, Ocupación y Desocupación, Gran Santiago, inscription No. 41275 (Santiago: March 1973), table 12, p. 24. The data for the December 1973 - March 1976 period are found in Universidad de Chile, Facultad de Ciencias Económicas y Administrativas, Departamento de Economía, Ocupación y Desocupación en el Gran Santiago, publication No. 32 (Santiago: March 1976), table 7, p. 19. The data for the June 1976 - June 1978 period are found in Universidad de Chile, Facultad de Ciencias Económicas y Administrativas, Departamento de Economía, Ocupación y Desocupación en el Gran Santiago, publication No. 58 (Santiago: June 1978), table 7, p. 17.

TABLE 11.6

Employed Population According to Occupational Status
Great Santiago, 1959-1978.
(Thousands of Persons)

Status	March 1959	June 1959	April 1960	June 1960	September 1960[1]	September 1960[2]	December 1960	March 1961	June 1961	September 1961
Total Employment	608,4	628,6	655,8	657,7	-	672,1	684,9	684,5	672,8	679,5
Employers	20,3	26,3	26,0	17,3	-	19,8	28,2	26,9	18,9	25,7
Own-Account Workers	118,5	121,0	131,8	142,5	-	126,7	122,4	116,6	128,1	119,4
Salaried Employees	181,5	171,2	179,6	178,3	-	211,9	210,8	217,6	212,9	217,2
Wage Employees	270,6	295,8	305,3	301,3	-	301,0	312,0	310,5	300,1	305,8
Unpaid Family Workers	17,5	14,1	12,9	18,0	-	11,6	11,2	12,9	11,9	11,4
No Data Available	-	0,2	0,2	0,4	-	1,1	0,3	0,2	1,1	0,2

Status	December 1961	March 1961	June 1961	September 1961	October 1962[3]	December 1962	March 1963	June 1963	September 1963	December 1963[4]
Total Employment	705,0	714,7	711,5	740,8	-	737,1	735,5	735,2	747,3	757,5
Employers	26,1	27,8	26,1	24,0	-	23,2	23,5	24,5	24,7	24,2
Own-Account Workers	127,3	133,7	139,5	143,8	-	138,8	135,3	141,0	142,0	138,6
Salaried Employees	221,3	213,3	215,4	232,9	-	242,9	233,2	228,9	248,1	254,5
Wage Employees	313,6	325,7	316,4	320,3	-	312,5	322,9	316,3	316,1	319,7
Unpaid Family Workers	16,5	14,2	14,0	19,4	-	19,8	19,9	23,5	16,4	19,7
No Data Available	0,4	0,2	0,2	0,5	-	-	x	1,2	-	0,8

1. Survey based on a sample designed in 1956.
2. Survey based on a sample designed in 1960.
3. Survey based on half of the sample interviewed in September of 1962.
4. Survey based on a sample designed in 1960.

TABLE 11.6 (Cont'd)

Employed Population According to Occupational Status
Great Santiago, 1959-1978.
(Thousands of Persons)

Status	December 1963[5]	March 1964	June 1964	September 1964[6]	September 1964	December 1964	March 1965	June 1965	September 1965
Total Employment	745,7	750,6	754,5	833,9	764,4	756,1	774,9	786,6	790,9
Employers	16,4	18,8	18,1	25,0	16,0	20,4	17,8	16,5	16,6
Own-Account Workers	136,5	138,1	139,2	153,4	134,7	139,9	137,9	147,9	141,6
Salaried Employees	227,4	232,7	236,0	274,4	238,2	246,5	248,7	243,1	258,6
Wage Employees	347,5	344,5	345,0	361,9	359,4	334,2	351,0	360,3	357,5
Unpaid Family Workers	17,9	17,3	16,3	19,2	16,0	14,4	18,6	18,9	16,6
No Data Available	-	-	-	-	-	-	-	-	-

Status	December 1965	March 1966	June 1966	September 1966	December 1966	March 1967[7]	March 1967[8]	June 1967	September 1967
Total Employment	806,1	801,8	803,6	828,1	846,7	850,6	822,5	845,8	861,8
Employers	18,5	19,2	17,2	19,9	19,5	18,7	17,3	18,6	19,8
Own-Account Workers	150,7	147,5	149,7	165,6	161,7	163,3	148,1	159,0	156,8
Salaried Employees	265,2	262,2	255,1	277,4	279,4	275,6	280,5	275,7	284,4
Wage Employees	351,5	360,D	359,0	351,9	369,2	376,8	362,7	378,1	383,5
Unpaid Family Workers	20,2	12,8	22,7	13,2	16,9	16,2	13,2	14,4	17,2
No Data Available	-	-	-	-	-	-	0,8	x	-

5. Survey based on a sample designed in 1963.
6. Survey with a special question about inactives.
7. Survey based on a sample designed in 1963.
8. Survey based on a sample designed in 1967.

TABLE 11.6 (Cont'd)

Employed Population According to Occupational Status
Great Santiago, 1959-1978.
(Thousands of Persons)

Status	December 1967	March 1968	June 1968	September 1968	December 1968	March 1969	June 1969	September 1969	December 1969
Total Employment	861,8	852,4	869,7	879,5	912,9	888,2	899,0	940,3	958,0
Employers	22,4	21,0	21,3	27,4	22,2	22,2	20,8	23,1	27,8
Own-Account Workers	146,5	145,3	168,4	156,4	166,7	160,8	176,6	167,9	179,3
Salaried Employees	301,6	295,6	304,8	310,5	338,3	318,9	313,2	330,4	364,4
Wage Employees	372,3	375,8	360,0	369,5	367,4	365,1	361,4	350,8	368,7
Unpaid Family Workers	18,1	14,5	15,3	15,8	18,3	20,4	27,2	15,1	17,8
No Data Available	x	0,2	-	-	-	x	-	-	-

Status	March 1970	June 1970	September 1970	December 1970	March 1971	June 1971	September 1971	December 1971	March 1972
Total Employment	920,0	951,9	955,3	948,8	946,4	1,018,0	1,011,1	1,019,3	1,010,2
Employers	19,2	21,9	19,4	19,5	22,3	24,8	24,6	22,5	26,6
Own-Account Workers	159,1	179,9	180,3	172,6	176,3	199,6	168,9	186,3	193,5
Salaried Employees	373,9	348,3	364,9	397,3	394,4	411,5	407,6	407,0	387,2
Wage Employees	351,3	379,5	366,8	337,5	329,6	353,5	391,1	380,3	381,1
Unpaid Family Workers	16,5	22,4	23,9	21,9	23,9	28,8	19,0	23,1	21,8
No Data Available	-	-	0,2	-	-	-	-	0,2	-

TABLE 11.6 (Cont'd)

Employed Population According to Occupational Status
Great Santiago, 1959-1978.
(Thousands of Persons)

Status	June 1972	September 1972	December 1972	March 1973	June 1973	December 1973[9]	March 1974	June 1974	September 1974
Total Employment	1,064,7	1,034,0	1,040,9	1,062,5	1,099,8	1,097,6	1,070,3	1,060,6	1,086,1
Employers	28,3	23,0	21,4	24,4	26,2	21,7	26,8	25,5	23,6
Own-Account Workers	205,8	195,1	198,9	214,4	231,4	251,4	213,4	231,6	223,8
Salaried Employees	450,2	418,3	447,5	453,4	454,9	403,1	389,1	385,4	415,6
Wage Employees	349,4	381,2	351,2	350,3	359,1	400,4	423,1	392,6	397,3
Unpaid Family Workers	30,8	16,5	21,8	20,0	28,2	21,0	17,1	22,8	24,1
No Data Available	-	-	-	-	-	-	0,7	2,7	1,7

Status	December 1974	March 1975	June 1975	September 1975	December 1975	March 1976	June 1976	July 1976	August 1976
Total Employment	1,109,3	1,067,2	1,029,5	1,019,9	1,041,2	1,041,1	1,093,0	1,074,6	1,071,9
Employers	23,0	25,9	22,9	21,6	23,6	25,2	34,9	27,1	23,5
Own-Account Workers	214,1	213,6	222,0	201,6	198,4	186,4	241,6	219,4	209,6
Salaried Employees	444,4	431,7	410,5	435,8	416,6	427,6	398,2	413,8	415,0
Wage Employees	409,0	374,7	349,3	340,4	383,5	380,8	390,2	387,2	408,1
Unpaid Family Workers	17,5	20,0	24,8	20,1	18,4	21,0	28,2	27,1	15,8
No Data Available	1,4	1,4	-	0,5	0,7	-	-	-	-

9. The figures for the period between December 1973 and March 1976 are those that were corrected in March of 1976.

TABLE 11.6 (Cont'd)

Employed Population According to Occupational Status
Great Santiago, 1959-1978.
(Thousands of Persons)

Status	September 1976	December 1976	March 1977	June 1977	September 1977	December 1977	March 1978	June 1978
Total Employment	1,089,2	1,138,3	1,151,4	1,190,4	1,195,6	1,193,9	1,208,9	1,244,8
Employers	32,0	28,4	24,8	29,5	28,1	30,9	19,9	32,8
Own-Account Workers	213,4	210,1	199,3	266,5	227,8	236,9	234,2	253,6
Salaried Employees	388,6	424,6	486,3	439,1	468,6	450,9	441,8	456,4
Wage Employees	438,4	452,5	423,2	464,3	446,9	454,3	488,9	479,1
Unpaid Family Workers	16,9	22,7	17,0	31,1	24,2	20,9	24,0	22,9
No Data Available	-	-	0,8	-	-	-	-	-

Sources: The statistical information for the period between March 1959 and June 1978 reflects corrected data given to the author directly by the Instituto de Economía. The time series of this table, which are the latest, revised and corrected ones prepared by the Instituto-Departamento de Economía of the University of Chile, differ, sometimes substantially, and especially for earlier time periods, from the statistical information presented in the sources listed below. The data for the March 1959 - June 1962 period are found in Universidad de Chile, Instituto de Economía, <u>Ocupación y Desocupación, Gran Santiago</u>, publication No. 48 (Santiago: June 1962), table 10, p. 26. The data for the September 1962 - December 1966 period are found in Universidad de Chile, Instituto de Economía, <u>Ocupación y Desocupación, Gran Santiago</u>, publication No. 91 (Santiago: December 1966), table 10, p. 27. The data for the March 1967 - March 1970 period are found in Universidad de Chile, Instituto de Economía y Planificación, <u>Ocupación y Desocupación, Gran Santiago</u>, publication No. 116 (Santiago: March 1970), table 14, p. 20. The data for the June 1970 - March 1973 period are found in Universidad de Chile, Instituto de Economía y Planificación, <u>Ocupación y Desocupación, Gran Santiago</u>, inscription No. 41275 (Santiago: March 1973), table 14, p. 26. The data for the December 1973 - March 1976 period are found in Universidad de Chile, Facultad de Ciencias Económicas y Administrativas, Departamento de Economía, <u>Ocupación y Desocupación en el Gran Santiago</u>, publication No. 32 (Santiago: March 1976), table 8, p. 20. The data for the June 1976 - June 1978 period are found in Universidad de Chile, Facultad de Ciencias Económicas y Administrativas, Departamento de Economía, <u>Ocupación y Desocupación en el Gran Santiago</u>, publication No. 58 (Santiago: June 1978), table 8, p. 18.

TABLE 11.7

Preferences for Work of Inactive Population
Great Santiago, 1964-1978.
(Thousands of Persons)

	December 1964[1]	March 1965	June 1965	September 1965	December 1965	March 1966	June 1966	September 1966	December 1966
Total Inactive Population	747,4	730,6	725,4	741,8	746,2	762,9	769,0	777,0	789,2
Persons Wishing to Work	-	124,2	140,0	140,9	125,4	143,4	137,3	143,7	152,3
A. Entire year 40 or more hours	-	33,6	37,7	37,8	36,6	45,8	48,9	46,6	42,6
B. Entire year from 20 to 39 hours	-	34,3	42,8	39,3	25,4	42,7	38,7	41,2	33,1
C. Entire year less than 20 hours	-	34,3	37,0	43,8	30,6	38,9	28,8	29,5	35,5
D. Unspecified schedule	-	-	-	-	-	0,8	1,5	-	0,8
E. Some months a year	-	21,2	20,3	20,0	32,8	15,3	21,0	25,6	40,2
Persons Without Desire to Work	-	599,1	585,4	598,6	619,3	617,9	622,2	630,1	634,5
No Data Available	-	7,3	0,7	2,2	1,5	0,8	9,6	3,1	2,4

	March 1967[2]	March 1967[3]	June 1967	September 1967	December 1967	March 1968	June 1968	September 1968
Total Inactive Population	811,2	799,0	785,8	800,8	821,3	826,0	823,1	849,3
Persons Wishing to Work	154,1	159,8	155,6	157,8	149,5	164,9	154,7	177,0
A. Entire year 40 or more hours	34,1	35,2	29,9	30,4	38,6	41,6	30,5	33,9
B. Entire year from 20 to 39 hours	25,1	35,2	28,3	27,2	28,7	37,3	26,8	32,3
C. Entire year less than 20 hours	24,3	33,6	29,9	23,2	14,8	20,3	26,7	26,0
D. Unspecified schedule	58,4	48,7	62,1	67,3	52,6	56,8	65,6	68,2
E. Some months a year	12,2	8,0	5,5	9,6	15,6	8,9	5,4	16,6
Persons Without Desire to Work	625,4	626,4	622,4	637,4	659,5	650,7	656,9	665,1
No Data Available	31,6	11,2	7,1	5,6	12,3	10,4	11,5	7,2

1. Survey based on a sample designed in 1963. It was since September 1964 that the surveys included a special question about inactives.
2. Survey based on a sample designed in 1963.
3. Survey based on a sample designed in 1967.

TABLE 11.7 (Cont'd)

Preferences for Work of Inactive Population
Great Santiago, 1964-1978.
(Thousands of Persons)

	December 1968	March 1969	June 1969	September 1969	December 1969	March 1970	June 1970	September 1970
Total Inactive Population	870,5	884,5	872,2	892,5	895,9	935,8	936,2	953,7
Persons Wishing to Work	192,5	180,4	191,4	182,1	178,8	179,4	204,6	235,9
A. Entire year 40 or more hours	41,5	31,8	31,1	27,7	33,2	27,5	30,8	32,5
B. Entire year from 20 to 39 hours	24,8	31,0	28,5	25,9	24,4	22,0	25,8	45,2
C. Entire year less than 20 hours	30,9	32,7	29,8	39,3	18,5	26,8	39,6	36,0
D. Unspecified schedule	70,4	78,7	86,8	79,4	86,0	87,0	100,5	104,0
E. Some months a year	24,9	6,2	15,4	9,8	16,7	16,0	7,9	18,3
Persons Without Desire to Work	673,0	699,6	669,6	704,2	712,5	751,8	725,5	708,9
No Data Available	5,1	3,5	11,3	6,2	4,6	4,6	6,1	8,9

	December 1970	March 1971	June 1971	September 1971	December 1971	March 1972	June 1972	September 1972
Total Inactive Population	958,4	977,0	979,9	1,012,6	1,006,1	1,052,8	1,070,1	1,085,7
Persons Wishing to Work	253,4	200,2	220,1	191,2	192,9	177,3	173,5	207,7
A. Entire year 40 or more hours	45,1	35,1	33,3	30,2	39,4	31,5	24,7	23,3
B. Entire year from 20 to 39 hours	33,0	37,7	45,9	47,7	28,4	41,1	28,0	52,9
C. Entire year less than 20 hours	36,7	31,3	41,1	23,9	29,7	29,8	31,4	14,8
D. Unspecified schedule	85,9	78,2	76,8	80,8	68,7	62,9	79,6	110,5
E. Some months a year	52,7	17,8	23,1	8,6	26,7	12,0	9,8	6,2
Persons Without Desire to Work	702,9	722,1	758,2	820,3	810,9	875,5	896,0	877,8
No Data Available	2,2	4,6	1,7	1,1	2,3	-	0,6	0,2

TABLE 11.7 (Cont'd)

Preferences for Work of Inactive Population
Great Santiago, 1964-1978.

	December 1972	March 1973	June 1973	December 1973[4]	March 1974	June 1974	September 1974	December 1974
Total Inactive Population	1,092,8	1,157,1	1,184,8	1,107,2	1,114,2	1,147,9	1,137,8	1,170,6
Persons Wishing to Work	245,1	242,3	246,4	254,5	219,5	233,1	214,9	199,2
A. Entire year 40 or more hours	31,1	36,4	35,8	65,8	37,3	49,3	40,9	61,5
B. Entire year from 20 to 39 hours	34,6	47,7	35,0	63,9	67,6	67,2	69,1	56,7
C. Entire year less than 20 hours	36,4	22,4	48,8	61,1	62,0	58,8	68,8	46,2
D. Unspecified schedule	95,7	127,3	111,4	43,8	52,6	57,8	36,1	34,7
E. Some months a year	47,4	8,5	15,4					
Persons Without Desire to Work	845,9	914,8	938,4	849,7	892,3	905,1	905,8	958,0
No Data Available	1,8	-	-	2,9	2,3	9,7	17,1	13,4

	March 1975	June 1975	September 1975	December 1975	March 1976	June 1976	July 1976	August 1976
Total Inactive Population	1,205,9	1,269,0	1,285,9	1,243,3	1,250,7	1,266,7	1,326,1	1,297,3
Persons Wishing to Work	179,4	174,8	150,6	228,1	208,9	212,9	118,3	140,5
A. Entire year 40 or more hours	40,9	40,8	33,6	64,5	58,2	59,8	37,5	39,3
B. Entire year from 20 to 39 hours	74,8	55,3	44,1	74,2	67,2	71,3	45,1	42,5
C. Entire year less than 20 hours	43,7	56,3	51,4	43,0	60,0	52,3	19,8	38,5
D. Unspecified schedule	20,0	22,4	21,6	46,5	23,5	29,5	15,9	20,2
E. Some months a year								
Persons Without Desire to Work	1,022,8	1,089,0	1,134,3	1,011,4	1,041,3	1,053,8	1,207,8	1,156,9
No Data Available	3,8	5,2	0,9	3,8	0,5	-	-	-

4. The figures for the period between December 1973 and March 1976 are those that were corrected in March of 1976. It appears that since December 1973, the information concerning item "E. Some months a year" has been deleted.

TABLE 11.7 (Cont'd)

Preferences for Work of Inactive Population
Great Santiago, 1964-1978.
(Thousands of Persons)

	September 1976	December 1976	March 1977	June 1977	September 1977	December 1977	March 1978	June 1978
Total Inactive Population	1,328,0	1,329,4	1,334,5	1,305,5	1,346,7	1,378,0	1,377,3	1,395,3
Persons Wishing to Work	141,7	164,9	144,4	137,0	133,8	148,7	190,3	172,8
A. Entire year 40 or more hours	44,0	48,4	36,6	37,0	36,9	56,3	51,2	45,3
B. Entire year from 20 to 39 hours	47,1	48,9	40,5	36,8	42,2	46,5	63,1	59,0
C. Entire year less than 20 hours	28,7	30,4	41,6	41,3	33,5	22,7	37,5	33,3
D. Unspecified schedule	21,9	37,3	25,6	21,9	21,2	23,2	38,5	35,2
E. Some months a year								
Persons Without Desire to Work	1,186,3	1,164,5	1,190,1	1,168,2	1,212,8	1,229,3	1,187,1	1,222,4
No Data Available	-	-	-	0,3	-	-	-	-

Sources: The statistical information for the period between December 1964 and June 1978 reflects corrected data given to the author directly by the Instituto de Economía. The time series of this table, which are the latest, revised and corrected ones prepared by the Instituto-Departamento de Economía of the University of Chile, differ, sometimes substantially, and especially for earlier time periods, from the statistical information presented in the sources listed below. The data for the March 1964 - December 1966 period are found in Universidad de Chile, Instituto de Economía, Ocupación y Desocupación, Gran Santiago, publication No. 91 (Santiago: December 1966), table 15, p. 39. The data for the March 1967 - March 1970 period are found in Universidad de Chile, Instituto de Economía y Planificación, Ocupación y Desocupación, Gran Santiago, publication No. 116 (Santiago: March 1970), table 19, p. 24. The data for the June 1970 - March 1973 period are found in Universidad de Chile, Instituto de Economía y Planificación, Ocupación y Desocupación, Gran Santiago, inscription No. 41275 (Santiago: March 1973), table 19, p. 31. The data for the December 1973 - March 1976 period are found in Universidad de Chile, Facultad de Ciencias Económicas y Administrativas, Departamento de Economía, Ocupación y Desocupación en el Gran Santiago, publication No. 32 (Santiago: March 1976), table 11, p. 25. The data for the June 1976 - June 1978 period are found in Universidad de Chile, Facultad de Ciencias Económicas y Administrativas, Departamento de Economía, Ocupación y Desocupación en el Gran Santiago, publication No. 58 (Santiago: June 1978), table 11, p. 23.

TABLE 11.8

Population of Great Santiago According to Sex and Employment Situation.
1966-1977 .

Period	Total	Sex		Under Twelve Years of Age	Twelve Years of Age and Over	Labor Force	Not Included in the Labor Force
		Males	Females				
	Absolute Figures (Thousands of Persons)						
Jul -Oct 1966	2,325,6	1,081,9	1,243,7	693,9	1,631,7	840,0	791.7
Nov 1966-Feb 1967	2,342,0	1,095,3	1,246,7	698,9	1,643,1	831,7	811,4
Mar -Jun 1967	2,368,8	1,107,1	1,261,7	711,5	1,657,3	832,0	825,3
Jul -Oct 1967	2,406,3	1,132,4	1,273,9	731,0	1,675,3	845,7	829,6
Nov 1967-Feb 1968	2,402,8	1,116,7	1,286,1	717,9	1,684,9	841,7	843,2
Mar -Jun 1968	2,432,5	1,144,0	1,288,4	737,5	1,695,0	842,8	852,2
Sep -Dec 1968	2,679,5	1,265,0	1,414,5	810,5	1,869,0	949,9	919,1
Jan -Jun 1969	2,691,5	1,273,7	1,417,8	818,0	1,873,6	920,7	953,0
Jul -Dec 1969	2,689,0	1,271,9	1,417,1	819,5	1,869,5	911,1	958,4
Jan -Aug 1970	2,739,2	1,291,4	1,447,8	818,9	1,920,3	929,5	990,8
Sep -Dec 1970	2,787,3	1,322,2	1,465,1	831,0	1,956,3	953,2	1,003,1
Jan -Jun 1971	2,829,1	1,317,0	1,512,1	843,4	1,985,7	935,4	1,050,4
Jul -Dec 1971	2,884,7	1,371,3	1,513,4	850,2	2,034,5	980,7	1,053,8
1972	2,954,2	1,397,3	1,556,9	873,8	2,080,4	994,1	1,086,3
1973	3,248,4	1,535,3	1,713,0	873,1	2,375,3	1,001,8	1,373,4
1974	3,345,0	1,566,3	1,778,7	839,5	2,505,5	1,059,0	1,446,5
1975	3,442,2	1,607,1	1,835,1	832,2	2,610,1	1,099,8	1,510,2
Jan -Mar 1976	3,508,8	1,617,8	1,891,0	804,0	2,704,8	1,147,8	1,557,0
Apr -Jun 1976	3,535,7	1,625,8	1,909,9	825,0	2,710,6	1,235,4	1,475,3
Jul -Sep 1976	3,509,0	1,620,7	1,888,3	809,7	2,699,3	1,219,9	1,479,4
Oct -Dec 1976	3,533,1	1,641,9	1,891,2	808,1	2,725,0	1,177,0	1,548,0
Jan -Mar 1977	3,557,4	1,652,9	1,904,5	806,8	2,750,7	1,183,6	1,567,0
Apr -Jun 1977	3,582,1	1,654,3	1,927,9	840,4	2,741,8	1,234,6	1,507,2
Jul -Sep 1977	3,606,6	1,672,2	1,934,4	817,7	2,789,0	1,203,3	1,585,6
Oct -Dec 1977	3,630,9	1,692,1	1,938,8	816,9	2,814,0	1,186,8	1,627,1

TABLE 11.8 (Cont'd)

Population of Great Santiago According to Sex and Employment Situation. 1966-1977.

Period	Total	Sex		Under Twelve Years of Age	Twelve Years of Age and Over	Labor Force	Not Included in the Labor Force
		Males	Females				
	Relative Figures (Percentages)						
Jul -Oct 1966	100.0	46.5	53.5	28.8	70.2	51.5	48.5
Nov 1966-Feb 1967	100.0	46.8	53.2	29.8	70.2	50.6	49.4
Mar -Jun 1967	100.0	46.7	53.3	30.0	70.0	50.2	49.8
Jul -Oct 1967	100.0	47.1	52.9	30.4	69.6	50.5	49.5
Nov 1967-Feb 1968	100.0	46.5	53.5	29.9	70.1	50.0	50.0
Mar -Jun 1968	100.0	47.0	53.0	30.3	69.7	49.7	50.3
Sep -Dec 1968	100.0	47.2	52.8	30.2	69.8	50.8	49.2
Jan -Jun 1969	100.0	47.3	52.7	30.4	69.6	49.1	50.9
Jul -Dec 1969	100.0	47.3	52.7	30.5	69.5	48.7	51.3
Jan -Aug 1970	100.0	47.1	52.9	29.9	70.1	48.4	51.6
Sep -Dec 1970	100.0	47.4	52.6	29.8	70.2	48.7	51.3
Jan -Jun 1971	100.0	46.5	53.5	29.8	70.2	47.1	52.9
Jul -Dec 1971	100.0	47.5	52.5	29.5	70.5	48.2	51.8
1972	100.0	47.3	52.7	29.6	70.4	47.8	52.2
1973	100.0	47.3	52.7	26.9	73.1	42.2	57.8
1974	100.0	46.8	53.2	25.1	74.9	42.3	57.7
1975	100.0	46.7	53.3	24.2	75.8	42.1	57.9
Jan -Mar 1976	100.0	46.1	53.9	22.9	77.1	42.4	57.6
Apr -Jun 1976	100.0	46.0	54.0	23.3	76.7	45.6	54.4
Jul -Sep 1976	100.0	46.2	53.8	23.1	76.9	45.2	54.8
Oct -Dec 1976	100.0	46.5	53.5	22.9	77.1	43.2	56.8
Jan -Mar 1977	100.0	46.5	53.5	22.7	77.3	43.0	57.0
Apr -Jun 1977	100.0	46.2	53.8	23.5	76.5	45.0	55.0
Jul -Sep 1977	100.0	46.4	53.6	22.7	77.3	43.1	56.9
Oct -Dec 1977	100.0	46.6	53.4	22.5	77.5	42.2	57.8

Source: National Institute of Statistics

TABLE 11.9

Labor Force in Greater Santiago by Occupational Group, 1966-1977.

Period	Labor Force in Greater Santiago				
	Total	Occupational Group			
		Employers, Self-Employed and Unpaid Family Workers	Salaried Employees	Wage Employees	Persons Seeking Work for the First Time
		Absolute Figures (thousands)			
Jul -Oct/66	840.0	187.0	277.3	362.1	13.6
Nov/66-Feb/67	831.7	191.6	261.3	371.9	6.9
Mar -Jun/67	832.0	191.1	273.6	361.7	5.6
Jul -Oct/67	845.7	204.0	277.9	359.1	4.7
Nov/67-Feb/68	841.7	196.0	263.5	376.8	5.4
Mar -Jun/68	842.7	209.7	264.0	362.9	6.1
Sep -Dec/68	949.9	-[1]	-	-	-
Jan -Jun/69	920.7	-[1]	-	-	-
Jul -Dec/69	911.1	-[1]	-	-	-
Jan -Aug/70	929.5	-[1]	-	-	-
Sep -Dec/70	953.2	-[1]	-	-	-
Jan -Jun/71	935.6	227.5	329.8	371.0	7.3
Jul -Dec/71	980.8	248.2	347.9	377.9	6.8
1972	994.1	244.7	377.9	365.2	7.1
1973	1,001.8	-[1]	-	-	-
1974	1,059.0	234.7	433.9	365.5	24.9
1975	1,099.8	236.5	445.2	379.1	39.0
Jan -Mar/76	1,147.8	253.1	449.1	402.4	43.2
Apr -Jun/76	1,235.4	284.4	467.9	425.9	57.2
Jul -Sep/76	1,219.9	288.7	440.3	448.1	42.8
Oct -Dec/76	1,177.0	312.8	417.3	405.1	41.8
Jan -Mar/77	1,183.6	269.6	453.7	411.6	48.7
Apr -Jun/77	1,234.6	294.3	457.3	434.6	48.4
Jul -Sep/77	1,203.3	279.4	441.5	446.4	36.0
Oct -Dec/77	1,186.8	298.5	421.5	441.6	25.2

TABLE 11.9 (Cont'd)

Labor Force in Greater Santiago by Occupational Group, 1966-1977.

Period	Total	Employers, Self-Employed and Unpaid Family Workers	Salaried Employees	Wage Employees	Persons Seeking Work for the First Time
		Relative Figures (percentages)			
Jul -Oct/66	100.0	22.3	33.0	43.1	1.6
Nov/66-Feb/67	100.0	23.1	31.4	44.7	0.8
Mar -Jun/67	100.0	23.0	32.9	43.5	0.6
Jul -Oct/67	100.0	24.1	32.9	42.5	0.5
Nov/67-Feb/68	100.0	23.3	31.3	44.8	0.6
Mar -Jun/68	100.0	24.9	31.3	43.1	0.7
Sep -Dec/68	100.0	-[1]	-	-	-
Jan -Jun/69	100.0	-[1]	-	-	-
Jul -Dec/69	100.0	-[1]	-	-	-
Jan -Aug/70	100.0	-[1]	-	-	-
Sep -Dec/70	100.0	-[1]	-	-	-
Jan -Jun/71	100.0	24.3	35.3	39.6	0.8
Jul -Dec/71	100.0	25.3	35.3	38.5	0.7
1972	100.0	24.6	38.0	36.7	0.7
1973	100.0	-[1]	-	-	-
1974	100.0	22.2	41.0	34.5	2.3
1975	100.0	21.5	40.5	34.5	3.5
Jan -Mar/76	100.0	22.0	39.1	35.1	3.8
Apr -Jun/76	100.0	23.0	37.9	34.5	4.6
Jul -Sep/76	100.0	23.7	36.1	36.7	3.5
Oct -Dec/76	100.0	26.6	35.4	34.4	3.6
Jan -Mar/77	100.0	22.8	38.3	34.8	4.1
Apr -Jun/77	100.0	23.8	37.1	35.2	3.9
Jul -Sep/77	100.0	23.2	36.7	37.1	3.0
Oct -Dec/77	100.0	25.2	35.5	37.2	2.1

Notes: 1. For this period there is no information available by occupational group.

Source: National Institute of Statistics.

Finally, the labor force in Greater Santiago by type of economic activity between 1966 and 1977 is presented in Table 11.10. One of the more disturbing trends revealed by Table 11.10 is the stagnation, in absolute terms, of the labor force in manufacturing – it was in December of 1977 slightly below its level on July-October 1966 – and the decline in the relative importance of the manufacturing labor force from 33.9 per cent of the total in 1966 to only 23.9 in October-December of 1977. The labor force (narrowly defined) in services, in contrast, almost doubled between 1966 and 1977 and the percentage importance of the labor force in services rose from 30.0 per cent in July-October 1966 to 41.6 per cent in October-December 1977. Thus, the process of servisalization described in (Mamalakis: 1976d) did not only continue but even was strengthened during the 1973-1977 period.

TABLE 11.10

Labor Force in Greater Santiago, by Type of Economic Activity, 1966-1977.

Period	Total	Agri-culture and Fishing	Mining and Quarry-ing	Manu-facture	Electri-city Gas and Sanitary Services	Con-struction	Trade	Transport Storage and Communi-cations	Services	Not Ade-quately Specified	Persons Seeking Work for the First Time
	Labor Force in Greater Santiago by Type of Economic Activity										
	Absolute Figures (In Thousands of Persons										
Jul -Oct/66	840.0	7.8	1.3	284.7	12.7	62.4	142.1	62.1	251.9	1.4	13.6
Nov/66-Feb/67	831.7	9.1	1.0	283.7	11.5	63.6	147.9	60.9	246.4	0.7	6.9
Mar -Jun/67	832.0	7.4	2.4	283.1	11.6	63.8	139.1	62.2	255.3	1.5	5.6
Jul -Oct/67	845.7	7.2	2.0	284.2	7.4	65.8	155.3	58.8	260.0	0.3	4.7
Nov/67-Feb/68	841.7	10.2	1.5	277.3	6.0	62.7	157.8	63.9	256.9	-	5.4
Mar -Jun/68	842.8	6.9	1.5	283.7	5.9	62.8	163.2	61.4	251.1	-	6.3
Sep -Dec/68	949.9[2]	-	-	-	-	-	-	-	-	-	10.8
Jan -Jun/69	920.7[2]	-	-	-	-	-	-	-	-	-	9.0
Jul -Dec/69	911.1[2]	-	-	-	-	-	-	-	-	-	4.3
Jan -Aug/70	929.5[2]	-	-	-	-	-	-	-	-	-	7.0
Sep -Dec/70	953.2[2]	-	-	-	-	-	-	-	-	-	4.9
Jan -Jun/71	935.7	9.7	2.2	297.5	6.8	69.5	162.8	89.3	289.4	1.2	7.3
Jul -Dec/71	981.2	10.9	3.2	317.2	6.6	77.7	159.0	97.6	300.1	2.1	6.8
1972	994.1	8.1	2.2	326.6	8.9	79.2	155.6	96.8	307.3	2.3	7.1
1973	1,001.8	32.7[1]	-	271.5	-	61.0	162.9	78.4	378.7	5.7	11.1
1974	1,059.0	13.5	6.6	273.9	12.6	73.3	177.8	82.4	391.8	2.3	24.9
1975	1,099.8	13.3	7.6	271.9	13.0	68.8	187.3	81.0	414.4	3.6	39.0
Jan -Mar/76	1,147.8	12.6	6.3	274.7	10.1	66.9	198.8	73.9	456.3	5.0	43.2
Apr -Jun/76	1,235.4	15.5	5.5	309.7	12.0	58.0	222.2	72.2	480.5	2.5	57.2
Jul -Sep/76	1,219.9	12.6	2.8	306.8	10.3	59.1	225.1	70.2	489.8	.5	42.8
Oct -Dec/76	1,177.0	14.3	5.6	287.7	9.8	56.9	231.4	68.0	461.4	.3	41.8
Jan -Mar/77	1,183.6	12.9	5.2	275.9	16.4	61.5	221.8	77.9	463.3	-	48.7
Apr -Jun/77	1,234.6	13.4	3.7	307.1	11.3	56.8	233.5	77.5	483.1	-	48.4
Jul -Sep/77	1,203.3	14.6	3.1	279.9	12.5	58.2	232.1	72.3	491.4	3.1	36.0
Oct -Dec/77	1,186.8	13.4	6.2	283.8	13.2	56.4	227.1	65.2	494.1	2.4	25.2

TABLE 11.10 (Cont'd)

Labor Force in Greater Santiago, by Type of Economic Activity, 1966-1977.

Period	Total	Agri- culture and Fishing	Mining and Quarry- ing	Manu- facture	Electri- city Gas and Sanitary Services	Con- struction	Trade	Transport Storage and Communi- cations	Services	Not Ade- quately Specified	Persons Seeking Work for the First Time
	Relative Figures (Percentages)										
Jul -Oct/66	100.0	0.9	0.2	33.9	1.5	7.4	16.9	7.4	30.0	0.2	1.6
Nov/66-Feb/67	100.0	1.1	0.1	34.1	1.4	7.7	17.8	7.3	29.6	0.1	0.8
Mar -Jun/67	100.0	0.9	0.3	34.0	1.4	7.6	16.7	7.5	30.7	0.2	0.7
Jul -Oct/67	100.0	0.8	0.2	33.6	0.9	7.8	18.4	6.9	30.7	0.1	0.6
Nov/67-Feb/68	100.0	1.2	0.2	33.0	0.7	7.4	18.8	7.6	30.5	-	0.6
Mar -Jun/68	100.0	0.8	0.2	33.7	0.7	7.4	19.4	7.3	29.8	-	0.7
Sep -Dec/68	100.0[2]	-	-	-	-	-	-	-	-	-	1.1
Jan -Jun/69	100.0[2]	-	-	-	-	-	-	-	-	-	1.0
Jul -Dec/69	100.0[2]	-	-	-	-	-	-	-	-	-	0.5
Jan -Aug/70	100.0[2]	-	-	-	-	-	-	-	-	-	0.7
Sep -Dec/70	100.0[2]	-	-	-	-	-	-	-	-	-	0.5
Jan -Jun/71	100.0	1.1	0.2	31.8	0.7	7.4	17.4	9.6	30.9	0.1	0.8
Jul -Dec/71	100.0	1.1	0.3	32.3	0.7	7.9	16.2	10.0	30.6	0.2	0.7
1972	100.0	0.8[1]	0.2	32.9	0.9	8.0	15.7	9.7	30.9	0.2	0.7
1973	100.0	3.3[1]	-	27.1	-	6.1	16.2	7.8	37.8	0.6	1.1
1974	100.0	1.3	0.6	25.9	1.2	6.9	16.8	7.8	36.9	0.2	2.3
1975	100.0	1.2	0.7	24.7	1.2	6.3	17.0	7.4	37.6	0.3	3.6
Jan -Mar/76	100.0	1.1	0.6	23.9	0.9	5.8	17.3	6.4	39.7	0.5	3.8
Apr -Jun/76	100.0	1.3	0.4	25.0	1.0	4.7	18.0	5.8	38.8	0.2	4.6
Jul -Sep/76	100.0	1.0	0.2	25.2	0.8	4.8	18.5	5.8	40.1	0.0	3.5
Oct -Dec/76	100.0	1.2	0.5	24.4	0.8	4.8	19.7	5.8	39.2	0.0	3.6
Jan -Mar/77	100.0	1.1	0.4	23.3	1.4	5.2	18.7	6.6	39.1	-	4.1
Apr -Jun/77	100.0	1.1	0.3	24.9	0.9	4.6	18.9	6.3	39.1	-	3.9
Jul -Sep/77	100.0	1.2	0.3	23.3	1.0	4.8	19.3	6.0	40.8	0.3	3.0
Oct -Dec/77	100.0	1.1	0.5	23.9	1.1	4.8	19.2	5.5	41.6	0.2	2.1

Notes: 1. Includes the following groups: Agriculture and Fishing, Mining and Quarrying, and Public Utility Services.
2. There is no information for the period September 1968-December 1970.

Source: National Institute of Statistics.

12
UNEMPLOYMENT AND JOBLESSNESS

INTRODUCTION

Statistical information on the labor force at the national level and in the Greater Santiago area was presented already in Chapters 10 and 11. Some of the tables of Chapters 10 and 11 also included information on unemployment and joblessness but only in a secondary manner. In the present chapter, in contrast, the focus is on presenting the most comprehensive information available on unemployment and joblessness both at the national level and for Greater Santiago.

Unemployment and Unemployment Rates at the National Level: 1960-1978

A summary picture of trends in unemployment and unemployment rates in Chile is provided by Table 12.1

TABLE 12.1

Employment and Population for the Whole Country. (thousands of persons)

Year	Total Population	% Change	Active Population	% Change	Employed Population	% Change	Unemploy-ment	Unemploy-ment Rate
1960	7,585.3	-	2,427.3	-	2,255.0	-	172.3	7.1
1961	7,773.3	2.5	2,474.6	1.9	2,276.6	1.0	198.0	8.0
1962	7,961.3	2.4	2,522.8	1.9	2,323.5	2.1	199.3	7.9
1963	8,147.3	2.3	2,572.0	2.0	2,379.1	2.4	192.9	7.5
1964	8,330.4	2.2	2,622.1	1.9	2,438.6	2.5	183.5	7.0
1965	8,509.9	2.2	2,673.2	1.9	2,502.1	2.6	171.1	6.4
1966	8,685.9	2.1	2,725.3	1.9	2,559.1	2.3	166.2	6.1
1967	8,858.9	2.0	2,778.4	1.9	2,647.8	3.5	130.6	4.7
1968	9,029.6	1.9	2,832.6	2.0	2,693.8	1.7	138.8	4.9
1969	9,199.1	1.9	2,887.8	1.9	2,714.5	0.8	173.3	6.0
1970	9,368.6	1.8	2,950.1	2.2	2,770.1	2.0	180.0	6.1
1971	9,539.1	1.8	3,020.9	2.4	2,906.1	4.9	114.8	3.8
1972	9,711.9	1.8	3,093.9	2.4	2,998.0	3.2	95.9	3.1
1973	9,887.9	1.8	3,167.6	2.4	3,015.6	0.6	152.0	4.8
1974	10,068.1	1.8	3,243.6	2.4	2,945.2	-2.3	298.4	9.2
1975	10,253.0	1.8	3,321.3	2.4	2,839.7	-3.6	481.6	14.5
1976	10,443.2	1.9	3,404.7	2.5	2,938.8	3.5	465.9	13.7
1977	10,639.0	1.9	3,490.2	2.5	3,046.9	3.7	443.3	12.7
1978*	10,840.5	1.9	3,577.8	2.5	3,187.4	4.6	390.4	10.9

Source: Sergio De Castro: 1979, 49.

Table 12.1 gives the total, active and employed population of Chile (as well as the annual percentage change in these variables) and the level of unemployment as well as the rate of unemployment between 1960 and 1978. This is the best summary table available.

Countrywide Employment-Unemployment Series: 1966-1976

The total population of Chile according to sex, age groups and employment situation in the labor force between 1966 and 1976 in both absolute and relative numbers is presented in Table 12.2.

In Table 12.2 the population of Chile is presented by sex and age (under 12 and 12 years of age and over). The population with 12 years of age and over is further subdivided into the labor force and those not included in the labor force. The labor force figures are further subdivided into employed and unemployed. The employed are classified into working and not working and the unemployed are classified into jobless and new entrants to the labor force. Those not included in the labor force are further subdivided into housewives, students and other.

As the absolute figures on employed persons of the labor force of Table 12.2 reveal, the total of persons employed in 1976 was below the total employed during 1969-1972 and very close to the figures of December 1969. Furthermore, both the absolute number of persons and the percentage of the labor force unemployed in 1975 and 1976 reached a high level that had existed in Chile before only during the depression years of the 1930s. The post-Allende unemployment figures are of catastrophic magnitude and a byproduct of the anti-inflation and economic reorganization policies of the Chilean government since 1973.

The Unemployment Debate of 1979

By 1979, even government economists admitted that unemployment had remained for six years so high and so pervasive that it could not be tolerated much longer. The social, economic and human costs were too high. And with inflation under control, booming copper prices, a balanced government budget, and a broad-based export boom, attention was concentrated on reducing, if not eradicating, unemployment. A debate developed about the optimum strategies needed in fighting unemployment and at the center of this debate were the unemployment figures.

Unemployment figures were being questioned in the following manner. The national as well as the Santiago figures on unemployment have been estimated on the basis of sample surveys undertaken by the National Institute of Statistics and the Department of Economics of the University of Chile. In order to obtain aggregate labor force, employment and unemployment numbers, the sample figures were "inflated" on the basis of estimated national and Santiago population figures. If the projected population figures were correct, the absolute unemployment, employment and related figures would also be accurate. However, as pointed out in earlier chapters, the official population estimates for 1978 and 1979 prepared jointly by ODEPLAN-INE-CELADE could have been overestimated because of underestimates of the decline in the country's birth rate and of international migration out of Chile. To the extent that the official population figures were inaccurate and inflated, the absolute unemployment figures would also be inflated and inaccurate. The percentage of unemployment, however, would not be affected since the sample figures used to calculate it were considered reliable. Since, however, the overestimate of the total population could not exceed 5-10%, the maximum overestimate of unemployment also could not be in excess of 10%. It was, thus, recognized that in order to make correct estimates of total unemployment it would be necessary to wait for the final population figures of the census of 1980 or undertake special surveys or studies to make new, independent population estimates.

The Santiago unemployment figures were further complicated by the fact that the Santiago population was estimated to grow, including the natural population increase, due to in-migration by 3.6 percent per year. To the extent that actual in-migration was smaller (or larger) than the estimated one, total population and unemployment figures would be over- (under)-estimated.

The issues discussed above become more real where the total population, active population, and employed and unemployed population figures of Tables 12.1 and 12.2 are compared. Both sets of statistics reflect official information but the figures of Table 12.1 are not only different but often also much higher than the corresponding figures contained in Table 12.2

TABLE 12.2

Total Population According to Sex, Age Groups, and Employment Situation in the Labor Force by Periods, 1966-1976.
(Thousands of Persons)

Periods	Total	Sex		Age Groups		Labor Force			
						Total	Employed		
		Male	Female	Under 12	12 & Over		Total	Working	Not Working
	Absolute Numbers								
Jul -Oct 1966	8,800.0	4,270.8	4,529.2	2,952.0	5,848.0	2,783.5	2,604.5	2,501.0	103.5
Nov 66-Feb 1967	8,883.9	4,312.8	4,571.1	2,987.1	5,896.8	2,799.2	2,659.3	2,539.1	120.2
Mar -Jun 1967	8,962.3	4,350.8	4,611.5	3,005.2	5,957.1	2,773.9	2,647.2	2,546.9	100.3
Jul -Oct 1967	9,046.1	4,396.8	4,649.3	3,032.1	6,014.0	2,804.3	2,660.3	2,558.0	102.3
Nov 67-Feb 1968	9,127.3	4,436.3	4,691.0	3,057.8	6,069.5	2,859.9	2,733.1	2,578.7	154.4
Mar -Jun 1968	9,208.3	4,487.2	4,721.1	3,084.6	6,123.7	2,755.5	2,639.1	2,543.8	95.3
Sept -Dec 1968	9,328.7	4,545.1	4,783.6	3,123.8	6,204.9	2,857.5	2,699.5	2,613.9	85.6
Jan -Jun 1969	9,434.0	4,600.3	4,833.7	3,157.4	6,276.6	2,869.2	2,725.5	2,602.4	123.1
Jul -Dec 1969	9,551.8	4,659.5	4,892.3	3,194.7	6,357.1	2,885.6	2,774.2	2,709.7	64.5
Jan -Aug 1970	9,697.5	4,733.5	4,964.2	3,242.8	6,454.7	2,913.0	2,816.6	2,709.5	107.1
Sept -Dec 1970	9,818.6	4,793.1	5,025.5	3,282.1	6,536.5	2,941.8	2,836.2	2,791.9	44.3
Jan -Jun 1971	9,920.1	4,843.6	5,076.5	3,314.9	6,605.2	2,980.7	2,845.0	2,726.2	118.8
Jul -Dec 1971	10,041.6	4,903.9	5,137.7	3,353.7	6,687.9	2,967.0	2,875.8	2,807.6	68.2
Jan -Jun 1972	10,184.5	4,971.8	5,212.7	3,400.9	6,783.6	2,981.0	2,887.9	2,762.7	125.8
1973[2]	-	-	-	-	-	-	-	-	-
1974[2]	-	-	-	-	-	-	-	-	-
1975	10,311.8	4,943.3	5,368.5	2,756.7	7,555.1	3,183.5	2,715.9	2,627.6	88.3
1976	10,529.9	5,069.7	5,460.2	2,789.8	7,740.1	3,151.3	2,741.7	2,672.3	69.4

TABLE 12.2 (Cont'd)

Total Population According to Sex, Age Groups, and Employment Situation in the Labor Force by Periods, 1966-1976.
(Thousands of Persons)

Periods	Labor Force Unemployed (1)			Not Included in the Labor Force			
	Total	Jobless	New Entrants	Total	Housewives	Students	Others
	Absolute Numbers						
Jul -Oct 1966	179.0	-	-	3,064.5	1,785.4	892.4	386.7
Nov 66-Feb 1967	139.9	-	-	3,097.6	1,844.6	662.1	590.9
Mar -Jun 1967	126.7	-	-	3,183.2	1,863.2	953.0	367.0
Jul -Oct 1967	144.0	-	-	3,209.7	1,870.9	970.4	368.4
Nov 67-Feb 1968	126.8	-	-	3,209.6	1,925.8	478.0	805.8
Mar -Jun 1968	116.4	-	-	3,368.2	1,946.6	1,029.3	392.3
Sept -Dec 1968	158.0	-	-	3,347.4	1,886.3	1,097.3	363.8
Jan -Jun 1969	143.7	-	-	3,407.4	1,926.1	852.6	628.7
Jul -Dec 1969	111.4	-	-	3,471.5	1,918.1	1,095.8	457.6
Jan -Aug 1970	96.4	-	-	3,541.7	1,953.0	954.2	634.5
Sept -Dec 1970	105.6	-	-	3,594.7	1,932.4	1,268.5	393.8
Jan -Jun 1971	135.7	-	-	3,624.5	1,926.5	934.6	763.4
Jul -Dec 1971	91.2	-	-	3,720.9	1,902.0	1,286.4	532.5
Jan -Jun 1972	93.1	-	-	3,802.6	1,961.8	1,123.0	717.8
1973[2]	-	-	-	-	-	-	-
1974[2]	-	-	-	-	-	-	-
1975	467.6	308.2	159.4	4,371.6	2,137.5	-	2,234.1[3]
1976	409.6	250.4	159.2	4,588.8	2,146.7	1,767.1	675.0

TABLE 12.2 (Cont'd)

Total Population According to Sex, Age Groups, and Employment Situation in the Labor Force by Periods, 1966-1976.
(Thousands of Persons)

Periods	Total	Sex		Age Groups		Labor Force			
						Total	Employed		
		Male	Female	Under 12	12 & Over		Total	Working	Not Working
	Relative Numbers								
Jul -Oct 1966	100.0	48.5	51.5	33.6	66.4	100.0	93.6	89.9	3.7
Nov 66-Feb 1967	100.0	48.5	51.5	33.6	66.4	100.0	95.0	90.7	4.3
Mar -Jun 1967	100.0	48.5	51.5	33.5	66.5	100.0	95.4	91.8	3.6
Jul -Oct 1967	100.0	48.6	51.4	33.5	66.5	100.0	94.9	91.2	3.7
Nov 67-Feb 1968	100.0	48.6	51.4	33.5	66.5	100.0	95.6	90.2	5.4
Mar -Jun 1968	100.0	48.7	51.3	33.5	66.5	100.0	95.8	92.3	3.5
Sept -Dec 1968	100.0	48.7	51.3	33.5	66.5	100.0	94.5	91.5	3.0
Jan -Jun 1969	100.0	48.8	51.2	33.5	66.5	100.0	95.0	90.7	4.3
Jul -Dec 1969	100.0	48.8	51.2	33.4	66.6	100.0	96.1	93.9	2.2
Jan -Aug 1970	100.0	48.8	51.2	33.4	66.6	100.0	96.7	93.0	3.7
Sept -Dec 1970	100.0	48.8	51.2	33.4	66.6	100.0	96.4	94.9	1.5
Jan -Jun 1971	100.0	48.8	51.2	33.4	66.6	100.0	95.4	91.4	4.0
Jul -Dec 1971	100.0	48.8	51.2	33.4	66.6	100.0	96.9	94.6	2.3
Jan -Jun 1972	100.0	48.8	51.2	33.4	66.6	100.0	96.9	92.7	4.2
1973[2]	-	-	-	-	-	-	-	-	-
1974[2]	-	-	-	-	-	-	-	-	-
1975	100.0	47.9	52.1	26.7	73.3	100.0	85.3	82.5	2.8
1976	100.0	48.1	51.9	26.5	73.5	100.0	87.0	84.8	2.2

TABLE 12.2 (Cont'd)

Total Population According to Sex, Age Groups, and Employment Situation in the Labor Force by Periods, 1966-1976.
(Thousands of Persons)

Periods	Labor Force: Unemployed (1): Total	Jobless	New Entrants	Not Included in the Labor Force: Total	Housewives	Students	Others
	Relative Numbers						
Jul -Oct 1966	6.4	-	-	100.0	58.3	29.1	12.6
Nov 66-Feb 1967	5.0	-	-	100.0	59.5	21.4	19.1
Mar -Jun 1967	4.6	-	-	100.0	58.5	30.0	11.5
Jul -Oct 1967	5.1	-	-	100.0	58.3	30.2	11.5
Nov 67-Feb 1968	4.4	-	-	100.0	60.0	14.9	25.1
Mar -Jun 1968	4.2	-	-	100.0	57.8	30.6	11.6
Sept -Dec 1968	5.5	-	-	100.0	56.3	32.8	10.9
Jan -Jun 1969	5.0	-	-	100.0	56.5	25.0	18.5
Jul -Dec 1969	3.9	-	-	100.0	55.2	31.6	13.2
Jan -Aug 1970	3.3	-	-	100.0	55.1	27.0	17.9
Sept -Dec 1970	3.6	-	-	100.0	53.8	35.3	10.9
Jan -Jun 1971	4.6	-	-	100.0	53.1	25.8	21.1
Jul -Dec 1971	3.1	-	-	100.0	51.1	34.6	14.3
Jan -Jun 1972	3.1	-	-	100.0	51.6	29.5	18.9
1973[2]	-	-	-	-	-	-	-
1974[2]	-	-	-	-	-	-	-
1975	14.7	9.7	5.0	100.0	48.9	-	51.1[6]
1976	13.0	7.9	5.1	100.0	46.8	38.5	14.7

Source: National Institute of Statistics

Notes:
1. Separate statistical information is lacking for the period between July-October 1966 and January 1972.
2. There does not exist statistical information at the national level for the periods between 1973 and 1974. This is so because the national employment survey was carried out only in some provinces during those years.
3. This figure lumps together students and other inactives.

Unemployment by Urban and Rural Zones

The rates of unemployment in 1975 and 1976 by province, region and urban and rural areas for 1975 and 1976 are presented in Table 12.3. The rates of unemployment among males and females in urban and rural areas in 1976 are presented in Table 12.4. Presented in Table 12.4 are absolute figures and percentages of the population of Chile of twelve years and over by sex and situation in the labor force and according to rural and urban areas. The statistics of Tables 12.2, 12.3 and 12.4 were collected and prepared by the National Institute of Statistics.

Detailed statistics on unemployment, employment and labor force according to economic activity, occupational category and urban and rural zones for the various regions of Chile are found in INE's national employment surveys (e.g., INE: 1977f to INE: 1977p).

Joblessness by Type of Economic Activity

Joblessness in the Greater or Great Santiago area by type of economic activity between 1956 and 1978 in thousands of persons is presented in Table 12.5. Jobless are defined as those persons who have lost their employment and are seeking a new job. Table 12.5 gives the figures for joblessness in goods producing activities, in service producing activities, in transportation, storage, communications and public utilities and in activities not adequately specified. Furthermore, joblessness in goods producing activities is subdivided into that found in (a) agriculture, hunting, forestry and fishing, (b) mining and quarrying, (c) manufacturing and (d) construction. Joblessness in service producing activities is subdivided into that found in (a) commerce, (b) governmental and financial services, (c) personal and housing-household services and (d) community and social services.

Joblessness in Santiago rises sharply between June 1973 (23.4 thousand) and March 1976 (191.7 thousand) declining subsequently to 134.3 thousand in June of 1978. The time series on joblessness presented in Table 12.1 are those compiled and published by the Institute of Economics of the University of Chile.

Joblessness According to Occupational Status

The Instituto de Economía time series on joblessness according to occupational status for the Greater Santiago area between 1959 and 1978 are presented, in thousands of persons, in Table 12.6. The occupational categories of Table 12.6 are those of employers, own account workers (self-employed), salaried employees, wage employees, unpaid family workers and no data available. What stands out in these figures is the more than seven-fold rise in Santiago joblessness between March 1973 and June 1976.

The National Institute of Statistics Time Series of Unemployment in Santiago

The population of Greater Santiago with twelve years of age and over according to the employment situation between 1966 and 1977 is presented in both absolute figures and in percentages in Table 12.7.

Unemployment rates by type of economic activity in the Greater Santiago area between 1966 and 1977 are presented in Table 12.8. The economic activities for which unemployment rates are given are those of agriculture and fishing, mining and quarrying, manufacturing, electricity, gas and sanitary services, construction, trade, transport, storage and communications and services. Standing out in this table is the high unemployment rate in construction and the apparent inability of the other sectors to grow rapidly enough to absorb the surplus labor within their sector and that found in construction.

TABLE 12.3

Rates of Unemployment in 1975 and 1976, by Province, Region and Urban and Rural Areas. National Employment Survey.

Province and Region	1975 Urban	1975 Rural	1975 Total	1975 Month of Survey	1976 Urban	1976 Rural	1976 Total	1976 Month of Survey
I Tarapacá	18.8	4,0	17,6	July	16.8	2.5	15.3	
II Antofagasta	12.8	2.4	12.4	August	14.0	0.9	13.5	
III Atacama	16.9	8.6	14.8	August	14.9	6.9	12.9	
IV Coquimbo	20.2	9.8	16.0	August	15.1	5.4	11.0	
V Aconcagua	17.1	17.3	17.2		11.3	6.2	8.8	
Valparaíso	19.2	12.5	18.2		11.0	7.4	10.6	
Total	18.9	14.3	18.0	October	11.1	6.9	10.3	December
VI O'Higgins	17.2	15.2	16.2		17.8	19.4	18.5	
Colchagua	8.9	9.1	9.0		12.7	12.0	12.2	
Total	15.4	12.7	13.8	October	16.5	16.3	16.4	October
VII Curricó	14.0	4.9	8.0		11.1	7.2	8.7	
Talca	19.9	5.1	12.8		18.1	5.8	12.5	
Maule	17.5	9.0	12.6		24.6	8.0	15.5	
Linares	17.6	5.6	10.5		10.9	2.9	6.4	
Total	18.2	5.7	11.2	December	16.0	5.6	10.5	
VIII Ñuble	18.0	9.0	12.9		21.0	12.0	16.4	
Concepción	18.1	14.4	17.6		15.6	12.0	15.1	
Arauco	14.9	7.8	11.5		16.9	12.3	14.8	
Bío-Bío	16.7	11.9	14.0		14.0	6.8	10.9	
Total	17.8	10.9	15.5	June	16.5	10.7	14.7	October
IX Malleco	20.8	10.0	15.5		16.5	14.9	15.4	
Cautín	19.1	7.5	13.5		12.5	4.6	6.8	
Total	19.6	8.3	14.1	December	14.6	9.8	11.2	
X Valdivia	15.1	9.6	12.5		17.3	6.5	11.4	
Osorno	10.8	2.7	6.8		12.0	4.4	8.4	
Llanquihue	17.2	6.2	11.2		14.5	6.6	10.3	
Chiloé	10.4	1.3	2.8		10.5	4.9	6.6	
Total	14.4	5.3	9.3	May	14.5	5.8	9.7	
XI Aysén	16.3	10.3	13.6	August	11.1	3.8	7.9	October
XII Magallanes	11.3	2.8	9.7	August	12.2	4.3	10.5	
Metropolitan Area	15.3	7.6	14.6	December				
Total	16.6	8.8	14.7	October 15	14.6	7.1	13.1	November 15

Source: National Institute of Statistics. National Employment Survey.

TABLE 12.4

Population of Chile with Twelve Years of Age and Over, by Sex and Situation in Labor Force and According to Rural and Urban Zones, 1976.
(Absolute Figures and Percentages)

Population by Sex and Situation in the Labor Force	Total Nacional		Zones			
			Urban		Rural	
	Persons	%	Persons	%	Persons	%
Total Population	10,529,900	100.0	8,238,180	100.0	2,291,720	100.0
Under 12 Years of Age	2,789,840	26.5	2,082,410	25.3	707,430	30.9
Population with 12 Years of Age and Over	7,740,060	73.5	6,155,770	74.7	1,584,290	69.1
Labor Force[1]	3,151,240	40.7	2,465,900	40.1	685,340	43.3
Not Included in the Labor Force	4,588,820	59.3	3,689,870	59.9	898,950	56.7
Labor Force	3,151,240	100.0	2,465,900	100.0	685,340	100.0
Employed	2,741,690	87.0	2,105,250	85.4	636,440	92.9
Unemployed	409,550	13.0	360,650	14.6	48,900	7.1
Males	5,069,750	100.0	3,888,390	100.0	1,181,360	100.0
Under 12 Years of Age	1,431,280	28.2	1,062,990	27.3	368,290	31.2
Population with 12 Years of Age and Over	3,638,470	71.8	2,825,400	72.7	813,070	68.8
Labor Force	2,277,290	62.6	1,700,710	60.2	576,580	70.9
Not Included in the Labor Force	1,361,180	37.4	1,124,690	39.8	236,490	29.1
Labor Force	2,277,290	100.0	1,700,710	100.0	576,580	100.0
Employed	2,013,650	88.4	1,473,750	86.7	539,900	93.6
Unemployed	263,640	11.6	226,960	13.3	36,680	6.4
Females	5,460,150	100.0	4,349,790	100.0	1,110,360	100.0
Under 12 Years of Age	1,358,560	24.9	1,019,420	23.4	339,140	30.5
Population with 12 Years of Age and Over	4,101,590	75.1	3,330,370	76.6	771,220	69.5
Labor Force	873,950	21.3	765,190	23.0	108,760	14.1
Not Included in the Labor Force	3,227,640	78.7	2,565,180	77.0	662,460	85.9
Labor Force	873,950	100.0	765,190	100.0	108,760	100.0
Employed	728,040	83.3	631,500	82.5	96,540	88.8
Unemployed	145,910	16.7	133,690	17.5	12,220	11.2

Notes: 1. The percentages were calculated taking as basis the population of twelve years of age and over.

Source: National employment survey for 1976 of the National Institute of Statistics.

TABLE 12.5

Joblessness by Economic Activity
Great Santiago, 1956-1978.
(Thousands of Persons)

Economic Activity	October 1956	June 1957	June 1958	March 1959	June 1959	April 1960	June 1960	September 1960[1]
Total Joblessness	37,8	32,0	54,2	62,5	43,3	44,3	47,4	-
Goods Producing Activities	23,6	20,6	31,0	37,2	21,7	25,8	26,0	-
Agriculture, Hunting, Forestry and Fishing	0,5	1,0	1,4	0,6	0,4	0,9	0,2	-
Mining and Quarrying	0,6	0,2	1,0	0,9	0,5	0,6	0,2	-
Manufacturing	13,4	11,4	17,0	24,7	12,5	16,1	17,7	-
Construction	9,1	8,1	11,7	11,0	8,3	8,3	7,9	-
Service Producing Activities	11,7	8,9	18,9	21,4	17,3	16,4	18,3	-
Commerce	3,3	2,8	5,1	7,1	5,3	5,0	4,6	-
Governmental and Financial Services	2,0	1,1	2,1	0,9	1,6	1,5	2,3	-
Personal and Housing Services	6,4	5,0	11,7	10,0	7,9	10,0	11,4	-
Community and Social Services				3,3	2,5			
Transportation, Storage, Communications and Public Utilities	1,9	1,9	4,1	3,7	4,4	2,0	3,1	-
Activities not adequately specified	0,6	0,5	0,2	0,2	-	-	-	-

1. Survey based on a sample designed in 1956.

TABLE 12.5 (Cont'd)

Joblessness by Economic Activity
Great Santiago, 1956-1978.
(Thousands of Persons)

Economic Activity	September 1960[2]	December 1960	March 1961	June 1961	September 1961	December 1961	March 1962	June 1962
Total Joblessness	44,6	45,8	45,7	43,6	42,8	31,5	36,2	35,3
Goods Producing Activities	23,6	22,6	25,1	24,3	21,7	18,4	20,2	19,3
Agriculture, Hunting, Forestry and Fishing	0,6	0,5	0,9	1,3	0,9	0,6	1,0	0,9
Mining and Quarrying	0,2	0,3	0,7	0,6	1,1	0,6	1,4	-
Manufacturing	14,6	13,0	15,4	14,9	13,4	12,1	12,6	12,8
Construction	8,3	8,8	8,1	7,6	6,3	5,1	5,2	5,7
Service Producing Activities	16,6	19,2	18,2	16,4	18,7	11,9	14,3	14,4
Commerce	5,5	5,2	5,5	3,8	6,0	4,4	4,3	5,0
Governmental and Financial Services	1,1	1,8	2,0	2,0	1,4	1,3	0,5	0,9
Personal and Housing Services	4,4	5,7	4,7	6,0	4,3	2,3	3,8	4,0
Community and Social Services	5,5	6,5	6,0	4,7	7,0	3,9	5,7	4,6
Transportation, Storage, Communications and Public Utilities	3,7	3,7	2,5	2,7	2,7	1,6	2,0	1,7
Activities not adequately specified	0,8	0,2	0,4	0,4	0,2	-	-	-

2. Survey based on a sample designed in 1960.

TABLE 12.5 (Cont'd)

Joblessness by Economic Activity
Great Santiago, 1956-1978.
(Thousands of Persons)

Economic Activity	September 1962	October 1962[3]	December 1962	March 1963	June 1963	September 1963	December 1963[4]	December 1963[5]
Total Joblessness	27,5	28,7	33,3	33,5	32,7	34,7	24,0	28,8
Goods Producing Activities	17,1	14,7	18,6	16,1	15,4	17,8	15,2	15,9
Agriculture, Hunting, Forestry and Fishing	0,9	0,6	0,4	0,5	1,2	0,5	0,2	0,3
Mining and Quarrying	0,7	0,6	0,2	0,2	-	0,3	0,2	0,3
Manufacturing	11,3	9,6	10,8	12,3	10,7	12,3	10,7	9,7
Construction	4,2	3,8	7,4	3,1	3,6	4,7	4,2	5,6
Service Producing Activities	9,2	12,1	12,5	16,2	14,3	13,4	6,7	10,7
Commerce	3,0	4,5	3,3	5,0	4,2	5,3	2,7	3,0
Governmental and Financial Services	0,5	-	1,5	0,8	1,2	0,8	-	0,5
Personal and Housing Services	1,5	3,5	2,6	4,3	4,2	2,4	1,7	3,0
Community and Social Services	4,2	4,1	5,1	6,1	4,7	4,9	2,3	4,2
Transportation, Storage, Communications and Public Utilities	1,5	1,6	2,3	1,3	3,1	3,2	2,2	2,0
Activities not adequately specified	-	0,3	-	-	-	0,2	-	0,1

3. Survey based on half of the same interviewed in September of 1962.
4. Survey based on a sample designed in 1960.
5. Survey based on a sample designed in 1963.

TABLE 12.5 (Cont'd)

Joblessness by Economic Activity
Great Santiago, 1956-1978.
(Thousands of Persons)

Economic Activity	March 1964	June 1964	September 1964[6]	September 1964	December 1964	March 1965	June 1965	September 1965
Total Joblessness	33,2	31,3	36,9	41,4	32,6	41,3	31,5	41,2
Goods Producing Activities	20,3	18,1	19,8	24,1	20,7	23,4	17,2	20,2
Agriculture, Hunting, Forestry and Fishing	0,5	0,5	0,9	0,2	0,5	0,3	0,5	1,1
Mining and Quarrying	0,3	0,3	-	0,5	0,5	0,3	0,2	0,2
Manufacturing	12,3	10,3	12,5	13,9	11,0	13,8	9,6	11,0
Construction	7,2	7,2	6,4	9,6	8,7	9,0	6,9	7,9
Service Producing Activities	11,9	10,9	15,1	15,6	10,2	15,1	11,8	18,2
Commerce	3,6	3,9	5,0	5,7	3,2	4,4	3,6	5,5
Governmental and Financial Services	0,8	1,3	1,0	0,5	0,8	1,1	0,3	1,4
Personal and Housing Services	2,7	3,0	3,1	4,4	2,3	3,8	2,8	5,5
Community and Social Services	4,8	2,8	5,9	5,0	3,9	5,8	5,1	5,8
Transportation, Storage, Communications and Public Utilities	1,2	2,4	2,1	1,7	1,7	2,8	2,6	2,8
Activities not adequately specified	-	-	-	-	-	-	-	-

6. Survey with a special question about inactives.

TABLE 12.5 (Cont'd)

Joblessness by Economic Activity
Great Santiago, 1956-1978.
(Thousands of Persons)

Economic Activity	December 1965	March 1966	June 1966	September 1966	December 1966	March 1967[7]	March 1967[8]	June 1967
Total Joblessness	33,0	32,0	40,2	39,3	38,5	40,7	46,5	44,0
Goods Producing Activities	17,5	15,9	20,9	21,4	19,3	22,2	25,9	26,2
Agriculture, Hunting, Forestry and Fishing	1,1	0,6	1,2	-	0,3	0,4	0,5	1,5
Mining and Quarrying	0,5	0,2	0,5	0,5	0,3	0,4	0,5	0,5
Manufacturing	10,2	10,4	12,9	11,4	10,7	14,2	13,6	13,8
Construction	5,7	4,7	6,3	9,5	8,0	7,3	11,4	10,6
Service Producing Activities	13,3	13,9	16,7	14,9	15,0	15,4	17,3	14,6
Commerce	3,7	5,2	6,0	4,4	4,9	4,6	4,7	4,5
Governmental and Financial Services	1,1	0,6	0,7	0,8	1,5	1,2	1,1	1,0
Personal and Housing Services	3,9	3,6	3,8	4,4	5,9	4,4	4,4	3,7
Community and Social Services	4,6	4,5	6,3	5,3	2,7	5,3	7,0	5,5
Transportation, Storage, Communications and Public Utilities	2,1	2,1	2,7	2,9	4,1	3,1	3,2	3,2
Activities not adequately specified	-	-	-	-	-	-	0,1	-

7. Survey based on a sample designed in 1963.
8. Survey based on a sample designed in 1967.

TABLE 12.5 (Cont'd)

Joblessness by Economic Activity
Great Santiago, 1956-1978.
(Thousands of Persons)

Economic Activity	September 1967	December 1967	March 1968	June 1968	September 1968	December 1968	March 1969	June 1969
Total Joblessness	45,7	48,8	40,8	48,3	52,2	43.4	64.8	53.2
Goods Producing Activities	24,2	27,9	22,3	28,2	29,2	23,4	26,6	23,7
Agriculture, Hunting, Forestry and Fishing	0,5	1,6	1,3	1,9	1,3	0,5	0,5	0,9
Mining and Quarrying	0,5	0,8	0,2	0,2	0,3	0,7	-	-
Manufacturing	13,8	17,6	12,7	13,8	16,5	12,2	15,9	13,2
Construction	9,4	7,9	8,1	12,3	11,1	10,0	10,2	9,7
Service Producing Activities	17,2	18,0	16,7	17,3	19,2	17,6	34,3	26,3
Commerce	4,1	4,1	5,5	5,4	6,4	5,1	8,2	6,4
Governmental and Financial Services	1,0	1,5	0,8	1,9	2,0	1,2	1,6	1,6
Personal and Housing Services	4,9	3,3	4,1	3,7	4,4	3,9	9,5	8,5
Community and Social Services	7,3	9,1	6,3	6,5	6,4	7,5	15,0	9,9
Transportation, Storage, Communications and Public Utilities	4,3	2,9	1,8	2,9	3,9	2,2	4,0	3,3
Activities not adequately specified	-	-	-	-	-	0,2	-	-

TABLE 12.5 (Cont'd)

Joblessness by Economic Activity
Great Santiago, 1956-1978.
(Thousands of Persons)

Economic Activity	September 1969	December 1969	March 1970	June 1970	September 1970	December 1970	March 1971	June 1971
Total Joblessness	43,7	44,0	52,6	57,3	54,1	68,2	63,9	43,2
Goods Producing Activities	21,7	22,7	29,0	30,3	28,2	36,7	38,6	24,4
Agriculture, Hunting, Forestry and Fishing	0,5	0,9	0,2	0,9	0,4	1,5	0,2	1,3
Mining and Quarrying	-	0,4	-	0,4	0,7	0,6	0,7	1,0
Manufacturing	14,3	11,1	16,9	17,7	14,8	17,9	22,3	13,2
Construction	6,9	10,4	11,9	11,3	12,3	16,8	15,5	9,0
Service Producing Activities	19,4	17,6	19,4	22,6	21,9	26,1	20,4	15,5
Commerce	5,1	4,0	4,4	5,4	5,6	6,2	3,7	5,4
Governmental and Financial Services	1,6	0,9	0,7	0,7	1,5	1,3	1,3	1,2
Personal and Housing Services	4,6	4,8	5,5	6,8	4,7	6,6	8,3	2,6
Community and Social Services	8,1	7,9	8,7	9,7	10,1	12,0	7,2	6,4
Transportation, Storage, Communications and Public Utilities	2,6	3,5	4,3	4,3	4,0	5,5	4,8	3,4
Activities not adequately specified	-	0,2	-	0,2	-	-	-	-

TABLE 12.5 (Cont'd)

Joblessness by Economic Activity
Great Santiago, 1956-1978.
(Thousands of Persons)

Economic Activity	September 1971	December 1971	March 1972	June 1972	September 1972	December 1972	March 1973	June 1973
Total Joblessness	38,3	29,7	38,8	24,9	23,3	29,7	27,3	23,4
Goods Producing Activities	19,2	15,5	18,9	11,8	11,3	16,3	12,5	10,0
Agriculture, Hunting, Forestry and Fishing	0,8	0,8	0,2	-	0,2	0,4	-	-
Mining and Quarrying	0,2	-	0,2	0,6	-	0,2	0,2	-
Manufacturing	9,9	8,1	13,0	7,3	7,6	10,8	8,7	8,4
Construction	8,3	6,6	5,5	3,9	3,5	4,9	3,6	1,6
Service Producing Activities	16,3	12,9	16,4	10,8	9,7	10,2	12,7	12,0
Commerce	5,1	3,2	3,1	3,3	4,3	3,5	2,8	4,4
Governmental and Financial Services	2,2	0,6	0,8	0,4	0,2	0,8	0,8	1,6
Personal and Housing Services	3,6	3,6	3,8	2,7	2,5	2,4	3,0	1,6
Community and Social Services	5,4	5,5	8,8	4,4	2,7	3,5	6,1	4,4
Transportation, Storage, Communications and Public Utilities	2,8	1,3	3,3	2,3	2,3	3,1	2,2	1,4
Activities not adequately specified	-	-	0,2	-	-	-	-	-

TABLE 12.5 (Cont'd)

Joblessness by Economic Activity
Great Santiago, 1956-1978.
(Thousands of Persons)

Economic Activity	December 1973[9]	March 1974	June 1974	September 1974	December 1974	March 1975	June 1975	September 1975
Total Joblessness	58,8	75,4	88,5	81,1	75,4	112,1	147,7	153,7
Goods Producing Activities	28,6	39,4	44,4	42,6	39,7	62,5	84,3	86,9
Agriculture, Hunting, Forestry and Fishing	1,1	0,9	2,2	2,4	2,2	1,9	2,0	1,2
Mining and Quarrying	0,9	1,9	1,7	0,5	0,5	0,5	1,0	0,9
Manufacturing	17,2	25,6	27,0	26,0	24,7	36,8	49,2	54,9
Construction	9,4	11,0	13,4	13,7	12,5	23,3	32,2	29,8
Service Producing Activities	23,9	30,1	37,9	29,8	30,9	43,2	54,8	53,8
Commerce	9.2	10,1	9,9	9,6	9.6	15.0	15,2	18,9
Governmental and Financial Services	1,6	2,1	4,0	3,1	3,4	5,0	6,9	6,2
Personal and Housing Services	8,9	12,0	16,9	12,0	11,5	17,1	24,3	19,4
Community and Social Services	4,2	5,9	7,2	5,1	6,5	6,2	8,4	9,2
Transportation, Storage, Communications and Public Utilities	5,4	5,9	6,2	7,9	4,3	6,2	8,6	13,0
Activities not adequately specified	0,9	-	-	0,7	0,5	0,2	-	-

9. The figures for the period between December 1973 and March 1976 are those that were corrected in March of 1976.

TABLE 12.5 (Cont'd)

Joblessness by Economic Activity
Great Santiago, 1956-1978.
(Thousands of Persons)

Economic Activity	December 1975	March 1976	June 1976	July 1976	August 1976	September 1976	December 1976	March 1977
Total Joblessness	176,6	191,7	178,6	152,4	161,0	157,0	131,6	126,6
Goods Producing Activities	92,1	101,7	98,4	83,1	85,4	87,3	68,9	60,2
Agriculture, Hunting, Forestry and Fishing	3,8	4,0	4,6	3,1	2,0	2,8	2,5	0,8
Mining and Quarrying	0,7	0,5	1,1	0,3	1,2	1,5	0,5	0,8
Manufacturing	54,1	59,7	60,3	49,0	51,1	48,8	43,7	39,5
Construction	33,5	37,5	32,5	30,7	31,1	34,2	22,2	19,1
Service Producing Activities	70,4	77,2	71,1	58,9	65,4	59,6	53,8	55,7
Commerce	21,0	26,5	23,9	18,5	23,9	16,8	14,8	18,6
Governmental and Financial Services	9,9	9,3	6,2	11,7	7,7	8,3	9,1	7,6
Personal and Housing Services	28,6	26,7	33,5	21,4	25,4	26,7	22,7	19,4
Community and Social Services	10,9	14,7	7,5	7,3	8,4	7,8	7,2	10,2
Transportation, Storage, Communications and Public Utilities	12,8	12,7	8,9	9,9	9,9	9,8	8,6	10,5
Activities not adequately specified	1,4	-	0,3	0,5	0,2	0,3	0,2	0,3

TABLE 12.5 (Cont'd)

Joblessness by Economic Activity
Great Santiago, 1956-1978.
(Thousands of Persons)

Economic Activity	June 1977	September 1977	December 1977	March 1978	June 1978
Total Joblessness	139,2	137,3	135,8	158,2	134,3
Goods Producing Activities	74,0	75,7	75,5	70,6	64,4
Agriculture, Hunting, Forestry and Fishing	1,9	3,5	2,4	1,9	3,0
Mining and Quarrying	1,1	1,1	1,8	1,6	0,5
Manufacturing	42,7	40,9	45,7	46,4	34,9
Construction	28,4	30,3	25,6	20,8	25,9
Service Producing Activities	56,5	53,6	51,5	78,4	61,4
Commerce	19,5	15,7	13,7	22,6	21,8
Governmental and Financial Services	8,6	7,7	7,9	11,1	11,7
Personal and Housing Services	19,5	18,9	16,1	29,9	17,2
Community and Social Services	8,9	11,4	13,7	14,8	10,6
Transportation, Storage, Communications and Public Utilities	8,1	7,2	8,7	8,6	8,2
Activities not adequately specified	0,5	0,8	-	0,5	0,3

Sources: The statistical information for the period between October 1956 and June 1958 reflects corrected data given to the author directly by the Instituto de Economía. The time series of this table, which are the latest, revised and corrected ones prepared by the Instituto Departamento de Economía of the University of Chile, differ, sometimes substantially, and especially for earlier time periods, from the statistical information presented in the sources below. The data for the March 1959 - June 1962 period are found in Universidad de Chile, Instituto de Economía, Ocupación y Desocupación, Gran Santiago, publication No. 48 (Santiago: June 1962), table 7, p. 21. The data for the September 1962 - December 1966 period are found in Universidad de Chile, Instituto de Economía, Ocupación y Desocupación, Gran Santiago, publication No. 91 (Santiago: December 1966), table 7, p. 19. The data for the March 1967 - March 1970 period are found in Universidad de Chile, Instituto de Economía y Planificación, Ocupación y Desocupación, Gran Santiago, publication No. 116 (Santiago: March 1970), table 9, p. 14. The data for the June 1970 - March 1973 period are found in Universidad de Chile, Instituto de Economía y Planificación, Ocupación y Desocupación, Gran Santiago, inscription No. 41275 (Santiago: March 1973), table 9, p. 21. The data for the December 1973 - March 1976 period are found in Universidad de Chile, Facultad de Ciencias Económicas y Administrativas, Departamento de Economía, Ocupación y Desocupación en el Gran Santiago, publication No. 32 (Santiago: March 1976), table 5, p.15. The data for the June 1976 - June 1978 period are found in Universidad de Chile, Facultad de Ciencias Económicas y Administrativas, Departamento de Economía, Ocupación y Desocupación en el Gran Santiago, publication No. 58 (Santiago, June 1978), table 5, p. 12.

TABLE 12.6

Joblessness According to Occupational Status
Great Santiago, 1959-1978.
(Thousands of Persons)

Status	March 1959	June 1959	April 1960	June 1960	September 1960[1]	September 1960[2]	December 1960	March 1961	June 1961	September 1961
Total Joblessness	62,5	43,3	44,3	47,4	-	44,6	45,8	45,7	43,6	42,8
Employers	0,6	0,2	-	-	-	0,3	0,5	-	0,2	-
Own-Account Workers	8,0	4,6	6,3	5,6	-	6,4	4,6	4,3	4,5	8,3
Salaried Employees	10,8	9,2	6,8	9,3	-	9,2	9,3	12,4	7,8	8,8
Wage Employees	43,2	29,4	31,2	32,6	-	28,2	31,4	29,0	31,2	25,6
Unpaid Family Workers	-	-	-	-	-	-	-	-	-	-
No Data Available	-	-	-	-	-	0,5	-	-	-	0,2

Status	December 1961	March 1962	June 1962	September 1962	October 1962[3]	December 1962	March 1963	June 1963	September 1963
Total Joblessness	31,5	36,2	35,3	27,5	-	33,3	33,5	32,7	34,7
Employers	0,4	0,7	0,2	0,2	-	0,4	0,2	0,5	0,2
Own-Account Workers	3,0	5,5	4,6	3,0	-	5,1	5,2	4,6	4,4
Salaried Employees	6,2	8,6	4,8	6,3	-	4,4	7,1	7,0	9,7
Wage Employees	22,1	21,4	25,8	18,1	-	23,2	21,1	20,6	20,3
Unpaid Family Workers	0,2	-	-	-	-	0,4	-	-	0,2
No Data Available	-	-	-	-	-	-	-	0,2	-

1. Survey based on a sample designed in 1956.
2. Survey based on a sample designed in 1960.
3. Survey based on half of the sample interviewed in September of 1962.

TABLE 12.6 (Cont'd)

Joblessness According to Occupational Status
Great Santiago, 1959-1978.
(Thousands of Persons)

Status	December 1963[4]	December 1963[5]	March 1964	June 1964	September 1964[6]	September 1964	December 1964	March 1965	June 1965
Total Joblessness	24,0	28,8	33,2	31,3	37,0	41,4	32,6	41,3	31,5
Employers	-	-	0,2	0,2	-	0,3	-	-	0,3
Own-Account Workers	1,8	2,9	4,1	1,7	3,1	4,1	3,5	5,2	2,7
Salaried Employees	6,7	4,6	5,1	6,2	9,2	7,2	4,7	9,0	5,6
Wage Employees	15,5	21,4	23,9	23,3	24,6	29,8	24,4	27,2	23,8
Unpaid Family Workers	-	-	-	-	-	-	-	-	0,2
No Data Available	-	-	-	-	-	-	-	-	-

Status	September 1965	December 1965	March 1966	June 1966	September 1966	December 1966	March 1967[7]	March 1967[8]	June 1967
Total Joblessness	41,2	33,0	32,0	40,2	39,3	38,5	40,7	46,5	44,0
Employers	0,8	0,3	-	-	0,2	-	-	0,1	-
Own-Account Workers	5,8	4,2	4,5	5,3	5,1	6,4	3,7	4,9	5,8
Salaried Employees	6,0	6,7	6,3	6,5	6,9	7,1	9,1	8,4	6,9
Wage Employees	28,6	21,8	21,1	28,5	27,1	24,8	28,0	33,1	31,4
Unpaid Family Workers	-	-	-	-	-	0,2	-	-	-
No Data Available	-	-	-	-	-	-	-	-	-

4. Survey based on a sample designed in 1960.
5. Survey based on a sample designed in 1963.
6. Survey with a special question about inactives.
7. Survey based on a sample designed in 1963.
8. Survey based on a sample designed in 1967.

TABLE 12.6 (Cont'd)

Joblessness According to Occupational Status
Great Santiago, 1959-1978.
(Thousands of Persons)

Status	September 1967	December 1967	March 1968	June 1968	September 1968	December 1968	March 1969	June 1969	September 1969
Total Joblessness	45,7	48,8	40,8	48,3	52,2	43,4	50,5	53,2	43,7
Employers	-	0,1	0,5	-	-	0,3	-	-	0,2
Own-Account Workers	5,7	7,4	5,1	8,0	5,9	6,1	4,5	8,5	6,2
Salaried Employees	6,4	8,6	7,4	8,4	7,6	8,7	11,9	11,3	7,4
Wage Employees	33,7	32,5	27,7	32,0	38,8	28,3	34,1	33,6	29,9
Unpaid Family Workers	-	0,1	-	-	-	-	-	-	-
No Data Available	-	-	-	-	-	-	-	-	-

Status	December 1969	March 1970	June 1970	September 1970	December 1970	March 1971	June 1971	September 1971	December 1971
Total Joblessness	44,0	52,6	57,3	54,1	68,2	63,9	43,2	38,3	29,7
Employers	0,2	0,2	0,2	0,4	-	-	0,4	0,4	0,4
Own-Account Workers	4,8	4,1	7,4	5,1	6,0	3,9	4,9	3,4	2,5
Salaried Employees	9,9	11,9	10,2	10,7	15,5	15,6	11,4	12,4	5,9
Wage Employees	29,2	36,4	39,6	38,0	46,7	44,3	26,6	22,2	21,0
Unpaid Family Workers	-	-	-	-	-	-	-	-	-
No Data Available	-	-	-	-	-	-	-	-	-

TABLE 12.6 (Cont'd)

Joblessness According to Occupational Status
Great Santiago, 1959-1978.
(Thousands of Persons)

Status	March 1972	June 1972	September 1972	December 1972	March 1973	June 1973	December 1973[9]	March 1974	June 1974
Total Joblessness	38,8	24,9	23,3	29,7	27,3	23,4	58,8	75,4	88,5
Employers	0,4	-	-	-	0,2	-	-	0,2	-
Own-Account Workers	3,3	0,8	1,7	1,4	3,4	2,4	8,9	11,7	10,7
Salaried Employees	12,6	8,7	6,4	9,0	8,5	9,4	14,3	16,9	24,3
Wage Employees	22,5	15,4	15,2	19,3	15,2	11,6	35,6	46,3	53,1
Unpaid Family Workers	-	-	-	-	-	-	-	-	0,2
No Data Available	-	-	-	-	-	-	-	0,2	0,2

Status	September 1974	December 1974	March 1975	June 1975	September 1975	December 1975	March 1976	June 1976	July 1976
Total Joblessness	81,1	75,4	112,1	147,7	153,7	176,6	191,7	178,6	152,4
Employers	0,2	1,0	-	0,5	0,2	1,2	0,3	0,5	0,8
Own-Account Workers	11,8	9,1	14,3	19,4	20,6	21,7	27,7	19,8	16,7
Salaried Employees	18,0	17,2	21,9	31,5	36,7	46,3	49,5	40,0	36,0
Wage Employees	50,5	47,2	75,5	96,1	96,2	107,2	114,0	118,3	99,0
Unpaid Family Workers	-	0,5	-	0,2	-	-	0,3	-	-
No Data Available	0,5	0,5	0,5	-	-	0,2	-	-	-

9. The figures for the period between December 1973 and March 1976 are those that were corrected in March of 1976.

TABLE 12.6 (Cont'd)

Joblessness According to Occupational Status
Great Santiago, 1959-1978.
(Thousands of Persons)

Status	August 1976	September 1976	December 1976	March 1977	June 1977	September 1977	December 1977	March 1978	June 1978
Total Joblessness	161,0	157,0	131,6	126,6	139,2	137,3	135,8	158,2	134,3
Employers	-	0,5	0,2	0,8	0,3	0,3	-	0,5	-
Own-Account Workers	20,2	20,4	10,4	10,2	14,9	14,1	14,8	14,6	13,6
Salaried Employees	30,1	31,5	27,9	39,0	28,1	30,0	36,5	44,7	38,5
Wage Employees	110,6	104,4	93,1	76,6	95,9	92,9	84,5	98,4	82,2
Unpaid Family Workers	-	0,3	-	-	-	-	-	-	-
No Data Available	-	-	-	-	-	-	-	-	-

Sources: The statistical information for the period between March 1959 and June 1978 reflects corrected data given to the author directly by the Instituto de Economía. The time series of this table, which are the latest, revised and corrected ones prepared by the Instituto-Departamento de Economía of the University of Chile, differ, sometimes substantially, and especially for earlier time periods, from the statistical information presented in the sources listed below. The data for the March 1959 - June 1962 period are found in Universidad de Chile, Instituto de Economía, Ocupación y Desocupación, Gran Santiago, publication No. 48 (Santiago: June 1962), table 12, p. 27. The data for the September 1962 - December 1966 period are found in Universidad de Chile, Instituto de Economía, Ocupación y Desocupación, Gran Santiago, publication No. 91 (Santiago: December 1966), table 12, p. 31. The data for the March 1967 - March 1970 period are found in Universidad de Chile, Instituto de Economía y Planificación, Ocupación y Desocupación, Gran Santiago, publication No. 116 (Santiago: March 1970), table 16, p. 21. The data for the June 1970 - March 1973 period are found in Universidad de Chile, Instituto de Economía y Planificación, Ocupación y Desocupatión, Gran Santiago, inscription No. 41275 (Santiago: March 1973), table 16, p. 28. The data for the December 1973 - March 1976 period are found in Universidad de Chile, Facultad de Ciencias Económicas y Administrativas, Departamento de Economía, Ocupación y Desocupación en el Gran Santiago, publication No. 32 (Santiago: March 1976), table 9, p. 22. The data for the June 1976 - June 1978 period are found in Universidad de Chile, Facultad de Ciencias Económicas y Administrativas, Departamento de Economía, Ocupación y Desocupación en el Gran Santiago, publication No. 58 (Santiago: June 1978), table 9, p. 20.

TABLE 12.7

Population of Great Santiago with Twelve Years of Age and Over According to Employment Situation. 1966-1977.

Period	Labor Force							Not Included in the Labor Force			
	Total	Employed			Unemployed						
		Total	Working	Not Working	Total	Jobless	New Entrants Without a Job	Total	Housewives	Students	Others
	Absolute Figures (Thousands of Persons)										
Jul -Oct 1966	840,0	780,0	736,4	43,6	60,0	46,4	13,6	791,7	451,9	238,4	101,4
Nov 1966-Feb 1967	831,7	783,8	737,5	46,3	47,9	41,0	6,9	811,4	461,8	196,0	153,6
Mar -Jun 1967	832,0	790,9	753,4	37,5	41,1	35,5	5,6	825,3	455,6	263,1	106,6
Jul -Oct 1967	845,7	802,3	769,5	32,8	43,4	38,7	4,7	829,6	459,5	259,9	110,2
Nov 1967-Feb 1968	841,7	803,1	733,9	69,2	38,6	33,2	5,4	843,2	470,7	133,5	239,0
Mar -Jun 1968	842,8	803,5	771,4	32,1	39,2	32,9	6,3	852,2	473,1	273,4	105,8
Sep -Dec 1968	949,9	895,8	865,2	30,6	54,1	43,3	10,8	919,1	497,4	320,7	100,9
Jan -Jun 1969	920,7	870,2	820,3	49,9	50,5	41,5	9,0	953,0	504,4	238,4	210,2
Jul -Dec 1969	911,1	878,2	855,2	23,0	32,9	28,6	4,3	958,4	498,2	325,9	134,3
Jan -Aug 1970	929,5	893,0	845,9	47,1	36,5	29,5	7,0	990,8	515,4	245,3	230,1
Sep -Dec 1970	953,2	911,8	895,7	16,1	41,4	36,5	4,9	1,003,1	517,6	373,8	111,8
Jan -Jun 1971	935,4	887,0	834,2	52,8	48,5	41,2	7,3	1,050,4	504,1	264,9	281,4
Jul -Dec 1971	980,7	948,7	925,0	23,7	32,1	25,3	6,8	1,053,8	513,7	388,6	151,5
1972	994,1	961,8	901,9	59,9	32,3	25,2	7,2	1,086,3	543,6	287,5	255,2
1973	1,001,8	953,6	890,1	63,5	48,2	37,1	11,1	1,373,4[1]			
1974	1,059,0	956,2	901,4	54,9	102,8	77,9	24,9	1,446,5	672,9	492,7	280,9
1975	1,099,8	934,4	882,4	52,0	165,4	126,4	39,0	1,510,2	695,0	477,2	338,0
Jan -Mar 1976	1,147,8	945,7	869,1	76,7	202,1	158,8	43,2	1,555,0	728,4	311,4	517,2
Apr -Jun 1976	1,235,4	998,7	948,0	50,7	236,7	179,5	57,2	1,475,3	649,1	644,3	182,0
Jul -Sep 1976	1,219,9	1,002,6	966,9	35,7	217,3	174,5	42,8	1,479,4	625,7	653,6	200,2
Oct -Dec 1976	1,177,0	1,016,5	983,7	32,8	160,5	118,7	41,8	1,548,0	634,6	538,9	374,4
Jan -Mar 1977	1,183,6	997,1	882,3	114,9	186,5	137,8	48,7	1,567,0	678,5	204,8	683,7
Apr -Jun 1977	1,234,6	1,050,6	1,007,4	43,2	184,0	135,6	48,4	1,507,2	649,0	633,3	224,9
Jul -Sep 1977	1,203,3	1,044,3	1,010,1	34,2	159,0	123,0	36,0	1,585,6	655,1	642,3	288,2
Oct -Dec 1977	1,186,8	1,050,2	1,026,3	23,9	136,6	111,4	25,2	1,627,1	695,3	568,1	363,8

TABLE 12.7 (Cont'd)

Population of Great Santiago with Twelve Years of Age and Over According to Employment Situation. 1966-1977.

Period	Labor Force							Not Included in the Labor Force			
	Total	Employed			Unemployed						
		Total	Working	Not Working	Total	Jobless	New Entrants Without a Job	Total	Housewives	Students	Others
	Relative Figures (Percentages)										
Jul -Oct 1966	100.0	92.9	87.7	5.2	7.1	5.5	1.6	100.0	57.1	30.1	12.8
Nov 1966-Feb 1967	100.0	94.2	88.7	5.5	5.8	5.0	0.8	100.0	56.9	24.2	18.9
Mar -Jun 1967	100.0	95.1	90.6	4.5	4.9	4.2	0.7	100.0	55.2	31.9	12.9
Jul -Oct 1967	100.0	94.9	91.0	3.9	5.1	4.6	0.5	100.0	55.4	31.3	13.3
Nov 1967-Feb 1968	100.0	95.4	87.2	8.2	4.6	4.0	0.6	100.0	55.8	15.8	28.4
Mar -Jun 1968	100.0	95.3	91.5	3.8	4.7	3.9	0.8	100.0	55.5	32.1	12.4
Sep -Dec 1968	100.0	94.3	91.1	3.2	5.7	4.6	1.1	100.0	54.1	34.9	11.0
Jan -Jun 1969	100.0	94.5	89.1	5.4	5.5	4.5	1.0	100.0	52.9	25.0	22.1
Jul -Dec 1969	100.0	96.4	93.9	2.5	3.6	3.1	0.5	100.0	52.0	34.0	14.0
Jan -Aug 1970	100.0	96.1	91.0	5.1	3.9	3.2	0.7	100.0	52.0	24.8	23.2
Sep -Dec 1970	100.0	95.7	94.0	1.7	4.3	3.8	0.5	100.0	51.6	37.3	11.1
Jan -Jun 1971	100.0	94.8	89.2	5.7	5.2	4.4	0.8	100.0	48.0	25.2	26.8
Jul -Dec 1971	100.0	96.7	94.3	2.4	3.3	2.6	0.7	100.0	48.7	36.9	14.4
1972	100.0	96.8	90.8	6.0	3.2	2.5	0.7	100.0	50.0	26.5	23.5
1973	100.0	95.2	88.9	6.3	4.8	3.7	1.1	100.0[1]			
1974	100.0	90.3	85.1	5.2	9.7	7.4	2.3	100.0	46.5	34.1	19.4
1975	100.0	85.0	80.3	4.7	15.0	11.4	3.6	100.0	46.0	31.6	22.4
Jan -Mar 1976	100.0	82.4	75.7	6.7	17.6	13.8	3.8	100.0	46.8	20.0	33.2
Apr -Jun 1976	100.0	80.9	76.8	4.1	19.1	14.5	4.6	100.0	44.0	43.7	12.3
Jul -Sep 1976	100.0	82.2	79.3	2.9	17.8	14.3	3.5	100.0	42.3	44.2	13.5
Oct -Dec 1976	100.0	86.4	83.6	2.8	13.6	10.1	3.5	100.0	41.0	34.8	24.2
Jan -Mar 1977	100.0	84.2	74.5	9.7	15.8	11.7	4.1	100.0	43.3	13.1	43.6
Apr -Jun 1977	100.0	85.1	81.6	3.5	14.9	11.0	3.9	100.0	43.1	42.0	14.9
Jul -Sep 1977	100.0	86.8	84.0	2.8	13.2	10.2	3.0	100.0	41.3	40.5	18.2
Oct -Dec 1977	100.0	88.5	86.5	2.0	11.5	9.4	2.1	100.0	42.7	34.9	22.4

Source: National Institute of Statistics

Notes: 1. It was impossible to subdivide the statistical information concerning the persons "not included in the labor force" into housewives, students and others.

TABLE 12.8

Unemployment Rates in Greater Santiago by Type of Economic Activity, 1966-1977.

Period	Total[1]	Unemployment Rates in Greater Santiago By Type of Economic Activity: Agriculture and Fishing	Mining and Quarrying	Manufacturing	Electricity Gas and Sanitary Services	Construction	Trade	Transport Storage and Communications	Services
July-Oct/66	7.1	7.6	-	5.0	1.5	14.9	4.2	7.4	4.0
Nov/66-Feb/67	5.8	3.2	-	4.0	5.2	13.9	4.6	7.8	3.0
Mar-June/67	4.9	4.0	8.3	4.3	-	13.1	3.3	5.3	2.4
July-Oct/67	5.1	-	-	4.7	-	13.2	3.6	5.4	2.9
Nov/67-Feb/68	4.6	6.8	20.0	4.0	-	8.9	4.4	4.2	2.2
Mar-June/68	4.7	2.8	13.3	4.5	3.3	12.1	2.0	4.3	2.3
Sep-Dec/68	5.7[2]								
Jan-Jun/69	5.5[2]								
July-Dec/69	3.6[2]								
Jan-Aug/70	3.9[2]								
Sep-Dec/70	4.3[2]								
Jan-June/71	5.2	6.1	13.6	5.1	-	13.2	3.0	5.3	2.0
Jul-Dec/71	3.3	8.2	9.3	2.4	-	7.2	2.2	2.0	1.7
1972	3.2	1.2	4.5	2.3	-	5.4	3.1	3.1	1.6
1973	4.8	5.6[3]	-	4.2	-	5.2	4.3	3.8	2.8
1974	9.7	12.6	15.7	8.8	6.8	14.5	6.8	7.3	5.4
1975	15.0	14.6	16.4	14.5	14.4	28.9	10.7	8.8	8.2
Jan-Mar/76	17.6	4.0	11.9	20.1	25.0	33.1	10.4	9.5	10.7
Apr/June/76	19.1	17.8	22.7	17.2	16.7	41.4	12.5	14.2	11.3
July-Sep/76	17.8	9.9	36.5	19.2	14.7	33.6	13.3	12.5	10.8
Oct-Dec/76	13.6	9.2	38.0	13.1	13.5	27.0	10.4	8.2	6.8
Jan-Mar/77	15.8	17.0	26.2	13.7	10.0	27.1	9.9	9.8	10.5
Apr-Jun/77	14.9	1.9	28.7	13.7	4.6	20.3	11.7	10.1	9.3
July-Sep/77	13.2	10.7	16.6	11.5	12.5	25.6	9.9	10.1	8.5
Oct-Dec/77	11.5	16.0	30.4	10.4	4.1	29.0	8.3	8.2	7.3

Notes: 1. The total unemployment rate includes persons seeking work for the first time. Figures for the 1972-1975 period also include unemployed in "activities not adequately specified".
2. There is no information covering this period.
3. Rates of global unemployment in Agriculture and Fishing, Mining and Quarrying, Electricity, Gas, Water and Sanitary Services activities.

Source: National Institute of Statistics.

Rates of Return to Education

The role of education in determining the flow of income over a person's active lifetime has been debated extensively in the literature. The rates of return to education by level and sex in the province of Santiago are presented in Table 12.9. A detailed analysis of sources and methods in calculating these returns can be found in Bruton (1968), Carnoy (1967), Corbo (1974), Harberger (1966) and Schiefelbein (1976).

TABLE 12.9

Rates of Return to Education by Level and Sex in the Province of Santiago.

Levels	Harberger Selowsky (1958)[1]	Carnoy (1958)	Bruton (1962) Males	M. Corbo[2] (1966-68) Males	M. Corbo[2] (1966-68) Females	Schiefelbein (1970) Males
Primary	24.0	11.6	18	5.2	4.9	14.0
Secondary	-	-	18	-	-	10.0
-Academic	16.9	12.3	-	13.2	12.8	-
-Technical	29.0	-	-	20.6	10.4	-
University	12.2	-	14	-	-	-

Notes: 1. The figures in parentheses underneath the name of the author give the year in which the information about incomes was compiled.
2. The study by Corbo distinguishes between public, private and mixed institutions. The figures in the present table are the simple average of the three rates of return calculated by Corbo.

Sources: A. Harberger and M. Selowsky, "Fuentes del Crecimiento Económico Chileno", Cuadernos de Economía N° 10, December 1966. M. Carnoy, "Tasas de Retorno a la Educación en América Latina", Cuadernos de Economía N° 13, 1967. H. Burton, "Productividad de la educación en Chile". Instituto de Economía y Planificación, 1968. M. Corbo, "Schooling Experience and Wages in Santiago, Chile", University of Chicago, 1974. E. Schiefelbein, "Diagnóstico del sistema educacional chileno en 1970", Departamento de Economía, Universidad de Chile, 1976. This table was obtained from (ODEPLAN: 1976, Table 10).

13
LABOR FORCE PARTICIPATION RATES

ACTIVE AND INACTIVE POPULATION: HISTORICAL CENSUS DATA

The basic statistical information about the economically active population (EAP) is provided by the population censuses. This information includes type of activity, individual occupation, type of economic activity and occupational category. According to type of activity, the economically active population is divided into the "economically active" and the "not economically active". In Chile, the lower age limit for a person to be included in the economically active population by the National Statistical Office is 12 years and the upper limit is 65 years (Tacla: 1975, 32).

The census of 1960 defined the economically active population as that population segment composed of all persons of both sexes who supply the labor force available for the production of goods and services (Tacla: 1975, 32). It included therefore the persons employed, the jobless and those seeking employment for the first time. The concept of the LABOR FORCE was introduced in the census of 1960 and it includes the employed as well as unemployed during the week preceeding the census.

The total population, the economically active population and the percentage of actives for the census years between 1907 and 1970 are presented in Table 13.1. Over the last seventy

TABLE 13.1

Chile: Total Population, Economically Active Population and Percentages of Actives. Censuses from 1907 to 1970.

Census	Total Population	Economically Active Population with 12 or More Years of Age	Percentage of Actives
1907	3,231,496	1,231,696	38.1
1920	3,731,473	1,243,373	36.0
1930	4,287,445	1,373,820	32.0
1940	5,023,539	1,621,000	32.3
1952	5,932,995	2,155,293	36.3
1960	7,374,115	2,388,667	32.4
1970	8,884,768	2,624,817	29.5

Source: Tacla, 1975, p. 33.

TABLE 13.2

Chile: Total Population and Economically Active Population, With 12 or More Years of Age, and Activity Rates

Census	Population With 12 or More Years of Age		Activity Rates %
	Total	Economically Active	
1907	2,410,741	1,231,696	51.1
1920	2,596,349	1,343,373	51.7
1930	2,976,879	1,373,820	46.1
1940	3,516,526	1,621,000	46.1
1952	4,103,713	2,155,293	52.5
1960	4,946,067	2,388,667	48.3
1970	6,018,543	2,624,817	43.6

Source: Tacla, 1975, p. 33.

years, an average of 33.8 per cent of the population corresponds to the economically active population (Tacla: 1975, 33). Major determinants of the share of the labor force in the total population include the age and sex profile of the population, the number of years in school, retirement system and opportunities, the employment opportunities available and the spectrum of labor compensation. The heavy historical dependence of Chile first on nitrate exports, income and government revenues and between 1935 and 1974 on copper exports and income has also influenced the relationship between active and total population. A lack of dynamism in the labor markets is revealed by these and the other statistics presented in Chapters 10, 11 and 12 and later on in the present chapter. Establishing a dynamic, flexible and stable labor market remains an unfulfilled goal in Chile.

The economically active as well as total population with twelve years of age and more and the activity or labor force participation rates for the census years between 1907 and 1970 are presented in Table 13.2. These statistics reveal a sharp and historically unique decline in the labor force participation rate from 52.5 per cent in 1952 to 43.6 per cent in 1970. As Tables 13.5 and 13.6 indicate this declining trend has continued into 1975 and 1976.

The size of the labor force is determined, as already mentioned, by demographic, economic and social factors. The most important demographic factor is the age and sex profile of the population since it determines the number of persons in active ages. In turn, this age and sex structure is determined by the nation's trends of fertility, mortality and international migration.

The age and sex specific labor force participation (activity) rates for Chile in 1960 and 1970 are presented in Table 13.3. The difference between male and female participation rates in both censuses is striking. In all age groups, the labor force participation rates of males exceeds that of females, retirement from economic activity is gradual and begins at age 35. In contrast, among females the participation rates rise sharply between 12 and 25 years of age, fall rather rapidly between 25 and 35 years of age, and subsequently decline more gradually. The pattern of female labor force participation rates is explained in part by their withdrawal from economic activity due to marriage and motherhood as well as statistical underestimates and lack of employment opportunities. Both male and female labor force participation rates experienced changes between 1960 and 1970.

A useful measure in comparing the participation of the population in economic activities is the duration of the average active life of a generation. Presented below are the major points of a study by Héctor Roldan Gutiérrez on "Aspectos Demográficos le la mano de obra" (Demographic aspects of the labor force) found in (Tacla: 1975, 36).

It is possible to calculate gross and net years of the active life. The "gross" measures the number of years a generation would participate in economic activity under the assumption that it is not affected by death before the age of retirement. The gross active life depends, therefore, only on the age

TABLE 13.3

Chile: Activity Rates by Sex and Age Groups. Censuses of 1960 and 1970

Age Groups	Activity Rates (percentages)			
	1960		1970	
	Males	Females	Males	Females
Total	77.5	20.9	70.0	19.2
12-14	11.8	3.9	5.1	2.1
15-19	61.7	23.5	44.0	16.3
20-24	91.6	32.4	83.5	31.1
25-29	97.0	27.9	95.0	29.0
30-34	97.5	23.8	96.5	25.0
35-39	97.0	22.5	96.3	24.1
40-44	95.7	22.2	95.0	22.5
45-49	93.4	21.3	92.2	20.8
50-54	88.0	19.4	86.4	19.0
55-59	83.7	16.8	80.4	15.0
60-64	76.8	13.7	70.0	10.6
65 and over	51.4	7.9	39.0	5.8
12-19	60.6	16.0	27.4	10.4
20-64	70.7	19.9	90.0	24.1
65 and over	51.4	7.9	39.0	5.8

Source: Tacla, 1975, p. 35.

people begin work and on the age they retire from economically active life. The limits used by Gutiérrez to determine active life were those of 15 and 70 years.

The "net" number of years of active life measures the years a generation would remain in economic activity taking into account the age of retirement from activity as well as the loss provoked by death among active persons of this generation before they reach retirement age.

According to Gutiérrez, in Chile, based on the male labor force participation rates of 1952, a male participates practically 50 gross years in economic activities between his 15 and 70 years of age and, according to the participation rates of 1960, this rate falls by two and a half years to a gross active life of 47.6 years. This value places Chile among the semi-industrialized nations.

The gross number of active years of females fell, according to Gutiérrez, from 14.5 years in 1952 to 11.7 years in 1960, that is, experimented a fall of almost three years (always based on the respective census labor force participation rates). Since, according to the United Nations, the gross number of active years of females is 16.8 for industrial nations and 15.4 for agricultural nations, it can be expected that the gross number of active years of females will rise in Chile. The figures presented in Table 13.3 show that the labor force participation rates for females showed a mild increase in 1970 over 1952 in the cohorts between 25 and 39 years of age.

LABOR FORCE PARTICIPATION RATES: REGIONAL, PROVINCIAL AND URBAN-RURAL DATA

The population of Chile of twelve years and over, the active population and participation rates by regions and according to urban and rural areas for the census of 1970 are presented, in thousands of persons and percentages, in Table 13.4. The participation rates are generally higher in rural than in urban areas. The participation rate for Chile as a whole in 1970 is 43.1 percent.

The Chilean population of twelve years and over, active population and participation rates by province, region, urban and rural areas in 1975, are presented, in thousands of persons and percentages in Table 13.5. The labor force participation rates for 1975 show a mild decline as compared to those of 1970 presented in Table 13.4. The labor force participation rates of the rural areas, however, remain above those found in urban areas.

The population of Chile of twelve years and over, the active population

TABLE 13.4

Population Twelve Years and Over, Active Population and Participation Rates
by Region and According to Urban and Rural Areas.
Census of April, 1970.
(Thousands of Persons and Percentages)

Regions	Total			Urban			Rural		
	Population 12 Years and Over	Active Population	Participation Rate	Population 12 Years and Over	Active Population	Participation Rate	Population 12 Years and Over	Active Population	Participation Rate
I Tarapacá	121,3	53,1	43.7	112,9	48,4	42.9	8,4	4,7	56.0
II Antofagasta	172,7	74,5	43.1	165,1	69,5	42.1	7,6	5,0	65.7
III Atacama	316,1	128,0	40.5	215,5	83,8	38.9	100,6	44,2	43.9
IV Coquimbo									
V Aconcagua									
Valparaíso									
Total of 5th Region	646,0	265,5	41.1	559,2	227,6	40.7	86,8	37,9	43.7
and San Antonio									
VI O'Higgins									
Colchagua									
Total of 6th Region	313,9	133,6	42.6	155,5	66,3	42.6	158,4	67,3	42.5
VII Curricó									
Talca									
Maule									
Linares									
Total of 7th Region	403,1	172,2	42.7	202,7	83,0	40.9	200,4	89,2	44.5
VIII Ñuble									
Concepción									
Aráuca									
Bío-Bío									
Total of 8th Region	937,3	383,3	40.9	637,9	250,9	39.3	299,4	132,4	44.2
and Malleco									
IX Malleco									
Cautín	278,9	115,1	41.3	147,6	57,2	38.8	131,3	57,9	44.1
Total of 9th Region									
less Malleco									
X Valdivia	284,7	120,2	42.2	165,9	66,1	39.8	118,8	54,1	45.5
Osorno									
Llanquihue	232,0	105,4	45.5	106,2	48,1	45.3	125,8	57,3	45.5
Chiloé and Aysen									
Total of 10th Region	516,7	225,6	43.7	272,1	114,2	42.0	244,6	111,4	45.5
and Aysén									
XI Aysén	-	-	-						
XII Magallanes	66,5	32,8	49.3	56,3	25,3	44.9	10,2	7,5	73.5

TABLE 13.4 (Cont'd)

Population Twelve Years and Over, Active Population and Participation Rates by Region and According to Urban and Rural Areas. Census of April, 1970. (Thousands of Persons and Percentages)

Regions	Total			Urban			Rural		
	Population 12 Years and Over	Active Population	Participation Rate	Population 12 Years and Over	Active Population	Participation Rate	Population 12 Years and Over	Active Population	Participation Rate
Metropolitan Area less San Antonio	2,276,2	1,023,5	45.0	2,159,9	970,1	44.9	116,3	53,4	45.9
Total for Chile	6,048,7	2,607,2	43.1	4,684,7	1,996,3	42.6	1,364,0	610,9	44.8

Source: This table was prepared by the Planning Office of the Presidency of the Republic of Chile by elaborating statistical information gathered by the National Institute of Statistics in its census of April, 1970.

TABLE 13.5

Population Twelve Years and Over, Active Population and Participation Rates by Province and Region, According to Urban and Rural Areas, 1975
National Employment Survey.
(Thousands of Persons and Percentages)

Regions	Total			Month of Survey	Urban			Rural		
	Population 12 Years and Over	Active Population	Participation Rate		Population 12 Years and Over	Active Population	Participation Rate	Population 12 Years and Over	Active Population	Participation Rate
I Tarapacá	161,0	75,4	46.8	July	150,5	69,4	46.1	10,5	6,0	57.1
II Antofagasta	202,9	87,0	42.8	August	195,8	83,6	42.7	7,1	3,4	47.9
III Atacama	128,7	54,3	42.2	August	98,4	40,4	41.1	30,3	13,9	45.9
IV Coquimbo	265,1	105,8	39.9	August	164,9	63,4	38.4	100,2	42,4	42.3
Atacama and Coquimbo	393,8	160,1	40.7		263,3	103,8	39.4	130,5	56,3	43.1
V Aconcagua	133,4	56,4	42.3	October	66,3	28,6	43.1	67,2	27,8	41.4
Valparaíso	706,4	305,0	43.1		612,3	259,1	42.3	94,1	45,8	48.7
Total of 5th Region	839,8	361,4	43.0		678,6	287,7	42.4	161,2	73,7	45.7
VI O'Higgins	244,6	106,1	43.4	October	121,0	52,8	43.6	123,6	53,3	43.1
Colchagua	126,5	51,7	40.9		37,2	14,9	40.0	89,3	36,8	41.2
Total of 6th Region	371,1	157,8	42.5		158,2	67,7	42.8	212,9	90,1	42.3
VII Curricó	96,0	43,2	45.0	December	35,1	14,8	42.2	60,9	28,4	46.6
Talca	192,1	90,3	47.0		102,8	47,1	45.8	89,3	43,2	48.4
Maule	66,2	27,1	40.9		29,5	11,5	39.0	36,6	15,6	42.6
Linares	146,5	58,3	39.8		62,0	23,7	38.2	84,6	34,7	41.0
Total of 7th Region	500,8	218,9	43.7		229,4	97,1	42.3	271,4	121,9	44.9
VIII Ñuble	231,6	88,6	38.3	June	100,4	38,3	38.1	131,1	50,2	38.3
Concepción	534,3	210,4	39.4		462,9	181,0	39.1	71,5	29,4	41.1
Aráuco	75,9	27,9	36.8		39,0	14,8	37.9	37,0	13,2	35.7
Bío-Bío	146.3	58,0	39.6		67,9	25,7	37.8	78,3	32,3	41.3
Total of 8th Region	988,1	384,9	39.0		670,2	259,8	38.8	317,9	125,1	39.4
IV Malleco	132,1	54,5	41.3	December	65,4	27,9	42.7	66,7	26,7	40.0
Cautín	312,0	126,5	40.5		165,1	65,3	39.6	146,9	61,1	41.6
Total of 9th Region	444,1	181,0	40.8		230,5	93,2	40.4	213,6	87,8	41.1
X Valdivia	215,4	93,1	43.2	May	114,6	48,8	42.6	100,7	44,3	43.9
Osorno	126,1	52,5	41.6		65,0	26,6	40.9	61,1	25,9	42.4
Llanquihue	155,3	70,3	45.3		71,6	32,2	45.0	83,6	38,1	45.6
Chiloé	92,3	45,0	48.8		17,3	7,4	42.8	75,0	37,6	50.1
Total of 10th Region	589,1	260,9	44.3		268,5	115,0	42.8	320,5	145,9	45.5
XI Aysén	41,9	20,5	49.9	August	23,1	11,0	48.9	17,9	9,2	51.4
XII Magallanes	82,2	38,5	46.8	August	70,5	31,0	44.0	11,7	7,5	64.1
Metropolitan Area	2,938,3	1,237,1	42.1	December	2,763,7	1,160,9	42.0	174,6	76,2	43.6
Total for Chile	7,555,1	3,183,5	42.1	Oct.15,1975	5,761,8	2,405,0	41.7	1,793,3	778,5	43.4

Source: This table was prepared by the Planning Office of the Presidency of the Republic of Chile by elaborating statistical information gathered by the National Institute of Statistics through its national employment survey.

and participation rates by province and region according to urban and rural areas in 1976 are presented in thousands of persons and percentages in Table 13.6. The active population in 1976 shows a decline as compared to the active population in 1975 while total population rises. As a consequence, the aggregate labor force participation rate shows a sharp decline from 42.1 per cent in 1975 to 40.7 percent in 1976. Both the population of 12 years and over and the active population in rural areas fall between 1975 and 1976 (the participation rate hardly changes) as a consequence of migration to urban areas. In view of the boom in agricultural, fishing, forestry and mineral exports since 1974, the decline in the rural active population is both puzzling and worrisome.

With employment opportunities being as scarce (if not more) in urban than in rural areas, the active urban population rises between 1975 and 1976 far slower than the population of twelve years and over with a consequent decline in the urban labor force participation rate from 41.7 percent in 1975 to 40.1 percent in 1976.

TABLE 13.6

Population Twelve Years and Over, Active Population and Participation Rates by Province and Region, According to Urban and Rural Areas, 1976 National Employment Survey.
(Thousands of Persons and Percentages)

Regions	Total			Urban			Rural		
	Population 12 Years and Over	Active Population	Participation Rate	Population 12 Years and Over	Active Population	Participation Rate	Population 12 Years and Over	Active Population	Participation Rate
I Tarapacá	158,2	76,2	48.2	145,4	68,1	46.8	12,8	8,1	63.3
II Antofagasta	214,4	86,7	40.4	207,6	83,5	40.2	6,8	3,2	47.1
III Atacama	131,1	55,3	42.2	102,9	41,7	40.5	28,2	13,6	48.2
IV Coquimbo	286,3	110,6	38.6	170,0	64,1	37.7	116,3	46,5	40.0
V Aconcagua	139,6	53,8	38.5	69,6	27,0	38.8	70,0	26,8	38.3
Valparaíso	744,9	291,8	39.2	667,0	256,9	38.5	77,9	34,9	44.8
Total of 5th Region	884,5	345,6	39.1	736,6	283,9	38.5	147,9	61,7	41.7
VI O'Higgins	246,0	99,4	40.4	131,9	52,3	39.6	114,1	47,1	41.3
Colchagua	132,6	50,1	37.8	45,3	17,0	37.5	87,3	33,1	37.9
Total of 6th Region	378,6	149,5	39.5	177,2	69,3	39.1	201,4	80,2	39.8
VII Curricó	93,1	38,3	41.1	38,8	15,0	38.7	54,3	23,3	42.9
Talca	193,6	86,3	44.6	106,3	46,8	44.0	87,3	39,5	45.2
Maule	66,9	26,3	39.3	31,2	11,9	38.1	35,7	14,4	40.3
Linares	151,2	55,9	37.0	67,7	24,2	35.7	83,5	31,7	38.0
Total of 7th Region	504,8	206,8	41.0	244,1	97,9	40.1	260,8	108,9	41.8
VIII Ñuble	237,8	88,4	37.2	114,7	43,5	37.9	123,1	44,9	36.5
Concepción	559,6	205,6	36.7	485,2	175,2	36.1	74,4	30,4	40.9
Aráuco	74,2	27,5	37.4	38,4	14,6	38.0	35,8	12,9	36.0
Bío-Bío	149,3	58,3	39.0	78,7	30,1	38.2	70,6	28,2	39.9
Total of 8th Region	1,021,0	378,9	37.2	717,0	263,5	36.8	303,9	116,4	38.3
IX Malleco	129,9	50,9	39.2	70,9	26,6	37.5	59,0	24,3	41.2
Cautín	328,0	123,6	37.7	171,9	62,2	36.2	156,2	61,5	39.4
Total of 9th Region	458,0	174,6	38.1	242,8	88,8	36.6	215,2	85,8	39.9
X Valdivia		94,5			42,9			51,6	
Osorno		55,5			29,3			26,2	
Llanquihue		73,0			33,8			39,3	
Chiloé		39,1			11,4			27,7	
Total of 10th Region		262,1			117,4			144,8	
XI Aysén	42,3	19,9	47.0	24,8	11,2	45.2	17,5	8,7	49.7
XII Magallanes	83,2	38,6	46.4	71,5	30,5	42.7	11,7	8,1	69.2
Total Metropolitan Area	2,725,0	1,177,0	43.2						
Total for Chile	7,740,1	3,151,2	40.7	6,155,8	2,465,9	40.1	1,584,3	685,3	43.3

TABLE 13.6 (Cont'd)

Population Twelve Years and Over, Active Population and Participation Rates by Province and Region, According to Urban and Rural Areas, 1976 National Employment Survey. (Thousands of Persons and Percentages)

Note: The employment survey for regions I to V was taken in December of 1976. The employment survey for regions VI to XII was taken in October of 1976. The employment survey for the metropolitan area was taken during October-December of 1976 and for the country as a whole on November 15, 1976.

Source: This table was prepared by the Planning Office of the Presidency of the Republic of Chile on the basis of data collected by the National Institute of Statistics through its national employment survey.

PART IV
WAGES, SALARIES, HEALTH AND SOCIAL SECURITY

14
WAGES AND SALARIES

Income determines the economic welfare of the population. Wages and salaries are a major component of total income. Over the last century, wages and salaries have accounted for approximately 40-45 per cent of total income (for a detailed examination of the relationship between wages, salaries and the distribution of income see Mamalakis: 1976d, 46-68, 212-221) in Chile. Although using wages and salaries as a measure of economic welfare has major limitations (transfers, subsidies, and taxes are ignored, workers have additional sources of income, and so forth), they are sometimes the only measure of economic welfare available.

In the present chapter the best available time series on wages, salaries, income of unincorporated enterprises and related statistics are presented. The statistics available are often good, however, better and longer time series are needed. Due to space limitations it is impossible to review the extensive literature on wages and salaries and make specific recommendations for future research on historical wage and salary time series. Such an undertaking would furthermore fall outside the immediate, direct objective of the present series on Historical Statistics of Chile. In addition, such a review of the literature already exists, at least in part. Scholars interested in Chile will benefit from consulting PISPAL, Inventario de Investigaciones Sociales Relevantes para Políticas de Población. Volumen III, Chile (Santiago, Chile: CELADE, Unidad Central Del PISPAL, FLACSO, 1977), pp. 1-433, which contains the author, title, place of publication, objectives and conclusions of 758 books/articles/working papers and so forth on Chile.

WAGES

Nominal and Real Sectoral Wages, 1940-1952

Average annual nominal wage earnings per laborer by industry in Chile between 1940 and 1952 are presented in Table 14.1. The time series on nominal wages of Table 14.1 are given for such major sectors as agriculture, fisheries, mining, industry, construction, utilities, commerce, finance and insurance, transportation and communications, government, and services. Some further subdivisions are made which are important to scholars.

Thus, agricultural laborers are divided into laborers proper and laborers miscalled salaried employees. This distinction is important in Chile since so many workers performing primarily manual labor (i.e. blue-collar workers) are classified as salaried employees in order to receive the higher income and other benefits stipulated by law. As the figures of Table 14.1 indicate, the nominal earnings of laborers miscalled salaried employees were generally double those earned by laborers proper.

Table 14.1 also contains more

detailed information on nominal wages per laborer in mining (large versus small and medium sized enterprises), industry (large versus small industries plus thirteen subsectors), government (central and municipal government, national health service, and government educational services) and for personal services (medical and private social welfare, domestic, private education, and hotels and other lodging places).

Average annual real wage earnings per laborer by sector for the period between 1940 and 1952 are presented in Table 14.2. Unlike Table 14.1, there are no real wage time series for subsectors in Table 14.2.

The high and rising differences in real wages between sectors from 1940 and 1952, which provide a statistical cornerstone of the Theory of Sectoral Clashes and Coalitions (Mamalakis: 1966a; Mamalakis: 1966b; Mamalakis: 1969; Mamalakis: 1971) are revealed by Table 14.2.

Minimum and Average Daily Wages

Minimum daily wages for agricultural laborers in the provinces of Tarapacá, Coquimbo, Santiago, Talca, Concepción, Arauco, Osorno and Magallanes between 1953 and 1967 are presented in Table 14.3. Average daily wages for agricultural workers in the same provinces as those of Table 14.3 for the period between 1965 and 1976 are presented in Table 14.4. Furthermore, average daily wages by type of economic activity of those insured (agriculture, mining, nitrate, copper, coal, oil, industry, construction and so forth) and working for an employer are presented for the period between 1946 and 1976 in Table 14.5.

Monthly Wages: 1944-1976

Average monthly registered wages quoted per capita by type of economic activity between 1944 and 1976 are presented in Table 14.6. In order to obtain these wages, total registered wages, which are presented in Table 14.7, are divided by twelve. Then, average monthly registered wages are divided by the number of workers insured to obtain the average monthly registered wages quoted per capita found in Table 14.6. Per capita wages in mining are further subdivided into wages in nitrate, copper, coal, oil and other mining for 1974, 1975 and 1976. These statistics reveal the high intra-mining wage differentials. For example, per capita wages in copper were ten times higher than wages in coal production in 1975 (only twice as high in 1976), while wages in petroleum production were approximately five times higher than wages in other mining in 1976.

Employment, Salaries and Wages in Manufacturing, 1957

Average employment, salaries and wages, man hours worked and family allowances are presented in Table 14.8. Internal industrial income per person employed, in 1950 prices, is presented in Table 14.9.

TABLE 14.1

Average Annual Nominal Wage Earnings, Per Laborer, By Industry, 1940-1952.
(Chilean Pesos)

	1940	1941	1942	1943	1944	1945	1946	1947	1948	1949	1950	1951	1952
Agriculture	3,422	3,852	4,046	5,026	6,165	6,256	8,310	9,132	10,640	12,802	14,221	16,426	21,564
Laborers Proper	3,114	3,575	3,672	4,518	5,330	5,684	7,402	8,122	9,490	11,452	12,625	14,656	19,249
Laborers Miscalled Salaried Employees	6,089	6,257	7,295	9,434	11,675	11,219	16,189	17,899	20,620	24,524	28,072	31,794	41,652
Fisheries	3,550	4,441	5,385	5,875	6,702	7,790	9,582	11,604	14,271	17,157	19,856	23,856	28,435
Mining	9,094	10,391	12,205	14,009	15,514	17,400	18,672	23,846	33,908	43,777	51,736	62,650	80,154
Large Enterprises	11,394	12,460	13,637	15,985	18,293	20,771	21,787	28,930	42,614	57,259	67,406	83,786	108,137
Small and Medium Size Enterprises	7,159	8,372	10,502	12,254	13,452	14,594	15,734	19,056	26,000	30,954	37,178	46,424	57,700
Industries	4,451	5,377	6,424	7,840	9,112	10,962	12,386	15,433	19,022	23,028	26,508	36,368	48,133
Large Industries	5,115	6,131	7,384	8,941	10,402	12,296	14,126	17,787	22,085	26,576	30,561	41,928	55,491
Small Industries	3,652	4,489	5,278	6,485	7,487	9,203	10,282	12,512	15,044	18,430	21,201	29,086	38,495
Nonmetallic Mine Products	4,703	5,678	6,924	8,791	9,326	13,426	11,981	15,780	20,096	23,491	27,376		
Glass Products	4,073	5,053	6,315	7,530	8,830	19,586	11,452	15,313	18,213	21,207	24,228		
Machine and Metallic Products	4,792	5,616	7,111	9,200	10,744	12,428	15,627	18,822	22,591	27,552	30,213		
Chemical Products	4,123	4,904	6,146	8,008	10,446	11,168	12,826	16,058	21,185	25,958	29,977		
Textile-Mill Products	4,320	5,291	7,330	8,253	10,172	12,586	13,589	20,049	24,403	29,420	33,837		
Paper Products and Printing	7,950	8,172	9,140	11,697	12,638	15,324	16,396	19,713	24,558	30,431	34,992		
Leather and Rubber Products	4,702	5,862	6,533	8,034	9,746	11,168	13,104	14,907	18,955	22,326	25,546		
Lumber and Cork Products	3,386	4,545	4,755	5,605	6,053	7,194	8,413	10,210	13,512	16,007	18,848		
Musical Items	4,675	6,578	8,675	8,908	5,153	5,256	8,958	9,973	11,305	15,826	20,661		
Food Products	4,952	5,924	6,980	8,156	9,206	10,462	12,429	14,783	17,697	22,115	25,704		
Beverages	4,086	4,868	5,704	7,098	8,807	9,741	12,174	15,179	18,824	23,028	27,910		
Tobacco Manufactures	5,287	6,808	8,342	9,942	10,379	12,796	17,724	22,662	33,044	39,247	45,117		
Clothing	3,008	3,869	4,342	5,123	6,666	7,376	8,935	10,977	12,376	14,637	17,327		
Construction	4,115	4,782	6,654	6,331	7,519	8,758	10,037	12,592	15,222	18,334	22,596	28,802	32,518
Utilities	7,180	10,774	10,786	11,503	12,614	14,832	18,086	25,491	30,842	38,899	45,290	57,628	82,908
Electricity and Gas	6,976	10,702	10,236	11,095	11,926	13,834	17,456	24,491	30,655	37,173	42,654	54,275	115,701
Water	9,346	11,724	16,516	13,584	15,827	18,890	20,670	29,307	31,551	43,694	51,953	66,102	95,117
Commerce	3,531	4,704	5,250	5,200	6,348	7,955	10,442	12,499	14,578	16,803	19,454	20,219	24,150

TABLE 14.1 (Cont'd)

Average Annual Nominal Wage Earnings, Per Laborer, By Industry, 1940-1952.
(Chilean Pesos)

	1940	1941	1942	1943	1944	1945	1946	1947	1948	1949	1950	1951	1952
Finance and Insurance	3,784	4,533	6,135	7,770	9,143	10,234	11,509	15,341	18,429	23,443	28,620	35,849	46,792
Insurance Companies	3,780	4,531	6,130	7,763	9,127	10,219	11,502	15,331	18,421	23,415	29,167	35,859	46,766
Financial Institutions	3,797	4,545	6,154	7,792	9,184	10,294	11,538	15,385	18,462	23,529	27,027	35,821	46,875
Transportation and Communications	8,517	10,504	11,493	14,090	15,230	18,943	19,394	26,186	29,214	30,918	41,836	48,027	58,872
Transportation	8,552	10,547	11,539	14,075	15,212	18,926	19,357	26,162	29,158	30,827	41,819	47,962	58,811
Communications	5,671	6,839	7,843	15,946	19,104	21,212	24,146	29,009	36,145	43,392	43,990	56,771	66,826
Government	4,235	4,790	5,483	6,350	8,024	9,060	10,614	12,019	15,761	16,645	20,478	28,500	28,883
Central Government	3,316	3,671	4,120	4,669	5,372	6,536	7,594	8,432	10,733	12,071	15,098	18,942	19,859
Municipal Government	5,761	6,905	9,343	11,808	13,920	15,581	17,487	23,380	28,399	30,360	38,042	63,767	82,876
National Health Service	4,984	5,960	6,459	7,453	8,643	10,449	11,757	15,170	16,514	19,439	24,958	28,138	33,264
Government Educational Services	3,637	3,731	5,229	6,235	7,569	8,094	8,759	12,031	15,751	16,783	18,214	25,491	30,245
Services	3,489	3,718	4,521	4,815	5,094	7,310	7,668	8,549	11,797	12,458	17,400	18,388	19,962
Medical and Private Social Welfare	4,984	5,960	6,459	7,453	8,643	10,449	11,757	15,171	16,514	19,439	24,959	28,138	33,265
Domestic Service (Household)	2,869	2,869	3,586	3,586	3,586	5,977	5,977	5,977	9,563	9,563	14,350	14,344	14,344
Private Education	3,628	3,727	5,212	6,227	7,584	8,094	10,219	12,018	15,714	16,780	18,241	25,441	30,329
Hotels and Other Lodging Places	7,355	8,252	10,877	13,022	14,218	15,447	18,166	23,135	27,658	30,970	36,471	43,572	57,098
Miscellaneous	4,954	5,956	6,458	7,451	8,636	10,451	11,747	15,168	16,524	19,439	24,949	28,151	33,263
All Industries, Per Laborer	4,353	5,009	5,649	6,661	7,694	8,894	10,348	12,261	15,349	17,987	21,405	26,131	32,535

Source: República de Chile, Corporación de fomento de la Producción, National Accounts, Annex XI of Agriculture and Transport Development Program (Santiago, Chile: CORFO, 1954), table 45.

TABLE 14.2

Average Annual Real Wage Earnings, Per Laborer, By Industry, 1940-1952.
(1940 Chilean Pesos)

	1940	1941	1942	1943	1944	1945	1946	1947	1948	1949	1950	1951	1952
Agriculture	3,422	3,344	2,730	2,986	3,279	3,058	3,496	2,884	2,847	2,285	2,783	2,629	2,824
Mining	9,024	9,020	8,434	8,324	8,233	9,505	7,856	7,530	9,073	9,863	10,122	10,027	10,499
Industries	4,451	4,668	4,440	4,659	4,847	5,358	5,211	4,873	5,090	5,189	5,186	5,821	6,304
Fisheries	3,550	3,880	3,736	3,406	3,577	3,824	4,033	3,652	3,831	3,880	3,886	3,755	3,734
Construction	4,115	4,151	4,598	3,762	4,000	4,281	4,222	3,976	4,074	4,138	4,421	4,009	4,259
Transporation and Communications	8,517	9,117	7,942	8,371	8,101	9,258	8,159	8,268	7,818	6,966	8,165	7,687	7,688
Utilities	7,180	9,352	7,461	6,830	6,717	7,243	7,617	8,030	8,257	8,758	8,859	8,216	10,855
Commerce	3,531	4,085	3,629	3,088	3,376	3,887	4,393	3,947	3,802	3,786	3,205	3,235	3,163
Finance	3,784	4,000	4,294	4,730	4,857	4,971	4,859	4,830	4,834	5,128	5,517	5,660	8,038
Services	3,489	3,226	3,125	2,661	2,709	3,573	3,226	2,699	3,157	2,307	3,400	2,943	2,613
Central and Municipal Governments	4,235	4,159	3,780	3,773	4,268	4,429	4,466	3,796	4,218	3,750	4,006	4,562	3,782
All Industries, Per Laborer	4,353	4,348	3,904	3,958	4,093	4,347	4,354	5,872	4,107	4,053	4,186	4,182	4,361

Source: República de Chile, Corporación de fomento de la Producción, National Accounts, Annex XI of Agriculture and Transport Development Program (Santiago, Chile: CORFO, 1954), table 46A.

TABLE 14.3

Minimum Daily Wages for Agricultural Laborers in Selected Provinces.[2]
(DFL 244 of July 1953) 1953-1967.
In Escudos.[1]

Years	Tarapacá	Coquimbo	Santiago	Talca	Concepción	Arauco	Osorno	Magallanes
1953-4	.090	.095	.100	.095	.075	.075	.095	.080
1954-5	.115	.120	.125	.115	.100	.100	.120	.110
1955-6	.184	.192	.200	.184	.160	.160	.192	.176
1956-7	.265	.280	.290	.265	.230	.230	.280	.255
1957-8	.350	.370	.380	.350	.300	.300	.370	.340
1958-9	.420	.445	.440	.420	.360	.360	.450	.410
1959-60	.579	.614	.634	.579	.496	.496	.621	.565
1960-1[3]	0.64	0.68	0.70	0.64	0.55	0.55	0.68	0.62
1961-2[4]	0.70	0.74	0.76	0.70	0.61	0.74	0.74	1.26
1961-2	0.82	0.86	0.89	0.82	0.71	0.71	0.86	1.47
1962-3	0.90	0.90	0.95	0.90	0.80	0.80	0.95	1.47
1963-4	1.28	1.28	1.35	1.28	1.14	1.14	1.21	1.14
1964-5	1.98	1.94	2.05	1.94	1.72	1.72	1.89	3.16
1965-6	3.26	3.26	3.26	3.26	3.26	3.26	3.26	3.26
1966-7	4.10	4.10	4.10	4.10	4.10	4.10	4.10	4.10

Notes: 1. All figures in the present table are expressed in escudos. The original figures were expressed in pesos up to 1959 and in escudos from 1960 onwards.

2. The minimum daily wages correspond to the agricultural year. As an example, for 1960-61, the figures are understood to correspond to the period between May 1, 1960 and April 30, 1961.

3. These figures refer to the minimum daily wage established May 1, 1961.

4. The former minimum daily wage was raised by 16.6% from July 1961 onwards.

Sources: Chile, Dirección de Estadística y Censos, Boletín No. 12, Deciembre Sinopsis 1962 (Santiago, Chile: DEC, 1963), p. 490 for the figures corresponding to the years 1953 to 1962. Banco Central de Chile, Boletín Mensual No. 448, June 1965 (Santiago, Chile: Impresora Gutemberg, 1965), p. 903 for the figures corresponding to the years 1963 to 1964. The figures on minimum daily wages for the years 1965 and 1966-67 were obtained from Banco Central de Chile, Boletín Mensual No. 465, November 1966 (Santiago, Chile: Impresones "Gutemberg", 1966), p. 1852.

TABLE 14.4

Average Daily Wages for Agricultural Workers in Selected Provinces. 1965-1976.
In Escudos Until 1973. In Pesos for 1974, 1975, and 1976.

	Tarapacá	Coquimbo	Santiago	Talca	Concepción	Arauco	Osorno	Magallanes
1965	3.23	2.21	2.33	2.05	2.14	1.96	1.96	6.58
1966	n.a.	n.a.	n.a.	n.a.	n.a.	n.a.	n.a.	n.a.
1967	9.44	4.41	4.63	3.88	4.70	4.25	3.94	12.67
1968	13.72	6.10	5.86	4.48	6.57	5.20	4.85	13.91
1969	18.97	8.30	8.29	7.03	7.84	7.08	6.90	18.72
1970	15.01	10.87	11.41	10.23	9.61	9.17	9.71	26.88
1971	37.87	17.19	19.04	16.28	17.01	15.90	16.22	45.02
1972	44.96	27.25	29.99	25.45	28.03	26.74	27.15	73.21
1973	83.00	61.00	75.00	56.00	86.00	67.00	65.00	256.00
1974	1.15	0.45	0.58	0.43	0.59	0.46	0.41	0.85
1975	2.56	2.81	2.88	2.20	2.69	2.35	2.49	3.18
1976	11.58	10.93	11.45	9.95	10.21	9.88	9.82	10.72

Sources: The figures for the year 1965 were obtained from República de Chile, Servicio de Seguro Social (SSS), Estadísticas 1965 (Santiago, Chile: SSS, 1965), p. 30. The figures for the year 1967 were obtained from República de Chile, SSS, Estadísticas 1967 (Santiago, Chile: SSS, 1967), p. 28. The figures for the year 1968 were obtained from República de Chile, SSS, Estadísticas 1968 (Santiago, Chile: SSS, 1968), p. 30. The figures for the year 1969 were obtained from República de Chile, SSS, Estadísticas 1969 (Santiago, Chile: SSS, 1969), p. 28. The figures for the year 1970 were obtained from República de Chile, SSS, Estadísticas 1970 (Santiago, Chile: SSS, 1970), p. 28. The figures for the year 1971 were obtained from República de Chile, SSS, Estadísticas 1971 (Santiago, Chile: SSS, 1971), p. 30. The figures for the year 1972 were obtained from República de Chile, SSS, Estadísticas 1972 (Santiago, Chile: SSS, 1972), p. 28. The figures for the year 1973 were obtained from República de Chile, SSS, Estadísticas 1973 (Santiago, Chile: SSS, 1973), p. 26. The figures for the years 1974 and 1975 were obtained from República de Chile, SSS, Estadísticas 1974-75 (Santiago, Chile: SSS, 1975), pp. 38-40. The figures for the year 1976 were obtained from República de Chile, SSS, Estadísticas 1976 (Santiago, Chile: SSS, 1976), p. 26.

TABLE 14.5

Average Daily Wages by Type of Activity of Those Insured and Working for an Employer.[3]
In Escudos from 1940 to 1973. In Pesos since 1974.

	1946[1]	1947	1948	1949	1950	1951	1952	1953	1954	1955
1. Agriculture	0.012	0.014	0.018	0.021	0.024	0.027	0.033	0.043	0.052	0.098
2. Mining[5]	0.037[2]	0.046	0.056	0.075	0.084	0.106	0.135	0.192	0.230	0.377
3. Nitrate	-	-	-	.068	0.076	0.089	0.103	0.135	0.192	0.282
4. Copper	-	-	-	-	-	-	-	-	-	-
5. Coal	-	-	-	0.052	0.060	0.071	0.095	0.137	0.202	0.344
6. Oil	-	-	-	0.057	0.105	0.127	0.203	0.296	0.381	0.624
7. Industry	0.032	0.039	0.049	0.059	0.071	0.083	0.103	0.136	0.180	0.303
8. Construction	0.028	0.035	0.042	0.049	0.060	0.070	0.087	0.118	0.151	0.255
9. Electricity, gas and water	-	-	-	-		0.120	0.155	0.176	0.245	0.426
10. Commerce	0.024	0.030	0.034	0.039	0.046	0.052	0.071	0.094	0.126	0.214
11. Transport	0.043	0.051	0.063	0.073	0.085	0.105	0.135	0.150	0.206	0.335
12. Domestic help	0.012	0.013	0.016	0.021	0.026	0.030	0.034	0.042	0.046	0.065
13. Other activities	0.028	0.033	0.040	0.049	0.059	0.065	0.080	0.100	0.131	0.211
14. Improperly indicated[4]	0.026	0.032	0.043	0.043	0.051	0.061	0.074	0.086	0.118	0.207
15. All activities	0.027	0.033	0.040	0.049	0.056	0.066	0.083	0.110	0.148	0.247

	1956	1957	1958	1959	1960	1961	1962	1963	1964	1965
1. Agriculture	0.185	0.260	0.330	0.390	0.430	0.590	0.690	0.920	1.32	2.17
2. Mining	0.673	0.960	1.290	2.080	1.530	2.070	2.250	2.980	3.97	6.14
3. Nitrate	0.388	0.820	1.090	1.270	1.980	2.060	2.510	3.390	4.97	7.64
4. Copper	-	-	-	-	2.370	3.810	4.920	6.090	8.67	12.64
5. Coal	0.529	0.670	0.920	1.100	1.340	1.660	1.890	2.540	3.52	5.44
6. Oil	1.034	2.060	2.780	2.660	2.520	3.960	4.800	5.740	9.52	13.61
7. Industry	0.510	0.710	0.930	1.270	1.490	1.880	2.240	2.620	3.89	6.01
8. Construction	0.453	0.690	0.880	1.110	1.240	1.320	1.470	2.170	3.07	4.98
9. Electricity, gas and water	0.744	1.050	1.460	1.930	2.150	1.800	1.840	4.360	6.65	9.05
10. Commerce	0.392	0.580	0.470	0.960	0.900	2.470	3.360	1.560	2.50	4.01
11. Transport	0.542	0.780	0.980	1.160	1.440	1.440	1.610	2.560	3.99	5.86
12. Domestic help	0.111	0.170	0.250	0.340	0.400	0.520	0.590	0.750	1.05	1.62
13. Other activities	0.383	0.570	0.750	1.030	1.220	1.560	1.730	2.070	2.86	4.53
14. Improperly indicated	0.340	0.490	0.670	0.910	1.000	1.290	1.420	1.770	2.57	4.05
15. All activities	0.413	0.590	0.750	1.020	1.190	1.460	1.840	2.350	3.35	5.13

TABLE 14.5 (Cont'd)

Average Daily Wages by Type of Activity of Those Insured and Working for an Employer. In Escudos from 1940 to 1973. In Pesos since 1974.

	1966	1967	1968	1969	1970	1971	1972	1973	1974[1]	1975	1976
1. Agriculture	3.28	4.37	5.47	7.63	10.53	17.74	28.23	72	.50	2.58	10.04
2. Mining	9.47	13.26	21.80	22.46	32.15	50.89	97.00	221	1.46	6.59	26.16
3. Nitrate	10.62	13.71	17.25	26.79	33.04	60.59	89.71	229	1.71	5.68	26.69
4. Copper	15.30	24.09	29.84	48.44	51.45	178.93	196.79	682	3.54	20.47	43.68
5. Coal	7.49	9.90	13.25	17.29	37.78	52.29	61.83	172	1.59	8.64	33.44
6. Oil	13.81	24.55	29.30	63.47	85.85	125.29	142.78	365	3.44	14.90	33.53
7. Industry	8.37	10.83	14.46	20.72	30.24	42.62	67.78	209	1.49	6.41	25.25
8. Construction	7.32	9.72	11.35	16.25	25.58	33.89	57.04	168	1.36	5.87	24.38
9. Electricity, gas and water	12.16	15.10	19.00	28.24	40.14	49.76	91.29	276	2.16	9.46	33.63
10. Commerce	5.54	6.13	9.24	14.95	19.36	24.69	39.44	114	1.16	5.26	19.36
11. Transport	7.57	10.94	14.81	18.08	22.67	33.46	57.21	164	1.54	5.82	22.84
12. Domestic help	2.31	3.07	4.66	6.48	8.44	14.81	24.90	68	0.44	2.23	8.81
13. Other activities	6.23	8.18	10.76	16.54	20.84	30.26	49.40	124	1.08	4.86	18.31
14. Improperly indicated	6.69	8.31	10.45	14.04	19.10	27.19	50.90	140	0.85	2.95	11.99
15. All activities	7.03	9.41	12.52	18.27	24.08	43.29	61.10	190	1.37	5.86	22.72

Notes: 1. The figures for the years between 1946 and 1973 are expressed in Chilean escudos. The figures for 1974, 1975, and 1976 are expressed in Chilean pesos, with one peso being equal to one thousand of escudos (\$1 = E°1,000, where E° stands for escudos). The figures until 1959 were originally expressed in pesos.

2. Detailed information on average daily wages by type of activity for all mining subsectors of nitrate, copper, coal, oil and other mining can be found only since 1960.

3. All figures refer to workers insured by an employer (apatronados). Self-employed workers are excluded. Information on independent workers is found in the year books listed in the sources.

4. The item "Improperly indicated" is expressed in a variety of ways in the Chilean sources. Thus, in the 1952-56 documents the term erroneously indicated (Mal Indicadas) is used. In the 1957-67 sources the term erroneously or not indicated (Mal o no Indicadas) is used. And, in the 1968-76 sources the term "not indicated" is used.

5. The activity termed "mining" is described as "mining" in the sources for the years 1952-65 and 1973 and as "other mining" in the sources for the years 1966-72 and 1974-76.

TABLE 14.5 (Cont'd)

Average Daily Wages by Type of Activity of Those Insured and Working for an Employer.
By Escudos from 1940 to 1973. In Pesos since 1974.

Sources: República de Chile, Caja de Seguro Obligatorio. Anuario Estadístico 1950 (Santiago, Chile: Imprenta de la Dirección General de Prisiones, 1952), pp. 14-15 for the year 1946. The figures for the year 1947-1951 were obtained from República de Chile, Caja de Seguro Obligatorio. Anuario Estadístico 1951 (Santiago, Chile: Imprenta de la Dirección General de Prisiones, 1952), pp. 18-19. The figures for the years 1952-1956 were obtained from República de Chile, Servicio de Seguro Social. Estadísticas 1952-1956 (Santiago, Chile: Editorial Universitaria, 1958), pp. 74-75. The figures for the years 1957-1958 were obtained from República de Chile, Servicio de Seguro Social. Estadísticas 1961 (Santiago, Chile: Imprenta del Servicio de Prisiones, 1961), pp. 30-31. The figures for the years 1959-1963 were obtained from República de Chile, Servicio de Seguro Social. Estadísticas 1963 (Santiago, Chile: Talleres Gráfico "Vera y Gianni", 1964), pp. 30-31. The figures for the year 1964 were obtained from República de Chile, Servicio de Seguro Social (SSS). Estadísticas 1964 (Santiago, Chile: SSS, 1964), p. 28. The figures for the year 1965 were obtained from República de Chile, SSS. Estadísticas 1965 (Santiago, Chile: SSS, 1965), p. 28. The figures for the years 1966-67 were obtained from República de Chile, SSS. Estadísticas 1967 (Santiago, Chile: SSS, 1967), p. 28-29. The figures for the year 1968 were obtained from República de Chile, SSS. Estadísticas 1968 (Santiago, Chile: SSS, 1968), p. 28. The figures for the year 1969 were obtained from República de Chile, SSS. Estadísticas 1969 (Santiago, Chile: SSS, 1969), p. 26. The figures for the year 1970 were obtained from República de Chile, SSS. Estadísticas 1970 (Santiago, Chile: SSS, 1970), p. 26. The figures for the year 1971 were obtained from República de Chile, SSS. Estadísticas 1971 (Santiago, Chile: SSS, 1971), p. 28. The figures for the year 1972 were obtained from República de Chile, SSS. Estadísticas 1972 (Santiago, Chile: SSS, 1972), p. 26. The figures for the year 1973 were obtained from República de Chile, SSS. Estadísticas 1973 (Santiago, Chile: SSS, 1973), p. 25. The figures for the years 1974-1975 were obtained from República de Chile, SSS. Estadísticas 1974-75 (Santiago, Chile: SSS, 1975), p. 36. The figures for the year 1976 were obtained from República de Chile, SSS. Estadísticas 1976 (Santiago, Chile: SSS, 1976), p. 25.

TABLE 14.6

Average Monthly Registered Wages Quoted Per Capita by Type of Economic Activity. 1944-1976.[2]

	1944	1945	1946	1948	1949	1950	1951	1952	1953	1954	1955	1956	1957	1958
Agriculture	0.16[1]	0.20	0.22	0.34	0.37	0.44	0.51	0.83	0.98	1.24	2.34	4.42	6.05	7.44
Mining	0.76	0.93	1.01	1.57	1.86	2.16	2.55	2.83	3.52	5.03	8.12	12.78	18.67	20.45
Industry	0.68	0.71	0.97	1.48	1.77	2.11	2.56	2.58	3.14	4.30	7.24	11.94	15.07	18.37
Construction	0.61	0.71	0.84	1.19	2.17	1.66	2.13	2.25	2.63	3.61	6.09	10.82	15.25	19.11
Electricity, Gas and Water								3.10	4.30	5.85	10.22	17.81	25.12	27.12
Commerce	0.63	0.74	1.01	1.42	1.09	1.92	1.61	1.78	2.16	3.01	5.11	7.76	10.60	12.24
Transport and Communications			-					3.17	3.77	4.91	7.98	12.87	17.89	19.34
Domestic Help	0.20	0.28	0.30	0.45	0.54	0.68	0.80	0.84	0.97	1.10	1.55	2.65	3.87	4.40
Other Activities	0.35	0.46	0.61	0.82	1.02	1.26	1.66	2.46	2.27	3.13	5.04	8.54	12.62	13.40
Not Indicated			-			-	-	-	-	*0.30	3.75	8.81	-	24.99
Total	0.41	0.50	0.59		1.04	1.24	1.43	1.85	2.19	2.98	4.97	8.38	11.38	13.58

	1959	1960	1961	1962	1963	1964	1965	1966	1967	1968	1969	1970
Agriculture	9.01	10.58	12.79	14.99	20.14	30.53	49.51	68.82	90.52	98.20	121.54	179.80
Mining	32.05	33.94	48.82	52.39	69.96	104.46	135.98	181.22	215.36	502.83	772.34	1,085.35
Industry	24.52	26.52	29.30	34.55	48.54	76.15	112.64	159.85	204.98	288.05	398.95	546.74
Construction	27.29	28.17	23.94	29.87	45.15	72.97	109.76	149.64	181.29	278.73	410.33	588.61
Electricity, Gas and Water	37.17	39.06	33.84	38.52	51.53	90.72	143.47	142.51	145.56	325.71	398.10	538.84
Commerce	18.11	21.45	25.92	32.20	41.15	58.85	75.89	99.06	130.34	236.87	291.45	384.25
Transport and Communications	20.94	24.07	26.06	23.76	31.95	48.32	93.13	118.26	156.30	147.78	205.50	291.76
Domestic Help	7.05	7.95	9.96	11.07	15.59	25.17	35.97	47.48	58.14	72.03	97.28	129.73
Other Activities	21.54	29.73	46.86	57.20	68.75	95.37	157.38	200.78	156.52	175.65	241.75	321.78
Not Indicated	45.39	32.13	-	-	-							
Total	18.82	20.93	24.10	28.25	39.28	60.56	88.32	120.02	148.82	245.14	279.75	389.35

Notes: 1. The average monthly registered wages quoted per capita (promedio de salario mensual cotizado per capita) is calculated in two steps. First, average monthly registered wages are calculated by dividing total registered wages by twelve. Second, average monthly wages are divided by the number of workers insured to obtain average monthly registered wages, quoted per capita. The complete statistical information on total registered wages is found elsewhere in the present volume and the number of workers insured is found in the references listed under sources of this table.

2. The figures for the years between 1944 and 1973 are expressed in Chilean escudos. The figures for 1974, 1975 and 1976 are expressed in Chilean pesos with one peso \$1=E°1,000, here E° stands for escudos.

TABLE 14.6 (Cont'd)

Average Monthly Registered Wages Quoted Per Capita by Type of Economic Activity. 1944-1976

	1971	1972	1973	1974	1975	1976		1974[3]	1975	1976
Agriculture	310.14	515.24	1,789	10.77	46.34	167.57	Nitrate	34.54	110.34	521.70
Mining	1,588.60	3,030.27	8,247	53.39	203.48	602.81	Copper	90.46	320.03	913.17
Industry	871.16	1,534.72	4,477	27.34	157.79	657.66	Coal	14.77	31.97	458.02
Construction	938.03	1,766.20	4,847	31.18	122.87	379.09	Oil	110.66	407.30	1,204.52
Electricity, Gas and Water	861.43	1,493.42	5,717	29.41	113.24	311.60	Other Mining	23.76	144.46	219.16
Commerce	598.40	990.99	2,901	17.92	64.68	286.91				
Transport and Communications	470.42	732.83	2,975	17.74	66.23	228.69				
Domestic Help	238.81	126.13	1,548	9.83	48.36	185.31				
Other Activities	537.53	1,035.99	2,933	18.69	71.95	263.22				
Not Indicated				4.73	34.07	80.10				
Total	623.88	1,107.37	3,595	22.36	93.58	331.39				

3. Detailed information on average monthly registered wages quoted per capita for nitrate, copper, coal, oil and other mining could be found only for 1974, 1975 and 1976.

Sources: República de Chile, Caja de Seguro Obligatorio, Anuario Estadístico 1946 (Santiago, Chile: Imprenta y Litografía Universo, S.A., 1948), p. 98, Table No. 2, for the years 1944-1946. República de Chile, Caja de Seguro Obligatorio, Anuario Estadístico 1948 (Santiago, Chile: Imprenta El Imparcial, 1949), pp. 9-94, for the year 1948. The figures for 1949 were obtained from República de Chile, Caja de Seguro Obligatorio, Anuario Estadístico 1949 (Santiago, Chile: Imprenta El Imparcial, 1951), pp. 11-114. The figures for 1950 were obtained from República de Chile, Caja de Seguro Obligatorio, Anuario Estadístico 1950 (Santiago, Chile: Imprenta de la Dirección General de Prisiones, 1952), p. 9. The figures for 1951 were obtained from República de Chile, Caja de Seguro Obligatorio, Annuario Estadístico 1951 (Santiago, Chile: Imprenta de la Dirección General de Prisiones, 1952), p. 13. The figures for the years 1952-1956 were obtained from República de Chile, Servicio de Seguro Social, Estadísticas 1952-1956 (Santiago, Chile: Editorial Universitaria, 1958), pp. 80-81. The figures for the years 1957-1959 were obtained from República de Chile, Servicio de Seguro Social, Estadísticas 1957-1959 (Santiago, Chile: Editorial Universitaria, 1959), pp. 66-67. The figures for the years 1960-1963 were obtained from República de Chile, Servicio de Seguro Social, Estadísticas 1963 (Santiago, Chile: Talleres Gráficos "Vera y Gianni," 1964), p. 27. The figures for the years 1964-1967 were obtained from República de Chile, Servicio de Seguro Social, Estadísticas 1967 (Santiago, Chile: SSS, 1967), p. 25. The figures for the year 1968 were obtained from República de Chile, Servicio de Seguro Social (SSS), Estadísticas 1968 (Santiago, Chile: SSS, 1968), p. 27. The figures for the year 1969 were obtained from República de Chile, SSS, Estadísticas 1969 (Santiago, Chile: SSS, 1969), p. 25. The figures for the year 1970 were obtained from República de Chile, SSS, Estadísticas 1970 (Santiago, Chile: SSS, 1970), p. 25. The figures for the year 1971 were obtained from República de Chile, SSS, Estadísticas 1971 (Santiago, Chile: SSS, 1971), p. 27. The figures for the year 1972 were obtained from República de Chile, SSS, Estadísticas 1972 (Santiago, Chile: SSS, 1972),

TABLE 14.6 (Cont'd)

Average Monthly Registered Wages Quoted Per Capita by Type of Economic Activity.
1944-1976

Sources (cont'd): p. 25. The figures for the year 1973 were obtained from República de Chile, SSS, Estadísticas 1973 (Santiago, Chile: SSS, 1973), p. 24. The figures for the years 1974-1975 were obtained from República de Chile, SSS, Estadísticas 1974-75 (Santiago, Chile: SSS, 1975), p. 35. The figures for the year 1976 were obtained from República de Chile, SSS, Estadísticas 1976 (Santiago, Chile: SSS, 1976), p. 24.

TABLE 14.7

Total Wages by Activities.
(Current prices in escudos from 1940 to 1973. In pesos since 1974)

Years	Total Activities	Agriculture	Nitrate and Petroleum	Copper and Coal	Other Mining	Industry	Construction	Electricity, Gas and Water
1940	2,578,854	479,382	170,241	84,307	241,061	756,465	207,143	-
1941	3,063,740	592,822	169,989	106,142	265,462	959,836	253,872	-
1942	3,602,023	660,981	178,597	127,597	317,515	1,208,814	286,140	-
1943	4,164,708	718,386	178,224	161,360	403,073	1,402,789	314,609	-
1944	4,865,032	755,223	181,058	183,770	392,930	1,701,215	395,584	-
1945	5,767,128	871,386	249,546	189,535	398,299	2,050,224	510,566	-
1946	6,825,687	1,003,386	300,281	196,521	383,202	2,447,248	640,542	-
1947	8,532,454	1,167,430	404,485	219,263	522,319	3,237,901	871,248	-
1948	10,375,036	1,453,018	494,509	316,456	632,208	3,991,463	927,193	-
1949	12,292,003	1,601,406	606,310	343,585	698,130	4,800,096	1,129,441	-
1950	14,599,825	1,897,873	639,820	417,290	760,637	5,773,895	1,355,786	-
1951	17,998,500	2,314,411	843,175	529,120	1,012,524	7,027,338	1,624,420	-
1952	23,929,671	2,825,025	1,106,695	1,900,379	627,847	9,042,762	2,579,555	309,097
1953	28,448,182	3,382,846	1,173,049	2,617,050	765,930	11,089,574	3,030,434	479,980
1954	39,174,257	4,449,331	1,821,481	3,546,748	1,028,349	15,711,767	4,376,688	709,401
1955	67,326,404	9,474,688	2,630,889	6,039,371	1,615,318	26,905,512	7,744,438	1,189,538
1956	115,343,721	17,742,773	4,423,683	9,867,241	2,761,616	43,331,737	14,619,429	2,179,568
1957	159,286,968	24,285,937	7,209,408	14,169,978	3,851,707	56,324,668	20,808,113	3,165,544
1958	194,104,005	30,227,452	8,007,326	16,123,771	4,387,903	70,496,811	26,579,875	3,644,546
1959	274,563,653	37,185,917	10,576,131	27,012,843	6,261,637	96,516,375	39,627,756	5,351,954
1960	311,370,729	43,921,147	10,669,703	30,167,700	7,221,940	108,540,228	42,924,819	6,093,099
1961	365,597,319	53,908,399	13,146,766	37,827,462	9,011,676	123,075,321	48,862,093	7,188,593
1962	437,673,293	63,847,713	15,373,799	39,789,599	9,779,767	149,332,404	60,137,112	8,967,819
1963	617,420,188	85,796,560	20,419,170	59,266,752	12,659,524	215,148,681	87,993,574	12,182,608
1964	973,876,665	131,544,892	32,169,005	88,606,459	22,002,848	346,504,446	146,660,749	20,466,750
1965	1,457,351,359	220,575,943				520,378,002	228,260,131	25,997,441
1966	2,030,791,421	319,036,046				738,700,124	326,665,815	26,507,627
1967	2,589,456,450	419,818,811				973,552,674	348,071,007	29,693,521
1968	3,446,655,708	524,384,737				1,281,706,088	447,871,347	52,374,581
1969	4,834,105,901	665,784,436				1,820,175,974	673,590,372	68,791,761
1970	6,896,238,835	1,009,317,398				2,556,787,473	990,280,266	95,697,214
1971	11,327,094,177	1,784,911,815				4,175,296,081	1,617,537,044	156,091,547
1972	20,464,199,205	3,018,465,369				7,488,227,969	3,100,742,692	275,984,797
1973	67,341,552,566	8,359,865,718				25,712,100,968	11,821,785,009	981,461,729
1974[1]	427,648,774	52,105,174				150,603,681	85,885,155	5,624,800
1975	1,726,332,933	255,728,067				573,792,418	308,651,362	23,536,443
1976	6,163,768,991	1,036,034,947				2,115,581,108	804,406,493	58,481,067

TABLE 14.7 (Cont'd)

Total Wages by Activities.
(Current prices in escudos from 1940 to 1973. In pesos since 1974)

Years	Trade	Transport and Communications	Domestic	Other Activities	Other, Not Properly Identified
1940	401,086	-	239,169	-	-
1941	464,457	-	251,160	-	-
1942	535,823	-	286,812	-	-
1943	627,969	-	277,797	80,501	-
1944	787,756	-	264,463	203,033	-
1945	908,645	-	357,169	231,758	-
1946	1,131,737	-	401,233	321,537	-
1947	1,278,167	-	452,295	379,346	-
1948	1,501,303	-	602,375	446,456	-
1949	1,702,539	-	787,843	600,373	-
1950	2,014,772	-	939,162	760,764	-
1951	1,767,460	-	1,174,546	1,705,506	-
1952	1,695,476	1,003,096	1,369,629	1,450,614	19,496
1953	2,071,444	786,246	1,604,353	1,445,596	1,680
1954	3,048,292	1,001,025	1,668,337	1,802,778	10,060
1955	5,018,001	1,551,874	2,060,884	3,086,902	8,989
1956	9,303,566	2,347,932	3,596,827	5,050,948	52,843
1957	12,998,184	3,500,064	5,295,966	7,663,147	14,252
1958	15,483,676	3,992,658	6,797,797	8,332,200	29,990
1959	23,909,670	4,522,152	9,811,680	13,624,121	163,417
1960	28,569,359	5,487,692	11,347,787	16,234,487	192,768
1961	34,217,462	5,940,566	13,602,360	20,638,897	177,724
1962	43,390,759	5,902,432	15,257,190	25,673,069	221,630
1963	64,049,310	7,553,657	19,610,311	32,422,378	317,663
1964	91,809,063	11,654,919	32,774,571	49,096,323	586,640
1965	133,965,100	18,440,292	48,685,422	69,875,474	427,555
1966	187,696,685	25,969,376	65,072,079	88,184,334	4,635,058
1967	276,833,767	37,512,452	79,959,215	120,398,922	6,421,233
1968	380,608,947	49,300,155	118,409,577	154,075,940	8,910,317
1969	478,450,175	71,020,630	163,084,115	212,934,182	
1970	646,461,457	103,282,724	222,923,497	290,764,371	
1971	1,031,886,840	171,043,110	420,679,545	497,970,736	
1972	1,739,773,863	270,885,187	739,732,029	975,899,162	
1973	5,461,590,803	833,535,036	2,192,063,229	3,039,609,162	
1974	36,330,102	6,106,457	13,539,870	15,727,714	452,496
1975	146,161,263	24,366,043	79,768,257	76,768,257	2,681,951
1976	605,917,112	82,079,606	311,615,896	350,571,904	7,497,632

TABLE 14.7 (Cont'd)

Total Wages by Activities.
(Current prices in escudos from 1940 to 1973. In pesos since 1974)

Note: 1. For the years 1974, 1975 and 1976 the figures are in pesos with $1 (one new peso) = E^{o} (escudos) 1,000.

Sources: The figures for the years 1940-1951 were obtained from República de Chile, Servicio de Seguro Social (SSS), unpublished statistical information. The figures for the years 1952-1956 were obtained from República de Chile, Servicio de Seguro Social, Estadísticas 1952-1956 (Santiago, Chile: Editorial Universitaria, 1958), pp. 80-81. The figures for the years 1957-1959 were obtained from República de Chile, Servicio de Seguro Social, Estadísticas, 1957-1959 (Santiago, Chile: Editorial Universitaria, 1959), pp. 66-67. The figures for the years 1960-1963 were obtained from República de Chile, Servicio de Seguro Social, Estadísticas 1963 (Santiago, Chile: Talleres Gráficos "Vera y Gianni", 1964), p. 27. The figures for the years 1964-1967 were obtained from República de Chile, Servicio de Seguro Social, Estadísticas 1967 (Santiago, Chile: SSS, 1967), p. 25. The figures for the year 1968 were obtained from República de Chile, Servicio de Seguro Social (SSS), Estadísticas 1968 (Santiago, Chile: SSS, 1968), p. 27. The figures for the year 1969 were obtained from República de Chile, SSS, Estadísticas 1969 (Santiago, Chile: SSS, 1969), p. 25. The figures for the year 1970 were obtained from República de Chile, SSS, Estadísticas 1970 (Santiago, Chile: SSS, 1970), p. 25. The figures for the year 1971 were obtained from República de Chile, SSS, Estadísticas 1971 (Santiago, Chile: SSS, 1971), p. 27. The figures for the year 1972 were obtained from República de Chile, SSS, Estadísticas 1972 (Santiago, Chile: SSS, 1972), p. 25. The figures for the year 1973 were obtained from República de Chile, SSS, Estadísticas 1973 (Santiago, Chile: SSS, 1973), p. 24. The figures for the years 1974-1975 were obtained from República de Chile, SSS, Estadísticas 1974-75 (Santiago, Chile: SSS, 1975), p. 35. The figures for the year 1976 were obtained from República de Chile, SSS, Estadísticas 1976 (Santiago, Chile: SSS, 1976), p. 24.

TABLE 14.8

Average Employment, Salaries and Wages, and Man-Hours in Manufacturing by Province, During 1957.

Provinces	No. of Establish-ments	Average Employment			Salaries and Wages			Man-Hours Worked by Workers (Hundreds)	Family Allowances[1] E° 100
		Total	Employ-ees	Workers	Total[1] E° 100	Employees E° 100	Workers E° 100		
Country Total	5,833	206,701	27,621	179,080	806,653.3	248,983.6	555,114.4	4,453,271	99,946.5
1. Norte Grande and Norte Chico	346	6,955	924	6,031	28,882.4	8,672.0	20,145.1	153,834	3,197.1
01 Tarapacá	76	1,889	241	1,648	8,062.1	2,372.8	5,662.7	37,098	804.9
02 Antofagasta	127	2,642	350	2,292	11,081.4	3,574.1	7,480.6	56,059	1,055.6
03 Atacama	50	768	96	672	4,325.9	963.5	3,350.4	27,151	531.5
04 Coquimbo	93	1,656	237	1,419	5,413.0	1,761.6	3,651.4	33,526	805.1
2. Central Nucleus I	3,967	153,561	21,056	132,505	598,448.1	185,369.3	410,893.0	3,357,384	70,555.7
11 Aconcagua	80	2,011	181	1,830	5,447.5	1,258.5	4,185.6	44,801	714.1
12 Valparaíso	596	23,436	3,639	19,797	107,557.8	36,497.7	70,794.6	521,256	11,786.6
13 Santiago	3,147	125,401	16,917	108,484	474,187.3	144,916.0	327,371.0	2,737,244	56,648.6
14 O'Higgins	104	1,894	211	1,683	8,331.2	1,829.0	6,485.6	38,177	1,051.5
15 Colchagua	40	819	108	711	2,924.3	868.1	2,056.2	15,906	354.9
3. Central Nucleus II	360	6,827	885	5,942	20,626.9	6,593.0	13,894.7	149,455	2,847.6
21 Curicó	45	612	80	532	1,582.1	402.5	1,120.1	12,747	257.0
22 Talca	120	3,606	535	3,071	12,786.1	4,627.3	8,140.7	75,931	1,441.4
23 Maule	24	201	6	195	528.3	47.2	451.1	4,442	64.2
24 Linares	60	923	108	815	2,458.0	708.3	1,746.5	20,945	540.4
25 Ñuble	111	1,485	156	1,329	3,272.3	807.7	2,436.3	35,390	544.6
4. Concepción and the Frontier	670	28,460	3,541	24,919	124,938.6	38,563.7	86,240.1	556,128	18,603.5
31 Concepción	332	22,405	2,873	19,532	108,153.7	33,742.6	74,294.3	433,327	15,958.8
32 Arauco	13	133	18	115	320.1	69.0	251.1	2,736	48.3
33 Bío-Bío	62	1,531	179	1,352	5,292.2	1,642.1	3,645.2	26,484	746.4
34 Malleco	62	1,348	170	1,178	4,439.5	1,452.6	2,984.9	27,559	600.5
35 Cautín	201	3,043	301	2,742	6,733.1	1,657.4	5,064.6	66,022	1,249.5
5. The Lake and Canal Region (Los Lagos y Los Canales)	490	10,898	1,215	9,683	33,757.3	9,785.6	23,941.5	236,470	4,742.6
41 Valdivia	163	4,977	557	4,420	15,551.9	4,800.9	10,750.6	111,073	2,495.1
42 Osorno	124	2,214	260	1,954	7,887.6	2,515.0	5,356.7	49,690	1,135.1
43 Llanquihue	95	1,666	171	1,495	3,977.1	963.7	2,994.5	36,051	666.0
44 Chiloé	17	140	12	128	227.0	44.0	182.2	3,290	13.5
45 Aysén	13	140	6	134	278.5	51.0	227.5	2,458	17.8
46 Magallanes	78	1,761	209	1,552	5,835.2	1,411.0	4,430.0	33,908	415.1
6. Economic Area of Valparaíso	480	18,506	2,955	15,551	84,286.4	29,176.1	54,860.0	420,259	9,138.4

TABLE 14.8 (Cont'd)

Average Employment, Salaries and Wages, and Man-Hours in Manufacturing by Province, During 1957.

Provinces	No. of Establishments	Average Employment			Salaries and Wages			Man-Hours Worked by Workers (Hundreds)	Family Allowances[1] E° 100
		Total	Employees	Workers	Total[1] E° 100	Employees E° 100	Workers E° 100		
7. Economic Area of Santiago	3,035	120,929	16,310	104,619	455,519.0	139,814.1	313,823.3	2,638,592	54,462.5
8. Economic Area of Concepción	294	21,192	2,737	18,455	102,390.4	32,388.9	69,894.3	407,351	15,251.0

Note: 1. The family allowances, called in Spanish cargas familiares, include actual payments to "workers in their own domicile".

Source: República de Chile, Ministerio de Economía, Dirección de Estadística y Censos III. Censo Nacional de Manufacturas, 1957 (Santiago de Chile: Dirección de Estadística y Censos, 1960), Table No. 10, p. 92.

TABLE 14.9

Internal Industrial Income Per Person Employed, in 1950 Prices (Escudos).

	1948	1954	1957
Valparaíso	156.7	145.6	229.0
Santiago	123.0	134.0	104.0
Concepción	129.7	177.0	173.1
Region I	131.3	134.7	123.6
Region II	120.7	159.4	165.4
Country	125.0	131.7	126.8

Notes: Region I includes the provinces of Aconcagua, Valparaíso, Santiago, O'Higgins and Colchagua. Region II includes the provinces of Ñuble, Concepción, Arauco, Bío-Bío and Malleco.

Sources: This information was obtained from Carlos Dodero H. Desarrallo Económico de la Region de Concepción 1948-1964 Memoria de Prueba. Facultad de Ciencias Económicas y de Administración, Universidad de Concepción 1963 (Concepción, Chile: Universidad de Concepción, 1963). Mimeographed. Table 7. The primary source used by Dodero to calculate the information of this table is S.N.E.C. Revista Industria (Santiago, Chile: S.N.E.C. various dates).

SALARIES

Basic Salaries in Santiago and Valparaíso, 1937-1977

Time series of the basic salary between 1937 and 1977 for the departments of Santiago and Valparaíso are presented in Table 14.10. These series cover scale A and scale B of the basic salary.

Basic Salaries by Province: 1937-1976

In Table 14.10 the time series for scales A and B of the basic salary (sueldo vital) were presented for the departments of Santiago and Valparaíso. Time series for the basic salary or vital salary or minimum wage rate for white-collar workers (these are synonyms) by provinces are presented in Table 14.11. There have been differences among basic salaries among provinces due to an effort to compensate for differences in the cost of living but these have been generally small.

Much of Chile's incomes policy as well as much of its labor-capital (class distribution), intra-labor (income distribution between workers and employees), and sectoral distribution of income between 1937 and 1973 were related to, if not partly determined, by the evolution of the basic salary. These statistics are also important because the basic salary assumed the role of a numeraîre during Chile's inflation and thus was intricately linked to monetary and fiscal policy.

Basic salaries by regions and the minimum hourly wage between 1976 and 1978 are presented in Table 14.12.

Salaries Per Employee by Sector: 1940-1952

Volume I on National Accounts of the Historical Statistics of Chile contains time series of real salaries by sector, 1940-1952 in millions of 1940 Chilean currency (Mamalakis: 1978c, table 47, 219-222). In the present section, average annual nominal salary earnings per employee by industry are given. These are found in Table 14.13. The information on annual nominal salaries per employee presented in Table 14.13 is supplemented by the information on average annual real salary earnings per employee by industry for the period between 1940 and 1952 presented in Table 14.14. The information presented in Tables 14.13 and 14.14 is not available anywhere else and is of a quality and coverage not reached by any subsequent time series.

TABLE 14.10

Basic Salary, 1937-1977.

Years	Months	Department of Santiago		Department of Valparaíso	
		Scale A	Scale B	Scale A	Scale B
1937	Jan.-Dec.	$ 420	$ 370	$ 400	$ 350
1938	Jan.-Dec.	$ 420	$ 370	$ 400	$ 350
1939	Jan.-Dec.	$ 445	$ 390	$ 460	$ 400
1940	Jan.-Dec.	$ 460	$ 448	$ 500	$ 430
1941	Jan.-Dec.	$ 600	$ 520	$ 580	$ 500
1942	Jan.-Dec.	$ 815	$ 710	$ 740	$ 660
1943	Jan.-Dec.	$ 1,050	$ 911	$ 1,000	$ 870
1944	Jan.-Dec.	$ 1,185	$ 1,030	$ 1,205	$ 1,070
1945	Jan.-Dec.	$ 1,320	$ 1,135	$ 1,300	$ 1,110
1946	Jan.-Dec.	$ 1,470	$ 1,280	$ 1,470	$ 1,270
1947	Jan.-Dec.	$ 1,995	$ 1,735	$ 2,065	$ 1,800
1948	Jan.-Dec.	$ 2,400	$ 2,084	$ 2,320	$ 1,991
1949	Jan.-Dec.	$ 3,040	$ 2,640	$ 2,900	$ 2,500
1950	Jan.-Dec.	$ 3,800	$ 3,300	$ 3,550	$ 3,100
1951	Jan.-Dec.	$ 4,670	$ 4,055	$ 4,460	$ 3,900
1952	Jan.-Dec.	$ 6,070	$ 5,270	$ 5,810	$ 4,950
1953	Jan.-Dec.	$ 7,550	$ 6,515	$ 7,270	$ 5,950
1954	Jan.-Dec.	$ 11,600	$ 10,009	$ 11,320	$ 9,300
1955	Jan.-Dec.	$ 18,400	$ 15,740	$ 18,320	$ 14,900
1956	Jan.-Dec.	$ 26,956	$ 23,059	$ 26,839	$ 21,829
1957	Jan.-Dec.	$ 35,086	$ 30,014	$ 34,934	$ 28,413
1958	Jan.-Dec.	$ 42,103	$ 36,017	$ 41,921	$ 34,096
1959	Jan.-Dec.	$ 57,550	$ 49,240	$ 57,310	$ 46,610
1960	Jan.-Dec.	$ 57,550	$ 49,240	$ 57,310	$ 46,610
1961	Jan.-June	E° 66.18	E° 56.63	E° 65.91	E° 53.60
	July-Dec.	E° 77.17	E° 66.03	E° 76.85	E° 62.50
1962	Jan.-Dec.	E° 80.91	E° 69.23	E° 80.58	E° 65.53
1963	Jan.-Dec.	E° 103.32	E° 88.41	E° 102.90	E° 83.68
1964	Jan.-Dec.	E° 150.23	E° 128.55	E° 149.62	E° 121.67
1965	Jan.-Dec.	E° 207.92	E° 177.91	E° 207.07	E° 168.39
1966	Jan.-Dec.	E° 261.77	E° 223.99	E° 260.70	E° 212.00
1967	Jan.-Dec.	E° 306.27	E° 262.07	E° 305.02	E° 248.04
1968	Jan.-Dec.	E° 373.34	E° 319.46	E° 371.82	E° 302.36
1969	Jan.-Dec.	E° 477.50	E° 408.59	E° 475.56	E° 386.72
1970	Jan.-Dec.	E° 617.41	E° 528.31	E° 614.90	E° 500.03
1971	Jan.-Dec.	E° 832.89	E° 712.69	E° 829.50	E° 674.54
1972	Jan.-Sept.	E° 1,016.96	E° 870.19	E° 1,012.82	E° 823.61
1972	Oct.-Dec.	E° 2,033.92	E° 1,740.38	E° 2,025.64	E° 1,647.22
1973	Jan.-Dec.	E° 2,033.92	E° 1,740.38	E° 2,025.64	E° 1,647.22
1974	Jan.-Apr.	E° 10,170.00	E° -	E° 10,128.00	E° -
	May -June	E° 13,200.00	E° -	E° 13,200.00	E° -
	July-Sept.	E° 15,900.00	E° -	E° 15,900.00	E° -
	Oct.-Nov.	E° 20,000.00	E° -	E° 20,000.00	E° -
	Dec.	E° 27,000.00	E° -	E° 27,000.00	E° -
1975	Jan.-Feb.	E° 27,000.00	E° -	E° 27,000.00	E° -
	Mar.-May	E° 36,000.00	E° -	E° 36,000.00	E° -
	June-Aug.	E° 62,000.00	E° -	E° 62,000.00	E° -
	Sept.-Nov.	$ 77.00	$ -	$ 77.00	$ -
	Dec.	$ 99.00	$ -	$ 99.00	$ -
1976	Jan.-Feb.	$ 99.00	$ -	$ 99.00	$ -
	Mar.-May	$ 131.00	$ -	$ 131.00	$ -
	June-Aug.	$ 180.84	$ -	$ -	$ -
	Sept.-Nov.	$ 227.86	$ -	$ -	$ -
	1° Dec.-31 Dec.	$ 268.87	$ -	$ -	$ -
1977	Jan.-Feb.	$ 268.87	$ -	$ -	$ -
	Mar.-June	$ 319.96	$ -	$ -	$ -

Notes: The symbol $ stands for pesos, old pesos until Jan.-Dec. 1960 and new pesos from Sept.-Nov. 1975 onwards. The symbol E° stands for escudos. The escudo was introduced in 1961 at a rate of E° = $1,000 (old pesos). The new peso was introduced in 1975 once again at a rate of $ (one new peso) = E° 1,000.
Source: National Institute of Statistics.

TABLE 14.11

Minimum Wage Rates for White-Collar Workers by Provinces[9].
(In pesos or escudos)[8]

Year	Tarapacá	Coquimbo	Santiago	Talca	Concepción	Arauco	Osorno	Magallanes
1937-8	480	360	420	409	420	323	432	425
1939	513	360	445	409	480	323	475	425
1940	530	380	460	420	500	360	490	455
1941	667	570	600	531	555	474	585	500
1942	800	730	815	750	752	620	650	730
1943	1,020	920	1,050	920	1,074	845	830	975
1944	1,140	1,170	1,185	975	1,206	947	1,000	1,200
1945	1,365	1,170	1,320	1,005	1,457	1,043	1,225	1,400
1946	1,595	1,500	1,470	1,200	1,482	1,142	1,265	1,620
1947	2,240	1,950	1,995	1,570	1,910	1,733	1,650	2,050
1948	2,490	2,250	2,400	1,900	2,300	1,922	1,950	2,400
1949	3,000	2,980	3,040	2,400	2,800	2,800	2,450	3,050
1950	3,600	3,550	3,800	2,775	3,400	2,822	3,000	3,600
1951	4,700	4,330	4,670	3,550	4,600	3,290	3,700	4,900
1952	6,200	5,550	6,070	4,550	6,302	4,580	5,000	6,250
1953	7,600	7,700	7,550	6,480	7,900	6,020	6,875	8,000
1954	11,700	11,000	11,600	11,000	11,950	7,710	10,000	12,000
1955	18,700	17,360	18,400	18,000	19,550	12,410	16,530	18,900
1956	27,396	24,432	26,956	26,370	28,641	18,181	24,216	27,689
1957	35,657	33,102	35,086	34,323	37,279	23,664	31,520	36,040
1958	42,791	39,722	42,103	41,188	44,735	28,397	37,824	43,248
1959	58,500	54,300	57,550	56,300	61,150	38,820	51,700	59,120
1961[10]	67.28	62.45	66.18	64.75	70.32	44.64	59.46	67.99
1961	78.44	72.80	77.17	75.49	81.99	52.05	69.32	79.28
1962	82.24	76.33	80.91	79.15	85.97	54.57	72.68	83.13
1963	105.93	97.47	103.32	101.07	109.78	69.69	92.81	106.16
1964	152.70	141.72	150.23	146.96	159.52	101.33	134.95	154.36
1965	211.34	196.14	207.92	203.39	220.91	140.24	186.77	213.63
1966	266.08	246.94	261.77	256.07	278.13	176.56	235.14	268.96
1967	311.31	288.92	306.27	299.60	325.41	206.58	275.11	314.68
1968	379.49	352.19	373.34	365.21	396.67	251.82	335.36	383.59
1969	485.37	450.45	477.50	467.10	507.34	322.08	428.93	490.61
1970	627.58	582.43	617.41	603.96	655.99	416.45	554.61	634.36
1971	846.61	784.58	832.89	814.74	884.93	848.84	784.17	855.75
1972	1,033.71	959.34	1,016.96	994.80	1,080.50	685.95	913.52	1,044.87
1973	2,067.42	1,918.68	2,033.92	1,989.60	2,161.00	1,371.90	1,827.04	2,089.74
1974[1]	20.00	19.00	20.00	20.00	21.00	21.00	18.00	23.00
1974[2]	27.00	26.00	27.00	27.00	29.00	29.00	25.00	31.00

TABLE 14.11 (Cont'd)

Minimum Wage Rates for White-Collar Workers by Provinces.
(In pesos or escudos)

Year	Tarapacá	Coquimbo	Santiago	Talca	Concepción	Arauco	Osorno	Magallanes
1975[3]	77.00	75.00	77.00	77.00	84.00	84.00	74.00	90.00
1975[4]	99.00	96.00	99.00	99.00	108.00	108.00	95.00	116.00
1976[5]	131.00	127.00	131.00	131.00	143.00	143.00	126.00	154.00
1976[6]	180.84	176.14	180.84	180.84	197.27	197.27	173.79	211.36
1976[7]	227.86	221.94	227.86	227.86	248.56	248.56	218.98	266.31

Notes:
1. These salaries (minimum wage rates for white-collar workers) correspond to the period from October 1 to November 30 of 1974.
2. These salaries correspond to the period from December 1 of 1974 to February 28 of 1975.
3. These salaries correspond to the period from September 1 to November 30 of 1975.
4. These salaries correspond to the period from December 1 of 1975 to February 29 of 1976.
5. These salaries correspond to the period from March 1 to May 31 of 1976.
6. These salaries correspond to the period from June 1 to August 31 of 1976.
7. These salaries correspond to the period from September 1 to November 30 of 1976.
8. The figures for the years between 1937 and 1959 are expressed in (old) pesos. The figures between 1961 and 1973 are expressed in escudos (E°) where E°1 = \$(old pesos)1,000. The figures for the years 1974-76 are in (new) pesos (1 = 1000 E°, where E° stands for escudos).
9. The minimum wage rate for white-collar workers (sueldo vital = vital salary) corresponds to the department in which the capital of the province lies.
10. There was no minimum wage for white-collar workers (vital salary) in 1960. A bonification was granted in 1959 which was incorporated to the salaries in 1961. From the 1st of July, 1961 a new vital salary was established.

Sources: Banco Central de Chile, Boletín Mensual No. 334, Diciembre de 1955 (Santiago: Imprenta Universitario 1956), p. 420, for the figures of the years 1937-8 to 1955. Banco Central de Chile, Boletín Mensual No. 425, Julio 1963 (Santiago: Impresora Gutemberg, 1963), p. 906, for the figures of the years 1956 to 1963. Banco Central de Chile, Boletín Mensual No. 448, Junio 1965 (Santiago: Impresora Gutemberg, 1965), p. 902, for the figures of the years 1964 and 1965. Banco Central de Chile, Boletín Mensual No. 534, Agosto 1972, (Santiago, Chile: BCC, 1972), p. 1066, for the figures of the years 1966-72. Banco Central de Chile, Boletín Mensual No. 560, Octubre 1974 (Santiago, Chile: BCC, 1974), p. 1353, for the figures of the year 1973. Banco Central de Chile, Boletín Mensual No. 575, Enero 1976 (Santiago, Chile: BCC, 1976), p. 156, for the figures of the year 1974. Banco Central de Chile, Boletín Mensual No. 583, Septiembre 1976 (Santiago, Chile: BCC, 1976), p. 1510, for the figures of the years 1975-76.

TABLE 14.12

Basic Salaries by Regions and Minimum Hourly Wage, 1976-1978.
(In pesos)

	1976[1]		1976[2]		1977[3]		1977[4]		1977[5]		1978[6]	
	Salary	Wage	Salary	Wage	Salary	Wage	Salary	Wage	Salary	Wage	Salary	Wage
I Region												
Arica	227.86	0.94	268.87	1.12	319.96	1.33	377.55	1.57	445.51	1.85	481.15	2.00
Iquique	227.86	0.94	268.87	1.12	319.96	1.33	377.55	1.57	445.51	1.85	481.15	2.00
II Region												
Tocopilla	266.31	1.10	314.24	1.30	373.95	1.55	441.26	1.83	520.69	2.16	562.35	2.34
Antofagasta	266.31	1.10	314.24	1.30	373.95	1.55	441.26	1.83	520.69	2.16	562.35	2.34
El Loa	266.31	1.10	314.24	1.30	373.95	1.55	441.26	1.83	520.69	2.16	562.35	2.34
III Region												
Chañaral	248.56	1.03	293.30	1.22	349.03	1.45	411.85	1.71	485.98	2.02	524.86	2.18
Copiapó	248.56	1.03	293.30	1.22	349.03	1.45	411.85	1.71	485.98	2.02	524.86	2.18
Huasco	248.56	1.03	293.30	1.22	349.03	1.45	411.85	1.71	485.98	2.02	524.36	2.18
IV Region												
Elqui	221.94	0.92	261.88	1.09	311.64	1.29	367.74	1.53	433.93	1.80	468.64	1.95
Limarí	221.94	0.92	261.88	1.09	311.64	1.29	367.74	1.53	433.93	1.80	468.64	1.95
Choapa	221.94	0.92	261.88	1.09	311.64	1.29	367.74	1.53	433.93	1.80	468.64	1.95
V Region												
Valparaíso	227.86	0.94	268.87	1.12	319.96	1.33	377.55	1.57	445.51	1.85	481.15	2.00
San Antonio	227.86	0.94	268.87	1.12	319.96	1.33	377.55	1.57	445.51	1.85	481.15	2.00
Quillota	227.86	0.94	268.87	1.12	319.96	1.33	377.55	1.57	445.51	1.85	481.15	2.00
Petorca	221.94	0.92	261.88	1.09	311.64	1.29	367.74	1.53	433.93	1.80	468.64	1.95
San Felipe	221.94	0.92	261.88	1.09	311.64	1.29	367.74	1.53	433.93	1.80	468.64	1.95
Los Andes	221.94	0.92	261.88	1.09	311.64	1.29	367.74	1.53	433.93	1.80	468.64	1.95
Isla de Pascua	227.86	0.94	268.87	1.12	319.96	1.33	377.55	1.57	445.51	1.85	481.15	2.00
Metropolitan Area												
Santiago	227.86	0.94	268.87	1.12	319.96	1.33	377.55	1.57	445.51	1.85	481.15	2.00
VI Region												
Cachapoal	221.94	0.92	261.88	1.09	311.64	1.29	367.74	1.53	433.93	1.80	468.64	1.95
Colchagua	227.86	0.94	268.87	1.12	319.96	1.33	377.55	1.57	445.51	1.85	481.15	2.00
VII Region												
Curicó	227.86	0.94	268.87	1.12	319.96	1.33	377.55	1.57	445.51	1.85	481.15	2.00
Talca	227.86	0.94	268.87	1.12	319.96	1.33	377.55	1.57	445.51	1.85	481.15	2.00
Linares	198.26	0.82	233.94	0.97	278.39	1.15	328.50	1.36	387.63	1.61	418.64	1.74
VIII Region												
Ñuble	221.94	0.92	261.88	1.09	311.64	1.29	367.74	1.53	433.93	1.80	468.64	1.95
Concepción	248.56	1.03	293.30	1.22	349.03	1.45	411.85	1.71	485.98	2.02	524.86	2.18
Arauco	248.56	1.03	293.30	1.22	349.03	1.45	411.85	1.71	485.98	2.02	524.86	2.18
Bío-Bío	218.98	0.91	258.39	1.07	307.48	1.28	362.83	1.51	428.14	1.78	462.39	1.92

TABLE 14.12 (Cont'd)

Basic Salaries by Regions and Minimum Hourly Wage, 1976-1978.
(In pesos)

	1976[1]		1976[2]		1977[3]		1977[4]		1977[5]		1978[6]	
	Salary	Wage	Salary	Wage	Salary	Wage	Salary	Wage	Salary	Wage	Salary	Wage
IX Region												
Malleco	221.94	0.92	261.88	1.09	311.64	1.29	367.74	1.53	433.93	1.80	468.64	1.95
Cautín	218.98	0.91	258.39	1.07	307.48	1.28	362.83	1.51	428.14	1.78	462.39	1.92
X Region												
Valdivia	218.98	0.91	258.39	1.07	307.48	1.28	362.83	1.51	428.14	1.78	462.39	1.92
Osorno	218.98	0.91	258.39	1.07	307.48	1.28	362.83	1.51	428.14	1.78	462.39	1.92
Llanquihue	218.98	0.91	258.39	1.07	307.48	1.28	362.83	1.51	428.14	1.78	462.39	1.92
Chiloé	218.98	0.91	258.39	1.07	307.48	1.28	362.83	1.51	428.14	1.78	462.39	1.92
XI Region												
Aysén	254.49	1.06	300.29	1.25	357.35	1.48	421.67	1.75	497.57	2.07	537.38	2.23
Gral. Carrera	254.49	1.06	300.29	1.25	357.35	1.48	421.67	1.75	497.57	2.07	537.38	2.23
Cap. Prat	254.49	1.06	300.29	1.25	357.35	1.48	421.67	1.75	497.57	2.07	537.38	2.23
XII Region												
Ultima Esperanza	266.31	1.10	314.24	1.30	373.95	1.55	441.26	1.83	520.69	2.16	562.35	2.34
Magallanes	266.31	1.10	314.24	1.30	373.95	1.55	441.26	1.83	520.69	2.16	562.35	2.34
Tierra del Fuego	266.31	1.10	314.24	1.30	373.95	1.55	441.26	1.83	520.69	2.16	562.35	2.34
Antártica Chilena	266.31	1.10	314.24	1.30	373.95	1.55	441.26	1.83	520.69	2.16	562.35	2.34

Notes: 1. These figures are valid for the trimester between September 1 and November 30 of 1976.

2. These figures are valid for the trimester between December 1 of 1976 and February 28 of 1977.

3. These figures are valid for the period from March 1 to June 30 of 1977.

4. These figures are valid for the period from July 1 to November 30 of 1977.

5. These figures are valid for the trimester between December 1 of 1977 and February 28 of 1978.

6. These figures are valid for the period from March 1 to June 30 of 1978.

Source: Banco Central de Chile, Boletín Mensual No. 601, February 1978 (Santiago, Chile: BCC, 1978), p. 410 for the figures of the years 1976 and 1977. Banco Central de Chile, Boletín Mensual No. 602, April 1978 (Santiago, Chile: BCC, 1978), p. 746 for the figures of 1978. These figures were reported to the Central Bank of Chile by the Comisión Mixta de Sueldos.

TABLE 14.13

Average Annual Nominal Salary Earnings, Per Employee, by Industry, 1940-1952.
(Chilean Pesos)

	1940	1941	1942	1943	1944	1945	1946	1947	1948	1949	1950	1951	1952
Agriculture	5,626	6,225	8,409	10,642	12,540	14,051	15,750	21,088	25,329	32,001	37,238	49,318	64,095
Fisheries	4,500	6,161	7,143	7,925	8,741	10,526	12,676	15,556	18,954	22,741	26,444	31,214	37,955
Mining	14,622	17,651	22,844	28,720	30,893	33,478	37,785	47,338	54,951	64,758	76,842	97,373	141,828
Large Enterprises	15,847	18,977	24,183	30,505	32,959	35,331	39,487	48,649	56,190	64,749	75,553	95,673	141,387
Small and Medium Size Enterprises	11,458	13,883	18,741	23,814	25,272	28,208	32,710	43,226	51,016	64,785	80,534	101,597	142,842
Industries	12,823	15,925	20,896	24,186	28,291	32,804	35,641	46,629	54,552	64,457	76,773	109,605	155,677
Large Industries	14,417	18,013	23,326	27,251	31,158	34,093	39,223	51,254	59,954	71,148	84,464	120,587	171,279
Small Industries	10,772	13,114	17,262	19,403	23,513	30,311	28,906	37,618	42,722	49,191	59,131	84,417	119,894
Nonmetallic Mine Products	13,464	13,826	17,538	18,287	26,545	29,847	28,896	40,351	46,304	55,909	66,656		
Glass Products	15,385	19,101	24,051	26,332	26,344	30,706	39,835	47,208	61,725	72,441	97,910		
Machine and Metallic Products	12,744	15,533	21,651	25,445	29,696	33,236	37,858	48,554	57,119	68,357	71,751		
Chemical Products	15,712	18,691	24,703	28,786	31,723	37,811	41,455	54,303	66,275	82,309	93,161		
Textile-Mill Products	17,457	19,622	24,554	32,240	34,681	38,483	47,505	59,761	68,750	80,734	95,098		
Paper Products and Printing	11,196	17,084	21,428	25,990	29,129	29,705	34,696	44,923	52,982	65,476	80,234		
Leather and Rubber Products	13,309	15,490	19,967	24,010	30,488	67,988	40,197	51,116	59,026	69,456	86,511		
Lumber and Cork Products	10,418	13,904	18,977	20,944	24,192	26,886	27,445	37,176	43,856	49,974	58,044		
Musical Items	14,721	16,583	25,000	26,791	36,000	31,034	36,585	50,000	31,250	48,000	57,692		
Food Products	12,912	16,233	20,172	22,409	26,166	27,401	33,325	41,883	50,720	57,980	75,892		
Beverages	16,014	17,934	24,701	28,631	31,055	33,011	36,837	58,519	61,130	68,863	83,952		
Tobacco Manufactures	15,625	19,022	25,785	27,126	31,981	37,123	40,089	69,231	77,618	93,688	117,235		
Clothing	9,081	12,981	17,608	20,484	24,325	25,800	32,883	39,675	44,870	49,911	61,777		
Construction	9,146	13,115	15,900	20,583	22,179	22,714	25,366	29,848	35,724	42,379	54,586	77,111	100,222
Utilities	15,417	20,041	23,036	28,144	28,411	31,631	41,033	52,042	60,079	72,694	109,946	142,874	202,264
Electricity and Gas	17,040	21,864	24,438	28,843	28,374	33,258	39,901	52,850	62,266	77,703	113,056	146,912	207,977
Water	9,850	13,158	18,094	26,156	28,531	26,573	39,501	49,484	53,199	56,258	100,125	130,123	184,224
Commerce	9,169	13,165	16,003	20,668	22,279	22,813	25,464	29,995	35,885	42,565	54,802	77,844	101,618
Finance and Insurance	14,393	17,237	23,359	29,495	34,818	38,992	43,712	58,458	70,281	89,018	104,240	136,867	177,968
Insurance Companies	14,216	17,037	23,050	29,131	34,340	38,438	43,142	57,691	69,350	89,018	109,805	134,938	175,392
Financial Institutions	14,421	17,270	23,412	29,554	34,895	39,079	43,797	58,574	70,414	89,018	103,258	137,088	178,215

TABLE 14.13 (Cont'd)

Average Annual Nominal Salary Earnings, Per Employee, By Industry, 1940-1952.
(Chilean Pesos)

	1940	1941	1942	1943	1944	1945	1946	1947	1948	1949	1950	1951	1952
Transportation and Communications	10,990	12,321	17,087	18,756	20,473	24,803	30,644	41,029	47,636	47,113	60,685	80,659	115,847
Transportation	9,438	11,058	14,150	17,774	19,991	25,932	29,279	36,864	43,211	48,023	61,575	75,342	120,434
Communications	15,203	15,973	25,811	21,008	21,661	22,070	34,193	51,608	57,866	45,033	58,992	94,039	106,060
Government	11,577	15,552	17,105	20,220	22,522	27,087	30,677	42,253	44,572	58,895	94,796	98,405	151,028
Central Government	12,662	15,545	17,601	20,877	22,370	27,423	29,705	48,089	46,697	60,234	116,126	106,488	203,030
Municipal Governments	10,513	12,601	17,047	21,549	25,394	28,434	31,911	42,676	52,016	63,600	84,484	133,564	173,582
National Health Service	6,421	6,912	9,862	11,012	12,886	14,283	22,671	25,233	26,170	43,791	46,979	77,633	78,068
Social Security and Similar Funds	10,662	10,982	15,162	16,533	19,592	20,468	28,594	34,396	41,010	49,706	69,896	79,683	91,686
Government Educational Services	11,416	20,922	19,522	23,609	27,572	32,961	37,018	37,103	48,553	63,782	74,506	87,756	78,997
Services	8,516	10,849	13,730	16,824	18,969	21,209	25,170	30,597	37,391	46,335	54,832	69,256	81,675
Medical and Social Welfare	6,409	6,908	9,872	11,013	12,911	14,191	22,627	25,255	26,196	43,868	46,913	77,706	78,173
Private Education	11,397	20,888	19,496	23,545	27,506	32,897	36,937	37,016	48,438	63,651	74,339	86,563	78,821
Religious	5,079	6,072	7,663	10,409	12,273	13,727	15,400	20,600	24,778	31,378	39,222	48,196	62,630
Hotels and Other Lodging Places	15,649	17,856	24,084	28,810	31,237	33,913	39,448	50,164	60,643	67,797	79,811	96,660	125,523
Miscellaneous	5,079	6,085	8,236	10,406	12,262	13,727	15,406	20,606	24,771	31,370	39,216	48,192	62,694
Per Salaried Employee	11,010	14,251	17,265	20,684	23,006	26,426	30,308	39,653	45,023	54,889	75,693	91,041	128,888

Source: República de Chile, Corporación de Fomento de la Producción, National Accounts, Annex XI of Agriculture and Transport Development Program (Santiago, Chile: CORFO, 1954), table 47.

TABLE 14.14

Average Annual Real Salary Earnings, Per Employee, By Industry, 1940-1952.
(1940 Chilean Pesos)

	1940	1941	1942	1943	1944	1945	1946	1947	1948	1949	1950	1951	1952
Agriculture	5,626	5,402	5,802	6,321	6,669	5,852	6,625	5,648	6,791	7,206	7,280	7,884	8,390
Mining	14,622	15,325	15,793	17,061	16,456	16,359	15,896	14,942	14,599	14,590	15,040	15,581	18,571
Industries	12,823	13,824	14,443	14,372	15,050	16,033	14,993	14,725	14,597	14,523	15,022	17,542	20,390
Fisheries	4,500	5,213	3,378	4,528	4,545	5,263	5,352	4,762	5,229	4,984	5,167	4,913	5,000
Construction	9,146	11,385	10,950	12,250	11,786	11,107	10,683	9,424	9,552	9,552	10,690	12,333	13,111
Transportation and Communications	10,990	10,693	11,807	11,145	10,591	12,122	12,892	12,955	12,747	10,616	11,874	12,909	15,184
Utilities	15,417	17,390	15,929	16,736	15,107	15,458	16,728	16,429	16,071	16,366	21,519	22,862	26,499
Commerce	9,169	11,427	11,058	12,281	11,850	11,151	10,712	9,472	9,503	9,591	10,722	12,459	13,311
Finance	14,393	14,960	16,140	17,525	18,517	19,060	18,392	18,458	18,806	20,060	20,397	21,905	23,310
Services	8,515	9,417	9,487	9,998	10,089	10,367	10,590	2,660	10,006	10,441	10,728	11,085	10,898
Central and Municipal Governments	11,577	13,500	11,821	12,014	11,980	13,238	12,906	13,342	11,927	13,871	18,548	15,750	19,781
All Industries, Per Employee	11,011	12,370	11,931	12,290	12,237	12,916	12,751	13,520	12,048	12,368	14,810	14,571	16,881

Source: República de Chile, Corporación de Fomento de la Producción, National Accounts, Annex XI of Agriculture and Transport Development Program (Santiago, Chile: CORFO, 1954), table 47-A.

Average Monthly Wages and Salaries, 1960-1977

Average monthly remunerations paid to blue- and white-collar workers between 1960 and 1977 are presented in Table 14.15. Also presented in Table 14.15 are the percentage variations in wages and salaries over the previous April and over a twelve-month period.

Average monthly remunerations paid to blue- and white-collar workers by sector (public utility services, mining, manufacturing, fiscal and semifiscal) for the period between 1960 and 1977 are presented in Table 14.16.

Indices of remunerations for white- and blue-collar workers for the period between 1960 and 1977 (April of 1959 = 100) are presented in Table 14.17. Combined indices for wages and salaries for public utility services, mining, manufacturing and the public sector for the period between 1960 and 1970 are presented in Table 14.18.

EARNINGS OF SELF-EMPLOYED

The unincorporated sector has played an eminent role in Chile's economic development. The proprietors of unincorporated enterprises, also referred to as self-employed, are considered as part of the capitalist class and their earnings are part of non-wage income. However, in Chile, as elsewhere, most of their earnings are remuneration for their labor and they do, quite often, earn "wages" often far below those earned in such industrial or mining subsectors as steel, petroleum and large-scale copper.

Earnings of Proprietors of Unincorporated Enterprises by Sector

Average annual nominal earnings of proprietors of unincorporated enterprises by sector and subsector between 1940 and 1952 are presented in Table 14.19. Average annual real earnings of proprietors of unincorporated enterprises by major sectors between 1940 and 1952 are presented in Table 14.20. Average real earnings of proprietors of unincorporated enterprises (or of self-employed or own-account workers) were below the real salaries per employee in all industries presented in Table 14.14 but at least twice as high as real wages per laborer in all industries in Table 14.2.

The incomes of self-employed workers (trabajadores por cuenta propia) subscribing to the social security service, by type of economic activity, between 1965 and 1977, are presented in Table 14.21.

MINIMUM EMPLOYMENT PROGRAM

The price stabilization, export and import liberalization, market- and private-enterprise based economic policies since 1973 have given rise to persistently high levels of unemployment in Santiago as well as in the provinces. The magnitude of the unemployment problem has been already examined in an earlier chapter. The last table of Chapter 14, i.e., Table 14.22, provides figures on the number of beneficiaries of the minimum employment program (programa del empleo minimo) introduced to alleviate some of the extreme suffering and poverty caused by the persistently high unemployment levels. Depending on the criterion used, the beneficiaries of the minimum unemployment program have been included with or excluded from the estimates of the unemployed. The figures of Table 14.22 are for 1975, 1976 and 1977 for the thirteen regions of Chile.

TABLE 14.15

Average Monthly Remunerations Paid to Blue- and White-Collar Workers, 1960-1977.

Period		Average Monthly Remunerations: Blue- and White-Collar Workers: Total	Blue- and White-Collar Workers: Percentage Variation: Over Previous Period	Blue- and White-Collar Workers: Percentage Variation: Over Previous April	Blue- and White-Collar Workers: Percentage Variation: Over 12 Months	Blue-Collar Workers: Total	Blue-Collar Workers: % Variation Over Previous Period	White-Collar Workers: Total	White-Collar Workers: % Variation Over Previous Period
						Chilean Escudos			
1960	April	91.34	-	-	-	66.77	-	144.08	-
1961	April	108.97	19.3	-	-	78.86	18.1	173.62	20.5
1962	April	123.86	13.7	-	-	89.00	12.9	198.54	14.4
1963	April	168.89	36.4	-	-	120.99	35.9	271.73	36.9
1964	April	227.03	34.4	-	-	169.17	39.8	351.25	29.3
1965	April	343.90	51.5	-	-	256.34	51.5	531.84	51.4
1966	April	465.99	35.5	-	-	348.81	36.1	717.52	34.9
1967	April	659.68	41.6	-	-	484.24	38.8	1,036.25	44.4
1968	April	799.69	21.2	-	-	626.46	29.4	1,171.54	13.1
1969	April	1,193.85	49.3	-	-	891.95	42.4	1,841.89	57.2
1970	April	1,748.30	46.4	-	-	1,279.02	43.4	2,755.62	49.6
1971	April	2,632.37	50.6	-	-	1,881.16	47.1	4,244.86	54.0
1972	April	3,658.49	39.0	-	-	2,804.34	49.1	5,491.90	29.4
1973	April	10,230.88	179.6	-	-	8,186.00	191.9	14,620.19	166.2
1974	April	67,146.65	556.3	-	-	51,563.18	529.9	100,596.53	588.1
						Pesos			
1975	April	338.76	404.5	-	-	246.08	377.2	537.69	434.5
1976	April	1,282.90	278.7	-	-	942.89	283.2	2,012.72	274.3
1977	April	3,617.21	182.0	-	-	2,656.88	181.8	5,678.59	182.1
1977	January	2,977.22	25.5	132.1	221.7	2,186.83	23.3	4,673.81	27.7
	April	3,617.21	21.5	182.0	182.0	2,656.88	21.5	5,678.59	21.5
	July	4,398.46	21.6	21.6	142.8	3,192.23	20.1	6,987.66	23.1
	October	4,614.63	4.9	27.6	94.5	3,396.30	6.4	7,229.79	3.5

Source: National Institute of Statistics.

TABLE 14.16

Average Monthly Remunerations Paid to Blue- and White-Collar Workers, By Sector, 1960-1977.

Period		Average Monthly Remunerations in the Sector Shown				
		Public Utility Services	Mining	Manufacturing	Fiscal	Semi-Fiscal
				Escudos		
1960	April	117.33	99.95	65.63	105.27	144.14
1961	April	146.50	120.86	76.10	123.84	177.05
1962	April	188.97	132.75	91.84	131.50	191.85
1963	April	253.27	189.80	124.29	199.68	241.65
1964	April	363.70	260.97	184.83	228.33	292.72
1965	April	503.19	379.08	262.15	365.63	506.41
1966	April	794.81	495.96	374.17	485.89	629.91
1967	April	1,158.18	782.81	473.78	802.94	886.89
1968	April	1,393.79	992.96	621.67	832.08	1,004.54
1969	April	2,277.46	1,467.06	861.92	1,401.23	1,547.50
1970	April	2,785.78	2,192.85	1,233.23	2,211.49	2,298.61
1971	April	4,580.04	3,397.30	1,776.00	3,286.95	3,568.30
1972	April	7,254.63	4,056.30	2,830.88	3,678.35	5,013.74
1973	April	17,804.97	12,130.01	8,490.22	10,660.51	11,773.23
1974	April	97,978.13	80,244.97	59,583.94	86,418.81	71,030.25
				Pesos		
1975	April	439.33	438.06	246.25	513.45	364.89
1976	April	1,857.05	1,615.26	976.65	1,808.88	1,357.61
1977	April	4,638.48	4,522.67	2,786.31	5,251.27	3,763.83
1977	January	3,920.46	3,708.59	2,310.63	4,282.27	3,069.35
	April	4,638.48	4,522.67	2,786.31	5,251.27	3,763.83
	July	5,555.77	5,271.13	3,368.76	6,564.65	4,726.67
	October	5,688.70	5,867.40	3,590.29	6,611.60	4,718.22

Note: This table shows average income per person derived from remunerations received by all workers in the various sectors included in the general salary index.

Source: National Institute of Statistics.

TABLE 14.17

Remuneration Indices of Blue- and White-Collar Workers, 1960-1977.

Period		Index of Wages and Salaries (April 1959=100): General				Blue-Collar Workers' Wages		White-Collar Workers' Salaries	
		Index	Variation (percentage)			Index	% Variation	Index	% Variation
			Over Previous Period	Over Previous April	Over 12 Months		Over Previous Period		Over Previous Period
1960	April	115.1	-	-	-	-	-	-	-
1961	April	132.5	15.1	-	-	-	-	-	-
1962	April	150.9	13.9	-	-	-	-	-	-
1963	April	205.7	36.3	-	-	260.5	-	210.5	-
1964	April	274.4	33.4	-	-	282.6	40.9	266.5	26.6
1965	April	422.6	54.0	-	-	432.5	53.0	413.0	55.0
1966	April	574.5	35.9	-	-	592.9	37.1	557.3	34.9
1967	April	817.2	42.2	-	-	816.5	37.7	817.8	46.7
1968	April	984.8	20.5	-	-	1,076.7	31.9	898.9	9.9
1969	April	1,478.4	50.1	-	-	1,510.0	40.2	1,448.8	61.2
1970	April	2,126.2	43.8	-	-	2,094.8	38.7	2,155.6	48.8
1971	April	3,253.5	53.0	-	-	3,184.3	52.0	3,318.2	53.9
1972	April	4,563.3	40.3	-	-	4,793.0	50.5	4,348.4	31.0
1973	April	12,601.8	176.2	-	-	13,878.1	189.5	11,408.0	162.3
1974	April[1]	8.1	546.2	-	-	8.4	508.3	7.9	589.4
1975	April	41.6	411.3	-	-	41.3	389.2	42.0	433.5
1976	April	158.6	280.9	-	-	158.7	284.4	158.4	277.7
1977	April	453.2	185.7	-	-	455.0	186.6	451.5	184.8
1977	January	373.1	27.0	135.2	227.7	375.8	25.2	370.6	28.8
	April	453.2	21.4	185.7	185.7	455.0	21.1	451.5	21.8
	July	553.4	22.1	22.1	146.2	548.2	20.5	558.2	23.6
	October	572.5	3.5	26.3	94.8	573.4	4.6	571.7	2.4

Note: 1. Starting in 1974 indices were simplified by 10,000 in order to facilitate reading, without altering the base. Variations have been calculated on the basis of original figures. These differ in some cases if calculated in respect of the simplified index.

Source: National Institute of Statistics.

TABLE 14.18

Index of Wages and Salaries by Sector, 1960-1977.

Period		Index of Wages and Salaries of Sector Indicated (Base April 1959=100)			
		Public Utility Services	Mining	Manufacturing	Public Sector[1]
1960	April	-	-	-	-
1961	April	-	-	-	-
1962	April	-	-	-	-
1963	April[2]	240.1	230.0	208.9	190.4
1964	April	344.9	317.4	310.7	231.5
1965	April	477.1	483.7	445.8	389.2
1966	April	753.7	630.2	640.9	496.1
1967	April	1,098.9	1,025.9	821.8	744.3
1968	April	1,321.6	1,376.2	1,082.4	813.2
1969	April	2,159.4	1,939.2	1,503.7	1,298.8
1970	April	2,641.4	2,677.4	2,110.8	1,979.4
1971	April	4,342.7	4,440.1	3,117.1	3,016.5
1972	April	6,878.6	5,405.5	4,927.8	3,876.1
1973	April	16,985.7	15,448.9	14,853.3	9,881.5
1974	April[3]	9.3	8.7	9.6	6.8
1975	April	41.7	53.6	43.8	37.7
1976	April	176.1	200.0	174.6	136.3
1977	April	439.8	609.9	500.7	386.9
1977	January	371.7	507.9	413.5	315.5
	April	439.8	609.9	500.7	386.9
	July	526.8	701.4	607.5	484.8
	October	539.4	737.4	646.2	486.2

Notes: 1. Formerly known as fiscal and semi-fiscal institutions.
2. According to law 15.163 of February 13, 1963 the wages and salaries of agriculture as well as those corresponding to the blue- and white-collar workers of the Large-Scale Mining Sector, of the Pacific Steel Company (CAP), of the National Petroleum Company (ENAP) and of the Pulp and Paper Manufacturing Companies were not included in the wage and salary index of the Chilean Housing Corporation (CORVI).
3. Starting in 1974 indices were simplified by ten thousand in order to facilitate reading of figures, without altering the base. Variations have been calculated on the basis of original figures. These, in some instances, differ if calculated in respect of the simplified index.

Source: National Institute of Statistics.

TABLE 14.19

Average Annual Nominal Earnings of Proprietors of Unincorporated Enterprises, By Industry, 1940-1952.
(Chilean Pesos)

	1940	1941	1942	1943	1944	1945	1946	1947	1948	1949	1950	1951	1952
Agriculture	8,554	10,267	13,892	17,557	20,697	23,164	26,000	34,770	41,796	52,811	61,436	81,329	105,703
Fisheries	5,975	7,439	8,958	9,934	11,135	13,018	15,956	19,358	23,801	28,602	33,114	39,010	47,405
Mining	10,168	12,154	16,502	20,840	24,561	27,437	30,832	41,245	49,560	62,547	72,772	96,373	125,257
Large Enterprises	11,364	11,628	16,216	21,212	20,000	27,273	30,303	41,860	48,936	62,500	72,549	95,918	125,862
Small and Medium Size Enterprises	10,133	12,170	16,513	20,830	24,712	27,442	30,848	41,221	49,587	62,549	72,784	96,391	125,226
Industries	7,297	9,056	11,158	13,559	16,504	18,529	21,558	29,345	32,726	40,826	47,116	65,995	86,013
Large Industries	10,194	12,240	16,475	20,828	24,505	27,474	30,707	41,250	49,542	65,692	73,710	103,243	134,552
Small Industries	7,157	8,914	10,882	13,224	16,151	18,149	21,274	28,971	32,067	39,793	46,021	64,462	84,016
Nonmetallic Mine Products	9,648	11,618	15,400	19,665	22,556	26,682	27,811	37.224	45.877	59,350	67,739		
Glass Products	10,000	12,069	15,493	20,130	23,313	26,554	29,457	40,260	48,125	63,077	70,659		
Machine and Metallic Products	9,094	11,202	14,714	18,293	21,393	23,855	29,086	37,758	44,495	56,472	62,912		
Chemical Products	9,540	11,531	16,124	18,835	24,858	25,684	26,910	37,024	45,454	59,298	61,232		
Textile-Mill Products	6,733	8,181	11,056	12,919	15,846	19,442	20,917	30,642	37,473	45,757	85,755		
Paper Products and Printing	11,231	12,465	16,041	20,559	24,189	27,244	30,376	40,300	49,152	64,815	74,876		
Leather and Rubber Products	9,336	12,141	16,402	20,756	24,101	26,866	30,614	38,371	45,777	60,135	66,829		
Lumber and Cork Products	7,511	9,864	11,880	14,458	16,380	18,925	21,296	27,343	35,927	45,796	54,630		
Musical Items	9,948	12,717	15,454	20,524	23,270	26,190	29,330	39,481	47,123	62,703	70,454		
Food Products	8,834	11,022	14,353	17,995	20,259	23,602	26,930	35,406	41,998	56,114	62,513		
Beverages	9,590	11,428	15,085	19,107	22,528	22,541	25,495	34,110	40,959	54,046	70,565		
Tobacco Manufactures	9,524	10,870	13,793	17,241	20,000	22,581	28,123	18,261	19,767	23,767	20,833		
Clothing	6,077	7,842	9,111	10,857	13,906	15,230	18,238	25,616	25,580	30,566	37,460		
Construction	26,147	20,519	27,082	33,197	41,663	41,361	51,631	51,060	68,838	75,989	90,365	107,556	136,415
Commerce	12,063	17,140	19,956	25,571	29,034	29,568	32,833	39,957	47,607	56,256	71,114	85,419	123,262
Finance and Insurance	18,340	21,047	23,442	30,807	31,901	37,805	45,806	55,837	59,467	62,620	74,786	87,279	110,596
Insurance Companies	18,675	21,682	24,098	31,200	32,360	39,183	48,156	58,466	61,820	64,440	74,773	86,918	108,866
Financial Institutions	16,438	17,450	19,737	28,571	29,299	30,000	32,515	40,964	46,154	52,326	74,857	89,326	121,547
Transportation and Communications	6,317	7,759	9,180	10,762	12,904	15,770	17,466	21,749	25,784	32,144	39,529	47,375	61,902

TABLE 14.19 (Cont'd)

Average Annual Nominal Earnings of Proprietors of Unincorporated Enterprises, By Industry, 1940-1952 .
(Chilean Pesos)

	1940	1941	1942	1943	1944	1945	1946	1947	1948	1949	1950	1951	1952
Services	7,843	10,403	13,373	17,224	19,484	20,915	23,367	29,480	36,433	46,001	55,441	68,275	88,901
Medical and Private Social Welfare	17,059	19,637	27,331	35,451	42,099	47,433	51,966	69,498	85,854	109,076	131,701	163,526	214,428
Domestic Service (Household)	11,602	14,136	19,095	25,923	27,982	31,679	35,565	47,200	57,088	72,181	90,210	110,702	144,089
Private Education	10,129	12,170	16,509	20,848	24,332	27,524	30,841	41,220	49,517	62,781	78,471	90,328	125,294
Hotels and Other Lodging Places	12,100	17,344	21,074	27,246	29,387	30,112	33,607	39,621	49,639	62,594	72,872	89,508	116,427
Miscellaneous	5,076	6,083	8,231	10,403	12,264	13,727	15,409	20,605	24,789	31,368	59,217	48,192	62,640
Per Proprietor	8,951	11,422	14,264	18,061	20,949	22,940	26,097	33,348	30,616	48,823	58,524	77,560	100,913

Source: República de Chile, Corporación de Fomento de la Producción, National Accounts. Annex XI of Agriculture and Transport Development Program (Santiago, Chile: CORFO, 1954), table 48.

TABLE 14.20

Average Annual Real Earnings of Proprietors of Unincorporated Enterprises, By Industry, 1940-1952.
(1940 Chilean Pesos)

	1940	1941	1942	1943	1944	1945	1946	1947	1948	1949	1950	1951	1952
Agriculture	8,554	8,913	9,600	10,432	11,009	11,322	10,959	10,979	11,185	11,900	12,020	13,017	13,845
Mining	10,168	10,519	11,334	12,353	13,078	13,448	12,929	12,996	13,292	14,139	14,257	15,432	16,390
Industries	7,297	7,863	7,698	8,057	8,773	9,056	9,069	9,266	8,757	9,199	9,219	10,563	11,266
Fisheries	5,975	6,449	6,196	5,848	5,919	6,356	6,704	6,101	6,360	6,436	6,473	6,242	6,206
Construction	25,147	17,810	18,721	19,718	22,157	20,217	21,721	16,120	18,425	17,125	17,744	17,810	18,134
Transportation and Communications	6,317	6,733	5,856	6,395	6,866	7,708	7,348	6,866	7,182	7,243	7,734	7,584	8,108
Commerce	12,063	14,878	13,791	15,195	14,912	14,452	13,812	12,616	12,740	12,676	13,914	15,272	16,145
Finance	18,340	18,228	16,222	18,270	17,001	18,480	19,263	17,647	15,911	14,148	14,666	13,989	14,487
Services	7,822	8,008	9,219	10,211	10,341	10,200	9,809	9,282	8,729	10,344	10,826	10,806	11,622
Total	8,982	9,912	9,897	10,728	11,138	11,212	10,981	10,332	10,605	11,007	11,368	12,275	12,988

Source: República de Chile, Corporación de Fomento de la Producción, National Accounts, Annex XI of Agriculture and Transport Development Program (Santiago, Chile: CORFO, 1954), table 49-A.

TABLE 14.21

Incomes of Self-Employed Workers Subscribing to the Social Security Service, by Type of Economic Activity, 1965-1977.[1]

Year and Month	Incomes Declared by Self-employed Workers									
	Total	Economic Activity								
		Agricul-ture	Mining	Manufact-uring Industry	Construc-tion	Electricity, Gas, Water, Sanitary Services	Trade	Transport-ation and Communica-tions	Domestic Services	Not Specified
	(In Millions of Escudos)									
1965	47.8	3.2	1.2	7.1	0.2	-	29.5	0.2	0.1	6.3
1966	76.6	6.8	1.5	12.3	0.3	-	44.8	0.3	-	10.6
1967	159.0	18.3	2.1	30.5	0.8	0.1	85.0	0.6	-	21.6
1968	222.8	16.2	2.3	44.9	1.8	-	125.1	0.5	0.2	31.8
1969	252.4	16.1	4.3	50.6	1.2	0.1	142.6	0.7	0.1	36.7
1970	275.8	19.6	6.4	33.9	1.6	-	163.2	0.8	0.1	50.2
1971	405.2	26.9	8.0	82.0	2.9	-	213.3	1.3	0.5	70.3
1972	592.4	38.4	12.5	124.2	2.5	1.6	265.7	4.6	2.3	140.6
1973	1,482.8	90.5	37.6	305.4	6.5	4.2	586.3	6.9	6.0	439.4
1974	16,936.4	1,222.7	370.2	3,852.4	176.5	19.5	6,828.8	137.6	12.0	4,316.7
	(In Thousands of Pesos)									
1975	72,098.0	5,159.3	1,529.9	16,279.0	731.1	209.8	29,227.1	549.4	47.6	18,364.8
1976	241,709.9	16,957.2	4,095.1	53,348.4	1,445.6	11.4	100,128.9	1,679.3	-	64,044.0
1977	588,165.6	68,516.2	6,557.2	140,774.8	2,303.0	-	190,513.3	4,919.2	-	174,581.9
January	45,960.1	5,101.6	1,286.9	9,789.5	137.9	-	16,683.5	91.9	-	12,868.8
February	31,836.1	3,533.8	891.4	6,781.1	95.5	-	11,556.5	63.7	-	8,914.1
March	40,660.1	4,513.3	1,138.5	8,660.6	122.0	-	14,759.6	81.3	-	11,384.8
April	40,992.9	5,001.1	246.0	11,068.1	164.0	-	13,322.7	491.9	-	10,699.1
May	45,753.0	5,581.9	274.5	12,353.3	183.0	-	14,869.7	549.0	-	11,941.6
June	57,433.4	7,006.9	344.6	15,507.0	229.7	-	18,665.9	689.2	-	14,990.1
July	42,740.0	5,214.0	256.0	11,540.0	171.0	-	13,891.0	513.0	-	11,155.0
August	58,653.0	6,592.0	476.0	13,315.0	219.0	-	18,563.0	696.0	-	18,792.0
September	56,189.0	6,545.6	564.3	12,927.2	240.9	-	17,359.4	713.2	-	17,838.4
October	53,261.0	6,392.0	325.0	11,402.0	172.0	-	16,394.0	682.0	-	17,894.0
November	61,899.0	7,175.0	362.0	15,019.0	384.0	-	18,860.0	126.0	-	19,973.0
December	52,788.0	5,859.0	392.0	12,412.0	184.0	-	15,588.0	222.0	-	18,131.0

Note: 1. This table does not include wages in the form of subsidies.

Source: Social Security Service and National Institute of Statistics.

TABLE 14.22

Beneficiaries of the Minimum Employment Program, by Regions. 1975-1977.

	Total	Beneficiaries of the Minimum Employment Program								
				REGIONS						
		Other Agree-ments	Total for Regions	First Tarapacá	Second Antofagasta	Third Atacama	Fourth Coquimbo	Fifth Valparaíso	Sixth O'Higgins
1975									
March	19,041	-	19,041	376	376	376	2,162	2,486	493
April	19,041	-	19,041	376	376	376	2,162	2,486	493
May	41,690	-	41,690	1,875	648	938	3,125	4,010	781
June	41,690	-	41,690	1,875	648	938	3,125	4,010	781
July	68,388	-	68,388	2,549	948	873	3,144	11,523	1,435
August	83,367	-	83,367	3,126	1,671	1,080	3,784	16,494	2,470
September	97,460	-	97,460	3,743	2,544	1,133	4,111	18,956	2,659
October	109,003	-	109,003	4,073	3,554	1,168	4,253	23,194	2,632
November	120,861	-	120,861	4,876	3,305	1,166	4,565	27,634	2,369
December	126,411		126,411	5,263	4,117	1,132	4,622	28,716	1,800
1976									
January	124,047	-	124,047	5,988	4,394	1,173	4,897	26,813	1,540
February	125,848	-	125,848	6,132	4,653	1,182	4,897	27,878	2,135
March	131,082	-	131,082	5,339	5,058	1,202	4,915	29,247	2,196
April	136,917	-	136,917	5,845	5,593	1,230	5,000	30,788	2,185
May	147,949	-	147,949	6,012	6,318	1,276	5,151	32,481	2,308
June	157,312	-	157,312	6,148	6,890	1,340	5,275	34,174	2,894
July	159,186	-	159,186	6,031	7,029	1,463	5,440	35,596	3,092
August	169,101	-	169,101	5,493	7,170	1,728	5,537	37,990	3,369
September	178,139	-	178,139	5,617	7,423	1,775	6,899	38,326	3,599
October	187,031	-	187,031	5,790	7,554	1,808	7,678	43,480	3,539
November	189,710	-	189,710	5,837	7,836	1,798	7,882	44,673	3,360
December	187,702	-	187,702	5,451	6,810	1,761	7,722	46,634	3,044
1977									
January	198,187	11,700	186,487	4,987	6,287	1,779	8,260	40,129	3,494
February	192,840	10,918	181,922	4,729	6,356	1,713	8,334	38,148	3,270
March	188,825	10,528	178,297	4,674	6,932	1,756	8,247	36,630	3,121
April	188,741	10,325	178,416	4,886	7,345	1,745	8,400	36,186	3,243
May	186,102	9,878	176,224	5,111	7,006	1,713	8,259	37,313	3,482
June	187,134	9,895	177,239	5,175	7,092	1,724	8,663	38,502	3,726
July	189,235	10,136	179,099	5,068	7,060	1,738	9,221	39,075	3,903
August	192,012	10,110	181,902	5,167	6,946	1,740	10,416	39,467	4,605
September	189,993	10,662	179,331	4,729	6,827	1,766	10,469	39,106	4,095
October	186,896	10,648	176,248	4,602	6,893	1,741	10,250	37,511	3,513
November	178,600	10,627	167,973	4,107	6,740	1,754	10,019	36,096	3,151
December	173,238	10,530	162,708	3,790	6,549	1,744	9,765	34,210	2,976

TABLE 14.22 (Cont'd)

Beneficiaries of the Minimum Employment Program, by Regions. 1975-1977.

	Beneficiaries of the Minimum Employment Program						
	REGIONS						
	Seventh Maule	Eighth Bío-Bío	Ninth Araucania	Tenth Los Lagos	Eleventh Aysen of General Carlos Ibañez	Twelfth Magallanes and Chilean Antartic	Santiago Metropolitan Region
1975							
March	1,021	3,754	823	1,959	249	218	4,748
April	1,021	3,754	823	1,959	249	218	4,748
May	2,031	6,041	1,667	5,209	417	365	14,583
June	2,031	6,041	1,667	5,209	417	365	14,583
July	7,082	8,918	1,525	7,853	584	671	21,283
August	5,224	10,127	2,371	10,757	846	716	24,701
September	6,777	11,876	3,153	13,582	1,200	1,104	26,622
October	7,264	14,058	3,792	14,830	1,384	1,163	27,638
November	7,416	16,164	5,124	16,620	2,049	1,225	28,348
December	6,790	17,003	6,700	18,424	1,917	1,219	28,708
1976							
January	6,692	16,045	6,694	18,800	2,055	1,113	27,843
February	5,266	16,256	7,279	18,993	2,066	1,023	28,088
March	6,469	17,012	7,433	20,768	2,100	980	28,363
April	7,056	17,263	8,058	19,169	2,086	1,072	31,572
May	7,706	18,905	9,386	19,879	2,210	1,227	35,090
June	7,799	21,197	10,845	20,619	2,184	1,451	36,496
July	7,956	20,801	11,170	20,056	2,443	1,769	36,340
August	8,308	22,519	12,432	22,246	2,392	1,984	37,933
September	8,559	23,696	13,252	25,761	2,459	2,073	38,700
October	8,774	24,138	14,313	26,225	2,390	2,100	39,242
November	8,055	25,269	14,759	26,701	2,043	1,910	39,587
December	7,483	24,371	14,664	26,707	1,643	1,675	39,737
1977							
January	6,748	23,526	17,241	30,913	1,863	1,523	39,737
February	6,661	22,867	16,041	30,924	1,755	1,362	39,762
March	6,420	22,839	15,606	29,400	1,654	1,177	39,841
April	6,640	22,339	15,385	30,000	1,407	991	39,849
May	6,899	21,596	14,809	29,270	1,513	939	38,314
June	7,017	21,344	15,484	29,748	1,523	946	36,295
July	7,133	21,357	15,738	30,292	1,630	962	35,922
August	7,326	21,631	15,870	30,384	1,678	925	35,747
September	7,435	21,163	15,336	30,771	1,656	855	35,123
October	7,426	21,695	15,286	31,217	1,593	756	33,765
November	7,079	19,596	14,843	30,247	1,508	658	32,175
December	6,983	19,194	14,673	29,936	1,586	605	30,697

Source: Ministry of Interior, Division of Community Services and Social Development, Chile.

15
HEALTH AND SOCIAL SECURITY

INTRODUCTION

The issues of private and public health, social security and welfare are central to the overall theme of economic development. Public and private health as well as public and private security and welfare affect the productivity of labor, determine the smoothness with which labor markets operate, are shaped by and shape both income distribution and capital formation and ultimately determine the structure and efficiency of production. Because of space limitations, only selected issues can be discussed and only a limited number of tables can be presented in this chapter. Because public health is so intimately related to deaths and causes of death, the first two sections of the chapter deal with these issues. In the third section the calorie and protein input of the Chilean population is presented. Statistics pertaining to Chile's National Health Service are presented in the fourth section.

Background information on health and social security in Chile between 1960 and 1970 can be found in ODEPLAN, 1971-76, Plan de la Economía Nacional: Antecedentes Sobre el Desarrollo Chileno-1960-70 (Santiago, Chile: ODEPLAN, 1971), pp. 308-321, 336-360. A comprehensive list of laws covering Chile's social security service is found in Departamento de Derecho del Trabajo y Seguridad Social, Universidad Católica de Chile, Guia de Leyes del Servicio Seguro Social (Santiago, Chile: Oficina Coordinadora de Investigación "Profesor Jaime Eyzaguirre, 1975), pp. 1-206.

Scholars interested in more detailed primary information concerning health than that presented in this chapter will find it in the following publications of the Ministry of Health: (1) Anuario (annual publication) Atenciones y Recursos, which contains statistics on medical and dental attention by physicians, nurses, midwifes and assistants, birth control assistance, level of nutrition by age and regions, diagnostic tests and laboratory examinations, milk distribution and so forth. (2) Anuario (annual publication) Accidentes del Trabajo y Enfermedades Profesionales which provides detailed statistical data on work accidents by region and type of economic activity, work accidents by type of disability (tipo de incapacidad), of accident occurrence according to day of week, by diagnostic group and so forth. (3) Anuario (annual publication) Defunciones y Causes de Muerte which supplies statistics on causes of death by location (region and province), by type of certification (medical, in or outside hospital or none), by sex and age, by month of occurrence, and so forth. (4) Anuario (annual publication) Enfermedades de Notificación Obligatoria, which provides detailed statistics of illnesses as causes of death for diseases for which medical notification is obligatory.

Deaths and Death Rates by Cause

Deaths and death rates by cause according to the 1955 revision of the abbreviated list of 50 causes for tabulation of mortality of the international statistical classification of diseases, injuries and causes of death is presented in Table 15.1. Death and death rates by cause according to the 1965 classification for the period between 1968 and 1972 are presented in Table 15.2.

General deaths according to cause according to the intermediate list of 150 causes for the period between 1964 and 1975 are presented in Table 15.3.

Tendencies and Causes of Mortality: 1955-1975

General and infant mortality in Chile have been already examined in Chapter 3. In the present chapter the emphasis is on public health and causes of death. Infant and general mortality tendencies, therefore, are examined here as they relate to public health and causes of death.

A comprehensive examination of infant mortality in Chile between 1930 and 1960 is found in Hugo Behm Rosas, Mortalidad Infantil y Nivel de Vida (Santiago, Chile: Universidad de Chile, 1962), pp. 1-134. In addition to an extensive methodological discussion, Behm analyzes the causes, trends and implications of Chile's infant mortality.

Also useful is the study of Hugo Behm, "Recent Mortality Trends in Chile" in Vital and Health Statistics, Series 3, Number 2. National Center for Health Statistics. U. S. Department of Health and Welfare. Washington, D.C. April 1964. Pp. 1-33.

The research on infant mortality between 1930 and 1960 by Hugo Behm has been brought up to date by Erica Taucher in two studies: (a) Erica Taucher, Chile: Mortalidad desde 1955 a 1975. Tendencias y Causas (Santiago, Chile: CELADE, September of 1978), pp. 1-83 and (b) Erica Taucher, "La Mortalidad en Chile desde 1955 a 1975: Tendencias y Causas" in Notas de Población, Revista Latinoamericana de Demografía, CELADE, Año VI, Diciembre de 1978, Nº18, pp. 113-142.

Mortality levels as well as the structure of mortality by cause of death have shown major improvements in Chile between 1955 and 1975. Even so, however, Chilean indices of mortality reduction are still far behind those of developed countries.

The paper by Taucher (1978b) suggests actions to achieve further reductions in mortality by drawing conclusions from past experience. After an analysis of the reliability of available statistics, Taucher is able through a description of mortality trends by age, sex and cause to identify those groups which were the main contributors to the reduction in mortality levels.

The Taucher analysis of the evolution of mortality and its structure by causes has two fundamental objectives: (a) to try and explain changes which have taken place in mortality rates between 1955 and 1975 and (b) to present information in such a manner that it can be used to direct action towards reducing mortality.

After reviewing the earlier studies on mortality, Erica Taucher decided to classify causes of death in a manner that would permit her to explain mortality changes in terms of contributing factors. As a first step, causes of death were divided into avoidable and unavoidable. In turn, avoidable deaths were grouped into the following four categories using as a criterion the actions that would most effectively lead to their reduction or elimination: (a) vaccines or preventive treatment; (b) advance medical diagnosis and treatment; (c) improvement in sanitary conditions; (d) combined actions. The remaining deaths were classified into (e) hardly avoidable with the present state of knowledge and technological development; (f) deaths due to ill-defined causes; (g) other.

Taucher's major tables and conclusions are presented below.

The structure by age at time of occurrence of expected, observed and avoided deaths and death rates observed in 1955-1956 and in 1974-1975 is presented in Table 15.4.

TABLE 15.1

Deaths and Death Rates by Cause According to 1955 Classification. 1952-1967[1].

Abbr. List Number	Causes of Death[7]	1952 Number	1952 Rate	1953 Number	1953 Rate	1954 Number	1954 Rate	1956 Number	1956 Rate
All	causes	81,966		80,068	1,263.7	84,519	1,281.2	84,199	1,212.6
B 1	Tuberculosis of respiratory system (001-008)	5,769		4,275	67.5	4,068	61.7	3,701	53.3
B 2	Tuberculosis, other forms (010-019)	1,027		667	10.5	540	8.2	516	7.4
B 3	Syphilis and its sequelae (020-029)	263		203	3.2	252	3.8	199	2.9
B 4	Typhoid fever (040)	323		214	3.4	207	3.1	199	2.9
B 5	Cholera (043)	-		-	-	-	-	-	-
B 6	Dysentery, all forms (045-048)	52		46	0.7	70	1.1	84	1.2
B 7	Scarlet fever and streptococcal sore throat (050-051)	8		34	0.5	17	0.3	16	0.2
B 8	Diphtheria (055)	177		144	2.3	178	2.7	167	2.4
B 9	Whooping cough (056)	745		489	7.7	535	8.1	756	10.9
B10	Meningococcal infections (057)	22		20	0.3	21	0.3	14	0.2
B11	Plague (058)	-		-	-	-	-	-	-
B12	Acute poliomyelitis (030)	98		86	1.4	100	1.5	120	1.7
B13	Smallpox (084)	-		2	0.0	4	0.1	1	0.0
B14	Measles (085)	273		498	7.9	785	11.9	579	8.3
B15	Typhus and other rickettsial diseases (100-108)	14		40	0.6	67	1.0	64	0.9
B16	Malaria (110-117)	-		-	-	-	-	-	-
B17	All other diseases classified as infective and parasitic (030-039, 041, 042, 049, 052-054, 059-074, 081-083, 086-096, 120-138)	571		565	8.0	680	10.3	634	9.1
B18	Malignant neoplasms, including neoplasms of lymphatic and haematopoietic tissues (140-205)	5,282		5,484	86.6	5,949	90.2	6,602	95.1
B19	Benign neoplasms and neoplasms of unspecified nature (210-239)	137		160	2.5	178	2.7	190	2.7
B20	Diabetes mellitus (260)	316		383	6.0	425	6.4	440	6.3
B21	Anaemias (290-293)	174		190	3.0	173	2.6	145	2.1
B22	Vascular lesions affecting central nervous system (330-334)	3,205		3,025	47.7	3,918	59.4	4,201	60.5
B23	Non-meningococcal meningitis (340)	1,182		755	11.9	513	7.8	573	8.3
B24	Rheumatic fever (400-402)	-		139	2.2	106	1.6	101	1.5
B25	Chronic rheumatic heart disease (410-416)	328		307	4.8	459	7.0	486	7.0
B26	Arteriosclerotic and degenerative heart disease (420-422)	1,884[3]		2,294	36.2	2,690	40.8	3,078	44.3
B27	Other diseases of heart (430-434)	7,736		5,755	90.8	1,627	24.7	1,578	22.7
B28	Hypertension with heart disease (440-443)			695	11.0	736	11.2	844	12.2
B29	Hypertension without mention of heart (444-447)	142		323	5.1	536	8.1	448	6.5
B30	Influenza (480-483)	965		1,464	23.1	1,249	18.9	973	14.0
B31	Pneumonia (490-493)	14,028		14,977	236.4	15,107	229.0	15,095	217.4

TABLE 15.1 (Cont'd)

Deaths and Death Rates by Cause According to 1955 Classification. 1952-1967.

Abbr. List Number	Causes of Death	1952		1953		1954		1956	
		Number	Rate	Number	Rate	Number	Rate	Number	Rate
B32	Bronchitis (500-502)	182		130	2.1	197	3.0	250	3.6
B33	Ulcer of stomach and duodenum (540-541)	241		222	3.5	255	3.9	258	3.7
B34	Appendicitis (550-553)	53		75	1.2	83	1.3	64	0.9
B35	Intestinal obstruction and hernia (560, 561, 570)	357		352	5.6	423	6.4	476	6.9
B36	Gastritis, duodenitis, enteritis, and colitis, except diarrhoea of the newborn (543, 571, 572)	3,063		2,409	38.0	2,473	37.5	2,468	35.5
B37	Cirrhosis of liver (581)	956		822	13.0	1,135	17.2	1,659	23.9
B38	Nephritis and nephrosis (590-594)	1,111		947	14.9	772	11.7	757	10.9
B39	Hyperplasia of prostate (610)	88		88	1.4	131	2.0	152	2.2
B40	Deliveries and complications of pregnancy, childbirth, and the puerperium (640-689)	706		725	11.4	764	11.6	743	10.7
B41	Congenital malformations (750-759)	319		366	5.8	786	11.9	594	8.6
B42	Birth injuries, postnatal asphyxia and atelectasis (760-762)	1,113		1,265	20.0	1,429	21.7	1,384	19.9
B43	Infections of the newborn (763-768)	2,965		2,492	39.3	2,286	34.7	2,738	39.4
B44	Other diseases peculiar to early infancy, and immaturity unqualified (769-776)	6,816		9,486	149.7	9,422	142.8	8,489	122.3
B45	Senility without mention of psychosis, ill-defined and unknown causes (780-795)	5,489[2]		6,577	103.8	10,572	160.3	9,168	132.0
B46	All other diseases (residual)	9,440[3]		5,965	94.1	7,269	110.2	7,635	110.0
BE47	Motor vehicle accidents (E810-E835)			129	2.0	216	3.3	3,037	43.7
BE48	All other accidents (E800-E802, E840-E962)	3,528		3,986	62.9	4,613	69.9	310	4.5
BE49	Suicide and self-inflicted injury (E963, E970-E979)			279	4.4	317	4.8	182	2.6
BE50	Homicide and operations of war (E964, E965, E980-E999)	818		519	8.2	186	2.8	2,031	29.3

TABLE 15.1 (Cont'd)

Deaths and Death Rates by Cause According to 1955 Classification. 1952-1967.

Abbr.List Number	Causes of Death	1957		1959		1960		1961	
		Number	Rate	Number	Rate	Number	Rate	Number	Rate
All	causes	91,506	1,285.1	91,348	1,150.8	95,486	1,241.9	91,348	1,162.5
B 1	Tuberculosis of respiratory system (001-008)	3,782	53.1	3,644	45.9	3,727	48.5	3,644	46.4
B 2	Tuberculosis, other forms (010-019)	405	5.7	360	4.5	313	4.1	360	4.6
B 3	Syphilis and its sequelae (020-029)	164	2.3	166	2.1	173	2.2	166	2.1
B 4	Typhoid fever (040)	221	3.1	170	2.1	193	2.5	170	2.2
B 5	Cholera (043)	-	-	-	-	-	-	-	-
B 6	Dysentery, all forms (045-048)	89	1.2	108	1.4	89	1.2	108	1.4
B 7	Scarlet fever and streptococcal sore throat (050-051)	14	0.2	40	0.5	22	0.3	40	0.5
B 8	Diphtheria (055)	168	2.4	333	4.2	415	5.4	333	4.2
B 9	Whooping cough (056)	468	6.6	189	2.4	362	4.7	189	2.4
B10	Meningococcal infections (057)	13	0.2	42	0.5	23	0.3	42	0.5
B11	Plague (058)	-	-	-	-	-	-	-	-
B12	Acute poliomyelitis (030)	81	1.1	119	1.5	117	1.5	119	1.5
B13	Smallpox (084)	-	-	-	-	-	-	-	-
B14	Measles (085)	986	13.8	1,904	24.0	2,052	26.7	1,904	24.2
B15	Typhus and other rickettsial diseases (100-108)	52	0.7	6	0.1	64	0.8	6	0.1
B16	Malaria (110-117)	-	-	-	-	-	-	-	-
B17	All other diseases classified as infective and parasitic (030-039, 041, 042, 049, 052-054, 059-074, 081-083, 086-096, 120-138)	647	9.1	607	7.6	700	9.1	607	7.7
B18	Malignant neoplasms, including neoplasms of lymphatic and haematopoietic tissues (140-205)	6,837	96.0	7,704	97.1	7,652	99.5	7,704	98.0
B19	Benign neoplasms and neoplasms of unspecified nature (210-239)	181	2.5	204	2.6	190	2.5	204	2.6
B20	Diabetes mellitus (260)	519	7.3	610	7.7	556	9.2	610	7.8
B21	Anaemias (290-293)	140	2.0	128	1.6	136	1.8	128	1.6
B22	Vascular lesions affecting central nervous system (330-334)	4,007	56.3	4,498	56.7	4,485	58.3	4,498	57.2
B23	Non-meningococcal meningitis (340)	480	6.7	689	3.7	620	8.1	689	8.8
B24	Rheumatic fever (400-402)	95	1.3	83	1.0	70	0.9	83	1.1
B25	Chronic rheumatic heat disease (410-416)	500	7.0	436	5.5	471	6.1	436	5.5
B26	Arteriosclerotic and degenerative heart disease (420-422)	3,235	45.4	4,181	52.7	3,767	49.0	4,181	53.2
B27	Other disease of heart (430-434)	1,605	22.5	1,584	20.0	1,665	21.7	1,584	20.2
B28	Hypertension with heart disease (440-443)	688	9.7	804	10.1	756	9.8	804	10.2
B29	Hypertension without mention of heart (444-447)	448	6.3	270	3.4	251	3.3	270	3.4
B30	Influenza (480-483)	4,702	66.0	1,602	20.2	1,512	19.7	1,602	20.4

TABLE 15.1 (Cont'd)

Deaths and Death Rates by Cause According to 1955 Classification. 1952-1967.

Abbr.List Number	Causes of Death	1957 Number	1957 Rate	1959 Number	1959 Rate	1960 Number	1960 Rate	1961 Number	1961 Rate
B31	Pneumonia (490-493)	16,719	234.8	15,759	198.5	16,820	218.8	15,759	200.5
B32	Bronchitis (500-502)	311	4.4	599	7.5	669	8.7	599	7.6
B33	Ulcer of stomach and duodenum (540, 541)	258	3.6	282	3.6	288	3.7	282	3.6
B34	Appendicitis (550-553)	73	1.0	100	1.3	97	1.3	100	1.3
B35	Intestinal obstruction and hernia (560, 561, 570)	506	7.1	526	6.6	501	6.5	526	6.7
B36	Gastritis, duodenitis, enteritis, and colitis, except diarrhoea of the newborn (543, 571, 572)	2,606	36.6	4,655	58.6	4,867	63.3	4,655	59.2
B37	Cirrhosis of liver (581)	1,378	19.4	1,944	24.5	1,984	25.8	1,944	24.7
B38	Nephritis and nephrosis (590-594)	726	10.2	736	9.3	755	9.8	736	9.4
B39	Hyperplasia of prostate (610)	152	2.1	214	2.7	212	45.3	214	-
B40	Deliveries and complications of pregnancy, childbirth, and the puerperium (640-689)	736	10.3	870	11.0	789	21.0	870	21.5[4]
B41	Congenital malformations (750-759)	590	8.3	747	9.4	719	9.4	747	9.5
B42	Birth injuries, postnatal asphyxia and atelectasis (760-762)	1,496	21.0	1,747	22.0	1,583	577.0[5]	1,747	616.3[5]
B43	Infections of the newborn (763-768)	2,804	39.4	3,443	43.4	3,352	1,221.7[5]	3,443	1,214.7[5]
B44	Other diseases peculiar to early infancy, and immaturity unqualified (769-776)	11,068	155.4	7,495	94.4	9,293	3,387.0[5]	7,495	2,644.3[5]
B45	Senility without mention of psychosis, ill-defined and unknown causes (780-795)	8,103	113.8	7,378	92.9	8,381	109.0	7,378	93.9
B46	All other diseases (residual)	7,757	108.9	7,954	100.2	8,068	104.9	7,954	101.2
BE47	Motor vehicle accidents (E810-E835)	496	7.0	695	8.8	670	8.7	695	8.8
BE48	All other accidents (E800-E802, E840-E962)	4,306	60.5	4,673	58.9	5,111	66.5	4,673	59.5
BE49	Suicide and self-inflicted injury (E963, E970-E979)	546	7.7	613	7.7	571	7.4	613	7.8
BE50	Homocide and operations of war (E964, E965, E980-E999)	348	4.9	437	5.5	375	4.9	437	5.6

TABLE 15.1 (Cont'd)

Deaths and Death Rates by Cause According to 1955 Classification.
1952-1967.

Abbr.List Number	Causes of Death	1962		1963		1964		1965	
		Number	Rate	Number	Rate	Number	Rate[2]	Number	Rate
All	causes	94,874	1,181.6	98,293	1,196.3	94,058	1,120.9	91,648	1,052.5
B 1	Tuberculosis of respiratory system (001-008)	3,572	44.5	3,942	48.0	3,405	40.6	3,182	36.5
B 2	Tuberculosis, other forms (010-019)	326	4.1	298	3.6	303	3.6	320	3.7
B 3	Syphilis and its sequelae (020-029)	119	1.5	128	1.6	106	1.3	131	1.5
B 4	Typhoid fever (040)	209	2.6	135	1.6	143	1.7	134	1.5
B 5	Cholera (043)	-	-	-	-	-	-	-	-
B 6	Dysentery, all forms (045-048)	41	0.5	28	0.3	50	0.6	56	0.6
B 7	Scarlet fever and streptococcal sore throat (050-051)	25	0.3	28	0.3	15	0.2	22	0.3
B 8	Diphtheria (055)	351	4.4	259	3.2	154	1.8	121	1.4
B 9	Whooping cough (056)	116	2.1	368	4.5	288	3.4	324	3.7
B10	Meningococcal infections (057)	5	0.1	14	0.2	35	0.4	16	0.2
B11	Plague (058)	-	-	-	-	-	-	-	-
B12	Acute poliomyelitis (030)	103	1.3	26	0.3	68	0.8	52	0.6
B13	Smallpox (084)	-	-	-	-	-	-	-	-
B14	Measles (085)	2,341	29.2	2,169	26.4	3,120	37.2	1,152	13.2
B15	Typhus and other rickettsial diseases (100-108)	10	0.1	14	0.2	22	0.3	62	0.7
B16	Malaria (110-117)	-	-	-	-	-	-	-	-
B17	All other diseases classified as infective and parasitic (030-039, 041, 042, 049, 052-054, 059-074, 081-083, 086-096, 120-138)	554	6.9	596	7.3	613	7.3	777	8.9
B18	Malignant neoplasms, including neoplasms of lymphatic and haematopoietic tissues (140-205)	7,835	97.6	8,283	100.8	8,447	100.7	8,547	98.2
B19	Benign neoplasms and neoplasms of unspecified nature (210-239)	358	4.5	291	3.5	186	2.2	224	2.6
B20	Diabetes mellitus (260)	586	7.3	666	8.1	568	6.8	593	6.8
B21	Anaemias (290-293)	138	1.7	115	1.4	153	1.8	200	2.3
B22	Vascular lesions affecting central nervous system (330-334)	4,486	55.9	4,991	60.7	5,035	60.0	5,335	61.3
B23	Non-meningococcal meningitis (340)	743	9.3	613	7.5	797	9.5	810	9.3
B24	Rheumatic fever (400-402)	81	1.0	50	0.6	27	0.3	18	0.2
B25	Chronic rheumatic heart disease (410-416)	389	4.8	494	6.0	422	5.0	479	5.5
B26	Arteriosclerotic and degenerative heart disease (420-422)	4,987	62.1	5,383	65.5	6,139	73.2	6,396	73.5
B27	Other disease of heart (430-434)	1,474	18.4	2,066	25.1	2,183	26.0	1,845	21.2
B28	Hypertension with heart disease (440-443)	351	4.4	581	7.1	628	7.5	711	8.2
B29	Hypertension without mention of heart (444-447)	325	4.0	392	4.8	256	3.1	270	3.1
B30	Influenza (480-483)	937	11.7	4,266	51.9	1,252	14.9	1,845	21.2
B31	Pneumonia (490-493)	15,953	198.7	14,905	181.4	14,053	167.5	13,418	154.1

TABLE 15.1 (Cont'd)

Deaths and Death Rates by Cause According to 1955 Classification.
1952-1967.

Abbr. List Number	Causes of Death	1962		1963		1964		1965	
		Number	Rate	Number	Rate	Number	Rate	Number	Rate
B32	Bronchitis (500-502)	481	6.0	715	8.7	581	6.9	905	10.4
B33	Ulcer of stomach and duodenum (540, 541)	277	3.4	321	3.9	297	3.5	290	3.3
B34	Appendicitis (550-553)	85	1.1	100	1.2	105	1.3	99	1.1
B35	Intestinal obstruction and hernia (560, 561, 570)	763	9.5	518	6.3	518	6.2	533	6.1
B36	Gastritis, duodenitis, enteritis, and colitis, except diarrhoea of the newborn (543, 571, 572)	7,413	92.3	6,001	73.0	5,344	63.7	5,317	61.1
B37	Cirrhosis of liver (581)	2,737	34.1	3,528	42.9	3,132	37.3	2,533	29.1
B38	Nephritis and nephrosis (590-594)	685	8.5	730	8.9	807	9.6	726	8.3
B39	Hyperplasia of prostate (610)	152	1.9	218	-	182	2.2	224	41.3[6]
B40	Deliveries and complications of pregnancy, childbirth, and the puerperium (640-689)	787	9.8	733	17.5[4]	721	8.6	787	...
B41	Congenital malformations (750-759)	694	8.6	729	8.9	695	8.3	956	11.0
B42	Birth injuries, postnatal asphyxia and atelectasis (760-762)	1,891	23.6	2,019	728.5[5]	2,008	23.9	1,947	709.1
B43	Infections of the newborn (763-768)	3,602	44.9	3,747	1,352.0[5]	3,976	47.4	3,567	1,299.1
B44	Other diseases peculiar to early infancy, and immaturity unqualified (769-776)	5,689	70.9	4,976	1,795.5[5]	5,982	71.3	5,187	1,889.1
B45	Senility without mention of psychosis, ill-defined and unknown causes (780-795)	8,311	103.5	7,540	91.8	6,806	81.1	7,070	81.2
B46	All other diseases (residual)	8,278	103.1	8,524	103.7	7,709	91.9	7,314	84.0
BE47	Motor vehicle accidents (E810-E835)	438	5.5			485	5.8	7,153	82.1
BE48	All other accidents (E800-E802, E840-E962)	5,456	68.0	6,793	82.7	5,799	69.1	-	0.0
BE49	Suicide and self-inflicted injury (E963, E970-E979)	529	6.6			249	3.0	-	0.0
BE50	Homicide and operations of war (E964, E965, E980-E999)	141	1.8			194	2.3	-	0.0

TABLE 15.1 (Cont'd)

Deaths and Death Rates by Cause According to 1955 Classification. 1952-1967.

Abbr.List Number	Causes of Death	1966 Number	1966 Rate	1967 Number	1967 Rate
All	causes	91,086	1,020.9	86,840	950.5
B 1	Tuberculosis of respiratory system (001-008)	3,183	35.7	2,912	31.9
B 2	Tuberculosis, other forms (010-019)	293	3.3	246	2.7
B 3	Syphilis and its sequelae (020-029)	120	1.3	111	1.2
B 4	Typhoid fever (040)	430	4.8	83	0.9
B 5	Cholera (043)	-	-	-	-
B 6	Dysentery, all forms (045-048)	41	0.5	46	0.5
B 7	Scarlet fever and streptococcal sore throat (050-051)	6	0.1	8	0.1
B 8	Diphtheria (055)	92	1.0	55	0.6
B 9	Whooping cough (056)	149	1.7	68	0.7
B10	Meningococcal infections (057)	16	0.2	8	0.1
B11	Plague (058)	-	-	-	-
B12	Acute poliomyelitis (030)	40	0.4	23	0.3
B13	Smallpox (084)	-	-	-	-
B14	Measles (085)	1,697	19.0	1,051	11.5
B15	Typhus and other rickettsial diseases (100-108)	54	0.6	50	0.5
B16	Malaria (110-117)	-	-	-	-
B17	All other diseases classified as infective and parasitic (030-039, 041, 042, 049, 052-054, 059-074, 081-083, 086-096, 120-138)	742	8.3	807	8.8
B18	Malignant neoplasms, including neoplasms of lymphatic and haematopoietic tissues (140-205)	8,849	99.2	9,110	99.7
B19	Benign neoplasms and neoplasms of unspecified nature (210-239)	305	3.4	241	2.6
B20	Diabetes mellitus (260)	617	6.9	656	7.2
B21	Anaemias (290-293)	200	2.2	199	2.2
B22	Vascular lesions affecting central nervous system (330-334)	5,408	60.6	5,525	60.5
B23	Non-meningococcal meningitis (340)	703	7.9	634	6.9
B24	Rheumatic fever (400-402)	28	0.3	38	0.4
B25	Chronic rheumatic heart disease (410-416)	487	5.5	499	5.5
B26	Arteriosclerotic and degenerative heart disease (420-422)	6,330	70.9	6,335	69.3
B27	Other diseases of heart (430-434)	1,528	17.1	1,559	17.1
B28	Hypertension with heart disease (440-443)	655	7.3	675	7.4
B29	Hypertension without mention of heart (444-447)	324	3.6	321	3.5
B30	Influenza (480-483)	1,297	14.5	783	8.6
B31	Pneumonia (490-493)	13,015	145.9	11,700	128.1
B32	Bronchitis (500-502)	1,005	11.3	942	10.3
B33	Ulcer of stomach and duodenum (540, 541)	271	3.0	311	3.4
B34	Appendicitis (550-553)	106	1.2	96	1.0
B35	Intestinal obstruction and hernia (560, 561, 570)	533	6.0	575	6.3
B36	Gastritis, duodenitis, enteritis, and colitis, except diarrhoea of the newborn (543, 571, 572)	5,240	58.7	4,577	50.1

TABLE 15.1 (Cont'd)

Deaths and Death Rates by Cause According to 1955 Classification. 1952-1967.

Abbr. List Number	Causes of Death	1966 Number	1966 Rate	1967 Number	1967 Rate
B37	Cirrhosis of liver (581)	2,933	32.9	3,359	36.8
B38	Nephritis and nephrosis (590-594)	747	8.4	704	7.7
B39	Hyperplasia of prostate (610)	221	39.8[6]	218	38.3[6]
B40	Deliveries and complications of pregnancy, childbirth, and the puerperium (640-689)	676	15.1[4]	630	...
B41	Congenital malformations (750-759)	885	9.9	922	10.1
B42	Birth injuries, postnatal asphyxia and atelectasis (760-762)	1,970	734.4	1,837	707.3[5]
B43	Infections of the newborn (763-768)	3,518	1,311.5	3,260	1,255.2[5]
B44	Other diseases peculiar to early infancy, and immaturity unqualified (769-776)	5,280	1,968.4	4,709	1,813.0[5]
B45	Senility without mention of psychosis, ill-defined and unknown causes (780-795)	2,556	28.6	6,396	70.0
B46	All other diseases (residual)	11,580	129.8	7,245	79.3
BE47	Motor vehicle accidents (E810-E835)	6,956	78.0	4,260	46.6
BE48	All other accidents (E800-E802, E840-E962)	-	0.0	390	4.3
BE49	Suicide and self-inflicted injury (E963, E970-E979)	-	0.0	253	2.8
BE50	Homicide and operations of war (E964, E965, E980-E999)	-	0.0	2,413	26.4

Notes:
1. Data exclude foetal deaths. In the present table, which corresponds to Part A of the table on deaths and death rates by cause published in the Demographic Yearbook of the United Nations, cause of death is classified according to the 1955 Revision of the Abbreviated List of 50 causes for Tabulation of Mortality of the International Statistical Classification of Diseases, Injuries and Causes of Death. Rates are the number of deaths from each cause per 100,000 population except for the rates for B39, B40, B41, and B43-44 where the base has been changed in order to relate the deaths more closely to the population actually at risk. The 1955 revision is not significantly different from the abbreviated list of 50 causes for tabulation of mortality of 1948, sixth revision, on which tabulations for earlier years were based.
2. Provisional data.
3. Other diseases of the circulatory system (467) are included in arteriosclerotic and degenerative heart disease (B26) rather than in all other diseases (B46).
4. Per 100,000 females.
5. Per 100,000 live-born.
6. Per 100,000 males of 50 years and over.
7. Data for this table are found in the U.S. Demographic Yearbook only up to 1967.

Sources: UN, Department of Economic and Social Affairs, Statistical Office, Demographic Yearbook 1957 (New York: U.N., 1957), p. 388 for the year 1952; 1955, p. 716 for the year 1953; 1956, p. 701 for the year 1954; 1959, p. 584 for the year 1956; 1960, p. 588 for the year 1957; 1962, p. 560 for the year 1959; 1963, p. 598 for the year 1961; 1964, p. 611 for the year 1962; 1965, p. 767 for the year 1964; 1966, p. 512 for the year 1960 and 1963; 1974, p. 729 for the years 1965, 1966 and 1967.

TABLE 15.2

Deaths and Death Rates by Cause According to 1965 Classification, 1968-1972[1].

Abbr.List Number	Cause of Death	1968 Number	1968 Rate	1969 Number	1969 Rate	1970 Number	1970 Rate	1971 Number	1971 Rate	1972 Number	1972 Rate
All	causes	84,433	902.9	84,336	881.7	63,014	939.6	83,456	844.7	87,429	899.3
B 1	Cholera (000)	-	-	-	-	-	-	-	-	-	-
B 2	Typhoid fever (001)	72	0.8	67	0.7	61	0.7	61	0.6	49	0.5
B 3	Bacillary dysentery and amoebiasis (004, 006)	21	0.2	13	0.1	15	0.2	23	0.2	13	0.1[3]
B 4	Enteritis and other diarrhoeal diseases (008, 009)	442	47.5	3,834	40.1	4,100	46.4	3,629	36.7	3,362	34.6
B 5	Tuberculosis of respiratory system (010-012)	831	30.3	2,498	26.1	2,103	23.8	1,945	19.7	2,042	21.0
B 6	Other tuberculosis, including late effects (013-019)	221	2.4	231	2.4	226	2.6	167	1.7	202	2.1
B 7	Plague (020)	-	-	-	-	-	-	-	-	-	-
B 8	Diphtheria (032)	43	0.5	35	0.4	46	0.5	60	0.6	83	0.9
B 9	Whooping cough (033)	92	1.0	100	1.0	114	1.3	59	0.6	89	1.0
B10	Streptococcal sore throat and scarlet fever (034)	6	0.1	5	0.1	11	0.1	5	0.0	4	0.0[3]
B11	Meningococcal infection (036)	12	0.1	8	0.1	5	0.1	7	0.1	1	0.0[3]
B12	Acute poliomyelitis (040-043)	32	0.3	27	0.3	36	0.4	21	0.2	12	0.1[3]
B13	Smallpox (050)	-	-	-	-	-	-	-	-	-	-
B14	Measles (055)	387	4.1	357	3.7	634	7.2	620	6.3	166	1.7
B15	Typhus and other rickettsioses (080-083)	51	0.5	40	0.4	23	0.3	4	0.0	-	-
B16	Malaria (084)	-	-	-	-	-	-	-	-	-	-
B17	Syphilis and its sequelae (090-097)	64	0.7	75	0.8	66	0.7	44	0.4	13	0.1[3]
B18	All other infective and parasitic diseases (remainder of 000-136)	453	15.5	1,506	15.7	1,602	18.1	1,446	14.6	1,680	17.3
B19	Malignant neoplasms, including neoplasms of lymphatic and haematopoietic tissue (140-209)	9,443	101.0	9,582	100.2	10,175	115.2	10,051	101.7	9,633	99.1
B20	Benign neoplasms and neoplasms of unspecified nature (210-239)	188	2.0	236	2.5	302	3.4	268	2.7	392	4.0
B21	Diabetes mellitus (250)	824	8.8	841	8.8	872	9.9	1,042	10.5	1,020	10.5
B22	Avitaminoses and other nutritional deficiency (260-269)	1,867	20.0	1,601	16.7	1,556	17.6	1,383	14.0	814	8.4
B23	Anaemias (280-285)	250	2.7	259	2.7	214	2.4	177	1.8	114	1.2
B24	Meningitis (320)	566	6.1	637	6.7	598	6.8	630	6.4	709	7.3

TABLE 15.2 (Cont'd)

Deaths and Death Rates by Cause According to 1965 Classification, 1968-1972.

Abbr.List Number	Cause of Death	1968 Number	1968 Rate	1969 Number	1969 Rate	1970 Number	1970 Rate	1971 Number	1971 Rate	1972 Number	1972 Rate
B25	Active rheumatic fever (390-392)	70	0.7	69	0.7	75	0.8	35	0.4	19	0.2[3]
B26	Chronic rheumatic heart disease (393-398)	582	6.2	649	6.8	542	6.1	575	5.8	590	6.1
B27	Hypertensive disease (400-404)	903	9.7	877	9.2	811	9.2	593	6.0	615	6.3
B28	Ischaemic heart disease (410-414)	5,132	54.9	6,080	63.6	5,933	67.2	6,255	63.3	6,339	65.2
B29	Other forms of heart disease (420-429)	3,631	38.8	3,101	32.4	3,577	40.5	3,553	36.0	2,941	30.3
B30	Cerebrovascular disease (430-438)	5,496	58.8	5,811	60.7	5,738	64.9	6,093	61.7	6,174	63.5
B31	Influenza (470-474)	1,960	21.0	1,752	18.3	1,372	15.5	888	9.0	1,016	10.5
B32	Pneumonia (480-486)	12,442	133.1	12,535	131.0	11,125	125.9	10,001	101.2	11,002	113.2
B33	Bronchitis, emphysema and asthma (490-493)	1,127	12.1	1,191	12.4	966	10.9	1,000	10.1	1,046	10.8
B34	Peptic ulcer (531-533)	332	3.5	293	3.1	292	1.3	341	3.5	325	3.3
B35	Appendicitis (540-543)	96	1.0	82	0.9	85	1.0	73	0.7	104	1.1
B36	Intestinal obstruction and hernia (550-553, 560)	512	5.5	485	5.1	497	5.6	409	4.1	389	4.0
B37	Cirrhosis of liver (571)	3,561	38.1	3,393	35.5	2,980	33.7	3,504	35.5	4,711	48.5
B38	Nephritis and nephrosis (580-584)	551	5.9	551	5.8	564	6.4	532	5.4	680	7.0
B39	Hyperplasia of prostate (600)	227	39.0[6]	255	42.8[6]	197	35.5[6]	63	...	218	...
B40	Abortion (640-645)	199	...	151	3.1[4]	150	3.5[4]	114	2.3[4]	106	...
B41	Other complications of pregnancy, childbirth and the puerperium. Delivery without mention of complication (630-639, 650-678)	351	...	303	6.2[4]	300	7.0[4]	221	4.4[4]	200	78.1[2]
B42	Congenital anomalies (740-759)	948	10.1	899	9.4	946	10.7	948	9.6	927	9.5
B43	Birth injury, difficult labor and other anoxic and hypoxic	2,159	867.3[5]	2,044	853.3[5]	2,267	865.3[5]	2,454	901.6[5]	2,982	1,164.4[2]
B44	Other causes of perinatal mortality (760-763, 769-771, 773-775, 777-779)	2,065	829.5[5]	2,078	867.5[5]	1,915	731.0[5]	2,113	776.3[5]	3,378	1,319.0[2]
B45	Symptoms and ill-defined conditions (780-796)	4,762	50.9	5,475	57.2	5,133	58.1	5,526	55.9	6,218	64.0
B46	All other diseases (remainder of 240-738)	7,218	77.2	6,879	71.9	7,245	82.0	8,133	82.3	7,773	79.9

TABLE 15.2 (Cont'd)

Deaths and Death Rates by Cause According to 1965 Classification, 1968-1972.

Abbr.List Number	Cause of Death	1968		1969		1970		1971		1972	
		Number	Rate	Number	Rate	Number	Rate	Number	Rate	Number	Rate
BE47	Motor vehicle accidents (E810-E823)	864	9.2	882	9.2	973	11.0	1,395	14.1	1,736	17.9
BE48	All other accidents (E810-E823)	3,747	40.1	4,197	43.9	2,711	30.7	1,771	17.9	1,880	19.3
BE49	Suicide and self-inflicted injuries (E950-E959)	419	4.5	486	5.1	482	5.5	514	5.2	529	5.4
BE50	All other external causes (E960-E999)	2,214	23.7	1,866	19.5	3,377	38.2	4,710	47.7	5,123	52.7

Notes: 1. Data exclude foetal deaths. In the present table, which corresponds to Part B of the table of deaths and death rates by cause published in the Demographic Yearbook of the United Nations, cause of death is classified according to the 1965 Revision of the Abbreviated List of 50 causes for Tabulation of Mortality of the International Statistical Classification of Diseases, Injuries and Causes of Death. Rate are the number of deaths from each cause per 100,000 population except for the rates for B39, B40, B43 and B44 where the base has been changed in order to relate the deaths more closely to the population actually at risk.

2. Per 100,000 live births.
3. Rates based on 30 or fewer deaths.
4. Per 100,000 females.
5. Per 100,000 live born.
6. Per 100,000 males of 50 years and over.

Sources: UN, Department of Economic and Social Affairs, Statistical Office, Demographic Yearbook 1974 (New York: U.N., 1974), p. 795 for the years 1968, 1969, 1970, 1971; 1976 for the year 1972.

TABLE 15.3

General Deaths According to Cause, 1964-1975.
(Intermediate List of 150 Causes)

Causes of Death International 'A' List 1965	General Deaths 1964	1965	1966	1967	1968	1969	1970	1971	1972	1973	1974	1975
Total	94,058	91,648	91,086	86,840	84,433	84,336	83,014	83,456	87,429	80,994	78,493	74,182
A 2 Typhoid fever	143	134	430	83	72	67	61	61	49	44	57	54
A 3 Paratyphoid fever and other salmonella infections	7	7	9	9	15	17	37	23	36	24	8	22
A 4 Bacillary dysentery and amoebiasis	50	56	41	46	21	13	15	23	13	7	22	20
A 5 Enteritis and other diarrhoea diseases	5,317	5,290	5,206	4,536	4,442	3,834	4,100	3,624	3,362	2,468	2,420	1,727
A 6 Tuberculosis of respiratory system	3,405	3,182	3,183	2,912	2,831	2,498	2,103	1,945	2,042	1,765	1,684	1,609
A 7 Tuberculosis of meninges and central nervous system	179	191	156	137	104	94	107	80	118	102	78	61
A 8 Tuberculosis of intestines, peritoneum and mesenteric glands	36	31	32	19	26	26	24	11	19	17	11	9
A 9 Tuberculosis of bones and joints	6	13	9	8	11	5	5	6	3	9	4	2
A10 Other tuberculosis, including late effects	82	85	96	82	80	106	90	70	62	57	76	62
A12 Anthrax	13	9	5	7	8	2	5	3	1	5	5	-
A15 Diphtheria	154	121	92	55	43	35	46	60	83	58	45	36
A16 Whooping cough	288	324	149	68	92	100	114	59	99	70	196	48
A17 Streptococcal sore throat and scarlet fever	15	22	6	8	6	5	11	5	4	-	-	3
A18 Erysipelas	11	352	12	10	3	6	6	7	5	3	3	5
A19 Meningococcal infection	35	16	16	8	12	8	5	7	1	1	5	-
A20 Tetanus	49	47	38	41	27	25	23	22	28	28	26	25
A21 Other bacterial diseases	185	1	348	411	1,040	1,106	1,201	1,072	1,272	1,229	1,261	1,378
A22 Acute poliomelitis	68	52	40	23	32	27	38	21	12	28	5	10
A23 Late effects of acute poliomelitis	4	6	5	7	2	2	1	-	1	1	-	-
A24 Smallpox	3,120	1,152	1,697	1,051	387	357	634	620	166	65	257	180
A27 Viral encephalitis	49	68	50	85	23	24	35	23	19	31	25	8
A28 Infectious hepatitis	50	67	65	67	50	73	49	46	89	100	79	76
A29 Other viral diseases	5	1	-	-	118	64	72	59	55	45	65	36
A30 Typhus and other rickettsioses	22	62	54	50	51	40	23	4	-	12	5	4
A32 Trypanosomiasis	-	-	-	-	6	4	5	12	7	7	3	7
A34 Congenital syphilis	57	48	51	49	45	45	43	34	13	12	12	13
A35 Early syphilis, symptomatic	1	-	-	-	-	-	-	-	-	-	1	-

TABLE 15.3 (Cont'd)

General Deaths According to Cause, 1964-1975.
(Intermediate List of 150 Causes)

Causes of Death International 'A' List 1965	General Deaths 1964	1965	1966	1967	1968	1969	1970	1971	1972	1973	1974	1975
A36 Syphilis of central nervous system	4	13	21	11	3	17	5	4	-	2	5	2
A37 Other syphilis	44	70	48	51	16	13	18	6	-	7	9	3
A38 Gonococcal infections	2	1	1	1	-	-	3	5	1	-	1	-
A39 Schistosomiasis	-	-	-	-	-	-	-	-	-	-	-	-
A40 Hydatidosis	36	52	48	37	59	59	44	47	50	57	67	56
A41 Filarial infection	5	-	-	-	-	-	-	-	-	-	-	-
A42 Ancylostomiasis	-	-	-	-	1	-	-	-	-	-	-	-
A43 Other helminthiases	14	13	18	10	17	13	8	9	14	11	10	7
A44 All other infective and parasitic diseases	183	153	143	122	84	111	113	118	102	90	86	95
A45 Malignant neoplasm of buccal cavity and pharynx	99	74	92	79	96	92	104	92	91	107	134	128
A46 Malignant neoplasm of oesophagus	408	447	417	461	526	500	523	547	464	488	484	500
A47 Malignant neoplasm of stomach	2,910	2,652	2,697	2,741	2,895	2,950	3,191	2,903	2,867	2,778	2,658	2,648
A48 Malignant neoplasm of intestine, except rectum	225	280	268	262	276	316	303	298	341	347	287	277
A49 Malignant neoplasm of rectum and rectosigmoid junction	130	127	120	136	140	135	95	165	173	147	142	173
A50 Malignant neoplasm of larynx	41	63	66	58	73	58	50	76	77	73	88	101
A51 Malignant neoplasm of trachea, bronchus and lung	519	534	598	644	680	692	731	787	740	775	756	783
A52 Malignant neoplasm of bone	98	133	108	132	93	89	99	121	73	93	112	95
A53 Malignant neoplasm of skin	60	49	57	67	66	62	50	67	68	72	49	64
A54 Malignant neoplasm of breast	262	317	356	324	409	378	438	445	426	480	445	479
A55 Malignant neoplasm of cervix uteri	394	360	445	441	491	483	567	566	576	635	651	621
A56 Other malignant neoplasm of uterus	290	263	257	255	230	228	216	213	209	219	183	171
A57 Malignant neoplasm of prostate	182	214	247	255	259	241	267	460	330	332	341	330
A58 Malignant neoplasm of other and unspecified sites	2,434	2,552	2,647	2,770	2,684	2,784	3,021	2,760	2,636	2,718	2,755	2,826
A59 Leukaemia	241	284	291	292	310	352	314	327	310	335	348	330
A60 Other neoplasms of lymphatic and haematopoietic tissue	154	190	183	193	215	222	206	230	252	237	258	268
A61 Benign neoplasms and neoplasms of unspecified nature	186	224	305	241	188	236	302	268	392	492	487	546
A62 Non-toxic goitre	1	1	2	4	2	13	6	5	4	1	5	3

TABLE 15.3 (Cont'd)

General Deaths According to Cause, 1964-1975.
(Intermediate List of 150 Causes)

Causes of Death International 'A' List 1965	General Deaths 1964	1965	1966	1967	1968	1969	1970	1971	1972	1973	1974	1975
A63 Thyrotoxicosis with or without goitre	2	-	6	5	7	6	6	5	5	4	2	1
A64 Diabetes mellitus	568	593	617	656	824	841	872	1,042	1,020	1,021	1,091	942
A65 Avitaminoses and other nutritional deficiency	279	232	215	280	1,867	1,601	1,556	1,383	814	1,614	1,298	1,346
A66 Other endocrine and metabolic diseases	416	588	673	614	72	99	100	81	87	94	137	113
A67 Anaemias	153	200	200	199	250	259	214	177	114	117	110	105
A68 Other diseases of blood and blood-forming organs					57	34	58	47	43	30	45	42
A69 Psychoses	113	117	87	65	96	140	112	137	111	89	105	151
A70 Neuroses, personality disorders and other non-psychotic mental disorders	435	374	426	452	312	303	232	304	323	251	254	278
A71 Mental retardation	81	74	36	23	15	17	10	20	25	15	15	47
A72 Meningitis	797	810	703	634	566	637	598	630	709	618	635	633
A73 Multiple sclerosis	3	-	8	-	7	8	9	-	6	13	12	15
A74 Epilepsy	354	271	306	332	290	338	334	364	305	317	314	316
A75 Inflammatory diseases of eye	6	3	1	1	4	2	1	1	1	2	4	3
A76 Cataract	-	-	-	-	-	1	1	-	--	-	-	1
A77 Glaucoma	-	-	-	1	-	1	-	1	-	-	1	-
A78 Otitis media and mastoiditis	83	62	76	69	59	58	55	38	47	31	40	33
A79 Other diseases of nervous system and sense organs	934	884	793	844	709	679	703	798	618	579	595	629
A80 Active rheumatic fever	27	18	28	38	70	69	75	35	19	11	12	7
A81 Chronic rheumatic heart disease	422	479	487	499	582	649	542	575	590	595	541	473
A82 Hypertensive disease	884	981	979	996	903	877	811	593	615	742	703	667
A83 Ischaemic heart disease	6,139	6,396	6,330	6,335	5,132	6,080	5,933	6,255	6,339	6,328	6,268	5,940
A84 Other forms of heart disease	2,183	1,845	1,528	1,559	3,631	3,101	3,577	3,553	2,941	2,569	2,287	2,507
A85 Cerebrovascular disease	5,035	5,335	5,408	5,525	5,496	5,811	5,738	6,093	6,174	6,057	6,005	5,001
A86 Diseases of arteries, arterioles and capillaries	1,059	1,081	1,083	1,095	1,477	1,520	1,617	1,465	1,236	1,296	1,162	1,225
A87 Venous thrombosis and embolism					129	131	154	141	239	154	164	138
A88 Other diseases of circulatory system	292	290	248	248	70	70	98	282	378	326	298	305
A89 Acute respiratory infections	361	311	277	165	648	457	510	739	624	404	502	420
A90 Influenza	1,252	1,845	1,297	783	1,960	1,752	1,372	888	1,016	511	910	446
A91 Viral pneumonia					2	7	9	10	8	19	26	55

TABLE 15.3 (Cont'd)

General Deaths According to Cause, 1964-1975.
(Intermediate List of 150 Causes)

Causes of Death International 'A' List 1965	General Deaths											
	1964	1965	1966	1967	1968	1969	1970	1971	1972	1973	1974	1975
A 92 Other pneumonia	14,053	13,418	13,015	11,700	12,440	12,528	11,116	9,991	10,994	7,864	8,088	6,545
A 93 Bronchitis, emphysema and asthma	581	905	1,005	942	1,127	1,191	966	1,000	1,046	928	1,014	907
A 94 Hypertrophy of tonsils and adenoids	1	3	2	3	1	1	-	1	-	2	1	2
A 95 Empyema and abscess of lung	105	82	68	87	70	59	65	75	66	61	55	59
A 96 Other diseases of respiratory system	484	424	448	431	348	272	372	329	281	331	323	316
A 97 Diseases of teeth and supporting structures	1	1	3	1	14	14	5	6	-	2	2	-
A 98 Peptic ulcer	297	290	271	311	332	293	292	341	325	309	337	323
A 99 Gastritis and duodenitis	27	27	34	41	35	19	17	27	42	39	17	30
A100 Appendicitis	105	99	106	96	96	82	85	73	104	119	103	87
A101 Intestinal obstruction and hernia	518	533	533	575	512	485	497	409	389	419	442	431
A102 Cirrhosis of liver	3,132	2,533	2,933	3,359	3,561	3,393	2,980	3,504	4,711	3,279	2,803	2,715
A103 Cholelithiasis and cholecystitis	471	563	605	564	669	620	663	680	742	617	682	579
A104 Other diseases of digestive system	1,537	1,168	5,423	1,208	1,183	1,109	1,194	1,546	1,573	1,234	1,089	1,091
A105 Acute nephritis	117	114	109	88	67	85	71	20	4	15	11	3
A106 Other nephritis and nephrosis	690	612	638	616	484	466	493	512	676	628	614	632
A107 Infections of kidney	128	142	174	142	167	161	175	180	215	190	201	221
A108 Calculus of urinary system	4	12	7	8	8	7	11	9	5	16	9	4
A109 Hyperplasia of prostate	182	224	221	218	227	255	197	63	218	264	275	242
A110 Diseases of breast	-	-	-	2	-	1	-	4	-	-	2	-
A111 Other diseases of genito-urinary system	177	187	191	169	370	332	340	460	453	333	358	399
A112 Toxaemias of pregnancy and the puerperium	70	54	42	48	57	68	51	29	24	25	27	27
A113 Haemorrhage of pregnancy and childbirth	99	151	112	123	78	57	67	60	45	50	47	40
A114 Abortion induced for legal indications					1	-	1	-	1	-	1	-
A115 Other and unspecified abortion	270	275	269	233	198	151	149	114	105	109	114	118
A116 Sepsis of childbirth and the puerperium	-	-	-	-	59	41	48	31	35	40	33	34

TABLE 15.3 (Cont'd)

General Deaths According to Cause, 1964-1975.
(Intermediate List of 150 Causes)

Causes of Death International 'A' List 1965	General Deaths											
	1964	1965	1966	1967	1968	1969	1970	1971	1972	1973	1974	1975
A117 Other compl. of pregnancy, childbirth and puerperium	6,391	5,705	5,514	4,957	138	137	127	101	96	85	91	87
A118 Delivery without mention of complication	-	-	-	-	19	-	8	-	-	22	-	-
A119 Infections of skin and subcutaneous tissue	97	107	89	113	67	94	84	109	83	65	73	65
A120 Other diseases of skin and subcutaneous tissue					79	81	79	62	75	59	77	46
A121 Arthritis and spondylitis	60	74	66	82	93	60	63	56	52	53	71	77
A122 Non-articular rheumatism and rheumatism unspecified	122	101	113	115	94	96	84	80	65	46	51	51
A123 Osteomyelitis and periostitis	9	15	19	19	13	11	9	21	10	9	14	13
A124 Ankylosis and acquired musculoskeletal deformities	4	4	8	3	7	8	4	2	4	3	5	3
A125 Other diseases of musculoskeletal system and connective tissue	90	144	127	100	54	57	74	54	55	47	72	65
A126 Spina bifida	32	47	87	61	69	49	46	43	26	32	47	56
A127 Congenital anomalies of heart	-	-	-	-	367	402	394	383	390	413	420	409
A128 Other congenital anomalies of circulatory system	363	453	424	430	13	8	13	9	4	10	12	19
A129 Cleft palate and cleft lip	-	-	-	-	21	23	17	15	10	12	10	12
A130 All other congenital anomalies	300	456	374	431	478	417	476	498	497	605	698	633
A131 Birth injury and difficult labor	868	886	953	849	813	675	554	632	832	788	769	683
A132 Conditions of placenta and cord					95	116	129	78	37	32	39	30
A133 Haemolytic disease of newborn	1,761	182	208	190	168	162	162	115	130	98	108	92
A134 Anoxic and hypoxic conditions not elsewhere classified	1,140	1,061	1,017	988	1,346	1,369	1,713	1,822	2,150	2,057	1,960	1,814
A135 Other causes of perinatal morbidity and mortality	3,673	3,174	3,329	3,048	1,802	1,800	1,624	1,920	3,211	2,911	2,674	2,716
A136 Senility without mention of psychosis	1,689	1,936	1,922	4,508	1,407	1,588	1,387	1,467	1,188	1,120	934	905
A137 Symptoms and other ill-defined conditions	5,117	5,134	634	1,888	3,355	3,887	3,745	4,059	5,030	5,173	5,799	5,835

TABLE 15.3 (Cont'd)

General Deaths According to Cause, 1964-1975.
(Intermediate List of 150 Causes)

	General Deaths											
	1964	1965	1966	1967	1968	1969	1970	1971	1972	1973	1974	1975
	639	785	833	1,078	811	961	762	762	612	533	374	391
	170	193	147	199	133	169	187	178	156	148	109	97
	180	195	175	211	151	167	216	204	168	180	163	168
	4	6	7	2	6	6	5	1	1	7	10	8
	-	1	340	1	4	3	3	2	-	5	2	2
	,822	1,651	1,854	1,529	1,917	1,652	1,816	2,436	2,823	2,827	2,164	2,011
missiles	342	925	1,182	1,243	1,457	1,403	1,342	1,343	1,990	2,753	1,444	1,218
AE145 Accidents mainly of industrial type	720	161	126	140	173	140	186	287	238	425	192	160
AE146 All other accidents	87	45	29	26	73	18	79	46	26	12	20	13
AE147 Suicide and self inflicted injury	139	185	173	193	173	235	239	324	406	393	399	409
AE148 Homicide and injury purposely inflicted by other persons; legal intervention	394	345	404	390	323	379	359	339	378	316	294	270
AE149 Injury undetermined whether accidentally or purposely inflicted	201	262	250	253	291	292	347	316	422	337	365	411
AE150 Injury resulting from operations of war	2,029	2,399	1,436	2,051	1,732	2,006	2,002	2,152	2,048	2,061	2,135	2,285
External Causes												
Total	6,727	7,153	6,956	7,316	7,244	7,431	7,543	8,390	9,268	9,997	7,671	7,443
AE138 Motor vehicle accidents	485	463	524	635	864	882	973	1,395	1,736	1,658	1,138	964
AE139 Other transport accidents	343	442	371	394	352	306	234	181	293	609	284	231
AE140 Accidental Poisoning	159	218	228	221	169	161	155	46	21	16	25	19
AE141 Accidental falls	472	754	681	618	173	237	209	217	169	236	120	103
AE142 Accidents caused by fires	90	78	86	125	311	338	335	338	345	289	280	259
AE143 Accidental drowning and submersion	993	1,039	1,122	1,013	461	209	308	104	29	174	150	135
AE144 Accident caused by firearm missiles	241	243	279	360	13	7	25	-	4	21	7	4
AE145 Accidents mainly of industrial type	336	290	330	260	162	134	111	92	116	230	119	80
AE146 All other accidents	3,165	3,295	2,954	3,342	2,106	2,805	1,334	793	903	748	647	605

TABLE 15.3 (Cont'd)

General Deaths According to Cause, 1964-1975.
(Intermediate List of 150 Causes)

Causes of Death International 'A' List 1965	General Deaths 1964	1965	1966	1967	1968	1969	1970	1971	1972	1973	1974	1975
AE147 Suicide and self inflicted injury	249	171	203	187	419	486	482	514	529	559	575	684
AE148 Homicide and injury purposely inflicted by other persons; legal intervention	194	160	178	161	254	327	305	365	416	560	278	260
AE149 Injury undetermined whether accidentally or purposely inflicted	-	-	-	-	1,960	1,539	3,072	4,345	4,707	4,509	3,891	4,011
AE150 Injury resulting from operations of war	-	-	-	-	-	-	-	-	-	388	157	88

Note: There exists information for the groups of causes of death from A117 to A135 for the years 1964 to 1968 but were not included in the present series due to changes introduced in the international classification of diseases, injuries and causes of death.

Source: National Institute of Statistics.

TABLE 15.4

Chile: Structure by Age at Time of Occurrence of Expected, Observed, and Avoided Deaths, and Rates Observed in 1955-1956 and in 1974-1975.

Age Groups (yrs)	Number of Deaths in the Two-Year Period 1974-1975 (yearly average)			Observed Rates (average)		Observed Reduction in Rates[c]
	Expected[a]	Observed	Avoided[b]	1955-1956	1974-1975	%
Under 1 year	34,888	15,584	19,304	137.8	61.6	55.3
1-4	9,197	2,395	6,802	9.3	2.4	74.2
5-14	3,373	1,672	1,701	1.4	0.7	50.0
15-24	4,981	2,627	2,354	2.5	1.3	48.0
25-44	14,205	7,322	6,883	5.5	2.8	49.1
45-64	22,555	15,887	6,668	15.9	11.2	29.6
65 and over	37,144	30,608	6,536	72.1	59.4	17.6
Total	126,343	76,095[d]	50,248	12.6	7.5	40.5

Notes: a. By applying 1955-1956 rates to 1974-1975 population figures.
b. Difference between expected and observed deaths.
c. In respect of two-year period 1955-1956.
d. Disregarding 138 deaths at ages unknown.

Sources: 1955-1956 National Institute of Statistics. 1973-1974 National Health Service. Taucher, 1978b, p. 118.

The mortality rates by age groups observed in Sweden in 1974 and in Chile in 1975 and observed and avoidable deaths in Chile are presented in Table 15.5.

TABLE 15.5

Mortality Rates by Age Groups Observed in Sweden, 1974 and in Chile, 1975, and Observed and Avoidable Deaths in Chile.

Age Groups (yrs)	Mortality Rates Per Thousand[a]		Deaths in Chile 1975			
	Sweden 1974	Chile 1975	Observed	Expected[b]	Avoidable Number	Avoidable %
Under 1 year	9.6	55.5	14,217	2,442	11,775	82.8
1-4	0.4	2.2	2,171	384	1,787	82.3
5-14	0.3	0.7	1,615	651	964	59.7
15-24	0.7	1.3	2,627	1,414	1,213	46.2
25-44	1.3	2.8	7,246	3,325	3,921	54.1
45-64	7.6	11.0	15,756	10,879	4,877	30.9
65 and over	54.6	58.1	30,412	28,581	1,831	6.2
CMR[d]	10.6	7.2	74,044[c]	47,676	26,368	35.5

Notes: a. Under one year per thousand live births and for the rest per thousand inhabitants.
b. Assuming Swedish rates ruling in Chile.
c. Disregarding 138 deaths at ages unknown. Data furnished by National Health Service.
d. CMR stands for crude mortality rate.

Sources: Sweden: Demographic Yearbook 1975. Chile: National Health Service, Death Yearbook. Taucher, 1978b, p. 119.

The averages of expected, observed and avoided deaths in 1974-1975, expected and observed rates in 1974-1975 and the decrease between the first and last biennium are presented in Table 15.6.

TABLE 15.6

Chile: Averages of Expected, Observed and Avoided Deaths in 1974-1975, Expected and Observed Rates in 1974-1975 and Decrease Between First and Last Biennium.

a. Average of Deaths During 1974-1975.

Cause Groups		Deaths			
				Avoided	
		Expected	Observed	Absolute Figures	Percentage
I } IX }	Infective Digestive[d]	20,341	11,878	8,463	16.9
II	Tumors	10,790	10,567	223	0.4
VI&VII	Nervous system and circulatory	23,623	17,151	6,472	12.9
VIII	Respiratory[e]	27,179	10,150	17,029	34.0
XV	Early infancy[f]	10,028	5,070	4,958	9.9
XVI	Ill-defined	15,698	7,488	8,210	16.4
XVII	Accidents and violence	8,382	7,600	782	1.6
Other		10,302	6,329	3,973	7.9
Total		126,343	76,233	50,110	100.0

b. Rates and Decrease Observed Between First and Last Period.

Cause Groups		Rates (per 100 thousand)		Decrease	
		1955-1956[b]	1974-1975	Absolute Figures	Percentage Figures[c]
I } IX }	Infective Digestive[d]	200.2	116.9	83.3	41.6
II	Tumors	106.2	104.0	2.2	2.1
VI&VII	Nervous system and circulatory	232.5	168.8	63.7	27.4
VIII	Respiratory[e]	267.5	99.9	167.6	62.6
XV	Early infancy[f]	98.7	49.9	48.8	49.4
XVI	Ill-defined	154.5	73.7	80.8	52.3
XVII	Accidents and violence	82.5	74.8	7.7	9.3
Other		101.4	62.3	39.1	38.6
Total		1,243.5	750.3	493.2	39.7

Notes: a. By applying 1955-1956 rates to 1974-1975 population.
b. Standardized by age.
c. With respect to 1955-1956 rates.
d. "Expected" include diarrhoea of the newborn.
e. "Expected" include pneumonias of the newborn.
f. "Expected" exclude diarrhoea and pneumonia of the newborn and inadaptation to the alimentary regime.

Sources: Deaths: National Health Service. Population: National Planning Office (ODEPLAN). Taucher, 1978b, p. 124.

The major groups of causes of death in Table 15.6 are the infective, digestive, tumors (neoplasms), of the nervous system, circulatory, respiratory, early infancy, ill-defined, accidents and violence and other.

Mortality rates for the three groups of the most important causes of death in Chile for 1955 and 1975 and the United States of America for 1974 by age groups are presented in Table 15.7.

TABLE 15.7

Mortality Rates for the Three Groups of the Most Important Causes of Death in Chile, by Age Groups. Chile, 1955 and 1975 and United States of America, 1974.

Age Groups and Causes	Chile 1955		Chile 1975		United States 1974	
	Rate[1]	Percentage	Rate	Percentage	Rate	Percentage
Under one year						
Infective and digestive	2,649.9	18.6	1,221.8	22.1	89.4	5.4
Respiratory	4,056.7	28.4	1,328.2	24.1	107.3	6.4
Early infancy	5,790.9	40.6	1,728.2	31.3	908.6	54.4
Sub-total	12,497.5	87.6	4,278.2	77.5	1,105.3	66.2
Total[2]	14,273.2	100.0	5,521.3	100.0	1,670.1	100.0
1-4 years						
Infective and digestive	311.3	32.6	41.9	19.1	4.6	6.2
Respiratory	384.0	40.1	52.0	23.8	7.0	9.4
Accidents	58.8	6.1	49.4	22.6	32.7	44.0
Sub-total	754.1	78.8	143.3	65.5	44.3	59.6
Total[2]	956.7	100.0	218.7	100.0	74.3	100.0
5-14 years						
Infective and digestive	25.0	17.9	6.6	9.9	1.0	2.6
Respiratory	36.6	26.3	7.2	10.7	1.9	5.0
Accidents	29.6	21.3	23.9	35.7	20.3	53.1
Sub-total	91.2	65.5	37.7	56.3	23.2	60.7
Total[2]	139.3	100.0	67.0	100.0	38.2	100.0
15-24 years						
Tuberculosis	52.1	19.7	6.6	5.1	0.1	0.1
Respiratory	33.8	12.8	6.5	5.0	2.9	2.4
Accidents	82.3	31.1	62.0	47.7	89.4	73.4
Sub-total	168.2	63.6	75.1	57.8	92.4	75.9
Total[2]	264.5	100.0	130.0	100.0	121.7	100.0
25-44 years						
Tuberculosis	95.6	16.9	18.0	6.5	0.7	0.3
Nervous and circulatory systems	95.6	16.9	36.5	13.2	44.6	21.9
Accidents	112.6	19.9	85.8	30.9	80.5	39.4
Sub-total	303.8	53.7	140.3	50.6	125.8	61.6
Total[2]	566.2	100.0	277.2	100.0	204.1	100.0
45-64 years						
Neoplasms	292.8	18.0	268.5	24.4	300.9	28.1
Nervous and circulatory systems	553.1	34.0	265.4	24.2	489.0	45.7
Digestive	165.9	10.2	153.0	13.9	67.8	6.3
Sub-total	1,011.8	62.2	686.9	62.5	857.7	80.1
Total[2]	1,628.4	100.0	1,098.5	100.0	1,068.9	100.0
65 years and over						
Nervous and circulatory systems	3,202.6	42.7	2,155.3	37.1	3,679.1	64.8
Respiratory	980.9	13.1	640.8	11.0	356.2	6.3
Ill-defined	1,322.8	17.6	897.0	15.4	60.3	1.1
Sub-total	5,506.3	73.4	3,693.1	63.5	4,095.6	72.2
Total[2]	7,498.1	100.0	5,814.2	100.0	5,677.1	100.0

Notes: 1. The rates are per 100,000 inhabitants.
2. Includes other causes.

Sources: Chile: Servicio Nacional de Salud, Anuario de Defunciones. United States: World Health Organization, "World Health Statistics", Vol. 1, 1977. Taucher, 1978b, pp. 126-127.

Deaths and death rates by avoidable causes, observed and expected in 1974-1975 are presented in Table 15.8.

The important decreases in mortality between 1955 and 1975, especially after 1963, can be attributed mainly to the decrease in infant mortality and mortality of children between one to four years of age.

In the lapse of twenty years, deaths due to causes considered avoidable have diminished by fifty per cent. This means that in the two year period 1974-1975, 33,340 yearly deaths were avoided, as compared with the two year period 1955-1956. Of these deaths, 28,844 (86.5%) correspond to decreases in mortality due to pneumonias, early infancy diseases and tuberculosis.

Deaths and causes of death which can be avoided through preventive action are, in relative terms, those that have experienced larger decreases.

Among deaths due to avoidable causes, accidents, pneumonia and early infancy diseases appear to remain the main problems. Altogether, they represent 22.7% of all deaths and 66.3% of avoidable deaths.

Accidents and violence constitute the more important causes between the ages of 5 and 44 years and would merit further analysis in order to adopt measures tending to reduce them. Pneumonia and bronchial pneumonia, which constitute 10% of all deaths, are also important in the cases of children under one year and under 28 days, in which groups they represent 23.7% and 13.1% of the death toll, respectively. Action to reduce these deaths would have the further effect of diminishing the high infant mortality rates.

Diseases peculiar to early infancy account for 32.5% and 59.7% of deaths of children under one year and under 28 days, respectively. The majority of these causes are related to control of pregnancy and childbirth care.

Diarrhoeal diseases continue to be important causes of death, particularly among children between 28 days and eleven months of age, representing in their case 22.2% of the total number of deaths.

An interesting research field which comes into view through Taucher's article is examination of some conditioning factors, within the framework of development policies. Infant mortality and some of its causes grouped under the caption "avoidable through combined measures" are the ones more susceptible to such study. The reason for this is that they cause a high number of deaths, they have experienced important reductions during the period under review and because they are linked to a country's development level. A breakdown of the factors that may affect these deaths, trying to quantify their individual contributions, would allow a better explanation of past evolution and the planning of future actions in public health, education and so forth (Taucher: 1978b, 140-141).

Calorie and Protein Intake

The daily per capita calorie and protein intake in Chile, both total and by main components, for selected years between 1948 and 1970, is presented in Table 15.9. Furthermore, the daily per capita calorie intake in special groups (military and civilian) for March-June 1960 is presented in Table 15.10.

National Health Service Statistics

Income and expenditures of the National Health Service between 1960 and 1967 are presented in Table 15.11. The subsidies A paid by the National Health Service between 1964 and 1976 are presented in Table 15.12. The subsidies called type A refer to payment orders, days and amount for maternity, lactation or curative medicine. The subsidies of the National Health Service called type B and presented in Table 15.13 for the period between 1964 and 1976 refer to payment orders issued, days and amount for preventive medical services, work accidents and professional illnesses and for services in day care centers (infant gardens under Law 17.301.

Social Security Service and Related Statistics

The number of subscribers (imponentes) and remunerations on which deposits made are based (remuneraciones imponibles) by pension plan institutions (institutiones previsionales) are presented in Table 15.14. Although the Spanish term "institutiones previsionales" has been translated here as "pension plan institutions", its meaning is much broader and could also be translated as "social security institutions." Also, the Spanish term "remuneraciones imponibles", which has been translated as "remunerations on which deposits made are based", refers to income subject to social security and related payments or withdrawals.

TABLE 15.8

Deaths and Death Rates by Avoidable Causes, Observed and Expected, in 1974-1975.[a]

Avoidable Causes	Number of Deaths		Avoidable Deaths	Percentage Change With Respect to Expected Avoidable Deaths	Rate Per 100 Thousand		
					Chile		United States 1974[b]
	Observed	Expected			Observed	Expected	
Through prevention	976	3,413	- 2,437	-71.4	9.6	33.6	3.95
Diphteria	40	195	- 155	-79.5	0.4	1.9	0.0
Whooping cough	120	948	- 828	-87.3	1.2	9.3	0.0
Measles	210	741	- 531	-71.7	2.1	7.3	0.0
Rheumatic diseases	544	944	- 400	-42.4	5.3	9.3	3.75
Venereal diseases	32	311	- 279	-89.7	0.3	3.1	0.2[c]
Other	30	274	- 244	-89.0	0.3	2.7	0.0
Through diagnosis and treatment	3,287	3,226	+ 61	+ 1.9	32.3	31.7	23.91
Ulcers and other	930	1,280	- 350	-27.3	9.1	12.6	3.97
Colecystopathis	596	493	+ 103	+20.9	5.9	4.8	0.74
Mammal carcinoma	481	327	+ 154	+47.1	4.7	3.2	9.31
Uterine carcinoma	850	855	- 5	- 0.6	8.4	8.4	3.03
Prostatic carcinoma	361	213	+ 148	+69.5	3.5	2.1	5.31
Skin carcinoma	69	58	+ 11	+19.0	0.7	0.6	1.55
By sanitary measures	2,944	3,797	- 853	-22.5	29.0	37.4	1.23
Salmonellosis	106	417	- 311	-74.6	1.0	4.1	0.0
Hepatitis and helm	133	153	- 20	-13.1	1.3	1.5	0.22
Diarrhoeas	2,705	3,227	- 522	-16.2	26.7	31.8	1.01
By combined measures	26,059	56,170	-30,111	-53.6	256.5	552.8	115.04
Tuberculosis	1,941	6,728	- 4,787	-71.1	19.1	66.2	1.00
Pneumonia and Bronchiopneumonia	7,592	24,168	-16,576	-68.6	74.7	237.9	14.90
Cirrhosis of liver	2,701	2,413	+ 288	+11.9	26.6	23.7	10.86
Maternal	331	1,121	- 790	-70.5	3.3	11.0	0.22
Early infancy	5,878	13,359	- 7,481	-56.0	57.8	131.5	22.72
Accidents and violence	7,616	8,381	- 765	- 9.1	75.0	82.5	65.34
Total	33,266	66,606	-33,340	-50.1	327.4	655.5	144.13

Notes: a. 1955-1956 rates standardized by age, considering as standard population that of 1974-1975.
b. United States rates standardized by age, considering as standard population that of Chile 1974-1975.
c. Rate not standardized for lack of information.

TABLE 15.9

Daily Per Capita Calorie and Protein Intake: Total and Main Components, Selected Years.

Period	Prewar[2]	1948	1951	1952	1954-56	1957	1957-59	1960	1961
Cereals	1,233	1,334	1,221	1,343	1,365	1,286	1,173	1,330	1,141
Potatoes and other starchy foods	141	153	112	123	145	176	145	173	148
Sugar and sweets	269	265	317	253	286	388	238	266	
Pulses and nuts	98	57	87	85	70	79	69	99	82
Vegetables	90	33	81	89	40	84	42	87	87
Fruits		54			39		40		
Meat	197	197	165	184	183	178	193	168	213
Eggs	7	8	19	18	16	16	10	17	11
Fish	11	16	23	33	40	34	37	38	30
Milk	76	159	183	183	199	150	192	158	156
Fats and oils	115	140	174	215	170	179	236	194	213
Total	2,237	2,420	2,344	2,488	2,550	2,570	2,380	2,530	2,420
Animal protein (grams per day)	21		24	26	26	26	29	28	28
Total protein (grams per day)	69		71	77	77	77	80	77	77

Period	1960-62[1]	1961-62[1]	1962	1963[1]	1963-65[1]	1966	1964-66	1967-69	1970
Cereals	1,146	1,183	1,153	1,227	1,347	1,513	1,166	1,189	1,172
Potatoes and other starchy foods	135	139	127	145	133	117	120	98	90
Sugar and sweets	331	340	246	335	328	348	338	346	332
Pulses and nuts	87	86	95	88	86	108	62	67	69
Vegetables	60	47	123	48	46	47	75	76	75
Fruits	74	68		67	64	65	62	69	68
Meat	216	228	206	196	217	209	203	237	253
Eggs	10	6	21	10	7	7	22	24	25
Fish	30	14	33	40	22	26	26	28	28
Milk	156	179	166	157	189	191	142	136	139
Fats and oils	189	192	197	246	206	201	218	264	308
Total	2,430	2,480	2,370	2,560	2,640	2,830	2,430	2,530	2,560
Animal protein (grams per day)	29	26	29	29	28	27	25	27	28
Total protein (grams per day)	77	71	79	81	85	82	65	65	66

TABLE 15.9 (Cont'd)

er Capita Calorie and Protein Intake: Total and Main Components, Selected Years.

nter-
Washington,

60-62, 1961-62, 1963, 1963-65 and 1966 are tentative.

n is for 1935-39. The F.A.O. obtains the information presented in this table from sheets prepared by governments with its collaboration. The "food balance sheet" which arrives at the estimated quantity of food and nutrient supplies available by deducting from the data of total food production, trade, and movement in stocks, animal feed, seed, and non-food purposes. The resulting figure is divided by the year to year information is not fully comparable because the estimates on farm and al stocks and quantities utilized for feed, seed, waste, and industrial uses, are conjectural.

3. In considering the reliability of food balance sheet data, some of which are found in the present table, and their comparability between countries and over time, some of the following main limitations should be taken into account: (a) The range, accuracy and classification of national statistics vary from country to country and over time. For a number of foodstuffs, official statistics of production and trade are frequently inadequate. Reliable information on the yearly changes in farm and commercial stocks is often nonexistent. The estimates made in such cases are of varying quality, based as they are on subjective knowledge. (b) Quantities utilized for feed, seed, waste, industrial uses and related technical conversion factors are frequently roughly determined in the absence of proper statistics on the utilization of individual commodities. (c) For a number of countries no proper statistical basis for population figures exists as yet. Even where population censuses and surveys have been taken, there may be appreciable errors in the estimates for postcensus years. (d) National figures on food composition are often not available and international data have to be used for the calculation of the nutritive value of food supplies. FAO Production Yearbook 1971, p. 718.

Source: Rome, Food and Agricultural Organization (FAO) of the United Nations, Production Yearbook (Rome, Italy: FAO). Various issues for the years 1951, 1955, 1957, 1961, 1962, 1963, 1964; Production Yearbook 1967, p. 427 for the 1960-62 figures; Production Yearbook 1966, p. 423 for the 1963 figures; Production Yearbook 1968, p. 441, for the 1966 figures; Production Yearbook 1969, p. 440, for the 1961-62 and 1963-65 figures; Production Yearbook 1971, p. 444, for the 1964-66, 1967-69 and 1970 figures. The information on calorie intake was obtained from table on "net food supply per caput-calories" in the aforementioned Production Yearbooks. The number of this table in the 1971 Yearbook is 136. The information on animal protein (grams per day) and total protein (grams per day) was obtained from the table on "net food supply per caput-proteins" in the aforementioned Production Yearbooks. The number of this table in the 1971 Yearbook is 137.

TABLE 15.10

Daily Per Capita Calorie Intake in Special Groups.
March-June 1960.

	Military	Civilian	Total
Mean calorie intake	3,300	2,300	2,700 (2,900-3,000)

Notes: The information of this table came forth from a nutrition survey of the Armed Forces and civilian population of Chile that was carried out by the combined U.S.-Chilean Nutrition Survey Team between March 20 and June 4, 1960. The nutrition survey had four major phases carried on concurrently as follows: 1. A study of agricultural production, food technology, and food distribution. 2. Clinical examinations of representative samples of the military and civilian populations predominantly urban and of the lower economic classes. 3. A dietary survey of the actual food intake of a representative sample of the military and of the civilian population examined and finally 4. Laboratory analysis of food, blood and urine samples from the populations and studies mentioned above for chemical constituents which correlate with various aspects of human nutrition.

The clinical examination studies involved the examination of 4,305 enlisted military personnel of Navy, Air Force, and Army involving most geographic areas. The military sample is believed to be truly representative of the military forces exclusive of commissioned officers. In addition, 5,374 civilians were examined in seventeen cities from Punta Arenas to Arica. Twelve hundred infants were examined in the hospitals of twelve cities and 140,000 school children were measured to determine growth status in eighteen cities. The civilian sample is representative of the urban population in the middle and lower income brackets but does not represent the wealthy groups. All ethnic groups except the Araucanian Indians and all geographic areas were included in the samples.

The data of the agriculture survey indicated that the total food available in Chile provides an estimated 2,700 calories per capita per day exclusive of wine consumption. Furthermore, it is very conservatively estimated that garden produce which is not accurately estimable, contributes 200-300 calories per person per day. The figures in parentheses in the present table give the total caloric intake per person per day while the first figure excludes garden produce. The U.S.-Chilean Nutrition Survey Team notes and 2,900-3,000 calories per person per day is a fairly accurate, or at least not overly optimistic approximation of the total food available for consumption in Chile in 1960. The present method which assumes that food is consumed can not estimate how much is actually eaten by individuals in various age categories and socioeconomic groups, how much is wasted in shipping and distribution, how much is canning waste, and how much is kitchen and plate waste.

The civilian dietary surveys (277 families) indicated the caloric intake per person per day to be slightly more than 2,200 calories. This figure, nevertheless, conceals geographical intake differences and among various socioeconomic groups. This intake was especially low in Santiago and Calama and highest in Punta Arenas and La Serena. On a socioeconomic level it appears that 37 percent of the families studied are receiving less than 2,000 calories per person per day and 28 percent are receiving less than 54 grams of protein per person per day (these families are largely in the low income groups). The military population consumes approximately 1,000 calories per day more than the civilian population. If its excess food consumed over that of the civilian population were equally divided, each civilian would receive less than 10 more calories per day. Ibid, pp. 1-7.

Source: Chile, Nutrition Survey, March-June 1960. A Report by the I[illegible] departmental Committee on Nutrition for National Defense [illegible] D.C.: U.S. Government Printing Office, 1961, 0-605281).

TABLE 15.11

Budgetary Balance of the National Health Service, 1960-1976.

Year	Budgetary Balance of the National Health Service		
	Income	Expenditures	Balance
	Millions of Escudos		
1960	113.7	113.7	0.0
1961	211.8	210.4	1.4
1962	132.5	132.5	0.0
1963	224.6	221.5	3.1
1964	297.6	293.4	4.2
1965	464.1	431.7	32.4
1966	640.9	625.5	15.4
1967	861.9	829.5	32.4
1968	1,097.4	1,167.0	-69.6
1969	1,599.1	1,649.7	-50.6
1970	2,301.9	2,398.1	-96.2
1971	3,953.5	3,999.6	-46.1
1972	8,149.5	7,933.4	216.1
1973	32,604.0	30,435.0	2,169.0
1974	234,892.1	221,502.6	13,389.5
	Thousands of Pesos		
1975	937,200.3	874,655.3	62,545.0
1976	2,780,250.7	2,755,166.2	25,084.5

Source: National Health Service and National Institute of Statistics.

TABLE 15.12

Subsidies-A Paid by the National Health Service, 1964-1976.

Year and Region	SUBSIDIES PAID: Payment Orders: Total	Payment Orders: Service: Maternity	Payment Orders: Service: Lactation	Payment Orders: Service: Curative Medicine	Days: Total	Days: Service: Maternity	Days: Service: Lactation	Days: Service: Curative Medicine
	Thousands of Escudos							
1964	397,126	45,483	10,189	280,571	6,160,045	767,587	267,166	3,657,397
1965[1]	425,235	45,350	8,954	305,481	6,366,356	774,565	234,566	3,852,638
1966	127,582	9,477	1,817	112,326	6,451,372	777,356	193,773	4,073,019
1967	125,118	10,425	2,231	108,794	6,773,089	899,382	234,548	4,286,856
1968	121,357	9,751	2,145	106,075	6,192,358	855,590	222,348	3,911,133
1969[2]	144,975	9,718	1,939	107,273	6,767,836	884,303	219,575	3,931,870
1970	132,270	9,023	1,829	99,654	6,527,287	814,591	186,102	3,949,089
1971	148,476	9,397	1,865	115,828	7,115,255	847,757	201,309	4,506,798
1972	172,131	9,753	1,853	138,494	7,879,821	903,510	170,962	5,215,126
1973	146,718	9,572	1,312	117,737	7,256,572	978,126	130,299	4,743,795
1974	128,671	9,464	1,120	103,653	6,289,662	1,102,613	113,289	3,963,005
	Pesos							
1975[3]	103,106	8,914	540	82,848	5,461,220	1,083,288	69,373	3,391,291
1976	90,875	7,961	297	74,062	4,586,582	935,588	36,513	2,827,039
I Tarapacá	2,430	368	-	1,862	124,318	44,821	-	51,251
II Antofagasta	3,411	399	-	2,783	183,835	48,011	-	115,073
III Atacama	1,890	87	-	1,464	79,353	11,395	-	39,083
IV Coquimbo	2,706	364	-	1,964	146,410	42,156	-	71,730
V Valparaíso	12,482	996	75	10,730	602,138	121,033	8,451	400,674
VI Of Liberator General Bernardo O'Higgins	4,094	219	-	3,558	185,202	26,503	548	134,690
VII Maule	3,658	303	-	2,725	196,651	35,984	-	113,756
VIII Bío-Bío	17,952	655	4	15,381	673,206	80,693	1,524	458,891
IX La Araucanía	2,736	157	-	2,149	180,624	18,266	-	120,607
X Los Lagos	5,337	272	-	4,445	245,475	31,898	30	165,302
XI Aysén of General C. Ibañez del Campo	391	13	-	247	16,490	2,666	-	9,009
XII Magallanes and Chilean Antarctic	1,563	86	-	1,389	63,224	9,037	-	39,212
Santiago Metropolitan Region	32,225	4,042	218	25,365	1,889,656	463,125	25,960	1,107,761

Notes: 1. The totals of the columns do not match the total of this table because they contain figures corresponding to Law 15.565 of municipalities which could not be split any further. The figures were: Number of orders, 641; number of days, 6,918; and amount, 51.9 (thousands of escudos).

TABLE 5.12 (Cont'd)

Subsidies-A Paid by the National Health Service, 1964-1976.

Year and Region	SUBSIDIES PAID: Amount: Total	Service: Maternity	Service: Lactation	Service: Curative Medicine
	Thousands of Escudos			
1964	14,633.7	1,616.4	179.8	8,886.7
1965[1]	22,698.3	2,366.2	210.2	13,793.6
1966	33,370.0	3,375.8	265.4	22,946.6
1967	46,846.8	5,481.3	426.3	32,853.1
1968	56,592.3	7,320.6	562.8	39,132.2
1969[2]	85,172.5	10,091.4	738.6	54,419.4
1970	116,689.8	12,932.9	905.1	78,066.1
1971	183,530.9	20,578.3	1,345.4	127,095.8
1972	323,479.7	33,956.1	2,324.3	230,223.3
1973	839,770.9	117,511.7	3,685.6	567,791.5
1974	4,584,730.7	738,503.2	18,946.6	3,122,753.9
	Pesos			
1975[3]	19,700,131.7	4,151,457.1	58,081.8	12,360,552.4
1976	66,948,912.0	13,700,113.4	158,751.1	42,678,846.0
I Tarapacá	2,062,896.8	684,841.4	-	1,011,731.7
II Antofagasta	2,636,924.4	429,501.8	-	1,848,792.6
III Atacama	1,131,036.6	106,675.5	-	623,821.8
IV Coquimbo	1,564,324.8	360,852.4	-	803,009.8
V Valparaíso	9,827,893.1	1,729,968.1	31,936.3	7,106,675.6
VI Of Liberator General Bernardo O'Higgins	1,786,881.6	229,056.0	1,021.6	1,358,427.3
VII Maule	2,197,514.6	479,797.7	-	1,170,270.3
VIII Bío-Bío	11,145,322.6	1,041,405.8	10,385.5	8,391,550.5
IX La Araucanía	1,727,032.0	196,369.2	-	1,118,271.6
X Los Lagos	3,146,545.5	415,981.9	437.2	2,221,330.7
XI Aysén of General C. Ibañez del Campo	218,891.2	33,020.2	-	105,657.2
XII Magallanes and Chilean Antarctic	1,354,435.9	120,177.6	-	951,082.8
Santiago Metropolitan Region	28,149,212.9	7,872,465.8	114,970.5	15,968,224.1

Notes: 2. Amounts in thousands of pesos were obtained from subsidy statistics and therefore do not match exactly with the budgetary results.

3. For administrative reasons zones III and XI were not included in the respective regions.

Source: National Health Service and National Institute of Statistics.

TABLE 15.13

Subsidies-B Paid by the National Health Service, 1964-1976.

Year and Regions	SUBSIDIES PAID: Payment Orders Issued			Days		
		Services			Services	
	Preventive	Work Accidents and Professional Illnesses	Law 17.301[1]	Preventive	Work Accidents and Professional Illnesses	Law 17.301[1]
	Thousands of Chilean Escudos					
1964	52,140	8,743	-	1,360,761	107,134	-
1965	54,460	10,349	-	1,374,447	123,222	-
1966	3,962	-	-	1,407,224	-	-
1967	3,668	-	-	1,352,303	-	-
1968	3,386	-	-	1,203,287	-	-
1969	3,016	23,029	-	1,028,729	703,359	-
1970	2,651	19,113	-	905,748	671,757	-
1971	2,769	18,617	-	877,793	681,598	-
1972	3,719	18,312	-	897,485	692,738	-
1973	2,749	14,881	467	816,096	577,738	10,518
1974	2,324	11,673	437	659,735	443,435	7,585
	Pesos					
1975	2,052	8,385	367	563,553	346,822	6,893
1976	1,726	6,466	363	495,775	285,436	6,231
I Tarapacá	67	107	26	24,159	3,863	224
II Antofagasta	57	172	-	13,750	6,997	4
III Atacama	46	293	-	19,019	9,856	-
IV Coquimbo	74	304	-	20,096	12,428	-
V Valparaíso	170	469	42	47,346	24,134	500
VI Of Liberator General B. O'Higgins	68	247	2	14,174	9,250	37
VII Maule	88	542	-	24,789	22,122	-
VIII Bío-Bío	302	1,574	36	68,321	63,243	534
IX Araucania	70	360	-	24,198	17,553	-
X Los Lagos	98	522	-	24,681	23,564	-
XI Aysén of General C. Ibañez del Campo	3	128	-	771	4,044	-
XII Magallanes and Chilean Antarctic	46	42	-	10,451	4,524	-
Santiago Metropolitan Region	637	1,706	257	204,020	83,858	4,932

TABLE 15.13 (Cont'd)

Subsidies-B Paid by the National Health Service, 1964-1976.

Year and Regions	SUBSIDIES PAID: Amount — Preventive	Services — Work Accidents and Professional Illnesses	Law 17.301[1]	Adjustment in Fees Under Preventive Medicine Law[2]
		Thousands of Chilean Escudos		
1964	3,000.5	950.3	-	-
1965	4,643.3	1,633.2	-	-
1966	6,218.0	-	-	554.2
1967	8,086.1	-	-	488.8
1968	8,948.7	-	-	628.0
1969	10,319.8	8,951.1	-	652.2
1970	12,780.9	11,187.1	-	817.7
1971	17,886.4	16,625.0	-	1,377.8
1972	27,537.9	27,175.1	-	2,265.0
1973	64,493.7	67,914.5	1,502.7	16,871.2
1974	366,413.5	330,892.9	7,220.6	106,002.0
		Pesos		
1975	1,732,402.7	1,363,891.0	33,746.7	243,340.5
1976	5,853,151.6	4,405,417.1	152,632.8	495,507.3
I Tarapacá	294,991.0	64,861.3	6,471.4	44,268.5
II Antofagasta	216,264.1	142,319.1	46.8	29,736.6
III Atacama	212,567.3	187,972.0	-	16,279.5
IV Coquimbo	225,191.6	175,271.0	-	26,528.4
V Valparaíso	591,769.2	354,045.1	13,498.8	33,589.0
VI Of Liberator General B. O'Higgins	95,882.4	101,702.3	792.0	24,555.5
VII Maule	242,734.9	304,711.7	-	10,319.8
VIII Bío-Bío	718,802.5	970,195.3	12,983.0	189,070.9
IX Araucania	214,231.0	198,160.2	-	33,854.3
X Los Lagos	214,342.2	294,453.5	-	20,894.3
XI Aysén of General C. Ibañez del Campo	4,606.7	75,607.1	-	-
XII Magallanes and Chilean Antarctic	181,649.7	101,525.8	-	6,358.7
Santiago Metropolitan Region	2,640,119.0	1,434,592.7	118,840.8	60,051.8

Notes: 1. Law 17.301 of 22.4. 1970, creating the National Board of Infants' gardens (Junta Nacional de Jardines Infantiles).
2. Adjustment in fees paid by National Health Service (not included in total figure).

Source: National Health Service and National Institute of Statistics.

Chile has had a maze of institutions where individuals could make pension payments or insure themselves against medical and other risks. As illustrated in Table 15.14, the Social Security Service (Servicio de Segure Social) has been the major but by no means the only provisional institution.

Excellent background information and a systematic presentation of the historical evolution of social security in Chile since independence can be found in Carmelo Mesa-Lago, Social Security in Latin America: Pressure Groups, Stratification and Inequality (Pittsburgh, Penn.: University of Pittsburgh Press, 1978), Chapter 2 "The Case of Chile", pp. 22-68.

For detailed statistical information concerning risks covered, family allowances, number of people insured, mortality of those insured, pensions granted, average duration of invalidity pensions, new inscriptions of insured, revenues and expenditures, origin of revenues and many other statistics see the annual publication (SSS: Estadísticas listed in the bibliography). For comprehensive information on the costs of social security see (Superintendencia de Seguridad Social: 1977), especially 21-22.

The number of subscribers (cotizantes) to the social security service by type of economic activity and according to sex is presented for the period between 1950 and 1976 in Table 15.15. The number of those insured (subscribers) is less than half of the labor force and has been stable since 1972. The majority of the insured are males (primarily engaged in agriculture and to a lesser extent manufacturing, construction and trade). Among females insured, the largest number is engaged in domestic services (household servants) and to a lesser extent manufacturing and trade.

TABLE 15.14

Number of Subscribers and Remunerations on Which Deposits Made are Based, by Pension Plan Institutions, 1967-1976.

Year	Total	Social Security Service	Private White Collar Workers Pension Plan	Auxiliary Organisms	Public Employees and News Sector Workers National Fund: Civil Service	Public Employees and News Sector Workers National Fund: News Workers	Chilean Police Force Pension Fund
	SUBSCRIBERS AND REMUNERATIONS — Pension and Provisional (Security) Funds						
	number of active subscribers						
1967	2,086,213	1,450,000	248,000	6,122	195,600	12,235	29,018
1968	2,087,155	1,406,000	257,000	5,999	214,506	12,235	29,791
1969	2,141,497	1,440,000	266,000	5,850	217,289	12,491	29,900
1970	2,232,043	1,476,000	275,000	5,753	261,260	12,838	29,735
1971	2,306,568	1,513,000	287,000	6,134	275,548	14,137	29,959
1972	2,362,584	1,540,000	310,000	6,819	268,651	14,594	29,946
1973	2,424,114	1,561,000	340,000	7,268	284,321	14,987	33,195
1974	2,507,278	1,594,000	361,000	7,231	291,615	12,358	33,248
1975 P	2,424,522	1,537,300	345,000	7,173	283,982	11,675	34,658
1976 P	2,431,817	1,550,000	350,000	6,922	273,362	12,875	35,510
	number of passive subscribers						
1967	469,028	291,255	15,118	1,796	46,440	9,680	27,973
1968	470,682	309,910	16,878	2,076	26,224	4,818	29,087
1969	487,485	320,481	19,086	2,196	28,149	5,033	29,686
1970	505,401	331,700	21,031	2,322	29,178	5,138	30,481
1971	529,394	347,949	23,045	2,633	30,971	5,063	31,200
1972	608,592	420,537	25,195	2,749	32,570	4,982	31,653
1973	645,810	447,779	27,942	2,862	33,979	5,188	32,376
1974	745,580	495,000	63,310	2,896	35,472	5,356	32,213
1975 P	760,988	509,365	69,149	3,271	41,269	5,917	32,959
1976 P	833,064	548,880	74,984	3,336	48,167	6,200	34,086
	amount of remunerations upon which deposits are made - millions of Chilean escudos						
1967	7,342.2	2,589.5	1,951.8	55.5	1,492.0	65.0	146.7
1968	9,550.4	3,446.7	2,553.6	75.4	1,847.1	117.2	153.4
1969	14,238.4	4,834.1	3,753.7	99.7	3,398.5	143.7	177.8
1970	20,255.5	6,896.2	5,740.3	129.3	3,969.6	200.7	264.0
1971	32,532.3	11,327.1	8,767.2	284.2	6,678.8	310.9	583.0
1972	57,977.3	20,464.2	17,016.8	516.0	9,937.5	641.0	1,116.3
1973	180,266.8	67,341.6	47,147.1	1,335.1	32,551.6	1,909.1	4,174.5
1974	1,333,722.2	420,648.8	368,871.4	11,811.1	293,651.1	9,993.8	37,918.0
	thousands of pesos						
1975	6,214,840.3	1,726,332.9	1,731,697.5	52,586.5	1,470,968.9	47,535.0	331,904.4
1976	21,678,232.9	6,163,769.0	6,605,519.5	170,772.9	4,922,634.8	124,850.6	592,772.9

TABLE 15.14 (Cont'd)

Number of Subscribers and Remunerations on Which Deposits Made are Based, by Pension Plan Institutions, 1967-1976.

Year	SUBSCRIBERS AND REMUNERATIONS — Pension and Provisional (Security) Funds								
	State Railroads Pension Fund	Water Service Employees and Laborers Pension Fund	National Defense Pension Fund	Flour Mills and Bakeries Workers' Indemnities Fund	Rural Association of Magallanes	Institutions: National Merchant Marine	Institutions: Municipal	Institutions: Horse Racing	Institutions: Banks
	number of active subscribers								
1967	26,512	1,334	41,596	-	-	34,589	19,226	4,019	17,962
1968	27,417	1,360	38,340	14,300	-	36,160	21,918	3,783	18,346
1969	28,790	1,495	41,431	15,500	-	36,920	23,564	3,756	18,511
1970	25,023	1,689	43,737	16,200	-	38,351	22,962	3,843	19,652
1971	26,528	1,819	48,260	16,500	-	40,761	22,466	4,033	20,423
1972	26,931	1,956	55,992	17,820	-	41,879	22,364	4,286	21,346
1973	26,845	1,821	44,816	18,500	-	43,773	22,469	4,180	20,939
1974	24,971	1,651	63,619	24,654	4	45,309	22,035	4,199	21,384
1975 P	21,991	1,479	67,388	20,199	4	48,519	20,322	3,809	21,023
1976 P	19,468	1,556	72,405	16,741	3	47,363	20,830	3,691	21,091
	number of passive subscribers								
1967	12,809	214	39,026	-	-	10,472	5,365	2,351	6,529
1968	12,197	295	39,896	2,500	-	9,521	8,246	2,400	6,634
1969	12,197	317	40,821	2,800	-	9,981	7,310	2,497	6,931
1970	12,870	366	41,481	3,000	-	10,362	7,599	2,609	7,264
1971	13,592	405	42,247	3,200	-	10,813	8,060	2,710	7,506
1972	13,720	447	42,799	3,456	-	11,316	8,567	2,949	7,652
1973	14,970	482	43,665	4,200	-	12,339	9,232	2,886	7,910
1974	32,336	501	44,060	-	-	12,568	10,285	3,260	8,323
1975 P	17,483	606	44,721	-	-	12,413	11,573	3,423	8,839
1976 P	17,021	740	45,386	15,693	-	12,931	12,421	3,698	9,521
	amount of remunerations upon which deposits are made - millions of Chilean escudos								
1967	150.5	17.6	245.4	-	-	164.1	159.5	19.2	285.4
1968	188.0	22.1	294.2	56.4	-	208.3	186.0	31.9	370.1
1969	243.7	37.7	364.0	80.2	-	296.7	257.2	40.2	511.3
1970	447.7	55.3	752.0	114.2	-	411.0	445.3	56.7	773.2
1971	585.3	82.2	1,141.1	165.8	-	702.1	615.0	126.5	1,163.1
1972	857.8	120.7	2,178.4	273.0	-	1,227.0	1,073.8	473.5	2,081.2
1973	2,988.8	356.2	7,033.2	764.7	-	3,803.1	3,075.6	2,043.6	5,742.8
1974	26,232.9	2,219.7	65,985.5	8,535.9	-	26,282.0	17,215.5	4,780.0	39,576.6
	thousands of pesos								
1975	92,057.0	7,965.8	322,844.6	46,211.0	27.5	110,176.4	83,970.2	8,395.3	182,167.3
1976	278,436.7	26,865.7	1,247,512.4	154,389.3	33.3	477,112.3	250,575.8	24,569.2	638,418.4

Source: National Institute of Statistics.

TABLE 15.15

Subscribers to the Social Security Service by Type of Economic Activity and According to Sex, 1950-1976.

Year and Sex	Total	Agricul-ture	Mining	Manufacturing Industry	Construction	Electricity Gas, and Water	Trade	Transport and Communications	Domestic Services	Other
		Subscribers to the Social Security Service By Type of Economic Activity								
Total										
1950[1]	984,700	363,200	71,600	228,600	68,000	-	87,500	-	115,500	50,300
1951[1]	1,048,000	377,500	78,100	228,600	63,700	-	91,300	-	123,000	85,800
1952	1,078,700	284,800	106,900	292,000	95,400	8,300	79,300	26,400	136,500	49,100
1953	1,083,700	287,400	107,900	294,800	96,200	9,300	80,100	17,400	137,600	53,000
1954	1,096,700	298,500	106,000	304,800	101,100	10,100	84,400	17,000	126,500	48,300
1955	1,128,200	337,200	105,600	309,800	106,000	9,700	81,800	16,200	110,600	51,200
1956	1,144,400	330,000	111,200	302,400	112,600	10,200	99,900	15,200	113,100	49,800
1957	1,166,000	334,600	112,600	311,400	113,700	10,500	102,200	16,300	114,100	50,600
1958	1,191,000	338,400	116,200	319,800	115,900	11,200	105,400	17,200	115,000	51,900
1959	1,216,000	344,000	114,000	328,000	121,000	12,000	110,000	18,000	116,000	53,000
1960	1,240,000	346,000	118,000	341,000	127,000	13,000	111,000	19,000	119,000	46,000
1961	1,264,000	351,300	102,400	350,000	163,100	17,700	110,000	19,000	113,800	36,700
1962	1,291,000	355,000	103,300	360,200	167,800	19,400	112,300	20,700	114,900	37,400
1963	1,310,000	355,000	110,000	369,400	162,400	19,700	129,700	19,700	104,800	39,300
1964	1,340,000	363,140	112,560	377,880	166,160	20,100	132,660	20,100	107,200	40,200
1965	1,375,000	371,300	116,900	385,000	173,300	15,100	147,100	16,500	112,800	37,000
1966	1,410,000	386,300	114,200	385,100	181,900	15,500	157,900	18,300	114,200	36,600
1967	1,450,000	386,500	115,000	395,800	160,000	17,000	177,000	20,000	114,600	64,100
1968	1,406,000	445,000	71,100	370,800	133,900	13,400	133,900	27,800	137,000	73,100
1969	1,440,000	456,500	73,400	380,200	136,800	14,400	136,800	28,800	139,700	73,400
1970	1,476,000	467,800	75,300	389,700	140,200	14,800	140,200	29,500	143,200	75,300
1971	1,513,000	479,600	77,200	399,400	143,700	15,100	143,700	30,300	146,800	77,200
1972	1,540,000	488,200	78,500	406,600	146,300	15,400	146,300	30,800	149,400	78,500
1973	1,561,000	389,360	89,730	479,749	203,245	14,307	156,891	23,345	118,013	86,360
1974	1,594,000	396,910	92,440	489,370	207,220	14,350	160,990	23,910	121,140	87,670
1975	1,537,300	409,440	105,310	421,430	185,080	18,730	168,800	28,190	125,260	75,060
1976	1,550,000	515,210	109,430	268,070	176,830	15,640	175,990	29,910	140,130	118,790
Males										
1966	1,088,500	372,400	112,900	275,700	174,600	14,900	94,400	18,100	6,600	18,900
1967	1,119,400	372,600	113,700	285,000	153,600	16,400	112,700	19,800	6,600	39,000
1968	1,085,200	429,900	70,300	276,600	128,500	12,900	87,000	27,500	8,000	44,500
1969	1,111,600	440,000	72,600	283,600	131,300	13,900	88,900	28,500	8,700	44,700
1970	1,139,600	451,000	74,500	290,700	134,600	14,300	91,100	29,200	8,300	45,900
1971	1,168,300	462,300	76,400	298,000	138,000	14,600	93,400	30,000	8,500	47,100
1972	1,189,000	470,600	77,600	303,300	140,400	14,900	95,100	30,500	8,700	47,900
1973	1,211,332	378,202	88,721	343,877	200,769	14,166	91,425	22,788	16,036	55,348
1974	1,236,410	385,540	91,400	350,770	204,700	14,200	93,810	23,340	16,460	56,190
1975	1,195,730	397,710	104,950	301,270	182,830	18,530	97,790	27,520	17,020	48,110
1976	1,213,500	505,750	108,540	196,230	175,660	15,510	101,090	29,310	14,190	67,220

TABLE 15.15 (Cont'd)

Subscribers to the Social Security Service by Type of Economic Activity and According to Sex, 1950-1976.

Year and Sex	Total	Subscribers to the Social Security Service By Type of Economic Activity								
		Agricul-ture	Mining	Manufacturing Industry	Construction	Electricity Gas, and Water	Trade	Transport and Communications	Domestic Services	Other
Females										
1966	321,500	13,900	1,300	109,400	7,300	600	63,500	200	107,600	17,700
1967	330,600	13,900	1,300	110,800	6,400	600	64,300	200	108,000	25,100
1968	320,800	15,100	800	94,200	5,400	500	46,900	300	129,000	28,600
1969	328,400	16,500	800	96,600	5,500	500	47,900	300	131,600	28,700
1970	336,400	16,800	800	99,000	5,600	500	49,100	300	134,900	29,400
1971	344,700	17,300	800	101,400	5,700	500	50,300	300	138,300	30,100
1972	351,000	17,600	900	103,300	5,900	500	51,200	300	140,700	30,600
1973	349,668	11,158	1,009	135,872	2,476	141	65,466	557	101,977	31,012
1974	357,590	11,370	1,040	138,600	2,520	150	67,180	570	104,680	31,480
1975	341,570	11,730	360	120,160	2,250	200	71,010	670	108,240	26,950
1976	336,500	9,460	890	71,840	1,170	130	74,900	600	125,940	51,570

Note: 1. Used for the years 1950 and 1951 is the old classification which does not contemplate a distinction between the activities of electricity and transportation.

Source: Social Security Service and National Institute of Statistics.

PART V
REGIONAL DISTRIBUTION OF POPULATION

16
DISTRIBUTION OF POPULATION BY REGIONS AND PROVINCES

Differences in climate, geography and natural resource and man-made capital endowments have contributed to a highly unequal regional and provincial distribution of the population of Chile. Without knowledge of the regional features of Chile, its long-term economic development process cannot be understood. And a viable strategy for removing poverty and improving labor productivity can hardly be established without increased emphasis on modernization of neglected areas, regions, provinces and sectors. It is hoped that sufficient statistical information is presented in Chapter 16 to reveal the central importance of regions and provinces in understanding the past and in charting a course for the nation's future.

Regional Distribution of the Population: North, Center, South

As Table 16.1 reveals, the Chilean population has been and still is concentrated in and around the agricultural, rich central valley -- often called the CENTER. The North, composed of the mineral-rich provinces of Tarapacá, Antofagasta and Atacama and with less than 9 per cent of the population, has always been a source of fabulous riches but has been and still remains overall an inhospitable region. An even smaller fraction of the population inhabits the three livestock and oil-rich provinces of Chiloé, Aysén and Magallanes of the South.

Population and Population Density by Provinces

The estimated population by provinces for June 30 of the years 1885, 1895, 1907, 1920, 1930, 1940, 1952, 1960, 1970 and 1975 is presented in Table 16.2. The population of each province has, in most instances, increased substantially over time. As the case of the province of Maule, however, indicates some provinces have even lost population. The information of Table 16.2 is complementary to that presented on migratory movements in the chapter on internal migration.

The population density of Chile by provinces for the census years between 1835 and 1970 is presented in Table 16.3. As revealed by this table, there are two population growth poles within what we referred to earlier as the CENTER of Chile. The one growth pole is comprised of the provinces of Valparaíso, Santiago and O'Higgins, where Chile's service-industrial base is found, and the other growth pole is the industrial-agricultural province of Concepción.

The classification of provinces of Tables 16.2 and 16.3 is the old one. Following the new political-administrative division adopted in recent years, Table 16.4 presents area, population and density according to regions and provinces for the census years of 1952, 1960 and 1970. The striking rise of population density in the provinces of

TABLE 16.1

Regional Distribution of the Population of Chile During Various Census Years, 1835 to 1970, and in 1975, in Percentages.

Census Year	Regions of the Extreme North (3 Provinces)	Central Regions (19 Provinces)	Regions of the Extreme South (3 Provinces)	Total
1835	2.8	92.9	4.3	100
1843	2.8	92.7	4.5	100
1854	3.5	93.0	3.5	100
1865	4.3	92.4	3.3	100
1875	3.4	93.4	3.2	100
1885	5.7	91.3	3.0	100
1895	7.2	89.7	3.1	100
1907	8.9	87.8	3.3	100
1920	8.7	87.6	3.7	100
1930	8.2	86.4	5.4	100
1940	6.7	90.0	3.3	100
1952	6.2	90.7	3.1	100
1960	6.2	91.0	2.8	100
1970	6.5	90.7	2.8	100
1975	6.6	90.7	2.7	100

Notes: Until the Census of 1885 the extreme North included Atacama only. Since that census Tarapacá and Antofagasta are also included. The region of the Extreme South includes the provinces of Chiloé, Aysén and Magallanes as well as the Antarctic Territory.

Source: XII Censo General de Población y I de Vivienda, 1952. (Chile: Servicio Nacional de Estadística y Censos), Tomo I. p. 132. (For the years 1835-1952): Población del País (Santiago, Chile: Dirección de Estadística y Censos, 1964), p. 1, Table 1. (For 1960). República de Chile, Ministerio de Economía, Fomento y Reconstrucción. Instituto Nacional de Estadísticas, Población 1960-1975, Total País, Provincias y Area Metropolitana, Estimaciones por Sexo y Grupos de Edad al 30 de Junio de Cada Año (Santiago, Chile: INE, 1977), pp. 1-232 (for 1970 and 1975).

TABLE 16.2

Estimated Population by Provinces for June 30 of the Years 1885, 1895, 1907, 1920, 1930, 1940, 1952, 1960, 1970, 1975.

Provinces	1885	1895	1907	1920	Years 1930	1940	1952	1960	1970	1975
Country	2,492,000	2,790,000	3,213,000	3,785,000	4,365,000	5,063,000	6,295,000	7,628,136	9,368,558	10,253,014
Tarapacá	54,334	101,086	120,308	118,918	115,381	104,915	109,061	127,492	185,015	209,889
Antofagasta	33,430	45,624	112,674	174,797	181,999	146,287	196,101	222,514	266,256	287,964
Atacama	63,749	61,797	63,602	49,106	62,204	84,974	85,001	118,774	160,978	179,173
Coquimbo	189,557	181,558	189,775	178,561	201,924	247,539	278,165	318,440	357,025	385,226
Aconcaqua	128,323	101,836	111,645	102,334	104,919	118,976	136,211	145,382	170,699	182,920
Valparaíso	203,318	229,614	280,965	325,870	367,011	428,404	528,655	637,542	779,365	854,965
Santiago	363,901	464,061	549,719	735,429	998,079	1,278,469	1,862,034	2,525,138		
O'Higgins	131,301	137,435	133,489	161,056	173,621	201,870	238,297	269,332	322,184	345,934
Colchaqua	109,707	114,858	113,317	121,030	122,731	132,279	148,045	164,243	178,381	183,686
Curico	63,424	71,052	72,959	75,722	77,383	81,823	94,889	111,377	120,168	125,681
Talca	122,372	123,002	122,817	127,816	144,792	158,375	184,291	313,532	245,025	259,400
Maule	91,464	94,323	81,246	85,430	75,729	71,051	76,585	82,424	86,699	89,024
Linares	109,824	105,168	108,339	120,634	125,312	136,028	155,189	176,978	199,306	209,206
Ñuble	209,842	215,488	218,170	228,202	236,085	245,095	266,678	295,711	332,523	347,035
Concepción	162,799	117,180	199,211	232,704	273,277	310,663	436,678	558,869	679,352	737,782
Arauco	69,626	62,432	62,369	62,535	62,179	66,626	76,700	92,721	103,669	106,383
Bío-Bío	99,350	90,567	96,224	106,127	115,442	128,312	146,730	173,868	203,400	214,773
Malleco	56,699	98,422	108,983	122,739	138,282	155,385	169,146	181,039	185,970	187,306
Cautín	52,589	92,585	176,471	254,789	320,967	377,602	387,387	408,507	444,574	462,563
Valdivia	38,925	55,069	80,932	120,727	151,716	193,147	246,842	265,147	292,294	304,222
Osorno	29,835	41,099	51,747	67,338	88,662	108,184	130,568	149,619	168,637	179,031
Llanquihue	33,406	40,692	53,713	71,175	94,202	118,146	148,527	172,489	209,559	228,974
Chiloé	72,153	79,721	87,094	110,902	93,733	102,505	106,830	102,543	116,866	119,380
Aysén	-	-	186	1,684	8,771	17,148	27,864	38,544	51,489	57,337
Magallanes	2,072	5,351	17,045	29,375	38,599	49,197	58,574	75,911	95,180	101,851

Notes: The information of this table was prepared by the following various steps. First, it was necessary to adapt the population distribution observed by the eight censuses taken in the years 1885, 1895, 1907, 1920, 1930, 1940, 1952, and 1960, to the administrative division in use at the time of the 1960 Census. Then the total official population of the country for those same years had to be redistributed to conform with the revised figures of the population by province. This way the population by provinces was obtained, in the middle of the year, for the eight population censuses, from 1885 to 1960, after accounting for the above mentioned administrative changes.

The attention of the reader is directed to the fact that the figures that appear for Aysén begin in the year 1907. The province of Aysén has its origin in the "Territory of Aysén" created by Law (DFL) 8582 of December 30, 1920, with territories belonging to the province of Llanquihue and to the territory of "Colonization of the Magallanes". The colonization of the region of Aysén dates to the beginning of the century. In the year 1900, its population had not reached 200 persons and since that period its size has increased gradually.

TABLE 16.2 (Cont'd)

Estimated Population by Provinces for June 30 of the Years 1885, 1895, 1907, 1920, 1930, 1940, 1952, 1960, 1970, 1975.

Source: Población Total por Provincias, Chile, 1885-1960 (Santiago, Chile: Dirección de Estadística y Censos, 1964), Table 1, p. 2, for the years between 1885 and 1960. República de Chile, Ministerio de Economía, Fomento y Reconstrucción. Instituto Nacional de Estadísticas, Población 1960-1975, Total País, Provincias y Area Metropolitana, Estimaciones por Sexo y Grupos de Edad al 30 de Junio de Cada Año (Santiago, Chile: INE, 1977), pp. 1-232 for 1970 and 1975.

TABLE 16.3

Population Density of Chile by Provinces for the Census Years Between 1835 and 1970.

Provinces	Surface in kms2	1835	1843	1854	1865	1875	1885	1895	1907	1920	1930	1940	1952	1960	1970
Republic	741,767	1.4	1.5	1.9	2.5	2.8	3.4	3.8	4.3	5.0	5.8	7.5	8.0	9.7	11.7
Tarapacá		-	-	-	-	-	0.9	2.1	2.3	2.3	2.1	2.0	1.9	2.1	3.0
Antofagasta		-	-	-	-	-	0.1	0.4	0.9	1.4	1.5	1.4	1.5	1.7	2.0
Atacama		0.3	0.3	0.6	1.0	0.9	0.8	0.9	0.8	0.6	0.8	1.0	1.0	1.5	1.9
Coquimbo		2.1	2.2	3.1	4.0	4.4	5.3	5.3	5.0	4.4	5.0	6.0	6.6	7.8	8.6
Aconcagua		10.9	10.5	14.2	16.9	19.7	8.9	9.0	9.0	8.4	30.9	11.4	12.6	14.2	16.3
Valparaíso		-	-	-	-	-	47.3	47.7	55.6	69.7	-	104.3	103.4	120.7	144.3
Santiago		10.2	9.9	13.3	16.8	18.4	24.4	29.7	35.2	44.9	57.0	99.5	100.7	137.8	182.7
O'Higgins		-	-	-	-	-	13.4	14.1	15.2	21.1	-	29.7	31.6	36.5	43.2
Colchagua		10.3	9.3	11.7	14.0	14.6	15.9	18.0	15.9	16.7	18.5	16.2	16.6	19.0	20.0
Curicó		-	-	-	-	-	13.3	15.5	13.8	13.7	-	15.5	15.6	20.1	21.8
Talca		6.7	7.1	8.3	10.0	10.4	14.0	14.9	13.2	13.4	14.2	16.5	18.0	20.3	22.9
Maule		5.0	6.5	8.2	10.4	13.4	16.4	21.5	17.2	15.6	12.8	10.8	12.8	14.0	14.5
Linares		-	-	-	-	-	12.2	11.2	10.7	11.6	-	12.9	14.9	18.2	20.1
Ñuble		7.1	8.1	10.4	12.4	13.5	16.3	19.7	18.8	18.8	16.3	15.7	17.7	20.5	22.7
Concepción		4.9	6.8	9.0	12.5	15.7	19.9	25.2	25.8	28.8	28.8	62.2	72.2	95.0	113.4
Arauco		-	-	-	-	-	4.5	10.8	9.6	10.6	-	11.7	12.6	17.1	18.9
Bío-Bío		0.6	1.4	2.4	3.8	6.0	9.5	7.7	7.2	7.7	11.3	11.1	12.3	15.2	17.4
Malleco		-	-	-	-	-	14.9	14.6	14.2	14.2	-	10.8	11.2	12.4	12.6
Cautín		-	-	-	-	0.3	-	5.2	9.2	11.7	14.1	18.5	21.0	21.5	23.0
Valdivia		0.3	0.8	1.1	1.5	1.9	2.4	3.3	5.5	7.5	8.5	9.9	11.1	14.1	15.0
Osorno		-	-	-	-	-	-	-	-	-	-	12.2	13.6	15.6	17.3
Llanquihue		-	-	-	-	-	3.1	0.8	1.1	1.5	-	6.3	7.6	9.2	10.9
Chiloé		1.3	1.5	2.0	2.4	2.7	7.1	4.1	4.0	6.1	5.6	3.8	4.3	3.7	4.1
Aysén		-	-	-	-	-	-	-	0.0	0.0	0.1	0.2	0.3	0.4	0.5
Magallenes		-	-	-	-	0.1	0.01	0.0	0.1	0.2	0.3	0.4	0.4	0.6	0.7

Source: República de Chile, XII Censo General de Población y Primero de la Vivienda of April 24, 1952 Tomo I. Resúmen del País (Santiago, Chile: Servicio Nacional de Estadística y Censos, 1956), Table 8, p. 43, for the data between 1835 and 1952. The information for 1960 was obtained from República de Chile, Dirección de Estadística y Censos, XIII Censo de Población, 29 de Noviembre de 1960, Serie A, Resúmen del País (Santiago, Chile: DEC), Table 1, p. 20. The figures on population density for 1970 were calculated by using the population data found in INE, Resultados Definitivos del XIV Censo de Población 1970. Total País (Santiago, Chile: INE, 1970), Table 5, p. 11 and the province-area figures found in the 1960 census publication cited above.

TABLE 16.4

Area, Population, and Density According to Regions and Provinces, 1952, 1960, and 1970: Census Data.

Regions and Provinces	Area km2	Population 1952 Census	Population 1960 Census	Population 1970 Census	Density (inhabitants per sq.km.) 1952 Census	Density 1960 Census	Density 1970 Census
Total[1]	2,006,626.34[2] (756,626.00)[3]	5,932,995	7,374,115	8,884,768	7.8	9.7	11.7
I. Tarapacá	58,072.70	102,789	123,070	174,981	1.8	2.1	3.0
Arica	16,924.60	30,307	51,947	95,902	1.8	3.1	5.7
Iquique	41,148.10	72,482	71,123	79,079	1.8	1.7	1.9
II. Antofagasta	125,306.30	184,824	215,219	251,906	1.5	1.7	2.0
Tocopilla	16,385.20	45,595	38,439	31,154	2.8	2.3	1.9
Antofagasta	65,987.00	94,666	119,520	147,900	1.4	1.8	2.2
El Loa	42,934.10	44,563	57,260	72,852	1.0	1.3	1.7
III. Atacama	78,267.50	80,113	116,235	152,616	1.0	1.5	1.9
Chañaral	24,659.80	16,576	27,056	36,880	0.7	1.1	1.5
Coplapó	34,542.00	34,158	48,403	63,233	1.0	1.4	1.8
Huasco	19,065.70	29,379	40,776	52,503	1.5	2.1	2.8
IV. Coquimbo	39,647.00	262,169	308,991	340,215	6.6	7.8	8.6
Elqui	15,290.30	110,708	135,958	166,339	7.2	8.9	10.9
Limarí	14,276.90	95,249	109,452	112,297	6.7	7.7	7.9
Choapa	10,079.80	56,212	63,581	61,579	5.6	6.3	6.1
V. Aconcaqua	16,378.20	670,399	817,729	967,369	40.9	49.9	59.1
Valparaíso	2,738.90	379,158	476,082	571,218	138.4	173.8	208.6
San Antonio	1,640.80	48,074	65,171	73,855	29.3	39.7	45.0
Quillota	1,613.30	102,911	122,616	145,344	63.7	76.0	70.1
Petorca	4,711.20	34,413	38,780	42,883	7.3	8.2	9.1
San Felipe	2,489.40	62,690	71,581	82,211	25.2	28.8	33.0
Los Andes	3,021.90	42,544	42,365	50,273	14.1	14.0	16.6
Isla de Pascua (Easter Island)	162.70	809	1,134	1,585	5.0	7.0	9.7
VI. Of the liberator General Bernardo O'Higgins	17,923.60	383,778	440,025	495,339	21.4	24.6	27.6
Cachapool	9,079.40	237,159	274,309	320,204	26.1	30.2	35.3
Colchagua	8,844.20	146,619	165,716	175,135	16.6	18.7	19.8
VII. Maule	30,518.10	481,563	563,042	619,130	15.8	18.4	20.3
Curicó	7,486.70	129,423	151,873	158,711	17.3	20.3	21.2
Talca	11,275.50	178,972	211,925	247,579	15.9	18.8	22.0
Linares	11,755.90	173,168	199,244	212,840	14.7	16.9	18.1
VIII. Bío-Bío	36,007.24	873,489	1,083,338	1,253,345	24.3	29.8	34.8
Ñuble	12,090.70	256,839	292,916	319,585	21.2	24.2	26.4
Concepción	3,305.90	355,414	475,604	576,836	107.5	143.9	174.5
Arauco	5,240.14	72,289	89,460	98,784	13.8	17.1	18.9
Bío-Bío	15,370.50	188,947	225,358	258,140	12.3	14.7	16.8

TABLE 16.4 (Cont'd)

Area, Population, and Density According to Regions and Provinces, 1952, 1960, and 1970: Census Data.

Regions and Provinces	Area km²	Population			Density (inhabitants per sq.km.)		
		1952 Census	1960 Census	1970 Census	1952 Census	1960 Census	1970 Census
IX. Of the Arucania	32,471.80	524,491	568,954	599,899	16.2	17.5	18.5
Malleco	14,095.10	159,419	174,300	177,089	11.3	12.4	12.6
Cautín	18,376.70	365,072	394,654	422,810	19.9	21.5	23.0
X. Of the Lakes	69,039.20	596,304	670,496	748,262	8.6	9.7	10.8
Valdivia	18,472.50	232,647	259,794	277,934	12.6	14.1	15.0
Osorno	9,236.30	123,059	144,005	160,159	13.3	15.6	17.3
Llanquihue	18,205.10	139,986	167,671	199,314	7.7	9.2	10.9
Chiloé	23,125.30	100,612	99,026	110,855	4.4	4.3	4.8
XI. Aisén of General Carlos Ibañez del Campo	107,153.40	26,337	37,955	49,197	0.2	0.4	0.5
Aisén	57,499.70	20,078	29,045	40,343	0.3	0.5	0.7
General Carrera	12,406.50	5,218	7,192	6,659	0.4	0.6	0.5
Captain Prat	37,247.20	1,041	1,718	2,195	0.0	0.1	0.1
XII. Magallanes and Chilean Antarctica	1,382,033.50	55,206	73,358	89,443	0.0	0.1	0.1
Ultima Esperanza	45,830.70	9,864	11,998	14,239	0.2	0.3	0.3
Magallanes	36,994.70	40,487	55,062	68,032	1.1	1.5	1.8
Tierra del Fuego	29,484.70	4,562	5,597	6,174	0.2	0.2	0.2
Chilean Antarctica	1,269,723.40	293	701	998	0.0	0.0	0.0
Metropolitan Region	13,807.80	1,691,533	2,355,703	3,143,066	122.5	170.6	227.6

Notes: 1. The present table contains area, population and density data classified according to the political-administrative division of Chile into regions, provinces, communities and districts prevailing on June 30, 1976 as well as on December 31, 1977. According to this new classification Chile was divided into twelve regions and the metropolitan area or region. Therefore, the information on population density of this table is more detailed and sometimes different than that presented in the table on population density of the country by provinces for the census years between 1835 and 1970.

2. It includes the Chilean Antarctic Territory.

3. It excludes the Chilean Antarctic Territory.

Source: National Institute of Statistics.

Valparaíso, Concepción and the Metropolitan Region of Santiago stands out as the most notable event between 1952 and 1970.

Rates of Population Increase by Province: 1885-1975

The annual rates of intercensal increase in population of the various provinces of Chile between 1885 and 1970 as well as during 1970-1975 are presented in Table 16.5. The annual rates of population increase show an overall rise in recent years but remain both variable and unequal.

It should be noted that the annual intercensal rate of population increase for the metropolitan area of Santiago during 1960-1970, and even more so during 1970-1975, presented in Table 16.5 is below, actually substantially below the rate of growth of population for Greater Santiago implicit in the employment-unemployment surveys of the Department of Economics of the University of Chile. The figures of Table 16.5 lend tentative support to the view that the Greater Santiago population, labor force, employment, unemployment figures for 1974-1978 have an upward bias.

Active Population and Participation Rates by Province and Region

Although the statistics on population of twelve years and over, active population and participation rates were presented primarily in Chapter 13 of the present volume, I decided to include Table 16.6 in the present chapter because of its focus on provinces and regions. Table 16.6 presents the population of Chile of twelve years and over, active population and participation rates by province and region for the 1960 and 1970 census years and for 1976.

TABLE 16.5

Annual Rates of Intercensal Increase in Population, by Provinces, Between the Censuses of 1885 and 1970 and Including 1975. Percentages.

Provinces	Years									
	1885-1895	1895-1907	1907-1920	1920-1930	1930-1940	1940-1952	1952-1960	1960-1970-A[1]	1960-1970-B[1]	1970-1975[1]
Country Total[3]	-	-	1.1	1.4	1.6	2.0	2.5	2.3	-	-
	1.14	1.18	1.27	1.44	1.49	1.83	2.43	1.88	2.13	1.82
Tarapacá	6.40	1.46	-0.09	-0.30	-0.95	-0.33	1.97	3.58	3.85	2.55
Antofagasta	3.16	7.82	3.44	-0.40	2.17	2.47	1.60	1.59	1.75	1.58
Atacama	-0.31	0.24	-1.97	2.39	3.17	-	4.27	2.76	2.94	2.16
Coquimbo	-0.43	0.37	-0.47	1.24	2.06	0.98	1.71	0.97	1.10	1.53
Aconcagua	-2.28	0.77	-0.67	0.25	1.26	1.14	0.82	1.69	1.50	1.39
Valparaíso	1.22	1.70	1.15	1.19	1.56	1.77	2.37	1.84	1.95	1.87
Santiago	2.46	1.42	2.26	3.02	2.59	3.19	3.88	2.93(ma)[2]	3.18(ma)[2]	2.67(ma)[2]
O'Higgins	0.46	0.42	1.45	0.75	1.52	1.39	1.57	1.19	1.82	1.43
Colchagua	0.46	-0.11	0.51	0.14	0.75	0.94	1.30	0.55	0.83	0.59
Curicó	1.14	0.22	0.29	0.22	0.56	1.24	2.02	0.44	0.87	0.90
Talca	0.05	-0.01	0.31	1.25	0.90	1.27	1.86	1.57	1.46	1.15
Maule	0.31	-1.24	0.39	-1.20	-0.64	0.63	0.92	0.95	0.67	0.53
Linares	-0.43	0.25	0.83	0.38	0.82	1.11	1.65	0.66	1.21	1.04
Ñuble	0.27	0.10	0.35	0.34	0.38	0.71	1.30	0.90	1.27	0.86
Concepción	0.85	0.98	1.20	1.62	1.29	2.88	3.13	1.95	1.94	1.67
Arauco	-1.08	-0.01	0.02	0.06	0.70	1.18	2.40	1.00	1.19	0.52
Bío-Bío	-0.92	0.50	0.76	0.84	1.06	1.13	2.14	1.47	1.71	1.09
Malleco	5.67	0.85	0.92	1.20	1.17	0.71	0.85	0.16	0.45	0.14
Cautín	5.82	5.52	2.87	2.34	1.64	0.22	0.67	0.69	1.25	0.80
Valdivia	3.53	3.26	3.13	2.31	2.44	2.07	0.90	0.68	1.02	0.80
Osorno	3.25	1.94	2.05	2.79	2.01	1.58	1.72	1.07	1.48	1.20
Llanquihue	1.99	2.34	2.19	2.84	2.29	1.93	1.88	1.74	2.15	1.79
Chiloé	1.00	0.74	1.88	-1.67	0.90	0.35	-0.51	1.13	1.36	0.43
Aysén	-	-	18.47	17.94	6.93	4.13	4.14	2.63	2.87	2.17
Magallanes	9.96	10.14	4.27	2.77	2.46	1.46	3.29	2.14	2.32	1.36

Notes: 1. Annual rates were calculated by means of the following formula:

$$r = [\sqrt[t]{P_t/P_o} - 1]\ 100 \text{ percent},$$

where r is the annual rate, P_t is total population in year t, P_o is total population in year 0, and t stands for time period (t-0).

2. The abbreviation (m.a.) stands for metropolitan area of Santiago which includes the department of Santiago with the communities of Santiago, Conchalí, Las Condes, Providencia, Ñuñoa, La Reina, La Florida, Maípu, Curacaví, Barrancas, Quinta Normal, Renca, Quilicura, Lampa, Til-Til, Colina;

TABLE 16.5 (Cont'd)

Annual Rates of Intercensal Increase in Population, by Provinces, Between the Censuses of 1885 and 1970 and Including 1975. Percentages.

Notes (cont'd):

the department of president Aguirre Cerda with the communities of San Miguel, La Granja and La Cisterna; the department of Puente Alto with the communities of Puente Alto, San José de Maipo and Pirque; the department of Talagante with the communities of Talagante, Peñaflor and Isla de Maipo; the department of Melipilla with the communities of Melipilla, María Pinto, El Monte, Alhué and San Pedro; the department of San Bernardo with the communities of San Bernardo and Calera de Tango; and, finally, the department of Maipo with the communities of Buín and Paine.

3. These figures on rates of population increase, which are presented here because they differ substantially, sometimes, from other official figures, are found in Odette Tacla Chamy, Panorama Demográfico de Chile y su Evolución en el Presente Siglo (Santiago, Chile: INE, 1975), table 2, p. 6.

Sources: The intercensus rates of population increase between the census of 1885 and the census of 1960 were obtained from Dirección de Estadística y Censos, 1964, Población Total por Provincias, Chile, 1885-1960 (Santiago, Chile: Dirección de Estadística y Censos, 1964), Table 2, p. 3. This document contains information for the country as well as for the provinces. There are two estimates of the intercensus rates of increase in the population between 1960 and 1970. The first estimate (1960-1970-A) was made by using as a basis the official census population figures published by the National Institute of Statistics. The second estimate (1960-1970-B) as well as the estimate for the 1970-1975 period were made by taking as a basis the corrected population figures found in Republica de Chile, Ministerio de Economía, Fomento y Reconstrucción. Instituto Nacional de Estadísticas, Población 1960-1975, Total País, Provincias y Area Metropolitana, Estimaciones por Sexo y Grupos de Edad al 30 de Junio de Cada Año (Santiago, Chile: INE, 1977), various pages. In this publication the concept of the province of Santiago has been abandoned and replaced by the concept of the Metropolitan Area (or Region).

TABLE 16.6

Population Twelve Years and Over, Active Population and Participation Rates by Province and Region in 1960, 1970, 1976. (Thousands of Persons and Percentages)

	1960 Census of November 29			1970 Census of April			1976 EDESEC[1]
	Population 12 Years and Over	Active Population	Participation Rate	Population 12 Years and Over	Active Population	Participation Rate	Participation Rate (July)
I Tarapacá	85,4	42,4	49.6	121,8	55,2	45.3	43.9
II Antofagasta	146,6	72,3	49.3	174,7	73,4	42.0	39.7
III Atacama	76,1	39,3	51.6	99,7	44,8	44.9	45.3
IV Coquimbo	196,4	88,4	45.0	220,0	86,1	39.1	41.1
Aconcagua	95,0	45,2	47.6	110,6	50,3	45.5	
V Valparaíso and	432,5	200,1	46.3	519,8	215,4	41.4	
San Antonio				36,6	14,4	34.3	
Total 5th Region			46.5	667,0	280,1	42.0	40.7
O'Higgins	168,0	79,9	47.6	205,5	71,8	34.9	
VI Colchagua	102,3	48,5	47.4	109,4	36,8	33.6	
Total 6th Region	270,3	128,4	47.5	314,9	108,6	34.5	42.0
Curicó	68,4	32,7	47.8	74,9	32,5	43.4	
Talca	133,7	65,3	48.8	153,4	66,5	43.3	
VII Maule	53,5	24,3	45.4				
Linares	111,4	53,9	48.4	123,2	53,2	43.2	
Total 7th Region	367,0	176,2	48.0	351,5	152,2	43.3	41.5
Ñuble	188,0	89,5	47.6	208,2	88,0	42.3	
Concepción	351,1	164,0	46.7	427,7	177,2	41.4	
VIII Aráuco	55,9	26,4	47.2	63,5	26,5	41.7	
Bío-Bío	108,9	53,0	48.7	123,2	53,1	43.1	
Total 8th Region	703,9	334,9	47.6	822,6	344,8	41.9	41.0
IX Malleco	113,1	51,5	45.5	115,1	37,4	32.5	
Cautín	260,6	120,0	46.0	281,1	113,6	40.4	
Total 9th Region	373,7	171,5	45.9	396,2	151,0	38.1	42.2
X Valdivia	166,9	81,4	48.8	179,7	76,6	42.6	
Osorno	95,4	48,6	50.9	105,3	46,8	44.4	
Llanquihue	107,8	52,7	48.9	128,6	56,7	44.1	
Chiloé	65,8	30,1	45.7	74,1	32,3	43.6	
Total 10th Region	435,9	212,8	48.8	487,7	212,4	43,5	45.7
XI Aysén	23,8	12,8	53.8	31,5	15,7	49.8	47.7
XII Magallanes	54,6	30,6	56.0	66,1	32,1	48.6	
Antarctic Territory	0,2	0,2	100.0				
Total 12th Region	54,8	30,8	56.2				47.9
				2,276,2[2]	1,023,5[2]		
Metropolitan Area	1,684,5	835,4	49.6	2,245,4		45.0	
Less San Antonio				36,6	14,4	39.3	
Total Metropolitan Area				2,312,8	1,037,7	44.9	45.0
Total for Chile	4,946,1	2,388,7	48.3	6,018,5	2,624,8	43.6	43.2

Notes: 1. EDESEC stands for encuesta demográfica-socioeconómica (demographic and socioeconomic survey).

2. These figures were obtained through an advance sample survey.

TABLE 16.6 (Cont'd)

Population Twelve Years and Over, Active Population and Participation Rates by Province and Region in 1960, 1970, 1976. (Thousands of Persons and Percentages)

Source: This table was prepared by the Planning Office of the Presidency of the Republic of Chile. The information for 1960 was prepared through the elaboration of data collected by the National Institute of Statistics in its census of November 29, 1960. The information for 1970 was prepared through the elaboration of data collected by the National Institute of Statistics in its census of April 1970. The participation rates for 1976 were calculated on the basis of information collected through the demographic and socioeconomic survey (encuesta demográfica-socioeconómica) carried out jointly by ODEPLAN (Planning Office of the Republic), CEDLADE (Latin American Center of Demography) and INGECOM (Empresa Consultera Ingenieros Comerciales = Consulting Firm Commercial Engineers). It should be noted that in Chile an economist is called a "commercial engineer".

17
URBANIZATION

Chile has been described as an export economy, as a mineral economy, as an agricultural latifundio economy and so forth. Each such description, even though not sufficient by itself to explain the complex Chilean economy, isolates a force or a set of forces that has shaped the distribution of its population between rural and urban areas.

THE NATIONAL URBANIZATION TREND

As the figures of Table 17.1 indicate, urbanization started early in Chile -- 28.6 per cent of the population was urban in 1865 -- and continued at a rapidly rising trend to reach in 1970 a level where urban population was 75.1 per cent of the total. Chilean economic development is intimately linked to urbanization with production, income distribution and capital formation shaping and being shaped by urbanization. Although it is recognized that Chile's urbanization process has been service- rather than industry-linked and service-, mineral-, export- and agriculture-based rather than industry-based (Mamalakis: 1972; Mamalakis: 1976a; Mamalakis: 1976b and 1976c; Mamalakis: 1976d) and that unless Chile's services and industry become more rural and rural-oriented economic development will be limited and partial (Mamalakis: 1977; Mamalakis: 1978b), a comprehensive, up-to-date analysis of the links between urbanization and economic development does not yet exist. Useful leads, however, to the existing literature on Chile's urbanization as well as valuable insights into the process of urbanization itself can be found in the excellent studies by Herrick (1965) and Hurtado (1966) as well as in the broad thesis by Hagerman (1978) and the numerous studies by CELADE (e.g. Ligua Herrera and Waldomiro Pecht: 1976).

Urban and Rural Population by Provinces and Regions: 1865-1980

Total population of Chile as well as the urban and rural population for all of its provinces between the census of 1865 and including the census of 1970 are presented in Table 17.2. Unfortunately, due to limitations of space, the percentages for the rural and urban population for each province and year could not be included in this chapter.

This deficiency is only partially corrected with inclusion of Table 17.3 which contains the population of Chile according to urban and rural areas and geo-economic regions in the census years of 1940, 1952 and 1960. Table 17.3 presents both the urban and rural population as well as the percentage of the urban in total population. The Northern Zone of Table 17.3 is composed of the Ist (Tarapacá and Antofagasta) and IInd Region (Atacama and Coquimbo). The Central Zone is composed of the IIIrd Region (Aconcagua and Valparaíso), the IVth Region (from Santiago to Colchagua) and the Vth Region (from Curicó to

TABLE 17.1

Percentage Distribution of Rural and Urban Population.
Census Years, 1865-1970 and 1975 and 1980.

	Total Population		Urban Population		Rural Population	
Year	Number of Persons	% of Total	Number of Persons	% of Total	Number of Persons	% of Total
1865	1,819,223	100.0	520,663	28.6	1,298,560	71.4
1875	2,075,971	100.0	725,545	35.0	1,350,426	65.0
1885	2,497,797	100.0	1,041,765	41.7	1,456,032	58.3
1895	2,687,984	100.0	1,223,407	45.5	1,464,577	54.5
1907	3,220,531	100.0	1,392,026	43.2	1,828,505	56.8
1920	3,714,887	100.0	1,723,552	46.4	1,991,335	53.6
1930	4,287,445	100.0	2,119,221	49.4	2,168,224	50.6
1940	5,023,539	100.0	2,639,311	52.5	2,384,228	47.5
1952	5,932,995	100.0	3,573,122	60.2	2,354,873	39.8
1960	7,374,115	100.0	5,028,060	68.2	2,346,055	31.8
1970	8,884,768	100.0	6,675,247	75.1	2,209,521	24.9
1975	10,253,014	100.0	8,009,833	78.1	2,243,181	21.9
1980	11,259,871	100.0	9,094,728	80.8	2,165,143	19.2

Sources: The data for the census years up to and including 1952 was obtained from República de Chile, Servicio Nacional de Estadística y Censos, XII Censo General de Población y Primero de la Vivienda of April 24, 1952. Tomo I, Resumen del País (Santiago, Chile: Servicio Nacional de Estadística y Censos, 1956), table 9, pp. 44-45. The 1960 figures were extracted from DEC, XIII Censo de Población 29 de Noviembre de 1960, Serie A Resúmen del País (Santiago, Chile: DEC, 1960), table 3, pp. 23-24. The information for 1970 was obtained from INE, Resultados Definitivos del XIV Censo de Población, 1970, Total País (Santiago, Chile: INE, 1975), p. 1. The figures for 1975 and the estimates for 1980 were obtained from INE, Anuario Estadístico 1976 (Santiago, Chile: INE, 1976), pp. 48-51.

TABLE 17.2

Chilean Urban and Rural Population by Provinces Since the Census of 1865 and Including the Census of 1970.

Provinces and Census Areas	1865	1875	1885	1895	1907	1920
Chile	1,819,223	2,075,971	2,497,797	2,687,984	3,220,531	3,714,887
Urban	520,663	725,545	1,041,765	1,223,407	1,392,026	1,723,552
Rural	1,298,560	1,350,426	1,456,032	1,464,577	1,828,505	1,991,335
Tarapacá	-	-	45,086	89,751	1,110,036	100,553
Urban	-	-	32,757	75,093	50,053	45,832
Rural	-	-	12,329	14,658	59,983	54,721
Antofagasta	-	-	21,213	44,085	113,323	172,330
Urban	-	-	16,465	36,291	61,766	80,002
Rural	-	-	4,748	7,794	51,557	92,328
Atacama	78,972	71,498	76,566	59,713	63,968	48,413
Urban	36,742	45,002	53,836	39,257	25,861	23,397
Rural	42,230	26,496	22,730	20,456	38,107	25,016
Coquimbo	145,895	157,977	176,344	160,898	175,021	160,256
Urban	42,275	69,279	96,371	87,225	52,498	54,625
Rural	103,620	88,698	79,973	73,673	122,523	105,639
Aconagua	124,828	132,799	144,125	113,165	128,486	116,914
Urban	23,541	42,454	60,899	50,208	36,556	37,696
Rural	101,284	90,345	83,226	62,957	91,930	79,218
Valparaíso	142,629	178,523	205,320	220,755	281,385	320,398
Urban	92,554	136,003	154,699	172,852	229,671	265,754
Rural	50,075	42,520	48,621	47,903	51,714	54,644
Santiago	341,683	365,940	329,753	415,636	516,870	685,358
Urban	141,535	185,710	227,626	300,082	363,187	546,812
Rural	200,148	180,230	102,127	115,554	153,683	138,546
O'Higgins	-	-	87,641	85,277	92,339	118,591
Urban	-	-	24,326	18,532	28,235	45,939
Rural	-	-	63,315	66,745	64,104	72,652
Colchagua	233,045	147,854	155,687	157,566	159,030	166,342
Urban	37,128	22,286	36,401	40,614	40,704	41,766
Rural	195,917	125,568	119,286	116,952	118,326	124,576
Curicó	-	92,858	100,002	103,242	107,095	108,148
Urban	-	16,808	31,806	24,463	30,902	27,635
Rural	-	76,050	68,196	78,779	76,193	80,513
Talca	100,575	110,388	133,472	128,961	131,957	133,959
Urban	25,832	30,782	39,930	45,733	47,742	47,516
Rural	74,743	79,606	93,542	83,228	84,215	86,441
Maule	187,983	118,761	124,145	119,791	110,316	113,234
Urban	26,961	21,090	24,714	25,963	30,848	26,048
Rural	161,022	97,384	99,431	93,828	79,468	87,183
Linares	-	118,474	110,652	101,853	109,363	119,284
Urban	-	19,550	19,704	22,535	27,509	30,330
Rural	-	99,211	90,948	79,323	81,854	88,954
Ñuble	125,409	136,871	149,871	152,935	166,245	170,425
Urban	27,582	34,517	49,747	51,877	57,653	59,419
Rural	97,827	102,354	100,124	101,058	108,592	111,006
Concepción	146,056	151,470	182,459	188,190	216,994	246,670
Urban	38,767	47,321	66,618	94,708	117,249	141,511
Rural	107,289	102,149	115,841	93,482	99,745	105,159
Arauco	71,901	51,307	93,625	59,237	61,538	60,233
Urban	12,832	9,212	13,343	20,259	17,324	11,931
Rural	59,069	42,095	80,282	38,978	44,214	48,302

TABLE 17.2 (Cont'd)

Chilean Urban and Rural Population by Provinces Since the Census of 1865 and Including the Census of 1970.

Provinces and Census Areas	1865	1875	1885	1895	1907	1920
Bío-Bío	-	76,498	101,768	88,749	97,968	107,072
Urban	-	14,409	23,589	18,609	20,259	26,506
Rural	-	62,089	78,179	70,140	77,709	80,566
Malleco	-	20,056	81,767	98,032	109,775	121,429
Urban	-	9,470	26,552	31,609	34,356	41,380
Rural	-	10,581	55,215	66,423	75,419	80,049
Cautín	-	-	-	78,221	139,553	193,628
Urban	-	-	-	17,718	42,363	54,190
Rural	-	-	-	60,503	97,190	139,438
Valdivia	23,429	30,525	41,987	60,687	118,277	175,141
Urban	4,124	7,165	12,864	24,625	43,511	52,918
Rural	19,305	23,360	29,123	36,062	74,726	122,223
Osorno	-	-	-	-	-	-
Urban	-	-	-	-	-	-
Rural	-	-	-	-	-	-
Llanquihue	37,601	48,492	62,809	78,315	105,043	137,206
Urban	4,564	5,592	7,703	13,187	15,302	31,501
Rural	33,037	42,900	55,106	65,128	89,741	105,705
Chiloé	59,022	64,538	73,420	77,750	88,619	110,348
Urban	6,028	5,975	20,965	8,740	6,238	8,442
Rural	52,994	48,561	52,455	69,010	82,381	101,906
Aysén	-	-	-	-	-	-
Urban	-	-	-	-	-	-
Rural	-	-	-	-	-	-
Magallanes	195	1,144	2,085	5,170	17,330	28,960
Urban	195	915	850	3,227	12,199	22,402
Rural	-	229	1,235	1,943	5,131	6,558
T. Antártico	-	-	-	-	-	-
Urban	-	-	-	-	-	-
Rural	-	-	-	-	-	-

TABLE 17.2 (Cont'd)

Chilean Urban and Rural Population by Provinces
Since the Census of 1865 and Including the Census of 1970.

Provinces and Census Areas	1930	1940	1952	1960	1970
Chile	4,287,445	5,023,539	5,932,995	7,374,115	8,884,768
Urban	2,119,221	2,639,311	3,573,122	5,028,060	6,675,137
Rural	2,168,224	2,384,228	2,359,873	2,346,055	2,209,631
Tarapacá	113,331	104,097	102,789	123,070	174,981
Urban	64,319	56,267	61,383	107,211	159,439
Rural	49,012	47,630	41,806	15,859	15,542
Antofagasta	178,765	145,147	184,824	215,219	251,906
Urban	89,212	76,686	165,005	203,997	243,286
Rural	89,553	68,461	19,819	11,222	8,620
Atacama	61,098	84,312	80,113	116,235	152,616
Urban	24,604	37,890	41,441	85,459	128,783
Rural	36,494	46,422	38,672	30,776	23,833
Coquimbo	198,336	245,609	262,169	308,991	340,215
Urban	63,376	85,392	103,230	160,148	205,025
Rural	134,960	160,218	158,939	148,843	135,190
Aconcagua	463,544	118,049	128,378	140,543	161,262
Urban	339,064	45,741	51,032	78,001	98,120
Rural	124,480	72,308	77,346	62,542	63,142
Valparaíso	-	425,065	498,254	617,510	738,336
Urban	-	352,314	424,799	548,481	676,096
Rural	-	72,751	73,455	69,029	62,240
Santiago	967,603	1,268,505	1,754,954	2,437,425	3,230,790
Urban	777,939	1,057,425	1,521,831	2,193,966	3,017,015
Rural	189,664	211,080	233,123	243,459	213,775
O'Higgins	-	200,297	224,593	259,470	306,870
Urban	-	71,787	90,827	138,315	173,033
Rural	-	128,510	133,766	121,155	133,837
Calchagua	295,971	131,248	139,531	158,509	168,516
Urban	81,889	28,388	36,501	51,823	61,917
Rural	214,082	102,860	103,030	106,686	106,599
Curicó	-	81,185	89,432	105,802	114,654
Urban	-	26,390	33,332	43,359	52,574
Rural	-	54,795	56,100	62,443	62,080
Talca	218,224	157,141	173,693	206,154	232,210
Urban	75,480	64,404	68,515	89,822	122,011
Rural	142,747	92,737	104,178	116,332	110,199
Maule	197,468	70,497	72,181	79,736	82,863
Urban	57,442	22,589	26,486	31,768	37,368
Rural	140,026	47,908	45,695	47,968	45,495
Linares	-	134,968	146,257	171,350	189,403
Urban	-	37,513	44,270	62,257	80,509
Rural	-	97,455	101,987	109,093	108,894
Ñuble	231,890	243,185	251,342	285,639	316,962
Urban	69,237	80,675	87,941	113,159	149,306
Rural	162,653	162,510	163,401	172,480	167,656
Concepción	329,495	308,241	411,566	539,521	644,091
Urban	185,390	208,443	313,297	440,770	549,772
Rural	144,105	99,798	98,269	98,751	94,319
Arauco	-	66,107	72,289	89,460	98,784
Urban	-	15,127	20,699	31,947	49,871
Rural	-	50,980	51,590	57,513	48,913

TABLE 17.2 (Cont'd)

Chilean Urban and Rural Population by Provinces
Since the Census of 1865 and Including the Census of 1970.

Provinces and Census Areas	1930	1940	1952	1960	1970
Bío-Bío	180,688	127,312	138,292	168,718	193,508
Urban	51,736	37,170	44,146	62,630	95,199
Rural	128,952	90,142	94,146	106,088	98,309
Malleco	-	154,174	159,419	174,300	177,089
Urban	-	52,508	61,647	78,350	91,756
Rural	-	101,666	97,772	95,950	85,333
Cautín	383,791	374,659	365,072	394,654	422,810
Urban	100,752	101,483	120,923	152,896	206,268
Rural	283,039	373,176	244,149	241,758	216,542
Valdivia	236,115	191,462	232,647	259,794	277,934
Urban	76,871	60,992	86,157	114,146	146,372
Rural	159,244	130,650	146,490	145,648	131,562
Osorno	-	107,341	123,057	144,005	160,159
Urban	-	32,747	49,773	66,417	86,696
Rural	-	74,594	73,286	77,588	73,463
Llanquihue	-	117,225	139,986	167,671	199,314
Urban	-	30,412	45,193	70,347	101,384
Rural	-	86,813	94,793	97,324	97,930
Chiloé	183,499	101,706	100,687	99,211	111,194
Urban	30,207	12,675	18,096	21,956	35,493
Rural	153,292	89,031	82,591	77,255	75,701
Aysén	9,711	17,014	26,262	37,770	48,858
Urban	2,051	6,344	11,677	19,966	31,249
Rural	7,660	10,670	14,585	17,804	17,609
Magallanes	37,913	48,813	55,199	73,156	89,443
Urban	29,652	37,950	44,921	60,869	76,595
Rural	8,261	10,863	10,198	12,287	12,848
T. Antártico	-	-	87	202	
Urban	-	-	-	0	
Rural	-	-	-	202	

Note: Due to lack of data by census areas, the population of the Department of Arica is not included in the province of Tarapacá for the census of 1885, 1895, 1907, and 1920.

Source: República de Chile, Servicio Nacional de Estadística y Censos. XII Censo General de Población y Primero de la Vivienda of April 24, 1952. Tomo I. Resumen del País (Santiago, Chile: Servicio Nacional de Estadística y Censos, 1956), table 9, pp. 44-45, for the census years up to and including 1952. The 1960 figures were extracted from: República de Chile, DEC, Población del País. Características Básicas de la Población (Censo 1960) (Santiago, Chile: Dirección de Estadística y Censos, 1964), table 2, p. 2. The 1970 census information was obtained directly from the National Institute of Statistics.

TABLE 17.3

Population of Chile According to Urban and Rural Areas, by Geo-Economic Regions. 1940, 1952, 1960.

	1940 Census			
		Urban		
	Total	Number	Percentage	Rural
Total	5,023,539	2,639,311	52.5	2,384,228
Northern Zone	579,165	256,234	44.2	322,931
Ist Region: Tarapacá and Antofagasta	249,244	132,953	53.3	116,291
IInd Region: Atacama and Coquimbo	329,921	123,281	37.4	206,640
Central Zone	2,586,955	1,706,551	66.0	880,404
IIIrd Region: Aconcagua and Valparaíso	543,114	398,055	73.3	145,059
IVth Region: From Santiago to Colchagua	1,600,050	1,157,600	72.3	442,450
Vth Region: From Curicó to Linares	443,791	150,896	34.0	292,895
Southern Zone	1,857,419	676,526	36.4	1,180,893
VIth Region: From Ñuble to Malleco	899,019	393,923	43.8	505,096
VIIth Region: From Cautín to Chiloé	892,573	238,309	26.7	654,264
VIIIth Region: Aysén	17,014	6,344	37.3	10,670
IXth Region: Magallanes	48,813	37,950	77.7	10,863

	1952 Census			
		Urban		
	Total	Number	Percentage	Rural
Total[1]	5,932,995	3,573,122	60.2	2,359,873
Northern Zone	629,895	371,059	58.9	258,836
Ist Region: Tarapacá and Antofagasta	287,613	226,388	78.7	61,225
IInd Region: Atacama and Coquimbo	342,282	144,671	42.3	197,611
Central Zone	3,227,273	2,297,593	71.2	929,680
IIIrd Region: Aconcagua and Valparaíso	626,632	475,831	75.9	150,801
IVth Region: From Santiago to Colchagua	2,119,078	1,649,159	77.8	469,919
Vth Region: From Curicó to Linares	481,563	172,603	35.8	308,960
Southern Zone	2,075,740	904,470	43.6	1,171,270
VIth Region: From Ñuble to Malleco	1,032,908	527,730	51.1	505,178
VIIth Region: From Cautín to Chiloé	961,451	320,142	33.3	641,309
VIIIth Region: Aysén	26,262	11,677	44.5	14,585
IXth Region: Magallanes	55,119	44,921	81.5	10,198

TABLE 17.3 (Cont'd)

Population of Chile According to Urban and Rural Areas, by Geo-Economic Regions. 1940, 1952, 1960.

	1960 Census			
	Total	Urban		Rural
		Number	Percentage	
Total[1]	7,374,115	5,028,060	68.2	2,346,055
Northern Zone	763,515	556,815	72.9	206,700
Ist Region: Tarapacá and Antofagasta	338,289	311,208	92.0	27,081
IInd Region: Atacama and Coquimbo	425,226	245,607	57.8	179,619
Central Zone	4,176,499	3,237,792	77.5	938,707
IIIrd Region: Aconcagua and Valparaíso	758,053	626,482	82.6	131,571
IVth Region: From Santiago to Colchagua	2,855,404	2,384,104	83.5	471,300
Vth Region: From Curicó to Linares	563,042	227,206	40.4	335,836
Southern Zone	2,433,899	1,233,453	50.7	1,200,446
VIth Region: From Ñuble to Malleco	1,257,638	726,856	57.8	530,782
VIIth Region: From Cautín to Chiloé	1,065,335	425,762	40.0	639,573
VIIIth Region: Aysén	37,770	19,966	52.9	17,804
IXth Region: Magallanes	73,156	60,869	83.2	1,287

Note: 1. The figures corresponding to total population and rural population in 1952 include 87 inhabitants surveyed in the Chilean Antarctic Territory. The figures corresponding to total population and rural population in 1960 include 202 inhabitants surveyed in the Chilean Antarctic Territory.

Source: República de Chile, DEC, Censo Población 1960. Resumen País (Santiago, Chile: DEC, 1960), pp. 23-24.

Linares). The Southern Zone is composed of the VIth Region (from Ñuble to Malleco), the VIIth Region (from Cautín to Chiloé), the VIIIth Region (Aysén) and the IXth Region (Magallanes). The classification of zones and regions provided by Table 17.3 is different from the classification of zones of Table 17.1 and of regions (the new introduced by the Military Junta since 1973) of Tables 16.4 and 16.6

The highest percentages of urbanization are experienced, in 1960, at the two extremes of the country (Magallanes with 83.2 per cent and Tarapacá and Antofagasta with 92 per cent) and the very center of the country (Aconcagua and Valparaíso with 82.6 per cent and from Santiago to Colchagua with 83.5 per cent).

Estimates of the population of Chile according to urban and rural areas by geo-economic regions for 1975 and projections for 1980 are presented in Table 17.4. It is likely that both of these sets of figures will undergo revisions as soon as the 1980 census figures become available.

TABLE 17.4

Population of Chile According to Urban and Rural Areas, by Geo-Economic Regions. 1975 and 1980.

	1975				1980			
	Total	Urban		Rural	Total	Urban		Rural
		Number	Percentage			Number	Percentage	
Total	10,253,014	8,009,833	78.1	2,243,181	11,259,871	9,094,728	80.8	2,165,143
I Region: Arica-Iquique	209,889	193,389	92.1	16,500	238,496	221,979	93.1	16,517
II Region: Tacopilla-Antofagasta-El Loa	287,964	278,998	96.9	8,966	312,080	303,364	97.2	8,716
III Region: Chañanal-Copiapó-Huasco	179,173	154,482	86.2	24,691	199,329	175,315	88.0	24,014
IV Region: Elqui-Limarí-Choapa	385,226	248,573	64.5	136,653	413,990	283,464	68.5	130,526
V Region: Valparaíso-San Antonio-Quillota-Petorca-San Felipe-Los Andes-Isla de Pascua	1,124,535	977,449	86.9	147,086	1,232,410	1,086,890	88.2	145,520
VI Region: Cachapoal-Colchagua	529,620	275,907	52.1	253,713	564,111	308,170	54.6	255,941
VII Region: Curicó-Talca-Linares	684,011	347,789	50.8	336,222	722,682	393,157	54.4	329,525
VIII Region: Ñuble-Concepción-Arauco-Bío-Bío	1,405,973	997,475	70.9	408,498	1,507,381	1,119,373	74.3	388,008
IX Region: Malleco-Cautín	649,869	353,065	54.3	296,804	672,389	395,922	58.9	276,467
X Region: Valdivia-Osorno-Llanquihue-Chiloé	831,607	448,393	53.9	383,214	883,073	515,043	58.3	368,030
XI Region: Aysén-General Carrera-Capitán Prat	57,337	38,704	67.5	18,633	64,300	45,635	71.0	18,665
XII Region: Ultima Esperanza-Magallanes-Tierra del Fuego-Antártica Chilena	101,851	87,825	86.2	14,026	111,119	96,963	87.3	14,156
Metropolitan Region	3,805,959	3,607,784	94.8	198,175	4,338,511	4,149,453	95.6	189,058

Note: The figures for 1975 and 1980 are estimates for June 30 of each year. 1980 are projections.

Source: República de Chile, Ministerio de Economía, Fomento, Reconstrucción. Instituto Nacional de Estadísticas, Chile, Anuario Estadístico 1976 (Santiago, Chile: Imprenta, INE, 1977), pp. 48-103.

18
SIZE AND GROWTH OF CITIES

It was already seen in Chapter 17 that urban population exceeded the rural population by 1940. In the present chapter statistical evidence is presented on the size and growth of the cities of Chile which have shaped Chile's urbanization process.

Cities With 100,000 or More Inhabitants

The population of Santiago and other Chilean cities with more than 100,000 inhabitants is presented in Table 18.1. The dominant role of the capital city of Santiago in shaping urbanization stands out. The size of the city of Santiago rises almost thirtyfold between 1865 and 1975 with its population amounting for approximately one-third of Chile's population in 1975. The port city of Valparaíso reaches a population of 100,000 by 1885. For fifty five years only Santiago and Valparaíso belong to this exclusive category of large cities. However, the growth of Santiago greatly outstrips that of Valparaíso throughout the 1885-1975 period.

Since 1940 more and more cities reach a population of at least 100,000. The industrial city of Concepción reaches this level by 1952 and the resort city of Viña del Mar by 1960. Three more cities reach this size by 1970 (Antofagasta, Talcahuano and Temuco) and four more by 1975 (Arica, Rancagua, Talca and Chillán).

Cities With 20,000 to 100,000 Inhabitants: 1854-1975

The population of cities with 20,000 to 100,000 inhabitants for the census years between 1854 and 1970 and for 1975 is presented in Table 18.2. This table includes cities with at least 20,000 and no more than 100,000 inhabitants during any year under consideration. The information presented in Table 18.2 complements that of Table 18.1. It shows the early growth of cities which by 1975 had graduated into the 100,000 city category and also shows which cities are most likely to enter the 100,000 category in the near future. Furthermore, it provides the number of medium-sized cities and trends in their population.

Cities or Localities with 1,000 to 20,000 Inhabitants

By 1975, the number of cities or localities with a population of at least 1,000 and no more than 20,000 inhabitants had grown substantially. I, therefore, decided to present two tables. The first, which is Table 18.3, presents the population of cities or localities of 1,000 to 20,000 inhabitants for the census years from 1854 to 1960. The second, which is Table 18.4, presents the long list of cities with 1,000 to 20,000 inhabitants on December 31, 1975. The figures of Table 18.4 are estimates made by the

National Institute of Statistics. Unfortunately, it was impossible to find data for 1970 to bridge the gap between Tables 18.3 and 18.4.

Chapter 18 concludes with Table 18.5 which presents Chile's population entities classified by categories in 1930. Population entities include cities (if the entity has more than 5,000 inhabitants), towns (with 1,001 to 5,000 inhabitants) and villages (with 201 to 1,000 inhabitants). Other entities included, all of which reflect Chile's diverse economic and political physiognomy, are isolated farm houses, airports, sulfur mining camps, borax mining camps, camps, railroad stations, radio stations, light houses, large scale farms, industries, islands, mineral mining camps, Araucanian reservations, salt mines, nitrate mining camps and dispersed.

TABLE 18.1

Population of Santiago and Cities of 100,000 or More Inhabitants, 1854-1975.

Census Year	1854	1865	1875	1885	1895	1907	1920	1930	1940	1952	1960	1970	1975[1]
City													
Santiago		115,377	129,807	189,332	256,403	332,724	507,296	712,533	952,075	1,350,409	1,907,378	2,861,900	3,229,800
Valparaíso				104,952	122,447	162,447	182,422	193,205	209,945	218,829	252,865	250,400	248,800
Concepción										120,099	148,078	178,200	170,300
Viña del Mar											115,467	179,600	234,300
Antofagasta												125,100	152,300
Talcahuano												148,000	187,000
Temuco												110,300	141,400
Arica													114,700
Rancagua													110,400
Talca													117,400
Chillán													103,800

Note: 1. The 1975 city population estimates are for December 31.

Sources: The statistical information for the 1865-1930 period was obtained from República de Chile, DGE, X Censo de la Población 1930 (Santiago, Chile: DGE, 1930), Vol. I, March 1931, p. 46, Table 4. The information for the 1940 and 1952 census years was obtained from República de Chile, XII Censo General de Población y I de Vivienda, 1952. Tomo I (Santiago, Chile: SNE, 1976), table 10, pp. 45-46. For the year 1960 the information was obtained from Chile, Ministerio de Economía, Dirección de Estadística y Censos. Población del País. Caraterísticas Básicas de la Población (Censo 1960) (Santiago, Chile: Dirección de Estadística y Censos, 1964), table 3, pp. 2-4. The information for 1970 was obtained from República de Chile, Instituto Nacional de Estadísticas, Características Básicas de la Población (Censo 1970). Resumen País (Santiago, Chile: INE, 1972), table 3, p. 4. The information for 1975 was obtained from República de Chile, Ministerio de Economía, Fomento y Reconstrucción, Chile Anuario Estadístico 1976 (Santiago, Chile: INE, 1976), pp. 18-19.

TABLE 18.2

Population of Cities of 20,000 to 100,000 Inhabitants by Census Years, 1854-1970 and 1975.

Census Years	1854	1865	1875	1885	1895	1907	1920	1930	1940	1952	1960	1970	1975[2]
Cities													
Antofagasta						32,496	51,531	53,591	49,106	62,272	87,860	*	*
Arica											43,344	87,700	*
Calama											26,166	45,900	60,600
Chillán				20,755	28,738	34,269	30,881	39,511	42,817	52,576	65,112	87,600	*
Concepción				24,180	39,837	55,330	64,074	77,589	85,813	*	*	*	*
Copiapo											30,123	45,200	56,700
Coquimbo										24,962	33,749	50,400	60,500
Coronel											33,870	37,400	39,400
Curicó									21,153	26,773	32,562	41,300	46,600
Iquique					33,031	40,171	37,421	46,458	38,094	39,576	50,655	64,500	73,800
La Serena								20,696	21,742	37,618	40,854	61,900	77,100
Linares											27,568	37,900	44,900
Los Andes											20,448	n.a.	26,200
Los Angeles									20,979	25,071	35,511	49,200	61,000
Lota								25,032	31,087	40,632	48,693	48,200	47,900
Magallanes (Punta Arenas)							20,437	24,307	29,883	34,440	49,504	61,900	71,400
Osorno									25,075	40,120	55,091	68,800	78,800
Ovalle											25,282	31,800	37,100
Puente Alto										22,482	43,557	n.a.	69,500
Puerto Montt									21,360	28,944	41,681	62,700	79,000
Quillota										24,782	29,447	36,500	43,100
Quilpue										20,268	26,588	40,200	51,900
Rancaqua								23,339	31,018	39,972	53,318	86,400	*
San Antonio											26,917	n.a.	60,800
San Bernando									20,673	37,221	45,207	n.a.	n.a.
San Fernando											21,776	28,000	33,300
Talca				23,432	33,232	38,040	36,079	45,020	50,464	55,059	68,148	94,500	*
Talcahuano							22,084	27,594	35,774	54,782	83,609	*	*
Temuco							28,546	35,748	42,035	51,497	72,132	*	*
Tocopilla											21,580	n.a.	23,000
Tomé											26,942	n.a.	34,000
Valdivia							26,854	34,296	34,496	45,128	61,334	82,400	98,900
Valparaíso	52,413	70,438	97,737	*[1]								*	*
Viña del Mar						26,262	35,441	49,488	65,916	85,281	*	*	*
Angol												23,500	27,900
Cauquenes												20,300	21,700
Coihaique[3]													22,700
Chiguayante													32,900
Chuquicamata													20,500

TABLE 18.2 (Cont'd)

Population of Cities of 20,000 to 100,000 Inhabitants by Census Years, 1854-1970 and 1975.

Census Years	1854	1865	1875	1885	1895	1907	1920	1930	1940	1952	1960	1970	1975[2]
La Calera													29,200
Melipilla													30,900
Penco													25,700
San Felipe												26,100	32,100
San Pedro													28,100
Talagante													20,200
Vallenar													36,000
Villa Alemana													38,100

Notes: 1. The asterisk means that by the year indicated the population of the city involved fell outside the 20,000 to 100,000 limits

2. The figures for 1975 refer to estimates for December 31 of the same year. Also, the additional cities with a size of at least 20,000 inhabitants in 1975 have been added to the earlier list of this table but not in alphabetical order.

3. Because no detailed information was available giving the size of all Chilean cities for 1970, it is possible that some of the cities had reached 20,000 inhabitants already in 1970 even though they are listed in the present table as having reached 20,000 in 1975.

Sources: The information for the years 1854-1952 was obtained from República de Chile, DGE, X Censo de la Población, 1930, Volume I (Chile: Dirección General de Estadísticas, March, 1931), table 4, p. 46, and República de Chile, SNE, XII Censo General de Población y I de Vivienda, 1952, Tomo I (Santiago, Chile: Servicio Nacional de Estadística y Censos, 1956), table 10, pp. 45-46. The information for 1960 was obtained from República de Chile, DEC, Población del País (Santiago, Chile: Dirección de Estadística y Censos, 1964), table 3, pp. 3-4. The information for 1970 was obtained from República de Chile, Instituto Nacional de Estadísticas, Características Básicas de la Población (Censo, 1970). Resumen País (Santiago, Chile: INE, 1972), table 3, p. 4. The data for 1975 was obtained from República de Chile, Ministerio de Economía, Fomento y Reconstrucción, Instituto Nacional de Estadísticas, Chile. Anuario Estadístico 1976 (Santiago, Chile: INE, 1976), pp. 18-19.

TABLE 18.3

Population of Cities or Localities of 1,000 to 20,000 Inhabitants by Census Years, 1854-1960.

Census Years	1854	1865	1875	1885	1895	1907	1920	1930	1940	1952	1960
Cities											
Tarapacá											
Iquique	-	-	9,222	15,391	*						
Arica	-	-	3,449	3,900	2,853	4,886	9,015	13,140	14,064	18,947	*
Antofagasta											
Antofagasta	-	-	-	7,588	13,530	*					
Calama	-	-	-	-	-	2,856	3,175	5,407	4,967	12,955	*
Taltal	-	-	-	4,761	5,834	11,456	8,404	7,835	5,659	4,901	
Tocopilla	-	-	-	1,816	3,383	5,366	5,207	15,305	15,516	19,353	*
Atacama											
Copiapó	12,425	13,381	11,432	9,816	9,301	10,287	9,834	10,747	15,693	19,535	*
Vallenar	3,823	4,562	4,948	5,129	5,052	5,561	6,348	7,378	8,472	9,677	
Coquimbo											
Coquimbo	-	7,138	5,077	8,440	7,322	12,106	15,438	17,121	18,863	*	
Ovalle	-	3,101	4,099	5,426	5,565	6,998	9,172	11,795	14,807	17,573	*
La Serena	-	13,550	12,293	17,230	15,712	15,996	15,240	*			
Aconcagua											
Los Andes	3,695	6,369	4,445	7,533	5,504	8,097	9,007	12,352	12,409	19,162	*
San Felipe	-	8,696	9,422	11,768	11,313	10,426	11,577	11,963	13,168	15,476	19,048
Valparaíso											
Viña del Mar	-	-	1,318	4,859	10,651	*					
Santiago											
Melipilla	-	3,564	3,431	3,341	4,286	6,265	6,225	8,730	9,316	11,525	
San Antonio	-	-	-	-	-	-	2,994	5,994	11,859	18,394	*
San Bernando	-	1,445	2,702	5,522	4,158	7,656	9,366	14,464	*		
O'Higgins											
Rancagua	-	5,508	4,051	5,757	6,665	10,380	17,188	*			
Sewell (mr)	-	-	-	-	-	-	6,307	7,556	11,761	9,009	
Colchagua											
San Fernando	4,676	5,883	5,177	6,959	7,447	9,241	10,753	13,016	14,419	17,598	*
Curicó											
Curicó	3,964	5,953	9,072	10,110	12,669	17,573	15,879	19,099	*		
Talca											
Molina	-	1,518	2,556	4,599	3,609	4,327	4,187	4,541	5,117	6,123	
Talca	14,144	17,900	17,496	*							
Maule											
Cauquenes	3,555	4,157	6,013	6,511	8,574	9,683	10,803	12,007	12,987	14,849	17,836
Constitutión	4,987	4,925	6,542	6,535	6,400	8,873	7,827	8,379	7,053	8,285	

TABLE 18.3 (Cont'd)

Population of Cities or Localities of 1,000 to 20,000 Inhabitants by Census Years, 1854-1960.

Census Year	1854	1865	1875	1885	1895	1907	1920	1930	1940	1952	1960
Cities											
Linares											
Linares	3,531	3,908	6,447	7,711	7,331	11,122	12,051	15,074	17,108	19,624	*
Parral	2,993	3,663	5,448	5,913	8,586	10,047	10,158	9,640	10,225	10,717	
Ñuble											
Chillán	12,665	14,665	19,044	*							
San Carlos	4,136	5,456	5,609	7,277	7,051	8,499	7,510	8,860	9,411	11,094	
Concepción											
Concepción	-	13,958	18,277	*							
Coronel	-	-	5,658	2,293	4,511	5,258	4,728	9,019	14,799	17,372	*
Talcahuano	-	2,062	2,495	5,030	10,431	15,561	*				
Tomé	-	5,291	3,529	5,530	3,977	4,739	5,774	5,039	10,722	18,228	*
Arauco											
Curanilahue	-	-	-			6,185	3,470	3,695	3,995	6,854	
Bío-Bío											
Los Angeles	2,497	3,960	4,570	8,279	7,868	11,691	13,274	17,202	*		
Malleco											
Angol	-	1,415	3,845	6,331	7,056	7,391	8,801	10,288	12,398	14,292	18,637
Curacoutín	-	-	-	-	588	1,821	4,437	4,491	5,740	9,201	
Victoria	-	-	-	2,550	6,989	9,840	7,181	8,585	9,039	10,671	
Cautín											
Carahue	-	-	-	-	1,247	2,251	3,056	3,125	4,341	5,012	
Lautaro	-	-	-	699	3,139	5,968	8,324	7,543	9,602	9,255	
Temuco	-	-	-	3,445	7,078	16,037	*				
Villarica	-	-	-	282	166	650	1,000	1,916	4,679	7,036	
Valdivia											
La Unión	-	720	913	1,454	2,830	3,449	4,510	5,735	7,234	9,830	
Río Bueno	-	-	1,160	1,144	1,453	3,001	4,593	4,388	4,852	6,259	
Valdivia	-	3,140	3,872	5,680	8,060	15,229	*				
Osorno											
Osorno	-	1,536	1,895	3,097	4,667	7,364	12,440	16,229	*		
Llanquihue											
Puerto Montt	-	-	2,137	2,787	3,480	5,408	9,751	16,150	*		
Chiloé											
Ancud	-	-	-	-	-	3,424	4,295	3,341	4,078	6,410	7,390
Castro	-	-	-	-	-	1,243	2,711	3,181	4,781	6,283	
Aysén											
Coihaique	-	-	-	-	-	-	-	-	-	5,870	

TABLE 18.3 (Cont'd)

Population of Cities or Localities of 1,000 to 20,000 Inhabitants by Census Years, 1854-1960.

Census Years	1854	1865	1875	1885	1895	1907	1920	1930	1940	1952	1960
Cities											
Magallanes											
Puerto Natoles	-	-	-	-	-	-	1,965	4,151	6,475	8,140	
Punta Arenas	-	195	915	850	3,227	12,199	*				

Note: The present table is incomplete because it includes only those cities of 1,000 to 20,000 inhabitants that are called major in the 1952 census. As far as I could determine, this meant that those cities were included that had a minimum of 5,000 inhabitants in 1952.

*The asterisk means that by the year indicated the population of the city involved fell outside the 1,000-20,000 limits.

Source: SNE, XII Censo General de Población y I de Viviendo. 1952, Tomo I. (Chile: Servicio Nacional de Estadística y Censos), Table 10, pp. 45-46. For 1960 see República de Chile, DEC. Población de País. Características Básicas de la Población (Censo 1960), (Santiago, Chile: Dirección de Estadística y Censos, 1964), Table 3, pp. 3-4.

TABLE 18.4

Cities With 1,000 to 20,000 Inhabitants.
Population Estimates for December 31, 1975.

City	Population	City	Population
Ancud	14,700	Molina	10,600
Andacollo	6,900	El Monte	8,100
Arauco	7,000	Mulchén	15,100
El Belloto	10,800	Nacimiento	9,800
Buín	18,400	Nueva Imperial	9,700
Bulnes	8,000	Paillaco	6,700
Cabildo	7,800	Panguipulli	6,300
Cañete	10,000	Parral	18,400
Carahue	5,400	Pedro de Valdivia	3,200
Casablanca	6,600	Peñaflor	18,900
Castro	13,700	Pitrufquén	8,700
Coelemu	6,100	Puchoco	4,800
Colina	12,200	Puerto Aysén	8,000
Collipulli	8,700	Puerto Natales	14,000
Constitución	13,100	Puerto Varas	12,100
Curacautín	9,900	Purranque	6,600
Curacaví	6,800	Quillicura	11,300
Curanilahue	13,800	Quintero	12,700
Chañaral	11,400	Rengo	13,300
Chimbarongo	6,400	Río Bueno	11,200
Freirina	3,200	Río Negro	6,600
Graneros	11,800	San Carlos	19,700
Illapel	13,400	San Fco. de Mostazal	7,700
Isla de Maipo	5,900	San Javier de Loncomilla	12,400
La Laja	15,800	Santa Cruz	10,900
Lanco	5,700	Schwager	10,900
Lautaro	13,500	Sewell	7,700
Lebu	18,700	Taltal	7,900
La Ligua	9,600	Tiltil	8,300
Limache	17,400	Traiguén	11,900
Lirquén	6,500	La Unión	18,400
Lo Barnechea	8,800	Victoria	19,100
Loncoche	8,900	Vicuña	6,000
Llanquihue	12,200	Villarrica	16,100
Llay-Llay	12,500	Yumbel	7,400
Machalí	8,600		
María Elena	3,600		
El Melón	6,200		

Source: República de Chile, Ministerio de Economía, Fomento y Reconstrucción, <u>Anuario Estadístico 1976</u> (Santiago, Chile: INE, 1976), pp. 18-19.

TABLE 18.5

Population Entities Classified by Categories in 1930.

Categories	No. of Entities	Population	Inhabitants by Entity	% of the Total Population
Cities (more than 5,000 inhabitants)	53	1,784,957	33,678	41.63
Cities of more than 50,000 inhabitants	4	1,020,616	255,154	23.80
Cities of 20,001 to 50,000 inhabitants	10	350,793	35,079	8.18
Cities of 10,001 to 20,000 inhabitants	18	261,502	14,528	6.10
Cities of 5,001 to 10,000 inhabitants	21	152,046	7,240	3.55
Towns (of 1,001 to 5,000 inhabitants)	162	334,264	2,063	7.80
Villages (of 201 to 1,000 inhabitants)	1,194	464,704	389	10.84
Isolated farm houses (caserías)(up to 200 inhab.)	5,198	297,646	57	6.94
Airports	6	437	73	0.00
Sulfur mining camps	5	810	162	0.00
Borax mining camps	1	19	19	0.00
Camps	151	9,975	66	0.02
Railroad stations	230	6,713	29	0.02
Radio stations	3	73	24	0.00
Light houses	11	185	17	0.00
Large scale farms (Fundos)	21,654	1,124,306	52	26.22
Industries	14	1,651	118	0.00
Islands	37	2,889	78	0.01
Mineral mining camps	300	59,020	197	1.38
Araucanian reservations[1]	1,510	98,703	65	2.30
Salt mines	6	181	30	0.00
Nitrate mining camps	163	88,083	540	2.05
Dispersed	-	12,829	-	0.30
Total	30,698	4,287,445	140	100.00

Note: 1. The Spanish term for it is Reducciones Araucanas.

Source: República de Chile, Dirección General de Estadística, X Censo de la Población of November 27, 1930, Volume I (Santiago, Chile: Dirección General de Estadística, 1931), table 8, p. 50.

www.ingramcontent.com/pod-product-compliance
Ingram Content Group UK Ltd.
Pitfield, Milton Keynes, MK11 3LW, UK
UKHW050952290926
15470UKWH00005B/1783